Praise for
Why the Right Went Wrong

"Dionne's expertise is evident in this finely crafted and convincing work . . . Lucid, pragmatic and buttressed by a parade of supporting facts."

—*Los Angeles Times*

"Talk about perfect timing. . . . An account of the GOP's internal tension . . . *Why the Right Went Wrong* is particularly interesting in its assessment of the past decade. . . . The book is up to the moment." —*Christian Science Monitor*

"Dependably intelligent . . . Dionne argues, with ample illustration decade by decade, that this right-wing populism would remain a Republican orthodoxy, latent or salient, throughout the time he covers. . . . Dionne comes closer to the facts with his tale of a ground bass of growls against moderation, swelling at times or diminishing, but continuously present."

—Garry Wills, *New York Review of Books*

"Dionne is right that America needs an intelligent conservative party, and the insights of this decent man who, as an award-winning journalist for the *Washington Post*, has unique access to politicians make wonderful reading."

—*Washington Post*

"Substantial . . . Dionne demonstrates his thesis with a wealth of historical examples. . . . Notably fair-minded." —*New York Times Book Review*

"So what went wrong? The question itself might seem provocative. The fact that Dionne is an avowedly liberal columnist for the *Washington Post* would redouble suspicion. Yet it would be hard to find a more sympathetic non-conservative to attempt an answer. He has covered every election since the 1970s and is liked and trusted by Republicans and Democrats. . . . [Dionne's] is a tempered book— suffused with the kind of moderation and balance he believes Republicans desperately need." —*Financial Times*

"Required reading for political insiders, for academics, for think-tank thinkers, for editorial writers." —*St. Louis Post-Dispatch*

"A sweeping, sophisticated and shrewd analysis of the radicalization of the Republican Party from the defeat of Goldwater to the rise of the Tea Party and the bizarre twists and turns of the GOP's presidential contest in the fall of 2015."

—*Pittsburgh Post-Gazette*

"To understand why the current conservative crackup so confounds and confuses the Republican establishment, you have to recognize that the party is facing two separate revolts taking place simultaneously: one led by Ted Cruz, the other by Donald Trump. The first is well described by E.J. Dionne in his important new book, *Why the Right Went Wrong*." —Fareed Zakaria, *Washington Post*

"Remarkably evenhanded . . . A policy wonk's delight . . . He demonstrates a delightful, low-key wit. . . . Dionne's book expertly delineates where we are and how we got there." —*Chicago Tribune*

"A terrific analysis . . . I recommend it without hesitation. . . . Very interesting and important." —Tom Hall, WYPR Radio, Baltimore

"A masterly account." —*Guardian*

"Masterful . . . In meticulous and chronological detail, Dionne recounts how since the 1964 landslide defeat of Barry Goldwater, the Republicans' ultra-conservative nominee for president, GOP candidates and even presidents have promised radical conservative action they could never deliver. . . . What makes his 468-page book so compelling and necessary for an understanding of today's GOP goes beyond the overarching analysis to the research, reporting and clarity with which he tracks the party's path. And this Republican presidential cycle, featuring the phenomenal popularity and resiliency of Donald Trump, makes Dionne appear especially prescient." —*Capital Times*

"His recounting in his new book of the last half-century of conservatism in America demonstrates expertise in public policy and polls, intimate familiarity with campaigns and the media, and an abiding interest in political ideas. He also stands out among his progressive peers for his willingness to at least acknowledge the value of 'conservatism's skepticism about the grand plans we progressives sometimes offer, its respect for traditional institutions, and its skepticism of those who believe that politics can remold human nature.'" —*Real Clear Politics*

"[Dionne] remains one of the best political writers in America. . . . The book makes the case that contemporary conservativism must reverse course on a calamitous step that conservativism took 50 years ago. There are 16 persuasive chapters, brimming with good analysis in *Why The Right Went Wrong*, that argue to this point. This is a book with great insight, attention to detail and beautifully researched." —*Buffalo News*

"An important pundit delivers a thorough exegesis of the stubborn recurrence of the fringe right wing in response to a sense of 'lost social status in a rapidly changing country.'" —*Kirkus Reviews*

ALSO BY E.J. DIONNE JR.

*Our Divided Political Heart: The Battle for the
American Idea in an Age of Discontent*

Souled Out: Faith and Politics After the Religious Right

*Stand Up Fight Back: Republican Toughs, Democratic
Wimps and the Politics of Revenge*

*They Only Look Dead: Why Progressives Will
Dominate the Next Political Era*

Why Americans Hate Politics

CONSERVATISM–

FROM

GOLDWATER

TO

TRUMP

AND BEYOND

WHY THE

RIGHT

WENT

WRONG

E.J. DIONNE JR.

SIMON & SCHUSTER PAPERBACKS

NEW YORK   LONDON   TORONTO   SYDNEY   NEW DELHI

Simon & Schuster Paperbacks
An Imprint of Simon & Schuster, Inc.
1230 Avenue of the Americas
New York, NY 10020

First Simon & Schuster trade paperback edition September 2016

SIMON & SCHUSTER and colophon are
registered trademarks of Simon & Schuster, Inc.

For information about special discounts for bulk purchases,
please contact Simon & Schuster Special Sales at
1-866-506-1949 or business@simonandschuster.com.

The Simon & Schuster Speakers Bureau can bring authors to your live event.
For more information or to book an event, contact the Simon & Schuster Speakers
Bureau at 1-866-248-3049 or visit our website at www.simonspeakers.com.

Interior design by Ruth Lee-Mui

Manufactured in the United States of America

1   3   5   7   9   10   8   6   4   2

The Library of Congress has cataloged the hardcover edition as follows:

Names: Dionne, E. J., author.
Title: Why the right went wrong : American conservatism—from Goldwater
to the Tea Party and beyond / E.J. Dionne, Jr.
Description: First Simon & Schuster hardcover edition. | New York : Simon & Schuster,
[2016] | Includes bibliographical references and index.
Identifiers: LCCN 2015027336
Subjects: LCSH: Conservatism—United States—History.
Classification: LCC JC573.2.U6 D57 2016 | DDC 320.520973—dc23 LC record
available at http://lccn.loc.gov/2015027336

ISBN 978-1-4767-6379-8
ISBN 978-1-4767-6380-4 (pbk)
ISBN 978-1-4767-6381-1 (ebook)

For Alice Mayhew

CONTENTS

    How W. United the Country, Then Divided It More than Ever

9. **THE NEW, NEW, OLD RIGHT**   236
    The Tea Party Explosion That Was Waiting to Happen

10. **DREAMS OF CELESTIAL CHOIRS**   261
    Barack Obama Hopes, but the GOP Doesn't Change

11. **THE LOGIC OF OBSTRUCTION**   291
    Why Conservative Opposition to Obama Was Inevitable

12. **THE TEA PARTY OVERREACHES AND REPUBLICANS WAGE CLASS WAR**   323
    The Making and Unmaking of Mitt Romney

13. **SAYING YES AND NO TO OBAMA**   365
    The Two Electorates and the Cycles of Dysfunction

14. **THE FEVER THAT WOULDN'T BREAK**   385
    When Winning Two Elections Isn't Enough

15. **REFORMING CONSERVATISM OR TRUMPING IT**   415
    A New Conservatism, a New Pizza Box,
    or Something Completely Different?

16. **UP FROM GOLDWATERISM**   443
    The Conservative Challenge and America's Future

    Afterword   469
    Acknowledgments   479
    A Brief Bibliographic Essay   487
    Notes   499
    Index   525

INTRODUCTION

What Happened to Conservatism?
Why Reforming the Country Requires Transforming the Right

The history of contemporary American conservatism is a story of disappointment and betrayal. For a half century, conservative politicians have made promises to their supporters that they could not keep. They offered stirring oratory that was not commensurate to what was possible. They described a small government utopia that was impractical and politically unsustainable because it required wrenching changes to government that most Americans didn't want. They denounced decades of change, pledging what amounted to a return to the government and the economy of the 1890s, the cultural norms of the 1950s, and, in more recent times, the ethnic makeup of the country in the 1940s. This proved to be far beyond the capacity of politics. Most Americans—including a great many who were neither very liberal nor radical, and especially the young—did not want to go back.

Conservatives have won many elections since their movement began to take control of the Republican Party more than a half century ago. But these victories produced neither the lasting electoral realignment that conservative prophets kept predicting nor the broad policy changes the faithful hoped for. For the rank-and-file right, the sense that their leaders had failed them and the political system had shortchanged them created a cycle of radicalization. We are living with its fruits today.

The Trumpification of Republican politics during the summer of 2015 provided gaudy confirmation that something is amiss. It's true that Donald Trump's unlikely insurgency reflected the complete fusion of the culture of celebrity with politics that the billionare builder, television star, birther, and self-promoter perfected. His rise could certainly be seen as part of a distemper that bred a mood of anti-Establishment protest across the world's democracies. But the deeper ideological force behind Trumpism is rooted in history. It was compactly summarized by Erick Erickson, editor of the popular right wing blog RedState. "The Republican Party created Donald Trump," he said, "because they made a lot of promises to their base and never kept them."

It is a problem that goes a long way back. Since 1968, no conservative administration—not Richard Nixon's, not Ronald Reagan's, and neither of the Bush presidencies—could live up to the rhetoric conservative politicians deployed to rally their supporters. Their appeals were rooted in the aspirations of the Goldwater movement that began reshaping American politics fifty years ago. The hopes Goldwater inspired were regularly frustrated. In response, movement conservatives advanced an ever purer ideology, certain that doing so would eventually bring them the triumphs that had eluded them over and over.

Consider the steady march rightward. The collapse of the Nixon presidency led to the rise of Ronald Reagan. The defeat of George H. W. Bush led to Newt Gingrich's revolution. The reelection of Bill Clinton pushed Republicans to impeach him. The partial exception to this pattern is George W. Bush. Yet by the time his second term was over, the cycle reasserted itself as his failures led to the rise of the Tea Party.

The second President Bush initially undertook a partial modernization of the right, preaching "compassionate conservatism" and seeking, in effect, a "Fourth Way" in response to Clinton's "Third Way" between left and right. But Bush's modernization project was incomplete, in many ways superficial, and short-lived. After carefully examining the reasons behind Bush's loss of the popular vote in 2000, Karl Rove, the architect of Bush's victories, concluded that moderation was a less effective political tactic than rallying the conservative faithful—and two wars eventually engulfed the administration, creating new sources of radicalism around national security questions and, for some on the right, attitudes toward Muslims.

Bush's difficulties, of course, might have led to a search for a more moderate conservatism. Instead, conservatives quickly defined Bush as an advocate of "big government" whose failures owed to his refusal to be conservative enough on spending, immigration, education, and Medicare. A return to the true faith was the only prescription on order. The result was the Tea Party, which was as much a reaction to Bush as to the election of Barack Obama. The long journey to the right continued.

This process has been self-reinforcing. The rise of cultural and religious conservatism, along with the emergence of the white South as the central pillar of the Republican Party, called forth a counter-realignment. As middle-of-the-road and progressive Republicans outside the South fled the party, it lost voters and leaders who would have supported moderate or moderately conservative candidates in primaries. The numbers tell the story: between January 1995 and January 2015, the proportion of Republicans who called themselves "very conservative" nearly doubled, from 19 percent to 33 percent. When even Eric Cantor, the very conservative former House majority leader, could be felled in a primary for being insufficiently faithful to the ideas of the right, no Republican could feel truly safe from challenge.

This is why the most important political development during Barack Obama's years in office was not the rise of a new progressive governing coalition that so many on the center-left anticipated when he swept the country in 2008. That coalition may yet become dominant. Demography is on its side, and it has proven its power in two consecutive presidential elections. But Obama's tenure also coincided with the climax of a half century of political agitation that transformed the Republican Party and American conservatism. The breakdown in American government and the dysfunction in our politics are the result of the steady radicalization of American conservatism—along with Obama's failure to anticipate it and his tardiness in dealing with it.

Obama's dreams of overcoming the divisions of red and blue America and of putting "unity of purpose over conflict and discord" were stillborn.

Obama eventually came to terms with the nature of the opposition he faced and acted accordingly. The substantial achievements of his final years in office were usually brought about unilaterally, without the support of Republicans—and, most often, in the face of their strenuous resistance. This was true of his steps toward immigration reform, his measures against climate change, the normalization of relations with Cuba, the nuclear deal he negotiated with Iran, and a host of other measures.

There are many accounts of Obama's presidency that lay the blame for his difficulties on personal failures—on his well-known reluctance to court and curry favor with Congress, his standoffishness, his reliance on a tight circle of personal aides, his tactical mistakes. Obama certainly had his shortcomings. But to assume that Obama was ever in a position to build broad support among Republicans for his program ignores their determination, from the very first day of his presidency, to prevent progressive policies from taking hold. More effective schmoozing and more invitations to the White House might have been nice, but they would not have solved Obama's problem. The fierceness of the opposition he faced had deep structural and historical roots in the long-term changes in conservatism and in the Republican Party.

This book offers a historical view of the American right since the 1960s. Its core contention is that American conservatism and the Republican Party did not suddenly become fiercer and more unyielding simply because of the election of Obama. The condition of today's conservatism is the product of a long march that began with a wrong turn, when first American conservatives and then the Republican Party itself adopted Barry Goldwater's worldview during and after the 1964 campaign.

Goldwater was personally appealing, principled, and candid. In the final years of his life, he became more moderate himself, uneasy with the direction in which many of his followers took the movement he did so much to build. Nonetheless, the radicalism of conservatism in our day is not primarily the product of the Tea Party. Rather, the Tea Partiers are the logical consequence of the ideology Goldwater preached. Goldwaterism, in turn, was rooted in the reaction of large sections of American conservatism to the New Deal in the 1930s, 1940s, and 1950s, and of a revolt against the efforts of more moderate conservatives to come to terms with the America FDR and his successors had created. The Tea Party was simply preaching the Goldwater creed in all its purity.

It is a mark of the success of the Goldwater movement that in the ensuing decades, it did more than simply drive liberals and then moderates out of the Republican Party. It also beat back alternative definitions of conservatism that were more temperate, more inclined to shape rather than resist cultural change, and more open to a significant role by government in solving problems.

One of the central purposes of this book is to argue that there was a road not taken by American conservatism. It was a path laid out by Dwight Eisenhower and the like-minded Republicans of his time. The moderation that characterized their approach is precisely the quality that American conservatism is now missing and badly needs. It is a disposition that the historian Clinton Rossiter described simply but insightfully, writing when the right was at its turning point in the 1950s and 1960s. Conservatives, he said, have the obligation to "steer a prudent course between too much progress, which throws us into turmoil, and too little, which is an impossible state for Americans to endure." Rossiter viewed conservatism's "highest mission" as fostering "the spirit of unity among . . . all classes and callings" in the name of "preserving a successful way of life." That Eisenhower and the Modern Republicanism he preached are now regarded as moderate or even liberal is a sign of how far to the right American conservatism has moved. Joe Scarborough, the former Gingrich-era congressman and television host, is one of the few contemporary conservatives to grasp that it's a mistake for conservatives to view Eisenhower "as a bland moderate, a figure of safety and accommodation, even a Democrat in Republican golf cleats whose conservatism could never equal that of Nixon or Reagan or George W. Bush." On the contrary, Scarborough argues, Eisenhower "knew how to win elections and how to govern conservatively. . . . We should learn from his example."

This book explores the history of contemporary conservatism to make the case that to move forward, today's conservatives must revisit and reverse the wrong turn their movement took fifty years ago. Understanding the long trajectory of the American right is also essential to understanding the severe constraints faced by those who would reform the conservative movement and revise its ideology.

As it has developed in the years since Goldwater, conservatism has come to operate almost exclusively on behalf of older, culturally conservative whites and a new class of wealthy Americans who see any impositions upon them by government as the work of a "taker" class intent on tearing down capitalism. This worldview is reinforced by an increasingly closed right-wing media system that disciplines those who depart from orthodoxy and screens out dissent, and also by an increasingly powerful donor class that the conservative writer David Frum has called "the radical rich."

As a result, the Republican Party is no longer the broad coalition of diverse groups that it once was. It has become instead what the political scientists Thomas Mann and Norman Ornstein have called "the insurgent outlier in American politics." Compromise becomes impossible when it is equated with selling out principle. Tactics such as government shutdowns and threats to the nation's credit in debt ceiling battles become routine. The opposing party's legislative achievements are neither accepted nor reformed. The contrast between the Republican Party's response to the enactment of Medicare and its reaction to the passage of the Affordable Care Act could hardly be more dramatic. Republicans rapidly came to terms with Medicare, even if they have in recent years tried to pare it back or partially privatize it. Obamacare, on the other hand, has been under constant attack from the right—on the floor of Congress, in the courts, and in many of the states Republicans control. Republicans talked of "repealing and replacing" the Affordable Care Act, but all their efforts focused on wiping it off the books.

If the United States had a multiparty system, the existence of a strong right-wing party drawing a substantial share of the vote would not be a problem for governing. The system itself would require such a party to reach coalition agreements with more moderate allies to produce a governing agenda. But in a two-party system with separated powers that frequently produces divided government, the radicalization of the right produces a zero-sum game. If it cannot take power, the GOP is committed, on principle, to preventing its adversaries from governing successfully.

The radicalization of conservatism is thus not solely an issue for the Republican Party, or for the movement itself. It is a problem for our efforts to reach compromise and common ground. It is a problem for how we govern ourselves. It is a problem for all of us. Reforming American conservatism is one of the most important tasks of our time.

★

It is not surprising that liberals are troubled by conservatism's current form. But radicalization is also creating long-term problems for Republicans themselves because their party has alienated the young, the country's rising Latino and Asian populations, and African-Americans.

It is one of history's ironies. The civil rights, cultural, and moral revolutions of the 1960s created the backlash that helped the conservative movement grow between 1964 and 1988, prompting the shift of white southerners to the GOP, the rise of the Reagan Democrats, and the birth of the religious right. Now conservatives are paying a price for these earlier victories. Over time, what might be termed "sixties values," in a more moderate form, have largely won in the broader culture. More openness about sexuality (and particularly the triumph of gay, lesbian, and transgender rights), racial and religious tolerance, environmentalism, gender equality—all have prevailed. They are nearly hegemonic among those under thirty-five years old.

When the Supreme Court declared marriage equality the law of the land in its historic decision of June 26, 2015, there were certainly protests on the right. Yet these seemed surprisingly muted when contrasted with the widespread celebration in the LGBT community and among the young—and also with the quiet acceptance of the decision among so many other Americans. Opposition to same-sex marriage did not disappear, and opponents fought rear-guard actions, defending local officials who refused to grant licenses on religious grounds. But the country broadly shared Justice Anthony Kennedy's view that same-sex marriage had come to represent another expression of "equal dignity in the eyes of law."

Southern states embraced the Confederate flag as a symbol of resistance to Civil Rights in the 1950s and early 1960s. In the decades that followed, conservative politicians were loath to challenge its prominence as part of southern state flags or in front of state capitols. These conservative leaders knew well that many on the right, particularly in the South, revered a standard that African-Americans saw as a symbol of slavery and racism. Then, in June 2015, nine African-American churchgoers were gunned down in a hideous massacre at a historic black church in Charleston, South Carolina. The killer was a white racist who had posed proudly in front of the flag of secession. Less than a month later, with the full support of the state's Republican and business establishments, the Conferederate banner that had first been raised in 1962 was lowered from its staff and removed from the South Carolina Capitol grounds.

It was a symbolic triumph, but a powerful one. It reflected, first, the power of African-American Chritianity and its witness on behalf of justice. But the lowering of the flag also spoke to the limits of the "southern strategy" Republicans had deployed since Goldwater's time to rally whites resistant to the advances of civil rights. It was the act of a nation that wanted to move on and move forward.

The gay marriage outcome and the Confederate flag episode demonstrated something else: that generational change could disrupt entrenched attitudes and habits, forcing the hands of even the most cautious politicians. A conservatism defined by the events and the arguments of fifty years ago is losing the battle for the loyalty of the young.

The Millennials are the only generation in which polls consistently find self-identified liberals matching or outnumbering conservatives, and they are driving a growing social liberalism among all Americans. A Gallup survey in May 2015 found that 31 percent of Americans described their views on social issues as liberal. It was the first time in Gallup's records that social liberals had achieved equality with social conservatives. As recently as 2009, social conservatives had outnumbered social liberals, 42 percent to 25 percent.

All of this reflects a central fact of American politics: the conservative movement is aging rapidly, a striking change from the relatively recent past. When conservatism was on the rise, it could count on a strong support from young Americans—the Reagan generation as personified by Michael J. Fox's character on *Family Ties*. No longer. In 1987, the Pew Research Center found that only 39 percent of conservatives were over fifty; in 2014, 53 percent were.

Demography is not always destiny, but over the long run, a party and a movement dominated by older white voters will face a significant handicap as the nation becomes increasingly non-white and as younger and less conservative voters join the electorate in full strength.

The dominance on the right of a sharp-edged ideological conservatism is also out of step with a fundamentally moderate country. "Moderation" has itself been seen as a bad word on the right since Goldwater demonized it in his 1964 speech to the Republican National Convention. And Republicans called "moderates" these days are, with a very few exceptions, quite conservative, moderate only in relation to their Tea Party colleagues and in their skepticism of extreme tactics such as government shutdowns. The clash between Tea Party and "Establishment" forces should thus not be mistaken for a fight between conservatism and moderation.

It's true that party stalwarts shrewdly managed the 2014 primaries to prevent extreme Tea Party candidates from spoiling the party's chances of retaking the Senate, as far-right nominees had in both 2010 and 2012. But in winning what was sometimes described as a civil war in the party, the Establishment paid the price of settling the ideological battle largely in the Tea Party's favor. The conservative writers Rich Lowry and Ramesh Ponnuru christened the Tea Party's ideological triumph with the revealing term "Establishment Tea." The Establishment had accommodated the right. It was no longer moderate and, in truth, no longer much of an Establishment. As the political scientists Jacob Hacker and Paul Pierson wrote after the 2014 elections, "based on voting records, the current Republican majority in the Senate is far more conservative than the last Republican majority in the 2000s." They noted the tendency of veteran conservative Republicans to be relabeled as "moderate" only because of their standing relative to the new hard-liners. "The long-timers aren't really moving left," they wrote, "they're being left behind as their party moves right."

But if Republicans and conservatives have moved so far from the political center, why did they do so well in the midterm elections of 2010 and 2014? After 2014, why did Republicans find themselves with more members of the House of Representatives and Democrats with fewer state legislative seats than at any time since 1928?

These elections did, indeed, demonstrate the Republican Party's staying power in Congress and in the nation's statehouses. The gerrymandering the party was able to execute after its victories in 2010 strengthened its hold on legislative districts at all levels. The Republicans are further advantaged because of the concentration of Democratic voters in urban districts, which Democrats win by landslide majorities. They thereby "waste" votes the party would prefer to have in more competitive districts. To understand the impact of this combination of gerrymandering and the geographic factors, consider that Barack Obama received some 5 million more votes than Mitt Romney did in 2012 yet carried only 209 House districts. Romney carried 226.

But more than maps and residential patterns were at play. Precisely because the Democrats overwhelmingly win the ballots of the young, African-Americans, and Latinos, they rely upon an electorate far more likely to turn out in presidential years than in midterm elections. Republicans won in 2010 and 2014 because some 40 million fewer Americans vote in midterms than in presidential elections, and a substantial majority of those 40 million is inclined toward the Democrats. Under a president who insisted that there was only one America, the growing demographic differences between the Republican and Democratic coalitions embedded two Americas into our political system: the America of presidential elections and the America of midterm elections. The 2014 elections confirmed what the 2010 elections had suggested.

This electoral pattern will only aggravate the country's difficulties in governing itself. A right-leaning Republican Party is in a strong position to rally a coalition of discontent among older white Americans who dominate the electorate in the off years. But absent a change in its approach, the conservative coalition is threatened with long-term minority status in presidential elections, where a younger, more culturally and ethnically diverse electorate holds sway.

And without a major political realignment, divided government of a dysfunctional sort will be built into our political system for some time to come. While periods of split-party control have led to constructive moments in policy and governance in the past, the new divided government holds no such promise.

Electoral outcomes, of course, are not preordained, and Republicans remain within hailing distance of winning the presidency. But the demographic odds are clear: Our current political system is most likely to produce Democratic presidents and Republican Congresses. The increasingly conservative character of the Republican Party makes fierce opposition to a Democratic executive inevitable.

The nature of our constitutional structure, particularly the makeup of the Senate, further fosters asymmetric parties by strengthening the forces of conservatism beyond their representation in the population as a whole. The Senate tilts strongly toward rural interests and conservative parts of the country: New York and California have the same representation as do Wyoming and North Dakota. Equal representation for the states gives Republicans a natural advantage. In the 2000 election, George W. Bush carried 30 of the 50 states even as he lost the popular vote to Al Gore. Translated into Senate votes, a minority share of the ballots would have yielded a filibuster-proof conservative majority based largely in the South and the Rocky Mountain West. The filibuster itself further increases the power of the smaller and mostly more conservative states: in principle, senators representing roughly 11 percent of the nation's population can produce the 41 votes now required to block action.

The importance of rural states in the Senate also means that Democratic majorities are not synonymous with liberal majorities. To win control, Democrats need to secure seats in more conservative states by nominating moderate and moderately conservative candidates. (Their losses in 2014 were concentrated in conservative states, most of them in the South.) This complicates the task of legislating even when Democrats outnumber Republicans, as the drawn-out battle over the Affordable Care Act demonstrated. The problem for progressives is especially acute when it comes to passing even broadly popular gun control measures such as background checks. By contrast, Republican senators, representing the most conservative parts of the country, are pushed further to the right because they have more reason to fear primary losses than general election defeats. Comparable pressures are at work in the House, where the vast majority of Republicans, because of the makeup of their districts, also have far more reason to fear defeat in primaries than in general election challenges from the center or left.

The alternative to the view I offer here is that political polarization affects both of America's political parties more or less equally—that the Democrats have moved as far to the left as the Republicans have moved right. But this comfortable claim flies in the face of the facts. Part of the story told in this book is how Democrats became a more moderate party in response to Ronald Reagan's victories and Bill Clinton's reconstruction efforts. Paradoxically, the most revealing marker of the Democrats' steady move toward the political center was Obama's health care plan, so often characterized by Republicans as extreme and "socialist."

The Affordable Care Act was, in truth, far more conservative than Clinton's health care proposal in the mid-1990s and more conservative still than the plans offered by Democrats in an earlier era. (It was also more conservative than Richard Nixon's health care initiatives in the early 1970s.) The Obama plan was based more on market-oriented ideas from the Heritage Foundation and Mitt Romney's approach in Massachusetts than on traditionally Democratic single-payer or "Medicare for all" concepts. It is one mark of radicalization that Republicans found themselves opposing ideas they once advanced themselves.

And the myth of equivalent polarization is belied by what the voters themselves say. In 2014, the Pew Research Center found that among Republicans, 67 percent called themselves conservative; only 32 percent said they were moderate or liberal. Among Democrats, by contrast, only 34 percent called themselves liberal; the vast majority, 63 percent, said they were moderate or conservative. The Republicans are an unapologetically ideological party. The Democrats are not. This difference leads to another: the sharply divergent attitudes of Republicans and Democrats toward the idea of compromise. In 2013, Pew asked whether respondents preferred elected officials who "make compromises with people they disagree with" or those who "stick to their positions." Among Democrats, 59 percent preferred compromise-seekers; among Republicans, only 36 percent did.

It is no great revelation that Democrats and Republicans don't like each other very much these days. But the antipathy of Republicans toward their partisan adversaries runs deeper. Pew found that 27 percent of Democrats saw Republicans "as a threat to the nation's well-being"—but 36 percent of Republicans said this of Democrats. Among Democrats who were consistently liberal, half said Republicans represented such a threat, but two-thirds of consistently conservative Republicans saw the Democrats in this dark light.

As it is with supporters of the parties, so it is with their politicians. In 2015, the *Washington Post*'s Christopher Ingraham reported that while both parties have sorted themselves ideologically, the Republicans have turned much more decisively away from moderation. Ingraham noted that beginning around 1975, "the Republican Party sharply turned away from the center line and hasn't looked back." The Democrats, he added, "have been drifting away from the center too, but nowhere near as quickly." Even more dramatically, Ingraham noted, the ideology scores computed by the political scientists Kenneth Poole and Howard Rosenthal in the spring of 2015 showed that "in the most recent Congress nearly 90 percent of Republican House members are *not* politically moderate. By contrast, 90 percent of Democratic members *are* moderates."

To understand what has happened to governance, it's essential to understand that polarization is *asymmetric*. As Hacker and Pierson demonstrated in their 2005 book, *Off Center*, on issue after issue Republican leaders and their rank-and-file alike have moved much further to the right of the median American view than Democrats have moved to its left. In their influential *It's Even Worse Than It Looks*, Mann and Ornstein, veteran and historically moderate academic analysts of Washington's ways, were simply reflecting the reality of the new Washington when they described the GOP as "ideologically extreme," "scornful of compromise," and "dismissive of the legitimacy of its political opposition." As a result, they wrote, the traditional Washington habit of seeking "solutions that move both sides to the center" is now "simply untenable" because "one side is so far out of reach."

This is not simply a view from the center or the left. David Frum, the former speechwriter for George W. Bush and the author of the president's famous "axis of evil" line, became a conservative apostate because of his urgent pleas calling his movement away from the philosophical precipice.

"Over the past five years," Frum wrote in the summer of 2014, "the American right has veered toward a reactionary radicalism unlike anything seen in American party politics in modern times."

What happened to conservatism?

★

I come at this question as an unapologetic liberal of social democratic inclinations and a temperate disposition. But I also ask it as someone who has
written—in my books *Why Americans Hate Politics* and *Our Divided Political
Heart,* and elsewhere—with a respect for the conservative tradition that is
rooted in my own experience. I grew up as a conservative in a conservative
family and still remember what it felt like as a twelve-year old to watch
Ronald Reagan's 1964 "A Time for Choosing" speech on behalf of Barry
Goldwater and to know at that moment that the right had finally found a
champion who could win someday. It's an experience I shared with millions
of conservatives, and I'll be noting the speech's electrifying effect later in
these pages.

Conservatism is thus not some exotic, irrational creed to me, even if
my own views moved toward the center-left many years ago. On the contrary, I offer this book in part because I continue to believe that a healthy
democratic order needs conservatism's skepticism about the grand plans we
progressives sometimes offer, its respect for traditional institutions, and its
skepticism of those who believe that politics can remold human nature. It's
true, as Corey Robin argued in his stinging critique, *The Reactionary Mind,*
that conservatism at its worst is primarily interested in preserving the power
of existing elites at the expense of "subordinate classes." In our history,
conservatives have, indeed, resisted movements on behalf of the rights of
African-Americans, workers, women, and other groups facing exclusion. But
at its best, as Philip Wallach and Justus Myers have written, conservatism
is a "disposition" that "has the most to offer societies that have much worth
conserving" and offers "incremental adaptation" as an alternative to radical
change. Conservatism of this sort tries to pull us back, as Edmund Burke
wrote, from "rage and frenzy" and prescribes in their place "prudence, deliberation and foresight."

My unhappiness with today's conservatism thus arises neither from a
visceral hostility to the tradition itself nor from a blindness as to why conservatism is so attractive to so many of my fellow Americans. I write instead
from a profound disappointment that has, at times, congealed into anger over

what the movement has become and how it is has made governing our country so difficult. Often, today's conservatives seem ready, even eager, to trade prudence and deliberation for the very rage and frenzy that Burke scorned.

Yet if I do not disguise my point of view, I try to tell the story straight. This book is in large part a work of history married to my own reporting through much of the period it covers. It brings together ideas and politics and is thus peopled by politicians and campaign advisers as well as thinkers and writers. I revisit some of the episodes I discussed in *Why Americans Hate Politics*, published in 1991, but often write about them in a different key. I hoped then that a modernized conservatism could rise in tandem with a liberalism being brought up to date for the twenty-first century. This book looks back on parts of that earlier history with the knowledge that conservatives chose to move in a very different direction.

My reporting includes a series of in-depth conversations and interviews with a group of conservative politicians, thinkers, and commentators carried out in 2014 and 2015 explicitly for this book. I say more about these discussions in my acknowledgments, but the insights these discussion partners shared were essential to this account and are reflected throughout. It was especially generous of them to give their time to someone who, they knew, held political views quite different from their own and was embarked on a project that would be critical of their overall perspective. Their openness suggests that it is still possible, even in our contentious time, for people of divergent views to engage in productive conversation.

This book appears in the midst of the 2016 presidential campaign. I certainly hope that readers will find its exploration of how modern conservatism has come to its current pass useful to the choices they will be making, and I discuss the early contours of the 2016 Republican presidential contest in the context of my overall story. This is not, however, a campaign book. Rather, it is an attempt to look back on the longer history of the American right and forward to a transformation of conservatism that I believe is essential to the well-being of our republic. The struggle for a new conservatism will long outlast this year's campaign and require political and intellectual initiatives that, with few exceptions, conservative politicians are not yet willing to contemplate. But only by correcting the path they are now on will Republicans and conservatives be able to break free of a narrative of disappointment that has held their party and their movement captive for a half century.

★

The book begins with a discussion of Ronald Reagan because all discussions of contemporary conservatism must start with the movement's ambiguous hero, but it then moves to Barry Goldwater's success in winning the 1964 Republican presidential nomination. The Goldwater campaign was the seedbed of Reagan's own career, and for the contemporary right, the theme of disappointment was present at the creation. Goldwater's victory was built on the conviction that the Republican Party's establishment had betrayed its conservative loyalists for a generation. Phyllis Schlafly's movement bestseller that year, *A Choice Not an Echo,* told the "inside story" of how "secret kingmakers" and "hidden persuaders" had repeatedly betrayed Robert Taft and his conservative loyalists by handing Republican nominations to apologists for Roosevelt's New Deal and his insufficiently anticommunist foreign policy. To examine the right-wing rebellion that led to Goldwater's nomination is to see that so much that we now regard as new on the right—in communications, in organization, in rhetoric and in ideology—was pioneered in the 1960s. It is also to understand how the conservative rebellion was directed at least as much against advocates of more moderate brands of conservatism—notably Eisenhower and the "Modern Republicanism" he preached—as it was against liberals and Democrats.

Fearlessly campaigning on a truly right-wing program—laid out unflinchingly in his bestselling *The Conscience of a Conservative*—Goldwater set a standard for the movement that future Republican presidents would be unable to live up to, even as they nodded to many of his themes.

The conservative emphasis on moral decay was previewed in the Goldwater campaign and he sowed the seeds of a religious right with which he later became so impatient. He spoke of crime and law and order. Above all, he broke the Republican Party's historic alignment with the interests of African-Americans and created a new Republicanism in the South built on a backlash against the civil rights movement. Race, discussed so frequently in relation to opposition to Obama, played a much earlier and essential role in creating the new conservatism. While conservatives now play down this part of their past, conservatives at the time (including the intellectuals and ideologists associated with *National Review*) were not shy about acknowledging the role of white reaction in building their movement.

Most accounts of the Goldwater crusade, particularly from conservatives themselves, emphasize its heroic role in establishing conservatism as a legitimate and popular creed. There is certainly truth to this. Since the Goldwater insurgency, conservatives have enjoyed major successes in changing the mainstream debate. They undercut assumptions that took hold in the New Deal era about the need for regulated markets, the efficacy of active government, the benefits of redistribution, and the importance of state-provided social insurance. They helped metaphors related to the market to become the intellectual currency not only of economics, but also of society, of psychology, even of love. They made the state anathema, and with it, high taxes.

Yet if the country moved right ideologically in important ways, it remained operationally moderate and, in many respects, liberal. It is this stubborn fact that set the conservative movement up for frustration. Those who rallied to the conservative cause in good faith believed that its promises—Goldwater's promises—would be kept someday. Instead there was a large disconnect between promise and achievement, between ideological affirmations and the actual behavior of conservatives in office. If Americans became somewhat more ambivalent about the moral world created by the New Deal and the Great Society, they did not want to destroy all that the New Deal and the Great Society had built. Conservative politicians could propagate conservative ideas; acting on them proved much more difficult.

Government remained large because the things it spends most of its money on—retirement and health care programs for the elderly, national defense and security at home, social insurance against unemployment and other personal misfortunes—are broadly popular, even among many who are part of the conservative movement itself. Conservatives could not cut taxes and balance budgets at the same time without undermining the government functions that most Americans support. And even the "intrusive regulations" the right attacked with such relish and effect won strong support when voters considered their concrete purposes: to keep the air and water clean; to protect Americans, particularly children, from unsafe products; to prevent injury and death in the workplace; and to regulate an economic system that can go off the rails at great cost to tens of millions, as the Great Recession showed.

Conservative politicians rallied millions of middle-class and working-class voters to their side with pledges to reverse cultural changes that began to take hold in the late 1950s and 1960s. Yet these changes were largely irreversible and cultural change continued—not because it was imposed from the top but because, as such change usually does, it bubbled up from below.

Nor could politicians reverse the fact that the United States had become an ethnically diverse nation in which white Americans will, over time, come to represent a minority of the population. It's true that these changes were set in motion by a political decision, the passage of the immigration act of 1965 that ended a pro-European tilt in our laws. But the immigrants who later flowed illegally across the country's southern border were not brought in by some liberal plot. They came to seek opportunity, to escape poverty (and, in some cases, violence) in their home countries, and they came because the American economy's demand for labor exceeded both population growth and the capacity of existing immigration rules to provide it.

The Goldwater campaign did more than create a powerful ideological legacy. It also transformed the Republican Party. Moderate and liberal Republicans were pushed out and alternative understandings of conservatism were rendered illegitimate. The reshaping of the Republican coalition took place so gradually and over such a long period that it's hard now to remember how different the present-day Republican Party is from its earlier incarnation. Until Lyndon Johnson championed the 1964 Civil Rights Act and Goldwater opposed it, African-Americans were a vital part of the GOP. Dwight Eisenhower won about 40 percent among nonwhite voters in 1956 and Richard Nixon secured about a third of their ballots in 1960. From 1964 on, African-Americans became the most loyal component of the Democratic coalition.

This was accompanied by the realignment of whites in the South, which in turn called forth a reaction from traditional Republicans elsewhere. As became obvious in the 1992 and 1996 elections, moderate white Republicans—in the Northeast especially, but also in the Midwest and on the West Coast—steadily abandoned the party. They become Independents or converted outright to the Democrats. The change was especially dramatic in the suburbs of around Philadelphia, Boston, Chicago, Washington, D.C., New York, and San Francisco. These once-loyal Republican bastions became purple or blue.

The result of the southern realignment and northern counter-realignment is easily measured. The Republican contingents elected to the House in 1960 and 2008 were of roughly equal size: Republicans won 174 seats in 1960 and 178 in 2008. But in 1960, 35 of those Republicans represented districts in New York and New England while only 8 hailed from the eleven states of the Old Confederacy. Among the 2008 Republican House members, only 3 came from New England and New York; 73 represented the old Confederate states. Even in the election of 2014, a banner year for Republicans nearly everywhere, the balance shifted only slightly: Republicans from the former Confederate states outnumbered those from New York and New England by 9 to 1. No wonder northern Republican congressional leaders like former House Speaker John Boehner could be described by a formula often applied to the pre–Civil War Democrats: these Republicans were often northern men of southern convictions. The South was now the dominant force in Abraham Lincoln's party.

Latinos have, on the whole, long been a Democratic group, but they have not been immune to appeals from Republicans. As recently as 2004, George W. Bush, a strong supporter of immigration reform, secured more than 40 percent of the Latino vote. But as the party's critics of liberalizing immigration statutes became louder and angrier, Latinos fled. In 2012, Mitt Romney won only 27 percent of their ballots. Even more surprising was Romney's paltry 26 percent among Asian-Americans, a group that had often been hospitable to Republican candidates.

Republicans have also suffered large losses among women, particularly the college educated. Until the 1980 election, there was no identifiable gender gap. To the extent that there were gender differences in voting, women tended to be more conservative than men. Now women vote consistently more Democratic. The defection of women means that conservatives and Republicans have lost yet another moderating influence—not only on social issues such as contraception and abortion but also on public spending, since women on the whole are more sympathetic to expenditures for safety net programs, education, and other public goods.

All these changes were first set in motion in 1964.

Goldwater's defeat was Richard Nixon's opportunity. Everything about Nixon is complicated, and this is certainly true of his relationship to American conservatives. They regarded him as a friend and an enemy at different moments in his political career, and never fully settled on a final judgment. The struggles within Nixon himself, among his 1968 campaign advisers, and inside his White House modeled the battles that would rage inside the Republican Party into our time. Nixon was a political entrepreneur and innovator who brought the party's Southern Strategy to fruition. He began creating the "New Majority" that Goldwater conservatives thought would be their legacy. Yet Nixon was also an instinctive moderate who signed a large stack of regulatory and environmental legislation that laid the basis for the new liberal state conservatives would rebel against. His foreign policy realism, especially his opening to Communist China, infuriated large parts of the right. Even Nixon's fall in the Watergate scandal produced ambivalence on the right. Some conservatives were inclined to defend him, if only to stand up to his enemies in "the liberal media" and among Democrats in Congress. Ronald Reagan stuck with Nixon to the end. Others, like Goldwater—he delivered the bad news to Nixon that his support in the Republican Party had collapsed—were appalled by his abuse of power. And many conservatives believed that Nixon simply got his comeuppance for having harvested conservative votes only to pursue liberal policies on a host of issues. The post-Goldwater cycle of disappointment had begun.

Nixon's Watergate travails provided an opening for Democrats, but it proved to be brief. They swept the 1974 elections with a new breed of "Watergate babies," many of them reform liberals whose rise signaled the party's slow transformation from a bastion of urban labor into a redoubt of suburban progressives. A then-obscure but resourceful Georgia governor named Jimmy Carter won the Democratic nomination in 1976 by being everyone's second choice. He beat all the party's factions, one by one—the old segregationists represented by George Wallace, the Cold War labor liberals (many of whom were or became neoconservatives) represented by Henry "Scoop" Jackson, and the middle-class progressives represented by Morris Udall. But this also meant that Carter lacked a strong base of his own in the party. He simultaneously alienated the Cold Warriors for being insufficiently bellicose, and the liberals for being insufficiently committed to their goals, notably national health insurance. The Cold Warriors defected to the Republicans and the liberals, led by Senator Edward Kennedy, challenged him in the primaries. As if he didn't have troubles enough, Carter was engulfed by gas lines, the Iranian hostage crisis, and the economic calamity of stagflation. The way was open for Reagan, the man conservatives always knew was destined for the White House.

If Nixon proved to be no conservative hero, Reagan was the conservative hero who, like Nixon, understood the limits on what he could achieve. The reemergence of a more radical right in our time would seem paradoxical because Reagan was thought to have accustomed conservatives to the disciplines of power. As president, he sanded some of the rough edges off the movement and pushed it away from conspiracy-mongering and intolerance. He left intact many of the legacies of the New Deal, the most important elements of Lyndon Johnson's Great Society, and large parts of the regulatory state that grew during the Nixon years. Conservatives rarely confess to disappointment over this. Instead, in a political version of displacement, they hold these sins against his successor, George H. W. Bush. By arguing that it was Bush, not Reagan, who betrayed their hopes, those at the right end of the Republican Party could continue to extol the purist Reagan of 1964, who had insisted that the battle was against those whose goal was "to impose socialism." They have been fighting "socialism" ever since.

The rebellion on the right against Bush's decision to sign a tax increase in 1990 created a new norm within conservatism: opposing all tax increases became the single most important test of philosophical loyalty. Bush's defeat in 1992 was a trauma for conservatives who assumed that Reagan's victory was the beginning of a long period of conservative dominance. It was an illusion that would reappear after George W. Bush's 2004 reelection.

The 1990s, to which I turn next, saw several turning points. Bill Clinton's election opened the way for a Democratic experiment that took account of conservatism's triumphs after the Johnson years even as it attempted to restore a centrist-leaning progressivism to dominance. Carter had tried to change the party along similar lines. But where Carter was seen by many of the Democratic factions as embarking on a hostile takeover—none of them saw him as one of them—Clinton was largely accepted as fostering changes from the inside. And the changes were much more readily accepted by the party after the intervening twelve years of Republican rule.

Fear that Clinton might well succeed in reengineering Democratic dominance was a central factor motivating unified Republican opposition to his designs. The attack was organized by a new and harder-line congressional leadership under Newt Gingrich, and the elections of the 1990s accelerated the ideological purification of the Republican Party. Clinton once mourned that his administration was pursuing the policies of Eisenhower Republicanism, but this did have political benefits. The Clinton years saw the conversion of many Republican moderates, who remembered Eisenhower fondly, into Democrats and staunch opponents of Gingrich's brand of conservatism.

The 1990s thus sped up the changes in the Republican Party and the conservative movement inaugurated in 1964. If moderate and progressive Republicans fled the party in large numbers during the Clinton years, southern conservatives took their place by moving decisively to the GOP in congressional contests, having long before declared allegiance to the party in presidential elections. In this context, the impeachment crisis becomes less surprising. A polarizing event was the natural consequence of a polarizing country. The impeachment of Clinton, far more than the moments of agreement between Clinton and his adversaries, defined the politics of the era and presaged the resistance Obama was to encounter.

Yet Clinton's presidency is now more often remembered primarily as a golden age of peace and prosperity, and both George W. Bush and Karl Rove, the architect of Bush's political career, understood the need to come to terms with the new, moderately progressive political center that Bill Clinton began building. I pay particular attention to the promise and failure of "compassionate conservatism" because the underlying instincts of its champions about where the right needs to go were sound, but their efforts were severely constrained by the philosophical commitments of the larger conservative movement. There are lessons here for a new generation of "reform conservatives," whose efforts also play a large role in these pages.

Nonetheless, Bush and Rove largely abandoned their modernization effort, their hands forced by the hostility to compassionate conservatism among many on the right. And the attacks of September 11, 2001, fundamentally and inevitably altered the Bush presidency. The public's eventual weariness with the Iraq War and the collapse of the economy in 2008 left the original Bush-Rove project in ruins. My account takes very seriously the claims of Tea Party conservatives and their allies that the origins of their rebellion should be traced to the failures of the Bush years and not be defined solely as a reaction to Obama.

In the end, Bush and Rove played a surprising, unexpected, and in some ways unintended role in the radicalization of the right. Bush not only missed an opportunity to create a more moderate and more broadly based conservative coalition; he also contributed—at times unintentionally—to the movement's rightward thrust. It was under Bush that slogans about "the real America" gained currency as part of an effort to marginalize the nonconservative parts of America in the Northeast and on the West Coast. In the Bush years, Fox News became the dominant cable news network. Its new prominence made it the principal adjudicator of conservative orthodoxy. And under Bush, the cleansing of the Republican Party of all moderate and progressive influences was nearly completed. The Tea Party would do the rest.

Bush, the ambivalent modernizer, was thus left with the worst of both worlds. Progressives continued to view his presidency as a series of right-wing misadventures. Yet the right itself mistrusted a man who would, on occasion at least, defend government's role in domestic policy, and insist upon the importance of a more culturally inclusive conservatism. The bitterness among conservatives deepened at the end of his term when he pushed for and then presided over a massive federal bailout of the banking system to prevent a financial collapse. Conservatives went into full rebellion.

Thus did American conservatism come full circle. Having made a variety of adjustments after Goldwater's landslide defeat—under Nixon, Reagan, and both Bushes—many conservative activists returned in frustration to the unvarnished and uncompromising version of their creed preached not only by the Arizona senator but also by groups on the farther reaches of the right such as the John Birch Society. The Tea Party and its media allies have regularly recycled ideas, charges, and conspiracy theories from the 1960s, the late 1950s, or even earlier.

I conclude by tracing how the fierce battles of the Obama years—both between Obama and the Republican Party and within the GOP itself—have created a politics of deadlock that will be broken only by fundamental change on the right.

There are conservatives who understand this, and I offer thoughts on a conservative reform movement that has at least begun to consider how the right might free itself from rhetoric about the "47 percent," antigovernment shibboleths, and an aversion to any form of redistribution. At a time of rising inequality and declining social mobility, some of these reformers accept that conservatism will make itself entirely irrelevant to the nation's challenges if it persists in its claims that capitalism's only problems are those created by government regulators and high taxes.

Yet the reformers are themselves constrained by history, by the current makeup of the Republican Party, and by the limits placed on the conservative imagination by the movement's continued fealty to the ideas of a half century ago. The shift away from the utopian dreams and sweeping rhetoric of Barry Goldwater and the Ronald Reagan of 1964 will have to be much bolder than most of the reformers are willing to contemplate.

Nor is it clear that Republican politicians will go even as far as the already restrained reformers would like. A few of the party's 2016 presidential candidates dabbled in reformist ideas, but they largely stayed within the confines of orthodoxy. A partial exception was Governor John Kasich. In the Republicans' first debate in August 2015, he was willing to break with party orthodoxy by offering an unambiguous defense of his push to have Ohio accept an expansion of Medicare under the Affordable Care Act. He offered a stirring defense of the interests of the working poor and seemed, for a moment at least, to be the incarnation of a compassionate conservatism coming back to life. In late October, Kasich excoriated his party's moves rightward on issues ranging from Medicare and Medicaid to the flat tax. "What has happened to our party?" he asked. "What has happened to the conservative movement?" They were the right questions.

But it was Donald Trump who took control of the Republican campaign during that summer of surprises, even if his poll numbers dropped in the fall. His excoriation of Mexican immigrants and his call for deporting the roughly 11 million who had come to the United States illegally quickly won him a substantial following, even as he pushed his rivals to harder-line positions that threatened to weaken the party's already dire standing with Latinos and Asian-Americans. Yet his attacks on the party's donor class and his occasional comments about the rich paying too little in taxes spoke to a different kind of frustration in the movement among its less affluent supporters. That an outsider who broke all the rules of conventional politics could emerge so quickly, could so disrupt his party, and could, for a spell, so dominate its discourse spoke to the crisis within conservatism. So did the turmoil that engulfed House Republicans after John Boehner stepped down as Speaker. Paul Ryan rose to the Speakership only after coming to terms with the party's right-wing rebels. Those who would save their tradition can no longer postpone the day of reckoning.

To end the cycle of disappointment and betrayal, conservatives will have to stop making promises they cannot keep. They will have to accept in practice what many acknowledge in theory: that to be successful and grow, a market economy requires a rather large government and a significant commitment to social insurance. They certainly do not have to embrace all cultural change uncritically, but they will need to accept its inevitability if they wish to preserve what is most valuable in our national tradition. And they would do well to acknowledge that the business of running a competent government in a racially and culturally diverse nation requires tolerance and compromise.

Doing these things is not antithetical to conservatism. On the contrary, these imperatives are in keeping with conservatism's historical mistrust of ideology and with the advice of Edmund Burke, who said that those who aspire to statesmanship must combine "a disposition to preserve and an ability to improve."

This history is thus offered as a plea to American conservatives from the other political shore. For the sake of their own cause but also for the good of the nation they revere, conservatives must recover the idea that extremism in pursuit of their political goals actually is a vice, and remember that moderation in approaching the problems of governing is a virtue.

1

THE AMBIGUOUS HERO

Ronald Reagan as Conservatism's Model and Problem

"You can choose your Reagan."

"I was 13 years old. . . . There was one afternoon my father called me into the room and he said, 'Listen, you've got to watch this. You've got to see what this man is saying.' And there in the TV was this former actor from California. And he looks right at me. He looked right at my father. But he was really speaking to an entire nation. And he said things to us that intuitively made sense. He talked about liberty and freedom. He talked about balanced budgets. He talked about traditional values and personal responsibility. And my father looked at me and said, 'Well, son, we must be Republicans.' And, indeed, we were, and are. That's the party I joined."

On a late June night in Mississippi in 2014, Chris McDaniel offered this warm invocation of the Gipper to open what most thought would be a concession speech. McDaniel had just lost a bitterly contested Republican runoff to incumbent senator Thad Cochran. The result came as a shock to McDaniel and his supporters. Just three weeks earlier, he had run first in the primary, only narrowly missing the majority he needed to avoid a second round. Incumbents forced into runoffs usually lose in Mississippi. Cochran won anyway.

As it happened, it was not a concession speech at all. McDaniel pledged to fight on and contest the outcome—in Reagan's name, of course—though his efforts ultimately failed. The decisive votes against McDaniel in the second round came from African-American Democrats who had crossed into the Republican contest (as they were allowed to under state law) to defend their state's seventy-six-year-old incumbent. "There is something a bit strange, there is something a bit unusual about a Republican primary that's decided by liberal Democrats," McDaniel insisted. "This is not the party of Reagan."

McDaniel had a point. The coalition Cochran put together and the way he did it was anything but orthodox by most conservative standards. McDaniel, a Tea Partier who embodied a kind of libertarian marriage with neo-Confederates, had a fair claim to being the new model of the old Reagan alliance. McDaniel's antigovernment fervor extended to refusing to say whether he would have voted for emergency assistance for his own state after Hurricane Katrina. "That's not an easy vote to cast," he had explained in an interview that came back to haunt him. The summer before, he had delivered the keynote address at an event sponsored by a chapter of the Sons of Confederate Veterans, a group that continues to think the wrong side won the Civil War. "The preservation of liberty and freedom was the motivating factor in the South's decision to fight the Second American Revolution," the group declares on its website. "The tenacity with which Confederate soldiers fought underscored their belief in the rights guaranteed by the Constitution." McDaniel added a strong dose of evangelical Christianity to his appeal. "There is nothing strange at all about standing as people of faith for a country that we built, that we believe in," he had declared in his nonconcession.

By virtually all reasonable standards, Cochran was a staunch Mississippi conservative. But he was also a proud appropriator who worked amicably with Democrats to pass budgets that included plenty of money for projects of local interest that knew no party affiliation. This was his sin, not only in McDaniel's eyes but also in the view of Washington-based antispending groups such as the Club for Growth and FreedomWorks. Both backed McDaniel.

Cochran's campaign, of necessity, turned into a textbook lesson in the contradictions of antispending conservatism. If the ideologues and some of the Washington-based groups disliked Cochran for his relaxed attitude toward the flow of Beltway dollars, many Mississippi Republicans, especially business groups and the politicians who ran local governments, were grateful for his genial approach to federal largesse, particularly in securing the billions that helped rebuild the Gulf Coast communities after Katrina.

"By God's grace, he was chairman of appropriations for two years during Katrina, and it made all the difference in the world," former governor Haley Barbour told me a couple of weeks before the primary. With Cochran slated to head up the Senate Appropriations Committee again if the Republicans took back the Senate, the state's establishment desperately did not want him to retire. "A whole lot of different people said, 'Thad, don't put yourself first. Put Mississippi first. You owe it to us to run again,'" Barbour recounted. When Cochran finally assented, the Barbour organization went to work.

Pause for a moment to consider that a state known for its deep antipathy to Washington—for having, as the Confederate veterans group would insist, a very particular view of "the rights guaranteed by the Constitution" to the states—just happens to get $3.07 back from the federal government for every dollar it sends in. It ranks number one among the states in federal aid as a percentage of state revenue. Big government in Washington might still have been the enemy in Mississippi, but its dollars were as welcome there as in any of the country's most liberal precincts.

The 2014 Republican Senate primary in Mississippi provided a particularly pointed lesson in the tensions and contradictions within contemporary conservatism. Federal spending is an evil, except when the money comes into your own state. African-Americans will be left to the other side, except when a conservative politician needs them. Since the GOP primary electorates are often too conservative to nominate a candidate with wide appeal beyond the Republican base, temporarily borrowing the other side's base is permissible in emergencies. And if you are a Republican, you can declare that whatever you are doing would have been blessed by Ronald Reagan.

Cochran's victory was an ironic tribute to the fiftieth anniversary of Freedom Summer and its drive to secure black voting rights. A Republican establishment initially built on white backlash against civil rights won an internal party contest only with the help of voters whose access to the ballot had been secured by the passage of the 1965 Voting Rights Act, a law that so many whites in Mississippi and in other states of the Deep South had so militantly resisted. Between the primary and the runoff, the *New York Times* concluded, "the increase in turnout was largest in heavily black counties, particularly in the Mississippi Delta." In Jefferson County, where African-Americans represent 85 percent of the population, turnout jumped by 92 percent—the largest increase in the state.

This is what infuriated McDaniel. "Today the conservative movement took a backseat to liberal Democrats in the state of Mississippi," he told his supporters. "In the most conservative state in the Republic this happened. If it can happen here, it can happen anywhere. And that's why we will never stop fighting."

But in truth, *all* sides in the Mississippi showdown saw themselves as fighting for Reagan's legacy. That is how protean it had become. When he had spoken to me before the primary, Barbour had proudly recounted his work as a political aide in Ronald Reagan's White House and insisted on the great philosophical continuity from Reagan to present-day conservatism. Now, as then, conservatives were still committed to "limited government, lower taxes, less spending, balanced budgets, rational regulation, peace through strength, open markets and free trade, tough on crime, strengthen families, welfare reform—that kind of stuff."

"That's the same stuff Reagan was for," Barbour said.

But McDaniel would have stoutly disagreed with something else Barbour told me that day. "In the two-party system," he observed, "purity is the enemy of victory." And there is the rub. Reagan can be seen as the champion of purity, and also as its enemy.

That both Chris McDaniel and Haley Barbour could reasonably claim to be following in Reagan's footsteps speaks to the ambiguous character of the Reagan legacy. There is the Reagan who excited the conservative movement before he became president and the chief executive who could govern in a pragmatic way and accept the limits imposed on him throughout his presidency by a House of Representatives led by Democrats. He campaigned thematically and governed realistically. The Reagan who made his name as Barry Goldwater's most effective advocate in 1964 was different from the Reagan who was governor of California or president of the United States.

When I explored this dilemma one day with Charles Krauthammer, the conservative columnist and Fox News commentator, he cut to the chase. "You can choose your Reagan," he said. Conservatives do it all the time.

Unraveling the riddles of the American right involves dissecting the twin and overlapping legacies of Reagan and Goldwater. I begin with the Reagan Condundrum because he remains the dominant figure of the conservative imagination and was a touchstone for Republican candidates during the 2016 campaign. Wisconsin Governor Scott Walker said he celebrated Reagan's birthday every year with "patriotic songs" and "his favorite foods— macaroni and cheese casserole and red, white and blue jelly beans." Senator Ted Cruz commissioned an oil painting of Reagan at the Brandenberg Gate in Berlin, and it hangs in his Senate office. There was no higher compliment to a candidate than to compare him to Reagan. Thus did conservative writer Paul Kegnor offer an extended essay in the *American Spectator* praising a May 2015 foreign policy speech by Senator Marco Rubio by arguing that he was "starting to sound like Reagan's heir."

Yet it has also become a habit of liberals, especially since the rise of the Tea Party, to say that the Reagan who served as president of the United States would have no chance of winning a Republican nomination and to cite his many apostasies. Jon Perr, a writer for the left-of-center Daily Kos blog, offered an impressive list. Reagan, he pointed out, raised taxes on a number of occasions (after first cutting them). He expanded the size of government. He strongly supported the redistributionist Earned Income Tax Credit. He offered amnesty to undocumented immigrants. He sought to eliminate nuclear weapons. And he approved some protectionist measures on trade.

This line of argument understandably irritates Reagan conservatives. "Those who write that Reagan would not now fit in the party he largely created make the mistake so many do in discussing Reagan," wrote his biographer and admirer Craig Shirley. "They confuse tactics with principles." And, yes, Reagan was also responsible for a steep cut in the top income tax rate— from 70 percent when he took office to 28 percent when he left. He broke the air traffic controllers union, helping set off a long decline in the private sector labor movement. He presided over a major military buildup.

Particularly in his first year in office, he aroused rage among liberals for steep cuts in domestic programs. One episode might serve as a reminder of how progressives felt about Reagan when he was in office: a 1981 Department of Agriculture regulation that declared ketchup a vegetable under the school lunch program. Liberals denounced this absurdity as representative of Reagan's overall approach to programs for the poor. The Gipper, ever the Haley Barbour–style pragmatist, eventually responded to the mockery by withdrawing the rule.

National security conservatives might concede merit to the pragmatic reading of Reagan's domestic record but insist that he was a rock when it came to standing up to the Soviet Union ("Tear down this wall!"). He went to great lengths to restore American military strength. His anticommunist credentials are certainly unassailable and the military spending he supported—totaling $2.8 trillion—is a simple fact. He did, indeed, initiate the Strategic Defense Initiative, popularly known as "Star Wars." And his success in persuading Western European nations to accept Pershing missiles in the early 1980s sent an important signal to the Soviet Union that its efforts to divide the Western alliance would fail. It may well have been the key step in the ultimate unraveling of the Soviet Union.

But viewing Reagan as a military interventionist misreads his record. In a deeply misguided decision, he sent American marines to Beirut, but then promptly withdrew them after 241 in their ranks were killed in a terrorist attack. The record suggests that he learned from this tragedy. He may have armed the Contras, who were fighting to undermine the leftist Sandinista regime in Nicaragua, but he resisted calls from Norman Podhoretz, William F. Buckley Jr., and other Cold Warriors to send troops to Central America. "Those sons of bitches won't be happy until we have 25,000 troops in Managua," Reagan complained to his chief of staff, Ken Duberstein. His more hawkish supporters were disappointed. Podhoretz, a founding neoconservative, grumbled that "in the use of military power, Mr. Reagan was much more restrained" than his loyalists had hoped. Reagan's intervention in Grenada was, to put it gently, a minor engagement—the American military against an army of six hundred. Still, as the writer Peter Beinart noted, Grenada gave him a military victory to brag about, at a very low cost. "Reagan's political genius," Beinart said, "lay in recognizing that what Americans wanted was a president who exorcised the ghost of Vietnam without fighting another Vietnam."

And when Reagan proved to be eager to achieve arms reduction with Soviet leader Mikhail Gorbachev, many conservatives were enraged. George F. Will, the conservative columnist and one of Reagan's most loyal defenders, grumbled that Reagan was "elevating wishful thinking to the status of political philosophy." In the negotiations, Will mourned, the administration had crumpled "like a punctured balloon."

Conservatives will almost always say it was Reagan's arms buildup that effectively bankrupted the Soviet Union and sped its collapse. But a strong case can be made that by dealing so openly and hopefully with Gorbachev, Reagan undercut Kremlin hard-liners and strengthened the forces of glasnost and perestroika. It can be argued, in other words, that the Soviet Union was brought down as much by Reagan the Peacemaker as by Reagan the Warrior.

The ambiguities in Reagan's record are not merely a matter of historical interest. They are vital to today's debates on the right. These "What Would Reagan Do?" moments occur again and again, but they are especially revealing when it comes to foreign policy, where his legacy is most secure. Consider the all-out brawl in the summer of 2014 between Governor Rick Perry and Senator Rand Paul about the Iraq War and the broader issue of when American troops should be deployed. Their whole exchange revolved around the Gipper.

Writing in the *Wall Street Journal,* Paul argued that Reagan was widely misunderstood and his legacy had been promiscuously misused. "Though many claim the mantle of Ronald Reagan on foreign policy, too few look at how he really conducted it," Paul wrote. "The Iraq war is one of the best examples of where we went wrong because we ignored that."

In defending his own caution about sending American forces abroad, Paul cited the doctrine offered by Reagan's defense secretary Caspar Weinberger laying down a very stringent set of tests for military intervention: that "vital national interests" of the United States had to be at stake; that the country would go to battle only "with the clear intention of winning"; that our troops would have to have "clearly defined political and military objectives" and the capacity to accomplish them; and that there must be a "reasonable assurance" of the support of U.S. public opinion and Congress. At the core of the Weinberger Doctrine, Paul said, was the principle that war should be fought only "as a last resort."

The Iraq War, Paul insisted, flunked the Weinberger test. And then he added what turned out to be fighting words: "Like Reagan," he wrote, "I thought we should never be eager to go to war."

Perry, then a contender for the party's 2016 presidential nomination, hit back the next month, charging that Paul had "conveniently omitted Reagan's long internationalist record of leading the world with moral and strategic clarity."

"Unlike the noninterventionists of today," Perry argued on the *Washington Post*'s op-ed page, "Reagan believed that our security and economic prosperity require persistent engagement and leadership abroad." Perry told the more familiar story: "Reagan identified Soviet communism as an existential threat to our national security and Western values, and he confronted this threat in every theater," he wrote. "Today, we count his many actions as critical to the ultimate defeat of the Soviet Union and the freeing of hundreds of millions from tyranny." And then came the swipe: Reagan had resisted those who "promoted accommodation and timidity in the face of Soviet advancement," Perry said, adding, "This, sadly, is the same policy of inaction that Paul advocates today."

Paul did not turn the other cheek. His lengthy counterattack in *Politico* carried the rather unambiguous headline: "Rick Perry Is Dead Wrong." Paul accused Perry (who ended his candidacy in September 2015) of offering "a fictionalized account of my foreign policy so mischaracterizing my views that I wonder if he's even really read any of my policy papers." And on the crucial Reagan point, Paul's Gipper was very different from Perry's Gipper:

Reagan ended the Cold War without going to war with Russia. He achieved
a relative peace with the Soviet Union—the greatest existential threat to the
United States in our history—through strong diplomacy and moral leadership.

Reagan had no easy options either. But he did the best he could with the
hand he was dealt. Some of Reagan's Republican champions today praise his
rhetoric but forget his actions. Reagan was stern, but he wasn't stupid. Reagan
hated war, particularly the specter of nuclear war. Unlike his more hawkish
critics—and there were many—Reagan was always thoughtful and cautious.

The substantive argument behind the name-calling over American intervention will be one of the great divides across the American Right in the coming
years. For a while at least, the more libertarian and anti-interventionist conservatives for whom Paul has become the leading spokesman—they included
many in the Tea Party—shed the inhibitions many of them felt during Bush's
presidency over fully expressing their unhappiness over wars of choice and
nation-building abroad. Indeed, for many conservatives, the Tea Party impulse was itself a reaction against the wars initiated by Bush. "Some of us as
conservatives were concerned about the war [and] how long the war had been
going on," Representative Raúl Labrador, elected to the House in the 2010
Tea Party wave, told me. Labrador said he was initially surprised to find himself agreeing with people well to his left who worried during Bush's second
term about the reappearance of an "imperial presidency" rooted in the sense
that "Bush had gone too far." Vin Weber, a former Republican congressman
from Minnesota who remains one of his party's most influential voices, is an
interventionist. But he, too, sensed a strengthening of isolationist feelings, on
the right and in the country at large. "After the Iraq War and the problems
in Afghanistan, and other things, and terrorism," Weber said, "there is a real
sense that the rest of the world is a place that we don't want to be."

Interventionism—reflected in Perry's orthodox interpretation of
Reaganism—remains a powerful impulse in the party. Polls showed that it
has never stopped being the majority Republican position, and it experienced

a revival in the final years of Obama's term with the rise of the Islamic State and the controversy over the president's negotiations with Iran. Most of the party's presidential aspirants, including Rubio, Chris Christie, Walker, and Jeb Bush, bet on this, for reasons explained by Whit Ayres, a Republican pollster and Rubio booster. "I cannot deny the historical isolationist feeling in America," he told me. "Nor can I deny that there's an increase in the Republican Party of that feeling." But he added: "I still believe that the dominant position in the Republican Party is, as Marco Rubio has said, 'problems don't go away just because we ignore them,' and that we are the only remaining superpower in the world, and that America has a responsibility to lead." Ayres's analysis was vindicated as the campaign progressed. Paul himself made tactical moves toward a more publicly hawkish position when he announced his presidential candidacy in April 2015, but his underlying skepticism of interventionism remained. While his view reflected a strong, if temporarily submerged, current on the right, Paul found himself falling behind his more hawkish rivals—though not Perry, whose campaign crumbled for other reasons.

The divide over how Republicans read Reagan's foreign policy is just one indicator of how unsettled the meaning of Reagan's legacy is. In one sense, it is a sign of Reagan's posthumous political success: everyone on the right wants to identify with him, and he thus plays a prophetic and, one might say, even a scriptural role. "All sides take as settled fact the premise that Reagan revealed the truth to the world in its entirety forever and ever," the liberal writer Jonathan Chait observed archly, "and any revisions to the Party canon must make the case that rival claimants have incorrectly interpreted the Reagan writ."

The argument over Reagan can run in an endless loop. Only if Reagan is entirely abstracted from the movement that created him can he be viewed as a moderate. Yet there can be no denying his pragmatic side. Both in his 1980 campaign and in the White House, he was careful not to push farther than American public opinion would allow. The movement builder, over time, became a politician. Yes, the true believer was always present. Krauthammer cited what might be seen as Reagan's Law—"government is the problem"—and insisted, "You can't get more radically anti–New Deal than that." But he added that Reagan "didn't govern that way, because you can't govern that way in a modern industrial society." Reagan, he said, understood that while the United States was "a center-right country," it was "not a right-wing country."

Is the Reagan who opposed the treaty giving the Panama Canal back to Panama the relevant Reagan? Or was it the Reagan who greeted Soviet leader Mikhail Gorbachev in November 1985 and said, "I bet the hard-liners in both our countries are bleeding when we shake hands"? Who matters most, the Reagan who uncompromisingly cut taxes in 1981, or the Reagan who happily compromised with House Speaker Tip O'Neill and raised social security taxes in 1983 to keep the system solvent? Do we pay attention to the Reagan who made Establishment pragmatist James A. Baker III his chief of staff, or the president who appointed Edwin Meese III, the staunch and long-time conservative, as his attorney general? Are Reagan's social views best understood by his opposition to abortion as president, by his decision to sign an abortion liberalization law as governor of California, or by his 1978 opposition to a California initiative that would have barred gays from teaching in public schools? ("Whatever else it is, homosexuality is not a contagious disease like the measles," Reagan wrote.)

When I spoke with William Kristol, the founder of the *Weekly Standard* magazine that sought to be for neoconservatism what *National Review* had been to conservatism, he hit on the dilemma in mid-thought. Noting that the pre-presidential Reagan had been out of the mainstream on a range of issues, including the Panama Canal treaty signed by Jimmy Carter—Reagan's opposition to it, Kristol said, "was, like, wacky," even to many conservatives—Reagan had managed to make the transition "from being a leader of protest to a plausible, governing conservative."

And then, on reflection, Kristol edited himself and suggested that the real contrast was between the Reagan who got elected and governed, and the Barry Goldwater who lost in a landslide. "Until the Tea Party can transition from being Goldwaterite to Reaganite," he says, "it has a big problem winning."

Yes, when many harder-line conservatives such as Chris McDaniel invoke Reagan, they really mean Goldwater—or, perhaps, Reagan at the moments when he most sounded like Goldwater. Far more than the Gipper, it was Goldwater who changed the trajectory of American politics. And Goldwater, in turn, was the product of a movement a long time in the making.

2

IN THE SHADOW
OF GOLDWATER

It Didn't Start with the Tea Party

"I have little interest in streamlining government or
making it more efficient for I mean to reduce its size."

Journalism, by its nature, focuses on discontinuities. What's new is, by definition, news. And so there was a breathlessness in much of the early coverage
of the Tea Party that treated the movement as an entirely novel form of spontaneous protest. It was said to represent a new populism with all the small-*d*
democratic legitimacy that word conveys.

Put aside that much of the protest was organized and well funded, not
spontaneous, and that what the Tea Party *opposed*—a government active
on behalf of economic equality—was precisely what the original American
populist movement was *for*. The important thing is that the rebellion on
the Republican right during and after George W. Bush's presidency was
not, in any way, philosophically or ideologically innovative. It wasn't new at
all. Most of the ideas it espoused were born in the 1930s and 1940s, as the
historian Kim Phillips-Fein wrote, "in the reaction against the New Deal,"

particularly among the businesspeople who formed the American Liberty League.

The organization's arguments sound stunningly familiar in our age. "You can't recover prosperity," said the chairman of the League's Illinois division, "by seizing the accumulation of the thrifty and distributing it to the thriftless and unlucky." Language about "job creators" and the "47 percent" is nothing new to American politics.

Right-wing ideas developed a deeper hold in the 1950s—in respectable anticommunism and in McCarthyism, in the conspiracy theories spun by the John Birch Society and its friends, and, for some, in fierce resistance to the rising civil rights movement and a liberal Supreme Court. Goldwater and Reagan broadly shared this outlook, although their pronouncements were sunnier and free of crude prejudices.

Rick Perlstein, the left's premier student of the right, was sufficiently bothered by the failure to see the continuities between the right's past and present that he took to the pages of the *Nation* in late 2013 to condemn the eagerness "to depict the Tea Party's brand of reactionary extremism as a new thing." On the contrary, he argued, the far right has been remarkably consistent with itself. To make his point, he cited conservative episodes over a span of seventy years that looked, felt, and sounded exactly like the obsessions and actions of today's right. "There is," he quipped, "little new under the wingnut sun."

Conservatives might not like Perlstein's way of saying it, but most of them agree with his underlying point: Very little of what today's right or radical right says is genuinely novel. Almost all of it was said in the lead-up to Goldwater's 1964 campaign and during the campaign itself. The roots of the politics of 2010 and 2015 reach back to 1964. What needs to be explored is why these old ideas came back to life with such ferocity.

As Perlstein showed in *Before the Storm*, his magisterial account with the well-chosen subtitle *Barry Goldwater and the Unmaking of the American Consensus*, breaking the hold that a consensual, centrist liberalism had on American politics was the central purpose of the Goldwater movement. It's no wonder that the Tea Partiers claim their lineage back to it.

Writers and intellectuals (perhaps because they are writers and intellectuals) pay disproportionate attention to the residents of one particular conservative neighborhood: William F. Buckley Jr. and the proudly dissident band he gathered around *National Review*. (I have often been guilty of this historical sin myself.) Buckley and his friends were determined to liberate the country from New Dealism and Dwight Eisenhower's Modern Republicanism alike, seeing little difference between them. Thus did the magazine proudly announce that it "stands athwart history, yelling stop."

The focus on Buckley and his friends is not entirely misplaced. A movement needs coherent doctrine and sprightly articulation. Buckley's project provided both. Simply by being smart, attractive, articulate, and, eventually, famous, Buckley gave heart to millions of conservatives tired of liberal know-it-alls and an arrogant consensus that regarded them as kooks. And the Buckleyites provided intellectual and at times moral discipline to the right, reading anti-Semites and Birchers out of the movement. (Buckley tried to read Ayn Rand out of the movement as well, but her hold on the libertarian-inclined, including a young Paul Ryan, was never broken.)

National Review also tried hard to resolve the contradictions of a movement that included antigovernment libertarians, traditionalists who put old values and old institutions ahead of the free market, and the robust anticommunists who might oppose small government but wanted the Pentagon to be supplied with as many tax dollars as it needed to roll back Soviet tyranny. The most important political contribution of the magazine was at the theoretical level: the development of what came to be known as "fusionism," the effort of Frank Meyer, *National Review*'s chief ideologist, to harmonize or at least rationalize the diverse strands of conservative thought into a coherent doctrine. He emphasized "two main strands of conservatism," wrote his biographer Kevin Smant: "the belief in order, transcendence, truth and the divine; and the belief that freedom was the highest *political* end, it being the only way for the individual legitimately to choose the truth."

Meyer shared with the traditionalists a belief in an "organic moral order" and in the importance of cultivating "virtue" in citizens. Lovers of liberty often did not appreciate how important a belief in an objective morality was to the task of preserving freedom, he argued. But traditionalists were sometimes too ready to confuse the authority they invested in tradition with the power they were willing to surrender to human rulers—to the state—to promote their idea of virtue. His conclusion: free markets were compatible with virtue and often promoted it, but virtue was the only proper end of freedom. Donald Devine, a conservative political scientist and Reagan administration official, summarized fusionism nicely: it meant "utilizing libertarian means in a conservative society for traditionalist ends."

Fusionism would never fully resolve the tensions within conservatism, and the movement, in our time no less than in Meyer's, would face the constant threat of conflict among its various wings. But as a rough-and-ready intellectual consensus, Meyer's idea was critical to conservatism's progress. It made it easier for competing factions to submerge their disagreements in the larger causes of opposing American liberalism and the more dire threat of communism.

But in understanding the Tea Party's lineage, an attention to the Buckley crowd misses right-wing precincts that were genuinely kooky—and also ignores the extent to which even the Buckley crowd was ready to throw in with the southern segregationists, who were key to building the new political majority they longed to create.

The Buckleyites rose side by side with an extreme right that included the Birch Society and other conspiracy-minded groups, as well as the South's archsegregationists resisting the civil rights push. *National Review* was set up to answer the *New Republic* and the *Nation*, and Buckley sought to bring the conservative cause to television, too. His *Firing Line* was a singularly successful public-affairs television program in which Buckley often debated leading liberals—among them John Kenneth Galbraith, Michael Harrington, and Al Lowenstein—who were eager to match wits with one of the nation's premier intellectual pugilists. Buckley was determined to "correct the sorry situation today where the liberal appears to have a monopoly on sophisticated information."

But people farther to his right had the same idea. In the late 1950s, H. L. Hunt, the Texas oil millionaire, set up the Life Line Foundation, which included a newsletter, television programs, and a book club. Its greatest influence came in its radio program. By the end of 1962, as the scholar Mary Brennan noted, it was being broadcast 342 times a day on roughly 300 radio stations in 42 states and the District of Columbia. There was also Dan Smoot, a former FBI agent turned right-wing pamphleteer and later a John Birch Society leader. He developed a substantial audience, with his radio program at one point reaching 150 stations and 16 million households weekly. Typical Smoot fare was his 1962 book, *The Invisible Government,* about the Council on Foreign Relations and its efforts to create "a one-world socialist system." It sold more than 2 million copies. Smoot believed that the key to political salvation could be found in the country's founding document. "We cannot re-establish Constitutional government and restore our free republic until a decisive number of Americans understand the Constitution and use it as a guide to political action," he said in one of his television broadcasts. "You should do your utmost to remove from public office every official who violates the Constitution's clear meaning if you want to save your own freedom and help restore your republic." Smoot died in 2003 at the age of eighty-nine, and if his words sound remarkably like a Tea Party broadcast, this helps explain why he has developed a modest new following in recent years, thanks to YouTube.

Before there was online fund-raising, there was direct mail. The Goldwater-era conservatives were its pioneers. Perlstein noted that whereas in 1960, 22,000 people made donations to John F. Kennedy's campaign and 44,000 to Richard Nixon's, "over a million gave to Barry Goldwater." The Goldwater mailing list became one of the hottest properties in conservatism, and throughout the 1970s and into the year of Reagan's triumph, direct mail specialists helped build a regiment of conservative organizations. The master of them all was conservative mail impresario Richard Viguerie.

Now in his eighties, Viguerie remains active in Tea Party politics. Direct mail, Viguerie once explained to me, served a double function. Its main purpose, of course, was to raise money. But it also created lines of communication among conservatives unimpeded by mainstream media, and the opportunity to highlight issues that were not on the mainstream's radar. The construction of ideological enclaves, so often bemoaned in the Bush and Obama years as major sources of polarization, is work that began in the 1950s and 1960s.

In our era, conservatives, particularly those associated with Fox News, are well-known for dominating bestseller lists. One week in late July 2014 was revealing: Hillary Clinton's memoir, *Hard Choices,* came in at No. 3 on the *New York Times* bestseller list, but it was one place behind *Blood Feud,* a book attacking her, and just one ahead of *One Nation,* written by Ben Carson, an African-American neurosurgeon who became a conservative hero for challenging President Obama at a White House prayer breakfast. Carson emerged in 2015 as a surprisingly strong GOP presidential contender.

But the proclivity of conservatives to buy movement books is not new. Their sales were simply never measured on the established bestseller lists because the right wing's punchy volumes tended to be paperbacks published by small presses, some of them set up to push out a single book, or self-published, as Smoot's was. The far right had networks of its own. Besides Smoot, other bestselling Birch authors included W. Cleon Skousen, who enjoyed a major revival in the Tea Party years. Skousen's eccentric view of the American founding, *The 5,000 Year Leap*, was a smash hit on Amazon in the early years of the Tea Party when talk show host Glenn Beck put it on the reading list of his one-day course on "The Making of America."

The Goldwater campaign was fueled by (and helped fuel) the sales of such tracts, the most important being *A Choice Not an Echo*. Long before she led the fight against the Equal Rights Amendment, Phyllis Schlafly was a heroine on the right for her self-published 126-page paperback, touted on its cover as "the inside story of how American presidents are chosen." The book's argument would be entirely familiar to today's Tea Party. She explained why the Republicans had consistently been "maneuvered into nominating candidates who did not campaign on the major issues"—meaning the right's issues.

"In each of their losing presidential years," she argued, "a small group of secret kingmakers, using hidden persuaders and psychological warfare techniques, manipulated the Republican National Convention to nominate candidates who would sidestep or suppress the key issues." Their goal was to make certain that "the New Deal–New Frontier foreign policy—in which they have a vested interest" was never "debated, investigated or submitted to voters." Thus was the defeat of the conservative champion Robert A. Taft at convention after convention—by Wendell Willkie, by Thomas E. Dewey (twice), and by Dwight D. Eisenhower—portrayed as a form of serial betrayal. Conservatives have been waging war on one "Republican establishment" or another ever since.

Especially instructive is the conservative columnist Ralph de Toledano's *The Winning Side: The Case for Goldwater Republicanism*, published in 1963. De Toledano shared with Schlafly—and in truth, with the entire right in the early 1960s—the conviction that conservatives had been blocked from the victory that would inevitably have been theirs had they only been given a chance to lead the Republican Party. "The dominant consensus of this country is and always has been of a conservative bent," de Toledano insisted. "This bent has failed to impose itself on the course of events because forces and individuals have deprived the American people of a choice."

Presciently (although not for 1964), de Toledano argued that "the Democratic coalition formed by Franklin Delano Roosevelt has begun to come apart" and that "a new conservative consensus has the potential strength to replace it." De Toledano made the case not only that Goldwater conservatism *should* win, but also that it *would* win—and was a more promising path to a Republican victory than Rockefeller-style liberalism.

The Winning Side was a mixed salad of ideological hope and political number crunching, some of it quite shrewd. At the heart of its argument was a belief that the South was destined to switch its allegiances from the Democrats to the Republicans, provided the Republicans embraced conservatism. "In its economic principles, in its devotion to Constitutional government, and in its abhorrence to any tyranny (whether of majorities or minorities), the South was akin to the Midwest, to the Mountain states, to the American countryside." Without any intended irony, he led off his list of conservative heroes with the Democrat who had been the outstanding political and intellectual defender of slavery before the Civil War. The South, de Toledano wrote, "was as Republican as John C. Calhoun, Robert A. Taft and Barry Goldwater." Abraham Lincoln would have been mystified and, one presumes, rather upset. With the civil rights push in full swing, de Toledano's mention of Calhoun and his reference to a tyranny of "minorities" made clear which side of the civil rights struggle he was on.

The Goldwater campaign and the backlash against Johnson's support for civil rights are often cited as the twin engines of the white southern defection from the Democratic Party. But to understand the deeply embedded role of race in the development of the conservative coalition, it's important to recognize that the Democratic coalition FDR built was *already* confronting severe pressures by the late 1930s around racial questions. As Ira Katznelson recounted in *Fear Itself: The New Deal and the Origins of Our Time,* southern Democrats in Congress were defecting from Roosevelt's program as early as the middle

1930s. Race was not an incidental factor in the new conservatism and the racial reaction so visible in the Obama years was part of a much older story.

To maintain segregation, the South always depended on the support or at least acquiescence of the rest of the country, and since the Civil War, the northern Democratic Party had been its natural ally in maintaining the racial status quo. But the New Deal's progressive economic measures upset the party's internal balances, aggravating the contradictions between the northern liberals who largely staffed the New Deal and southern segregationist voters, particularly southern elites.

Although New Deal programs, because of southern influence, were far less generous to nonwhites than to whites, they nonetheless empowered African-Americans and altered their political loyalties. Under Roosevelt, African-American voters outside the South began switching their allegiances from the party of Lincoln to the party of FDR. (In the South, most of them couldn't vote at all.) As economic change swept the South, millions of African-Americans migrated from southern farms to northern industrial jobs, bolstering the black vote and rendering it even more important to the Democrats in key states such as Michigan, New York, Ohio, Illinois, and Pennsylvania. The electoral interests of northern and southern Democrats began to diverge.

The rise of the labor movement, facilitated by the Wagner Act, further alarmed southern Democrats. As Katznelson points out, CIO unions in particular "cultivated African-American membership" and "quickly became the most racially integrated institutions in American life." Senator James Byrnes of South Carolina, a Democrat who later served as Harry Truman's secretary of state, warned in 1938 that the Democrats had fallen under the influence of "the Negroes of the North" and he complained that the New Deal's policies on unions and wages were undermining southern racial arrangements. He concluded that the South—meaning the white South—had been "deserted by the Democrats."

A reaction to Roosevelt's "court packing" plan to expand the size of the Supreme Court and then the onset of recession were decisive in moving southern Democrats to seek alliances with like-minded Republicans, as the historian James T. Patterson noted. In late 1937, Senator Josiah Bailey, a North Carolina Democrat, joined with leading Republicans to produce a conservative manifesto that criticized high levels of public spending and called for tax cuts, particularly in capital gains, "to free funds for investment and promote the normal flow of savings into profitable and productive use." Here again were old ideas that would be pronounced new in the 1980s and again in our time. The manifesto also attacked organized labor and the CIO's sit-down strikes. "We insist upon constitutional guarantees of the rights of person and of property," the conservatives wrote, "the right of the worker to work, of the owner to possession, and of every man to enjoy in peace the fruits of his labor."

The "conservative coalition" of most congressional Republicans allied with almost all of the southern Democrats was born. From 1938 until Lyndon Johnson's 1964 landslide, it largely controlled Congress, even though it was nominally under Democratic leadership during most of those years.

Southern segregationist intellectuals and activists were already envisioning a new politics around race in the 1940s, as the political scientist Joseph Lowndes showed in *From the New Deal to the New Right*. In 1947, Charles Wallace Collins, a southern lawyer and segregationist, published *Whither Solid South? A Study of Politics and Race Relations*. Wallace, who saw how resistance to racial equality would ally naturally with a broadly conservative view of economics and federal power, might be seen as the first theorist of a southern political realignment. As Lowndes notes, Collins was no crackpot. Born into a planter family in Alabama, he studied law, then Semitic languages and archeology at the University of Chicago, and finally politics and economics at Harvard.

Collins argued that the South was distinct from the rest of the country because "the doctrine of white supremacy is akin to a religious belief" in the region, "rooted in the very fiber of the southern soul." If the Democratic Party had been the South's bulwark before the 1930s, the New Deal had fundamentally altered the party's role, turning it into a friend of concentrated power in Washington and an enemy of states' rights. "Centralization has brought national planning and with it new words, and new meanings to old words."

Collins was particularly upset with the transformation of the word *democracy*. Under the New Deal, it had come to refer to "moral and spiritual values," including racial equality that would be imposed by the state. Therefore, he saw "the whole Negro program" as "infected with the deadly virus of stateism." This was one of the earliest marriage proposals between Confederate ideas and contemporary libertarianism.

Collins, as Lowndes notes, had taken heart in the 1940s from the opposition of many Republicans to the creation of a permanent Fair Employment Practices Commission. If the South opposed the new body in order to maintain white supremacy, many conservative Republicans opposed it for interfering with the prerogatives of private employers. And here is where Collins proved prophetic. In the short run, he said, the South should seek to gain the balance of power between national Democrats and Republicans in the Electoral College. This was the case for what became the States' Rights Democratic Party, the "Dixiecrats" who nominated Senator Strom Thurmond against Democrat Harry Truman and Republican Thomas E. Dewey in 1948 and carried Louisiana, South Carolina, Alabama, and Mississippi. But in the longer run, Collins saw the issues of personal freedom, local self-government, and support for private enterprise as creating the common ground on which Democrats in the South would come together with conservative Republicans everywhere else. This coalition, he predicted, could become "the strongest party in the country, provided that the issue of Negro equality was left to the sponsorship of a new Liberal Party."

It would take sixteen years for Collins's dream to move from the Dixiecrat experiment to the Goldwater realignment. The rise of the civil rights movement would not only tear the Democratic Party apart, but also fracture a Republican Party that had once been the African-Americans' best ally.

By the 1950s, sympathy for the South's resistance to civil rights extended beyond the far edges of the conservative movement. While Buckley was often a defender of tolerance, witnessed by his opposition to anti-Semitism, he and his magazine supported southern resistance to civil rights. Their views were characteristic of a significant body of conservative opionion at the time. The August 24, 1957, issue of *National Review* published "Why the South Must Prevail," an editorial that explicitly defended white supremacy. The editorial asked "whether the White community in the South is entitled to take such measures as are necessary to prevail, politically and culturally, in areas where it does not predominate numerically?" Its response: "The sobering answer is Yes—the White community is so entitled because, for the time being, it is the advanced race."

Buckley took up the argument in his own name in his 1961 book, *Up from Liberalism*, declaring flatly that "yes, there are circumstances in which the minority can lay claim to preeminent political authority, without bringing down on its head the moral opprobrium of just men." Buckley went on:

> In the South, the white community is entitled to put forward a claim to prevail politically because, for the time being anyway, the leaders of American civilization are white—as one would certainly expect given their preternatural advantages of tradition, training and economic status. . . .
>
> A conservative feels sympathy *for* the Southern position which the Liberal, applying his ideological abstractions ruthlessly, cannot feel. If the majority wills what is socially atavistic, then to thwart the majority may be the indicated, though concededly undemocratic, course. It is more important for the community, wherever situated geographically, to affirm and live by civilized standards than to labor at the job of swelling the voting lists.

Buckley suggested that the South could strengthen its case if it applied "voting qualification tests impartially, to black and white." It could then be accused of being undemocratic, but not racially discriminatory—and being undemocratic, in Buckley's eyes, was by no means the worst sin: "The democracy of universal suffrage is not a bad form of government; it is simply not necessarily nor inevitably a good form of government," he once wrote. "Democracy must be justified by its works."

Buckley later said that he and his magazine had been mistaken in opposing civil rights legislation in 1964 and 1965, and he endorsed the idea of a national holiday in honor of Martin Luther King Jr., whom he came to admire. But resistance to civil rights in the name of states' rights and even white supremacy was both mainstream on the right and central to the reorganization of conservatism in the 1960s. It is a key to grasping what would come later. Richard Nixon is credited with successfully executing the "Southern Strategy" in his 1968 and 1972 campaigns, and he did. But that strategy was outlined first by those touting the electoral promise of Goldwaterism before the 1964 campaign.

In the February 12, 1963, issue of *National Review,* William A. Rusher, the magazine's publisher and a leader of the Draft Goldwater movement, offered an article titled "Crossroads for the GOP." It was republished for separate distribution, and Rusher proudly noted in his memoir that it "became one of the most popular reprints ever published by *National Review*." Rusher's opening assumption was that any Republican could carry "the GOP's Midwestern heartland, and such peripheral fiefs as northern New England and certain mountain states, accounting in all to perhaps 140 electoral votes." This proved wildly optimistic in light of Goldwater's actual performance in 1964. But his next point was key: "Goldwater and *Goldwater alone*... can carry enough southern and border states to offset the inevitable Kennedy conquests in the big industrial states of the North and still stand a serious chance of winning election."

Already, then, conservatives were intent on writing off the northeastern states, which had been part of the Republican coalition from Lincoln to Dewey to Eisenhower, and replacing them with a southern bastion. This would have the advantage for conservatives of replacing their northeastern liberal foes inside the GOP with conservative former Dixiecrats who would be their allies. It was a form of political reengineering that would permit the virtual southern takeover of the Republican Party.

In *The Winning Side*, de Toledano offered his own case for the Southern Strategy by way of explaining why Goldwater would be a stronger candidate than New York Governor Nelson Rockefeller. By de Toledano's estimate, Rockefeller would lose to Kennedy in the Electoral College, 371–153. But by sweeping most of the Deep South, Goldwater would beat Kennedy, 284–248. (For some reason, he didn't call the state of Delaware, leaving out three electoral votes.) De Toledano's final numbers bore no relationship to the outcome of the Johnson-Goldwater election, yet his map (while slightly too optimistic for Republicans in some places and too pessimistic in the South and border states) was prophetic—and remarkably close to the final outcome of the 2004 election, when George W. Bush defeated John Kerry, 286–251. The Goldwater dreamers were on to something.

★

Goldwater and Reagan, both as historical figures and as heroic ideological symbols, must be seen in the context of the politics roiling the right in the

1960s, a time when both were viewed in much the same way as today's Tea Partiers are. But where the Tea Party has been fighting an Establishment that is essentially conservative, the Goldwaterites were pushing the Republican Party away from an Establishment that reflected the liberalism of Nelson Rockefeller and the moderate brand of conservatism preached by Dwight Eisenhower.

The central goal of the new conservative movement was preventing Eisenhower's ideology, which he came to label as "Modern Republicanism," from becoming the party's dominant disposition. Buckley was particularly scornful of Ike. "It has been the dominating ambition of Eisenhower's Modern Republicanism to govern in such a fashion as to more or less please more or less everybody," Buckley said. "Such governments must shrink from principle: because principles have edges, principles cut; and blood is drawn, and people get hurt. And who would hurt anyone in an age of modulation?" The "Eisenhower program," Buckley went on, is "an attitude, which goes by the name of a program, undirected by principle, unchained to any coherent idea as to the nature of man and society." Notice that for Buckley, "modulation" was a grave sin.

As for Rockefeller, he was beyond the philosophical pale and uninhibited in taking the fight to the internal enemy. He condemned those he labeled as "extremist groups, carefully organized, well-financed, and operated through the tactics of ruthless, roughshod intimidation." Republicans, he said, were "in real danger of subversion by a radical, well-financed and disciplined minority." If he mentioned "well-financed" twice, it wasn't just because his own wealth made him conscious of such things. Then, like now, the right had plenty of money.

The Goldwater who later supported the Panama Canal treaty that Reagan opposed during Jimmy Carter's presidency—and who came to speak in moderate tones about abortion and homosexuality—was not the Goldwater who excited Schlafly and Rusher, de Toledano, Buckley, and Thurmond. The Goldwater who set off a convulsion in the Republican Party laid out the new conservative creed boldly—and, for a future presidential candidate, recklessly—in his 1960 book, *The Conscience of a Conservative*. Ghostwritten by Brent Bozell, Buckley's brother-in-law, it would make good reading at any Tea Party gathering in 2015. Indeed, *The Conscience of a Conservative* provided the movement with its talking points and principles for the next half century. To read it now is to realize how much of the intellectual arsenal of today's Tea Party and how many lines from the campaign speeches of the typical conservative candidate in 1994 or 2016 were provided by Goldwater.

Here was the heart of Goldwaterism:

I have little interest in streamlining government or making it more efficient for I mean to reduce its size. I do not undertake to promote welfare for I propose to extend freedom. My aim is not to pass laws, but to repeal them. It is not to inaugurate new programs but to cancel old ones that do violence to the Constitution, or that have failed in their purpose, or that impose on the people an unwarranted financial burden.

He backed this up with plenty of specifics—enough to cause him no end of trouble when he faced LBJ in 1964. Goldwater called for an end to the farm program, an end to grants-in-aid to states (he called them "a mixture of blackmail and bribery"), an end to the graduated income tax (it was, he said, "repugnant to my notions of justice"), and steep and regular budget cuts ("The root evil is that government is engaged in activities in which it has no legitimate business"). On foreign policy, the goal was victory over communism without any fear of risking war. "A craven fear of death is entering the American consciousness," he wrote. He insisted that Americans "must affirm the contrary view"—begging the question of what exactly was the "contrary view" of fearing death. The cornerstone of our foreign policy, he said, should be this: "that we would rather die than lose our freedom." This meant ridding ourselves of our terror over nuclear war, so he proposed to "perfect a variety of small, clean nuclear weapons" that could be used on a battlefield.

The book was a sensation—helped along by wealthy businessmen, including members of the board of the John Birch Society. Perlstein notes that just as the book was being readied for public sale, Bozell dropped by a Birch Society board meeting to encourage bulk sales. Fred Koch, father of the brothers who would become famous as bankrollers of the Tea Party and other right-wing and libertarian causes, immediately ordered 2,500 copies "to be circulated to every library, newspaper and VIP in Kansas."

To ignore how genuinely and fearlessly radical Goldwater was, for his time and for ours, is to miss the whole reason he inspired such passion, why he created a vast movement—and why he suffered such a crushing defeat in 1964.

Decades before "compassionate conservatism" made its appearance, Goldwater objected to the idea that there was anything wrong with conservatism that required corrective adjectives or nouns. In the first paragraph of the book's first chapter, he specifically targeted statements by his party's two most important leaders: the incumbent president, and the vice president who would be its presidential candidate the year the book was published:

> I have been much concerned that so many people today with Conservative instincts feel compelled to apologize for them. Or if not to apologize directly, to qualify their commitment in a way that amounts to breast-beating. "Republican candidates," Vice President Nixon has said, "should be economic conservatives, but conservatives with a heart." President Eisenhower announced during his first term, "I am a conservative when it comes to economic problems but a liberal when it comes to human problems." Still other Republican leaders have insisted on calling themselves "progressive" Conservatives. These formulations are tantamount to an admission that Conservatism is a narrow, mechanistic, *economic* theory that may work very well as a bookkeepers' guide, but cannot be relied upon as a comprehensive political philosophy.

Goldwater begged to differ.

Of the Supreme Court's 1954 school desegregation decision in *Brown v. Board of Education,* he declared: "I am firmly convinced not only that integrated schools are not required but that the Constitution does not permit any interference whatsoever by the Federal government in the field of education." While he said he believed it "both wise and just for negro children to attend the same schools as whites," he added: "I am not prepared to impose that judgment of mine on the people of Mississippi or South Carolina, or to tell them what methods should be adopted and what pace should be kept in striving for that goal." The white voters of Mississippi and South Carolina would later return his graciousness.

Other themes that would, again and again, be touted as new departures in conservatism were already there in Goldwater's canonical book. In the 1990s and once more in the Tea Party years, the right would invoke the Tenth Amendment as a broad mandate to dismantle the federal programs and agencies that had proliferated since the Progressive Era. The amendment reads: "The powers not delegated to the United States by the Constitution, nor prohibited by it to the states, are reserved to the States respectively, or to the people." For Goldwater, its mandate was unmistakable. The Tenth Amendment, he said, was "a prohibitory rule of law."

"Nothing could so far advance the cause of freedom as for state officials throughout the land to assert their rightful claims to lost state power," he wrote, "and for the federal government to withdraw promptly and totally from every jurisdiction which the Constitution reserves to the states."

If the habit of labeling Barack Obama a "socialist" seemed bizarrely inappropriate in light of the roaring comeback of capitalism and stock market prices on his watch, seeing all liberals as "socialists," in fact if not in name, was central to Goldwater's argument. He is at pains in *Conscience* to argue that while socialists had acknowledged "the bankruptcy of doctrinaire Marxism" and of direct government ownership of "productive property," their new approach was actually more insidious because it could prove to be more effective.

"The collectivists have not abandoned their ultimate goal—to subordinate the individual to the State—but their strategy has changed," he wrote. "They have learned that Socialism can be achieved through Welfarism quite as well as through Nationalization." Goldwater added: "Socialism-through-Welfarism poses a far greater danger to freedom than Socialism-through-Nationalization precisely because it *is* more difficult to combat."

Decades later, conservatives would warn against the Clinton and Obama plans to expand the federal government's role in health insurance because they feared these programs would become popular and entrenched—precisely what happened with Medicare, which both Goldwater and Reagan stoutly opposed in the 1960s.

One mark of how today's American conservatism has reverted back to Goldwaterism is the contrast between two views of *Conscience*, separated by twenty-five years, offered by George F. Will, perhaps the most influential conservative columnist of his generation. Will's 2007 introduction to a new edition of Goldwater's book published by Princeton University Press was almost entirely laudatory. "He knew that popular government rests on public opinion, which is shiftable sand," Will wrote of Goldwater. "With this book, and with his public career that vivified the principles herein, he shifted a lot of sand."

"Goldwater," Will declared, "lost 44 states but won the future."

But in a 1982 essay, Will took sharp issue with aspects of Goldwater's approach, singling out a passage in *Conscience* laying out a conservative ideology that was, on principle, unresponsive to social and economic changes. "The laws of God, and of nature, have no dateline," Goldwater wrote. "The principles on which the Conservative political position is based have been established by a process that has nothing to do with the social, economic and political landscape that changes from decade to decade and century to century."

To which Will replied: "'Nothing'? Surely most conservatives would insist that conservatism has everything to do with prudent accommodation to perpetually changing social, economic and political landscapes, and that the essence of unconservative approaches to politics is the attempt to apply fixed doctrine to a world forever in flux."

Will questioned Goldwater's assertion that conservatism's overriding concern "will always be: *Are we maximizing freedom?*" No, Will argued, "the distinguishing virtue of the conservative mind is suspicion of politics organized around one single overriding concern." And he criticized those "who fancy themselves conservatives and who cherish the cozy purity of the 'movement' (as they understand it) more than they desire influence and responsibility."

The differences between the two essays reflected a movement in Will's own thinking over the years from a communitarian and traditionalist brand of conservatism to a much more robust libertarianism. But the shift was also representative of changes within conservatism itself. If Bill Buckley gave the world a book called *Up from Liberalism*, a conservative writing at the end of the Bush years or during Obama's term might well pick the title *Back to Goldwaterism*.

In 1964, at least, Goldwaterism was anything but popular. Goldwater's pronouncements in *Conscience* and many of the other positions he took—he called for privatizing Social Security and said of Medicare, "Where in the Constitution is the federal government given the right to become a Federal doctor?"—gave Lyndon Johnson and the Democrats all the ammunition they would need to win one of the great landslides in American history. For many conservatives it was an instructive experience, simultaneously dispiriting and exhilarating. Vin Weber, who would be elected to Congress in 1980 at the age of twenty-eight and was one of Newt Gingrich's closest allies, was captivated by Goldwater and jokes that it was a sign of "a dysfunctional childhood that I formed a teenage Republican club when I was 11 years old." He read Goldwater's books and campaigned hard for him, but also learned the limits of his hero's appeal, even within his loyally Republican family. When he tried to get his great-aunts to put Goldwater signs in their yards, they were not enthusiastic. "Well, we'll put something out that says 'Republican,' but not 'Goldwater,'" they told him. Why? "He says that he would cut Social Security," they explained. Weber calls it his earliest lesson about "the perils that conservatives face if they really produce an undistilled conservative ideology."

The surge rightward that de Toledano and Rusher had predicted did not materialize. On the contrary, the surge went the other way. Goldwater's 27,177,838 votes reflected a loss of nearly 7 million ballots from Richard Nixon's total of 34,106, 671 four years earlier. The complete collapse of the Republican vote in New England and the Northeast was beyond anything imagined even by conservatives who had been prepared to write off those regions. Vermont and Maine, two of the most loyally Republican states since the party's formation in 1854—only they had held out against Franklin Roosevelt's 1936 landslide—were indicative of the mass exodus of moderate Republicans. In Vermont, Nixon won 98,131 votes, 59 percent. Four years later, Goldwater won just 54,942 votes, 34 percent. The Republican story was even worse in Maine, where the GOP tally went from 240,608 and 57 percent for Nixon to 118,701 and 31 percent for Goldwater. More than half of the Republican vote in Maine disappeared. There were steep drops all across the Northeast and Midwest. In the rest of the country, Goldwater salvaged only his home state of Arizona—barely, by a single percentage point.

Republicans were decimated in Congress, dropping from 176 to 140 seats in the House, and from an already paltry 34 seats in the Senate to 32. No wonder George F. Gilder and Bruce K. Chapman, two young progressive Republicans (they would later become Reaganites), titled their book on the 1964 election *The Party That Lost Its Head*.

But there was one consolation: the Deep South delivered for Goldwater, just as his strategists had predicted. Georgia voted Republican for the first time in its history; Alabama, Mississippi, and South Carolina did so for the first time since Reconstruction; Louisiana, which had voted for Eisenhower in 1956, voted Republican again. And these still overwhelmingly white electorates—the Voting Rights Act was not to pass until the next year—gave Goldwater overwhelming majorities: 87 percent in Mississippi, 70 percent in Alabama, 59 percent in South Carolina, 57 percent in Louisiana. Only in Georgia, where Goldwater won 54 percent, did LBJ come close—and not that close.

Few at the time realized that the Goldwater rout would be the New Deal coalition's last hurrah. Just four years later, Richard Nixon would take the White House, facing a Democratic Party torn left and right by the Vietnam War and civil rights.

For the conservative movement—and for the long-term trajectory of American politics—the most important things that happened in 1964 were, with a single exception, not obvious to anyone except the conservatives.

The exception was the decisive southern realignment, too big for anyone to miss. Here Rusher's 1963 *National Review* article was largely on target. He had asked whether the GOP would be best served by "turning its back on the new, conservative and increasingly Republican South and gumming blintzes with Nelson Rockefeller" or "by nominating a candidate who—win or lose—will galvanize the party in a vast new area, carry fresh scores and perhaps hundreds of Southern Republicans to unprecedented local victories, and lay the foundations for a truly national Republican Party, ready to fight and win in 1968 and all the years beyond?" He wanted them to skip the blintzes. They did, and reaped their southern dividend.

Turning the interplay between morality, race, and crime into political capital was another contribution of the 1964 Goldwater campaign to the

American right. In Salt Lake City on October 10, Goldwater gave the speech that won him an unambiguous *New York Times* headline: GOLDWATER HITS U.S. MORAL "ROT."

"With your help and with God's blessing," Goldwater declared, "I pledge my every effort to a reconstruction of reverence and moral strength, those great pillars of human happiness in our land." Rehearsing themes that would be heard from conservatives for the next half century, Goldwater condemned the U.S. Supreme Court for its ban on prescribed prayer in public schools—and the Democrats for failing to mention God in their platform. "You will search in vain for reference to God or religion in the Democratic platform," he said. "This is a matter of even greater regret, when we realize that this platform, with its utter disregard of God, was written to the exact specifications of Lyndon Johnson." Exactly the same issue would be raised against the Democratic Party's draft platform in 2012. After an outcry, President Obama's operatives got the convention to put God into the document before it was adopted.

Calling for a constitutional amendment to overturn the Supreme Court decisions, Goldwater said that "nothing is more tragic than to speak of drift and decay in your native land." Crime and what he called the "erosion of the honor and dignity of our nation and of the individuals who compose it" were caused by the "rot and decay" in the nation's moral fiber and by "something basic and dangerous" that was "eating away at the morality, dignity and re-spect of our citizens, old as well as young, high as well as low." He condemned the "recent wave of rioting"—"much of it of a racial character," as the *Times* diplomatically noted—and concluded: "My fellow Americans, is this the time in our nation's history for our Federal Government to ban [the] Almighty?"

The Goldwater campaign's most extraordinary contribution to the politics of morality and race blew up in its face. Goldwater had authorized two of his lieutenants, Russ Walton and F. Clifton White—the brilliant architect of the original Draft Goldwater movement—to produce a half-hour documentary to highlight what he called the "morality issue." What they came up with by late October was at once crude and sophisticated, appalling in its appeal to base instincts and far ahead of its time as a video production destined to stir strong emotions. They called it "Choice."

Right from the start, viewers knew they were watching something different. It might have been called "postmodern" if the term had been popular at the time. The first several minutes of the film is all quick cuts with a jazz track appropriate for a strip club. "Choice" opens with images of a reckless, speeding Lincoln Continental careening down a road, and the film keeps coming back to the car. It was intended to symbolize Lyndon B. Johnson's power-hungry carelessness, and lest there be any doubts, at one point an empty Pearl beer can flies out of its wondows. It was a reference most viewers probably got, since Johnson had received some very bad publicity for an episode in March during which he led journalists on a 90-mph tour of his ranch, sipping a Pearl beer as he went. When *Time* magazine published an account of the episode, the historian Robert Dallek noted, it "strengthened the impression of him as a Texas wheeler-dealer who played fast and loose with the rules and gave less thought to the national well being . . . than to his own self-indulgence."

National self-indulgence was the theme that "Choice" drove home again and again in black-and-white. It was soft porn as politics, with rapid-fire cinematography showing partiers doing the twist, many of them pretty women, occasionally in bikinis, sometimes half naked, with lots of shots of gyrating bottoms. There are cuts to a criminal resisting arrest and to a civil rights protest. Back and forth the images go, portraying a country that, in the eyes of God-fearing (and white) Americans at least, is obviously falling apart. Then the scene changes to images of patriotic comfort: hundreds of very cute boys and girls reciting the Pledge of Allegiance, shots of the Statue of Liberty and the Constitution, and finally an announcer who gets to the point.

"Now there are two Americas," the actor Raymond Massey intones off-camera. "One is words like *allegiance* and *republic*. This America is an ideal, a dream. The other America is no longer a dream but a nightmare. Our streets are not safe. Immorality begins to flourish. Violence pits American against American. We don't want this."

And on and on it goes, rehearsing themes that would become part of the conservative campaign canon for the next generation. Always there was the contrast between the old, rugged Christian America and the dissolute, undisciplined nation that was coming to be. "Brave men passed on a revolutionary code of justice, morality and freedom. . . . Virgin land—they cut it, built it, marked it with a Cross."

But suddenly "the bottom began to fall out across America." Over scenes of black rioters, the announcer speaks of "demoralization, chaos." And: "Over eight short months, there are more riots in the United States than in the last eight years." The country was threatened with "mobocracy"—and the courts were siding with the lawbreakers. "By new laws, it is not the lawbreaker who is handcuffed. It is the police." Thus: "Justice becomes a sick joke."

The outcry against "Choice" was such that Goldwater, who didn't see the film before it went out, wound up denouncing his own campaign's production as "sick" and "racist." The ad and the way it was handled hurt Goldwater in 1964. But a template was created. "Choice" was a preview of coming political attractions. Almost all of its themes would become a permanent part of conservative demonology—and a resource for the makers of countless thirty-second campaign spots for decades to come.

The most consequential moment of the Goldwater campaign had absolutely no impact on the outcome. It was an event that the gifted journalist Theodore H. White didn't even mention in *The Making of the President, 1964*, the second volume of his popular and innovative series of campaign books. Goldwater's key moneymen had amassed a large sum in a separate campaign account called "TV for Goldwater-Miller." They insisted, against the wishes of the Goldwater hierarchy, that some of the money be used to put an actor named Ronald Reagan on national television for half an hour, offering what had become known in right-wing circles as "The Speech." And since they controlled the cash, they got their wish.

Even before Reagan had opened his mouth, an important milestone had been reached. The TV account was flush in part because some of the long-form ads it sponsored closed with an appeal for donations. The Goldwater faithful were eager to send their checks to a post office box in Los Angeles. It was the beginning of the small-donor world. But it was something else as well: long before the campaign money system was first reformed and then deregulated by the Supreme Court, long before the age of the Super PACs and superdonors, Goldwater's rich business backers were in a position to insist that they have their way. The era of the campaign within a campaign had begun.

It is in no way an exaggeration to say that Reagan's speech, titled "A Time for Choosing," changed the course of history. When Ronald Reagan appeared in conservative living rooms on the night of Tuesday, October 27, 1964, a week before Goldwater's coming rout, millions in their ranks realized that they had found the leader who would pick up where Goldwater left off—and could deliver their message far more powerfully than the man they were about to vote for.

It is unlikely that the speech changed many minds about the election, but it did present the conservative vision in what later became familiar as the classic Reagan style. There was always a concreteness to Reagan's rhetoric, and he was always trying to advance an argument. He blended the telling (if often misleading) statistic with the cheerful quip and the homely parable.

"Well," he said, deploying his favorite word to signal his informality, "the trouble with our liberal friends is not that they're ignorant; it's just that they know so much that isn't so."

"Actually," he said at another point, "a government bureau is the nearest thing to eternal life we'll ever see on this earth."

These were Reagan classics. But he also pioneered many arguments—about government spending and government power—that the right would use into the present day. "Welfare spending," he said, is "10 times greater than in the dark depths of the Depression. We're spending 45 billion dollars on welfare. Now do a little arithmetic, and you'll find that if we divided the 45 billion dollars up equally among those 9 million poor families, we'd be able to give each family 4,600 dollars a year. And this added to their present income should eliminate poverty.

"Direct aid to the poor, however, is only running only about 600 dollars per family," he added, and then offered the sort of light little dig that became his trademark: "It would seem that someplace there must be some overhead." Statistics of this sort (arresting but also misleading because they lumped so many different forms of spending together) would be cited again and again by critics of the welfare state—right on through to Paul Ryan in the Obama years.

Reagan's criticisms of Social Security would be heard again when George W. Bush pressed—unsuccessfully—to privatize part of the program. "A young man, 21 years of age, working at an average salary—his Social Security contribution would, in the open market, buy him an insurance policy that would guarantee 220 dollars a month at age 65," Reagan said. "The government promises 127. He could live it up until he's 31 and then take out a policy that would pay more than Social Security."

"A Time for Choosing" is largely Reagan speaking to the conservative faithful, yet there were glimpses of how he would later move the country as a whole by putting the rhetoric of the New Deal with which he was so familiar to work on behalf of its unraveling.

His warnings against the onset of socialism under the name of liberalism were clear enough. "Last February 19th at the University of Minnesota, Norman Thomas, six-times candidate for President on the Socialist Party ticket, said, 'If Barry Goldwater became President, he would stop the advance of socialism in the United States.'" And then the clincher: "I think that's exactly what he will do." Barack Obama was not the first Democrat to be accused of socialism.

There was Reagan the Warrior, echoing *The Conscience of a Conservative* by putting life in second place behind liberty, but in terms utterly accessible to a broad audience. "You and I know and do not believe that life is so dear and peace so sweet as to be purchased at the price of chains and slavery," he said, dismissing those who believe that "nothing in life is worth dying for" and asking if Moses should "have told the children of Israel to live in slavery under the pharaohs."

"Should Christ have refused the cross?" he went on. "Should the patriots at Concord Bridge have thrown down their guns and refused to fire the shot heard 'round the world? The martyrs of history were not fools, and our honored dead who gave their lives to stop the advance of the Nazis didn't die in vain."

He closed with an echo of FDR, almost shocking in the context of the rhetorical war on his legacy that Reagan had just waged. "You and I," he declared, "have a rendezvous with destiny." And then the formulation that would serve him well for the next two decades: "We'll preserve for our children this, the last best hope of man on earth, or we'll sentence them to take the last step into a thousand years of darkness."

Reagan, history would show, made his career with that evening's broadcast. But in its time, "The Speech" was a sermon of affirmation for the faithful, not a closing argument that would assuage widespread doubts about Goldwater. Reagan lifted himself up, but there was nothing he could do for his candidate.

★

Goldwater's defeat was so comprehensive that the smart punditry of the time assumed the right wing was buried for good. "No modern precedent exists for the revival of a party so badly defeated, so intensely discredited, and so essentially split as the Republican Party is today," Gilder and Chapman wrote, reflecting a widespread view.

In light of the polemics around race and politics during the Obama years, it should be noted that in the more progressive regions of the party, loud cries of alarm were raised at the prospect of the GOP becoming the party of southern reaction. In 1966, Edward W. Brooke, the forty-seven-year old Republican attorney general of Massachusetts, published *The Challenge of Change,* a liberal Republican manifesto. He was direct about the dangers of a white southern takeover of the party:

> Personally, I would be deeply discouraged were the Republican Party to alter its position in order to accommodate itself to the attitudes of the traditional deep South. For that would mean a realignment of all of our thinking, a rejection of the better part of Republican ideals and tradition. Republicanism oriented toward segregation and racism would have nothing in common with the origins and history of the party. Still—the argument goes—it *would* have a permanent base of political support, and we cannot afford to ignore practical political considerations in favor of our personal penchants.

The argument was, indeed, personal for Brooke, who would go on that year to become the first African-American to be popularly elected to the United States Senate. In his book, Brooke challenged the Southern Strategy on practical as well as moral grounds. The conservative southern votes the GOP right was seeking, he argued, would prove to be "fool's gold" because an appeal to the Old South would eventually hurt Republicans in the region's rising (and moderate) metropolitan areas. Brooke's argument would not prevail, but it would finally win some vindication in 2008 when the metropolitan areas of Virginia, Florida, and North Carolina tilted those states toward the country's first African-American president.

Theodore H. White, the master chronicler of presidential campaigns, used a down-to-earth metaphor to describe the "desperate condition" of the party:

> Someone had said that an American political party is so low-grade a zoological organism that, like a worm, if it is chopped in two, one or the other half can wriggle away and thereafter regenerate itself. In 1964 the Republican Party has indeed chopped itself in two—yet in all the months since then, to the day of this writing, no one can tell whether the two halves can sew themselves together, or whether enough vitality remains, in one or the other half, to find a direction in which they can invite the American people to move.

Yet White acknowledged that it was hard to know which aspects of the election might "intrigue future storytellers." He added that "looking back, they might find in the election of 1964 the seed-names of some entirely new era." Reagan, of course would be most important of those, but countless young conservatives—Vin Weber and George Will (twenty-three years old that year) among them—would be inspired by a glorious defeat that would change history and provide the right with templates it would use for the next half century.

The era saw the first start-ups in creating alternative means of communication for conservatives—through books, broadcasts, and mail. The core ideas laid out in Goldwater's short book would mark the movement, too: ideas about liberalism as a path to socialism, about free markets and individual liberty, about the need for militancy against the communist threat. The political power of white backlash first became obvious in 1964, as Brooke feared it would, and the Republican Party began the long transition that would make it the champion of a new Solid South. The paranoid style of the farther reaches of the right and the popularity of conspiracy theories would endure, as well. Republicans and the broader conservative movement would continue to be torn, as the GOP was at the 1964 convention, between their obligations to resist extremism and the temptation to harness the political energy of the far right. "The future of the Birch Society and the radical right will very largely be shaped by the way business, conservatives, and the Republican Party police the boundaries of their movement," Alan F. Westin, a Columbia University professor, wrote in 1962. Those boundaries were to become quite porous with the rise of the Tea Party.

But Goldwater's experience was also a cautionary tale, not only for Republican politicians but also for conservatives themselves, as the eleven-year-old Vin Weber had noticed. It was not possible to ride roughshod rhetorically over government programs that were firmly rooted in American life. In this sense, New Deal liberals had become the party of conservatism, measured as the preservation of a status quo that included many benefits from government. Goldwater had characterized farm programs as a "mess of oppression"—and he was trounced in traditionally Republican farm states. As White put it, "Forced to choose, the American farmer went along with what government had given him." The elderly, as Vin Weber's great-aunts had taught him, did not welcome a form of "economic freedom" that would leave them without Social Security. And in a nuclear world, Americans were uneasy with a politician who spoke of the utility of smaller nuclear weapons and was so quick to say "that we would rather die than lose our freedom." In a pinch, most Americans might well believe that. But it was a choice they preferred to avoid.

And so conservatives would go through a long two-steps-forward, one-step-back period. They would hold to Goldwater's creed but learn from his mistakes. They might compromise a bit, here and there. The compromises would never sit quite right with many of the rank and file and would, over time, feed a new sense of disappointment. But the conservatives were also realists, and did not want to reproduce Goldwater-size margins of defeat, election after election.

Workaday Republican politicians recalibrated. They came to accept that conservative activists were now an important part of their party even as the party regulars worked to prevent the right-wing enthusiasts from pushing the party toward the father shoals of unelectability.

The two politicians who learned these lessons best—from very different starting points—were Richard Nixon and Ronald Reagan.

Nixon, once an Eisenhower-style Modern Republican, could count votes. He knew that conservatives could block his last chance at the presidency, and he moved shrewdly to co-opt them where he could and to defeat them where he had to. He also understood that white southern votes were up for grabs, and he intended to make them his.

Reagan had an ideologue's faith but a practical temperament. He would always be the movement's hero, but he would not let the movement dictate his choices, either over how to reach power or on what to do once he secured it.

In succession, Nixon and Reagan would seek practical ways of bringing to life the conservative majority that de Toledano, Rusher, and the South's Charles Wallace Collins insisted was there for the creation. Both of them, Nixon especially, would also leave many of the conservatives' dreams unfulfilled.

3

FROM RADICALISM
TO GOVERNING

How Nixon Failed Conservatives, Reagan Thrilled
Them—and Then Left Them Hanging

"Government hasn't been radically rolled back. The Reagan
gains are pretty evanescent from a certain point of view."

If Barry Goldwater's campaign began the transformation of the Republican
Party and American conservatism, its short-term effects were catastrophic
for scores of Republican politicians, who went down to defeat in the LBJ
wave. American was clearly not yet ready for the new conservatism. But 1964
was a very good year for Richard Nixon. He was the one Republican who
figured out precisely where to position himself in relation both to the new
conservative movement and to the older middle-of-the-road part of his party
that would be searching for a savior four years later. Nineteen sixty-four was
also the breakthrough year for Ronald Reagan. For many conservatives, the
eventual disappointments of the Nixon years came as no great surprise. Those
of the Reagan era did, which is why they try to overlook them.

Richard Nixon's 1968 victory and, even more, his 1972 landslide were the first harbingers of what his lieutenants labeled, quite simply, "the New Majority." Since Republicans won five of the six presidential elections from 1968 to 1988, Nixon's partisans were not deluded in thinking they created something new. A brilliant young Nixon campaign aide named Kevin Phillips assembled all the numbers, charts, and maps to make the case for what was coming in *The Emerging Republican Majority,* published a year after Nixon's victory. It was shrewd and persuasive—and it petrified Democrats.

Still, Nixon's "new majority" never extended to Congress, which remained under Democratic control throughout his time in office. Indeed, after Nixon was forced from power by Watergate, Democrats vastly enhanced their congressional dominance in the 1974 election. The "Watergate babies" elected that year were to help Democrats hang on to the House for another two decades.

Certainly Ronald Reagan's two triumphs, followed by the election of his vice president, George H. W. Bush, in 1988, were seen as a mark of the permanence of what came to be known as the Reagan Coalition. Reagan picked up the party from the wreckage of Watergate and the narrow defeat of President Gerald Ford by Jimmy Carter in 1976. He helped crack the Democrats' twenty-six-year lock on control of the U.S. Senate in 1980, when the Republicans picked up twelve seats. Eventually, after the 2000 election, George W. Bush would become the first Republican president since 1952 to preside over a Congress in which both houses were controlled by Republicans.

There are two other moments when hopes for Republican dominance seemed, for the short term, justified. Newt Gingrich's Republican Revolution of 1994 deserves to be seen as the most durable of all the GOP's breakthroughs. Until Gingrich, Democrats controlled the House for forty consecutive years—and, more astoundingly, for 58 of the 62 years since FDR's 1932 victory. Reestablishing competitiveness in the contest for control of the House is an enduring achievement.

And there was one promise of a new Republican era that differed from all the others. It anticipated the GOP's long-term success *not* as a victory for the right or center-right but as a triumph that would be earned by way of a journey down the middle of the road. During Dwight Eisenhower's presidency, Arthur Larson, one of Ike's advisers, coined the term "Modern Republicanism" to codify what he saw as Ike's underlying philosophy of moderation. Essentially, Larson wanted the party to do over the long term what Eisenhower had done in office: to come to terms with the New Deal and the welfare state—to support "as much government as is necessary," as Larson put it, "but not enough to stifle the normal motivations of private enterprise."

Had Richard Nixon defeated John F. Kennedy in 1960, he might well have turned Modern Republicanism—the very approach that Buckley, Goldwater, and their conservative allies loathed—into his governing philosophy. Nixon, after all, waited a long time before he identified himself as a conservative, and was never fully comfortable doing so. Chris Matthews's joint biography of Kennedy and Nixon reminds us that when the two were first elected to Congress in 1946, it was Kennedy who ran as the "fighting conservative" while Nixon proclaimed his allegiance to "practical liberalism."

No one talks much about "Modern Republicanism" anymore, yet it may have been the great missed opportunity of American politics.

Still, 1960 was a consensual time and 1968 was not. The Nixon who had been a supporter of civil rights became the Nixon of law and order, pursuing the votes of southern whites and northern working-class voters, particularly Catholics in the big cities. The very structure of the 1968 contest made Nixon the man in the middle—between the liberalism of Hubert Humphrey, already weakened by his association with LBJ and the increasingly unpopular Vietnam War, and George Wallace, the outspoken segregationist Alabama governor. Nineteen sixty-eight was the year of the Democratic Party crackup as the party's left revolted against Johnson on the Vietnam War, even as its right, in the South and in white ethnic neighborhoods in the Northeast and Midwest, revolted around the questions of desegregation, crime, and welfare.

Nixon's conservative advisers, including Phillips and Pat Buchanan, his young personal emissary to the party's right, knew that the path to a future Republican majority was not down the middle road. It would be built by converting Wallace's Democrats and Independents into Republicans. Nixon was never going to be a hero to the left, they argued. His hope lay in a "silent majority" anchored on the right.

The failure of three different realigning moments—four if one includes the Gingrich Revolution of 1994—helps explain the slowly building rage on the right end of American politics.

Over and over, the conservative rank and file was promised that *this* victory would be the decisive one. It was the conservative version of "the final conflict" that Marxists sang about. At each juncture, conservatives felt they had finally created a long-lasting governing majority in the tradition of the New Deal coalition, only to see those hopes disappointed.

Samuel Lubell, the public opinion analyst, wrote in 1952 of the existence of a dominant party he called the "sun" party, and a minority party he referred to as the "moon" party. "It is within the majority party that the issues of any particular period are fought out," he said, "while the minority party shines in reflected radiance of the heat thus generated."

But every time the conservative movement sensed it might finally be part of the sun party, its sun would set, prematurely. Today's rage on the right is the culmination of decades of broken dreams.

"These are people who grew up voting for Reagan and winning twice, and then Bush [wins], and feeling like the country was kind of moving in their direction," said William Kristol. And then conservatives started losing elections—four of six after 1992, and five of six in the popular vote.

"And they lose on certain cultural fights—marriage and others," he continued. They win "mild victories" in the Supreme Court, "but ultimately . . . *Roe v. Wade*'s not getting overturned. And the country's more secular. . . . I don't know. Why wouldn't they be unhappy with the way things are going? I mean, you can say, you know, they were optimists then and now they're pessimists, but that's just another way of saying they've lost a lot of fights. That's just objectively true, I think. Government hasn't been radically rolled back. The Reagan gains are pretty evanescent from a certain point of view."

Indeed they are. And the pattern began with Richard Nixon.

★

The struggles inside Nixon himself and within Nixon's 1968 campaign provide a template for the battles that would rage within Republicanism into our time. Almost alone among Republican politicians, Nixon managed to remain on decent terms with all wings of the GOP. He personally embodied the full range of a party's sensibilities as few other politicians ever have. Although his own career seemed at an end after he lost a 1962 campaign for governor of

California and gave an angry postelection performance at what he called his "last press conference," Nixon still harbored hopes of being nominated for president again in 1964. But he remained at the sidelines as Goldwater and Rockefeller tore each other apart. And when Goldwater won the nomination, Nixon did not walk away, as so many moderate and liberal Republicans did, but campaigned for Goldwater all over the country. Nixon won gratitude on the right and Goldwater's enduring loyalty—broken only when the Arizona senator decided that Nixon's actions during and after Watergate demanded his resignation. In the 1966 midterm elections, Nixon campaigned for Republican candidates of every ideological stripe and received a share of the credit when the GOP picked up forty-seven seats in the House, the clear signal that the era of the Great Society was over, just two years after Johnson's landslide.

The 1966 elections also strengthened the hand of those who favored a Southern Strategy and saw new openings around racial issues. Republican House and Senate candidates, the historian Julian Zelizer noted, "were determined to capitalize on the underlying fragility of the liberal victories in 1964 by exploiting the tensions that had arisen over housing, the War on Poverty, civil rights and other issues the liberals had pushed." While most Republican candidates "didn't believe that opposing civil rights or even focusing on urban unrest was their best strategy," Zelizer noted that many in the party—including Ronald Reagan in his 1966 campaign for governor of California—actively campaigned against open housing laws that had created a backlash among white homeowners.

By 1968, Nixon was again the nation's dominant Republican. His principal rival for the nomination, Governor George Romney of Michigan, dropped out of the contest after telling reporters he had been "brainwashed" into supporting the Vietnam War by American government officials there. It was an unfortunate term that was unfairly invoked to question Romney's psychological stability. It carried heavy baggage in a Cold War era when communists were alleged to have brainwashed American POWs. George Romney's campaign was largely dismissed by history until his son won the Republican nomination in 2012. But Geoffrey Kabaservice, the definitive chronicler of the downfall of moderate Republicanism, is right in asserting that "Romney was the GOP moderates' last and best chance to elect one of their own to the presidency, which in turn would have preserved the long-term viability of the moderate movement." Never again would a moderate Republican of progressive instincts start out with a real chance of winning the party's nomination. Representative John Anderson's fight for the Republican nomination in 1980 would prove the point: a politician of his inclinations was far too progressive for the party. Anderson eventually ran for the presidency as an Independent, taking a rump of Republican moderate activists with him.

Even after Romney's fall, Nixon's nomination did not go uncontested. As was his wont, he was the middle man, opposed from the left by Rockefeller and from the right by Ronald Reagan's late entry after less than two years as California's governor. And it was the South, more than any other region, that delivered for Nixon at the Republican convention in Miami Beach. He won 78 percent of its delegates, including, critically, the support of Senator Strom Thurmond and his South Carolina delegation. In 1948 Thurmond bolted from the Democratic Party to run as a Dixiecrat candidate opposed to Harry Truman's civil rights policies. In 1964 he had switched to the Republican Party in response to the civil rights bill and Goldwater's candidacy. In 1968 he held southern conservatives for Nixon. The southern strategy was alive and well.

What's intriguing in retrospect is that Nixon was not fully sold in 1968 on building a new coalition of southern whites and urban Catholics around hard-edged issues related to crime, campus disorder, and, indirectly, race. In his memoir about Nixon's 1968 campaign, *The Greatest Comeback*, Pat Buchanan described a split in the campaign along ideological lines. The research-and-writing team—he was part of it—strongly urged an appeal to what Buchanan called the "gut vote" of middle-class constituencies angry about crime, a liberal Supreme Court, and student dissidents on college campuses. On the other side were moderates, including Leonard Garment, who was later Nixon's White House counsel; William Safire, the future *New York Times* columnist; Robert Ellsworth, a progressive former Republican House member from Kansas; and Ray Price, former editorial page editor of the *New York Herald Tribune*, one of last bastions of liberal Republicanism.

Typical from the Buchanan camp was a two-thousand-word memo written by conservative writer Jeffrey Bell arguing that the Nixon campaign was so fearful of mistakes that it had settled on a timid, "not taking chances" strategy. When Nixon did say something that caught public attention (Bell's examples included his comments on the Columbia University student protests, the Supreme Court, and the crime issue) "the initial flurry of protests from the liberal press has often caused it to be modified—if not dropped."

Bell urged Nixon to tough it out on such occasions. "Liberal commentators will accuse us of demagogy whenever we do something that is appealing," Bell wrote. "I think we must steel ourselves to that fact." In the margin, Buchanan reports that Nixon wrote the word "Right."

Yet Nixon was torn, drawn as he was to his man-in-the-middle role. As Buchanan writes:

> He seemed of two minds: One responded instinctively, viscerally, positively, in margin notes to what Jeff [Bell] had written. That Nixon wanted a fighting campaign. But wary of backlash, the other Nixon would heed the counsel of those who warned that he was risking becoming another Goldwater, that he was resurrecting the "old Nixon" of the McCarthy Era and the Helen Gahagan Douglas days. The battle for the soul of the Republican Party between a robust and rising conservative movement and a Rockefeller-Javits-Lindsay wing in eclipse was raging inside the Nixon staff of 1968. *Courage and Hesitation* was the title of a book novelist Alan Drury would write about Nixon in 1972. The title fit the candidate of 1968.

Buchanan's description nicely captures how Nixon continued to behave as president. The "liberal" Nixon presided over the creation of the Environmental Protection Agency and the Occupational Safety and Health Administration. He approved the indexing of Social Security benefits to inflation. Urged on by dissident Democrat Daniel Patrick Moynihan, he pushed for the Family Assistance Plan, an attempt to establish a minimum guaranteed income for poor families. His economic policies infuriated free marketers. They included wage price controls and a scrapping of the twenty-seven-year-old Bretton Woods currency system.

On foreign policy, he was a realist rather than an ideologue. He did not end the Vietnam War quickly. He authorized the invasion of Cambodia, and he continued to bomb North Vietnam. All of this infuriated the antiwar movement. But he slowly withdrew American troops—his "Vietnamization" policy—which seemed to satisfy middle-ground opinion. He also launched the opening with China and his détente policy with the Soviet Union. Both enraged the anticommunist right.

Yet following Buchanan's lead, Nixon ran unabashedly in pursuit of George Wallace's voters. He strongly opposed school busing to achieve integration; attacked student protesters who burned American flags; proclaimed himself the champion of the "silent majority" of his fellow citizens who devoted themselves to family and work; criticized the drug culture; and continued to push law and order. When Democrats turned left and nominated George McGovern in 1972, Nixon's task became easier. McGovern was tagged as the candidate of "acid [as in hard drugs], amnesty [for draft resisters] and abortion." (It came to light years later that the phrase was invented not by a Republican but by Democratic senator Thomas Eagleton in a conversation with conservative columnist Robert Novak. McGovern later chose Eagleton as his running mate, then dropped him after it emerged that Eagleton had undergone electroshock therapy. Novak did not reveal the source of the line until after Eagleton's death.)

This eclectic mix was Nixonism. It was certainly coherent when it came to Nixon's political needs and personal instincts, but it satisfied few who were in search of consistency as defined by either conservatives or liberals of the time.

The conservative ideologues, who had stood with Nixon early in his term, began to pull away. On August 10, 1971, *National Review* published an unusual "Declaration" signed by twelve prominent conservatives, including Buckley, Rusher, and Jeff Bell, in which they "resolved to suspend our support of the Administration." It was a careful choice of words, signaling less than a clean break. The declaration was modestly critical of Nixon on domestic affairs (they accused him of continuing "excessive taxation and inordinate welfarism"). But the conservative rebels hit him hard on foreign policy, including "his overtures to Red China done in the absence of any public concessions by Red China to American and Western causes," and for presiding over a "deteriorated American military position."

In late December, Representative John Ashbrook of Ohio, one of the early Draft Goldwater organizers, decided to take the cause of the Republican conservative dissidents to the voters—and received all of 9.7 percent of the vote in the New Hampshire primary, less than half the vote won by Representative Paul "Pete" McCloskey, a California Republican who challenged Nixon from the left on the Vietnam war. Nixon, again the man in the middle, won 68 percent. By the summer, most conservatives, including Buckley, returned to the Nixon fold, but not Rusher. He took to the op-ed pages of the *Los Angeles Times* to announce he would vote for neither Nixon nor McGovern. Nixon, he charged, "has not only traduced almost all of conservatism's basic principles; he has, for the time being, largely silenced its leaders, confused or seduced a good part of its following and effectively paralyzed the whole conservative movement." It was an eloquent complaint from a betrayed conservative—of a sort that would be heard again and again in the coming years.

Rusher took some satisfaction in including this lengthy polemic in his memoir, published a decade after Nixon's departure, noting that "in the more genial light of hindsight . . . we know the grim price that America, the conservative movement, and the Republican Party would all shortly have to pay for their willingness to settle for Richard Nixon."

It is hard to know what would have happened to Nixon's "New Majority" absent the Watergate scandal. Despite Rusher's frustration, he acknowledged that Nixon's 1972 landslide certainly seemed like the realignment that conservatives had been waiting for and that he had foreseen years before in his "Crossroads" essay. After he left office, Nixon wrote that he had fully intended to build a durable new conservative electoral alliance.

Savoring in retrospect his moment of triumph before his fall, Nixon wrote in his 1978 memoir, *RN*, "I won a majority of every key population group identified by Gallup except the blacks and the Democrats. Four of these groups—manual workers, Catholics, members of labor union families and people with only grade school educations—had never before been in the Republican camp in all the years since Gallup had begun keeping these records.

"Now I planned to give expression to the more conservative values and beliefs of the New Majority throughout the country. . . . I intended to revitalize the Republican Party along New Majority lines."

Nixon had seen the Promised Land but, because of Watergate, he wouldn't enter.

Conservatives were in a state of raging ambivalence. They were certain that Nixon had been brought down by a liberal media that both he and they loathed. ("I never really cared for Nixon until Watergate," quipped the conservative columnist and movement founder M. Stanton Evans.) They knew that a New Majority—*their* New Majority—had been foiled by the press's connivance with congressional Democrats, liberal judges, and establishment Republicans who went soft and forced Nixon out. Nixon had not been out of office a year when Pat Buchanan published a book on this theme, *Conservative Votes, Liberal Victories*. Conservatives insisted that Nixon had been held to standards in Watergate far higher than those against which liberal heroes like FDR and JFK had been judged. Ronald Reagan, by then the governor of California, shrewdly gauged the temper of his party: he stuck with Nixon until the end was obvious. Like Nixon's campaigning for Goldwater in 1964, Reagan's loyalty to Nixon would stand him well.

And yet the right knew that Nixon was not one of them—or, as Buchanan suggested, that only half of him was. Many of the fervent anticommunists could not abide his foreign policy and were especially wary of the role Henry Kissinger played in pushing Nixon toward pragmatism and realism. There was an irony here, since liberals had long regarded Kissinger as a conservative. But he was a conservative of the old school of balance-of-power politics. Further, many conservatives knew that Nixon's approach to economics was a long way from Milton Friedman's or Friedrich von Hayek's. And having railed against excesses of presidential power since the days of Roosevelt, a significant number of conservatives felt a need to be consistent with themselves in standing up to Nixon's abuses. Thus was Barry Goldwater an early voice for Nixon's resignation, which endeared the prime mover of the conservative insurgency to liberals for the rest of his life.

Instead of a New Majority, Nixon ushered in an internecine battle among conservatives of differing temperaments. It was fought out in 1976 between President Gerald Ford, the genial congressional Republican whom Nixon had chosen as his vice president in 1973 upon the resignation of Spiro Agnew, and Reagan himself. When he succeeded Nixon, Ford, a classic midwestern conservative, had bowed to the GOP's moderate wing by choosing Nelson Rockefeller, the scourge of Goldwaterism, as his vice president. It was a popular choice among liberals outside the party, but it enraged the right and undercut Ford's legitimate conservative credentials.

The battle of 1976 was different from the fights of the 1960s, involving open contests between progressive and conservative Republicans. Buchanan shrewdly observed: "The liberal wing of the Republican Party is a spectator now. It lacked the numbers to advance its own candidate, or the will to save its own champion, the Vice President. The civil war in the GOP is between conservatives—militant and moderate."

★

Buchanan's reflection is a reminder that the purge of progressive Republicans that began in 1964 continued right through the Nixon years and beyond. This is true even though liberal Republicans did well in the 1966 midterm elections, which provided the setting for Nixon's vigorous campaigning. *Time* and *Newsweek* put the same six Republican winners on their postelection covers: Governors Rockefeller, Reagan, and Romney, and Senators-elect Mark Hatfield, Edward Brooke, and Charles Percy. All but Reagan were progressives.

It was a false dawn. Gradually, but with great determination, conservatives waged war on the party's progressives—and after a while, many liberal Republicans gave up and switched parties, or retired from politics.

One of the earliest post-Goldwater victims was Senator Thomas Kuchel, a liberal Republican who had been appointed by California governor Earl Warren in 1953 to fill Richard Nixon's seat. Kuchel lost his California primary in 1968 to the state's conservative education superintendent, Max Rafferty, a very early critic of progressive education. Rafferty was a defender of phonics, a foe of sex education, and a champion of assigning old children's classics in schools; his books included *What They Are Doing to Your Children*. There was no doubt about the ideological affinities of the "They." Rafferty swept past Kuchel in the same conservative Southern California counties that two years earlier had allowed Reagan to defeat a moderate Republican and then seize the governorship from Democrat Pat Brown. Kuchel learned of his defeat on the same evening that Robert F. Kennedy was assassinated in Los Angeles after claiming victory in the Democratic presidential primary. Rafferty, however, also gave Republicans an early lesson in the costs of nominating conservatives whom voters regarded as extreme. Democrat Alan Cranston defeated Rafferty and began a long Senate career. No Republican since Kuchel has won the seat.

A year later, New York City mayor John V. Lindsay, one of the most liberal Republicans in the country, lost his Republican mayoral primary to John Marchi, a conservative state senator who made himself the voice of Catholic ethnic outer-borough voters against the dashing former congressman from Manhattan's silk stocking district. Lindsay won reelection on a third-party Liberal ticket, became a Democrat, and ran unsuccessfully for president in the 1972 primaries. Conservatives were happy to be rid of Lindsay, whom Bill Buckley had opposed from the right in a raucous 1965 campaign on the Conservative Party ticket. Buckley's challenge kept conservatives in the national news following Goldwater's defeat, led him to produce one of his most engaging books, *The Unmaking of a Mayor*, and indirectly led to the election of his brother Jim to the United States Senate in 1970.

Jim Buckley also ran on the Conservative Party line. Lindsay won in 1969 because the Democrats had nominated a conservative named Mario Procaccino, who split the right-of-center vote with Marchi. Buckley profited from a split vote on the left between Democratic congressman Richard Ottinger and Senator Charles Goodell, a liberal Republican (and the father of the future National Football League commissioner). The Nixon White House targeted Goodell—one of the few times Nixon supported a purge of a liberal in his own party. Spiro Agnew, Nixon's always rhetorically creative vice president, referred to Goodell as the "Christine Jorgensen of the Republican Party," a reference to one of the first Americans to undergo a sex change operation. In an interview for this book, Buchanan, who was close to Agnew, explained that the administration feared that Ottinger would defeat Buckley and so the Nixon forces set out to boost Goodell among liberals by attacking him. The strategy succeeded brilliantly, drew votes away from Ottinger, and elected Buckley.

Party switching picked up speed in the 1970s. As southern Democrats switched to the Republican Party, northern Republicans responded in kind. Congressman Ogden Reid of the *Herald Tribune* family became a Democrat, and so did Congressman Don Riegle of Michigan. First elected in the GOP class of 1966, he went on to become a Democratic U.S. senator. Primaries from the right ended the careers of two of the party's most outspoken liberals: Clifford Case of New Jersey in 1978 (Buckley's magazine called him "Hopeless Case" as far back as 1959) and Jacob Javits of New York in 1980.

The rise of Newt Gingrich and the Republican takeover of the House in 1994 led to a further rout of the progressive Republicans—this time at the hands of Democrats. Moderate and even liberal voters in the Northeast and Midwest, particularly in suburban districts, once proudly sent progressive Republicans to Washington. But the increasing dominance of southern conservatives in the party of Lincoln made such voters wary of electing Republicans of any stripe and handing control of Congress to a Republican Party dominated by the right. In the 1990s and 2000s, one middle-way Republican after another was defeated by a Democrat. The fallen included representatives such as Connie Morella in Maryland, Jim Leach in Iowa and Chris Shays in Connecticut, along with Senator Lincoln Chaffee in Rhode Island. These politicians lost not because their constituents stopped liking them—on the contrary, they maintained high approval ratings—but because their identity as Republicans turned them into enablers of right-wing congressional leaders.

All this happened gradually, until there were no liberals and only a few moderates left. The shape of what was coming could have been discerned in 1976.

★

Reagan's 1976 campaign was a triumphant defeat. His rise to the White House began not in 1980 but in 1976. That's when he established himself as not only the undisputed leader of the conservative movement but also the most popular figure in his party. He gave conservatives a rallying cry they would use for decades by "raising a banner of no pale pastels but bold colors which make it unmistakably clear where we stand." In introducing his account of Reagan's glorious loss, *Reagan's Revolution: The Untold Story of the Campaign That Started It All*, conservative activist and writer Craig Shirley observes: "Without Reagan's 1976 campaign, Americans would not have witnessed the reordering of the two major political parties and the shift in our political universe. . . ."

Ford had hoped to rout Reagan, and the accidental incumbent did well in the early primaries. But mid-campaign, Ford ran head-on into the power of the conservative movement in the person of Jesse Helms in the North Carolina primary. Reagan rolled to a series of subsequent primary victories, particularly in the South, and briefly went ahead of Ford in the delegate count.

Three aspects of the Ford-Reagan battle are instructive for what would come later. First was the power of single-issue politics—and, in particular, the ability of conservatives to use a single issue to dramatize a larger point or drive home a broader attack. For Reagan, it was opposition to turning over the Panama Canal to Panamanian control. (The issue would later serve him well against Jimmy Carter, too.) "When it comes to the Canal," Reagan would say, to raucous approval from his crowds, "we bought it, we paid for it, it's ours." Few politicians had anticipated that the issue would be decisive, and even conservatives such as Barry Goldwater approved of making a deal with Panama. But as Rick Perlstein noted in *The Invisible Bridge,* the issue also stood for something else. He cited David Keene, a Reagan organizer who would play a large role in the conservative movement. Keene was surprised by the power of the canal question, which was getting very little play in the newspapers. It would not be the first time that conservatives would respond to a cause that the mainstream media had seen as marginal. For Keene, the canal stood in for larger fears about American loss of influence in the world—a logical conclusion after the Vietnam debacle. "The issue I sense," Keene said, "is 'The empire is in decline.'" Such feelings were at the heart of conservative and right-wing critiques of Kissingerian diplomacy: a belief that Ford and Nixon, under Kissinger's tutelage, were accommodating decline rather than reversing it. (In 2015, Donald Trump would appeal to the same impulses by using a Reagan slogan, "Make America Great Again," as his own.) The Panama issue gathered force during Jimmy Carter's administration when American hostages were seized in Iran and the Soviet Union invaded Afghanistan. Reagan would establish himself then as the champion of renewing the United States' global power.

Nineteen seventy-six also brought the first indications of the intensity of the right's opposition to abortion. *Roe v. Wade* was only three years old, and the early stirrings of religious activism against the decision would lead to the rise of the Christian Right. Abortion would, for some time, be the premier single issue, with gun rights close behind.

In struggling for the Republican nomination, Ford was continuously required to accommodate his more conservative foes. He had already dumped Rockefeller as his vice president, announcing a year in advance that he would choose a different running mate. "The conservative challenge drove Ford to the right," Kabaservice wrote. "For many moderates, his rhetoric on school prayer, busing, government spending and abortion began to sound uncomfortably like Reagan's." Ford even distanced himself from his own approach to international affairs. "We are going to forget the use of the word *détente*," he said. Fearing that whatever they might do would only weaken Ford and help Reagan, "progressive Republicans were largely paralyzed," recalled Senator Charles "Mac" Mathias of Maryland, a lion of liberal Republicanism (who, at the age of eighty-six, a little more than a year before he died, would endorse Barack Obama in his first campaign for president).

To further mollify Reagan's forces, Ford let through a platform plank on "Morality in Foreign Policy." It was a barely veiled rebuke to his own policies and a calculated insult to Kissinger, his secretary of state. When it came to selecting a running mate, Ford would have preferred William Ruckelshaus, the former head of the Environmental Protection Agency, or Senator Howard Baker, who rose to fame for his even-handedness during the Senate's Watergate hearings. But to satisfy Reagan and the right, Ford picked Senator Bob Dole. Dole was then seen as a fighting conservative, though like so many others of traditional conservative inclinations, he would later be regarded as a moderate.

A pattern was set: even when moderate conservatives won, they secured their victories only by appeasing the militants.

Yet there was one discordant note for Reagan early in the campaign that spoke to the difficulty conservatives faced in translating their principles into practical and popular policies. Reagan might have won the nomination in 1976 but for one particularly bold idea, a plan "to cut $90 billion from the federal budget and slash income taxes while simultaneously balancing the budget, all of this to be achieved by transferring spending authority to the states." For the right, it had everything: budget cuts, tax cuts, and enhanced states' rights. But there was a catch, as Kabaservice noted: "This would also transfer a massive taxation burden to the states, which New Hampshire residents quickly realized would end their freedom from state income and sales taxes." Ford won the New Hampshire primary, narrowly, and built a lead that Reagan's later surge could not overcome.

Extremism in defense of liberty may be no vice, but radical changes in the structure of benefits and taxes, even in the name of conservative principles, are often viewed skeptically by voters. They reflect a different kind of "conservatism," temperamental rather than ideological, and wary of radical changes. It was, as Goldwater had already learned, often at odds with the philosophical demands of the conservative movement.

For Reagan, 1976 was a temporary setback. He came very close to winning, and he learned a great deal in the process. He would prove himself quite capable of flexibility when success demanded it.

It is easy to forget that in defeating Ford, Jimmy Carter came close to overturning the entire conservative electoral project. Dealing a mighty blow to the Republicans' southern hopes, Carter swept the South, winning every former Confederate state except Virginia. In the thirteen elections from 1960 to 2012, Carter would be the only Democrat to carry Mississippi and Alabama. Carter carried Texas and South Carolina, something no Democrat would do again through the 2012 election. Carter's southern coalition, moreover, fulfilled the populists' dream from the 1890s by drawing a class line across the South, allying African-Americans with whites of more modest income. Key southern counties that had voted for George Wallace in 1968 and Richard Nixon in 1972 voted overwhelmingly for Carter in 1976. Because of Carter's strength in the rural South, he was the last Democrat to carry a majority of the nation's counties: 1,711. In 2012, Barack Obama won a slightly larger share of the popular vote than Carter. But since his support was concentrated in metropolitan areas, Obama carried only 692 of the nation's 3,113 counties.

But Carter's breakthrough was short-lived. His presidency was not without real achievements. The peace treaty between Israel and Egypt is one of the enduring legacies of his years in office. The Panama Canal treaty created political problems for Carter, but it, too, was enduring and helpful to American relations with Central and South America. Carter's emphasis on human rights in American foreign policy helped pave the way for some of the successes Reagan enjoyed later. By associating the United States with this cause, Carter helped undo the damage done to America's image during the Vietnam years and weakened the Soviet Union in the global ideological struggle. He also pushed the pace of democratization in South America. The move toward economic deregulation began under Carter, not Reagan, and so too did the military arms buildup.

But these last achievements did Carter little good among liberals (even if some of them, including Ted Kennedy, supported deregulatory moves in the interest of consumers). Carter disappointed the left by failing to push for national health insurance and was cool to labor law reform that might have strengthened the union movement. Kennedy's challenge to Carter in the 1980 presidential primaries was a sign of liberal frustration, but Kennedy also picked up blue-collar votes in many states that would eventually transfer to Reagan. In any event, Carter was hit by a series of crises—stagflation, the energy crisis, soaring interest rates, the Iranian hostage crisis, and the Soviet invasion of Afghanistan—that would have made his reelection difficult even with a more unified party.

There were also forces at work not entirely within Carter's control, and these would shape conservatism in important ways. The inflation of the 1970s, later accompanied by rising unemployment to produce "stagflation," had a double effect. It undercut confidence in traditional Keysenian economics because its prescriptions no longer seemed to be working. It also led to sharp increases in taxes on moderate-income families. The first resulted in the rise of supply-side economics, which were really very old-fashioned conservatism in attractive new clothes. The second set off a tax revolt.

The most celebrated example, California's Proposition 13 enacted by the voters themselves in 1978, was, in part, an unintended consequence of long-term prosperity. The state's growth led to astonishing increases in property values: between April 1974 and April 1978, the price of the average house in

Los Angeles County rose by 120 percent. The higher values were translated into higher property taxes. Inflation also drove nominal (but not necessarily real) incomes higher, pushing middle-class voters into tax brackets never intended for them. "When inflation blended with tax schedules to push up rates," wrote the liberal economics writer Robert Kuttner, "hard-pressed consumers were in no mood to tolerate rising taxes, as they might have been a decade earlier when times were good."

On the surface, the 1978 mid-term elections rendered a mixed political verdict. Democrats suffered a net loss of only three seats in the Senate, for example, because most of the Republican pickups were offset by Democratic gains. But Republicans cut into Democratic territory and did well in contested terrain. They picked up two seats in Minnesota (one in a special election called after the death of the liberal giant, Hubert Humphrey) and also defeated Democratic incumbents in Maine, New Hampshire, Iowa, and Colorado. These shifts, combined with the roiling discontent over taxes epitomized by the Proposition 13 campaign, were a harbinger of what would come two years later.

In the meantime, conservatives used their time out of power to strengthen their institutions and to foster an intellectual offensive through newly empowered think tanks. This created a new narrative that proved popular across the media: liberals were out of ideas while conservatives were enjoying a policy renaissance. That many of the conservative ideas were rooted in the worldview of Calvin Coolidge was acknowledged by some conservatives—there was a vogue, particularly among supply-siders, for neckties bearing Coolidge's image—but less noticed elsewhere.

Reagan's 1980 victory over Carter was overwhelming, a crushing 489–49 triumph in the Electoral College. In a three-way race, with John Anderson representing the old liberal Republicanism as a third-party candidate, Reagan secured 50.8 percent of the vote, to 41 percent for Carter and 6.6 percent for Anderson. Reagan's election felt like an earthquake because it was. The twelve seats the Republicans gained in the Senate suggested that this was more than a personal victory, a view underscored by the defeat of a who's who of Democratic liberals—George McGovern, Frank Church, Birch Bayh, Warren Magnuson, and Gaylord Nelson.

During the Republican primaries, Anderson had received wide attention but few votes—12 percent of the total. Moderate Republicans tended to prefer George H. W. Bush to Anderson and he ran second to Reagan. In a shrewd move aimed at uniting the party, Reagan picked Bush as his running mate, even though Bush had described Reagan's supply-side tax cut plan as "voodoo economics."

Realizing his views had no future in his own party, Anderson set off on his Independent path. Despite his relatively weak national showing, Anderson won between 10 and 15 percent of the vote in the six New England states, and also had pockets of strength in upstate New York, in the upper Midwest, and on the West Coast. (In light of the vacation habits of Democratic presidents, it's worth noting that two of Anderson's top three counties in the country—the third was part of his Illinois congressional district—were Dukes County, which most know as Martha's Vineyard, and Nantucket in Massachusetts. In both, Anderson won more than 20 percent of the vote.) Anderson's support serves as a marker for the steady defection of the progressive Republicans from their party. If George Wallace was a way station for southern Democrats on their way to becoming Republicans, Anderson served, in a less spectacular fashion, as a transfer point for northern Republicans moving toward the Democrats.

But the vote for Anderson also reflected the impatience of many liberals with Carter, visible in the third-party candidate's strength in relatively liberal and normally Democratic states such as Massachusetts and New York. Liberals who voted for Anderson were willing to risk a Reagan victory because they were so fed up with Carter.

If Reagan's victory was thus impressive, his share of the popular vote was less so. Of Reagan's 489 electoral votes, 222 of them were secured in states in which he won less than 50 percent of the popular vote. In a fair number of these states, Reagan was not far below half the vote and many of them would likely have tipped Reagan's way even if Anderson had not been on the ballot. But these figures put his Electoral College sweep in context. The map revealed but also exaggerated the extent of his triumph.

Reagan was elected not because he turned the whole country conservative, but because he persuaded enough swing voters frustrated over stagflation, the Iranian hostage crisis, and the seemingly (and misleadingly) rising power of the Soviet Union that he was not the conservative ideologue of old. Reagan played down his more right-wing positions—deflecting, for example, Carter's attack on his past opposition to Medicare with the most memorable line of their only debate: "There you go again."

Reagan's 1980 acceptance speech at the Republican National Convention in Detroit was one of the best of the genre, and a sign of things to come. Although Reagan pledged to reduce the size of government and was specific on one issue—he called for "a 30 percent reduction in income tax rates over a period of three years" with a 10 percent "down payment" in his first year—it was a speech aimed at an audience much larger than the conservative faithful. Reagan addressed all who shared "a community of values embodied in these words: family, work, neighborhood, peace and freedom."

He promised that "everything that can be run more effectively by state and local government we shall turn over to state and local government," but, perhaps remembering the difficulties his $90 billion devolution plan caused him in 1976, added the words "along with the funding sources to pay for it." Gone was any talk of privatizing Social Security. On the contrary, Reagan declared that "it is essential that the integrity of all aspects of Social Security be preserved." This would be no Goldwater campaign. And while conservatives would always love him, his presidency would not be dedicated to fulfilling their more extravagant hopes.

The two Reagan traditions that Republicans can choose to identify with, the aspirational and the pragmatic, reflect the complexity of his actual political project, his personality, and his way of governing. Reagan is often cast as a relatively simple man. He wasn't.

Our current political turmoil and the ongoing discontent on the right grows out of this essential fact: *Reagan changed the terms of the American political debate without changing the underlying structure of American government.*

Reagan's genius lay in his skill at making a sustained, compelling argument for conservative positions. It is precisely this talent that captured conservative imaginations on that October evening in 1964 when he rallied the faithful, if not many others, to Barry Goldwater. Reagan understood the New Deal argument inside out, having once been a New Dealer himself and never giving up his admiration for Franklin D. Roosevelt. As a result, he could speak to a national consensus shaped by New Dealism with an eye toward changing it—though less so than most of his core supporters hoped.

The transformation of the debate in the Reagan years is unmistakable. Perhaps appropriately in light of Reagan's past, the shift can be illustrated by way of one of the most beloved movies of the 1940s, *It's a Wonderful Life*. The film captures the underlying values of the New Deal Era by pitting the socially oriented capitalism of George Bailey against the cold banking calculations of Mr. Potter. Bailey's commitment is to broadly shared prosperity, reflected in the success of his savings and loan in turning so many people in Bedford Falls into homeowners. Potter is a man of the bottom line, for whom Bailey's behavior is mere sentimentalism. Moreover, the movie makes the case that "traditional values"—warm and loving home lives, the patriotism of George's war hero brother, the intimate ties of a tightly knit community—are rooted in economic arrangements that guarantee everyone a stake. In the movie's alternative universe—the world as it would have been without George Bailey and the opportunities he created—Bedford Falls becomes "Pottersville," a nasty gambling town where prostitution thrives and social bonds are shattered.

Reagan's project might be seen as turning *It's a Wonderful Life* on its head. In the world of the 1980s, entrepreneurs and bankers—the Mr. Potters of the world—became heroes as conservative persuaded Americans that Potter's analysis of capitalism was right: getting rich was good because when some people got rich, everyone prospered. There was an underlying morality and even spirituality to capitalism, captured well by two popular books of the early Reagan era, *Wealth and Poverty* by George Gilder (the onetime liberal Republican who had written about 1964 Republicanism as "the party that lost its head"), and Michael Novak's *The Spirit of Democratic Capitalism*. The condemnations of Mr. Potter had things all wrong.

"Capitalism begins with giving," Gilder insisted. "Not from greed, avarice or even self-love can one expect the rewards of commerce, but from a spirit closely akin to altruism, a regard for the needs of others, a benevolent, outgoing and courageous temper of mind." Novak similarly linked capitalism to spiritual growth. "The highest goal of the political economy of democratic capitalism is to be suffused by *caritas*," he wrote. "Within such a system each person is regarded as an originating source of insight, choice, action and love. Yet each is also a part of all the others."

In this telling, the free individual's greatest calling is to be entrepreneurial, to use a word that came back into vogue in the Reagan period. Gilder linked the disorders of family life to high inflation and high marginal tax rates, which had the tendency "to penalize the family that depends on a single earner who is fully and resourcefully devoted to his career."

In the meantime, the rise of the counterculture in the 1960s drove a wedge between traditional values and New Dealism. The morally tidy world of Bedford Falls was not under threat from Mr. Potter or from economic injustice. It was being challenged by new values, including feminism, sexual license, an attack on religion, the drug culture—and, as Gilder suggested, excessive taxation.

Government plays a limited role in *It's a Wonderful Life*, although the state's bank examiners are cast as friendly rather than threatening figures when they tear up their complaint against Bailey and toss a contribution into the community fund that Bailey's wife raises to get George out of bankruptcy. But Reagan built on the disaffection with government unleashed by the Vietnam War, Watergate, and the hyperinflation of the late 1970s to create a new, long-term view of the state as bumbling, incompetent, and ultimately oppressive. In their sleep, conservatives can recite the Reagan catechism, preached in his Inaugural Address: "Government is not the solution to our problem. Government is the problem."

What's not fully appreciated is that Americans did not hold this view of government until the late 1970s and early 1980s. Government was seen from the Great Depression forward as the force that ended the Depression, won World War II, and built the nation up through the Public Works Administration, the Works Progress Administration, the Interstate Highway System, and countless other public investment projects. In 2011 Rachel Maddow, the MSNBC host, filmed a promotional spot in front of the Hoover Dam that harks back to the New Deal worldview and captures it quite precisely:

I feel like we have sort of an amazing inheritance in terms of what our grandparents and our great-grandparents thought to leave us when they were building the infrastructure that is the spine of this country—they knew that the benefit of it would redound to us—they knew it. What are we doing?

It shows us how much Reagan changed the prevailing assumptions. Maddow insists that generational responsibility should be defined by the public investments earlier cohorts of Americans made that benefited those who came after. This was the New Deal view. But when generational responsibility is invoked now, it is almost always done to criticize the public debt being left behind for later generations to pay off. For Maddow, government was part of the solution. The Reagan view that it is part of the problem is still with us—even though we have had two long Democratic presidencies since Reagan left office. Neither Bill Clinton nor Barack Obama fully undid Reagan's ideological inheritance.

The federal government certainly tilted in different directions in the Reagan era—toward employers and against unions, toward companies and away from environmentalists, toward extractive industries and away from renewables, toward laissez-faire and away from consumer protection, employee health and safety, and financial regulation. In the financial field, Clinton approved measures that pushed deregulation even further.

Yet the underlying structure of government changed little. The historian Joshua Freeman summarizes Reagan's fiscal legacy:

> The political arithmetic of the budget made it impossible for the Reagan administration to reduce nonmilitary spending sufficiently to meet its goal of ending deficits. It could do nothing about debt payments, and Reagan ruled out substantial cuts in the popular Medicare, veterans', school lunch, Head Start and summer youth programs. Social Security made up a major component of the budget, but Reagan's one effort to reduce its cost backfired, when his proposal to further reduce benefits for people who chose to retire early led to a Congressional uproar, forcing him to retreat. . . . What remained were the discretionary domestic programs that made up 17 percent of federal spending, which the Reagan Administration tried to slash.

Even here, Reagan made less of a dent than his budget director, David Stockman, had hoped. Stockman wanted to cut "weak claims, rather than weak claimants." Instead, the weak claims largely survived and the cuts hit weak claimants. As Freeman notes, Reagan failed to make a significant dent in agricultural subsides and the Export-Import Bank, along with "tobacco subsidies, the NASA budget [and] subsidies for nuclear fuel plants." Spending on "local bridges and roads" survived, too. All of these reductions were defeated or contained "as affected groups and local political interests mobilized resistance."

That left spending for "the poor and the urban working class, groups with little clout in the White House or the new Congress." So Reagan did manage to reduce or eliminate "child nutrition programs, CETA [spending under the Comprehensive Employment and Training Act], food stamps and mass transit subsidies." The budget of the Department of Housing and Urban Development fell by 57 percent between 1981 and 1987, and social spending, "which had risen under each of the previous five presidents, fell at an average annual rate of 1.5 percent under Reagan."

In retrospect, one can understand why the Reagan years left both liberals and small-government conservatives dissatisfied. The cuts that were real and visible hit programs for low-income Americans. This is the Reagan progressives remember. And he fundamentally altered the nation's tax structure. Tax rates have gone up since Reagan's time, but the top marginal tax rate is still far lower than it was when he took office. This is an achievement that still shapes (and, from a progressive point of view, bedevils) our fiscal debates.

But at the end of Reagan's eight years, the federal apparatus was not only left standing; it was spending more than ever. Reagan had promised to balance the budget, but the federal government ran a deficit of $100 billion or more every year of his term. The national debt rose from $907 billion in 1980 to $2.8 trillion in 1989. In his 1980 Republican convention speech, Reagan had pledged to "work to reduce the cost of government as a percentage of our gross national product." As a share of gross domestic product (GDP), federal spending had stood at 21.1 percent in 1980, the last full year of Jimmy Carter's presidency. By 1987, it had been cut to 21.0 percent, virtually no change. It fell back further to 20.5 percent in 1989, but the post-Reagan recession pushed it back up to 21.7 percent in 1991, higher than its level at the end of the Carter years.

Of course, the mix of spending changed, with Reagan pushing his military buildup. And here is one of history's ironies. There was indeed a strong economic recovery that helped Reagan win his landslide reelection. But as Freeman notes, the theory that conservatives put forward to explain the boom didn't match the reality. Reagan's large tax cuts did not boost personal savings, which fell under Reagan, nor did they lead to massive investment in plant and equipment, "which even during the recovery remained below the rate of previous decades." But the tax cuts and the military spending together did act "as a vast Keynesian stimulus program." In other words: high deficits and government spending saved the economy. The very theory the supply-siders rejected came to Reagan's rescue and was immensely helpful to his political standing.

None of this meant that Reagan was unpopular. In fact, his flexibility and his personality were keys to his success in winning over voters who did not necessarily share his worldview. But his administration created an enormous disconnect between movement expectations and reality.

Libertarians were especially alive to this while Reagan was in office. Ed Crane, the founding president of the Cato Institute, an early Koch family venture that promoted the purest strains of libertarian thinking, edited and published volumes on the promise and reality of the Reagan presidency that found it falling short. Crane still feels that way.

"I remember when Reagan was elected, the Heritage [Foundation] folks were going all on about how, well, the battle is over, we won," Crane told me. "I'm looking around and thinking: This is the same government. We didn't get rid of anything after eight years of Reagan. . . . It's this upward ratcheting of programs and spending that never ended. I guess Reagan slowed it down, but what did he abolish? He added to departments and didn't get rid of any."

In short: no politician has made the case for smaller government and lower taxes more effectively than Reagan did. That is why his ideological legacy endures. Yet a smaller government is precisely what he did not deliver. That is why conservatives remain frustrated. All these years later, House Republicans are still trying to get rid of the Export-Import Bank.

What made Reagan a success, Crane argued, were his gifts in responding to a country that badly needed a morale boost after the Carter years. "Reagan was a remarkable motivator," Crane said. "The American people loved the idea: here's this guy saying this is a great country, don't tell me about malaise."

When Perlstein published *The Invisible Bridge* in 2014, he was criticized by some reviewers for presenting Reagan as a kind of flimflam artist who prospered by telling the American people how good they were. Perlstein's key line: "People want to believe. Ronald Reagan was able to make people believe."

Perlstein's view of Reagan is far richer than his critics have allowed because it in no way diminishes Reagan to view his presidency as successful precisely because, as Crane suggests, the country wanted and needed an injection of optimism at that moment. One might, indeed, summarize the politics of the period 1980–2000 by saying that Ronald Reagan stole optimism from FDR and the Democrats, and Bill Clinton stole it back.

And this is where Reagan is so confounding, to friend and critic alike: Reagan was an ideologue in his speeches, particularly before he became president, and he really believed the conservative gospel. But he was also intent on being both successful and popular. He would test limits, but not push beyond them if the political traffic could not bear what he had originally hoped for. This was obvious when he was governor of California. As Perlstein observed, when his proposal for a 10 percent across-the-board cut in every department's budget proved impractical, "he changed course, moved on, learned, adjusted, gladly dropping right-wing orthodoxy when more pragmatic solutions presented themselves." Reagan wanted "to chalk up accomplishments." Perlstein notes that some conservative "purists" were so frustrated with Reagan that they launched a recall movement against him in 1971. It came to nothing—and did little to dent Reagan's image in the eyes of conservatives around the nation.

It's true that Reagan could live with a good deal of cognitive dissonance between his public statements and his practice. Reagan, as Freeman notes, "thrived on . . . contradictions, declaring himself against abortion but doing nothing to end it; calling for a constitutional amendment to require balanced budgets while creating the largest peacetime deficits in history; and extolling family and community while promoting a deregulated free market that eroded both."

But he could also make real choices. He was, for example, willing to pull back a third of his tax cut in 1982, courtesy of the attractively named Tax Equity and Fiscal Responsibility Act. At the time, as the historian Sean Wilentz notes, true-believing supply-side conservatives felt they had been "stabbed in the back" by "perfidious forces within the White House," suggesting that Stockman and Chief of Staff James Baker were "purposefully undermining the president's supply-side intentions."

As Wilentz noted, they were "utterly mistaken." Reagan was "fully involved in these decisions." He was "governing as he had done since his days in California, holding out as long as possible, compromising when necessary, protecting his important gains while preparing to fight another day." Reagan's central interest was in preserving his cut in the top marginal tax rate from 70 percent to 50 percent, and he did.

Reagan showed flexibility in other areas, as we've seen, dropping his Social Security cuts and instead creating a bipartisan commission with House Speaker Tip O'Neill to make the system more solvent. The combination of modest tax increases with modest benefit cuts passed without controversy.

No doubt Reagan was more moderate than he might have been, both as governor and as president, because he had to work with Democrats in the legislative branch. But his willingness to do so, celebrated by Chris Matthews in his book *Tip and the Gipper*, is a part of his legacy that contrasts so sharply with the approach of today's Tea Party right.

★

By his second term, Reagan had run out of agenda. The historic tax reform passed in 1986 was at least as much a congressional and Democratic initiative (spearheaded by Senator Bill Bradley and Representative Richard Gephardt) as it was a White House plan. And while it was markedly "Reaganite" in bringing the top income tax rate down even further, to 28 percent, it was progressive in not only dumping loopholes but also shifting the tax burden from individuals to corporations. In a distinctly anti-supply-side move, the reform raised the capital gains tax from 20 percent to 28 percent by treating capital gains as ordinary income. It is difficult to see any conservatives agreeing to such a change at this point in the twenty-first century.

The electoral magic of the Reagan Coalition disappeared in the 1986 midterm elections as Democrats retook the Senate. It was the first election in which the "Reagan Class" of Republican senators from 1980 was on the ballot, and its members fared badly. Republicans gave up their 1980 gains in Florida, Alabama, Georgia, North Carolina, both Dakotas, and Washington State. The conservative realignment seemed further away than ever. It was not so much a repudiation of Reagan as a sign of his increasing irrelevance. He had no new program to offer, and his themes were old. Democrats, in the meantime, focused on the parts of the country where Reagan's "Morning" had not yet arrived. They attacked the "Swiss-cheese economy"—it was an economic recovery full of holes—and the "bicoastal economy," a way of championing the cause of the heartland and turning old conservative charges of East Coast–West Coast liberal elitism on their head.

An upstart Republican congressman from Georgia named Newt Gingrich drew a lesson from 1986 that would stick with the right for many years to come. "If voters see a race as a nice-guy Republican against a nice-guy Democrat, we lose," Gingrich said. Republicans had not drawn the issues sharply enough and had been far too soft. It's not a mistake they would make again.

Two years later, Reagan's vice president, George H. W. Bush, won a solid victory over Governor Michael Dukakis of Massachusetts by running anything but a nice-guy campaign. It looked like the triumph that would cement the new majority in place. It proved to be its undoing.

4

THE END OF THE REAGAN MAJORITY

George H. W. Bush, Bill Clinton, and the Politics of Deadlock

"I hope you're all aware we're Eisenhower Republicans here."

When the history of modern conservatism is recounted and old war stories are told, Lee Atwater is well remembered by the political cognoscenti of a certain age. But his role in building a conservative majority and keeping it alive in 1988 is often underplayed or even forgotten. Atwater's political career came to an abrupt and tragic end when he was diagnosed with a brain tumor that took his life in 1991, at the age of forty, just three years after he helped make George H. W. Bush president. Atwater, the crafty campaign manager, was not there when Bush had to face the voters again in 1992. His absence was felt.

Because Atwater's political tactics were unapologetically hard-edged, many in Bush's governing inner circle preferred not to highlight how important this brash, blues-guitar-playing South Carolinian had been to Bush's 1988 victory. Bush himself drew a sharp line between campaigning (the sometimes ugly things you had to do to gain power) and governing (the re-

sponsible things you try to do once you have it). Atwater was entirely associated with the first, grubbier imperative.

In my days as a day-to-day political journalist covering campaigns, and
particularly the campaign of 1988, I confess to having had warm feelings
toward Atwater personally, even if I was appalled by so many of the things he
did. Typically (though not always), he owned up to his bare-knuckle tactics.
More than that: he took responsibility when others ran away.

When the criticism of Bush's 1988 attacks against Democrat Michael
Dukakis got increasingly fierce, many of Bush's friends expressed dismay and
some of his aides held their tongues. Not Atwater. He was quite ready to
claim full ownership of the campaign's nastier side, to explain why the assaults
made tactical and strategic sense, and to be clear on his own role in formulating them. Atwater's close associates were disturbed that he had to take much
of the blame for the campaign's negative cast while the campaign chairman,
James A. Baker III, took credit for its success. Atwater, who had been working for years on a Ph.D. thesis on the dangers to candidates of high negative
ratings in the polls, insisted this never bothered him.

There could be no denying Atwater's brutal side. In 1980, his candidate
for Congress, Representative Floyd Spence, a South Carolina Republican,
was opposed by Tom Turnipseed, a former campaign official for George Wallace and one of the more rococo figures in southern politics. Atwater report-
edly planted a reporter at a Turnipseed press briefing who said he understood
Turnipseed had once had psychiatric treatment and electroshock therapy.

When Turnipseed attacked Atwater for spreading the report, Atwater
told a journalist he did not want to comment on a statement by someone who
was once "hooked up to jumper cables." Atwater later apologized, though he
insisted that he never set the reporter up to ask the question. "That would be
an insult to the press," he told me when I asked him about this in 1988. He
said it with a chuckle, although that summer there had been nothing funny
about rumors spreading all over Washington that Dukakis had once had psychiatric treatment. Dukakis vehemently denied this, and Atwater said he was
not responsible for them.

But beneath the proud, tough-guy image, Atwater was very sophisticated
in understanding where the conservative movement stood in 1988, and how

it got there. He also understood his own candidate's shortcomings and challenges. Bush was in no way a movement conservative, and there was mistrust of him on the right; as Reagan's main rival in 1980 he had been critical of Reagan's views on taxes and economics.

Atwater knew exactly how much the Republican Party had been changed by Reagan—but also how Reagan had been changed by governing and by having to lead the whole GOP. "What we had in 1988 was a party that Ronald Reagan had brought more to the right, and in effect there was no longer a classic moderate wing of the party," he explained at a postelection campaign manager's conference at Harvard's Institute of Politics in late 1988. "But by the same token, the party brought Reagan more to the center. The new nominating wing of the party would be what I termed, for lack of a better word, the mainstream wing of the party, which would be about 70 percent of the vote."

Immunizing Bush started with an embrace of Reagan, but didn't end there. "I felt there were only two things Bush needed to do other than stick with Reagan that would preempt anybody from ever being able to get to him on the right," Atwater said. "One was to be hard-core on taxes, which as you all know he was. Number two was to be hard-core on the anticommunist cluster of issues. If he did those two things, no one could ever move out on him on the right. . . ."

Atwater was also clear about what Bush needed to do to defeat the Democrats. He was under no illusions that the Republican majority in the country was secure—the 1986 midterm elections had cured party realists of such fantasies. Atwater's view was that most Democrats who had strayed to Reagan in 1984 wanted to go home to their old party. The swing voters, he believed, were "conservative populists," responsive to Democrats on lunch bucket economics but to conservatives on social and cultural issues. If such voters did not see great differences between Bush and Dukakis, Atwater said candidly, "Guess what? They would have gone back and been Democrats again." This squared with what he had told me during the campaign itself: "Our task," he had said, "is to show that there are differences."

And this is what the Bush campaign did.

The primaries played out as Atwater had predicted. The three movement conservatives who were on the ballot—Representative Jack Kemp for the supply-siders, Pat Robertson for the religious right, and Governor Pierre S. "Pete" du Pont of Delaware for libertarian-light conservatism—got in each other's way and could not claim the direct ties to Reagan that Bush had by virtue of his office.

Bush's victory was a tactical marvel. He dispatched Bob Dole, his main opponent, by accusing him of harboring a wish to raise taxes—Bush pledged that he would never do such a thing—and labeling Dole a "straddler" on the issue that was the conservative litmus test. In the primary in New Hampshire, one of the most tax-sensitive states in the country, this was enough. Dole never recovered.

In the general election, Bush embraced Reagan's successes but tried to soften Reaganism by promising to be "the education president" and "the environmental president." For good measure, he pledged to create a "kinder, gentler" America. But toward Dukakis there was neither kindness nor gentleness. Proving there was still some juice in the old conservative social issues, Bush relentlessly went after Dukakis as a "liberal"—it had become a bad word in the 1960s—who favored repealing the death penalty, had vetoed a bill requiring students to say the pledge of allegiance, and backed gun control. To undermine Dukakis's national security credentials, the campaign also featured an ad that included footage of the Massachusetts governor waving from a tank and wearing what the journalist Dorothy Wickenden diplomatically called an "unfortunate helmet." Atwater gleefully said it made Dukakis look like Rocky the Flying Squirrel.

The most emotionally resonant assault of the campaign involved the oldest kind of racial politics, conveniently tied to crime policy. The Bush forces assailed Dukakis for sponsoring a weekend prison furlough program that a convicted killer named Willie Horton had taken advantage of. While out of prison, Horton committed assault, armed robbery, and rape. Horton was African-American. Susan Estrich, Dukakis's campaign manager, said flatly what many (including most Democrats) believed. "It was very much an issue about race and racial fear," she told the Harvard conference. "Look, you can't find a stronger metaphor, intended or not, for racial hatred in this country than a black man raping a white woman. And that's what the Willie Horton story was." Atwater, a southerner well schooled in the politics of race, was fully aware of the ad's implications but denied the ad was about race. He insisted that the furlough program itself "defied common sense." But in an interview shortly before his death, Atwater apologized for the whole thing. "In 1988, fighting Dukakis, I said that I 'would strip the bark off the little bastard' and 'make Willie Horton his running mate,'" Atwater said. "I am sorry for both statements: the first for its naked cruelty, the second because it makes me sound racist, which I am not."

But at the time, it worked. Bush's attacks on Dukakis kept the movement conservatives in line, even if he never inspired them. Bush swept the South and held on to enough of the Reagan Democrats to carry the key industrial states of Pennsylvania, Ohio, Illinois, and Michigan. It helped Bush that the economy was on track again: GDP growth hit 4 percent in 1988.

Viewed one way, Bush's 53 percent of the popular vote was the Reagan Coalition at sustainable cruising speed. He didn't win by the blowout Republican margins of 1972 or 1984, but he won solidly enough.

Yet especially in retrospect, Dukakis's showing can be seen as the beginning of a Democratic recovery. His nearly 46 percent of the popular vote was the second-best Democratic showing in two decades (after Jimmy Carter's narrow 1976 victory). In the Midwest, Dukakis won back about 60 percent of the Reagan Democrats, and about half of them in the Northeast. But in the South, the Reagan Democrats split toward Bush, a sign of the continuing realignment.

Bush's 426–111 Electoral College margin was depressing for Democrats, yet the contours of future Democratic victory maps began to come into view as Dukakis picked up states the Democrats would need in the Northeast, the upper Midwest, and the Pacific Northwest. This, however, can only be seen in retrospect. At the time, Democrats simply saw their fifth defeat in six presidential elections. It pushed many of them—notably a young governor in Arkansas named Bill Clinton—toward intense rounds of introspection.

★

Bush's presidency might have ushered in a more moderate and durable form of conservatism, and for much of his time in office, this seemed an entirely realistic possibility. His two main domestic achievements, a new Clean Air Act and the Americans with Disabilities Act, were broadly progressive and they passed with Democratic support. His management of the end of the Cold War and the reunification of Germany was masterly. And in moving a huge American fighting force to the Middle East to reverse Saddam Hussein's August 1990 invasion and occupation of Kuwait, he won acclaim across the partisan and ideological divides. Bush's approval rating hit an astonishing 89 percent in a Gallup poll completed in early March 1991 and remained in the 60s and 70s through late October.

It was a paradox: although the vote to authorize the intervention closely divided Congress, the Gulf War proved to be an unusually unifying conflict. No doubt some of its popularity owed to a simple fact: the fighting to free Kuwait from Saddam Hussein's forces ended quickly, and in an unambiguous American victory. But it's also true that the first President Bush was respectful in how he approached Congress in seeking ratification of his policies. He did not ask for a war vote during the 1990 midterm election campaign but waited until afterward, thus keeping it out of electoral politics. While he was seeking authorization, he never used the war as a domestic political cudgel. And Bush himself showed resolve, discipline, and restraint. Once he declared in August 1990 that Saddam's aggression against Kuwait "will not stand," he patiently built up American forces in the region—to a peak of over 500,000. There was never an imbalance between American ends and means. His secretary of state, James A. Baker III, painstakingly built broad international support for the American mission.

And after the victory in Kuwait, Bush resisted calls to invade Iraq and overthrow Saddam. His reasoning was explained best by his secretary of defense, Dick Cheney, who would take a different view of the matter a decade later. "We'd achieved our objective," Cheney said in 1992, "and we were not going to get bogged down in the problems of trying to take over and govern Iraq."

But in the end, it was not the war but domestic politics that defined Bush's political standing. After his 1991 highs, Bush's approval rating fell steadily from the fall of 1991 onward, hitting a low point of 29 percent in early August 1992. His central problem was a recession that began in July 1990. Economists placed its end date at March 1991, but the recovery was very slow, and when the Democrats held their convention in July 1992, unemployment still stood at nearly 8 percent. It's no wonder that James Carville, Bill Clinton's brilliant and offbeat political maestro, became known for a quip that was also a strategic insight: "It's the economy, stupid."

Almost as damaging, and far more consequential to the future of conservatism, was Bush's decision to reach a budget deal with Democrats who controlled Congress. With the deficit spiraling upward again, Bush sought spending cuts. To get Democrats to agree, he was willing to raise taxes. Bush's presidency never recovered from his decision to make this concession, and the conservative movement has never been the same.

Bush's efforts to defeat Dole and to paint Dukakis as a liberal—or, as Atwater liked to put it, "the typical, New Deal, northeastern, Kennedy-type liberal"—included his firm pledge never to raise taxes. Perhaps the most memorable and certainly the most concrete line of his 1988 speech accepting the Republican presidential nomination was "Read my lips: No new taxes." For supply-side conservatives who remembered Bush's assault on Reagan's "voodoo economics," it was a signal of Bush's conversion to the true faith.

But Bush was never a real convert, and he felt a sense of responsibility that had long been a characteristic of old-guard conservatives: it was worth breaking a campaign promise to bring the budget closer to balance and avert a crisis.

His mix of tax increases and budget cuts seemed to fall under the traditional definition of fair and balanced, and Bush thought the deal he initially worked out ought to appeal to supply-side conservatives because it excluded any increases in taxes on income or capital gains. It resembled nothing so much as the tax increase Reagan had agreed to in 1982. The initial deal included nearly $300 billion in spending cuts, notably in Medicare, and $133 billion in tax increases on gasoline, alcohol, expensive cars, boats, jewelry, and furs. It also reduced tax deductions on upper-income taxpayers.

By that time, Representative Newt Gingrich had been narrowly elected as House Republican whip. He was best known as a bomb-thrower who had derailed the Democratic Speakership of Jim Wright in 1989 and spent much of his energy assailing Democrats with words such as "bizarre," "pathetic," "lie," "cheat," "corrupt," "sick" and "traitors." Gingrich sat with Bush administration officials, including the man he would make his nemesis, Budget Director Richard Darman, as they negotiated with Democrats. (Darman, also old-fashioned about responsible budgeting, had tried and failed to knock the "no new taxes" pledge out of Bush's 1988 speech.) And then, when the deal was reached, Gingrich denounced it and corralled Republicans to buck their own president on the House floor.

The result on October 5, 1990, was a humiliation for Bush. A president whose approval rating was still positive saw his budget design overwhelmingly rebuked in the House, 254–179, and it was opposed by majorities in both parties. Only 71 of Bush's own Republicans supported it, while 176 of them joined Gingrich in voting no. Only 108 of the 258 Democrats supported the deal. Most of them voted no because they opposed the cuts, or saw the tax package as regressive—or both.

Given Republican opposition to any tax increases, Bush was forced to make further concessions to Democrats to get a deal through. The final package, signed by Bush in early November, violated a core Republican commitment by increasing the top income tax rate from 28 percent to 31 percent. And the final roll call in the House reflected this political reality: Only 10 of the 173 Republicans voting supported it. Democrats, on the other hand, backed it 217–40.

It was a watershed moment. Gingrich earned the lifelong disdain of George H. W. Bush, who, thirty-two years later, would allude to the episode when he endorsed Mitt Romney over Gingrich in the 2012 Republican primaries. The elder Bush didn't directly mention the events of two decades earlier. He simply described Romney as "mature and reasonable—not a bomb-thrower."

But Gingrich's move was, in personal terms, political genius. He set himself up as the leader of conservative forces in the House, the essential step toward his Speakership after the 1994 elections. More important for the long run, he and his conservative troops had transformed Republican and conservative politics. It was no longer possible to balance the movement's two priorities—fiscal prudence and lower taxes. Taxes were now a trump card.

The right could not forgive Bush for a sin they had barely noticed when

Reagan committed it because conservatives believed—no, they *knew*—that the Gipper did not have his heart in it. If Reagan did such a thing, it absolutely had to be the last resort. Of Bush they believed no such thing. Many on the right had always suspected him of being a moderate who had adjusted rightward only because he was an able judge of political reality. To them the budget deal showed that Bush had never really recanted his condemnation of "voodoo economics."

It's said that Reagan established tax-cutting as a central—perhaps *the* central—tenet of Republican and conservative dogma. That's only partly true. As on so many matters, Reagan himself was not dogmatic on taxes. It was the ritual political punishment of George H. W. Bush on the tax issue by conservatives that established there could be no heresy of any kind on the question. The line was drawn on October 5, 1990, in a House vote that might be seen as the first Tea Party roll call. For more than three decades, it would define the GOP.

Paradoxically, given Reagan's flexibility, that moment also established what it meant to be a true Reaganite. George H. W. Bush and his aides saw his administration's task as the *consolidation* of Reaganism—by correcting it in certain areas such as education and the environment; by establishing long-term fiscal solvency, preferably through consumption taxes, while leaving in place, as much as possible, Reagan's commitment to relatively low taxes on income and capital; by preserving Reagan's devotion to pro-business entrepreneurialism; and by emphasizing the achievement of social welfare through voluntarism, thus Bush's "thousand points of light."

One might see Bush's approach as the old "modern Republicanism" of the Eisenhower era pushed a bit further right. And, indeed, Bush's father and George W.'s grandfather, Senator Prescott Bush, had been a champion of the Eisenhower approach. "It is a philosophy of progressive moderation, as the president has called it, or of moderate progressivism, as others name it," Prescott Bush explained in a Lincoln Day speech in the 1950s. Neither word—"progressive" or "moderate"—was popular anymore in the GOP, and George H. W. Bush's effort to inject some moderation into Reaganism failed.

A group of younger Bush aides shared Gingrich's belief that consolidation was a strategy for accommodation and defeat. Conservatism could prosper, in their view, only by continuing to push forward: against taxes, government, regulation, and bureaucracy. It was the conservative version of a theory of permanent revolution. Gingrich saw a narrower discussion of exactly how much government should do to solve particular problems as conceding the terms of the debate to liberals and Democrats. They would win such arguments because voters typically turned toward the center-left when they wanted government to engage in problem solving. The only acceptable conservative solutions (vouchers for education, for example) would be those that further weakened the public sector, decreased the number of public employees, and empowered new private initiatives.

Bush made a spectacular recovery from his October budget setback with his Gulf War triumph. But by the fall of 1991, memories of war victory faded and the economy continued to struggle. Domestic politics returned with a vengeance. Bush seemed directionless, the staunchest conservatives remained restless, and Bush was confronted with a surprisingly robust challenge in the 1992 Republican presidential primaries from Pat Buchanan, who ran boisterously to his right. On February 18, Buchanan shocked the Bush apparatus by winning 38 percent of the vote in the New Hampshire primary and holding Bush to 53 percent. It proved to be the beginning of the end of the Bush presidency.

★

"Richard Nixon was the last president of the liberal era," Robert Borosage, the veteran progressive activist, told me one day over lunch in the 1990s. "Bill Clinton was the last president of the conservative era."

There was hope mixed with analysis here, a reflection of Borosage's desire for an end to the conservative ascendancy that Reagan had announced. But it was a shrewd observation. For most of his career, Nixon operated in the shadow of the New Deal. Arthur Larson's "Modern Republicanism" reflected an acceptance of the America that FDR had created. Nixon's own record included many progressive departures. To win over the working-class voters whose support he so prized, Nixon needed to reassure them that he would not undo the many aspects of the Roosevelt-Truman legacy they prized. Reagan himself was eventually forced to give up on plans of replacing Social Security and scrapping Medicare, LBJ's popular extension of FDR's social insurance state.

Clinton, on the other hand, was reacting to a set of conservative triumphs—to the five Republican election victories since 1968. He understood that the progressive project and the Democratic Party's strategy needed to adjust. A child of the sixties (he had helped run Texas for George McGovern's campaign in 1972), Clinton was acutely aware of how first Nixon and then Reagan had pried working-class votes away from the Democrats. They had done so not by touting Hayek's economic theories or traditional right-wing arguments about "constitutionalism," but by using those "gut" issues that Buchanan and his conservative colleagues on the Nixon campaign championed in 1968: crime, welfare, race, rights, and taxes. These were the issues that had produced what Thomas and Mary Edsall described as a *Chain Reaction*, the title of their perceptive book published in 1992.

Guided by his own instincts and the polling of Stanley Greenberg, who had conducted elaborate studies of Reagan Democrats in the Detroit suburbs of Macomb County, Clinton launched his project to create "New Democrats" in conjunction with the Democratic Leadership Council, a centrist group formed in response to Democratic defeats. The New Democrats' answer to Reagan's paean to "family, work, and neighborhood" was "opportunity, responsibility, and community." Clinton would be tough and smart on crime, and unwavering in supporting the death penalty. He proposed welfare reform, signaling to hard-pressed blue-collar whites who had drifted from the Democrats that he would stand against what he called a "something for nothing" approach to social insurance that those whites saw as promoting indolence. But the design of the Clinton approach, heavily influenced by the progressive Harvard economist David Ellwood and his book *Poor Support*, would be more generous to the needy than the existing system. Clinton's policy balance was also a political balance: "No one who works full time and has children at home should be poor anymore," he'd say. "And no one who can work should stay on welfare forever."

Yet there was also left-of-center populism at the heart of Clinton's appeal. He assailed the Republicans as the party of "the rich and special interests" and spoke of declining pay and the millions of Americans who were "working harder for less," even as business executives pulled down "outrageous salaries." It's likely that no one would have understood what Clinton was doing better—or, in professional terms, appreciated it more—than Lee Atwater.

Clinton's political genius lay in his gifts for juxtaposition and synthesis. He was America's dialectical politician, skilled at drawing on seemingly opposed insights to create something new. He could be seen as trying to re-create the old New Deal alignment by emphasizing a politics of class over race and economics over moral and religious issues. His formula on abortion—it should, he said, be "safe, legal, and *rare*"—was designed to keep pro-choice votes on the Democratic side without alienating too many pro-lifers. His approach was highly satisfactory to the large share of the Americans whose views on abortion were ambivalent and who were altogether tired of the prominence the issue enjoyed.

The historian Sean Wilentz captured the nature of Clinton's politics as well as anyone, and, in keeping with Borosage's insight, he included his account of the Clinton years in a volume titled *The Age of Reagan*. Clinton, Wilentz said, "was not one thing or another, but many things at the same time, and somehow they all hung together." He was presented with political tasks that "required continual bobbing and weaving, compromising and negotiating, retreating in order to advance." He "figured out a great deal on the run." Clinton*ism*, Wilentz added, contrary to what both his staunchest friends and archest critics might have said, "turned out to be neither a set of public positions nor a psychological dysfunction, but an evolving, sometimes improvised, pragmatic politics, informed by liberal values and worked out on the job." Wilentz's last point about Clinton being informed by "liberal values" is important and a fact often ignored both by critics to Clinton's left and by journalistic detractors who saw him as a mere opportunist. Surely there was opportunism, but it was opportunism with a purpose. Paradoxically, Clinton's conservative critics who suspected him of being a stealth progressive may have understood this best.

In the absence of Atwater, Bush's advisers made the great mistake of not taking Clinton seriously in 1992. They saw him as an Arkansas governor who won the Democratic nomination only because so many Democratic heavyweights passed up the race, assuming that Bush would win reelection easily. It was only much later that most political professionals realized Clinton was, in fact, the political heavyweight of his generation. There were a few who did understand Clinton's skills, especially among his fellow governors and old friends from past campaigns. They formed the core of Friends of Bill: the informal, national, and largely invisible political machine he had been building since his college days at Georgetown.

If Bush was hit early from his right by Buchanan, he was the subject of what was a kind of sneak attack from the center, courtesy of the eccentric and very rich Ross Perot. Perot harbored a personal dislike of Bush, an obsession with the budget deficit, and a deep mistrust of free trade. One of his best-known phrases referred to the "giant sucking sound"—of jobs being drawn out of the country. He was the perfect protest candidate of the middle. His budget talk appealed to a certain kind of conservative, his opposition to free trade appealed to blue-collar union members and economic nationalists of the Pat Buchanan stripe, and his discussion of class divisions in the country drew some support on the left. "A disturbing trend has emerged from the decade of greed, the era of trickle-down economics and the period of capital gains tax manipulation," Perot declared, long before the days of Occupy Wall Street. "We are headed for a two-class society." His personal values were obviously conservative, yet his stands on issues such as abortion were moderate or even liberal. At a time when the religious conservatives were a rising force in the Republican Party, Perot did best with more secular voters, including conservatives who were not particularly religious.

Perot entered the race at a moment when both Bush and Clinton were hemorrhaging support, and he was briefly the front-runner, a sign of how utterly unsettled American politics had become and how great the yearning for change was. A Gallup poll in early June 1992 showed Perot at 39 percent, with Bush at 31 and Clinton at 25. But the unpredictable Perot dropped out of the race in July, in the midst of the Democratic National Convention. He declared that his candidacy might no longer be needed "now that the Democratic Party has revitalized itself." There could not have been a move better calculated to hurt Bush. Clinton soared in the polls after a strong convention performance and his choice of a young fellow southerner, Al Gore, as his running mate.

Perot altered the content of the political debate in a way that undercut Bush and unsettled conservatism. Bush's major calling card was a well-executed foreign policy. Conservatives since the time of Goldwater—and especially in the McGovern-Nixon and Carter-Reagan contests—had relied on their reputation for strength in military and foreign affairs as a major asset against liberals whom they regularly accused of being weak. But Perot, capturing the country's post–Cold War mood, announced a new era. "The people are concerned that our government is still organized to fight the Cold War," Perot said. "They want it reorganized to rebuild America as the highest priority." Barack Obama did not invent the idea that "nation building begins at home."

Perot came back into the race in October. He regained his original core support, added liveliness to three televised debates, but never threatened Clinton. And Election Day left Nixon's New Majority and Reagan's coalition shattered.

Bush's 37.4 percent of the popular vote was the lowest Republican share since the 1912 election, when Theodore Roosevelt split the GOP and ran as a Progressive. Bush received nearly 10 million fewer votes than he had won in 1988, and 15 million fewer than Ronald Reagan had received in 1984. He lost particular ground in suburban areas outside the South that had long been a source of Republican strength. Clinton would extend those Democratic suburban gains four years later, and Democrats have largely maintained them since. And even the Republicans' conservative bedrock in the South became competitive again as Clinton picked up 4 of the 11 states of the Old Confederacy and ran Bush close to even in the southern popular vote. Clinton's 43 percent of the popular vote nationally was actually less than Dukakis's share four years earlier. But in a high-turnout contest, Clinton received over 3 million more votes than Dukakis had.

Republicans always insisted that Perot had split the Republican vote and they used Clinton's status as a president elected with well under 50 percent of the vote as part of an effort to undercut his legitimacy. But the truth was that Perot's vote was drawn equally from both parties, and he brought new voters to the polls who would not have shown up had he not run. Exit polls showed that if Perot had not been on the ballot, 38 percent of his supporters would have voted for Bush, 38 percent would have voted for Clinton, and the rest would not have voted at all. Clinton would have won an outright majority if Perot had not rejoined the contest.

Because the "Perot voters" are, into our day, a touchstone of political analysis (an iconic group like the "Wallace voters" or the "Reagan Democrats"), it's important to remember that Perot drew his support from the middle of the middle. Among voters who called themselves both moderate and independent, Perot ran second, ahead of Bush. He did best among voters with middle levels of education—those who attended college but didn't get a degree. He did better in the heart of the middle class than among those who were the best or worst off. He was stronger with men than with women, and 94 percent of his supporters were white.

But the political analyst Ruy Teixeira pointed to two factors that made Perot voters substantially different from Clinton voters. Perot voters were far more skeptical than Clinton's of government spending and government activism. And Perot's partisans had suffered more severe wage losses than comparable voters who shared their demographic backgrounds. This combination of skepticism about government and anger about the economy would matter to the outcome of the midterm elections two years later.

For conservatives, losing badly was a political trauma. After a series of elections that seemed to promise them a long run in power, conservatives watched with alarm and disdain as their standard bearer was reduced to a share of the vote not seen since William Howard Taft in 1912, Herbert Hoover in 1932, and Alf Landon in 1936. A large number of conservatives treated Clinton's election as less than legitimate, not only because of his minority share of the popular vote but also because in the face of his victory, Republicans had gained seats in the House of Representatives. The Republican gains were taken on the right as the true measure of the country's continuing conservatism. Moreover, details of Clinton's irregular personal life had already been aired during the campaign. He was the first president to reach maturity in the 1960s and controversies over his approach to his marriage, to the draft during the Vietnam era, and to marijuana use ("I didn't inhale") were all central to the right's view of who he was. "Not only did he epitomize to many conservatives the things they found distasteful about how the country had changed since the 1960s," Joshua Freeman wrote in his history of the period, "but even more importantly his ascent broke what many conservatives had come to see as their rightful control over the reins of power."

Political oppositions, of course, are by definition opposed to whoever holds office. And charging liberal administrations with being less than fully "American" is by no means a new habit on the right. As far back as 1944, even a progressive Republican like Thomas E. Dewey had linked Franklin Roosevelt to communism. John Bricker, his running mate that year, was more explicit. "First the New Deal took over the Democratic Party and destroyed its very foundation," Bricker had said in a speech in Boston shortly before the election. "Now, these Communist forces have taken over the New Deal and will destroy the very foundations of the republic." McCarthyism had its precedents.

But the Clinton years would establish a new template for the right. Democratic presidents would not simply be opposed. They would face an unprecedented degree of challenge to their authority. This pattern began not with Obama but with Clinton. As Freeman wrote: "From the moment he took office, Clinton faced a well-funded conservative effort to weaken or destroy his presidency by uncovering and publicizing his personal transgressions." No one in 1993 imagined how far it would all go.

The wall of legislative opposition formed early. From the start there would be no Republican votes for Clinton's balanced budget deal, which included, as he had promised during the campaign, a substantial tax increase on the best-off Americans. If Bush had bumped up the top income tax rate to 31 percent, Clinton raised it all the way to 39.5 percent. For the supply-side conservatives, this was both an outrage and a menace. "I believe this program is going to make the economy weak," declared Senator Phil Gramm, who as a conservative Texas Democrat had been a lead sponsor of the Reagan economic program and then became a Republican. "I believe hundreds of thousands of people are going to lose their jobs. I believe Bill Clinton will be one of those people."

"Clearly this is a job killer in the short run," declared Representative Dick Armey, who would later become the Republican majority leader. "The revenues forecast for this budget will not materialize; the costs of this budget will be greater than what is forecast. The deficit will be worse, and it is not a good omen for the American economy."

Once again, conservatives placed their biggest bet on the tax issue. Clinton's plan passed with only Democratic votes. The economy soared through the rest of the decade. The Republicans' economic predictions proved flatly wrong. But in the short run, they were rewarded politically.

For the budget as enacted was a less populist document than the design Clinton had promised during the campaign. Shortly before Clinton took office, Bush disclosed that the deficit had grown by $60 billion. Clinton's advisers of centrist inclinations and Wall Street roots insisted that he make cutting the deficit his highest priority. Only lower interest rates could spur the economy, and cutting the deficit was essential to reassuring the bond market to get those rates down. No wonder James Carville was heard to say that if he were reincarnated, "I want to come back as the bond market. You can intimidate anybody."

In his determination to stand with the budget balancers, Clinton made three tactical errors that served to strengthen his conservative foes. Having failed to get a larger increase in energy taxes in the hope of promoting conservation—it was foiled by the opposition of oil-state senators in his own party—he should have punted on the small four-and-a-half-cent gas tax increase he eventually agreed to. This added a regressive element to an otherwise wholly progressive tax package without raising much money. The move made it easier for Republicans to attack the Clinton plan for hitting all taxpayers, even though its levies were overwhelmingly on the best-off.

Second, Clinton failed to include at least a nod to the promise of a middle-class tax cut he had made in the 1992 campaign. As Bush could testify, voters remember pledges on taxes. Reconfiguring his budget package to include at least a down payment on this tax cut would have served Clinton well in the long run.

Third, he failed to include enough money in his budget to finance a more generous welfare reform. The key to welfare reform was always to combine a work requirement (a worthy goal in itself and a political counter to conservative charges that the welfare state encouraged sloth) with far more generous assistance to the poor. With some liberals already balking, a shortage of funds made it impossible for Democrats to enact a welfare bill—and the measure that finally did pass after Republicans took over Congress was far less generous than Clinton's original design envisioned.

All the measures that went by the wayside had been a direct response to the rise of the right, an effort to defang the "race, rights, and taxes" issues. They fit the Napoleonic axiom that Karl Rove would often cite: "The whole art of war consists in a well-reasoned and circumspect defensive followed by rapid and audacious attack." Clinton temporarily gave up on major components of his well-reasoned defensive.

The battle over the deficit and the influence of financial industry stars like Robert Rubin, Clinton's top economic adviser who later became Treasury secretary, revealed Clintonism's deep tensions. It wasn't simply a matter of "new" and "old" Democrats. There were also overlapping stresses between a working-class strategy and a financial industry strategy; between a desire to appeal to Washington's middle-of-the-road elites and a will to stand as a proud outsider; between a campaigning Clinton and a governing Clinton; between his obligations as a deficit scourge and his aspirations as a policy innovator; and between business-friendliness and support for labor.

During the 1992 campaign, Clinton could fudge some of these choices. He waited until a month before the election to endorse the North American Free Trade Agreement, and his speech announcing his stand was so full of warnings about the damage the treaty could cause without broader policy changes that it barely sounded like an endorsement at all. He called for "supplemental agreements" with Mexico and Canada on environmental and worker safety issues, and for legislation to assist workers and farmers who might be hurt by the treaty. But once he was president, it was an up-or-down matter, despite the side agreements. The fight over NAFTA badly split his party, alienated labor, and delayed the legislative battle over his health care law.

Underlying all the tensions was an uncertainty about whether the Clinton project was primarily reactive or forward-looking—even if Clinton, following Rove's motto about war, would argue that defense and offense went hand in hand. Clinton certainly saw his overall purpose as blazing a new trail, and his aspirations to a Third Way between "the brain dead politics of both parties" had an international aspect. In alliance with British prime minister Tony Blair and moderate social democrats in Europe, Clinton hoped to create a new politics that accepted the dynamism of the market but saw a critical role for government in investing in education, health care, job training, and other public goods while providing social insurance to sustain those whom the market would temporarily leave behind. Blair and Clinton were unrepentant about thinking Big Thoughts and partisans of their approach often referred to their dreams and plans as simply "The Project." When Clinton's friends spoke the words, you could always hear that the *T* in the word *The* was capitalized. It denoted that what they were up to was, to use a favorite Clinton phrase, "a big deal."

But those less enamored of The Project—to its left as well as its right—saw Clinton and Blair as engaged in a holding action that effectively ratified the new conservative era that Reagan and Margaret Thatcher had inaugurated. Critics saw Clinton and Blair as more engaged in making concessions than in breaking new ground. Above all, they seemed to accept the pro-market intellectual and policy revolution that writers like Gilder and Novak had announced, and did little to undo the go-go spirit among the rich that took hold in the 1980s. Peter Mandelson, one of the central architects of British New Labor, captured the spirit of the time (at least in the eyes of his left-of-center critics) when he declared in 1998 that he was "intensely relaxed about people getting filthy rich." In good Third Way fashion, he had appended "as long as they pay their taxes." In the United States, the rich did pay more in taxes—but they still got richer.

Clinton himself may have been the shrewdest judge of how the American political world was realigning. As Republicans moved right, Democrats occupied more and more of the center ground. Seen one way, the Democrats had made a wise and necessary political adjustment. But it came at a cost as Clinton surveyed his own work, with some frustration, in April 1993. He told his advisers, unhappily: "I hope you're all aware we're Eisenhower Republicans here," he said. "We're Eisenhower Republicans fighting the Reagan Republicans. We stand for lower deficits and free trade and the bond market." Clinton's remark was a rather precise description of what would happen to the country's electoral politics in the course of his time in office as the moderate Republican vote in the Northeast and Midwest moved out of the Republican Party. These GOP moderates saw a kindred spirit in Clinton, recognizing the Eisenhower Republicanism in his program, even if they liked this orientation rather more than Clinton did.

Clinton, for his part, saw at least one big thing he could do for those who had elected him and on whose behalf he had intended to govern—a big, traditionally *Democratic* thing. After his confession to becoming an Eisenhower for the 1990s, he had added: "At least we'll have health care to give them, if we can't give them anything else."

But in the end, he couldn't give them health care. Clinton's health care reform effort failed for a complex of reasons, including splits among Democrats over how market-oriented the system should be, fights over how it would be paid for, and a much stronger coincidence of interest among opponents of reform than among its potential supporters. The long-term decline in confidence in government that fed the Reagan Revolution and was then pushed along by it meant that the balance between fear and hope titled toward fear: many Americans worried they had more to lose than gain from a new approach to health care. And Clinton ran into the problem Obama would face later: how intricate any new system must be if it tries simultaneously to use government to expand coverage while keeping some semblance of the private health insurance market intact. As the first mover, Clinton did not have the experience of defeat that Obama would learn from. The Clinton plan was actually more ambitious in scope than Obamacare proved to be. Obama gave more ground—and settled for something less than universal coverage—partly because of the lesson many took from Clinton's failure: when it came to dealing with all the interests involved in the health care system, a great deal of compromise was necessary to get anything done.

But for the purposes of understanding the trajectory of conservatism, a memo written by William Kristol in December 1993 may be the most revealing part of the episode. It baldly laid out the political stakes in *all* battles over government-guaranteed universal coverage. It explained why conservatives have consistently resisted efforts to have the United States follow every other industrialized country in establishing such a guarantee. Nearly two decades before the fact, it showed why Republicans resisted the Affordable Care Act, and have continued to make its repeal one of their highest political priorities.

While Kristol nodded to various policy objections to the Clinton plan, the thrust of his argument was unapologetically political and ideological. In a sense, he paid Clinton the highest possible compliment from a political activist, calling the president's health plan "a serious political threat to the Republican Party."

Why? Because it would upend the core commitments of conservative ideology. "It will relegitimize middle-class dependence for 'security' on government spending and regulation," Kristol explained. "It will revive the reputation of the party that spends and regulates, the Democrats, as the generous protector of middle-class interests. And it will at the same time strike a punishing blow against Republican claims to defend the middle class by restraining government."

For this reason, Kristol condemned Republicans who were seriously considering negotiating with the administration to get a compromise plan through. He didn't name them, but he was clearly thinking of moderates such as Senator John Chafee and legislative warhorses like Senate Minority Leader Bob Dole, a conservative who was also a legislator of the old school. Kristol wrote:

> Any Republican urge to negotiate a "least bad" compromise with the Democrats, and thereby gain momentary public credit for helping the president "do something" about health care, should also be resisted. Passage of the Clinton health care plan, in any form, would guarantee and likely make permanent an unprecedented federal intrusion into and disruption of the American economy—and the establishment of the largest federal entitlement program since Social Security. Its success would signal a rebirth of centralized welfare-state policy at the very moment we have begun rolling back that idea in other areas.

Kristol drew on the work of Clinton pollster Stanley Greenberg, whose views were a mirror image of Kristol's. Greenberg wanted the health care plan to succeed for the same reasons Kristol wanted it to fail. As Green-berg put it later, "this initiative offered the prospect of renewed confidence in this political community's capacity to promote both the individual welfare and the nation's growth." Its passage would be a victory progressives could build on, demonstrating simultaneously the possibility of collective action and the benefits that could flow from it. This is precisely why Kristol insisted that the only logical goal for Republicans was "the unqualified political defeat of the Clinton health care proposal." Such an outcome would be a thoroughly cheerful prospect for conservatism. "Its rejection by Congress and the public would be a monumental setback for the president," he predicted, "and an incontestable piece of evidence that Democratic welfare-state liberalism re-mains firmly in retreat."

Kristol was right about the monumental nature of the setback. The bill died in the fall of 1994 as the midterm election campaign was being joined in earnest. This gave the Republicans new momentum, fostering an impres-sion that Clinton and the Democrats couldn't govern. True, Clinton and the Democrats could brag about their budget, but Republicans largely succeeded in encouraging the public to ignore everything about it except its tax in-creases. In 1994, the economy enjoyed its greatest growth in a decade, but it didn't *feel* like growth. As the *Los Angeles Times* reported, the year "begot the worst stock market since 1990 and the worst bond market in more than 60 years." The core Democratic constituencies at the middle and bottom of the economy were still not feeling the full effects of what was in the process of becoming one of the great boom times in American history.

Clinton had won approval of the North American Free Trade Agree-ment, but he did so only because a large majority of Republicans had voted for it; a majority of his own party voted no. It was not, in any event, an issue that would mobilize either Democrats, particularly its usually reliable labor constituencies, or Perot's voters. On the contrary, many Democrats held his battle for the agreement against Clinton. Perot was highly visible in opposing the treaty and debated it on CNN's *Larry King Live* with Vice President Al Gore. Gore was generally seen as the much crisper debater and the encoun-ter helped his personal standing. But pitting the No. 2 administration figure against the leader of 19 million swing voters was not a wise tactical choice for Democrats. They would need Perot voters in the 2014 midterm elections. They wouldn't get them.

The final big congressional confrontation before the election was over a crime bill that Democrats hoped would shore up their reputation for toughness against lawlessness, a matter still on their mind from Dukakis's defeat. The crime bill contained draconian penalties that made many Democrats uneasy—and would come under sharp attack two decades later for leading to massive over-incarceration, particularly of African-American men. At a critical moment, enough Democrats defected to to derail the bill temporarily. This was taken, correctly, as a major defeat for Clinton. The bill eventually passed but Republicans shrewdly went after it on two fronts. They charged that it was laden with social service pork, and their emblematic attack on a small appropriation for "midnight basketball" programs in inner cities carried unmistakable racial connotations. And they assailed the gun control measures in the bill, which included an assault weapons ban. This mobilized the National Rifle Association for the fall campaign. Thus, even when Clinton and his party followed the New Democrat playbook to defuse those Buchanan "gut" issues, they managed to divide themselves even as Republicans found ways to undercut them. For conservatives, it was another new dawn.

The 1994 Republican takeover of the House is the stuff of conservative legend, and deservedly so. The Republicans gained 54 seats for a 230–204 seat majority on the basis of a 52–45 percent lead in the popular vote. This represented a 6.8 percent swing to the GOP. Republicans gained nine seats in the Senate for a 52–48 majority—and, adding insult to defeat, two Democratic senators, Ben Nighthorse Campbell of Colorado and Richard Shelby of Alabama, padded this advantage by switching to the GOP.

Perot's voters played an important role in the Republican sweep. Two years earlier they had split their votes almost evenly between Republican and Democratic House candidates. In 1994 the Perot voters who went to the polls backed the Republicans by a 2–1 margin. There was talk that it had been the year of "angry white men" for a reason: white men were central to the Republican victory. They had long been somewhat more Republican than other groups. In 1992, 51 percent of them had voted Republican for the House; in 1990, 52 percent of them had. But in 1994, 63 percent of white men voted for the GOP.

Especially alarming for Democrats were their losses in the white working class and middle class. Among white male high school dropouts, the Democratic share of the House vote dropped 10 points between 1992 and 1994; for white male high school graduates who did not go on to college—a classic pollster's definition of who constituted the "working class"—the Democrats dropped an astonishing 20 points, from 57 percent to 37 percent. The lunchbucket vote that had been the linchpin of Democratic majorities in the New Deal era was now part of the conservative coalition.

The 1994 election was not simply a major Republican victory. It also changed American politics in ways that help explain much of what would happen later—in elections, in government, and in the conservative movement. Key to the Republican triumph was the completion of their southern realignment. The Republicans had already picked up some southern seats when Clinton was elected in 1992, partly because of reapportionment plans that packed predominantly Democratic African-American voters into a limited number of southern seats. This increased black representation but also created new, overwhelmingly white and conservative districts. The 1992 tremors were a harbinger of the 1994 earthquake, and the election was the final answer to Charles Wallace Collins's 1947 question: *Whither Solid South?* The white South was now solidly Republican.

Thus: In 1990, Democrats had controlled 83 House seats in the South (the 11 states of the Old Confederacy plus Oklahoma and Kentucky) to 46 for the Republicans. After 1994, Republicans outnumbered Democrats in the South for the first time since Reconstruction: 73 southern House members were Republican, only 64 were Democrats. Republicans also came out of 1994 with a majority of southern U.S. Senate seats and governorships. The overall Democratic vote among southern whites collapsed, too. In 1990, 50 percent of white southerners had voted for Democratic candidates for the House; in 1994, only 36 percent did.

This was the year when American politics was both nationalized and polarized. The process took three forms: congressional voting was brought into line with presidential voting; partisan allegiances were brought into a tighter relationship with how voters actually cast their ballots; and ideological sympathies and partisan sympathies came to overlap to a larger degree than ever.

Going into 1994, Democrats held 51 seats in districts that had voted for

George H. W. Bush in both 1988 and 1992, most of them in southern or border states; in Clinton's first midterm election, they lost 27 of these. They also lost 21 of the 77 seats they held in swing districts that had voted for Bush in 1988 but Clinton in 1992. On the other hand, they lost only 8 of the 128 seats that had voted Democratic for president in both elections. Voters often said they were tired of partisan politics, but in 1994, they made choices that divided the country along the now-overlapping lines of partisanship and ideology more rigidly than ever.

This was true at the level of the individual voter as well. In the 1990 midterm elections, 23 percent of voters who called themselves Republican nonetheless voted for Democratic House candidates; in 1994, only 8 percent of Republicans voted for Democrats for the House. The same was true ideologically: 37 percent of self-described conservatives voted Democratic for the House in 1990; only 19 percent did in 1994. The sorting by party and ideology was nearly complete: In 1990, fully 22 percent of those who described themselves as conservative and Republican voted Democratic in House races; only 5 percent did in 1994. On the other side, liberal Democrats were one of the only groups in the country that gave *less* support to the Republicans in 1994 than they did in 1990: 16 percent of liberal Democrats voted for Republican House candidates in 1990; four years later, the figure was cut in half.

The sorting was virtually complete by 2010, when only 2 percent of conservative Republicans and 3 percent of liberal Democrats voted for candidates of the opposing party. And the white South continued to move away from the Democrats; by 2010, their share of the white southern vote in House races was down to 27 percent. But political developments that were later described as the product of the Obama years—particularly the polarization that was the topic of such obsessive conversation—were actually set in motion when Clinton was president.

The rise of a competitive House after years of Democratic dominance created strong new political incentives for confrontation. In keeping with Lubell's theory of "sun" and "moon" parties, a minority party accepting the likelihood of a long period out of power is more likely to deal and compromise with a dominant majority than a party that sees defeat as only temporary and is constantly on the lookout for an edge to win a majority in the next election.

When Obama's top political adviser David Axelrod would quip that "in Washington, every day is Election Day," he intended it as a knock on the city's (and particularly the media's) lack of interest in governing. But in truth, the ongoing, closely fought nature of both House and Senate elections, a legacy of 1994, meant that for congressional leaders in both parties, *treating every day as Election Day was an entirely rational choice.* It was a form of rationality that would lead to gridlock, polarization, and even impeachment.

Newt Gingrich was always proud of the "Contract with America," the program for action in the new Congress that almost all Republican candidates signed on to in the fall of 1994.

It's not that the Contract was actually electorally decisive. "The notion that we won because of the Contract with America was never valid," said Vin Weber two decades later. It was, rather, "a useful tactic." Since "a candidate running for federal office for the first time doesn't always know what to say," Weber observed, "the contract gave them all something to talk about."

And the existence of what was cast as a governing document helped soften the Republicans' image. Having resisted every major component of Clinton's program, Gingrich's band wanted to insist that they were more than a party of the very loud "No!" They had ideas for where they would take the country.

In fact, the Contract was highly revealing about the nature of Republican and conservative priorities. It came in two parts. The first pledged to enact immediately a series of rules changes aimed at taking advantage of disaffection (particularly among Perot voters) with how Democrats had run the House. Democratic leaders were cast as tired, out of touch, high-handed, and suffering from an arrogant sense of entitlement. Most of the ideas were crowd-pleasers, among them: requiring that Congress be subjected to all laws applied "to the rest of the country," reducing the number of House committees and applying term limits to all committee chairs, launching audits to discover "waste, fraud, or abuse" in Congress, and requiring all committee hearings to be made public. There was only one rules change that affected substantive legislation. It required a three-fifths majority to pass a tax increase—which meant empowering a conservative minority to override the majority's view on the one issue that, as George H. W. Bush learned, had developed a near-sacred standing for conservatives.

Next, it listed ten specific bills that House Republicans promised to enact during their first hundred days in power. Five of them involved tax cuts or tax limitations of one sort or another. There was a tough-on-crime bill, another to cut welfare, and a potpourri of socially conservative initiatives ("The Family Reinforcement Act") that included child support enforcement, anti-pornography measures, and more tax benefits to promote adoption and care for elderly parents. The "National Security Restoration Act" included a classic right-wing attack on the United Nations ("No U.S. troops under U. N. command") along with military spending increases. Another promised bill, aimed at securing the votes of senior citizens, repealed the tax increases on Social Security benefits passed as part of Clinton's budget package. Two other bills, "The Job Creation and Wage Enhancement Act" and "The Common Sense Legal Reform Act," were business wish lists. And for those who despised Congress as a general matter, there were term limits for House members.

The Contract was a politically clever (and carefully focus-grouped) document. The journalist Ronald Brownstein aptly saw the document as one part Reagan, one part Perot, and one part William Bennett, the last a reference to social conservatism's informal culture czar. One might amend this to say that it was more like two or three parts Reagan, given its emphasis throughout on lower taxes and smaller government and its bows to the corporate sector with its talk of tort reform, deregulation, and various business tax breaks.

The Contract was also a tribute, simultaneously, both to Clinton *and* to Clinton's failures. Its proposed tax credit for parents and children was a Clinton idea (his old middle-class tax cut) that blended relief for working-class and middle-class voters with a mild pro-family social traditionalism. It was a rebuke to Clinton for having allowed the middle-class tax cut to go by the wayside when he shifted his emphasis to budget reduction. The Republicans' welfare reform measures were far harsher than Clinton's—but the failure of Clinton and Democrats in Congress to enact a plan of their own opened a path for the GOP's more punitive approach. As for the Perot voters, Clinton had promised a variety of political reforms, including campaign finance reform, but these were killed by Democrats in Congress who had become accustomed to generous political action committee contributions. The short-sightedness of Democrats on this issue became clear with lightning speed. Business interests that had contributed generously to Democrats when they seemed likely to control the House indefinitely now massively shifted their funds to Republicans, with whom they had far more ideological affinity.

Decades after the fact, it's easy to forget the import of 1994. It is not simply that the structural changes in our politics that the election ushered in are still with us. The election also helped discredit one conservative approach and ratify another. Gone was George H. W. Bush's hope to create a conservatism that would consolidate the movement's gains while making concessions to middle-ground opinion on the environment and education. Gone also was acknowledgment of the need for more revenue to run a government that provided benefits American voters wanted. On the rise was the claim by Gingrich and his allies that a tougher, bolder approach that held the line on taxes and pushed the boundaries of conservatism rightward would be more successful. That Bush lost in 1992 and Gingrich won in 1994 sent a powerful message as to which approach held more promise.

In the meantime, Clinton's supporters were disappointed in their hope that his Third Way politics would not only create a broad center-left majority but also eventually force the Republicans and the conservative movement to pursue a more moderate path. This was by no means a foolish bet. It is precisely what happened in Britain when the Conservative Party, after three successive defeats at the hands of New Labor, modernized itself under David Cameron.

But rather than ratify center-left gains, the 1994 election upended them. The parts of the progressive coalition that leaned toward the center still had profound differences with the parts that leaned left, trade being emblematic of some of the deepest tensions. Later in the decade, arguments over deregulating the financial industry would sharpen these divisions. And the difficulty Democrats had in bringing the white working class back into the fold—a problem since Nixon's days—limited their ability to create a durable majority of their own. This set up an ongoing battle of two populisms, with conservatives relying on social issues (again, "race, rights, and taxes"), and progressives trying to develop what Greenberg called "a renewed bottom-up vision" rooted in economic inclusion.

In 1994, the initiative passed to the conservatives' side. They would not keep it for long.

Since the rise of Reagan, conservatives have always foundered on the interrelated issues of taxing, spending, and popular attitudes toward government. The cause of their difficulty was first explained in 1967 by two wise students of public opinion, Lloyd Free and Hadley Cantril. In what has become a hallowed formulation among political scientists, journalists, and politicians alike, Free and Cantril argued that Americans are, at one and the same time, "ideological conservatives" and "operational liberals." Americans tend to express conservative views at a general or philosophical level but seek rather a lot from government and usually welcome its efforts to solve problems.

Free and Cantril help explain the voter, often mocked by liberals, who tells a politician to "keep the government's hands off my Medicare." It is, of course, an absurd statement on a substantive level. Yet this citizen was probably a Free-and-Cantril sort who liked the government program in question just fine but so mistrusted government he could not imagine that something he appreciated so much was actually a state-run program.

Ever since the rise of supply-side economics, conservatives have saddled themselves with commitments that are difficult to square. It's true that they have been able to have them add up in theory, as Paul Ryan has done by proposing budgets with steep spending cuts designed to make possible the large tax cuts he favors. But even if the public either did not mind or welcomed the reductions in taxes—though tax cuts for the wealthy are not, in fact, broadly popular—they want core public services (particularly those they benefit from) and resist most program reductions. This is why Reagan could manage steep cuts only in the modest part of the budget that goes primarily to the very poor.

Conservatives often compound their difficulty by supporting large increases in military spending, as Reagan did and Ryan does. The growth in the libertarian wing of the Republican Party reflects a partial coming to terms with this challenge. Rand Paul and his allies want to cut defense budgets along with everything else. But libertarians, in the end, face the same overall political problem: defense aside, voters still want far more from government than the libertarians are willing to provide. And, as Paul's political difficulties showed, they remain a minority within the broader conservative movement.

Related to this problem is conservative fealty to "small government" as a moral imperative. Again, as an abstraction, this is popular. Calling for an end to "government intrusion" and "excessive regulation" brings cheers—until an environmental catastrophe strikes, an unsafe product kills people, or an inadequately inspected plane goes down. The definitive observation on the subject was offered by a Republican in the midst of the Gingrich Revolution in 1996, after the crash of an airliner flown by a now-defunct company called ValuJet. "Government is the enemy," said Senator William Cohen of Maine, "until you need a friend." Reflecting the direction many moderates were moving in, Cohen, a classic Eisenhower Republican, later joined the Clinton administration as secretary of defense.

The Republicans' budget and regulatory conundrums revived Bill Clinton's political fortunes. But his political resurrection set loose the conservative furies.

5

THE GINGRICH REVOLUTION AND CONSERVATISM'S SECOND CHANCE

M2E2 and the Right's Achilles' Heel

"I was determined to hold them to the laws of arithmetic."

Clinton was shell-shocked by the Republicans' 1994 gains and his reaction was comprehensive. He went into a period of introspection and shook up his operations. A key move was bringing back into his fold a consultant from earlier in his career. Dick Morris had become increasingly conservative with the years and was known as a political Svengali who did what it took to win. Clinton reasoned that Morris would be more in tune with what seemed to be a growing conservative mood in the country. Clinton also pushed aside Greenberg, who believed in a populist approach to the middle class, and brought in Mark Penn and his partner Doug Schoen. Both had a passion for seeking and finding the political center.

As Clinton explained in his memoir, Morris's "main advice was that I had to practice the politics of 'triangulation,' bridging the divide between Republicans and Democrats and taking the best ideas of both." Thus did a new word enter the American political lexicon. Clinton put a positive spin on the idea, but it also meant that he could run *against* both Republicans and Democrats when doing so was convenient. He was at pains after his presidency to insist that "while many liberals and some in the press corps" saw triangulation as "compromise without conviction, a cynical ploy to win re-election," he saw it differently—as a continuation of his DLC-style politics and the sort of thing he had done as governor of Arkansas. "I had always tried to synthesize new ideas and traditional values, and to change government policy as conditions changed," he insisted.

Whatever "triangulation" was, Clinton's rebound owed at least as much to what Republicans did as to his own strategy. The GOP, particularly in the House, gave Clinton plenty of maneuvering room, and he noted elsewhere in his memoir that his belief the GOP would overreach was a source for his confidence that he would survive politically after 1994. He'd be helped by steady economic improvement, but also by the fact that "the new Congress, especially the House, was well to the right of the American people." Republicans, he predicted, "would soon be proposing cuts in education, health care, and aid to the environment to pay for their tax cuts and defense increases."

"It would happen," he added, "because that's what ultra-conservatives wanted to do, and because I was determined to hold them to the laws of arithmetic." Salvation through math: it would work again and again whenever liberals confronted a resurgent conservatism.

Before the fight, however, came Clinton's nod to conciliation. His 1995 State of the Union address contained many bows to the new Gingrich dispensation—with little digs thrown in for the future. "I think we all agree that we have to change the way the government works. Let's make it smaller, less costly, and smarter; leaner, not meaner," Clinton said.

The congressional crowd noticed the "not meaner" line and chuckled. Clinton was doing what he could to triangulate the Republicans' way rhetorically while still defending core Democratic propositions.

First came the bow to the Republican victory:

Our government, once a champion of national purpose, is now seen by many as simply a captive of narrow interests, putting more burdens on our citizens rather than equipping them to get ahead. The values that used to hold us all together seem to be coming apart. . . . Our job is to get rid of yesterday's government so that our own people can meet today's and tomorrow's needs. And we ought to do it together.

Then the Democratic pivot:

But I think we should all remember, and almost all of us would agree, that government still has important responsibilities. Our young people—we should think of this when we cut—our young people hold our future in their hands. We still owe a debt to our veterans. And our senior citizens have made us what we are. Now, my budget cuts a lot. But it protects education, veterans, Social Security and Medicare, and I hope you will do the same thing. You should, and I hope you will.

He was setting the Republican revolutionaries up.

The Republicans busily went about passing their Contract—for the new congressional majority, it served the useful postelection function of creating discipline in a raucous caucus—but this would not prove to be the 104th Congress's main act. The Republicans and Clinton negotiated on the budget through the end of the fiscal year on September 30, 1995, and the government continued to operate on a continuing resolution (they're known to budgeters as "CRs") until mid-November. On November 10, as Clinton recounted, Congress sent him "a new CR that increased Medicare premiums 25 percent, cut funding for education and the environment, and weakened environmental laws." Clinton wouldn't go for it. On Veterans Day, he continued to insist he wanted to work with Republicans to balance the budget but in a way that was "consistent with our fundamental values" and "without threats and without partisan rancor." Clinton did not leave it to the media to get the message across. After Labor Day, Democrats started running television ads criticizing the GOP's cuts, especially in Medicare and Medicaid. This infuriated Gingrich and his colleagues, who had not expected as much resistance from the triangulating Clinton.

After a fruitless and angry negotiating session on November 13 (Clinton reports that House Majority Leader Dick Armey complained that the Clinton TV ads had "frightened his elderly mother-in-law"), Clinton vetoed both the CR and a bill raising the debt ceiling that was also packed with objectionable Republican measures. The shutdown began on November 14 and 800,000 federal workers were sent home. Shutdowns continued off and on until January 6, 1996, when Republicans finally reached a deal that gave Clinton most of what he wanted. The Gingrich revolutionaries in the House felt intense pressure from Senate Majority Leader Bob Dole, who was running for president. Dole had always harbored doubts about the shutdown strategy, and he knew his association with Gingrich was hurting him. In all, the government was shut for twenty-seven days.

In the long saga, Republicans made a series of errors that were characteristic of problems that conservatism would continue to confront. The most basic miscalculation was one that Clinton took pleasure in, recounting in his memoir. "'We made a mistake,'" he quotes Gingrich as saying during a budget meeting shortly before a deal was reached. "'We thought you would cave.'"

It was not an entirely foolish blunder. Clinton himself was uncertain early on as to whether he could win a shutdown fight. Morris believed the administration needed to reach an accord with the Republicans and thus sent signals—not intended to be misleading—that there was an agreement to be had. But as the fight went on, Clinton realized he was on the high ground. His political resurrection, he realized, would depend on standing strong and not capitulating.

The strength of Clinton's position owed to a more fundamental miscalculation by his opponents, one rooted in conservative ideology. Forgetting the Free and Cantril insight, Republicans assumed that voters had handed them a mandate to shrink the size of government and that this abstract goal was more important to voters than the particulars of the cuts it would take to achieve the objective. Clinton zeroed in on four areas where majorities welcomed public spending. "Medicare, Medicaid, Education, and the Environment" became a Clinton litany repeated so often that that the administration's defenders gleefully turned it into a would-be character from the *Star Wars* movie: M2E2. Clinton reduced Gingrich to the role of Darth Vader. In the name of the Conservative Empire, the Speaker was endangering the good that government did.

Their philosophical blinders led the staunchest conservatives in Gingrich's ranks to miscalculate how the public would respond to the shutdown itself. Government was so unpopular, they assumed, that Americans wouldn't much notice its absence. "Have you missed the government?" Senator Phil Gramm, asked on ABC's *This Week with David Brinkley,* certain that he knew the answer. The reply of many Americans was, "Yes, we do."

Representative David Funderburk from South Carolina shared Gramm's certainty and believed the shutdown proved the point conservatives wanted to make about government. "We have had 800,000 Federal workers on furlough. Can the liberals continue to argue that these Federal workers and the thousands of idle programs they administer are critical to the health and safety of our country?" he declared. "Americans don't miss these programs on Federal holidays and they certainly don't miss them today." But miss them they did.

The 1995–96 shutdown battle also brought home the contradiction between the Republicans' stated desire for a balanced budget and the higher priority they placed on tax cuts. The GOP revolutionaries made a large mistake: their proposed $245 billion in Medicare cuts almost exactly matched the size of their tax cuts. This made it easy for Clinton and the Democrats to argue that conservatives were not paring back Medicare in the name of fiscal responsibility. They were cutting a popular program to finance their ideological obsession. Polls consistently showed that given a choice, voters preferred protecting Medicare to cutting taxes—Free and Cantril, again. And at crucial moments, both Gingrich and Bob Dole managed to remind voters that most Republicans (including, it should be said, Ronald Reagan, with considerable passion) had opposed Medicare in the first place.

In an unusually candid editorial published as the negotiations wound toward their troubling end for Republicans, the conservatives at *National Review* grappled with the tension that would vex conservatives again and again. "The balanced budget is more important as symbolism than as accounting," the magazine admitted editorially. "What matters now is that the government be clearly put on a path of reduced improvidence." Suddenly the goal that closed the government for nearly a month and created political chaos was no more than a symbol.

"Republicans have stopped talking about the positive aspects of their program," *National Review* complained, "because they are so preoccupied with the essentially defensive message of 'reducing the rate of growth' of government programs. Balancing the budget is consuming every issue that comes near it."

National Review's recipe was for the Republicans to give in to President Clinton on many of the numbers as long as conservatives got major policy changes in return. There was nothing wrong with throwing another $70 billion at Medicare, the magazine's editors said, as long as Republicans preserved their medical savings accounts, which would severely undercut Medicare and represented "a radical departure from the Great Society model of government." Throw more money at Medicaid, they said, but don't let the White House preserve its "entitlement status" as the medical program of last resort for the poor. Unsurprisingly, there was only one issue on which the magazine counseled "intransigence." The Republicans, the editors advised, should insist on their entire $245 billion tax cut.

Here was the clincher from the bellwether of conservative opinion. "Their most important accomplishment this year," the magazine said of congressional Republicans, "is not potentially balancing the budget—an elusive goal still nearly a decade away—but scrapping huge chunks of the federal entitlement state." (To nearly everyone's surprise, balance would be reached far sooner, for reasons having very little to do with the Battle of the Shutdown.)

In one essay, the magazine neatly explained why the Republicans had such difficulty in fashioning a coherent and unified negotiating strategy, and why they were in disarray. The balanced budget was for some Republicans a vital goal and for others merely a front for the underlying conservative agenda. And so it would be two decades later.

★

In the midst of the budget wrangling, a devastating tragedy would cause the nation to pause and consider the implications of the abrasive antigovernment rhetoric that had taken hold on the far right. At 9:02 a.m. on April 19, 1995, a truck bomb exploded outside the Alfred P. Murrah Federal Building in Oklahoma City. The attack killed 168 people and injured nearly 700. Within a sixteen-block radius, 324 buildings were damaged or destroyed.

Initial speculation saw the attacks as the work of Arab or Muslim terrorists, which only increased the nation's shock when it learned that the bombing was the work of two Americans, Timothy McVeigh and Terry Nichols. McVeigh had been inspired by the racist and antigovernment writings of William Luther Pierce, a white supremacist who wrote under the pseudonym Andrew McDonald. His 1978 novel, *The Turner Diaries*, described the overthrow of the American government and a resulting nuclear war and race war that culminated in the extermination of Jews, gays, and nonwhites. Two pages from the book describing plans for the bombing of the FBI building in Washington were found in McVeigh's getaway car. McVeigh made clear that he was responding to the FBI's fifty-one-day siege of a compound in Waco, Texas, occupied by a cult known as the Branch Davidians. The siege ended on April 19, 1993—two years to the day before the Oklahoma City attack—with the burning of the compound and the death of seventy-six people, including the group's leader, David Koresh. For many on the far right, Waco became the symbol of an oppressive federal government. In a letter to Fox News' Rita Crosby a week after the Oklahoma City attack, McVeigh spoke the language of a soldier doing battle against an enemy.

"I chose to bomb a federal building because such an action served more purposes than other options," he wrote. "Foremost, the bombing was a retaliatory strike; a counter attack, for the cumulative raids." The federal government had grown "militaristic and violent," he said, and the bombing was "a pre-emptive (or pro-active) strike" against its "command and control centers within the federal building."

"When an aggressor force continually launches attacks from a particular base of operation, it is sound military strategy to take the fight to the enemy."

The "enemy" was the government of the United States.

For Clinton, whom Republicans had cast as a big-government advocate despite his New Democrat exertion, the bombing was an occasion for a direct and forceful challenge to right-wing rhetoric. "People should examine the consequences of what they say," he said, "and the kinds of emotions they're trying to inflame." He urged Americans to resist "the purveyors of hatred and division" and "the promoters of paranoia." Sensing the danger, Newt Gingrich shot back at liberals who saw links between McVeigh's extremism and the standard rhetoric of the right. "It is grotesque," said Gingrich, "to suggest that anybody in this country who raises legitimate questions about the size and scope of the federal government has any implication in this." The contrast between the two statements suggests who was on offense after the attack, and who was on defense.

In a moving speech in Oklahoma City on April 23, Clinton stayed away from politics and spoke comforting words steeped in religious faith. "It was the nation's first exposure to Clinton as mourner in chief," Michael Waldman, his chief speechwriter, wrote later. "In fact, it was the first time Clinton had been a reassuring figure rather than an unsettling one." But if Clinton was subtle, he did not miss the chance to make a case against extremism. "Let us let our own children know that we will stand against the forces of fear," he declared. "When there is talk of hatred, let us stand up and talk against it. When there is talk of violence, let us stand up and talk against it. In the face of death, let us honor life."

And in honoring the dead, he offered an image of government workers far removed from conservative attacks on distant bureaucrats or McVeigh's denunciations of federal officials as "militaristic and violent." The public employees killed in the bombing were fellow citizens, Clinton said, "who served the rest of us—who worked to help the elderly and the disabled, who worked to support our farmers and our veterans, who worked to enforce our laws and to protect us. Let us say clearly, they served us well, and we are grateful."

In the ensuing years, historians and journalists have debated whether Clinton's response to Oklahoma City was even more important to rescuing his presidency than the budget battles with Gingrich and the Republicans. The *New York* magazine writer Peter Keating made one of the best cases for this view fifteen years after the bombing. He argued that Clinton "found his voice" after Oklahoma City and that his response "gave Clinton the chance to pull his presidency together." Both are true.

Keating cites a memo from Dick Morris eight days after the attack suggesting that Clinton could use "extremism as issue against Republicans," not by "direct accusations," but via a "ricochet theory," since some Republicans would be pushed by some of their supporters to defend right-wing militias that had been organized to oppose a federal government they looked upon much as McVeigh did. Clinton, as Keating notes, never went as far as Morris suggested, but he did write in his memoir: "The haters and extremists didn't go away, but they were on the defensive, and, for the rest of my term, would never quite regain the position they had enjoyed after Timothy McVeigh took the demonization of government beyond the limits of humanity."

Clinton brought the links between various parts of his message home at his 1996 State of the Union speech when he invited Richard Dean, a Vietnam veteran who had worked in the Murrah Federal Building and, as Keating noted, "re-entered the building four times to rescue people after it blew up." But Clinton was not simply praising a hero. He was also making a point about the government shutdown. "This last November," Clinton said of Dean, "he was forced out of his office when the government shut down. And the second time the government shut down, he continued helping Social Security recipients, but he was working without pay. . . . I challenge all of you in this chamber: Never, ever shut the federal government down again."

Keating concluded: "That's how much Clinton got it: He explicitly linked the terror of Oklahoma City to the federal shutdown, and both to the Republican Congress. After that, Clinton barely needed to look over his shoulder to get reelected."

However one judges the Oklahoma City effect, it's clear that Clinton's budget victory was a setup for a triumphant election year that finally saw a complete economic revival. Jobs were up by 2.6 million. Both the index of consumer confidence and the sale of new homes were up by 11.5 percent. The economy's momentum was such that in 1997 growth would hit an astonishing 8.2 percent. By the end of Clinton's term, incomes were growing even for those who found themselves at the bottom of the class structure and who had long suffered from stagnating incomes. (It would not be long before they were stagnating and falling again.) The Roaring Nineties had hit their stride.

In his 1996 State of the Union message, Clinton arrived at the apotheosis of triangulation in two sentences. "The era of big government is over," he declared. "But we cannot go back to the time when our citizens were left to fend for themselves." He made a giant (and both unnecessary and inaccurate) ideological concession in the first sentence, and then pulled it back.

For conservatives, there was an odd disconnect between the Gingrich Revolution and the battle for the Republican presidential nomination. Senator Bob Dole was the front-runner but he was also caught up in the congressional mayhem, and his involvement with the shutdown would hurt him in the fall contest with Clinton. "If Dole wins and Gingrich runs Congress," ran the tagline on one Clinton ad, "there'll be nobody there to stop them." It was simple, and devastating, given the collapse of Gingrich's popularity.

Yet in the primaries, Dole was in no way a representative of the new conservative rebels. On the contrary, he was the voice of an older style of congressional politics. A staunch conservative, the man who had knocked Nelson Rockefeller off the Republican ticket sixteen years earlier was now cast as a Rockefeller Republican.

Dole narrowly won the Iowa caucuses, with Pat Buchanan coming in a very close second. Buchanan had never stopped running after 1992. His Republican convention speech four years earlier declaring the country in the midst of a "culture war" and a "religious war" did George H. W. Bush much harm among swing voters. But it solidified Buchanan's standing with the social conservatives who loomed large in Iowa Republican politics. Combining this with Perot-style economic nationalism made Buchanan a powerful force but ultimately doomed him in a party whose pro-business wing strongly favored free trade.

Buchanan's strength helped Dole in the long run because it dispatched two other conservatives who might have posed a more significant challenge later. Millionaire publisher Steve Forbes ran in favor of flat taxes, while Phil Gramm was the closest thing to a Gingrich revolutionary on the ballot.

By edging out Dole in the New Hampshire primary, Buchanan caused the front-runner a temporary embarrassment, but he also fatally wounded the one candidate who might have beaten Dole and run a Clinton-style campaign against Clinton himself. Lamar Alexander, the former education secretary, had also served as Tennessee's governor and his profile was similar to Clinton's, a young New South figure who had focused on improving education in his state. Yet the mood in the party created an odd set of incentives for Alexander that showed how difficult it was to offer a governing agenda: a campaign video simultaneously touted Alexander's achievements as secretary of education—and called for the abolition of the very department he had led. A strong Alexander challenge to Dole (and, if he had won the party's nomination, to Clinton) can be seen in retrospect as a path-not-taken for contemporary conservatism. Alexander had the potential of being a conservative modernizer, marrying Clinton's pragmatic style to a center-right ideology. But when the votes were counted in New Hampshire, the result at the top was a three-way split: 27 percent for Buchanan, 26 percent for Dole, and 22 percent for Alexander. Having also finished third in Iowa, Alexander was finished in the campaign. There was room for one Establishment candidate. There was room for the ideological enthusiasms of Buchanan and Forbes. There was not room for an innovator.

The topsy-turvy nature of politics on the right was captured by a poignant moment in February 1996 when Dole visited the eighty-seven-year old Barry Goldwater at his home in Arizona's McDowell Mountains. Dole was there to get Mr. Conservative's blessing, and the scripted part of the visit went just fine. Goldwater vouched for Dole as the heir to "the Barry Goldwater, Ronald Reagan legacy of conservatism," while condemning Buchanan for offering a "fearful and divisive" message.

But then, with reporters present, the two old warhorses could not resist ruminating on how much their party had changed. Dole, always irrepressible, went completely off the talking points. "Barry and I—we've sort of become the liberals," Dole cracked.

Goldwater agreed. "We're the new liberals of the Republican Party," he said with a laugh. "Can you imagine that?"

It is difficult to find a more revelatory statement about what had happened to conservatism. The shift rightward was, indeed, breathtaking.

Dole eventually secured the nomination and chose Jack Kemp as his running mate. In doing so, Dole was reaching back to one of the most powerful strands of Reaganism, but also forward to what would later become compassionate conservatism.

Kemp's story is revealing about what conservatism had become, but also about the turn it had yet to take. No politician was so identified with supply-side economics and its vigorous tax cutting, which reinforced Dole's call for a 15 percent across-the-board tax cut. No one was as evangelical as Kemp was about the power of rewarding "work, savings, and investment." (I saw this in my own mail; Kemp regularly sent me good-natured admonishments when I wrote in favor of tax increases.) The Reagan tax cuts were honored in short-hand as "Kemp-Roth," after Kemp and Delaware Senator Bill Roth.

Yet as a former NFL quarterback who had worked in the racially inte-grated environment of professional sports, Kemp was passionate about the need for Republicans and conservatives to reach out to African-Americans and to others in need. He had been an activist secretary of housing and urban development under Bush, giving life to a department Republicans so often treated as a backwater. He was always in search of ways to benefit inner-city residents through policies rooted in his low-tax, entrepreneurial philosophy. He pushed, for example, for the sale of public housing units to tenants, and extolled enterprise zones, where taxes would be waived to encourage invest-ment. For Kemp there was no conundrum about tax cuts and deficits: he was plainly not worried a bit about the latter. He assumed that the high growth rates he was certain his tax cuts would promote could finance all the social spending he did not want to cut. There were epithets in Kemp's world for Republicans who cared about deficits too much. He'd say they were propos-ing unnecessary painful "root canal" economics because they were obsessive "green eyeshade" people who looked only at budget numbers. Kemp devoutly believed in the obligation to create a world without pain—and sometimes, in his rejection of trade-offs, he seemed to imagine that such a world already existed.

Kemp, who died in 2009, had only one speed: enthusiasm. He was as sunny and ebullient as any politician who ever walked the halls of Congress. He was as loved by liberals for his ferocious opposition to racism as he was by conservatives for his in-season-and-out devotion to tax reduction and entre-preneurship. Paul Ryan has honored the Kemp tradition by repeatedly speak-ing of him as a role model and a hero.

But Kemp's highly vocal dedication to the interests of African-Americans and Latinos, including immigrants, has never caught on with a large share of the conservative movement. Kemp realized this and was openly and regularly impatient with his party and his ideological comrades. This tripped him up in the sole vice presidential debate that fall with Al Gore. When asked at one point about affirmative action, Gore set a trap for Kemp by complimenting him. "I want to congratulate Mr. Kemp for being a lonely voice in the Republican Party over the years on this question," Gore said, seemingly graciously. "It is with some sadness that I refer to the fact that the day after he joined Senator Dole's ticket, he announced that he was changing his position and was . . . thereafter going to adopt Senator Dole's position to end all affirmative action."

Kemp bristled. "My position on affirmative action has been clear ever since I left the professional football career for Congress in 1970," he insisted, and then repeated his mantra about the urgency of "extending access to credit and capital, job opportunities, educational choice in our inner cities." He also gave one of his classic sermons on inclusiveness. "It is so very important for Americans, white and black, Jew and Christian, immigrant and native born," Kemp said, "to sit down and talk and listen and begin to understand what it's like to come from that different perspective."

What Kemp did not do—conservatives noticed this and they were angry—was challenge Gore for singling him out as "a lonely voice in the Republican Party" on issues related to race. Nor did he defend Dole, presumably his main job as his running mate. Gore's description of his debate opponent ran too close to the way Kemp saw himself. Kemp remains a touchstone for conservatives eager to see their movement take the path toward inclusion. But his reaction that night suggested he realized how long the journey would be.

As 1996 went on, Clinton and Republican leaders in Congress—perhaps especially Gingrich—realized they might share common interests, after all, as Morris thought they would. Republicans were desperate to hold their majority, which they sensed was imperiled by the Clinton sweep that seemed in the offing. Their largest joint achievement, to the fury of many liberals, was welfare reform. The true cost of the Democrats' failure to enact a more generous version of welfare reform when they controlled Congress became clear when Republicans passed their own, far more punitive versions. Clinton vetoed Republican welfare bills twice, but in the summer decided to sign the third version they sent him, after a fierce internal debate that divided his administration.

The ambivalence in the Clinton camp was summarized by two cabinet officers who offered their views at a White House meeting. Treasury secretary Robert Rubin, according to the journalist John Harris's fine account of the Clinton years, said, "signing would be safer." Then he added, "I wouldn't sign it." Housing secretary Henry Cisneros declared: "My head says yes, my heart says no." No sentence better summarized the divided conscience of American liberal pragmatism in the 1990s.

Clinton defended his decision to go along with the Republicans by noting that the bill included some $14 billion for child care. Yet he was sensitive to criticisms from his left. He cast the new law as the beginning rather than the end of a process. And he suggested that liberals should be pleased that it would become far harder to demagogue the issue. As it turned out, the politics of "makers" and "takers" that would emerge in the Obama years showed that no single bill, however tough, would ever prevent welfare, by whatever name, from being demonized.

"When I sign it, we all have to start again," Clinton said. "And this becomes everybody's responsibility. After I sign my name to this bill, welfare will no longer be a political issue. The two parties cannot attack each other over it. Politicians cannot attack poor people over it. There are no encrusted habits, systems, and failures that can be laid at the foot of someone else."

Liberals were not persuaded, and their somewhat unlikely champion was Senator Daniel Patrick Moynihan of New York, the man who had served Richard Nixon and was the architect of Nixon's Family Assistance Plan. One of the original neoconservatives, Moynihan made the classic conservative case for a liberal position. He highlighted the law of unintended consequences, a favorite neocon theme, and argued that the new system of public assistance was the very sort of social engineering the right typically warned against. "We are putting those children at risk," Moynihan thundered, "with absolutely no evidence that this radical idea has even the slightest chance of success."

Clinton's centrist and New Democrat advisors were not persuaded. They defended the merits of the bill and also argued that he could not keep vetoing

Republican welfare reform bills when he had made welfare reform his political calling card four years earlier. Besides, it was an election year.

Dole never had a chance, and as the election got nearer, House Republicans geared their strategy around a Clinton victory. Gone was a bold quest
for political realignment. They hoped to hang on by casting themselves as a
check on Clinton.

Clinton was looking forward to winning a clear majority so he could finally rid himself of the minority president tag. It was not to be. In the final
Pew poll, Clinton had 52 percent to 38 percent for Dole and 9 percent for
Ross Perot, who ran again. But Clinton's vote was held down by a fund-
raising scandal that broke in the fall involving Asian money illegally flowing
into Democratic coffers. A particularly odd episode involved a fund-raising
visit by Gore to a Buddhist temple in California. The Pew survey had found
that among Clinton's supporters, 7 percent said the scandal raised doubts
about him. Some of them clearly defected or chose not to vote in what was an
unusually low-turnout contest. In the end, Clinton won 49.2 percent to 40.7
percent for Dole and 8.4 percent for Perot, who got in the race late and said,
among other things, that Clinton would be "totally occupied for the next two
years in staying out of jail."

The failure to go over 50 percent mattered not in the least to the outcome, but it did matter to Clinton. "It was a blowout victory, but the number
rankled even so, and would for years to come," wrote Harris. "It is a reminder
of the precarious state of Clinton's fortunes for most of his term that the man
regarded as the most skilled Democratic politician of his generation never
commanded more than a plurality in a national election."

The Republican vote was up only slightly from Bush's disastrous 1992
showing. And by becoming the first Democratic president since Roosevelt to
be reelected, Clinton put an exclamation point on the idea that the Reagan
Coalition was dead. Clinton won 379 electoral votes, nine more than in 1992.
He lost three states he had carried in 1992, Montana, Colorado, and Georgia,
but picked up Arizona and Florida. Just eight years before, the vogue in punditry was to describe a long-term Republican "Electoral College lock." Clinton picked it. Only 16 states voted Republican in both 1992 and 1996, while
29 voted Democratic in both contests. In the Electoral College, Democrats

were beginning to build what political writer Ron Brownstein would later call their "blue wall." Clinton's own analysis pointed in that direction. He noted that between 1992 and 1996, his margin rose, often sharply, "in less culturally conservative or more economically sensitive states." Most of the Northeast and the West Coast fell into the first category, the Midwest into the second.

But the fund-raising scandal—along with the GOP's closing put-a-check-on-Clinton pitch and his failure to campaign heavily for House candidates—helped the Republicans keep their House majority. They also kept control of the Senate.

The House was a closely run thing. In the popular vote, Democrats actually edged the Republicans by 60,000 votes out of 87 million cast, and they picked up a net of nine seats. There was a 3.7 percent swing away from the Republicans from 1994, and 18 Republican incumbents were defeated. But these losses were offset by 3 Democrats who lost their seats, and by Republican gains in open seats: 29 Democrats and 21 Republicans retired, and these districts produced a net 6-seat gain for the GOP.

What the elections did underscore was a continuing shift of power in the Republican Party toward the South. John F. Cogan and David W. Brady of the Hoover Institution nicely summarized what went on:

> In the Northeast and Midwest the vote swing against Republican congressional candidates from 1994 to 1996 was on average about 5 percent. In terms of lost seats the swing translated into a six-seat loss in the Northeast and a four-seat loss in the Midwest. In the southern and border states the swing against Republicans was only 1 percent, and in this region Republicans picked up four seats. In the West the swing was 3 percentage points against the Republicans, and they lost three seats. *Overall, the Democrats picked up thirteen seats in nonsouthern regions, while in the southern and border states, Republicans gained four seats* for a net loss of nine seats. (Emphasis added)

The Republicans were no longer the party of Willkie, Dewey, and Rockefeller. Indeed, they were barely the party of Bob Dole, newly self-declared as one of the "liberals." Conservative southerners were now the most dynamic force in the GOP.

★

The second Clinton term can be divided into triumph, disgrace, and survival. In the same period, Newt Gingrich's approach went from statesmanship to overreach to defeat. And the conservative movement demonstrated its proclivity for brinksmanship, its refusal to accept that the decisive realignment to the right was not going to happen, and its desire to refight the battles of the 1960s over and over again.

Clinton's 1996 victory, the Republicans' near loss of the House, and a soaring economy created a very temporary Era of Good Feelings. When boom times pour money into federal coffers, win-win budget compromises are easy. It seemed that Washington had finally figured out how to make divided government work.

It was a sign of how starved Washington was for achievement that the 1997 budget deal was touted as being so grand. House Budget Committee chairman John Kasich pronounced it "a dream come true" while Clinton proclaimed it "the achievement of a generation." The deal itself was not particularly objectionable, but neither did it justify the high-fiving, chest-thumping, boy-are-we-great triumphalism of Democratic and Republican politicians alike.

The bargain was a political classic of the sort passed routinely in state legislatures at moments when the economy is hot and revenue pours in. Difference splitting is easy, because everything can be topped up—some money to new programs, some to tax cuts. Democrats are then allowed to point to the good things they are spending money on while Republicans can talk about the burdens they are removing from businesses and hardworking taxpayers.

At the time the agreement was reached, the federal budget was moving toward balance all by itself. "The economy is the champion here," observed the notoriously honest Ben Cardin, a Democratic House member from Maryland who would later go to the Senate. Clinton did have a right to claim credit for the return of fiscal sanity—but because of his 1993 budget, not the latest one. You could sense that Clinton felt a trifle guilty claiming the new bargain as a big deal, especially since so many Democrats had lost their seats in 1994 after walking the plank for Clinton on the earlier, painful fiscal plan. "The budget agreement that we announce today," Clinton acknowledged, "would not be possible had it not been for the tough vote taken in 1993 to set us on the right path." He might have added that George H. W. Bush deserved some credit, too. The 1990 budget deal that caused him such grief had begun closing the big hole. By contrast to 1990 or 1993, the 1997 deal was easy because Clinton and the Republicans had money to spread around.

Some of it was even well spent. Clinton finally got a significant down payment on expanding health coverage. The $24 billion, five-year children's health program (crafted by the famed bipartisan Senate deal makers Ted Kennedy and Orrin Hatch) extended health insurance to 3–5 million children. It was the largest expansion of health coverage since Medicaid and Medicare and was as close as anything in the grand bargain to being worthy of the label "historic."

The bill also contained a few improvements to make the new welfare system a bit more generous, and its $500 per-child tax credit was good for middle-income families and resembled Clinton's original promise of a "middle class tax cut." But that progressive measure was stuffed in with a cut in capital gains taxes that conservatives always sought. Citizens for Tax Justice, a liberal group, found that the bill's tax cuts were, on net, heavily tilted toward the wealthy. What this meant is that pro-market conservatives got what they needed out of the deal.

But not all on the right were satisfied. As soon as the agreement was announced, the Heritage Foundation issued a scathing analysis that, not accidentally, bore a great deal of similarity to statements Heritage and other groups aligned with the Tea Party would make in the Obama years.

Under the headline "The Return of Big Government," Heritage's statement argued that the agreement masked "substantial growth in the size and scope of the federal government," and it plainly accused Republicans of selling out. Heritage noted that "while the President's agenda is revealed explicitly in the documents accompanying the agreement, the congressional agenda is left largely up to the imagination."

"Taxpayers," Heritage complained, "are being asked to accept bigger government in exchange for the promise of a 'balanced budget' and a small cut in their taxes."

Making clear yet again that balancing the budget mattered far less to conservatives than hacking away at government, Heritage concluded: "The real test of a balanced budget plan is whether it actually leads to smaller, less costly government and leaves more money in the pockets of working families. The available evidence shows that this budget deal fails on nearly every count and that, in most cases, the policies it reflects may be worse than doing nothing."

Gingrich, however, was effusive in praising Clinton for responding to his reelection victory by choosing "to reach out a hand and say, 'Let's work together.'" And as reporters noticed at the time, he appeared chastened at his party's near loss of the House. The deal, he said, showed that "the American constitutional system works, that slowly, over time, we listened to the will of the American people, that we reached beyond parties, we reached beyond institutions, and we find ways to get things done."

As a young man, Gingrich first became active in politics as a Rockefeller Republican. For a time, it seemed, he was willing to work with the reluctantly self-described Eisenhower Republican in the White House.

When 1998 began, Clinton seemed poised to make the reach for greatness he had always envisioned. He was as popular as ever. A Gallup poll in mid-January found that 60 percent of Americans approved of his performance, and only 30 percent disapproved. The era of deficit politics was over as surpluses started rolling in, which gave Clinton fiscal room to take the initiative. And Republicans, as Gingrich's comments on the budget agreement showed, were still smarting from Clinton's successful attacks on them, and from the failure of their more revolutionary phase. Clinton had plans, including an effort to continue to move the country toward universal health care coverage through gradual steps rather than in one large fight. Building on the children's health bill, he now wanted to allow the near-elderly to buy into Medicare. He was also looking to pass a $21.7 billion child care program and sought new federal spending for school construction and to hire 100,000 more teachers, matching his initiative that financed local governments to hire 100,000 cops. "We lived and learned and took our environment as we had it," Gene Sperling, the president's senior economic adviser, told me at the time. "We're now in clearer waters."

And then, in a matter of days, came the tidal wave. The United States

Supreme Court had set it all in motion on May 27, 1997, when it ruled that the president could not avoid testifying in a civil suit brought by Paula Jones that accused Clinton of harassing her sexually six years earlier, before he was elected president. The details of the encounter had been revealed in an article in the conservative *American Spectator* magazine in January 1994. The reporting on Clinton's personal life had been financed by Richard Mellon Scaife, a conservative multimillionaire who ultimately gave the magazine close to $2 million specifically for what became known as the "the Arkansas Project" designed, in the careful language of the *New York Times*, "to unearth damaging information about President Clinton." Not for nothing did Hillary Clinton later speak of a "vast right-wing conspiracy."

Jones's lawsuit was also financed by conservative groups, and Clinton hoped he would be able to avoid testifying in the case until after his term was over. But in ruling that Clinton could not use his office to avoid a deposition, the Supreme Court offered what turned out to be one of the worst predictions ever made by any judicial body, anywhere. It rejected the idea that testifying in the case might "place unacceptable burdens on the President that will hamper the performance of his official duties." Justice John Paul Stevens wrote for the unanimous Court that it "appears to us highly unlikely to occupy any substantial amount of petitioner's [Clinton's] time."

It's worth pausing briefly over the concatenation of events that led to Clinton's impeachment. Doing so is a reminder of how thoroughly bizarre the episode was, how reckless the president was, and the lengths to which his enemies would go in their attempts to drive him from office.

The government shutdown had the utterly unintended consequence of setting up the circumstances for Clinton's relationship with Monica Lewinsky, a twenty-three-year-old White House intern. In a largely deserted White House being run by a skeleton staff, Clinton and Lewinsky found each other alone on November 15, 1995, and that's when their sexual relationship began. It continued until April 1996, when Evelyn Lieberman, Clinton's shrewd deputy chief of staff, arranged, initially without Clinton's knowledge, to transfer Lewinsky to the Pentagon. There Lewinsky was to make a friend named Linda Tripp. Even after the transfer, Clinton and Lewinsky stayed in touch through racy phone calls.

The Jones case and the president's affair collided on Saturday, January 17, 1998, the day Clinton gave his deposition in the Jones case. Unbeknownst to the president, Ken Starr, the special prosecutor investigating the Whitewater land deal Clinton had been involved in when he was governor of Arkansas, got a tip. Starr sought and received Justice Department approval to expand his investigation into possible obstruction of justice in the Jones case. Lewinsky had confided her affair with Clinton to Tripp, and Tripp secretly recorded phone calls with Lewinsky about the relationship with Clinton. She later turned them over to Starr. The Jones lawyers were fully briefed on the Lewinsky affair by a literary agent named Lucianne Goldberg, with whom Tripp had discussed the whole matter in the hope of getting a book contract. On the day before Clinton gave his deposition—indeed, while he was preparing for it—agents for Starr's office surrounded Lewinsky at the Pentagon City Mall, where she was meeting with Tripp. They detained her for several hours and questioned her.

Clinton then proceeded to deny the affair with Lewinsky during his deposition, which ultimately opened him up to the perjury and obstruction charges that became the centerpiece of the impeachment articles. Adding to the chance absurdities of the case, Lewinsky had intended to dry-clean a dress stained with the president's semen, but Tripp talked her out of it, thereby preserving the evidence that would undercut his claim that his encounters with Lewinsky had not been sexual.

The story of Starr's new investigative focus and Clinton's new problem leaked quickly, again with help from Goldberg. She had arranged for Tripp to tell her story to *Newsweek*'s Michael Isikoff. When *Newsweek* editors chose not to run the story, Goldberg informed the fledgling *Drudge Report* of the magazine's internal debate. Drudge, an increasingly influential voice on the right, played the story big, and by Tuesday night, January 20, the *Washington Post* and ABC News reported what Isikoff had been trying to get into *Newsweek*.

The response in Washington was electric—and among the president's own supporters, the range was from dismay to rage. I described the reaction of Clinton partisans in my own column that Friday, January 23: "Their fury is in some cases about morality but in all cases about the prospect of such extraordinary irresponsibility on the part of the leader they had vouched for. Why, they ask, would he risk his whole presidency for such an affair? If this is true, how dare he bring aid and comfort to their Limbaugh-listening friends? If he knew this story was there, why didn't he settle the Paula Jones case?" Even though Clinton's friends and allies eventually rallied to oppose impeachment, these are questions Clinton supporters still ask themselves.

For a few days, Clinton attempted qualified rather than outright denials, but they weren't working. Clinton had been on the phone with Dick Morris, who advised him that voters at that point would accept nothing less than a complete denial. Clinton's famous reply to Morris: "Well, we just have to win, then." Winning meant lying—or, to put the most charitable spin on the matter, accepting Clinton's rather narrow definition of "sexual relations" as meaning only intercourse.

And so on Monday, January 26, appearing with the first lady and Al Gore to talk about child care policy, he issued the statement that would never be forgotten: "I want you to listen to me. I'm going to say this again. I did not have sexual relations with that woman, Ms. Lewinsky. I never told anyone to lie, not a single time—never. These allegations are false. And I need to go back to work for the American people."

As a political matter, Morris was probably right: Clinton had to issue a full denial because the Lewinsky revelations had so shocked official Washington that pressure would likely have built very quickly for Clinton's resignation. Clinton needed to buy time, to rally his own supporters, and to hope that his enemies would overplay their hand.

Which is exactly what they proceeded to do. Here was a case—and the pattern would repeat itself often in the coming years—where conservatives mistook their own opinions for the views of the vast majority of the country. And the impeachment period heightened the tendency of conservatives to talk mostly to themselves. This is not a habit unique to conservatives, of course, but it was an especially devastating inclination on a matter that a majority of the country viewed with some distaste.

It's striking that throughout 1998, Clinton's approval rating in the Gallup poll stayed high, ranging from 59 percent (toward the beginning of the year) to an astonishing 73 percent at the end of the year, *after* the House had voted to impeach him. It's worth remembering what the traditional poll question asks; if voters approve or disapprove of how an incumbent "is handling his job as president?" Americans were responding to how Clinton was doing as *president*, and they were happy with his stewardship of *public* affairs. Most were also uncomfortable that his private life, however flawed, would be blown up into a national crisis.

Conservatives could not understand how the country could take such a relaxed view of the matter. It seemed to many on the right that the sixties really had corroded the country's moral sense. The more conservatives talked to each other, the more outraged they were—and as the polls rolled in, they were increasingly unhappy with the American people. Wasn't it the liberals who always spoke of the evils of sexual harassment, of powerful men taking advantage of young women? Wasn't the hypocrisy here perfectly obvious? Conservatives went back and forth, at times emphasizing Clinton's personal immorality, at others insisting the scandal wasn't about sex at all but about *public* acts of perjury and obstruction. They did have to grapple with the fact that the lawsuit in which these charges came up was a civil matter about private behavior, pushed along and financed by conservatives hoping to take Clinton down. No matter, the conservatives insisted: It was not they who had the relationship with an intern and lied about. Even if a trap was set for Clinton, his own actions led him into it.

The most extended expression of the conservatives' frustration was William Bennett's book *The Death of Outrage: Bill Clinton and the Assault on American Ideals*, published at the end of 1998. Bennett, who served as education secretary under George H. W. Bush, had assembled *The Book of Virtues* six years earlier, a popular collection of traditional stories teaching moral lessons. He thus established himself as the premier conservative moralist. He used his standing not only to condemn Clinton but also to express frustration over the failure of so many Americans to be—his title was significant—as outraged as he was. His brisk dismissal of Clinton's defenders (and, indeed, the way he characterized their arguments) spoke to the chasm between perceptions and attitudes on the right and those of much of the country. Bennett is worth quoting at some length because he so perfectly summarized how conservatives felt at the time:

It is said that private character has virtually no impact on governing character; that what matters above all is a healthy economy; that moral authority
is defined solely by how well a president deals with public policy matters;
that America needs to become more European (read: more "sophisticated")
in its attitude toward sex; that lies about sex, even under oath, don't really
matter; that we shouldn't be "judgmental"; that it is inappropriate to make
preliminary judgments about the president's conduct because he hasn't been
found guilty in a court of law; and so forth. If these arguments take root in
American soil—if they become the coin of the public realm—we will have
validated them, and we will come to rue the day we did. These arguments
define us down; they assume a lower common denominator of behavior and
leadership than we Americans ought to accept. And if we do accept it, we will
have committed an unthinking act of moral and intellectual disarmament.
In the realm of American ideals and the great tradition of public debate, the
high ground will have been lost. And when we need to rely again on this high
ground—as surely we will need to—we will find it drained of its compelling
moral power. In that sense, then, the arguments invoked by Bill Clinton and
his defenders represent an assault on American ideals, even if you assume the
president did nothing improper.

But most Americans simply did not see the Clinton episode as rising to
the level of the grand, world-historical event that Bennett described. Their
reaction was neither "an assault on American ideals" nor "an unthinking act
of moral and intellectual disarmament." Sexual transgressions among the
powerful were not a novelty, and the fact they were covered up came as no
surprise. The majority of Americans saw Clinton's behavior as tawdry but also
commonplace. It wasn't that most Americans were indifferent to his personal
behavior, let alone that they sanctioned it. Most were, in fact, appalled at what
Clinton had done—many for moral reasons, almost all for his sheer irresponsibility. The popular word among Democrats who were *defending* Clinton
against impeachment was that his behavior was "reprehensible."

The fact that most Americans turned hard against those who would remove him from office did not mean that they suspended judgment. It reflected a kind of moral realism linked with what can only be called a deeply

conservative instinct: private life is called "private" for a reason, and Americans did not want private behavior to become a dominant public issue. Most Americans were well aware that many other politicians, in both parties, had led far from exemplary family lives, no matter how often they invoked "family values." (This fact would boomerang on some Republican politicians later.) They sensed hypocrisy and came to see the scandal as more about politics than about sexual irresponsibility—or obstruction of justice, or perjury. The tangled web among conservative funders and right-wing journalists (and among Tripp and Goldberg and Starr) fed suspicions that Hillary Clinton was on to something when she spoke of "the vast right-wing conspiracy." On the whole, the majority just wished the whole thing had never come up.

In a sense, then, Clinton was rewarded for his initial (and untruthful) denial. The more time Americans were given to reflect and the longer they watched the behavior of Clinton's opponents, the more they were inclined to support his remaining in office.

The perception gap, not only between conservatives and liberals but also between the right and the rest of the country, was widened by the rise of new conservative media, and it was during the Clinton scandal that conservative radio and television became major growth industries. Rush Limbaugh began national syndication in 1988 and the conservatives' disdain for Clinton had already been a boon to his business. A decade later, the Lewinsky scandal would enhance Limbaugh's reach and influence, and he spawned many imitators. Over time, many local radio stations would prosper by turning over nearly all of their broadcast day to conservative talk.

Even more important was the boost the scandal gave to Fox News. Fox was a relative novelty then. It went on the air in October 1996 and at its launch reached only 10 million households. By 2000, after the boost it received during the impeachment controversy, it was available in 56 million homes. It became a mark of loyalty to the conservative cause to tune in to Fox, and it was in this period that CNN began to lose ground to Roger Ailes's upstart network.

The Clinton-Lewinsky saga also indirectly laid the groundwork for the rise of liberal cable television. MSNBC, then a neutral news source formed in an alliance between NBC and Microsoft, brought in Keith Olbermann, a popular sports journalist, to host a program in its 8–9 p.m. time slot. Known as *The Big Show*, a name he brought over from ESPN, the program became a go-to place during the Clinton scandal. But Olbermann said the whole episode depressed him, and he left MSNBC in 1998 to return to sports (ironically, in light of subsequent events, to Fox Sports Net). He returned to MSNBC at the end of March 2003 and his *Countdown* program, over time, came to reflect his appalled response to those who had pushed for Clinton's impeachment. Later, Olbermann would strike a nerve among liberals as he became increasingly outspoken against both Fox News and George W. Bush. One of his popular regular guests was the liberal radio host Rachel Maddow, and she was eventually given a program of her own in the 9 p.m. slot. The network realized it had found a niche and moved toward progressive programming across much of its schedule. (It was to take some steps back from its liberal role in 2015.) Olbermann left the network in 2011, but he had created the template for its success during the Bush and early Obama years. All of this began during the impeachment mess.

The summer of 1998 was, in one sense, a set of victories for Ken Starr as he closed in on Clinton and put one key Clinton staffer after another before his federal grand jury. At the end of July, Starr worked out an immunity agreement with Lewinsky and her family. The next day, Clinton agreed to testify voluntarily before the grand jury.

Yet that summer also damaged the prosecutor and his cause. In June, for example, the respected journalist Steven Brill alleged that Starr had been leaking information to the media, and reported that Starr had admitted to the leaks. Starr called Brill "reckless" and "irresponsible" and said he had misinterpreted their interview. The notion of an out-of-control investigation was planted deeper when CNN reported that three FBI agents had given evidence of a plan to wire Lewinsky's conversations, which refuted Starr's public denials of such a plan.

In a sense, both Clinton and Starr lost that summer. Clinton was finally forced by the evidence Starr had assembled to admit he had lied. On August 17, he testified before the grand jury and that night gave a five-minute address to the nation. "I did have a relationship with Miss Lewinsky that was not appropriate," he said, speaking from the Map Room in the White

House. "In fact, it was wrong. It constituted a critical lapse in judgment and a personal failure on my part for which I am solely and completely responsible."

He also acknowledged he had lied, without using that word. "I know that my public comments and my silence about this matter gave a false impression," he said. "I misled people, including even my wife. I deeply regret that."

Yet even as he sealed Starr's victory, he went on offense against his enemies, including the special prosecutor. "I intend to reclaim my family life for my family," he said. "It's nobody's business but ours. Even presidents have private lives. It is time to stop the pursuit of personal destruction and the prying into private lives and get on with our national life."

As it turned out, this second line of argument had the greater staying power, even if it seemed petulant that evening. By September—and with the midterm elections approaching—congressional Democrats had coalesced around a strategy of calling for Clinton to be censured by Congress. It was a clever form of "triangulation" by those who had once been triangulated against. Censure allowed Democrats to offer strong condemnations of Clinton's behavior even as they also denounced Republicans for putting the country through an impeachment process it did not want. The Democrats had found a middle ground that matched where a majority in the country stood.

Gingrich saw none of this coming. He confidently predicted major and possibly sweeping gains for his party that November. "If everything breaks against us, my guess is we'll be about plus 10 [seats]," he told the *Atlanta Journal* shortly before Election Day. "If everything breaks for us, [it] will be much closer to plus 40." Gingrich himself, the historian Steven Gillon reported, had been worried about a backlash against Republicans on impeachment and even complained toward the end of the campaign that it was the media that had a "maniacal fixation" with the Lewinsky scandal. But the Republicans' congressional campaign arm launched a tough ad campaign, "responding," as Gillon wrote, "to pressure from conservatives, who felt the party failed to lay down clear ideological markers for the public."

"Unable to get ideological traction on standard Republican issues," Gillon added, "conservatives believed the party needed to make Clinton's character and behavior the central issue." The anti-Clinton ads did not get a wide run, but Democrats leaped on them and the media saw them as a sign of Republican weakness. "Gingrich looked to Monica as his deliverance from having to come up with a new Republican agenda," wrote *Time* magazine's Margaret Carlson.

But the ads mattered less than the fact that Clinton's enemies kept impeachment in the news throughout the fall campaign. It was another instructive example of how what the conservative Republicans were hearing from their core supporters badly misled them about the temper of the nation as a whole. The presumption on the right was that the more Americans were exposed to Clinton's outlandish and even criminal behavior, the more they would rally to the cause of removing him from office. Instead, the piling on produced a backlash.

Ken Starr delivered his 445-page report on September 9 and it was released two days later. "It revealed, in graphic detail," wrote Gillon, "that over a fourteen-month period beginning in November, 1965, Clinton had nine sexual encounters with Lewinsky, and fifteen phone-sex conversations, and then lied about it to his aides, to his country, and under oath." Starr seemed to realize that some readers might pull back in horror over the report's purple language and that they would find the extraordinary amount of storytelling about sex offensive. The report itself was thus defensive in insisting that "the details are crucial to an informed evaluation of the testimony, the credibility of witnesses, and the reliability of other evidence. Many of the details reveal highly personal information; many are sexually explicit. This is unfortunate, but it is essential."

But many Americans were dismayed that a government investigation of a president of the United States could be so focused on the toting up of such tawdry facts. They concluded that Starr could have proved Clinton perjured himself without competing with Jackie Collins or Jacqueline Susann. The Starr Report had the effect of making exactly the opposite case from the one conservatives wanted to put forward. They argued that the episode was about perjury and obstruction of justice, not sex. The Starr Report unintentionally sent the signal that it was really all about the sex.

Nonetheless, the Republicans decided to double down. If the Starr Report didn't persuade the public, then surely the public release of Clinton's grand jury testimony would do the trick. It went public on September 21. An estimated 22 million Americans watched the president on television as he parried questions about his private behavior, carefully maintaining his composure and presenting himself as contrite and ashamed.

I was covering an event with Clinton on the day the video was streaming across the nation's television screens. It was, all at once, a poignant, telling, and absurd moment. Clinton had traveled to the New York University School of Law for what, under other circumstances, might have been a triumphant celebration of his approach to politics. The occasion was a conference titled "Strengthening Democracy in the Global Economy," but Washington policy types had simply dubbed it "The Third Way Meeting." Its purpose was to champion the approach to politics that Clinton had made his own and sought to spread around the democratic world. The supporting cast could not have been more impressive, including as it did Clinton's main Third Way partner, British prime minister Tony Blair, along with Italian prime minister Romano Prodi and other world leaders.

As Clinton's testimony was being broadcast on television screens elsewhere at the school, Clinton and Blair gamely talked about their achievements and the Big Idea they hoped would sweep the world. Blair, who loved synthesizing concepts and sometimes opposites as much as Clinton did, pronounced their approach as an "alliance between progress and justice." It was an effort to "take the basic value structure" of old progressive faith "minus the dogma."

For his part, Clinton spoke with the breezy informality he had used during living-room get-togethers in countless New Hampshire towns when he was first battling reports about his personal life during the primaries in 1992. Third Wayers, he said, wanted to be "modern and progressive," to avoid "false choices designed to divide people to win elections," to have an America that would stand up for "collective responsibilities beyond our borders" and would "moderate boom-bust cycles."

As the highly advanced information systems that Third Wayers extolled were feeding the president's testimony to millions, it fell to Hillary Rodham Clinton to preside over a morning discussion among the Third Way intellectuals. Her words were those of a stoic, and they had more than one meaning that day. "We have to take the world as we find it," she said, "and do what we can to improve upon it."

Although the collision of the conference and the broadcast was happenstance, it provided a revealing juxtaposition. The very success Clinton had enjoyed politically in advancing an alternative to Reaganism is what marked him out as a dangerous enemy to those who had looked forward to an ascendant conservatism. Clintonian Third Way, New Democrat politics had undercut conservative politicians accustomed to running and winning campaigns against traditional liberals. This is not to say that the horror grassroots conservatives expressed over Clinton's behavior was contrived or insincere. Nor does it diminish Clinton's responsibility for what he did. But the very successes Clinton and Blair celebrated that day at NYU meant that the stakes involved in Clinton's career and his presidency were very high.

And while it seemed strange that Clinton would be talking about education, health care, economics, and job training while television screens showed him discussing his sex life, a rather large majority of Americans made their choice about impeachment on the basis of that very contrast. They had elected Clinton because of what they hoped he would do about these practical concerns that had a bearing on their own lives, not because they regarded him as a moral paragon.

This became clear when they cast their ballots in the midterm elections. Shockingly for Gingrich and the Republicans, the Clinton scandal helped rather than hurt Democrats in November. Instead of losing seats, the Democrats picked up five. It was a much bigger defeat for the Republicans than the small number might suggest. Not since 1934 had the party out of the White House failed to gain seats at midterm. And not since 1822 had the out-party failed to gain seats in midterms held during a president's second term in office.

An election that might have cost Clinton the presidency instead cost Gingrich the Speakership. On November 6, three days after the election, Gingrich announced he was stepping down. Even his own longtime supporters told him it was time to go. Given Gingrich's association, particularly in the minds of liberals, with a rather rabid brand of conservatism, what is striking in retrospect—and important for understanding today's right—is that many conservatives had soured on Gingrich precisely because he seemed so ready to work with Clinton after the failure of the shutdown strategy. He had survived earlier efforts to push him out led by his colleagues Tom DeLay and Dick Armey. At the time of the earlier coup, many on the right expressed unhappiness not with Gingrich's ideological zeal but with his moderation. A young Florida congressman named Joe Scarborough, who would later host MSNBC's morning news program, summarized how they felt. "Quite a few members are obviously concerned over the direction that the leadership has taken," Scarborough said. "We have a concern that our leadership remains shell-shocked from the government shutdown a year and a half ago. Most of us are ready for them to start leading again rather than sitting back and reading from Clinton's song sheet."

When Gingrich finally fell, ideology was not the only factor, perhaps not even the central cause. Republicans were simply exhausted with a very complicated man. "Too much drama, too many headaches," as Bill Kristol put it sixteen years later. If conservatives were glad to see him go, it turned out that Clinton would miss him, especially in the coming weeks.

Clinton hoped the 1998 election would be the end of impeachment. It wasn't. With Gingrich out, power shifted toward Henry Hyde, the House Judiciary Committee chairman, and House Whip Tom DeLay. Both were determined to push through to impeachment, even though the voters had just said no—and even though any effort to remove Clinton was destined to fail in the Senate, where 45 Democrats would block the required two-thirds majority. For the same reasons conservatives had come to mistrust Gingrich, Clinton's lieutenants felt he would have found a practical way out. But the passion in the GOP was to mark Clinton permanently as a president who had been impeached. And the majority view in the country had little impact on the Republican majority that would make the decision—for a reason that would continue to foster polarization for years to come. As Gillon observed, since "most GOP members represented districts with high concentrations of Republican voters . . . most representatives felt they could pursue the case for impeachment without fear."

Before it was over, the saga produced another political casualty. Representative Bob Livingston of Louisiana had been elected unopposed by his Republican colleagues to replace Gingrich as Speaker. But in the culture war that accompanied impeachment, *Hustler*, the pornographic magazine founded by Larry Flynt, was eager to demonstrate Republican hypocrisy on sexual matters. Learning that Flynt was about to publish a story on his extramarital affairs, Livingston publicly apologized and announced his resignation. He urged Clinton to follow his example to "heal the wounds you have created."

On December 19, the House voted two articles of impeachment, the first charging him with committing perjury in his grand jury testimony, the second accusing him of obstructing justice. It voted down two others, linked to perjury in the Paula Jones lawsuit and alleged abuses of power in covering up the Lewinsky affair. The House action forced a reluctant Senate to take up the matter. When it finally acted on February 12, 1999, it rejected the obstruction of justice article on a 50–50 vote, while the perjury article received only 45 votes. Five Republicans voted to reject both articles and an additional five voted for the first but against the second. It was a small dose of bipartisanship at the end of a wild partisan ride.

The Clinton impeachment battle was one of the most bizarre and distasteful episodes in American political history. It formally involved charges of perjury and obstruction of justice. For some conservatives, those will always be the issues. Yet the episode was also the staging ground for a series of overlapping cultural and political trials involving issues and sensibilities that went beyond these legal questions. For many, the values of the 1960s were on trial. Bill Clinton stood in for everything they saw wrong about this formative era, and his sins were the sins of a permissive value-neutrality that was bringing the nation low. For many liberals, the conservative Congress—and, yes, the "vast right-wing conspiracy"—were on trial. Organized conservatism and organized conservative money instigated and financed a series of investigations, lawsuits, and press reports designed to bring Clinton down, by any means necessary. For many Americans, politicians as a group were on trial, and few of them, left or right, came out of the struggle with much credit. The whole thing seemed a terrible waste of time, energy, and money.

It's also possible to see the imbroglio as the first clear sign of a crisis in the political system with which we are still living. Since the collapse of the liberal consensus in the 1960s—it came under attack first from the Goldwater right and then from a New Left appalled by the Vietnam War and a spirit of conformity—American politics has involved a fierce and relatively evenly matched struggle for power. For conservatives, who thought first in 1980 and then in 1994 that they had finally gained the upper hand, it was a long era of dashed hopes. The ferocity of the response to Clinton reflected the view of many in their ranks that his victories were based on trickery, manipulation, and slickness. And when they thought they had him cornered, he escaped— with the help of voters who, when given a choice between a flawed but reasonably successful president and his enemies, chose against his enemies.

For contemporary conservatism, the 1990s were a formative decade. They began with George H. W. Bush's failure to reshape conservatism into a more middle-of-the-road philosophy. Bush had come to accept that the Republican Party of his age was no longer the party of his father's era, and the very locus of his political career had forced him to acknowledge that Eisenhower could no longer be the model of a popular Republicanism. If Prescott Bush had been elected to the Senate from Connecticut, where Eisenhower-style Modern Republicanism sold well, his son built his electoral career in Texas, which demanded a much fiercer loyalty to conservatism. Out of political necessity, Bush thus acknowledged the GOP's new imperatives long before Reagan's rise.

Yet Bush was the least doctrinaire of politicians and he never thought he was establishing a creed. This led to some missed opportunities. By failing to engage seriously with Jack Kemp's ideas on poverty rooted in "empowerment," he lost a chance to renovate conservatism in a way that might have broadened its appeal. While Bush was resisting new ideas, Bill Clinton was turning his party into a laboratory for innovation—to the point, as Kristol pointed out, that some dissident conservatives inside Bush's own administration quietly opened a dialogue with Clintonian New Democrats.

For all that, George Herbert Walker Bush was an instinctive moderate who seemed to share his father's instincts. Bush 41 was about turning Reaganism into a fiscally sustainable and practical proposition. That Bush did not seem to understand the rebellion he was courting when he agreed to tax increases in the 1990 budget deal said a lot about him.

For conservatives, it said that he wasn't one of them. As Kristol put it many years later, conservatives were struck by the "cavalier" way in which Bush broke his no-new-taxes promise. They sensed, he said, that when Reagan raised taxes, he did so unhappily and "under pressure." Because Bush drew such a sharp distinction between what might be said during a campaign to get elected and what it took to govern, he didn't seem bothered at all by his apostasy.

Seen from another perspective, Bush was simply a realist who accepted what Clinton would call "the laws of mathematics" on budgeting and believed that conservatives were more likely to consolidate their gains if they used power in prudent ways—paradoxically, as we have seen, much as Reagan had done most of the time.

Had Bush succeeded, a consolidated and moderated form of conservatism may well have taken hold. Instead, Gingrich's 1990 rebellion, Bush's defeat, and Gingrich's triumph four years later put a more aggressive, ideological conservatism back at center stage.

The Gingrich sweep was built on a shift toward much more party-line voting in congressional elections, and it tightened the grip of southern conservatism on the party as a whole. The influence gained by a highly ideological conservative media in those years, particularly during the Clinton scandal, would further empower the right wing while creating an increasingly inward-looking conservative echo chamber. This led to the party's miscalculation of the public's response to impeachment, and it would have a comparably distorting impact on conservative perceptions and strategies in the coming years.

Bill Clinton's victory, in the meantime, created a new set of political alignments that endure to this day. In 1992, Clinton broke the coalitions that Nixon and Reagan had built. Starting with Bush's defeat, Republicans were to lose the popular vote in five of the next six presidential elections. New England, much of the rest of the Northeast, and the West Coast became increasingly closed to the Republicans. The upper Midwest, which had been friendly to Republicans in presidential elections even during the Roosevelt and Truman eras, now consists of either swing states or states that are reliably Democratic.

Clinton bequeathed the Democrats valuable legacies, in foreign policy and domestic policy. These were nicely summarized by Hillary Clinton, who liked to ask: "Which part of peace and prosperity didn't you like?" Clinton's ideological innovations gave Republicans fewer targets on such issues as crime and welfare. His balanced budgets made future attacks on Democrats as profligate "big spenders" problematic. Clinton sent a clear message, as the political scientist Steven Teles observed, that Democrats were now "unwilling to serve as hapless victims of the Republican campaign playbook."

Nonetheless, the loss of the House and Senate in 1994 and the impact of the Lewinsky scandal after his reelection diminished Clinton's ability to reorder American politics in a more fundamental way. There were limits to his New Democrat project, as Clinton signaled himself when he invoked populist arguments against excessive cuts in public programs and in taxes on the wealthy. He drew on the traditions of New Deal and Great Society liberalism even as he was revising them.

Parts of the business-friendly agenda that both he and Tony Blair pursued, particularly the deregulation of the finance industry, were seen in a much harsher light after the financial implosion of 2008 than they were as the economy roared forward in the late 1990s. The harsh criminal penalties that were part of his crime program led to widespread overincarceration, particularly of African-Americans, and came under sharp attack in the Obama years. Clinton himself acknowledged this in a May 2015 interview with CNN. Because of the way the law was "written and implemented," he said, "we cast too wide a net and we had too many people in prison."

Some of Clinton's rhetorical concessions to the right, notably his declaration that "the era of big government is over," also weakened already porous liberal defenses while strengthening the conservatives' public argument.

Clinton underscored his own role in moving the political spectrum rightward with his impatient declaration about becoming an Eisenhower Republican. Democrats had taken over the role once played by moderate and liberal Republicans and this had the effect of pushing the real Republican Party toward even greater philosophical homogeneity.

Occupying this ground did not hurt Clinton politically, and neither did the state of the economy. As his term ended, he was a very popular figure. His approval ratings in the Gallup poll throughout his last full year in office stayed within a range of 56–66 percent, consistently ahead of the scores

Americans gave the Republican Congress. The Gingrich Revolution failed to achieve the degree of change conservatives had hoped for—and failed to drive Clinton from office. If Clinton had not achieved all that he might have, he nonetheless turned back what had once seemed an unstoppable conservative wave.

How could conservatives regroup and create the durable majority that kept eluding them? A Texas governor named George W. Bush and Karl Rove, his brilliant field general, had some ideas about this, and conservatives would initially embrace them. But that white whale of a conservative realignment would not only remain elusive; it would soon move farther out of reach.

6

PUT ON A COMPASSIONATE FACE

The Promise and Limits of Compassionate Conservatism

"People think oftentimes that Republicans are mean-spirited folks. Which is not true, but that's what people think."

"Bush was the measure of how hungry Republicans were to get back to power," says Mike Gerson, who signed up as a Bush speechwriter in 1999 for the coming campaign.

Trim, compact, and both gentle and deliberate of speech, Gerson has the demeanor of someone who would be very comfortable as a professor. His intensity while parsing theological or ideological concepts matches that of any Marxist at a living room gathering debating the dialectics of *Capital*. Yet he is at ease challenging his own last thought or his own side's assumptions. An evangelical Christian, he is fervent in faith but intellectually open and curious, a disposition he developed early. He says he was a contrarian in the strict Calvinist environment of his youth and observes that his father-in-law, an elder in his church, was almost removed from his position for singing in a choir at a Billy Graham revival. His in-laws' very strict brothers and sisters in faith did not take well to Graham's openness to Catholics. "Very conservative Calvinists wanted to fight the Reformation every day," Gerson observes. He says this with a smile. He clearly still respects the deep commitment of his Calvinist cobelievers, but their view of Catholics is utterly alien to him as a Protestant admirer of Popes John Paul II and Francis.

Gerson adds that his mother "was never that conservative" and became part of the charismatic renewal that affected both Protestants and Catholics around the country in the 1970s and was especially strong in the St. Louis area. It was a movement of the spirit that emphasized joy and conversion rather than heretic-hunting. It was an orientation to faith that clearly influenced Gerson. He would remain a faithful contrarian, loyal to his party and to those for whom he worked, but not without the dissidence that led his father-in-law to sing in Billy Graham's choir.

It says something about Gerson that the first presidential candidate he actively supported was not a Republican but a Democrat, a fellow evangelical named Jimmy Carter—and against Ronald Reagan in 1980.

Gerson was sixteen years old at the time, and he made the case for Carter in a high school debate. "There wasn't much to recommend the Republicanism of Nixon and Ford when it came to evangelicalism," said Gerson, noting that Carter, by constrast, had appeared on the cover of *Time* when the magazine published a story about his born-again Christianity. The future president's religious orientation was treated by the media at the time more as an anthropological oddity from a distant land than as a vibrant chord of the American religious chorus. "These were things that were revolutionary in political discourse at that time," Gerson recalls. By 1984, the Democrats' firm support for abortion rights and what Gerson came to see as their hostility to religion converted him to Reagan and the Republican Party. But his earliest independence from conservative Republicanism marks him out from so many movement conservatives for whom either Goldwater (nominated the year Gerson was born) or Reagan defined a lifetime of commitment.

Gerson, by temperament and early experience, seemed destined to the almost Sisyphean undertaking of reforming and transforming the causes to which he pledged his fidelity. What attracted Gerson to George W. Bush was precisely his new candidate's willingness to do things "purposefully and early in the campaign" to distance himself and his party "from both cultural pes-simism and libertarian ideology." In the Bush campaign, he says, "I found a perfect environment with a party that was uniquely poised to accept a candi-date like this." Bush, he said, "was not reflecting some broad consensus within the Republican Party; he was challenging the consensus within the party." Many conservatives were willing to back the son of a president they consid-ered an apostate—and as someone who seemed to be seeking a new direction for the conservative movement—simply because they wanted to win.

Gerson was a real catch for the Bush campaign. Having left politics for a brief and happy stint as a writer for *U.S. News & World Report,* he was well known and liked within the journalistic class Bush would be courting. But Gerson's hiring was itself a symbol of Bush's apparent determination to do things in a new way.

Gerson was a compassionate conservative before Bush made the term popular. A movement that Bush himself is often credited with inaugurating, it began its life in the mid-1990s under Clinton. One of its leading promoters was Senator Dan Coats, an Indiana Republican for whom Gerson had also written speeches.

The compassionate conservatives were quite conscious of conservatism's shortcomings. They worried about the sense of indifference their allies often conveyed toward the poor and to the social pain the budget cuts they cham-pioned might create. "We should not ignore the potential for suffering in our cities when government retreats," Coats said at the time. "There is not—and could never be—a government plan to rebuild civil society. But there must be ways to actively take the side of people and institutions who are rebuilding their own communities and who often feel isolated and poorly equipped."

The roots of compassionate conservatism could be traced to a 1977 mani-festo issued by the sociologist Peter Berger and the Lutheran pastor Richard John Neuhaus, *To Empower People.* (Neuhaus later became a Catholic priest and, having started his political life on the left, became a conservative who grew close to Bush during his presidency.) Berger and Neuhaus highlighted "those institutions standing between the individual in his private life and the large institutions of public life." They emphasized neighborhoods, families, churches, and voluntary associations. Their book might be seen as laying the philosophical foundations for the implicit ideology of working-class Reagan Democrats. Reagan's emphasis in 1980 on family, work, and neighborhood bore Berger and Neuhaus's inspiration.

But this approach had little impact on the actual policies of the Reagan administration, and while Jack Kemp preached a similar gospel when he was George H. W. Bush's housing secretary, the elder Bush took little interest in it.

Clinton showed more signs of engagement in these ideas than did either of his immediate Republican predecessors. The welfare reform bill he signed included a provision authored by Senator John Ashcroft, a Missouri Republican of deep evangelical conviction, establishing "charitable choice," which eased the flow of government money to religiously based social welfare efforts. Thus was the first "faith-based center" at a federal agency established by Clinton. Appropriately, in light of Kemp's earlier interest in "empowerment," it was set up at the Department of Housing and Urban Development, and it was headed by a progressive Catholic priest. Bill Kristol's observation that Clinton-style Democrats were often more open to new conservative initiatives than Republicans or conservatives themselves applied to compassionate conservatism.

Its rise in the 1990s coincided with a growing interest on both the right and the left in the idea of "civil society." Civil society thinkers focused on institutions that were independent of the state but not organized, as businesses are, primarily as actors in the economic market. These were the places, as the theme song from the television show *Cheers* put it, "where everybody knows your name," and a good deal else about you, too. They were churches and synagogues and mosques, Little League, bowling leagues and soccer clubs, Shriners, Elks, and Rotary clubs, book clubs, neighborhood watch groups, and countless other organizations that brought people together. The left insisted that trade unions were also classic examples of civil society, a position that conservatives found easier to accept when the unions were in communist Poland than in the United States. In fact, the idea of civil society became especially popular after the fall of communism in Eastern Europe. By maintaining underground and then increasingly public opposition movements to repressive regimes, the Eastern European rebels—personified by Vaclav

Havel in Czechoslovakia and typified by the Solidarity union movement in Poland—showed that even the most vigorous police states could not stamp out all vestiges of independent social life that survived in cafés and churches, workplaces and families. Progressives (particularly the community organizers among them) championed these grassroots activists. So did conservatives, who saw civil society as an alternative to the state.

"For too long in modern America," wrote Coats and Senator Rick Santorum of Pennsylvania in 1998, "politics and public debate has tended to focus on the role of government and the rights of individuals. It has neglected the layer of institutions that raise our children, enforce an informal order in our neighborhoods, and even reclaim our lives when we fall and fail."

The imperative, Coats and Santorum wrote, was to "take the side of people and institutions who are rebuilding their own neighborhoods, and who often feel isolated and poorly equipped." Civil society, they argued, "can be coaxed and nurtured, not engineered. It will not be rebuilt by government. Nor will it be rebuilt by 'no government.' But it must be encouraged to rebuild itself."

It was easy enough for liberals to be skeptical of the compassionate conservatives, who sometimes seemed to be suggesting that you could solve any social problem by throwing a church at it. They spoke so much about personal pathologies that needed healing they made it easy to forget that most poor people had perfectly good values and worked very hard for very little. Even the most organized, most churched, and most moral communities can't make it with little income and with shrinking tax bases—and enterprise zones could do only so much.

Nonetheless, it would be a mistake to write off compassionate conservatism as simply a gimmick. It was, to begin with, an attempt on the part of some of its sponsors to reestablish Republican and conservative bonds with minority communities, and particularly with African-Americans. Many of the most committed compassionate conservatives acknowledged that the southern strategies pursued from Goldwater to Nixon to Reagan (and even the first President Bush with his Willie Horton campaign) were built on white reaction to civil rights, and at times, on racism itself. Conservatives who rallied to this new set of ideas insisted that their movement and the Republican Party would never make progress with African-American voters until this legacy was shed. Jack Kemp would tell any audience that would listen: "No one cares what you think until they think you care." The compassionate conservatives wanted to reverse this history, their hopes captured well by the scholar Steven Teles: "Instead of embracing racial resentment, compassionate conservatism preached, Republicans should rebrand themselves as the party of racial solidarity—the allies of the moralizing agents of the inner cities."

Compassionate conservatives were also willing to accept the legitimacy of progressive goals and progressive issues—the need to alleviate poverty, combat racism, and expand opportunity—while insisting that their solutions were sounder than those embodied in the liberal welfare state. Teles noted that "compassionate conservatism sought to advance traditionally liberal ends by conservative means" and its partisans often looked to the two core principles of Catholic social thought for guidance: "subsidiarity" and "solidarity." Subsidiarity embodied "the principle that power should be held by institutions as close to the individual as possible." Solidarity referred to "the idea that a society must be measured by how it treats its weakest and neediest members." Teles noted that compassionate conservatives consciously drew on a notion made popular by Clinton's New Democrats—that government's task was to "steer, not row." It's a reminder that the period between Clinton's reelection and the country's descent into the impeachment imbroglio offered occasional moments of ideological cross-pollination.

As a practical matter, compassionate conservatives divided into two broad groups.

On the one side were those whose primary motivation was a deep and authentic concern for the poor. These members of the tribe combined a profound impatience with conservative indifference to the needy and the cause of social justice with a sharp critique of the failures of traditional welfare programs.

An emblematic figure in this group was David Kuo, a committed Christian who worked as a Capitol Hill staffer and as an aide to both Kemp and William Bennett. (He later worked in the Bush White House's Office of Faith-Based and Community Initiatives and then founded his own anti-poverty group.) Writing in 1997, Kuo argued that liberals and conservatives needed to learn from each other, which in today's political climate seems a thoroughly radical idea.

Kuo's lesson to liberals was simple enough: "Faith matters." Yes, he said, liberals usually understood that faith was "a matter of importance," and some acknowledged that the "liberal welfare tradition . . . had its roots in religious revival." Yet liberals who might acknowledge this were still prone to "ignoring" or "being actively hostile to" the role of faith "as a catalyst for radical change in people's lives." Liberals needed to embrace the work of private, not-for-profit groups and the success of "social entrepreneurialism." They also needed to abandon their belief "that true compassion is directly related to federal spending on welfare."

Conservatives, in turn, needed to accept something very hard for many of them to say outright: "Governmental programs can do—and have done—good." Kuo pointed to the success of food stamps in alleviating hunger and of Social Security in slashing poverty rates among the elderly. Further, conservatives needed to acknowledge that "[p]overty in America is real." It was not "just an invention of the left," Kuo wrote, and not "mostly a matter of sloth and bad bookkeeping." In words that still resonate, he added: "Conservatives will have more success undoing the welfare state if they abandon arguments that all of America's poor are either 'undeserving' or 'non-existent.'"

The other wing of compassionate conservatism was interested in devolving responsibility for social action to churches and other civil society groups as a way of shrinking the size of government. The more aggressive iteration of this approach was popularized by Newt Gingrich when he championed the writings of Marvin Olasky, a University of Texas journalism professor who later became a Bush campaign adviser.

Olasky was, like Kuo and Gerson, deeply religious, but his faith led him to different conclusions about the role of the state. Olasky argued that religious charities had always been, and would always be, more effective in helping the poor than any government program. The upshot, to exaggerate a little: government should drop dead to bring the religious charities to life. He argued in a 1996 book, *Renewing American Compassion,* that in an ideal world, Congress would simply abolish the federal safety net. "It is time for Congress to increase the pressure by phasing out federal programs," he wrote, "and pushing states to develop ways for individuals and community-based institutions to take over poverty-fighting responsibility." Olasky saw the old conservative doctrine of states' rights much as liberals did: as a pathway for dismantling the social protections that had been built since the days of Theodore Roosevelt and the Progressive Era. But if this likely outcome is why liberals are skeptical of states' rights arguments, it is precisely why Olasky embraced them. He called for "placing in the hands of state officials all decisions about welfare and the financing of it and then pressing them to put welfare entirely in the hands of church- and community-based organizations." A radical formula, really: smash the state in the name of God.

There were overlaps between these two wings of compassionate conservatism, of course. It was possible to be disillusioned with the welfare state because it had failed the poor. Gerson and Kuo certainly felt this way. Both shared the conservative view that "government bureaucracies are blunt and ineffective instruments," as Gerson put it in his memoir of the Bush years. "'Take a number and wait' compassion has little to offer men, women and children in spiritual and emotional crisis."

Nonetheless, their passion for the poor, animated by their Christian faith, led both Kuo and Gerson to become sharp critics of antigovernment conservatives. Tensions between those who wanted to build a new faith- and community-based approach to poverty within government and those who were most deeply committed to getting government out of the way would make compassionate conservatism a problematic guide to governing. Splitting the difference between these two poles was impossible.

On the other hand, the existence of these camps reflected how powerful compassionate conservatism could be as a coalition-building tool. The idea had the potential of bringing together three political strains: religious conservatives generally, who welcomed the emphasis on the power of faith; moderates and moderate conservatives who welcomed an acknowledgment of the need for creative social policy; and an antigovernment right that embraced the movement's critique of government welfare programs and saw it as a way of reducing or eliminating them.

For a variety of personal and philosophical reasons, some growing out of his own religious faith, George W. Bush was genuinely drawn to compassionate conservatism. But he and Karl Rove also understood its political power. The movement was taking hold at the very moment when the Republican establishment and the conservative movement alike were ready to turn to him for leadership.

In light of how divisive and unpopular Bush became, it's important to re-member what a gifted politician he could be and how shrewd he was in grap-pling with the new landscape Clinton had created. Mike Gerson was far from alone in his party in viewing Bush as the GOP's natural leader at the end of the Clinton era. During his campaign for reelection as governor of Texas in 1998, journalists, conservative intellectuals, and Republican operatives de-scended on Texas to check out the man whose skills and instincts might get the Republicans back into power. The political cognoscenti gave Bush the sort of rave reviews that had greeted Clinton's pre-campaign rollout in 1991. Tough, gimlet-eyed political reporters and power brokers came close to gush-ing about him: He had a new Republican message. He had learned from Clinton, his father, and Ronald Reagan alike. He could talk about religion without scaring people. He sounded oh-so-much better than the crowd in Washington. And in his reelection campaign, he was running 40 points ahead in the polls.

In late October of that year, I was part of the media swarm that visited with Bush on the campaign trail, and got a chance to interview him at length. What I saw—at a winery in the appropriately named town of Grapevine, Texas, and at stop after stop that day—was a natural retail politician who understood his strengths and seemed comfortably aware of his weaknesses. During a reception held among rows of great oak casks, Bush offered bear hugs and kisses, handshakes and shoulder pats. He looked people in the eye. A rambunctious smile lit his face. He clued in quickly to the particular thing that made the person in front of him tick. At the winery, he didn't talk too long. He seemed more eager to work the crowd, to put an arm on friends, to remember things about their kids. He knew what he did best.

"He's not looking over your shoulder at the next guy's name tag," said Tom

Craddick, a Republican state representative, offering the mirror compliment to the criticism so often directed at Washington operators. Bush conveyed a merry irony about the very political game he took so seriously. He was like Bill Clinton, yet very, very different. Bush didn't feel your pain; he let you in on the joke.

When I asked people why they liked him, they talked much more about who he was than what he had done as governor. The phrases rolled off their tongues: He was "down to earth," "not a politicians' politician," someone who "brings people together."

"He's an inspiration," Paula Day, a cochair of his campaign in Tarrant County, told me that day. "He represents a positive attitude, an optimistic attitude, that you can do it, you can achieve." She seemed to be speaking of a motivational specialist, not a politician.

Bush's stump speech reflected this. He did address what he'd done and what he'd do with a second term in Austin, but this is not what moved his crowds. They most liked his inspirational words and moral talk—yet his sermons did not sound the least bit like those of Pat Robertson or Jerry Falwell.

At a juvenile justice center in Dallas that day, he pledged "to make sure that there are consequences for bad behavior in our state." To a reporter for a local Spanish-language television station, Bush said—in Spanish—"Love and discipline go hand in hand."

At a rally at Collin County Community College in Plano, he touted his program to get all children to read and spoke of the one in five Texas kids who couldn't. "That means somebody's got low hopes, low standards, low expectations," he said. These were serious sins in George W.'s world.

Striking about Bush's paean to reading was the way he tied his message of personal responsibility to a call for social action while leaving government's role quite blurry. "There is a responsibility to love your neighbor like you want to be loved yourself," he told the well-scrubbed Plano crowd. "The best juvenile justice program is to make sure the children of Texas know how to read."

At the time, I spoke with the man Democrats had chosen to run a race they knew he and they were going to lose. Garry Mauro, the Texas land commissioner, was the first to acknowledge that Bush was "a good politician," someone who "knows how to get along with the state Legislature" and "hires good people and listens to them."

Mauro argued that while Bush was not a man of ideas, he did know where to find them. "He didn't spend a lot of time doing something innovative or different. He picked up a lot of other people's ideas and made them his own. That's a pretty smart thing to do."

Of late, Bush had spoken of his passion for reading and new efforts to promote literacy. Mauro was a skeptic. "If he thought remedial reading was so important, why didn't he propose it two years ago?" Mauro asked. His judgment on Bush? "The last thing I would call George Bush is an ideologue," Mauro said. "I don't believe George Bush has strong feelings about anything." Karl Rove was happy at the time to hear people describe Bush as a nonideologue, exactly the kind of candidate who could win the supposedly postideological Clinton era. But a decade later, Bush's critics on the right would say much the same thing, and not so charitably.

In the buildup to his presidential campaign, Bush was quite brilliant in presenting different sides of himself to different people. Many Texas Democrats I spoke with then called Bush a centrist who agreed with them on many things. "George has been at odds with some of the leading Republican figures in the state," said one Democratic state legislator who didn't want his name used, for fear of offending Bush and his fellow Democrats simultaneously. "You talk to him in private, and there are a lot of things that, as a Democrat, you agree with him on. He's a moderate."

Yet conservative Bush fans said exactly the opposite: that he was a true conservative who knew how to talk moderate. "More conservative than his father, George W. has a proven record of conservative accomplishment that the media have largely ignored," Ralph Reed, former executive director of the Christian Coalition, wrote in *National Review* in July 1998. "A Bush victory in November 2000 would be a conservative triumph, not a moderate one." Reed's view may have been colored by the fact that he was then a Bush consultant paid to help win over the religious right. But Reed was echoing what other conservatives were saying.

Among progressives, Bush profited from being a Republican in Texas, where you could be very conservative and still look very middle-of-the-road compared with your fellow partisans. Liberals were accustomed to conservative tough guys like Tom DeLay, Dick Armey, and Phil Gramm. Compared with them, Bush was a sweetie. State representative Glen Maxey, an openly gay member of the Texas legislature and a Democrat who was one of Bush's most articulate critics, said a funny thing to me back then: "As a liberal gay activist in the Texas House of Representatives, I say: He's not as bad as he could be."

Some endorsement. And yet Maxey went on: "This place can be very mean. It can be very mean-spirited. There are many of us who are so pleasantly surprised that he's AWOL on issues that could be so detrimental to Texas." Far better to be AWOL than nasty.

Here's Bush in one of his TV ads of the time: "Whether for government or individuals, I believe in accountability and responsibility. For too long, we've encouraged a culture that says if it feels good, do it, and blame somebody else if you've got a problem. We've got to change our culture to one based on responsibility." Those who hated the 1960s loved this stuff, yet it was not at all Pat Buchanan's culture war. I heard Bush say over and over that he wanted to be "a uniter, not a divider" because "dividers can't lead."

This was the music of compassionate conservatism to which Gerson would provide the words. Rove traced Bush's embrace of the idea to an interview during the 1998 governor's race when Bush had described himself as a "conservative with a heart," unconsciously echoing the old Nixon line that had vexed Goldwater. The phrase, Rove recalls in his memoir, caught the interest of his other top aide, Karen Hughes. In preparing Bush's 1998 election night address—he'd win 68 percent of the vote against Mauro—Hughes "refined" Bush's words "into 'compassionate conservative' and repeated the alliterative phrase in his draft victory speech—four or five times." Bush, Rove recalls, "said it just once that night and then repeated it in response to a question at a news conference the next morning."

"Still," he added, "we had our mantra."

Later in his book, Rove records proudly that "Bill Clinton later told Bush that when he heard the Texas governor first use the term, he knew Democrats were in trouble." It says something about Clinton's standing as a master politician that Rove would brag on winning the Clintonian imprimatur.

Rove may remember compassionate conservatism as a late entry into the

Bush lexicon, but, as his own account suggests, Bush was beginning to work with the idea long before it went into his victory speech. What Bush told me when I interviewed him then made clear he was thinking a good deal about how to win back moderates who had strayed to Clinton and Ross Perot.

When I asked him what the Republican Party had done wrong since 1994, he had a ready answer. "It hasn't put a compassionate face on our conservative philosophy," he replied during an interview in his uncluttered wood-paneled office in the state capitol in Austin. "People think oftentimes that Republicans are mean-spirited folks. Which is not true, but that's what people think."

Notice: Bush said his party needed to put on a compassionate *face*. That's not the same as transforming it. His message was that there nothing wrong with the Republican Party that a different face wouldn't cure. He had a certain face in mind.

At the time, I was trying to figure out how Bush could be all things to all people, whether it was really true that he lacked deep beliefs or whether, instead, he was hiding something from somebody. I was also fascinated by his open talk about his religious faith. It seemed quite authentic, yet it could also be viewed skeptically, as his very personal way to get right with the religious conservatives without sounding scary to the less religious.

He was very aware of such dangers as he spoke that day. He wanted his listener to realize that he knew how embarrassing it would be if he laid his faith on too thick. He suggested that his religious experiences were not something he liked to talk about—and then willingly talked about them at length.

"First of all, I generally don't spend a lot of time talking about my religion unless I'm asked," he says, "or unless there's a purpose." The nice reluctance. Then: "I was raised in a Christian household by a mother and father who really gave me the greatest gift of all, which is unconditional love.

"But I think everybody has to come to terms with their own religion," he continued. "And I always say God works in mysterious ways and I renewed my spirit. It means precisely that I've accepted Christ as my savior, that's what that means."

The language was deeply evangelical, and evangelical Christians always regarded Bush as one of them. They stuck with him much later when he was tumbling in the polls after Iraq went sour and his response to Hurricane

Katrina was widely panned. His was an old-fashioned ethic that emphasized self-improvement through self-discipline. Faith seemed to have a very functional, twelve-step-program quality for a man who acknowledged he once had a drinking problem.

"For me, it means understanding and accepting whatever comes with life," he told me. "I mean, it helps prepare me for my own daily struggles and my own thinking. I believe in prayer. I read the Bible. It helps strengthen me as a person. It helps me understand the priorities in life of family and faith."

In talking about his sense of responsibility, he managed to take an oblique but tough shot at Clinton. There is, he said, "a certain maturation that happens when you assume the responsibility of being a father and a husband. . . . I mean, I take solemn oaths very seriously and I can remember when our twins were born. I remember feeling how much my life changed the moment they were born and in anticipation how much it was going to change over time. And there's no question that if you assume your responsibility as a dad as seriously as we should, it changes your life."

From there Bush moved easily to answering questions about his brand of compassionate conservatism. "In terms of government policy," he said, "probably the most profound impact that religion has had on me has led me to help, in our state, forge this relationship between church, synagogue and mosque and people who need help . . . and [we] have welcomed people of faith into the public arena to help people. I mean, the theory is that let's change your heart first, and good results will follow."

The way Bush talked about his religious faith solved three problems at once. In speaking with compassion about the poor, he made conservatism sound softer and more moderate. His faith talk allowed him to relate easily to Christian conservatives without talking about any of the specific issues that had a downside on the left and in the center. And discussing his conversion allowed Bush to draw a sharp line between his self-described "young and irresponsible" past, and his presidency-seeking present. He cast himself as the prodigal son, the repentant sinner, the transformed man.

When I put this suspicious view to him—it bordered, admittedly, on the downright cynical—Bush got testy for the only time in our chat and dismissed the idea. "People will see through that in a minute," he said.

Over the years, no one I have encountered who knew Bush ever doubted the sincerity of his faith, and this was true even among his staunchest political opponents. Nor did anyone question that his life did seem to change when he turned forty in 1986. But the content of his faith has always been much harder to pin down. The evidence, especially of his own words, was that it was less an intellectual calling than a matter of feelings and the will. When I asked him about favorite passages in the Bible, his answers were vague and general—"Well," he said, "the Beatitudes are great. I mean a lot of the Bible."

"Religion is a very personal matter to me—as it should be to everybody," he explained. "I also understand that everybody comes to have religion different ways. All I know is—I know the pathway for me is what I know. And I'm not going to try to tell you the pathway for you." It was very nonjudgmental, end-of-the-century, good-vibes religion.

Compassionate conservatism Bush-style was clearly rooted in personal experience, in the notion that religious faith offered the most effective path to solving problems—very much what David Kuo was talking about. It could be parodied as a kind of New Religious Deal: government would, somehow or other, help every American who wanted one to have a religious experience. Nonetheless, Bush conveyed great sincerity when he talked about his hopes.

"I ask the question, 'Does it work?'" he said. "And to answer your question, from firsthand knowledge I know that changing your heart can work. It's worked for me. Will it work for everybody? Probably not. But, for example, if in fact we've reduced recidivism by changing hearts first, the state of Texas and, for that matter, America ought to say, 'Thank you, Lord, let's do more.'"

Religious language enabled Bush to move hard, controversial political questions to the more comfortable ground of personal obligation and faith. He didn't talk about social justice, minimum wages, unions, or monopoly power. He simply preached everybody's obligation—well, to be kinder and gentler, to create a thousand points of light.

"Getting tough on crime is easy, compared to loving our neighbors as ourselves," said the man who presided over 152 executions, more than any previous governor in American history. (His successor, Rick Perry, would break that record.) "The truth is," Bush went on, "we must turn back to God and look to Him for help." Bush's compassion talk was never about the failure of the economic system, or the rights of those who are poor, or systematic injustices. He always came back to individuals.

Those who saw Bush as unsophisticated might pay close attention to what he said next. "I know many conservative thinkers and people who adhere to the notion of heralding the individual and individualism and less federal government are people who really do care about the future," he said. "Because they know what I know: Government can't make people love one another. There have really been a lot of false promises over the last 30 years as well: 'Oh don't worry, you know, we'll make you love each other.' Well, unfortunately it doesn't happen that way. Love comes from a more powerful source."

What's fascinating here is how Bush justifies a fundamentally libertarian view in the name of compassion. Social justice brought about by government action—or, for that matter, by the needy organizing themselves in their own interest—recedes as an issue. Love, of both the human and divine sort, becomes the key to change.

With this move, Bush made it easy to parody liberalism as a creed that proposed to use government to "make people love one another." Never mind that liberalism was about a different, more achievable, and less abstract claim: that government could make the world a bit more just and ease the burdens on those down on their luck or short of opportunity. What Bush was doing here was squaring the circle between Gersonian and Olasky-style compassionate conservatism. He had plenty of compassion, but the dig against liberals was just what small-government conservatives wanted to hear. He seemed to be proposing God, not government. Or, at the least, religious charity would make smaller government possible.

And government in Texas, under Bush and since, was very small. In 1999, *National Journal* magazine had ranked Texas as 50th among states in total per capita government spending, and 35th in per capita education spending. At the time he was governor, Texas had a minimum wage of $3.35 an hour, one of the lowest in the country and $1.80 lower than the national minimum.

Bush's words underscored the ambiguities of compassionate conservatism and its divided character. I tried to get at this tension by asking Bush about his take on Olasky's ideas. He did not defend his adviser's every proposition but he did embrace him in a more general way. "I think that our society can change one heart, one soul, one conscience at a time. That's what I believe," he said. "And I believe that Olasky understands that, and I believe that many people of faith understand that, and I'm proud that Olasky wants to try to figure out ways to make society respond to the call."

Bush was certainly more aggressively antigovernment before he announced his candidacy for president than he was afterward. In April 1996, for example, he declared: "As government did more and more, individuals were required to do less and less, and they responded with a vengeance. Dependency and laziness are easy when someone else is to blame. We became a nation of victims. Blame it on the parenting, the Prozac, the bossa nova—take your pick." And he picked up on a favorite theme of the right by going back to the Founders and the Tenth Amendment. "We must reduce the role and scope of the federal government," he said, "returning it to the limited role our forefathers envisioned when they wrote the 10th Amendment to the Constitution, giving the states all power not specifically granted to the federal government."

Compassionate conservatism was always a work in progress and had the capacity to be different things to different people. At times Bush genuinely seemed to struggle between Olasky-style antistatism on the one side, and Gerson's more state-friendly thinking on the other. Nine months after I talked to him, he gave his definitive speech on compassionate conservatism in Indianapolis. His address in July 1999 was largely Gerson's work, and it tilted more in his direction. Bush memorably proposed to unleash the faith-based "armies of compassion," but he was far more careful to defend a role for government and to insist that his private legions could not fully substitute for the state. "There are some things that government should be doing—like Medicaid for poor children," he said, adding that "government cannot be replaced by charities."

By turns attacking and defending government, Bush managed to straddle the entire field. He was ingenious at devising formulas that could be read as friendly by pro- and anti-government voters alike. "My guiding principle," he once said, "is government if necessary, but not necessarily government." Those words might, in principle at least, be spoken as easily by Ted Kennedy as by Jesse Helms.

But for all of Bush's warm invocations of "mercy" and "love," there remained a hard—or, if you prefer, tough-love—side to his compassion. I asked Bush why people are poor, and he spoke almost entirely about their shortcomings. "Oftentimes people are poor because of decisions they make," he says. "Oftentimes people are poor because they didn't get a good education . . . [and aren't] making right choices and staying in school and working hard in school."

Were there any social reasons for poverty, I asked? "I think if you grow up in an impoverished world that's full of drugs and alcohol, it makes it very hard to break out of the environment which you're in," he replied.

Again: drugs and alcohol. Perhaps it was too much to expect a probusiness Republican to offer an answer that might include references to market failures, capitalism's injustices, racism, or joblessness. But Bush's answer underscored why compassionate conservatism was such a useful idea to the right.

A focus on personal shortcomings pointed to the need for individual conversion and self-help. A focus on conversion and self-help led to an emphasis on faith and charity, not government or justice. Kuo was right, of course, that it was possible to care about both sets of concerns. Gerson was right that Bush was not a radical libertarian who proposed the wholesale dismantling of the state, and Bush would make other nods to his progovernment side as the campaign proceeded. Nonetheless, the deeply conservative implications of compassionate conservatism as Bush described it were impossible to miss. Structural changes in the economy or the health system or in the relationship between workers and employers were not on the Bush agenda.

What conservatives seemed to understand is that Bush's compassion was rooted in the very old Republican doctrine that voluntary action is better than government action.

Here is what Bush said in his inaugural address after he was reelected as governor: "Reducing problems to economics is simply materialism," he declared. "The real answer is found in the hearts of decent, caring people who have heard the call to love their neighbors as they would like to be loved themselves. We must rally the armies of compassion in every community of this state. We must encourage them to love, to nurture, to mentor, to help and thus to offer hope to those who have none."

Now consider another speech: "Our national resources are not only material supplies and material wealth but a spiritual and moral wealth in kindliness, in compassion, in a sense of obligation of neighbor to neighbor, and a realization of responsibility by industry, by business and by the community for its social security and its social welfare. . . . We can take courage and pride in the effective work of thousands of voluntary organizations for the provision of employment, for the relief of distress, that have sprung up over the entire nation."

The words are Herbert Hoover's, spoken in 1932 in the midst of the Great Depression. When Bush insisted that he truly was a conservative, he had a good case to make and a powerful pedigree to invoke.

A riddle wrapped in a mystery inside of an enigma: Churchill's description of Russia in 1939 seemed quite apt to the way Bush presented himself as he prepared his presidential campaign. In 1999, I wrote a magazine piece for the *Washington Post* based on my interview with Bush and some of the reporting reflected here. I concluded that based on who Bush said he was—and on the contradictory ways others described him—it was impossible to know how he intended to govern. It was possible that he would prove to be the man who brought his party back to a modulated view of government that his grandfather would understand. Yet it was equally possible that he would parade into office under the banner of compassion and turn out to be one of the most conservative presidents in recent history.

There was also this: Bush had absolutely no interest in resolving the matter until the presidential campaign was over.

It was an enviable place for a candidate to be at the outset of a presidential campaign.

7

DOUBLE-EDGED "STRATEGERY"

George W. Bush, Karl Rove, and the Search for a Fourth Way

"All the ingredients are in place for this epic disaster in 2008."

The word "strategery" began its life on *Saturday Night Live* on October 7, 2000, a month before the election. The brainchild of veteran *SNL* writer Jim Downey, the word was used by Will Ferrell to parody Bush's on-again, off-again war with the English language and his tendency to garble old sayings and mispronounce words. Noting that people regularly "misunderestimated" him is a Bush classic.

Rather than bristle or complain, the Bush team embraced and ran with the concept. They secured the White House, after all, so whatever "strategery" was, it had worked. Bush aides came to speak of a White House Office of Strategery and regularly used the word with tongue-in-cheek pride.

Parsing the difference between normal strategy and "strategery" became a party game among political junkies and management experts. Dan Simon, writing in *Forbes*, distinguished between "strategy," a carefully planned, long-term approach, and "strategery," which entailed seat-of-the-pants gambits, often designed under pressure. "If you're writing it on a plane, train or the back of a car," Simon explained, "it's strategery."

Strategery, constant improvisation, is precisely what Bush and Karl Rove were required to do over a decade during which they tried to build a narrow but enduring conservative majority in rapidly changing circumstances and in an overall climate that was pushing against conservatism.

Sometimes nimble and sometimes clumsy, they sought to stay ahead of events, pursuing different approaches at different moments—often, until 2006, with real success. Bush's complex dance with the right and the middle that began with his 1998 reelection campaign for governor won him the 2000 Republican nomination. His 2004 reelection with a popular vote majority— the only majority Republicans managed between 1992 and 2012—was the high point. But the costs were high. Bush simultaneously created long-term problems inside the conservative coalition and alienated a large part of the political center that Rove had hoped to move rightward.

Understanding the Bush years in all their complexity is essential to grasping why conservatism and the Republican Party radicalized in the Obama years. The second President Bush's political project began as an effort to come to terms with Clintonism and to seize enough of the political center to offer Republicans a chance at long-term dominance. Yet Bush found himself dependent on the party's conservative base at crucial moments, notably when John McCain endangered his campaign for the Republican presidential nomination. And after 2000, Karl Rove came to see the limits of an appeal to voters in the political center: there were fewer of them than he originally thought. He returned to older Republican strategies involving polarization and the use of hard conservative issues to increase turnout among loyalists. In the wake of the attacks of 9/11, Bush expanded the repertoire of base-mobilizing issues to include appeals built around the war on terror. In doing so, he retooled charges of Democratic "softness" toward a foreign adversary that were a trademark of Richard Nixon's career and were a key to his 1972 landslide victory over George McGovern. If Bush began his national career with an eye toward moderating conservatism, he was forced by the logic of the contemporary right to a strategy of polarization.

In the end, Bush's strategery created the worst of all worlds: His polarizing strategies infuriated Democrats and liberals while his moves toward moderation alienated the right. Progressives saw a socially conservative president who cut taxes on the rich, pushed the country to war on false pretenses, and bogged it down in Iraq. Conservatives saw a "big-government" Republican who turned surpluses into deficits, was far too "multicultural," far too open to immigration reform, and far too eager to federalize education policy. When the catastrophic economic collapse came in 2008, both sides took it as a ratification of their respective negative verdicts on Bush's stewardship.

The events of 9/11 also meant that Bush's presidency did not, in the end, resemble the one he originally had in mind. He had hoped that, like Clinton, he would enjoy a sojourn overseeing peaceful and prosperous times. His time in office came to be defined instead by the attacks of September 11, 2001, his subsequent decision to invade Iraq, and economic mayhem.

Critical to Rove's planning for the 2000 election was his acceptance of the successes of Clintonism and the failures of the 1994 Republican revolution. His approach was based on a realistic assessment of the advances Democrats had made and the continuing weaknesses of conservatism as a brand. He knew it was not 1980 anymore.

Bush and Rove also knew that Clinton's image as an amiable compromiser who would do what it took to get things done played well against the Republican Congress, and Gingrich in particular. Clinton seemed devoted to uniting the country. His Republican opponents seemed determined to divide it, and impeachment served as Exhibit A of their indifference to national concord. Bush's refrain heard during his reelection campaign about being a "uniter not a divider" became a maxim of his presidential quest, a clear signal that he was not like those annoying congressional Republicans whom so many voters disliked.

At the same time, Rove saw the Clinton scandal as a useful foil. It was the one aspect of Clinton's tenure that upset swing voters, even if they had opposed impeachment. Regular, subtle reminders of the Lewinsky affair appealed to a Republican base, particularly the religious conservatives who continued to loathe Clinton. Without mentioning the forty-second president, Bush regularly promised to "restore honor and dignity to the White House." Bush could remind the religious conservatives of Clinton's sins as a reason for voting Republican again without harping on issues such as abortion or gay rights. Bush broadly agreed with the social conservatives, particularly in their views on the right to life. But he didn't make his opposition to abortion a central part of his campaign because he had no intention of losing those suburban women whose votes he was courting so ardently.

Having it both ways on Clinton became a Bush trademark as he separated himself from the divisive impeachers while taking full advantage of the country's sour response to the Clinton affair itself. And the approach had a side benefit: only at the very end of the 2000 campaign did Al Gore finally find a way to embrace Clinton's successes while distancing himself from Clinton's personal behavior.

The problem posed by the scandal (and Bush's use of it) was "almost paralyzing" to Gore, wrote John Harris, Clinton's biographer. Gore "oddly came to believe that to embrace any part of the Clinton record was to embrace all of it." If Gore's ambivalence arose from an entirely understandable—if, in a political context, dysfunctional—anger over what Clinton had done, he was also responding to a comparable ambivalence in parts of the public that Bush took advantage of.

Yet Rove also sought to apply affirmative lessons he learned from Clinton on the need to broaden a party's appeal, something that was already obvious in Bush's reelection campaign and the compassionate, unifying image he so carefully cultivated before he announced for president. Bush's strong support for immigration reform, a cause also endorsed by the pro-business right, was the most successful aspect of the effort. Bush bolstered his formal position on the issue with warm words about immigrants themselves. "Not only do immigrants help build our economy," Bush said at one point, "they invigorate our soul." Bush won upwards of 40 percent of the Latino vote in both 2000 and 2004. The political costs of his support for immigration reform on the right end of the party would emerge only after he had been safely reelected.

The emphasis on compassionate conservatism was part of this larger endeavor, and Bush was occasionally willing to take Republicans in Congress to task for being insufficiently mindful of the poor. In late September 1999, for example, Bush criticized a GOP proposal to restructure and cut the Earned Income Tax Credit (EITC), which subsidizes the incomes of the working poor. Bush echoed, word for word, a critique of Republican budgeters on which Democrats thought they owned the copyright. "I don't think they ought to balance their budget on the backs of the poor," Bush said.

Such forays into the political center won Bush early and favorable notice from journalists. A few days after his comments on the EITC, Dan Balz, the *Washington Post*'s top political reporter, described Bush as having "stolen a page from President Clinton's political playbook" by "distancing himself from the unpopular congressional wing of the Republican Party in the same way Clinton played off congressional Democrats." Two could play the triangulation game.

Yet Balz shrewdly noticed something else: the "reality" that "Bush has not strayed dramatically from conservative orthodoxy—from abortion to guns to tax cuts to school vouchers." Bush seemed to be making small nods to the center (the EITC proposal he opposed amounted to only $8 billion in budget reductions) while making the hard commitments the right demanded. The tensions and contradictions that were obvious in 1998 did not go away.

As Rove explained the strategy to *Washington Post* reporter Thomas B. Edsall, the more divisive approaches used by Nixon and even Bush's father in 1988 were "old paradigm," and in the new millennium, "voters are more attracted . . . by a positive agenda than by wedge issues."

The heavy stress Bush put on education in the 2000 campaign is an example of Rove's audacity in trying to seize an issue from the Democrats. Since Bush had attempted to reform the way Texas financed its public schools, he came to the question with some credibility, even if his reform effort had been defeated. In having Bush talk regularly about schools, Rove was very clear about the target voters he had in mind. Education, he wrote in his memoir, "was a major concern with suburban independents, especially women, and soft Republicans." By ceding the issue to Democrats, Rove argued, Republicans threw away votes that could be theirs. He noted that voters who considered education their top voting issue in 1996 had supported Clinton over Dole by 62 points, 78 percent to 16 percent. It was thus a matter of great pride to Rove that "[a]fter Bush talked about education endlessly during his 2000 presidential campaign, he received 44 percent of the vote from those for whom education was their top issue." Bush reduced the 62-point Democratic advantage on education to just 4 points.

One thing Rove's 1999 strategy did not anticipate was the early strength of John McCain's insurgency in the Republican primaries. McCain's campaign was exciting and caught the imagination of the media. McCain sometimes referred to journalists, not inaccurately, as part of his "base." Bush may never have been in as much jeopardy from McCain as he seemed to be the night he was defeated by the Vietnam War hero in the New Hampshire primary in an astonishing 49 percent to 30 percent landslide. For if McCain's Straight Talk Express was fueled by the fascination his breezy but edgy candor created in the media and among political independents and some Democrats, Bush's campaign was a large and sturdy all-terrain vehicle not easily thrown off its center-right course. Despite all of his careful repositioning, the Bush campaign's ballast was on the right: against McCain, at least, Bush became the favorite of the GOP's conservative wing.

Even in the face of Bush's defeat in New Hampshire, the numbers were telling. The state allowed independents to vote in either party's primary, and they flooded into the Republican contest to support McCain, who won them 61 percent to 19 percent over Bush. Independents built the McCain landslide. McCain was so strong in New Hampshire that he carried Republicans as well, but by a narrower, 44-to-36 percent, margin, and conservatives split their ballots almost evenly, 37-to-36 percent for McCain over Bush.

McCain's relative weakness among conservatives even in his New Hampshire stronghold explained why Bush would go on to overwhelm him in the next, decisive and also vicious contest in South Carolina. Wooing a very conservative primary electorate in one of the most conservative states in the union, Bush ran unapologetically to McCain's right. Bush's first stop after his New Hampshire defeat was a boisterous rally at Bob Jones University. He was later attacked by McCain and the Democrats for visiting a college that banned interracial dating and labeled Catholicism as a "Satanic counterfeit" of Christianity. But the visit and other appeals to evangelicals (along with a variety of below-the-radar attacks on McCain) had their effect. In his memoir, Rove explicitly asked: "Was it a mistake to go to Bob Jones?" He seemed to have few regrets, given how things turned out. "It was a big venue, a major stop for GOP candidates, and a large and enthusiastic crowd the day after a bad defeat," Rove wrote. Fully embracing the moderate and compassionate remake of conservatism would have to wait until the base and the nomination were secure.

Thus did Bush's campaign suggest "directly and indirectly," as the *New York Times*' R. W. Apple Jr. put it, "that McCain was a closet liberal, or at least unreliably conservative." The payoff was large. Conservatives in South Carolina backed Bush over McCain, 65 percent to 29 percent. Not only did conservatives make up a much bigger part of the Republican electorate in South Carolina than they did in New Hampshire; they were also conservatives of a different kind. Religious conservatives made up only 16 percent of New Hampshire GOP voters, but accounted for 34 percent of the Republicans who cast ballots in South Carolina—and they went overwhelmingly to Bush.

The political to-and-fro—from center to right and then back to the middle again—is a mark of Rove's tactical flexibility, but also a sign of what an intricate contraption his game plan was. Bush and Rove knew the damage the party's conservative congressional wing had done to Bob Dole in 1996 and to the party's standing with moderate and suburban voters, particularly outside the South. But they also knew that the party was more conservative than it had been when Republicans had nominated Bush's father. This dictated corrections here and there while staying true to the right on the key questions, as Balz had noticed. It also meant that the man who would write a laudatory book about his dad in 2014 showed surprising caution when discussing his father's legacy when I interviewed him in 1998. Asked about his family's tradition of public service, Bush was surprisingly circumspect. "Obviously it's a proud tradition," he said—and then immediately put distance between his father's achievements and what he and his brother Jeb, then governor of Florida, were doing. "I believe we have that sense of service," W. said, "but I believe that we're both driven as well by ideas and philosophy. That we have come to realize, particularly in our respective roles as governors, how powerful an idea can be. And that it's important to serve but it's also important to achieve results: To set goals, clear and measurable goals, and to lead."

Being "driven as well by ideas and philosophy" was Bush's polite way of saying that he and his brother understood the importance to the Republican base of *conservative* ideas and philosophy in a way their dad had not.

Bush knew from having worked with religious conservatives during his father's campaign that they were a key force in GOP nominating politics. Led by Pat Robertson, the Christian Right had almost upended his father's campaign in the 1988 caucuses in Michigan and pushed him into third place in Iowa. This would not happen to the son.

At the same time, the younger Bush was a corporate and business Republican by temperament and experience. He had paid $600,000 for his share of the Texas Rangers baseball team and sold his stake a decade later for nearly $15 million. It was no surprise that he loved capitalism and his business friends, or that talk of creating "an environment in which people are willing to risk capital" would routinely cross his lips.

This Bush was acutely aware of the problems supply-side tax cutters had with his father. The son would avoid the father's mistakes in this area, too, and made a $1.3 trillion tax cut a centerpiece of his campaign program.

Looking back in 2014, David Frum, the Bush speechwriter and future conservative apostate, explained why Bush's strategery had its moments of real success but ultimately failed to produce the enduring conservative majority that was Rove's goal. Frum argues that it's important to see that Rove and Bush were primarily interested in solving a "political problem," and "not in devising a broad new policy approach." As short-term politics, Frum saw their approach as "very brilliant" because it did manage to "rebrand and repackage conservatism, to make it more acceptable to educated women."

But he added pointedly: "They do not solve the policy problem." The Bush-Rove correction was primarily "stylistic," he said, designed to make Republicans look "less argumentative and contentious."

Moving education to the center of his agenda may have been a substantive change, but there was no such change on taxes, where Bush offered supply-side cuts while "jettison[ing] the supply side argument" for them. As Frum observed, the Clinton surpluses allowed Bush to argue that he could simultaneously pay for his priorities, pay down the debt, and then and only then cut taxes. He could cast this as "prudent management of extra money after we do the basics."

"They don't win a landslide," Frum concluded, "but it was good enough for government work."

The problems Frum described emerged over time. But an immediate hitch with the Rove strategy emerged on election night: Bush not only failed to win a majority; he actually lost the popular vote to Gore. And Bush's Electoral College victory was secured only through the intervention of five conservative justices on the Supreme Court who stopped the recounting of ballots in Florida. The Republicans' harsh, personal attacks on Gore for seeking recounts—any candidate for any office would have asked for a recount in a similarly close contest—and justices who used arguments they had rejected in the past to make Bush president created a bitterness among Democrats that would never go away. Gore was repeatedly told that in trying to get an honest count, he was putting his own interest before the country's, as if the national interest depended on allowing Bush to become president as quickly as possible. The conservative *Weekly Standard* was representative in referring to Gore's recount efforts as "The Gore Coup." Bush (through surrogates, of course) was perfectly willing to be a "divider" if that's what it took to win the recount fight. The chasm between the two parties that marked Bush's presidency through all but the months immediately following the 9/11 attacks was opened first in Florida's recount halls and in courtrooms, not on Iraq's battlefields.

While publicly battling Gore during the Florida episode, Rove was privately upset that his strategy had fallen far short of his expectations of a clear and uncontested victory. He commissioned Matt Dowd, the campaign's pollster, to undertake a study to explain Bush's disappointing showing. Dowd's conclusion was explosive: the true swing, independent part of the electorate—the voters who had so preoccupied Rove—had shrunk from roughly a quarter of the electorate in the Reagan years to a mere 6 percent in 2000. The upshot, as the historian Gary Gerstle put it, was that "Bush's pursuit of the 'phantom middle' of the electorate had cost him votes among hard-core Republicans, especially those who described themselves as evangelicals."

After Dowd's statistical revelations, polarization and mobilization became the watchwords. What Rove had called the "old paradigm" was new again. As Edsall put it, Dowd's memo "allowed Republican leaders and strategists to return to the kind of wedge issues and polarizing tactics that had worked so effectively in the decades following the 1960s."

Rove did not give up on the political center entirely. But as Gerstle noted, the strategy that emerged from Rove's dual quest—to convert moderates and to mobilize the base at the same time—"was inherently difficult to execute, for it required balancing contradictory ambitions, broadening the party's appeal while persuading the conservative base that the party was a vehicle for their views alone." Even with the best strategery, it was not a feat he could pull off.

★

With the unpleasantness of Florida out of the way, Bush immediately set about to keeping his core campaign promises. With a Republican Congress backing him up, Bush would not allow the disputed character of his election to get in the way of his program.

His short and elegant inaugural address was pure and explicit compassionate conservatism. "America at its best is compassionate," he declared. "In the quiet of American conscience, we know that deep, persistent poverty is unworthy of our Nation's promise. And whatever our views of its cause, we can agree that children at risk are not at fault."

Bush defended government's role, but he also defined it parsimoniously, referring to its "responsibilities for public safety and public health, for civil rights and common schools." He then offered a nicely hedged view of the state that both pro- and anti-government compassionate conservatives could cheer. "Yet, compassion is the work of a nation, not just of government," he said. The limiting word "just" suggested some role for government, even as the emphasis of the rest of the passage was on actors far removed from the bureaucracies. "And some needs and hurts are so deep," Bush went on, "they will only respond to a mentor's touch or a pastor's prayer. Church and charity, synagogue and mosque lend our communities their humanity, and they will have an honored place in our plans and in our laws." If liberals put government at the center of their struggle for a more just society, Bush put religious Americans at the center of his plan to create a more caring country.

A president whose administration would, in just eight months, come to be defined by an act of terrorism and two wars devoted exactly two paragraphs in a thirty-paragraph address to foreign policy. And both were vague, including a promise "to build our defenses beyond challenge, lest weakness invite challenge."

His first major order of business was cutting taxes. It was not just that Bush wanted to draw a clear line between himself and his father; he was also a sufficiently conventional pro-business conservative to believe that tax cuts would boost an economy beginning to sag. Moreover, Clinton's surpluses allowed Bush to tell citizens that he was simply giving them some of their money back.

In truth, the rationale for the tax cuts kept shifting. Initially, they were affordable because the economy was booming. Later, they were necessary because the economy was stalling. No matter what was happening with the economy, it was always time for a tax cut.

First came the Economic Growth and Tax Relief Reconciliation Act of 2001, a classic across-the-board, supply-side measure. The top income tax bracket for the best-off was cut from 39.6 percent to 35 percent; the 36 percent bracket went down to 33 percent, and so on down the line. The estate tax cut was cut incrementally over a decade and set to be repealed entirely in 2010. The revenue cost of the bill was estimated at the time at $1.35 trillion. Because budget rules limited the amount that could be added to the deficit after the first decade of a law's life, the bill contained a "sunset" provision that automatically repealed the entire measure on January 1, 2011. It was a gimmick designed to permit a much larger tax cut than would otherwise have been possible.

Particularly as it related to the estate tax, this gamesmanship created perversities—or, as the *New York Times* columnist Paul Krugman mischievously wrote, "some interesting incentives." As the law was written, the estate tax would be zero on December 31, 2010, but jump back up to 55 percent on January 1, 2011, a startling difference for those looking forward to large inheritances. Krugman came to refer to the law as the "Throw Momma From the Train Act of 2001."

This was not the only tax cutting Bush would do. The Jobs and Growth Tax Relief Reconciliation Act of 2003 cut the main capital gains tax rate from 20 percent to 15 percent, and reduced taxes on dividends, preciously treated as ordinary income, to 15 percent. The second tax cut was tilted even more heavily toward the wealthy than the first and cost the Treasury another $350 billion in revenue over a decade. Liberals were not alone in being enraged by a tax cut for the rich in the middle of a war. John McCain was also at full throttle. Ridiculing claims that the law would promote economic growth, McCain said that "the only thing growing . . . will be the tax breaks for the wealthiest citizens of this country." Adding to the liberal rage was Dick Cheney's sense of entitlement in pushing ahead with more tax cutting. Since Republicans had won the 2002 midterm election, he was quoted as saying, "it's our due."

In the long run, as David Frum observed, "the Bush domestic economic program really doesn't work as advertised."

"There was a big tax-cut, but it doesn't ignite the level of growth that was hoped for," he said. "The level of growth does not translate into rising personal incomes, which is an even bigger problem, and then inadvertently, you generate this huge debt bubble as consumers facing stagnant income try to increase their consumption by taking extra debt. . . . [T]he credit markets become ever-more willing to provide credit in lieu of income for people."

"All the ingredients are in place for this epic disaster in 2008."

But even in the short run, Bush did not get the political jolt out of his first tax cut victory that he had counted on. It was immediately overshadowed by what was, in Washington terms at least, a monumental political event. The tax cuts passed on May 23, 2001, and the next day, Senator James Jeffords of Vermont quit the Republican Party, declared himself an Independent, and announced that he would be caucusing with the Democrats. The Senate had been split 50–50, with Vice President Cheney's vote giving Republicans the right to manage its business. Jeffords switch gave the Democrats 51 seats and control of the Senate. Immediately, committee chairmanships switched parties and Democrats were in control of what happened on the floor.

Jeffords, who in 1981 had been the only Republican to vote against the Reagan tax cut, joined the long line of moderate and progressive Republicans who had abandoned the GOP because they felt abandoned themselves in its steady journey rightward. He explained that he had finally accepted the GOP for what it had become and could no longer be part of it.

"Increasingly, I find myself in disagreement with my party," Jeffords said.

"I understand that many people are more conservative than I am, and they form the Republican Party. Given the changing nature of the national party, it has become a struggle for our leaders to deal with me and for me to deal with them."

Conservatives denounced Jeffords in bitterly personal terms for abruptly upending Republican control of the Senate. "Why isn't everyone talking about what a big baby Jeffords is?" complained the *Wall Street Journal*'s editorial page in a snappish tone that was typical of reaction on the right. The *New York Post* portrayed the senator in colonial garb under the headline: "Benedict Jeffords."

Still, *National Review,* the guardian of conservative orthodoxy, recognized the logic of Jeffords's position. After all, it was the same logic the magazine had embraced since its inception to argue for purifying the Republican Party of progressives and the followers of Dwight Eisenhower. "He is a liberal," the magazine said of Jeffords, and his conversion "makes it clear that the Republicans are the conservative party and the Democrats are the liberal party." His choice, *NR* added, was "clarifying." And so it was.

Two other major pieces of domestic legislation enacted under Bush underscored the philosophical and political ambiguities of the Bush-Rove project.

The No Child Left Behind Act, passed at the end of 2001 and signed into law in January 2002, was the most genuinely bipartisan achievement of the Bush years. It was enacted not with stray votes from a handful of moderate and conservative Democrats, but after extensive negotiations between the Bush administration and two of Congress's leading liberals, Ted Kennedy in the Senate and George Miller in the House. John Boehner, the chair of the House Education Committee, was closely involved in the negotiations. This fed hopes later on—largely disappointed until his final act as Speaker in the fall of 2015, by which he avoided another shutdown through a budget and debt ceiling agreement—that he would be a deal maker.

The later transformation of Boehner from the No Child Left Behind committee chair to the Republican leader who lived in fear of a Tea Party rebellion is one of the most powerful indicators of the acceleration of change within the party. Boehner eventually gave up in the fall of 2015. The chaos involved in trying to replace him put an exclamation point on the party's radicalization.

The new education law was an authentic achievement consistent with Bush's past. It combined ideas popular among Republicans, to hold schools and teachers accountable, with the Democrats' insistence that reform cost money and that the federal government needed to provide more of it for poor school districts. The law passed the House overwhelmingly, 381 to 41. It's telling that 33 of the "no" votes came from conservative Republicans, many of them concerned about federal interference in state and local education decisions. These concerns would grow as the party marched rightward.

And as was the case with the tax cut, this Bush policy triumph also failed to have the enduring effect he and Rove had hoped for. It did not take long for Democrats and Republicans to begin battling over the matter of money. By October 2003, as Jim VandeHei reported in the *Washington Post*, Democrats were already blaming Bush and congressional Republicans "for shortchanging the law by billions of dollars." This allowed Bush's foes on the left to pick up on a favorite Republican talking point: that Washington was "slapping unfunded mandates on states that cannot afford them."

Bush's tax cuts also had unintended consequences for the states. Since many of them linked their tax rates to those of the federal government, VandeHei wrote, the Bush-sponsored federal reductions thus cut tax rates in these states and "drained revenue from state coffers that otherwise would have helped fund education."

VandeHei cited the findings of David Winston, a pollster for congressional Republicans, showing them trailing Democrats 50 percent to 36 percent on the education issue, "a 14-point drop since the measure was signed in January 2002." Bush's reversal of the Democrats' advantage on the education issue, so prized by Rove, proved to be short-lived.

The prescription drug benefit under Medicare, signed into law in December 2003, was the most intricate piece of policy politics Bush engaged in, and it divides the right to this day. As a simple matter of policy, covering prescription pharmaceuticals was a long-overdue and logical step in modernizing Medicare, a program established long before the age of expensive (and essential) drugs. Politically, the drug plan delivered a valuable benefit to the elderly, a key, high-voting constituency, and reflected another Bush foray into ground traditionally held by Democrats. Medicare was a proud Democratic achievement and had been a key issue in helping Clinton defeat the Gingrich Congress. Neither Bush nor Rove was prepared to leave the drug issue to the Democrats, especially at a time when the passing of the New Deal generation made senior citizens increasingly open to the Republican Party.

But where Bush wanted his benefit to be structured in a free-market way that would also appeal to the insurance and pharmaceutical industries, liberals wanted drug coverage paid for directly by Medicare. Because the government represented so many beneficiaries, it would be able to bargain with the pharmaceutical companies for lower prices. Bush, by contrast, pushed a plan that would provide Medicare subsidies to support the purchase of private insurance for drug coverage, offering insurance companies the opportunity to create scores of plans geared to different groups of seniors.

The Medicare Modernization Act was thus crafted to divide Democrats while bringing around enough conservatives to secure its passage. And it accomplished exactly that, though toward the end of the winding legislative process, the approach proved to be almost too clever. Extraordinary and highly controversial legislative tactics were ultimately required to push it through because so many conservative Republicans continued to believe that their party should *never* be in the business of expanding a major Federal entitlement program.

The Democratic split was real and could hardly have been more dramatic, pitting the party's two leading experts on health care—and two of its historic figures—against each other. Senator Hillary Clinton strongly opposed the bill and summarized the Democrats' dilemma in a June 2003 speech on the Senate floor: "Do we support legislation that we know is not the best for our seniors, but view it as a step in the right direction? Or do we vote it down because it fails to deliver more promise than perils for our seniors?" Democrats, she insisted, should oppose Bush's design and fight for a better bill. Ted Kennedy reached exactly the opposite conclusion on the basis of Clinton's logic. If a Republican president and a Republican Congress were willing to back off grand plans for Medicare privatization and were also prepared to put $400 billion on the table as a "down payment" toward solving the prescription drug problem, Kennedy reasoned, Democrats should grab the deal.

As the Republican leadership kept adding provisions aimed at satisfying conservatives still uneasy over such an expansive measure, Kennedy's doubts about his initial approach deepened. In its final version, the bill included Medicare privatization experiments, big subsidies for HMOs, and Health Savings Accounts. These and other changes pushed Kennedy to withdraw his support and he led a last-ditch fight against the final version of the bill. In the end, to the fury of most of their Democratic colleagues, Senators Max Baucus of Montana and John Breaux of Louisiana broke off from their party and negotiated a final deal with Bush. Strategery in this case dictated legislative maneuvers at odds with those Bush had pursued to pass No Child Left Behind: when he lost the chance to deal with the Democratic mainstream, Bush was happy to split the Democratic Party and do business with its most conservative members. It was indicative of a long-term challenge for Democrats, particularly in the Senate, and a reason why the Democrats would maintain a substantial moderate wing even as the Republican Party became more homogeneous. Democratic politicians, particularly senators from conservative states, were under far more pressure to cooperate with Republicans than Republican politicians were to deal with Democrats. Democrats worried more about losing general elections to Republicans; Republicans feared losing primaries to more conservative fellow Republicans.

The bill finally went through the House on November 22, 2003, on one of the most dramatic and bitterly contested evenings in the body's history. In the early hours of the morning, the bill appeared to have lost by two votes at the end of the customary fifteen-minute roll call. Rather than accept defeat, House Whip Tom DeLay kept the roll call open for an unprecedented two hours and fifty-one minutes. After much arm-twisting, cajoling, and at least one charge that a vote was virtually purchased, the bill passed 220 to 215. "I don't mean to be alarmist," thundered Representative Barney Frank, "but this is the end of parliamentary democracy as we have known it." Among the "no" votes were 189 Democrats, mostly liberals, the independent socialist Bernie Sanders of Vermont—and 25 of the most conservative Republicans in Congress. One of the ironies of this episode is that the structure of the drug benefit, relying heavily on the private insurance market, resembled what would become Obamacare.

To this day, many conservatives regret voting for the bill. One of them is Chris Chocola, then a member of Congress and later president of the Club for Growth, which would support many conservative challenges to more moderate Republicans that would make big news in the Tea Party years. Chocola told me in 2014 that he voted for the bill because, at the time, he regarded Bush's approach as "the most conservative alternative" to providing the benefit. Now he cannot be more emphatic in declaring his vote a mistake. "It was a bad vote, it was a wrong vote, I regret that vote today," he said.

Chocola's retrospective judgment is an instructive marker on the GOP's post-Bush road to the right. Although only twenty-five House Republicans actually voted against the drug benefit, it became increasingly common for conservatives to look back on the program as a budget buster—even if, in practice, conservative legislators have not actually tried to take this benefit away from the older voters who dominate their coalition. On prescription drugs for the elderly, Republicans politicians were conservative in theory but liberal in practice.

The combination of a tax cut, an education bill that drew support from liberals, a market-oriented drug benefit, and a steady flow of compassionate rhetoric defined the median point of the center-right that Rove was trying to create. It was an amalgam that had the potential of disorienting Democrats while creating sufficient unity on the right to give Bush room for continuing maneuver. Yet Democrats would eventually find their voices. And what began as quiet doubts on the right about Rove's strategery would become louder as Bush's position became weaker.

In 2007, Princeton University Press republished Barry Goldwater's *The Conscience of a Conservative* and asked conservative columnist George Will to write a new foreword. Bush's program gave Will the ammunition he needed to offer a reverie on "the impotence of books." Will wrote:

This edition of *The Conscience of a Conservative* comes after a Republican-controlled Congress, abetted by a Republican President, passed in 2001 the largest federal intervention in primary and secondary education in American history. And in 2002 enacted the largest farm subsidies. And in 2003 enacted the largest expansion of the welfare state—the prescription drug entitlement added to Medicare—since Lyndon Johnson, the president who defeated Goldwater in 1964, created Medicare in 1965.

For many conservatives, it is this view that would come to define Bush.

In the summer of 2001, Bush was preoccupied with a matter that faded quickly behind more exigent issues. Embryonic stem cell research was an issue that posed a real threat to Rove's coalition building. The abortion issue was also divisive, but many pro-choice voters did not cast ballots on the issue because they believed that abortion rights were already protected by *Roe v. Wade*. But stem cell research aroused sympathy even among some pro-life voters and legislators because of the possibilities it opened for medical break-throughs. Nonetheless, the staunchest pro-lifers believed that "harvesting" embryos for research was inherently and profoundly immoral.

After an extensive review of policy, Bush sided with the pro-lifers on this principle: "We do not end some lives for the medical benefit of others." But he tried to find a middle way that finessed the politics of the issue by de-clining to ban privately funded stem cell research and announcing that the federal government would fund research involving existing stem cell lines, but no others. This, Bush said in a nationally televised address from his Texas ranch on August 9, 2001, would allow scientists to "explore the promise and potential of stem cell research without crossing a fundamental moral line by providing taxpayer funding that would sanction or encourage further destruc-tion of human embryos that have at least the potential for life."

The speech did not satisfy supporters of stem cell research, who questioned whether Bush's fine distinctions had the moral consistency he claimed for them. Even Gerson, a strong defender of Bush's position, acknowledged that "the practical effect of the president's stem-cell policy was limited," though Gerson insisted that the president had "introduced a large philosophic debate into a political argument" by rejecting "utilitarianism."

Yet as he was devoting the bulk of his energies that month to the stem cell decision and speech, an ominous portent crossed his desk. On August 6, 2001, the morning's presidential daily brief from the intelligence agencies included the heading "Bin Laden Determined to Strike in U.S."

8

"I CAN HEAR YOU"

How W. United the Country, Then Divided It More than Ever

"The Bushes have always underestimated the depth
of the base's dissatisfaction with their policies."

Bush's initial response to the attacks of September 11, 2001, was hardly reassuring, and his aides knew it. He got the news while reading *The Pet Goat* to a second-grade class at the Emma E. Booker Elementary School in Sarasota, Florida. After he finished with the schoolchildren, Bush was rushed to the airport. His plane went first to Barksdale Air Force Base in Louisiana for refueling; there he spoke briefly to the nation. "Freedom itself was attacked this morning by a faceless coward, and freedom will be defended," he said. He told Americans that he was "in regular contact with the Vice President, the Secretary of Defense, the national security team, and my Cabinet" and that they had taken "all the necessary security precautions to continue the functions of your government." He concluded: "We will show the world that we will pass this test." Then he was whisked off to a bunker in Nebraska.

Rove acknowledged in his memoir that the president's initial response was less than satisfactory. "The president had vital matters on his mind, and his best wordsmiths, who would have helped him shape more reassuring and stronger messages for use in Florida and Louisiana, were stuck in Washington, huddled in D.C. office buildings, or hunkered down in a bunker under the South Lawn."

Rove was at pains to note that Bush was unhappy that he was not in Washington, and in his own memoir, Bush makes clear it was he who insisted on returning to the capital. During a videoconference from Nebraska, Bush wrote, "I put my foot down. I had decided to speak to the nation and there was no way I was going to do it from an underground bunker in Nebraska."

The speech Bush gave that evening when he finally did get back to Washington did not go much better in the view of one of those "best wordsmiths." Gerson saw the address as "unequal to the moment—too much sentiment, not enough resolve, too much forced word play." One line that came in for critique: "These acts shattered steel, but they cannot dent the steel of American resolve." In his book *Heroic Conservatism,* the usually loyal Gerson concluded: "The president looked stiff and small. . . . The first day of the crisis had not been a good day for the president."

Bush did not find his voice and his footing until September 14. In the morning, he gave a powerful speech that was more of a sermon at the Washington National Cathedral. "Just three days removed from these events, Americans do not yet have the distance of history," he said. "But our responsibility to history is already clear: to answer these attacks and rid the world of evil." Gerson, conscious of subsequent criticisms of Bush for apocalyptic rhetoric, went out of his way later to note that Bush was not supposed to have claimed that he would rid the world of *all* evil. The text of the speech had referred to "*this* evil," a narrower promise. Gerson observed that "the president had misspoken." Despite the error, it was one of the best speeches of his presidency, but it was a telling error nonetheless.

Later that day came Bush's signature moment, when he visited Ground Zero in New York City, stood among the ruins of the World Trade Center towers, and spoke through a bullhorn. When the crowd shouted, "We can't hear you!" Bush shouted back: "I can hear you. And the rest of the world hears you. And the people who knocked these buildings down will hear all of us soon." Thus began the heroic phase of Bush's tenure.

There was genuine statesmanship in one of Bush's earliest acts after the attacks. Two days after his bullhorn moment, Bush visited the Islamic Center of Washington, D.C., and gave one of the remarkable speeches of his presidency. He declared:

> The face of terror is not the true faith of Islam. That's not what Islam is all about. Islam is peace.... America counts millions of Muslims among our citizens.... Muslims are doctors, lawyers, law professors, members of the military, entrepreneurs, shopkeepers, moms and dads. And they need to be treated with respect.... Moms who wear head cover must not be intimidated in America. That's not the America I know. That's not the America I value.... Those who feel like they can intimidate their fellow citizens to take out their anger don't represent the best of America, they represent the worst of human-kind, and they should be ashamed of that kind of behavior.

The nation's Muslims, Bush added, "love America just as much as I do."

Over the years, as we'll see, large parts of the right began to forget the lessons Bush taught about the dangers of anti-Muslim feeling—particularly after the nation elected a president whose middle name was Hussein, and when a group of Muslims sought to build a community center near Ground Zero. But Bush deserves to be remembered for standing up for the rights of American Muslims when doing so was essential.

It was, indeed, possible to see a "new Bush" after 9/11, as he grew into his new role. Bush seemed to lose some of his partisanship and returned to his "uniter" role. Democrats gave him good reason to do this, rallying to Bush and avoiding questions they might well have asked about why the administration had not seen the attack coming. This would not happen until later. A $40 billion antiterrorism appropriation sped through Congress, as did a resolution authorizing retaliation for the attacks. Republicans even accommodated some Democratic amendments. "They could have rolled over us," a very partisan Democratic congressional leadership aide told me at the time, appreciating the fact that the Republicans didn't.

The 9/11 attacks produced one of the most stunning changes in a president's approval rating in the history of polling. In the Gallup poll taken from

September 7 to September 10, Bush's approval stood at 51 percent. In the next survey, taken on September 14 and September 15, his approval soared to 86 percent. It would rise to 90 percent a week later and stay between 86 and 89 percent for the rest of the year. Not until March 2002 did it fall into the 70s and not until August and September 2002 would it gradually settle into the 60s. When Bush sent troops into Afghanistan on October 7, 2001, to take on the Taliban and through them al-Qaeda, the country cheered across ideological and partisan lines. Gallup found that Americans endorsed the war by a margin of 80 percent to 18 percent.

The survey, however, contained important clues that pointed to future divisions. Fully 22 percent of Americans supported the war but were classified by Gallup as "reluctant warriors" because they said they would not have supported the Afghanistan action in the absence of the September 11 attack. This group felt that military force should be used only as a last resort. At the other end of the spectrum, another 22 percent were classified by Gallup as "hawks" because they said they would have favored using force in Afghanistan even absent the September 11 attacks—and, as a broader matter, they felt that the United States should use military force as readily as diplomatic and economic pressure in pursuit of foreign policy goals. The rest supported the Afghanistan action but were not readily classifiable as either hawks or doves.

It's worth pausing over these numbers because they call into question the widespread view at the time, repeated again and again in the media, that "everything changed" on September 11. Many who believed this were surprised when normal politics based on pre-9/11 political alignments returned so quickly. Some were also taken aback when support for military action, particularly in Iraq, began falling away even before the end of Bush's first term.

The Gallup numbers make clear that 40 percent of Americans either opposed to the war in Afghanistan or were among those "reluctant warriors." Even at a moment of national unity, there were clear partisan and ideological differences in attitudes toward the use of force: 49 percent of Democrats and 54 percent of liberals fell into one of these dovish or relatively dovish groups, but only 31 percent of Republicans and 33 percent of conservatives did. And even if conservatives were more hawkish than liberals, only a minority of them, 28 percent, took the strongly hawkish view as defined by Gallup (compared with 14 percent of liberals).

The reemergence later of anti-interventionist views on the right is easier to understand when one considers that at the height of support for the use of American power, only a little over a fifth of conservatives were enthusiastic about the regular deployment of American forces. The large middle group that supported the Afghanistan action willingly but did not share the ideological certainties of the hawks might be seen as the "swing voters" on the matter of military intervention. They were likely to judge wars by how they were prosecuted and what outcomes they produced. The Bush administration would have been wise at the time to notice that just over a month after 9/11, Americans were not willing to offer even a popular president battling in a broadly unifying cause a blank check. They should have understood that the support he enjoyed was more tentative than it seemed at the moment. It was clear that if a war went badly or came to be seen as disconnected from the battle against terrorism, opinion would shift rapidly.

Some Republicans hoped that Bush would use his new standing and the ad hoc coalition of national unity that had assembled behind him to change the Republican Party. Representative Tom Davis, who possessed one of the GOP's shrewdest political minds, saw the president as having the opportunity "to reshape the image of the party from the top down." It was possible at the time to imagine that a new version of Eisenhower Republicanism might create the enduring majority that Rove had always envisioned by encompassing broad parts of the middle ground of American opinion rather than simply the center-right.

But other voices saw a different opportunity: to take Bush's newly won popularity and deploy it to win enactment of as much of the conservative agenda as possible. Eight days after 9/11, the *Wall Street Journal* urged Bush to use the moment to push through every policy change he had been seeking, since "the bloody attacks have created a unique political moment when Americans of all stars and stripes are uniting behind their president." The *Journal* wanted to get approval for oil drilling in the Arctic, to speed up tax cuts (even as the country was spending billions more for security), and to push for the confirmation of conservative judges. The *Journal*'s editorial page reached back, as it often does, to the successful liberal campaign in 1987 to block the Supreme Court nomination of Robert Bork. "Democrats in the Senate," the editors wrote, "will hesitate to carry our borkings that clearly undercut Mr. Bush's leadership." Not only was it untrue that "everything changed" after the attacks. For some, nothing had changed at all—except, perhaps, that the response to the attacks had created new openings for old ideas.

Partisanship on the right quickly emerged in another way: even as Democrats resisted the immediate temptation to ask why Bush had not been more aware of the impending danger, conservatives showed no compunction about blaming the tragedy on . . . Bill Clinton. "We have no choice but to address the policies and decisions, made at the very highest levels of our government, which helped bring us to this point," Rush Limbaugh wrote in the *Journal* on October 4. Such a sentence might well have been written about Bush, but for Limbaugh, the issue was that Clinton "didn't do enough to stop terrorists." Senator Richard Shelby, the Alabama Republican, blamed Clinton for the CIA's restrictions on the recruitment of informants overseas. "The Clinton curbs," he said, "have hindered the work of our human intelligence agents around the world."

Over time, 9/11 was used as a weapon to discredit the very peace and prosperity that characterized the Clinton years. The conservative Charles Krauthammer coined what would become an enduring phrase on the right, dismissing the Clinton era as a "holiday from history" in a November 2001 article in the *Weekly Standard*. "During the Clinton years," he wrote, "while the United States engaged in (literally) paperwork, the enemy was planning and arming, burrowing deep into America, preparing for war."

Krauthammer came back to this idea again and again, writing in 2003: "We now pay the wages of the 1990s, our holiday from history. . . . The chief aim of the Clinton Administration was to make sure nothing terrible happened on its watch. Accordingly, every can was kicked down the road."

The eagerness of conservatives to blame Clinton for 9/11 was matched by their resistance to any effort to hold Bush to account for what happened—or even to explain why American intelligence had not raised more alarms about the threat. As the journalist Brian Montopoli reported, Vice President Dick Cheney called Majority Leader Tom Daschle in January 2002, while the Senate was preparing closed-door hearings on intelligence failures before 9/11. Cheney warned Daschle that if Democrats called for wider and more open hearings, they "would be met by accusations that they were hampering the war on terror."

The call for a bipartisan commission to investigate the attacks was championed by three of the least partisan members of Congress, Senators John McCain and Joe Lieberman and Representative Tim Roemer, a moderate Indiana Democrat. Their effort gained ground when the families of those who met their deaths on 9/11 joined the call for an independent inquiry. But even the families could not, initially at least, move the administration off its opposition, with Cheney telling Fox News that an investigative commission was "the wrong way to go." The administration's stonewalling eventually enraged McCain. "No one has lost their job, no one has been even reprimanded, nothing has happened as a result of Sept. 11," McCain said. "Unless responsibility is assigned, then we can't cure the problem."

Eventually the commission was set up—but only after the 2002 midterm elections.

As 2002 went on, Bush and the Republicans were more and more willing to use national security issues as a political cudgel. They supplemented the old attacks around social issues, race, rights, and taxes with the charge that Democrats were soft on terror. It was a made-to-order issue in Rove's post-2000 effort to mobilize the conservative base and another way in which Bush's move toward moderation in the 1998 to 2000 period fell by the wayside. When Democrats challenged Bush on any aspect of the war on terror, they were beaten back with accusations that they were undermining patriotism at a moment that required unity. Cheney denounced "incendiary" commentary by the opposition as "thoroughly irresponsible and totally unworthy of national leaders in a time of war."

A window into Rove's thinking about how the war on terror might transform American politics was a congratulatory letter he wrote to Melinda Lawson, an academic historian, about her book *Patriot Fires*, which described the new sense of nationhood forged during the Civil War. Lawson wrote of "the partisan construction of national identity" and of how Republicans in Lincoln's day stoked the "the tendency to conflate Republicanism with

loyalty and Democracy [as the Democrats were often called then] with treason." Lawson quotes George Julian, the influential Indiana Republican congressman, who said in 1863: "Loyalty and Republicanism go hand-in-hand
throughout the Union, as perfectly as treason and slavery." It's possible, of
course, that Rove, a lover of American history, simply admired Lawson's fine
work on how the Civil War changed the way in which Americans understood
their country. But it seems likely that in the post-9/11 atmosphere, Rove also
saw how a new national trauma and Bush's leadership could have political effects comparable to those left behind by the Civil War and Abraham Lincoln.

The gradual escalation of partisan warfare continued through 2002, but
reached an entirely different level when the administration began to make
the case for the war in Iraq that summer. There was no evidence that Saddam
Hussein was connected with the 9/11 attacks, and he was a known foe of
al-Qaeda and Osama bin Laden. Many leading Republicans with close ties
to the elder President Bush were dubious of the Iraq venture. They included,
privately, Secretary of State Colin Powell, and, publicly, Brent Scowcroft, the
first president Bush's top foreign policy adviser and one of his closest friends.
Scowcroft took to the pages of the *Wall Street Journal* on August 15, 2002, to
issue a prophetic warning under the unambiguous headline: "Don't Attack
Saddam."

Arguing that "there is scant evidence to tie Saddam to terrorist organizations" and that "Saddam's goals have little in common with the terrorists
who threaten us," Scowcroft undercut the administration's central rationale
for war. A war against Saddam, he said, "would not be a cakewalk," "undoubt-
edly would be very expensive," and would have "serious consequences for the
U.S. and global economy." Any campaign against Iraq, he added, "is certain to
divert us for some indefinite period from our war on terrorism."

The public was ambivalent. While 56 percent of Americans told ABC
News pollsters they supported military action to depose Saddam, a quarter of
those supporters fell away when asked if they would still take this view in the
face of opposition from America's allies.

That September, I spoke with a number of Republican members of Congress who had quiet but profound doubts about the impending war. "My
sense from talking to people here is that the case hasn't been made," said Rep-

resentative Dave Camp, who represented a solidly Republican district in central Michigan. His constituents, he said, were "concerned about a go-it-alone strategy, and that included going it alone without the American people."

Representative Thomas Petri, whose Wisconsin district was also loyal to the GOP, said his voters had expressed "concern about whether we know what we're doing or how we're going to do it." That both Camp and Petri used the word "concerned" nicely captured the mood: most of the country was not ready to take on the president, but they were not persuaded that he was on the right path. The observations of these Republicans were consistent with the message of the Gallup poll on Afghanistan a year earlier: Americans wanted a tough response to terrorism, but they were reluctant warriors.

The rise of the war issue made the midterm elections more bitter—and sowed confusion and division among Democrats. When Bush went to Congress that fall for approval of a resolution to put the country on a path to war, he made Iraq and the terror issue central to the campaign. It was a marked departure from his father's approach. The first President Bush delayed asking Congress for authorization to go to war with Iraq over Saddam's occupation of Kuwait in 1990 until after that year's midterm elections. He thus gave away political advantage, but in the process allowed for a nonpartisan debate that fostered national concord. The second Bush would gain the political upper hand, but at significant cost to national unity later.

George W. Bush moved on two fronts that fall. He sought a strong United Nations resolution that called for new weapons inspections but also threatened force if Iraq refused to comply. At the same time, he asked Congress to authorize military action. The first move pushed aside criticism that Bush was trying to go it alone without allies or international sanction—something his administration had earlier claimed it could do. The second put Democrats on the spot.

And they quickly split. The war resolution won strong support from Representative Richard Gephardt and Senators Joe Lieberman and John Edwards. All three would eventually seek the 2004 Democratic nomination, as would Senator John Kerry. Kerry also supported the resolution but criticized the administration's "hasty war talk" and stressed the need for support "from the region and our allies . . . for the far tougher mission of ensuring a future democratic government after the war." Its other backers included Senator Hillary Clinton, whose decision would haunt her politically. Strong opposition came from outside the ranks of potential presidential candidates, including Senators Ted Kennedy and Paul Wellstone. Although few paid much attention at the time, another opponent was a young Illinois state senator named Barack Obama. "What I am opposed to is a dumb war," he said in a speech at a Chicago antiwar rally on October 2, 2002. "What I am opposed to is a rash war." He upbraided "armchair, weekend warriors in this administration" who would "shove their own ideological agendas down our throats, irrespective of the costs in lives lost and in hardships borne."

Democratic senators Carl Levin and Dick Durbin sought a middle-ground solution that would give Bush support in his effort to rally the world against Saddam without having Congress authorize war. Levin and Durbin resisted conflating the question of whether the United Nations should require coercive inspections to determine if Saddam had weapons of mass destruction with a direct congressional endorsement of armed conflict. Democrats, they said, were perfectly ready to strengthen Bush's hand at the UN. But they insisted the decision to go to war should be debated separately, and later.

Levin and Durbin showed courage and ingenuity, but they failed to slow the rush to war. For his part, Bush himself mocked those whom he characterized as saying, "I think I'm going to wait for the United Nations to make a decision." He went on: "It seems like to me that if you're representing the United States, you ought to be making a decision about what's best for the United States. If I were running for office, I'm not sure how I'd explain to the American people—say, 'Vote for me, and oh, by the way, on a matter of national security, I'm going to wait for somebody else to act.'"

Such comments turned Iraq into a 2002 campaign issue, embittered his opponents, and left Bush with no safety net when his Iraq policy went off the rails later. But in the short term, Bush was successful, both in getting the war endorsement and in winning the midterms.

The war resolution passed the House on October 10, 297 to 133. The Senate passed it a day later, 77 to 23. Only seven Republicans, six House members, and Senator Lincoln Chafee of Rhode Island opposed it. (Chafee later left his party to become first an Independent and then a Democrat.) The

Democrats were sharply split. In the House, 82 Democrats voted in favor of the resolution while 126 voted against it. Senate Democrats divided 29 to 21 in support of the resolution. The newly independent Jeffords also voted no.

In the face of the most important decision of Bush's presidency, the political opposition found itself speaking with many voices. Some Democrats supported Bush on principle, but many later regretted not speaking out more forcefully against the war. They would harden their stances later. These feelings of guilt and regret—combined with anger among grassroots Democrats at the party's failure to stand up against Bush—would be immensely helpful to Barack Obama in 2008.

The impact on the campaign trail was plain. Most Democrats were very cautious that fall, inclined to follow the advice of political consultants who said their party's strategic task was to get the war debate out of the way so the campaign could "move back to the economy." Republicans held the opposite view, but for the same underlying reason: they hoped the war and terror issues could move the discussion *away* from a sagging economy—and corner their Democratic opponents.

There were a few Democrats who were willing to campaign against the war, the most notable being Paul Wellstone. Up for reelection, he took his case against intervention to Minnesota's voters with his characteristic verve and energy. I visited with Wellstone on October 23 at a campaign rally on the University of Minnesota campus in Crookston, near the North Dakota border. He was buoyant (he was almost always buoyant) because his principled vote against the war brought him far more admiration than opposition. "I thought maybe that vote would be it, and I don't think it is," Wellstone told me that day. "I've never had so many people come up to me and be so respectful even if they didn't agree." This was partly a point about Iraq policy but also a tribute to the benefits of being a conviction politician.

Two days later, Wellstone was dead. He and his wife, Sheila, were killed in a plane crash while on another campaign swing. His tragic passing gave an already larger-than-life figure special standing in his party. His campaign song, "Stand Up, Keep Fighting," became a rallying cry for progressives unhappy with their party's caution in the face of Bush's policies. Wellstone's death would also cost the Democrats a Senate seat. When a Wellstone memorial service came to look like a campaign rally—it had not been planned that way—Republicans who had only recently been attacking Wellstone attacked the supposed politicization of his death. In the election for Senate on November 5, Republican Norm Coleman narrowly defeated former vice president Walter Mondale, who had been drafted to stand in for Wellstone.

More typical was the contest in Indiana's 2nd Congressional District, one of the election's premier battlegrounds, where the Republican strategy played out exactly as the GOP hoped it would. I visited the district that fall and it was where I first met Chocola, the Republican candidate against Jill Long Thompson, a Democrat who had served in Congress from a nearby district before she was swept out in the 1994 Republican landslide.

In light of how unpopular the war in Iraq became, what Chocola told me then is striking: he was counting on the war issue to win him the election, he said, and would focus his criticism on Long Thompson's votes in Congress against the first Iraq war and defense spending, as well as her endorsement by a peace group. Bush campaigned on Chocola's behalf, which, the candidate said, "sent the message loud and clear that there is only one candidate who would stand with the president consistently."

During that trip, I met up with Long Thompson at an afternoon tea for voters at the stately Queen Anne Inn in South Bend. She was very clear about the issues on which she'd contest Chocola—and about where she wouldn't go. "It's on domestic issues," she said; "it wouldn't be international." Judging by the tenor of the questions from the generally sympathetic group of voters who turned out to meet her, they were looking for criticism of Bush's war plans. She didn't oblige. When asked about Iraq, she began by noting her husband's twenty-three-year career in the military and the reserves, called for UN participation in war, but stressed her support for Bush. She explained her answer to me later. "I think people are very uneasy about a potential strike on our part," she said, "but we are very patriotic in the Second District, and we will support our president, and we will support our troops."

Her response pointed to a reality about the Bush presidency that would have a long-lasting effect: in the period from 9/11 through John Kerry's 2004 presidential campaign, Republicans were prepared to pummel Democrats who broke with Bush as bordering on unpatriotic and as insufficiently alive to the need to protect the nation against terrorism. Bush's partisan invocation of patriotism and security set a pattern that would affect Tea Party politics after he left the White House.

Chocola won the race, 50 percent to 46 percent, and his brief congressional career perfectly matched the trajectory of the politics of the Bush era. With Bush leading the ticket in 2004, Chocola was easily reelected over Democrat Joe Donnelly. But when Donnelly ran again in 2006, Chocola became a casualty of a Democratic sweep fueled by disillusionment with Bush, and with the war that had initially advanced Chocola's career.

Bush picked another national security fight in 2002 that gave Republicans additional campaign fodder. Although he had initially resisted the creation of a new Department of Homeland Security, he changed course in early summer but still found a way to take issue with the Democrats. Criticizing them for affording the new department's employees various union and civil service protections, he argued these would make it more difficult to dismiss employees for reasons related to national security, insubordination, or incompetence. Republican senators filibustered all efforts to reach a compromise and Bush charged that the Senate (meaning its Democratic majority) was "not interested in the security of the American people."

It can fairly be said that the battle over DHS definitively broke whatever had survived the post-9/11 bipartisan spirit. One particularly vicious Republican advertisement would be cited by Democrats years later as the signpost for when everything became partisan again. In Georgia, Republican Saxby Chambliss pilloried Democratic senator Max Cleland by using pictures of Osama bin Laden and Saddam Hussein to accuse Cleland of being soft on terrorism because he had supported the DHS union and civil service rules. The ad claimed that Cleland had voted against Bush's "vital homeland security efforts 11 times," which simply meant that in all of the procedural maneuvering, Cleland had supported the Democrats' approach over Bush's. What made the visual association of Cleland with Saddam so galling to Democrats was Cleland's standing as a Vietnam War hero who had lost an arm and both of his legs in a grenade explosion near the end of his tour. "I served my country and don't have to prove my patriotism to anybody," said an angry Cleland, who noted that Chambliss had used four student deferments to escape service before being released because of "an old football knee."

Cleland lost and months after the election, Durbin captured the mood of so many of the defeated senator's colleagues. "This is something that gnaws at us," Durbin said. "A decorated and disabled Vietnam veteran would be discredited because of his stand in the homeland security debate?"

As Georgia and Indiana's 2nd District went, so went the country. It was a remarkable election for Bush, Rove, and the Republicans because it marked only the third time since the Civil War that a president's party had gained seats in a midterm contest. The other two were 1934, a ratification of FDR's New Deal, and 1998, which, as we've seen, reflected a backlash against Republican efforts to impeach Bill Clinton. (A partial exception: 1902, after the size of the House was expanded and both parties gained seats.) Republicans picked up eight seats in the House, and netted two in the Senate, which returned them to control after the Jeffords interlude. The exit polling pointed to a 9/11 effect. Compared with the election two years earlier, Democrats lost more ground with women than with men, particularly married women. This fed the idea that a new Republican electoral group, "security moms," had taken the place of the old pro-Clinton group, "soccer moms." The Democratic vote fell more sharply in the East, the region directly affected by 9/11, than elsewhere. The Republicans gained more ground among higher-income voters than among others—perhaps a response to Bush's tax policies but also likely a 9/11 effect. And Republican House candidates had their best election in some time among party members who described themselves as moderate or liberal. Such Republicans had often given Democrats a significant minority of their ballots. It was a glimmer of the possibility for an alternative coalition rooted in the center ground—an approach that Bush and Rove ultimately rejected. By 2008, most of these swing moderate and liberal Republicans had moved away from their party again.

The notion that Democrats and liberals were weak on terror, less than patriotic, and not part of the "real America" never fell out of the conservative playbook. It would play later into attacks on Obama as less than fully American, as "a Muslim" who had been "educated at a madrassa" and as "a Kenyan anti-colonialist." Talk of the red states as representing the "real America," opposed to a counterfeit nation in the Northeast and on the West Coast, had a similarly long-term impact on the right, which embraced this trope, and on the left, which was enraged by it.

At the 2004 Republican convention, it fell to a Bush-supporting Democrat, former Georgia governor Zell Miller, to offer the most inflammatory speech of the conclave. "Today's Democratic leaders see America as an occupier, not a liberator," Miller declared. "In their warped way of thinking, America is the problem, not the solution. They don't believe there is any real danger in the world except that which America brings upon itself through our clumsy and misguided foreign policy."

There was also this, of Bush's opponent: "Senator Kerry has made it clear that he would use military force only if approved by the United Nations." It was an odd thing to say, since Kerry had just a few weeks before delivered an acceptance speech in which he explicitly declared: "I will never give any nation or international institution a veto over our national security."

Nor was Miller's rhetoric a one-off. It would persist throughout Bush's presidency. Speaking to the New York State Conservative Party in July 2005, Rove himself declared: "Perhaps the most important difference between conservatives and liberals can be found in the area of national security. Conservatives saw the savagery of 9/11 and the attacks and prepared for war; liberals saw the savagery of the 9/11 attacks and wanted to prepare indictments and offer therapy and understanding for our attackers."

Republicans would continue to deploy such rhetoric about alleged Democratic weakness into the Obama years.

★

The first Gallup poll taken after the November 2002 elections put Bush's approval rating at 68 percent, but over the next two years his popularity came back down to earth. On May 1, 2003, Bush, appearing in an aviator's uniform, announced the end of major combat operations aboard the USS *Abraham Lincoln* in front of a banner that read MISSION ACCOMPLISHED.

It was an astonishingly ill-considered bit of public relations, and as the war dragged on with the mission not at all "accomplished," both Bush's popularity and support for his Iraq policy collapsed. Every prediction the administration had offered went awry—about the war's costs, about the number of troops it would require, about the duration of the conflict, about the likelihood of concord among the Shiites, the Sunnis, and the Kurds, and, of course, Vice President Cheney's certainty that "we will be greeted as liberators." The reason most Americans gave their ascent to the war was the administration's claim that Iraq had weapons of mass destruction. "We don't want the smoking gun to be a mushroom cloud," said Condoleezza Rice, Bush's national security adviser who later became his secretary of state, in one of the pithiest and most evocative versions of the case. But when it turned out that Saddam did not have such weapons, the reluctant hawks felt betrayed.

By 2004 the country was once again as divided about Bush as it had been in 2000. His approval rating had fallen to 49 percent at the beginning of February, and for the rest of the year, it hovered between 46 percent and 55 percent. He hit this higher number only in late November, after his reelection.

Rank-and-file Democrats were increasingly impatient with both the party's failure to stand against the war at the outset and the continued hedging on Iraq among its leading presidential candidates. Howard Dean, who ended his twelve years as governor of Vermont in 2003, jumped into the 2004 presidential race as an unapologetic antiwar candidate and created a sensation. He brought on-line fundraising to an entirely new level, building up a large cadre of small donors eager to talk back to the Democratic establishment, and to Bush. Barack Obama would later expand on what Dean had started. Yet Dean, briefly the pundit favorite going into the Iowa caucuses, faltered as he and Gephardt, deemed his major rival, discredited each other with a barrage of back-and-forth negative attacks. This opened the way for Kerry, who finished a strong first in Iowa.

Democratic primary voters came to see Kerry, a decorated Vietnam veteran, as especially dangerous to Bush. If patriotism was the Republicans' trump card, the party would finesse it by nominating a war hero. Kerry turned the 2004 Democratic National Convention into a martial celebration of the nation and his own service record, while the young African-American Democratic Senate nominee from Illinois gave a keynote address on national unity and Republican efforts to divide the nation that instantly turned him into a Democratic star. Barack Obama's life changed that night.

It was thus a shock to Kerry and the Democrats that the Republicans quickly moved to turn his greatest asset into a liability. The Democratic convention ended on July 29, and a Pew survey in early August gave Kerry a narrow lead over Bush. Then, on August 5, a group called Swift Boat Veterans for Truth went on the air with the first in a series of ads attacking Kerry's Vietnam War record, his veracity, and his fitness to lead. Regnery, the conservative publishing house, issued a volume called *Unfit for Command: Swift Boat Veterans Speak Out Against John Kerry*. It became an instant bestseller. Thus did the term *swift boating* enter the political lexicon. The Kerry campaign was slow to respond, failing to anticipate how quickly the attacks would take hold and dominate the news. Theoretically, the Swift Boaters were an independent group, though it later emerged that its leading funders were prominent Republicans, among them Bob J. Perry, a longtime Bush supporter who contributed more than $4 million to the effort. T. Boone Pickens Jr. gave $2 million.

Over time, media accounts discredited the charges—among them, that Kerry had exaggerated his war record and didn't deserve the medals he won. Most of those who served closely with Kerry backed him up. And it was clear that many of Kerry's foes were continuing a vendetta dating back to the early 1970s against a decorated veteran who came home and actively opposed the Vietnam War. ("How do you ask a man to be the last man to die for a mistake?" Kerry had asked the Senate Foreign Relations Committee in 1971.) A lengthy *New York Times* investigation found that the Swift Boat accounts were "riddled with inconsistencies," and that "material offered as proof by these veterans is undercut by official Navy records and the men's own statements." The *Los Angeles Times* editorialized flatly that "these charges against John Kerry are false." But much damage was done.

In the meantime, Rove continued to be attentive to the lessons of Matt Dowd's polling and the need to shore up the Republican base. Rove had estimated that some 4 million evangelical Christians had failed to vote in 2000; in 2004, he was determined to bring them out. The Bush campaign engaged in unprecedented organizing efforts in the conservative churches. And when the Massachusetts Supreme Judicial Court in 2003 legalized gay marriage in the state, he was handed the issue around which he could keep the religious right mobilized. Bush made "traditional marriage" a key campaign theme, declaring marriage between a man and a woman "the most fundamental institution of civilization." He endorsed a federal constitutional amendment banning gay marriage in early 2004, and Rove encouraged referenda on state constitutional amendments enshrining traditional marriage in key battlegrounds, notably Ohio.

Bush's move against same-sex marriage had the desired result in mobilizing social conservatives. But Representative Mick Mulvaney, elected to the House from South Carolina in the 2010 Tea Party wave, argued that it was also a sign of weakness. "I knew what Rove was doing," Mulvaney told me in a 2014 interview. "He was trying to gin up support within the Christian conservative base for a lackluster candidate. He was trying to create enthusiasm for a Republican candidate because the Republican candidate couldn't do it on his own." Already, Mulvaney said, many on the right had their list of grievances against Bush, beginning with the most basic: "He had spent too much money." Because Bush's lieutenants "thought they were going to lose . . . they did something that violates our core conservative principles in order to drive people to the polls."

Mulvaney's position on the issue—he supported traditional marriage but believed the matter should be settled by the states—was a minority view on the right at the time, but his analytical point about Rove's strategy is instructive about the early rumblings of conservative discontent.

Such doubts about Rove's approach were not widely shared in 2004 because whatever its shortcomings, his strategy worked. If the 2000 election carried a taint from Bush's loss of the popular vote and the Supreme Court's intervention, the 2004 result was a clear, if still narrow, triumph.

The contours of the results were not radically different from those of 2000. Only three states switched sides: New Mexico and Iowa from Gore to Bush, and New Hampshire from Bush to Kerry, netting Bush a 286-to-251 victory in the Electoral College. But in the popular vote, Bush went from a 500,000-vote deficit to Gore to a 3-million-vote lead over Kerry. Especially striking were the successes of Bush's campaign operation in turning out voters in far suburban, exurban, and rural counties. In Ohio, the state both sides rightly identified as the key to the election, a well-organized Kerry operation hit the campaign's targets in the major cities. But these Democratic turnout gains were more than offset by Bush's successes in the less heavily settled, whiter, and more socially conservative parts of the state.

The election also strengthened the Republicans' hold on Congress with three additional seats in the House and four in the Senate. Significantly, five of the Senate Republican pickups came in the South, a further step toward the party's southernization, even as they lost contests in Illinois (the seat was won by Barack Obama) and Colorado. But the Republicans' biggest and most symbolically important prize was South Dakota, where Senate Democratic leader Tom Daschle was narrowly defeated. It was the first time that a sitting party leader had lost since 1952, when a forty-three-year-old Phoenix city council member named Barry Goldwater ousted Democratic majority leader Ernest McFarland in Arizona.

Rove's efforts with evangelicals (and with conservative Catholics) had exactly the impact he had hoped for. A single exit poll finding launched thousands of essays: 22 percent of voters said the issue that mattered most to their choice was "moral values," and they backed Bush, 80 percent to 18 percent. The survey also found that 8 percent of voters said a candidate's "strong religious faith" was the personal quality that mattered most to them, and they backed Bush 91 percent to 8 percent.

But while turnout among social conservatives certainly mattered, Bush won the election in the middle of the electorate because of the lingering power of the terror issue. Bush increased his share of the vote among women from 43 percent in 2000 to 48 percent in 2004. As in 2002, the results suggested the existence of a "security mom" constituency. The exit polls found that one-tenth of Al Gore's 2000 voters switched to Bush, and among these switchers, more than 8 in 10 thought the war in Iraq was part of the war on terrorism, a key indicator of support for Bush's global view.

It's easy to forget in light of subsequent events that Bush's 2004 victory was widely hailed on the right as the decisive realignment that conservatives had been waiting for since Bill Rusher had laid out its contours for *National Review*'s readers in 1963 and Richard Nixon proclaimed his "new majority" in 1972.

Writing in the *Weekly Standard* under the headline "Realignment, Now More than Ever," a pun on Nixon's 1972 slogan, the conservative journalist Fred Barnes gave Rove credit for achieving his dream. The facts, Barnes argued, were clear: "Republicans now have both an operational majority in

Washington (control of the White House, Senate, and the House of Representatives) and an ideological majority in the country (51 percent popular vote for a center-right president). They also control a majority of governorships, a plurality of state legislatures, and are at rough parity with Democrats in the number of state legislators."

Barnes's conclusion: "Rove says that under Bush a 'rolling realignment' favoring Republicans continues, and he's right. So Republican hegemony in America is now expected to last for years, maybe decades."

The new conservative majority endured less than two years.

★

Bush was nothing if not bold in response to his reelection. "I earned capital in the political campaign," he famously declared the day after his victory, "and I intend to spend it." He betrayed no sense that there might be something fragile about his 50.7 percent majority or that it was built with votes borrowed from the other side—the security moms and the Gore defectors who had no particular sympathy with the ideological right. Such voters had decided, for the time being, that Bush was the stronger leader more likely to keep the country safe.

Bush and Rove were determined to use their victory to reshape the political economy in ways that would keep their realignment rolling. Their main vehicle would be a redesign of Social Security, the great achievement of the New Deal era. A program that had taught millions of Americans that government could protect them from some of life's uncertainties would, in their vision, become a vehicle for enlarging the "investing class" and reducing voters' dependence on government. If Huey Long had described an America in which every man was a king, Bush and Rove wanted to make every man and woman a capitalist.

Bush was certain that his reelection had given him a mandate for his partial privatization plan. He had mentioned it regularly in the campaign, even if it was hardly his central argument to voters. He wanted to allow workers to take part of their Social Security tax payment and invest it instead in a private retirement account. Since Bush promised those at or near retirement that they could keep their existing pensions, the transition costs of the plan—because of the lost revenue from the redirected tax money—were estimated to run to about $1 trillion. This did not deter Bush, because he argued that over the long run, Social Security payments would be reduced. The wonders of the marketplace would create a whole new class of small investors who would, over time, become conservatives and Republicans. No longer worried about getting benefits from Washington, they would watch the stock ticker. So, at least, went the theory.

This was a serious, if utopian, hope of many conservatives. The Bush program, wrote Stephen Moore, then of the Club for Growth, "would empower millions of working class Americans to become owners of stocks and bonds for the first time in their lives. They would, in short, move out of the dependency class and into the shareholder class."

Where privatization was concerned, Bush's big investment of his political capital went bust. Bush never actually put forward a plan of his own in the face of opposition not only from Democrats but also from many inside his own party. The more it was discussed, the less popular the plan became. Most Americans, it turned out, valued the "security" in the program's title and were understandably wary of giving up the one part of their retirement that was not dependent on the ups and downs of the market or their own ability to save. The steady move in the private sector away from defined-benefit pension plans made the old-fashioned guarantees of traditional Social Security all the more attractive.

Many Republicans in Congress understood this. Having to face the voters every two or six years, they were not willing to gamble their seats on a theory of long-term political realignment. Here again was a bold promise to the political right that was bound to be unkept—not because of liberal scheming but because the vast majority of voters were deeply skeptical of where the conservative dreamers wanted to go.

Responding to the privatization idea in 2006, Tom Davis, the Republican congressman, offered one of the most backhanded compliments ever bestowed upon a president. "I guess you could argue that if it gets Iraq off the front page, it was probably a good thing at this point," he said of Bush's plan. He then rendered the political judgment that so many of his GOP colleagues also reached. A White House push on the issue, Davis said, "is not going anywhere. This president never likes to back down. I think he's putting it on the table, but I don't think anybody's going to pick it up." The privatization idea died without ever getting a vote.

To his credit, Bush continued to follow through on his promise for immigration reform, and his efforts were thoroughly bipartisan—partly because they had to be. Large parts of Bush's own party and the conservative movement stoutly opposed anything that was, or even looked like, "amnesty for illegal immigrants." Opposing the bipartisan immigration bill became a central cause of right-wing talk radio, particularly Rush Limbaugh and many of Fox News' personalities.

When the Senate voted in June 2007, supporters of reform could not even muster a majority on a procedural motion to proceed with a bill. In the end, only 46 senators voted to move forward; 53 voted against. Bush lobbied hard, but only 12 of the Senate's 49 Republicans stuck with him. Most of the support came from Democrats, more than two-thirds of whom—including the young first-termer Barack Obama—voted yes.

Senator Jeff Sessions, an Alabama Republican, was a leading opponent of the bill, as he would be a vociferous critic seven years later of Obama's executive action to give relief to millions of undocumented families. Sessions pinpointed the organizing force behind the opposition in the Bush years. The bill's supporters, he explained, had wanted to pass a bill quickly, "before Rush Limbaugh could tell the American people what was in it." Talk radio, he told the *New York Times*, was "a big factor" in derailing immigration reform.

The death of the immigration bill, even more than the failure of Social Security privatization, signaled the implosion of the Bush-Rove drive for a new conservative majority that depended heavily on winning a significant share of Latinos for the GOP, as Bush did in both of his campaigns. The party's obvious role in killing immigration reform would lead to the collapse of the Republican Latino vote. And Bush's failure to move his party on the issue was a sign that his talk of a newly compassionate conservatism did little to change the underlying rightward tilt of a party whose base was still almost uniformly white and conservative.

The historian Gary Gerstle offered an exceptionally shrewd analysis of both Bush's hopes and his failures. The very religious president had tried to initiate what Gerstle called a "multiculturalism of the godly," welcoming the hardworking, family-oriented, and God-fearing of all races and creeds. On the questions of "immigration and diversity," Gerstle wrote, "Bush was worlds apart from Patrick Buchanan and the social-conservative wing of the Republican Party that wanted to restore America to its imagined Anglo-Saxon and Celtic glory." Bush offered "groups of minority voters reason to rethink their traditional hostility to the GOP" by showing he "was comfortable with diversity, bilingualism, and cultural pluralism as long as America's ethnic and racial subcultures shared his patriotism, religious faith, and political conservatism."

For the significant sections of the right fiercely opposed to amnesty for illegal immigrants, strongly in favor of English-only laws, and alarmed by the proliferation of new Spanish-speaking neighborhoods all over the country, this amounted to betrayal. The rejection of the 2007 immigration law that Bush championed, said the conservative columnist Christopher Caldwell, "was the clearest sign he was losing the ear of his party."

And these feelings persisted long after Bush left office. In explaining Republican House majority leader Eric Cantor's June 2014 defeat by a Tea Party candidate, Sean Trende, the perceptive, conservative-leaning writer for *RealClearPolitics*, pointed to the enduring hostility to Bush on substantial parts of the right.

"The Republican base is furious with the Republican establishment, especially over the Bush years," Trende wrote. "From the point of view of conservatives I've spoken with, the early- to mid-2000s look like this: Voters gave Republicans control of Congress and the presidency for the longest stretch since the 1920s. And what do Republicans have to show for it?" It would be an enduring theme.

Even the old social issues stopped working for Republicans. In a reversal whose speed had little precedent in the history of public opinion, gay marriage became steadily more popular, particularly among Millennial voters, who were a growing part of the electorate. The Supreme Court's ratification of same-sex marriage in 2015 was an instance of judges following the public rather than leading it.

Conservatives also miscalculated badly on end-of life issues. In March

2005, Bush strongly supported and signed a bill to overturn a Florida state court decision allowing the husband of Terri Schiavo to remove her feeding tube. In a tragic episode that won wide attention around the country, Schiavo had suffered severe brain damage after a potassium imbalance caused a heart attack in 1990, and she went on life support. Since 1998, her husband, Michael, and her parents had battled in court over whether the feeding tube should be withdrawn. The law Bush signed effectively sided with the parents, even though the measure flatly contradicted conservative claims to be the champions of states' rights. To the surprise of many on both sides of the debate, the move also enraged a majority of the public. Most Americans saw end-of-life decisions as tragic, difficult, and not the business of politicians to decide. The federal courts affirmed the state judicial ruling and Schiavo died on March 31, 2005, ten days after Congress acted. An autopsy contradicted the claims of those who had denied the severity of Schiavo's impairment, concluding, as the *Washington Post* reported, that she had "suffered severe, irreversible brain damage."

The episode did far more damage to Bush and the Republican Congress than was obvious at the time. It was the most extreme case of Rove's dual strategy backfiring. Efforts to mollify and mobilize the religious right could not be undertaken in isolation. Middle-of-the-road voters would be turned off by the very moves designed to turn on a powerful minority inside the GOP.

And there was no coming back for Bush after his administration's botched response to Hurricane Katrina. The failure of the relief effort hurt Bush on two levels. There was the simple rage and disappointment over the incompetence of the Federal Emergency Management Agency, on display in the country's living rooms day after day in televised reports by correspondents increasingly outraged by the suffering they encountered. But the episode was especially damaging politically because it undercut the primary source of Bush's political success: his claim that he could protect his fellow Americans. Leadership, strength, and security were Bush's calling cards. These were lost in the surging waters of New Orleans.

Things got no better as the situation in Iraq worsened. From the perspective of the Bush camp, Gerson (he left the White House in June 2006) saw the growing unpopularity of the Iraq War as playing an indirect role in strengthening conservative opposition to Bush. The party's right did not publicly turn against the war, but as Bush "lost altitude" because of it, Gerson said, conservative found other reasons "to go after him," "to distance themselves," and "to express frustration." Many on the right, Gerson believed, "clearly wanted to humiliate the president," and they gave their dissidence "an ideological context" by arguing that theirs was actually a "revolt against big government conservatism." This would become a major Tea Party rallying cry.

Gerson pointed to two episodes of early conservative unrest. In 2005, conservatives rose up against Bush's nomination of Harriet Miers, his White House counsel, to the Supreme Court. Some questioned her credentials, but the right's central objection was to her ideological profile: she didn't have one. Conservatives worried that she would turn out to be a stealth moderate or even moderately liberal justice in the mode of David Souter, nominated by the first President Bush. Miers withdrew on October 27, 2005, in response to the conservative pressure, just twenty-four days after Bush named her. The right got what it wanted when the president named Samuel Alito to the Court. He became one of its most reliable conservative votes.

In February 2006, conservatives in large numbers joined leading Democrats in rebelling against the sale of a port management company to a state-owned firm in the United Arab Emirates, Dubai Ports World. Critics claimed the deal would weaken U.S. port security. It was eventually scuttled, to Bush's embarrassment.

The Dubai Ports controversy pointed to the tensions within Bush's strategy of using the fear of terrorism to advance his political interests. Bush hoped to court Muslim and Arab allies and favored free trade and open international markets. The ports deal fit with both commitments. Yet if "protecting the homeland" against the terrorist threat was the nation's highest priority, the backlash against Arab ownership of a company responsible for the flow of American shipping was hardly surprising. Democrats embraced opposition to the Dubai Ports deal with a gleeful opportunism. Having been the victims of antiterrorism politics, Democrats were happy to turn the tables on Bush. They were joined by many conservatives who were determined not to cede any ground on the issue that had helped them win elections.

In the fall of 2006, voters handed control of both the House and Senate to the Democrats. The growing unpopularity of the Iraq War turned the security issue into a reverse wedge against Bush and the Republicans. Resistance in the GOP to immigration reform enraged Latinos, and Republican losses were especially severe among Hispanic evangelicals, the linchpin of Bush's Latino support and key players in his "multiculturalism of the godly."

The rebuke to Bush previewed many of the trends that would help elect Barack Obama two years later. The youth rebellion against the Republicans began not in 2008 but in 2006. In the 2002 midterms, Democrats had won a bare 51 percent majority among voters under 30; four years later, they won 61 percent. Suburbanites, the ultimate swing voters, swung hard: from 41 percent Democratic in 2002 to 51 percent in 2006. And among self-described moderates, the Democratic vote rose from 54 percent to 61 percent. For Bush, the middle was collapsing.

The irony of George W. Bush's impact on American politics is that in trying to do too much—to mobilize the right at the same time he was trying to build support in the center—he ended up alienating both parts of the center-right alliance he was trying to create. His moderate "big-government" moves—pushing through No Child Left Behind and the Medicare prescription drug benefit—angered significant parts of the right, as did his push for immigration reform. Yet his embrace of the conservative social issues alienated moderates. Rising deficits, the result of tax cuts in tandem with war and stepped-up security spending, alienated budget-balancing moderates and conservatives alike. The wars themselves, in Afghanistan but especially in Iraq, distracted Bush from his domestic goals and created a backlash that transcended normal left-right lines.

In his 2014 interview, Frum offered an instructive epitaph to Bush-Rove strategery. He contrasted their efforts with the reforms of the British Labour Party instituted by Tony Blair and the adjustments in the British Conservative Party's approach inaugurated by David Cameron.

Both Blair and Cameron, Frum argued, made "substantive" changes to their party's ideologies and policies. Blair jettisoned traditional Labour socialism while Cameron embraced certain ideas associated with progressives, including gay rights and efforts to halt climate change. Bush and Rove, by contrast, "tried to preserve most of conservative policy" and declined to revise conservatism in any fundamental way. They were looking for "just enough change ... to rebrand the product, but not so much that you frighten and alienate the members of your traditional constituency."

Under pressure, both halves of the strategy fell apart.

The Bush years are central to understanding why conservatism took such a hard right term during the Obama years—because of what Bush did, and because of what he failed to do. He had two opportunities to remake conservatism. His initial forays into compassionate conservatism opened the possibility of a broader Republican and conservative coalition, particularly because of their potential to appeal to Latinos and to strengthen the Republicans' hold on the white working class. A more ambitious compassionate conservatism might also have transformed conservative policy strategies, introducing a somewhat more secular version of European Christian Democracy into the repertoire of the American right. Bush might thus have broadened the focus of religious conservatism to include issues related to social justice. But this would have required a compassionate conservatism that was something more than the simple recognition of the acts of mercy and kindness undertaken by the churches, synagogues, and mosques. It would have demanded that Bush opt unequivocally for the more progovernment versions of the idea reflected in the thinking of Kuo, Gerson, and John DiIulio, the first leader of Bush's Office of Faith-Based and Community Initiatives, over the Christian libertarianism of Olasky. Making this choice would have required issuing a fundamental challenge to contemporary conservatism, something Bush was unwilling to do.

Of course 9/11 changed Bush's priorities in fundamental ways, but the post-9/11 period represented his second lost opportunity. Bush's high approval ratings for months after the attacks reflected something that transcended politics: the desire of a nation traumatized by horror to come together and to give every benefit of the doubt to its commander in chief. Bush grew into the unifying role, and the endurance of his good poll numbers reflected what, early on at least, was his sensitivity to what the new situation demanded. Bush had a chance to respond to the new spirit of patriotism by issuing a broad call to national service. He could have abandoned tax cutting for the duration, and resisted using security issues as political wedges. And, of course, he could have followed Brent Scowcroft's advice and avoided the war in Iraq.

Here was the opportunity to create a moderate conservatism in the Eisenhower mold that would have dovetailed with compassionate conservatism. Eisenhower's ideology is recalled as being far more secular than the conservatism that took hold after the rise of the religious right and is thus typically seen as out of synch with today's social issues right. But as the historian Kevin Kruse has shown, Eisenhower-style conservatism, like Bush's, was religiously inflected, and it was during Ike's time in office (and with his support) that the phrases "One Nation Under God" and "In God We Trust" became part of the country's civic liturgy. Any conservatism now would likely stand to the right of where Eisenhower—still a figure of the New Deal era—or Bush's grandfather stood. Nonetheless, a shaken nation was open to a unifying approach to politics. By the fall of 2002, Bush had made other choices.

In the end, both Bush and Rove decided that maintaining the traditional conservative coalition and activating conservative voters were their most practical political options. They were responding to the conservatism the country had, not a conservatism some might wish we had. The changes in the movement since Goldwater had reduced what Republican politicians perceived to be their margin of maneuver. When it came to short-term politics, Bush and Rove found their calculations justified by the elections of 2002 and 2004. But an opportunity to create a more lasting, if more moderate, conservative majority was lost, and Bush's complicated ideological dance left conservative activists, liberals, and many in the middle ground dissatisfied and, in many cases, angry.

Chris Chocola and Mick Mulvaney speak for Tea Party and libertarian conservatives in insisting, with passion and conviction, that Bush failed because he advocated big government: large deficits, a prescription drug benefit under Medicare, and the further centralizing of power over the nation's schools through the No Child Left Behind law. Bush was not averse to new federal spending—for education, part of his deal with Ted Kennedy to get No Child passed, or for his ambitious initiative to help the victims of AIDS in Africa. Many on the right resented his talk of a compassionate conservatism, seeing the adjective itself, as Barry Goldwater had in a different time, as a putdown implying that normal, unqualified conservatism must somehow be mean and callous. Others on the right never forgave Bush his strong advocacy of immigration reform and his embrace of America's Latino community.

Trende offered the familiar litany: "Temporary tax cuts, No Child Left Behind, the Medicare prescription drug benefit, a new Cabinet department, increased federal spending, TARP, and repeated attempts at immigration reform. Basically, despite a historic opportunity to shrink government, almost everything that the GOP establishment achieved during that time moved the needle leftward on domestic policy."

"The icing on the cake for conservatives," Trende added, "is that these moves were justified through an argument that they were necessary to continue to win elections and take issues off the table for Democrats. Instead, Bush's presidency was followed in 2008 by the most liberal Democratic presidency since Lyndon Johnson, accompanied by sizable Democratic House and Senate majorities." What conservatives saw as political opportunism was bad enough; that it didn't work made it unforgiveable.

Since the defeats of Robert Taft, "Mr. Conservative," in the 1940s and 1950, the narrative of betrayal had deeply embedded itself in the conservative psyche. It was taken up with a vengeance when George W. Bush's presidency ended with Obama's election.

George W. Bush's most enduring betrayal in the eyes of Tea Partiers and free-market purists was the $700 billion bank bailout during the financial crisis in the fall of 2008. Judged with the benefit of historical hindsight, this could be viewed as Bush's most courageous act, a step that was painful, in many ways unjust, but also necessary to keep the economy from collapsing. It was an enormous affront to Bush's own stated beliefs, which made it a brave choice and also enraged many Republicans and conservatives. Their rage only grew with time, as fears of an economic meltdown receded.

The fight over the bailout is especially instructive about the complexity of Bush's political legacy. Conservatives who just four years earlier had hailed Bush as the architect of a new majority for their movement turned hard against his bank rescue. Yet much of the political blame for Bush's proposal was ultimately shouldered by the Democrats.

In light of the fierce attacks on the bailout from both right and left, it's important to remember how ambivalent the country was about it at the time. Two polls, conducted at the same time, produced what appeared to be contradictory results that, in fact, accurately captured how torn Americans were about rescuing the institutions that many of them blamed for the crisis.

The Pew Research Center's survey, taken from September 19 to September 22, 2008, asked: "As you may know, the government is potentially investing billions to try and keep financial institutions secure. Do you think this is the right thing or the wrong thing for the government to be doing?" By a margin of 57 percent to 30 percent, Americans declared it the right thing to do.

On the same dates, Bloomberg and the *Los Angeles Times* asked: "Do you think the government should use taxpayers' dollars to rescue ailing financial firms whose collapse could have adverse effects on the economy and market, or is it not the government's responsibility to bail out private companies with taxpayers' dollars." This more pointed and arguably loaded inquiry (with its two references to "taxpayer dollars" and no mention of the soothing word "investing") produced an almost exactly opposite verdict: 55 percent were against this, while 31 percent were in favor.

Americans wanted the government to save the economy. They just didn't much like getting it done by way of sending their dollars to Wall Street firms and banks. And in an era during which we have become accustomed to opinions being tethered closely to the loyalties of red and blue, attitudes on the bailout transcended party lines. Substantial majorities of Republicans, Democrats, and Independents gave affirmative responses to the Pew question and negative responses to the Bloomberg/*Los Angeles Times* question.

But party lines were clearer in the House vote on September 29. Even though Bush was pushing his party to support the rescue, two-thirds of House Republicans opposed it, and their opposition defeated the bill. Among Democrats, on the other hand, two-thirds voted with a president so many of them loathed. The market response to the House failure to pass the bailout was instantaneous: the Dow Jones industrial average dropped 778 points, losing 7 percent of its value.

The arguments of the conservative opponents heard that day would echo through the Obama years. Representative Jeb Hensarling, a Republican of

Texas, said the bailout would put the nation on "the slippery slope to socialism" and create "the mother of all debt." Representative John Culberson, his fellow Texas Republican, took a populist tack. "This legislation is giving us a choice," he said, "between bankrupting our children and bankrupting a few of these big financial institutions on Wall Street that made bad decisions." Thus was small-government conservatism, which had favored deregulating financial markets, able to adopt an anti–Wall Street idiom when the time of reckoning arrived—all the while inveighing against socialism. Attacks on "corporate socialism," long a staple of the left, soon became a Tea Party calling card.

Four days later, some changes in the bill, but mostly sheer terror over the consequences of inaction, led 33 Democrats and 24 Republicans to switch their votes and pass the rescue plan. But even on the second, successful vote, Republicans still split against the bill, 91to 108, while most Democrats, including Obama, then running for president, voted for it. Democrats would wind up with political ownership of a Republican president's Wall Street bailout.

The conservative critique of Bush, of course, did nothing to persuade progressives to accept what to them was an absurd notion: that Bush was a closet moderate. Here, after all, was a man whose presidency was tainted from the start by an act of outlandish judicial activism. As many progressives saw it, five conservative justices effectively appointed him as president in *Bush v. Gore*. Thousands affixed "Re-defeat Bush" bumper stickers to their cars to memorialize the injustice and vow revenge. Liberal anger over the willingness of conservatives to go to the brink on impeachment became all the more ferocious after *Bush v. Gore*.

Bush's principal domestic achievement, in the liberal view, was tax cutting—and more tax cutting. His policies not only squandered the surplus left by Bill Clinton but, when combined with the cost of the wars in Afghanistan and Iraq, plunged the nation back into deficits that made it harder for his successor to respond to the economic collapse when it came.

Here the right and left converged to a degree, though their respective views about what caused the deficits and why they might be a problem diverged sharply. The right saw them as created by more big-government spending. The left saw them as a barrier to needed programs to expand health coverage and to relieve poverty and inequality. Liberals located the cause of the red ink not in a domestic spending spree—as Gerson pointed out, nonsecurity domestic discretionary spending grew by only 2 percent between 2001 and 2006 under Bush—but in an unnecessary war and Bush's largesse toward the wealthiest Americans.

Although it's unusual for a liberal to say so, Bush's failure might be seen as something of a tragedy, particularly by those who long for a less divisive and more moderate approach to politics and governing. Bush's willingness to embrace a federal responsibility in education and in the expansion of health care pointed to the possibility of a conservatism that went beyond antigovernment broadsides. Yet as Frum suggested, Bush never sought to challenge conservative assumptions and thereby left his initiatives as policy orphans. Supporters of a more moderate brand of conservatism were isolated and ripe for attack from the Tea Party that would soon rise.

If Bush and the Republican Party were unrelenting and at times demagogic in using national security issues for political purposes, his embrace of the nation's Muslim community and his warnings against religious bigotry were among his greatest acts of statesmanship. He never abandoned his insistence on the rights of American Muslims. But this concern faded behind other priorities, and when Bush left office, significant parts of the right felt much less constrained in their anti-Muslim campaigning. In 2010, attacks on the proposed Muslim Cultural Center in lower Manhattan, routinely referred to on Fox News as "the Mosque at Ground Zero," became a rallying point for the right. Gerson lamented that in demanding that President Obama oppose a mosque, his conservative allies were forgetting the lessons of his old boss's speech at Washington's Islamic Center just days after 9/11. "No president, of any party or ideology, could tell millions of Americans that their sacred building desecrates American holy ground," he wrote. Joe Scarborough, the *Morning Joe* host and former conservative congressman, denounced "elements of our party that are marching through the fevered swamps of ideology." But Gerson and Scarborough were minority voices in a movement shaped by the "real America" rhetoric that took hold under Bush and continued to do its work of exclusion.

The failure of compassionate conservatism is another cause for regret, even if it was destined to founder as long as Bush refused to resolve its inherent tensions. The movement could claim one major monument: the President's Emergency Plan for AIDS Relief, known as PEPFAR. Gerson, the compassionate conservative pioneer, opens *Heroic Conservatism*, his book about the Bush years and the future of his cause, with a description of the Oval Office meeting where Bush approved the program. Gerson then moves his narrative to an AIDS clinic at a squatter's camp in Uganda, and offers an uplifting take on what politics can sometimes achieve. "In that Oval Office meeting, and in the slums outside Kampala," he writes, "I saw one of the high points of political idealism in American history: an American president, out of moral and religious motivations, pledging billions to save the lives of non-citizens, with no claim to American help other than their humanity."

Yet Gerson was under no illusions, and his book, while a defense of Bush's Iraq project, was also a protest against what he saw as a rise in cynicism and a collapse of idealism. "A retreat from idealism and ambition, at this point in our history," he warned, "would be a disaster for Republicans, for conservatives, and for America."

Compassionate conservatism never won traction among Republicans in Congress except when it could be used a battering ram against liberals for their supposed hostility to government partnerships with faith-based groups. (In fact, Obama would direct more money to faith-based groups than Bush did.) Compassion was transformed into a rationalization for cultural warfare—yet even this was not enough to excite the conservative base. As Gerson told me, Republican leaders like Dick Armey and Tom DeLay, as well as committee chairs, "were not interested in seriously considering the domestic policy approaches the Administration might have on things that might be considered 'compassionate conservatism,' particularly if they cost money. . . . You had a lack of enthusiasm on Capitol Hill and a gradual diminishing enthusiasm in portions of the White House out of frustration."

David Kuo, who worked at Bush's faith-based office and left in disappointment, offered a tougher assessment. "From tax cuts to Medicare, the White House gets what the White House wants," he wrote in 2005. "It never really wanted the 'poor people stuff.'" In 2006, he wrote a scathing book called *Tempting Faith: The Inside Story of Political Seduction*, expanding this critique and offering evidence that faith-based grants were used for political purposes to shore up Bush's evangelical base. Kuo, who died of cancer in 2013 at the age of forty-four, said he could not get away from the idea that there was something wrong with "taking Jesus and reducing him to some precinct captain, to some get-out-the-vote guy."

There is a plaintive quality when Gerson looks back to 1999 and his devout hope then that Bush could transform conservatism by "challenging the consensus within the party." It turned out, he says, that Bush "was not reflecting some broad consensus within the Republican Party" for change. Bush's 2000 moment, he says, "really reflected a party that wanted to win, not a party that had been persuaded."

"I came to believe," Gerson concluded, "that Bush's victory didn't change the party."

Indeed it had not. The party's core constituencies continued to move rightward and faced steadily weaker internal opposition. Moderates tended to come from swing districts and were thus disproportionately represented among the Republicans who went down to defeat in the Democratic wave elections of 2006 and 2008.

The energy in the party, Steven Teles observed, was still organized around tax cuts and smaller government. Noting that 9/11 and the war in Iraq had given Republicans a new national security strategy for reaching swing voters, he argued that compassionate conservatism "again became an answer to an electoral question that no one was asking" and "never captured the commitment of the party's core factions, and was viewed skeptically by many of them."

"Whereas tax cuts, regulatory relief, gun rights, and opposition to abortion have large mobilized interests able to enforce party orthodoxy through credible threats of electoral retribution," he continued, "compassionate conservatism does not."

And then came the financial crisis that Frum called the "epic disaster in 2008." It discredited conservative economic doctrine in exactly the way the Great Depression had nearly eighty years before. Tax cuts had not shored up the economy. Financial deregulation—approved by the Gingrich Congress, but signed, it should be said, by Bill Clinton—had opened the way for Wall

Street chicanery. The rising inequality aggravated by conservative policies led to stagnating or declining blue-collar incomes which, in turn, encouraged families to take on additional debt to maintain their standards of living. Prosperity based on growing debt rather than rising incomes proved to be a very fragile flower. Ironically, the crash was one of just two factors that the *Weekly Standard*'s Fred Barnes had said could get in the way of the Republican realignment he had predicted four years earlier, but he quickly dismissed its likelihood. Citing Walter Dean Burnham, the great academic specialist on realignments, Barnes had written: "For Republicans to slip into minority status again, he says, it would take a monumental party split like that in 1912 or 'a colossal increase in the pain level' of Americans as happened with the Great Depression. Neither is likely."

In fact, the second came to pass. And while the GOP did not formally split, it found itself divided and disillusioned.

Activist conservatives truly believed that blame for their travails rested with Bush and not their doctrine. Mulvaney says his decision to seek elective office in 2006 was "fueled with the disappointment I had with the Bush administration." For moderate conservatives such as Representative Steve LaTourette of Ohio, who left Congress in 2012, it was a source of mystery and frustration that his more right-wing colleagues attributed the party's thrashing in the 2006 elections and its subsequent defeats to big-government conservatism and Bush's philosophical inconsistencies. The facts, he told me, pointed elsewhere. "I looked at the data, and I think the data shows that everybody that was a Republican showed up and voted for Republicans, everybody that was a Democrat did the same, and we lost 58 percent of the independents because of the war was pretty unpopular by 2006, because George W. Bush was pretty unpopular, because it was the six-year-itch election for a president. I thought that was it."

But many of his colleagues felt differently. "I can remember going down to my first meeting of the Republican Conference" after the election, LaTourette said, "and I thought I'd landed on another planet because the conservative guys were flying to the microphone saying, 'It's because we weren't conservative enough. It's because we didn't stand up enough on the abortion issue, on the gun issue, on the spending issue, and so our people stayed home, and we have to find our way again.'"

"That's not what the numbers showed me," LaTourette said, but the post-election fury on the right was "the first sign of open warfare."

Many Republicans shared LaTourette's coolly realistic view of what happened to Bush and the party. But it became far more convenient, both for the party's ideologues and, over time, its leadership, to locate the problem elsewhere. Thus did a combination of honest disillusionment among rank-and-file conservatives and a shrewdly fought interpretive battle allow the right to escape responsibility for Bush's failures. If Obama's victory and large-scale Democratic gains in Congress could be explained by the ideological apostasy of Bush and Republican congressional leaders, then the logical next steps for the movement would be obvious: return to the true faith and battle for smaller government and lower taxes. This approach allowed conservatives to avoid any concession that the country was shifting toward the center or center-left and any hint of a strategy geared toward moderation. The party's leaders and its activists didn't want to go there.

It might seem surprising that the collapse of the economy did not create more soul-searching on the right. The financial crisis of 2008 represented a wholesale rout of conservative ideas on taxes and deregulation. The tax cuts of the Bush years had produced, at best, a modest recovery in the mid-2000s—and, when combined with war and national security spending, they had turned the large Clinton surpluses into deficits. The economic growth of the Bush years, such as it was, did little to boost wages or median income. Even at its peak in 2007, median income in the Bush years was still below where it had stood in Clinton's final two years in office. In Bush's first term, job growth was negative. For the entirety of his eight years in office, the economy under Bush produced a net 1.1 million new jobs—compared with 22.7 million new jobs in the Clinton years. And the paltry Bush-era job gains were wiped out in the first few months of Obama's term as the costs of the collapse that began on the forty-third president's watch mounted. Supply-side policies had failed, and only Keynesian policies pulled the country out of free fall. A conservative president was forced to turn to big government to save the banking system and the economy.

Yet if all of this seemed obvious to conservatism's critics, it's no shock that conservatives resisted the diagnosis. Wholesale philosophical reversals, after all, are rare.

Conservatives did what they could to blame the financial collapse on policies in which they had, at best, a limited stake, including efforts under both Clinton and Bush to expand home ownership to lower income Americans and problems at Fannie Mae, the government-backed enterprise that supported mortgages. That many Clinton-era Democrats were complicit in financial deregulation facilitated conservative buck-passing. Since the full costs of the Great Recession were not felt until after Obama took office, it was easy to shift responsibility to the Democrats—especially since congressional Republicans let Democrats provide the bulk of the votes needed for the Wall Street rescue. So this Bush policy could be hung on the Democrats, too.

After 2008, the conservative critique of the Bush years was broadly adopted by the party's rising political generation. It's worth briefly jumping ahead in our story to record the triumph of this narrative as reflected in a campaign book published in advance of the 2010 elections. It was offered by three prominent younger House members, Paul Ryan, Eric Cantor, and Kevin McCarthy. All would rise to leadership positions, although Cantor and McCarthy would suffer at the hands of the very movement they helped to build. Their problems would open the way for Ryan to become Speaker, a job he didn't really want. The book's title, *Young Guns: A New Generation of Conservative Leaders,* was telling both about their own self-image and how they would sell Republican candidates that fall.

As might be expected, the volume was largely a critique of Obama and the Democrats. But its most revealing moments were those in which three prominent members of Congress—two of whom, Cantor and Ryan, had served during the entirety of Bush's time in office—sought to separate themselves from the previous eight years of conservative governance.

"Don't get me wrong," Cantor wrote. "We're proud Republicans. We just believe that our party has at times lost sight of the things we believe in, ideas like economic freedom, limited government, the sanctity of life, and putting families first. . . . Republicans controlled Washington from 2001 to 2006. They did some good things, but they also did a lot to give conservatism a bad name." Republicans, he added, "had become the party of Washington—instead of the party that wanted to change Washington." Cantor's words seem ironic in retrospect, since he would lose his 2014 primary to a Tea Party candidate who made exactly this argument.

Ryan, for his part, spoke of "the corruption that occurred when Republicans were in the majority," and what he had in mind were "earmarks" that involved the special spending projects favored by individual members of Congress. Without naming names, Ryan offered this rather searing indictment of his party: "They brought in more machine-like people," he wrote. "And I think our leadership changed and adopted the position that we beat the Democrats' machine, now it's time to create a Republican machine to keep us in the majority. And out of that came this earmark culture." Somehow, Ryan, the veteran member of Congress, managed to cast himself as independent of the "they" who brought in those "machine-like people."

McCarthy, who would replace Cantor as majority leader in 2014 but whose quest for the Speakership would be upended by the Republican right in October 2015, was first elected in the face of the Democrats' 2006 sweep. He wrote that his travels during that miserable GOP year persuaded him of "a deep disconnect between what Republican leaders in Washington were saying, and what I, as a first-time congressional candidate, was hearing." The voters, he said, "were talking about the party's failures—our failures—from high-profile ethical lapses to the inability to rein in spending or even slow the growth of government." And for McCarthy, as for his colleagues, earmarks loomed as a sin so grievous it qualified as original. "The Republican base," he wrote, "was angry about the way the party had betrayed its principles with earmarks that lacked the transparency and accountability that the public expected when taxpayer dollars were spent."

What's remarkable is that the book contained no second thoughts about policies and actions that had plainly hurt the Republicans in 2006 and 2008: the Iraq War, the Schiavo case, the handling of Hurricane Katrina, the tax cuts and the other economic policies that ended in the Great Recession. Yes, McCarthy said, the "first step was admitting how the party had lost its way." But his indictment involved only a single count: "Under Republican leadership in the early 2002, spending and government got out of control."

Meet the new Republican orthodoxy. It was the same as the old Republican orthodoxy, but held even more fiercely, in the manner of the penitent.

Skepticism about the George W. years would haunt Jeb Bush's campaign for the 2016 Republican presidential nomination from its inception.

Jeb, rather bravely, courted some of the opposition he faced from the right by declaring that a Republican candidate needed to be willing "to lose the primary to win the general" and insisting that he would refuse to "fake anger to placate people's angst." He told a party not eager to hear it that it needed to embrace immigration reform and the reality of a diverse America—and chose to deliver part of his announcement speech in Spanish. For some in the party, Jeb Bush seemed to promise the necessary course correction from its Tea Party detour, much as George W.'s 2000 campaign tried to pull the party back from the excesses of the Gingrich Congress.

Yet Jeb's posture only aggravated his problem of being seen by many on the right as the embodiment of all that went wrong with both Bush presidencies. "The Bushes have always underestimated the depth of the base's dissatisfaction with their policies," Laura Ingraham, a conservative talk radio host, told the *Washington Post* in June 2015, when Jeb's effort hit a low point, "and they take the criticism personally." A McClatchy-Marist poll of Republicans and Independents who leaned Republican in March 2015—taken at a moment when Bush was running relatively well—confirmed his weakness at the right end of the party. He drew 26 percent against the rest of the Republican field among moderates, 18 percent among conservatives, but only 7 percent among those who called themselves very conservative.

When Jeb formally announced his candidacy on June 15, 2015, his mother, Barbara, was there. His father and his brother were not. And his campaign logo, "Jeb" plus an exclamation point, did not include the word "Bush." His campaign clearly realized the problems his family legacy created for him. And no one took more gleeful advantage of Jeb's weakness with the right than Donald Trump, who made him the target of some of his harshest and most derisive barbs. After a poor performance in a CNBC debate in late October, Jeb fell to as low as 4 percent in some national polls.

George W. Bush did too little to change the party and the movement, but just enough to provoke a fierce reaction on the right. Barack Obama would win election because of Bush's failures—and soon became the object of the backlash they provoked.

But it was not just Obama's election or Bush's failures that created the Tea Party. There were deeper forces at work pushing conservatism in new directions—and also back toward the right-wing radicalism of the 1960s.

9

THE NEW, NEW, OLD RIGHT

The Tea Party Explosion That Was Waiting to Happen

"This change taking place in the country is really scary to me."

The surprise is that the Tea Party was a surprise. When the Bush presidency ended, the country was angry and frightened, and the conservative movement was in shock. The elation over the election of Barack Obama among the young, African-Americans, and Democrats was matched by the disappointment and, in some cases, horror in the parts of the country that did not identify with the nation's young and urbane president. This discontent was bound to find an outlet. More than a third of the country is reliably conservative, and at least a fifth of it regularly identifies with views well to the right of center. History suggested that the far right is always less constrained when liberals are in power—and when the failure of a conservative regime stokes suspicions that its concerns had never really been taken seriously.

Before picking up the narrative from the end of the Bush presidency, it's important to see that much was happening only barely beneath the surface of politics, outside the boundaries of Rove's game plan and not much noticed by liberals. The forces of conservative rebellion, barely kept in check at the end of the Bush years, were ready to march.

Traditional conservative politicians tried to explain the rise of this New, New Right—how many "new's" are required can be debated—as a reaction to specific policies pursued by the new Obama administration. Doing so made it easier to corral the protesters into traditional forms of politics. Thus was the Tea Party seen primarily as a reaction to soaring deficits created by the recession itself and by the stimulus program Obama initiated to revive a staggering economy. It was also cast as a revolt against a new health care law that expanded a welfare state that so many conservatives already considered too big. Tea Partiers themselves gave these explanations plausibility, since the stimulus and Obamacare were always at the top of their own lists of grievances.

But many discerning politicians on the right understood that something deeper and less easily explained by individual issues was at work. For the Tea Party was largely a movement of older Americans, almost all of them white. Most were loyal to very traditional social views and unhappy with cultural changes that its members saw as taking the country away from them. Some were bothered by the election of the first African-American president and many more were upset by the forces he represented: the young and the urban, the secular and the sophisticated, the vast new populations of Latinos and Asians, and a scientific and technical class that seemed to own the future even as factories closed and blue-collar jobs disappeared.

Vin Weber, a loyal conservative since his days as the young Goldwater enthusiast, captured the vague but powerful sense of discontent. "I think people look at television and fashion and movies, and maybe particularly older people . . . and they say: 'This is not good. It's not the way I grew up,'" he said. "You take all that together and older, largely white, but not entirely white, people, think, 'This change taking place in the country is really scary to me.'"

Haley Barbour, the former governor of Mississippi and a Reagan-era veteran, encountered the same fears. "I'll tell you the expression I heard starting in 2009 and '10 that I never heard before in my life," he said. "'I'm afraid my children and grandchildren are not going to inherit the same country I inherited.'"

And former representative Tom Davis, one of the party's best political strategists, suggested that the feelings made manifest in the summer of 2009 reflected an explosive combination of social unease and economic rage.

"Look at these people economically," Davis said of the Tea Party's supporters. "These are the people who are still struggling. They haven't seen any benefit under Bush or Obama. Their wages have been stagnant. They watch their country go through two failed wars, and now you've got an economic meltdown coming at the end of [Bush's] term. The world's changing around these people. There's going to be a reaction to this."

Obama, Davis said, couldn't reach this group, but he also argued that the new president didn't seem to try. "He's not talking to those people," Davis said. "He's talking to a different alienated group."

It was a telling observation: Americans were now divided even in their alienation.

★

That the Tea Party had a powerful political impact is obvious. But as we began to see in Chapter One, it was far more *a new form of something old* than an altogether innovative political venture. *New York Times* reporter Kate Zernike published a fine, fast-off-the-mark journalistic account of the Tea Party movement in 2010 titled *Boiling Mad*. A year later, the British academic Dominic Sandbrook published a good book of his own called *Mad as Hell*. But Sandbrook's volume was not about the Tea Party. Its subtitle summarizes its story: *The Crisis of the 1970s and the Rise of the Populist Right*. Alan Crawford, a conservative, wrote *Thunder on the Right: The "New Right" and the Politics of Resentment*, to warn that in its efforts to exploit popular fears and anxieties, "the Right had been transformed into an institutionalized, disciplined, well-organized, and well-financed movement of loosely-knit affiliates." His book was published in 1980. Large parts of the conservative movement had been angry for a long time.

The Tea Party was the newest manifestation of an old set of political habits. Academic analysts moved quickly to train the big guns of social science on the movement and concluded that the economic and cultural components could not be separated. In a sense, "economic issues" had become "cultural issues."

The political scientists Christopher Parker and Matt Barreto were most explicit among the scholars in linking the new forms of right-wing activism to the oldest strains of the American far right. In *Change They Can't Believe In: The Tea Party and Reactionary Politics in America*, Parker and Barreto invoked theories from the 1950s and early 1960s, advanced by the historian Richard Hofstadter, the sociologist Seymour Martin Lipset, and others, tracing movements of "the radical right" to anxieties over lost social status in a rapidly changing country. Groups facing such displacement, Parker and Barreto argued, "will use any means at their disposal to forestall what they believe is a loss of social prestige as social change takes root." They were far from alone, particularly on the left, in using Hofstadter's famous essay, *The Paranoid Style in American Politics*, to explain the Tea Party. They noted Hofstadter's description of the citizen who saw himself as "spied upon, plotted against, betrayed, and very likely destined for ruin."

"We believe that people are driven to support the Tea Party from the anxiety they feel as they perceive the America they know, the country they love, slipping away," they wrote in 2013, "threatened by the rapidly changing face of what they perceive as the 'real' America: a heterosexual, Christian (mostly) male, white country." They added: "They not only wish to halt change; if we are correct, Tea Party supporters wish to turn the clock back." Parker and Barreto noted the repeated insistence of Tea Party members that their movement was not racist, but concluded that "true believers in the Tea Party tend to harbor *much, much* more group-based hostility than true skeptics of the movement." They used italics to underscore how strongly they believed their data pointed in this direction.

In *The Tea Party and the Remaking of Republican Conservatism*, Theda Skocpol and Vanessa Williamson used their interviews with grassroots Tea Party activists to show that the movement was not, in fact, opposed to all government programs. Unsurprisingly because so many of the movement's members were past or near retirement age, Tea Partiers strongly supported government programs such as Medicare and Social Security, but opposed most others, particularly Obama's health care expansion. Seen one way, the Tea Partiers were engaged in simple, self-interested behavior, protecting "their" programs while condemning government spending on behalf of people unlike themselves. But Skocpol and Williamson's respondents had a rationale for the distinction they drew: They saw traditional New Deal benefits as earned through a lifetime of hard work. What concerned them, Skocpol and Williamson wrote, was "being stuck with the tax tab to pay for 'unearned' entitlements handed out to unworthy categories of people." These "unworthy" groups—"freeloaders"—included immigrants, low-income Americans, and the young. Skocpol and Williamson go out of their way to avoid blanket charges of racism against the movement, and cite data and their own interviews suggesting that many of its members held complex views on race. Nonetheless, the two scholars noted that a "sense of 'us versus them' along racial and ethnic fault lines clearly marks the worldview of many people active in the Tea Party."

Skocpol and Williamson were careful not to pretend that the Tea Party could be understood simply as a spontaneous eruption. It also reflected long-term changes in the structures of influence on the right. "Grassroots activists, roving billionaire advocates, and right-wing media purveyors—these three forces, together, create the Tea Party and give it the ongoing clout to buffet and redirect the Republican Party and influence broader debates in American democracy."

If the Bush years prepared the ground for this new, particularly aggressive round of fury on the right, the new factors Skocpol and Williamson identified gave it its shape and reach. It was Goldwaterism and, in some cases, Birchism on steroids.

The new forms of conservative media were essential to the rise of a newly militant right and allowed its ideas to become part of the mainstream discussion in an unprecedented way. Conservative ideas gained traction in an interaction among an expanding conservative broadcast industry, a substantial presence on the Web, and large conservative inroads in publishing. All this gradually played back into the traditional media.

It's common to focus on conservative radio and television, but conservative books also played an important part in transforming the movement, as we saw initially in Chapter One. The right-wing bestsellers of the 1950s and 1960s, often issued by publishing houses set up for the sole purpose of pushing particular volumes, were never recognized on the formal bestseller lists. But from the 1970s on, mainstream publishers came to realize how hungry the right and far right were for books. It was one of many ways in which American conservatives defied liberal clichés about them. Once marginal—and marginalized—ideas found new audiences.

The conservative publishing boom was enabled by the vast expansion of conservative broadcast media, an interactive process exemplified by Glenn Beck's role in championing old John Birch Society books. We've already seen that conservatives had long sought to penetrate radio and television through far-right programs like H. L. Hunt's *Life Line* and *The Dan Smoot Report* in the 1950s and 1960s and Bill Buckley's sophisticated, lively, and mainstream *Firing Line.* But the end of the Fairness Doctrine during the Reagan administration freed stations from the need to provide alternative viewpoints. Conservatives quickly colonized large parts of the AM radio dial, which was in search of new programming as music migrated to FM in the late 1960s. Rush Limbaugh was the father of them all, starting his syndicated radio show in 1988. His success spawned many imitators. Conservatives who already believed that the mainstream networks media were biased against them finally had their own voices—and treasured them. It is no accident that conservatism's steady movement back to the ideological purity of the Goldwater years parallels the rise of conservative radio. Radio talkers on the progressive side of politics never developed the loyalty or reach of the conservatives— liberals seemed to prefer news programs—even as progressives such as Bill Press charged that conservative owners of radio chains favored conservative talk over moderate or liberal alternatives. Whatever the cause, conservative on-air minutes now outnumber liberal minutes by a ratio of at least 10-to-1.

Roger Ailes, who helped Richard Nixon learn how to use television in 1968, tried for a while to turn Limbaugh into a television star. It was not to be. But rather than give up on his ambition, Ailes simply went bigger. He founded Fox News in 1996 and, as we saw in Chapter Four, the network took off during the Clinton impeachment saga. It got another push in the Bush years, particularly after the attacks of 9/11. In January 2002, it passed CNN as the number-one cable news network. It has stayed number one ever since, even if it suffered some viewership declines during parts of the later Obama years. It was on the upswing again during the Trump Summer of 2015 and the Republican presidential debate the network sponsored in August 2015 drew an astonishing 24 million viewers. It was, *Ad Week*'s "TV Newser" website reported, "the highest non-sports cable program of all time" and "the highest-rated cable news program of all time."

It is impossible to overstate the importance of the rise of Fox in strengthening forces on the right of the Republican Party, and on the right end of conservatism itself. "Ailes built Fox into an entire political universe," wrote Gabriel Sherman in his biography of Ailes, *The Loudest Voice in the Room*. It was political innovation on a large scale. Before Fox News, there had never been an explicitly ideological television network. And its ideology was closely linked to Republican politics. As Sherman noted, after Fox hired Sarah Palin in the fall of 2009, Ailes had five prospective Republican presidential candidates on his payroll: Palin, Mike Huckabee, Rick Santorum, Newt Gingrich, and John Bolton. Santorum and Gingrich would go on to become Mitt Romney's most durable challengers for the Republican nomination in 2012.

Fox turned Glenn Beck, with all of his touting of old Bircher ideas, into a national celebrity. Even Ailes was surprised at how quickly Beck caught on. "I've never seen anyone build an audience this fast," Ailes told his executives, according to Sherman. At his peak, Beck reached over 3 million viewers a day.

Fox has played a unique role in politics because of the unusually close relationship rank-and-file conservatives have developed with the network. Liberals have no comparable devotion to any broadcast outlet, including MSNBC, Fox's progressive prime-time rival, which began losing audience share after the 2012 election and softened its liberal leanings in 2015. A PRRI/Brookings Institution survey in June 2014 underscored how different the left and the right are in their media loyalties. Asked which broadcast news source they trusted most, Republicans issued an unambiguous verdict: 53 percent of them said Fox News, and no other alternative came close. The traditional broadcast networks were second at 22 percent, with CNN a distant third at 9 percent. Among self-described conservatives, the numbers were comparable: 49 percent chose Fox, 19 percent the broadcast networks, and 13 percent CNN. And among conservative Republicans, 56 percent chose Fox.

By contrast, there was no dominant broadcast source for Democrats and liberals. Only 10 percent of liberals and Democrats, and just 11 percent of those who identified as both liberal and Democratic, listed MSNBC as their most trusted source. The old broadcast networks came in first (31 percent of Democrats, 24 percent of liberals), followed among Democrats by CNN at 26 percent and public television at 14 percent. Among liberals, second-place choices scattered—*The Daily Show* with Jon Stewart and public television both came in at 17 percent, CNN at 16 percent.

Not only does no network on the left or center play the dominant role that Fox does on the right; Fox also appears to have a strong impact on the views of its audience. At the least, since cause-and-effect are difficult to establish, those who most trust Fox constitute the most right-wing part of the Republican Party. Fox News Republicans were far more likely to regard themselves as members of the Tea Party movement (35 percent) than non-Fox Republicans (15 percent). Only 42 percent of Republicans who most trusted Fox News supported a path to citizenship for immigrants living in the country illegally, compared with 60 percent of other Republicans. Fox News Republicans were far more forceful in their opposition to same-sex marriage: 76 percent were opposed to it, including 47 percent who were strongly opposed. Among non-Fox Republicans, only 57 percent opposed same-sex marriage, and only 31 percent did so strongly. The Fox difference was not confined to social issues. Fox News Republicans, for example, opposed increasing the minimum wage to $10.10 an hour by a margin of 64 percent to 33 percent. Non-Fox Republicans favored the wage increase, 56 percent to 41 percent.

Fox would eventually play a central organizing role in the Tea Party rebellion, prodding the movement along, serving as a bulletin board for its demonstrations, broadcasting its successes in the summer of town meetings in 2009, and mounting a sustained attack on Obama and his presidency. Its commentators did not always trouble themselves over whether an accusation was true. Thus did the network "report" that Obama had attended a "madrassa" as a child in Indonesia. (He hadn't.) The network gave expansive play to the idea that Obama had not been born in the United States and could not produce a birth certificate, a cause championed with particular energy by Donald Trump. (When the president did produce his birth certificate, he shut down some but not all of the birthers. Trump, for one, continued to express skepticism.) Fox regularly amplified charges from the conservative Web, often taken at face value without much, if any, checking.

A singularly revealing and disgraceful instance of the power of the conservative media to influence the actions of even a Democratic administration came in July 2010. The episode involved Shirley Sherrod, an Agriculture

Department employee who was forced to resign after a video of her making supposedly "racist" comments about discriminating against a white farmer was posted on the Breitbart website. The video was broadcast over and over by Fox, and its commentators took the mainstream media to task for not covering the story. It was a remarkably successful tactic on the right.

For good measure, the NAACP, which typically did not follow Fox's or Breitbart's lead, condemned Sherrod's comments. When the mainstream media did cover the story, they discovered that the parts of the video that had been posted wildly distorted what Sherrod has said: she had actually been offering a *critique* of stereotypes of whites. Sherrod was vindicated. But she had no interest in returning to her job and both the NAACP and the Obama administration were embarrassed. It was a media moment that simply would not have happened before the rise of Fox.

Perhaps the height of "tell them what they want to hear" journalism was Fox's coverage of the lead-up to the 2012 election, during which many of the network's commentators repeatedly assured their audience that, despite the public polls, Mitt Romney would defeat Barack Obama.

Romney, said Dick Morris, the former Clinton adviser turned conservative pundit, "is going to win by more than five points." The polls, he insisted, were overestimating Democratic turnout. "You have me back on the show," he told Fox's Greta Van Susteren. "You hold me accountable." He told Fox's Bill O'Reilly that Romney would win by a "landslide," and said a 10-point popular vote margin was possible. Morris did face accountability. He was fired by Fox, and, to his credit, acknowledged that the loss of his contract was appropriate. "I was fired because I was wrong," he said. "I was wrong and I was wrong at the top of my lungs."

But Morris was not alone in predicting a Romney win. Others who took this view included Fox regulars Karl Rove (although more cautiously than Morris), Charles Krauthammer, Fred Barnes, Michael Barone, and others. In a remarkable demonstration of how conservatives had constructed a reality of their own, conservatives took to "unskewing" the polls, applying their own corrective to surveys that, they insisted, overestimated how many Democrats would turn out to vote. This statistical form of voter suppression was no more successful in 2012 than the real thing.

It fell to David Frum to call out Fox and conservative radio and, in the process, to invent a term. "Republicans have been fleeced and exploited and lied to by a conservative entertainment complex," Frum declared after the election on MSNBC's *Morning Joe*. Joe Scarborough joined in, arguing the Right's radio/television/website complex profited by offering a distorted view of reality. "That's not an electoral strategy," Scarborough said, "that's a business strategy for them." It proved to be a durable business. That central challenge of the right-wing media to conservatism's long-term future was captured by the title of a paper by Jackie Calmes of the *New York Times*: " 'They Don't Give a Damn About Governing': Conservative Media's Influence on the Republican Party." Published in July 2015 by Harvard's Shoreinstein Center on Media, Politics and Public Policy, Calmes's paper offered a detailed look at how the party's leaders had been forced to cede power to conservative talkshow hosts and outlets. "If leaders of the Republican Party are not setting its agenda, who is?" Calmes asked. Her answer: "Once allied with but now increasingly hostile to the Republican hierarchy, conservative media is shaping the party's agenda in ways that are impeding Republicans' ability to govern and to win presidential elections."

No political figure demonstrated the loss of control by party leaders more comprehensively than Donald Trump, who won support from key conservative talkers even as he dominated the mainstream media by being outrageous, interesting, and a celebrity. Trump proved to be the first conservative figure powerful enough to survive a confrontation with Roger Ailes and Fox News. Trump attacked one of the the network's most important stars, Megyn Kelly, in boorish and sexist terms because she had asked him some probing—and journalistically normal—questions during the Fox News debate. At first, Ailes worked out an accomodation with Trump (and Kelly went on an unplanned vacation), the first indication of Trump's media power. When Trump went after Kelly again, Ailes had no choice but to criticize him and defend Kelly. Yet none of this hurt Trump's standing in the polls at the time, a rare moment when the network found itself outdone by a conservative politician. "They really didn't know what to do because their audience loves Trump," Sherman told the conservative website-turned-network NewsmaxTV. Ailes, he said, "has really never really faced an adversary like Donald Trump. Donald Trump is not predictable, and Roger Ailes is used to Republicans coming to kiss his ring. They all bow down to Fox News. But Donald Trump does not play by those rules and so Ailes essentially doesn't know how to act." Suddenly, Fox needed to look over its own right shoulder and worry that the movement the network helped build might be radicalizing even beyond the network's own standards. Over time, in the face of continued provocations from Trump, Ailes would toughen his stand.

The libertarian writer Julian Sanchez took the term "espistemic closure" from philosophy to describe the effect of the conservative media system. "Reality is defined by a multimedia array of interconnected and cross-promoting conservative blogs, radio programs and of course, Fox News," he wrote. "Whatever conflicts with that reality can be dismissed out of hand because it comes from the liberal media and is therefore ipso facto not to be trusted."

The conservative media and epistemic closure were not the only forces at work promoting ideological purity. Skocpol and Williamson's shorthand reference to "roving billionaire advocates" pointed to another essential ingredient to the Tea Party revolt: the proliferation and radicalization of conservative money.

Rich donors are not new to the right. Reagan's "A Time for Choosing" speech, after all, was aired precisely because Goldwater's moneymen insisted on doing so. When he founded the John Birch Society, Robert Welch relied on conservative businessmen, including the Wichita, Kansas, oil executive Fred Koch. Ronald Reagan's Kitchen Cabinet of millionaires included Justin Dart, Holmes Tuttle, Alfred Bloomingdale, and Joseph P. Coors.

But in Goldwater's time, business money was, on the whole, pragmatic. While many business leaders continued to fight the New Deal, many others had made their peace with a set of economic arrangements that produced widespread prosperity. The idea of spreading purchasing power to workers, even through unionization, made sense to many who became wealthy themselves as part of a broad burst of growth based on Keynesian economics. The quintessential business organization of the postwar consensus, as John Judis argued in his book *The Paradox of American Democracy*, was the middle-of-the road, consensual Committee for Economic Development, many of whose founding members had been on FDR's Business Advisory Council during World War II. Even when the Establishment was conservative and Republican, it instinctively leaned against a more radical right. Indeed, the core complaint of Phyllis Schlafly in *A Choice Not an Echo* in 1964 was precisely that Establishment Republicans were effectively allies of New Dealism who regularly foiled the hopes of the conservative grass roots. On this, she spoke for many in her movement.

But in reaction to the regulatory advances pushed by a new consumer movement led by Ralph Nader—a large number of them signed into law by Richard Nixon—business began to embrace much harder antigovernment positions. In the 1970s, as Judis noted, many "corporate leaders and bankers abandoned their commitment to disinterested public service and to a politics that transcended class." They "turned against union organizers, environmentalists and consumer activists with the same resolve that an older generation of business leaders had turned against the AFL, the IWW and the Socialist Party."

This was the era when corporations and trade associations began creating political action committees on a large scale. It's also when corporate philanthropy and large donors began building new free-market think tanks, reviving older ones, and developing strong ties with universities. A Virginia lawyer named Lewis Powell, whom Nixon would appoint to the Supreme Court, wrote a memo for the U.S. Chamber of Commerce that became a manifesto for the new business activism. "The American economic system is under attack," Powell declared. "The overriding first need is for businessmen to recognize that the ultimate issue may be *survival*—survival of what we call the free enterprise system. . . ."

Powell was obsessed with the influence Nader had accumulated (calling him the "single most effective antagonist of American business") and he urged business leaders to finance sympathetic professors, to monitor school textbooks and the media, and to demand "equal time" for pro-capitalist speakers.

The future Supreme Court justice was knocking on an open door, and the 1970s saw the birth of the Heritage Foundation, the revitalization of the American Enterprise Institute, and the establishment of the Business Roundtable. The same period saw the rise of K Street as Washington's lobbying center. As Judis noted, the number of businesses with registered lobbyists in Washington rose from 175 in 1971 to 2,445 in 1982. The number of corporate offices increased from 50 in 1961 to 500 in 1978, to 1,300 by 1986. Between 1978 and 1986, the number of trade associations nearly doubled, from 1,800 to 3,500, and the number of people they employed doubled from 40,000 to 80,000. Beginning in the 1970s, Washington became a very different place.

The shift of business groups to the right continued in the 1990s when business found itself under pressure from Republicans in Congress to take firmer ideological positions. Even before the Republican takeover of the House in 1994, a signal moment came during the battle over Clinton's health care proposal. Initially, leading business groups, including the National Association of Manufacturers and the Chamber of Commerce, were prepared to work with the administration on behalf of reform. Since so many businesses—particularly large manufacturers of cars and steel—provided coverage for their employees, reform could be seen as being in their interest. Employers who offered coverage often subsidized, through family policies, employers who didn't. But business support crumbled because of pressure from two directions. In an odd turn, conservative Republicans lobbied the business lobbyists to push them away from reform. Upstart conservative business groups, such as the National Federation of Independent Business, launched assaults and membership raids on the Chamber of Commerce, pushing it away from Clinton. The national Chamber has since become even more loyal to Republican positions, although local Chambers are often less ideological. And businesses opposed to Clinton's reforms, including the smaller insurance companies and enterprises such as restaurants and fast-food chains that hired thousands of low-wage workers, were far more vocal in opposing Clinton's plan than were businesses that supported it—often with qualms going in.

The growing power of finance had a complicated relationship to the new stream of antigovernment feeling. It was not initially obvious that Wall Street, the hedge funds, and the venture capitalists would be a force for conservatism. Democrats raised substantial funds from the financial world, both because many in its ranks were liberal, particularly on social issues, and because the Clinton administration was broadly sympathetic to financial deregulation. But after the 2008 crash, the performance of Wall Street came under heightened attack from the left. Democrats proposed higher taxes on the wealthy (ironically, back to the levels under Clinton, who was nonetheless seen as more friendly to business than Obama), including increases in the low capital gains tax rates enacted under Bush. Curiously, the wealthiest people in the country came to see themselves as beleaguered and ostracized—even as their share of national income continued to grow.

Conservative and Republican money took a further turn rightward as political campaigns became more expensive and various barriers to money's penetration of politics—in custom and in law—began to fall. The *Citizens United* decision by the Supreme Court in 2010 was the Magna Carta of big money in politics. In principle, these changes were ideologically and politically neutral: rich Democrats could increase their influence alongside rich Republicans. In practice, not only are there more rich Republicans, but the most ideologically committed conservatives were far more prepared to invest resources on a large scale to influence the political debate. Moreover, wealthy Democrats were, on the whole and with some notable exceptions, more interested in social and environmental issues than in progressive economic policies. Wealthy conservatives, on the other hand, were passionate advocates of deregulation and opponents of anything that smacked of "socialism."

Thus did the inclination to purify and purge the Republican Party of liberal influence affect donors no less than the rank-and-file. If liberals had largely been driven out of the party by the time of the Gingrich Revolution, the new imperative was to drive out moderates and even politicians who were moderately conservative, lest they use their influence to do business with Democrats. As the Republicans who voted in primaries became more uniformly conservative, the purges became easier to execute.

The Club for Growth, one of the innovative new-style conservative groups, focused primarily on punishing Republican apostasy on the tax issue. "We want to be seen as the tax cut enforcer in the party," said Stephen Moore, a conservative writer and activist. Moore founded the group with Thomas L. "Dusty" Rhodes, who worked on Wall Street and served as president of *Na-*

tional Review, and Richard Gilder, a longtime supply-sider who made his fortune in the securities industry. As the pedigree of the group's founders suggests, keeping taxes on investment income low is the Club's priority.

The Club made its first big splash in 2004, backing Representative Patrick Toomey's primary challenge to Senator Arlen Specter in Pennsylvania. Specter barely survived, with 51 percent of the vote, and he needed the support of the entire Republican establishment, including President Bush, to pull off his narrow victory. After his defeat, Toomey took over as president of the Club, serving until he launched his second Senate race in 2010. The threat of the primary drove Specter out of the Republican Party. In the fall, Toomey finally got his Senate seat, winning narrowly in the Republican tide.

The poster brothers for the new right-wing money were Charles and David Koch, Fred Koch's children. The Brothers Koch had a long history of financing libertarian ventures and spent many years operating outside the confines of the GOP. They provided the funding to establish the Cato Institute in 1977 and it became a respected intellectual redoubt for libertarian thinking. Its philosophical consistency gave Cato a nonpartisan feel. It was quite critical of the Reagan administration both on foreign policy (Cato was noninterventionist) and in the domestic sphere (Reagan-era spending, particularly on the military, was still far too high for the taste of Cato's scholars). In 1980, David Koch joined the Libertarian Party ticket led by oil executive Ed Crane. Since the Supreme Court had ruled that candidates for office could spend as much on their own campaigns as they wished, running for vice president freed Koch from any limits on his contributions to the Libertarian campaign.

The Koch brothers' centrality to so many forms of libertarian philanthropy in the 1970s led their critics to dub them "the Koch-topus," a term Brian Doherty, the leading historian of the movement, mocked as referring to "a supposedly strangling, controlling monster of multiple limbs." In his book *Radicals for Capitalism*, Doherty noted that the Kochs, working closely with Ed Crane (he had been Ed Clark's campaign manager and served for many years as president of Cato) were the primary funders of not only Cato and the Libertarian Party, but also of two impressively edited magazines, *Inquiry* and the *Libertarian Review*. They also financed Students for a Libertarian Society, a group that sought to capture some of the feel of the sixties New Left's Students for a Democratic Society, and many other libertarian enterprises. Crane came in for his share of criticism, too. When libertarian dissidents were not criticizing the Koch-topus, they were attacking the "Crane machine."

In light of the Koch brothers' subsequent history, this period is fascinating because it marked a time when libertarians saw an opening on the *left* side of the political spectrum, a strategy the Koch's were underwriting. *Inquiry*, for example, drew on the adversary culture of the left, included many liberal-leaning writers in its pages, and emphasized libertarian issues—from civil liberties to social liberalism to noninterventionism in foreign policy—that appealed to progressives. For a time, libertarians believed that their path to power (or, since they were libertarians, to *dismantling* state power) passed through an alliance with the individualist currents on the left.

This strategy had the potential of working on particular issues. But given the devotion of liberals to regulation and the welfare state, it was bound to be a dead end, as the Koch brothers came to realize. Over time, they moved toward alliances with like-minded Republicans, not only libertarian purists such as Ron Paul but also top political figures such as Dick Armey, the House majority leader under Newt Gingrich. In the 1990s, Koch-allied organizations fought the Clinton administration on regulatory issues, energy policy, and health care.

That the Kochs' fortune came from oil put them in a long tradition of right-wing funders: in American history, the extractive industries were almost always allied with the right, even when they received substantial benefits from government. This alliance was strengthened in the George W. Bush years, when large parts of the administration's energy program, its authorship overseen by a task force led by Vice President Dick Cheney, amounted to the oil and gas industry's wish list. Fearing a backlash against the administration's ties to Big Oil, Cheney and Bush's aides fought to keep the task force's deliberations secret. A 2007 *Washington Post* report confirmed what the critics had suspected: the task force had, indeed, relied heavily on officials of the major energy companies for advice.

With Obama's election, the Koch infrastructure and Koch dollars were there to take the lead in organizing the opposition. In the summer of 2010,

New Yorker writer Jane Mayer made the Kochs famous (much to their dismay) by chronicling the central role played by Koch-supported groups in lending logistical and financial support to the Tea Party insurrection. The town-meeting strategy in the summer of 2009 would have been impossible absent the backing of well-financed groups such as FreedomWorks, headed by Armey, and the Koch-organized Americans for Prosperity.

Mayer described a visit to Washington by David Koch "to attend a triumphant Americans for Prosperity gathering." From the Kochs' point of view, she wrote, it was a heady time:

> Obama's poll numbers were falling fast. Not a single Republican senator was working with the Administration on health care, or much else. Pundits were writing about Obama's political ineptitude, and Tea Party groups were accusing the President of initiating "a government takeover." In a speech, Koch said: "Days like today bring to reality the vision of our board of directors when we started this organization, five years ago. . . . Thankfully, the stirrings from California to Virginia, and from Texas to Michigan, show that more and more of our fellow-citizens are beginning to see the same truths as we do."

She quoted David Axelrod, Obama's senior adviser, in frustration over media coverage of the Tea Party that tended to overlook the sources of its financing. "What they don't say," Axelrod observed, "is that, in part, this is a grassroots citizens' movement brought to you by a bunch of oil billionaires."

Charles and David Koch, thanks to Mayer's article and subsequent attacks on them from Democrats, became the most visible symbols of the new conservative money machine. But they were by no means alone, and it was not only liberals who were calling attention to their role in transforming the right. Writing in *Foreign Affairs* magazine, Frum described the rise of a group he called "The Radical Rich."

Who were they? One of them was the venture capitalist Tom Perkins. He had written for the *Wall Street Journal* "from the epicenter of progressive thought, San Francisco" about "the parallels of fascist Nazi Germany to its war on its 'one percent,' namely its Jews, to the progressive war on the American one percent, namely the 'rich.'"

Perkins was not the only wealthy American offering Nazi analogies. As

Frum noted, the financier Stephen Schwartzman "equated Obama's attempt to raise taxes on hedge funds with Adolph Hitler's invasion of Poland," while Kenneth Langone, one of Home Depot's cofounders, "warned that liberal arguments about income inequality reminded him of Nazi propaganda."

The radical language reflected radical views. Mitt Romney's "gaffe" about 47 percent of the country falling into a hopeless dependency on government, Frum argued, was not a gaffe at all. "Wealthy Republicans had been talking that way all through the Obama years," he said. During the 2012 campaign, "the radicalization of Republican donors propelled the party to advocate policies that were more extreme than anything seen since Barry Goldwater's 1964 campaign."

"One would normally expect wealthy Republicans to value predictability and stability," Frum concluded. "But if they perceive their country to be predictably and stably hurtling toward socialist oppression, then even the richest will demand massive resistance by any means necessary."

Americans wearing Revolutionary War costumes and shouting about the president's birth certificate did not build the Tea Party all by themselves. Earnest, less flamboyant middle-class ideologues who were persuaded that liberty was under threat were not alone, either. A radicalized conservatism also had support—essential support—from wealthy, highly successful Americans just as intent on taking their country rightward.

There were, finally, more subtle ideological and demographic changes that scrambled received wisdom about the forces at work on the right.

For decades, the conservative movement was easily enough described as a coalition of free-market advocates, including libertarians, social traditionalists, and anticommunists. The great achievement of Buckley, *National Review*, and Frank Meyer's "fusionism," as we've seen, was to patch together an ideology that held these forces together in one movement. But fusionism was always in jeopardy of flying apart. The libertarian revolt of the 1970s reflected the impatience of free-market advocates who shared neither a belief in tradition nor faith in the foreign-policy interventionism that the robust anticommunists demanded. And many of the traditionalists did not share the near-absolute faith in capitalism that animated the economic conservatives. Russell Kirk, traditionalism's great expositor and defender, could be disdainful of this view. "Conservatism is something more than mere solicitude for tidy incomes," he wrote, and he insisted that "economic self-interest is ridiculously inadequate to hold an economic system together, and even less adequate to preserve order." Some of these tensions emerged again in the debate over compassionate conservatism.

Free enterprise and anticommunism were the dominant keys of Goldwaterism, even if the themes of the controversial campaign film "Choice" and some of Goldwater's own speeches offered hints of a strong strain of traditionalism just below the surface of his movement. It was not until the late 1970s that traditionalism got a strong mass base and organizational muscle with the rise of the religious right.

The new religious movement was, first and foremost, a reaction against the gains of social liberalism in the 1960s and a cry of protest from parts of America that felt disrespected and ignored by cultural and coastal elites. At a minimum, these white evangelical Christians wanted respect and acknowledgment. "The religious person is entitled, if not to prevail, at least to be heard," the conservative writer Terry Eastland insisted in 1981. These Christians were enraged by liberal victories in the 1960s and 1970s across a broad front: Supreme Court decisions banning prescribed prayer in public schools, new legal tolerance for pornography, and the *Roe v. Wade* decision legalizing abortion (although many evangelicals were, early on, far less hostile to the decision than Catholics). The sociologist Nathan Glazer captured the spirit of the new religious conservatives well in a 1982 essay. The religious right, he wrote, "may be on the offensive, but it is, if I may use the phrase, a 'defensive offensive,' meant to get us back to, at worse, the 1950s, and even that is beyond the hopes, or I would think the power, of Fundamentalist faith." On the other hand, viewed from the point of view of progressives trying to preserve victories for civil rights, women's rights, and social tolerance, pushing the country back to the 1950s seemed a very aggressive move indeed.

The religious right was not simply a spontaneous eruption. Leaders of the conservative movement were searching in the 1970s for ways to mobilize new voters—and to split off constituencies from the old New Deal coalition. "The

New Right is looking for issues that people care about," said Paul Weyrich, a major movement figure who was one of the founders of the Heritage Foundation. "Social issues, at least for the present, fit the bill."

The Supreme Court's *Roe v. Wade* decision legalizing abortion angered many Catholics and mobilized the Catholic hierarchy. Working-class Catholics had begun to defect from the Democrats in substantial numbers in the 1950s, returned en masse to John F. Kennedy in 1960, largely stuck with Lyndon Johnson in 1964, but began defecting again in 1968. In 1972, Richard Nixon narrowly defeated George McGovern among Catholics. The *Roe* decision created new reasons for them to view the Republicans warmly. The conservative political class was ready to encourage them and sought to link conservative Catholics and conservative evangelicals in common cause. In 2004, Bush engaged in an unprecedented effort to target conservative Catholics on social issues alongside white evangelicals.

The sense of cultural isolation felt by evangelicals and fundamentalists went back to the *Scopes* trial of the 1920s. Most of them supported Franklin Roosevelt and the New Deal, but FDR ushered in a quiet social revolution that saw power shift to Catholics, Jews, and the big cities, whose cultural preoccupations could hardly have been more distant from the rural and small-town ethos revered by theologically conservative Protestants. The Supreme Court's decision ending prescribed prayer in public schools had a particular resonance because while the prayers were typically nondenominational, they tended to reflect the country's Protestant origins. The end of public school prayer was another signal that Protestant civic influence was on the decline.

More generally, religious conservatives sensed that religion was being pushed out of public life by increasingly influential secular forces, creating what Rev. Richard John Neuhaus, the progressive-turned-conservative, famously called *The Naked Public Square*, the title of his influential 1984 book. Day-to-day culture was changing, too, most visible to tens of millions in the move on network television from celebrations of traditional domesticity such as *Leave It to Beaver* or *Father Knows Best* to more daring offerings. In many localities, social conservatives invoked the language of the New Left about controlling the decisions that affected their own lives by demanding that school textbooks, written by academics far away and published by big publishers in major cities, be replaced with volumes sensitive to their own values.

In many places, the religious conservatives who started out as a pressure group became integrated as part of regular Republican organizations, something Karl Rove was acutely aware of when he planned both of Bush's campaigns.

The religious right caused such commotion in the 1970s and 1980s that it is often ignored how many of the voters whom it motivated to pledge allegiance to the Republican Party had already made their first moves to the GOP (in their voting behavior if not always their formal party affiliations) in the 1960s—and in some cases, back in the late 1940s and 1950s. A large share of the energy on the religious right came from white southerners who began voting Republican in 1964, or for segregationist third parties in 1948 or 1960, in reaction to civil rights. The followers of Jerry Falwell and later Pat Robertson were the same sorts of voters that Rusher and de Toledano had targeted when they imagined a conservative majority.

An episode in the 1970s underscored that among white southern conservatives, race and religion were not always easily separated. The *Brown v. Board of Education* decision in 1954 desegregating southern schools led to the creation of private schools, popularly known as "segregation academies," for white students fleeing multiracial classrooms. In one of the many ironies associated with Richard Nixon's administration, the attack on their tax status began during his presidency. Robert Finch, a progressive Republican who was secretary of the Department of Health, Education and Welfare for seventeen months under Nixon, announced in January 1970 that he would ask the Treasury Department to end these schools' tax exemptions.

Nixon was characteristically ambivalent. His first reaction, as the historian Joseph Crespino notes in his fine account of the controversy, was impatience with the often liberal Finch. "Tell him to do the right thing for a change," Nixon told his aide John Ehrlichman. "Whites in Mississippi can't send their kids to schools that are 90 percent black; they've got to set up private schools."

But Nixon eventually relented and ordered the Internal Revenue Service to follow Finch's approach. The issue kicked around for several years and did not come to a head until August 1978, when the IRS during Jimmy Carter's presidency laid out clear guidelines ordering a review of the tax status of schools that "were formed or substantially expanded at or about the time of desegregation of public school" and had "an insignificant number of minority students." The reaction among conservative (white) Christians, Crespino noted, "bordered on the apoplectic." An attack on segregation was cast as an assault on Christian education. The IRS battle, said Richard Viguerie, the New Right leader and direct mail maestro, "kicked the sleeping dog. It galvanized the religious right. It was the spark that ignited the religious right's involvement in real politics." Weyrich said the move "shattered the Christian community's notion that Christians could isolate themselves inside their own institutions and teach what they pleased."

Reagan seized on the issue in the 1980 campaign. In a January speech at Bob Jones University—then fighting the IRS for having lifted its tax exemption because of the school's ban on interracial dating—Reagan called for "a spiritual revival" and denounced "the evil character of racial quotas." The 1980 Republican platform pledged to "halt the unconstitutional regulatory vendetta launched by Mr. Carter's IRS commissioner against independent schools," ignoring, as Crespino noted, that it was the Nixon administration that had set the whole process in motion.

The episode certainly does not prove that the religious right was simply cover for an older politics of segregation. Many of the Christian conservatives were, indeed, animated by other questions, from abortion to school prayer. But the battle over the Christian academies does underscore how often reactions connected to race were linked with other forms of social conservatism. It helps explain why white southerners and African-Americans who typically shared similar Christian religious commitments and conservative social and theological views divided sharply at election time. Particularly (though not exclusively) in the Deep South, issues connected to civil rights and racial equality remained the decisive questions.

The interaction between race and other forms of social conservatism is also instructive for what would happen in the Obama years. The subject of race and Obama has been discussed with both excessive delicacy and sweeping certainty. It's obviously not true that all or even most opposition to Obama could be explained by race, given that so many of the same groups and individuals who voted against and at times loathed Barack Obama had also voted against and at times loathed Bill Clinton. Ideology mattered most. But there can be no denying that racial feeling played an important role in explaining opposition to Obama—and in the conservative ideology that many of these voters held. And it's clear that particularly in the South and across Appalachia, a significant number of whites who had been open to other Democrats opposed Obama because he is black.

The *New York Times* published what would become a famous map showing which counties had become more Democratic between 2004 and 2008, and which had become more Republican. Not surprisingly, given Obama's substantial victory, he ran ahead of John Kerry in 78 percent of the nation's counties. But the 22 percent of American counties where he ran behind Kerry, the *Times* noted, "tended to be lower income, less educated, more rural, less diverse, and Southern." The map portrayed what some Democrats took to calling "the red slash." It was the grouping of counties that defied the national trend by shifting Republican between the two elections. The slash started in western Pennsylvania, worked its way through West Virginia, eastern Kentucky, much of Tennessee, and northern Alabama. It took in almost all of Arkansas, large parts of Louisiana and Oklahoma, and many counties in northern and eastern Texas. The cultural feel of red slash counties was captured by this statistic: in 1,173 counties, Obama received 10 percentage points or more of the vote than John Kerry did, and these counties were only 6 percent Southern Baptist; but in the 225 counties where Obama ran 10 percentage points or more behind Kerry, 32 percent were Southern Baptist.

Nationwide, Obama captured 43 percent of the white vote, but in Louisiana his share was only 14 percent; in Mississippi, 11 percent; and in Alabama, 10 percent. David Bositis, senior political analyst at the Joint Center for Political and Economic Studies, noted to the *Times'* Adam Nossiter that the 18 percent share of whites that voted for John Kerry in Alabama was almost cut in half for Mr. Obama. "There's no other explanation than race," he said.

There can also be no denying that the racial attitudes of Tea Party supporters are distinctive. In April 2010, a *New York Times*/CBS News poll designed to study the Tea Party phenomenon asked a classic survey question designed to gauge racial attitudes: "In recent years, do you think too much has been made of the problems facing black people, too little has been made, or is it about right?" Among those who were not Tea Party loyalists, only 19 percent said "too much." But among Tea Party supporters, 52 percent said "too much."

As important as the direct effect of race on politics was the growing interaction between racial, cultural, and economic conservatism. This is why efforts to explain the Tea Party as a new, more libertarian alternative to the religious right were mistaken. It's true that the public issues on which the Tea Party focused most were the bank bailout, Obamacare, rising deficits, "big government" in the abstract, the centralization of power in Washington, and the need for a return to "constitutional government." But as Skocpol and Williamson's research showed, opposition to big government did not extend to two of the federal government's biggest programs, Medicare and Social Security, which disproportionately benefited the older voters who gravitated to the Tea Party. Moreover, the Tea Party's libertarianism did not extend to immigration. On the contrary, polls consistently showed that opposition to illegal immigration was one of the motivating issues for Tea Party supporters—and one of the central causes of its alienation from Bush.

Far from being an alternative to the religious right, the Tea Party was an overlapping form of political organization that gave voice to many of the same forms of social traditionalism that had animated followers of Jerry Falwell and Pat Robertson. A PRRI/Brookings Institution survey taken shortly before the 2010 elections made the overlap clear: fully 47 percent of those who identified as members of the Tea Party said they also considered themselves part of the religious conservative movement. The overlap was even greater when it came to specific issues on which Tea Party members were conservative, not libertarian: 63 percent said abortion should be illegal in all or most cases, and only 19 percent supported gay marriage. Some 55 percent of Tea Party supporters said they considered America a "Christian nation," compared with 42 percent of the general population. Among all Americans, 48 percent said that immigrants were a burden on the country "because they take jobs, housing and health care"; among Tea Party supporters, 65 percent said this.

There were moments during the Tea Party rebellion when the overlap of conservatism, race, and nativism was stark. At a 2010 Tea Party meeting, former representative Tom Tancredo of Colorado drew cheers when he declared that in the 2008 election, "something really odd happened, mostly because I think that we do not have a civics literacy test before people can vote in this country. People who could not even spell the word 'vote,' or say it in English, put a committed socialist ideologue in the White House, name is Barack Hussein Obama." Rarely has a politician strung together so many resentments so economically. Tancredo's mention of literacy tests, the phony devices developed in the Jim Crow years to disenfranchise African-American voters in the South, brought a certain brand of conservative politics full circle.

★

Consider the political and social changes (and shocks) since the rise of the Goldwater movement. They include the increasing ideological homogeneity of the Republican Party, the country's growing racial and ethnic diversity, the rising cultural fears of older white voters, the political mobilization of conservative Christians, the expansion of a new conservative media, the shift of business rightward, the collapse of restrictions on big money in politics, the growing influence of the "radical rich," widespread popular frustration after two long and inconclusive wars, and an economic collapse that made the nation's foundations tremble. Any one of these would have shaken politics. Taken together, they guaranteed a political explosion on the right. It was all the more powerful because of the disillusionment at the end of the Bush years.

The politics of disappointment and betrayal meant that a young president who had pledged himself to ending divisions in the country between red and blue would be thwarted in his hopes and resisted with a ferocity that few fully anticipated. Most surprised of all, it seemed, was Barack Obama.

10

DREAMS OF CELESTIAL CHOIRS

Barack Obama Hopes, but the GOP Doesn't Change

"Maybe I've just lived a little long, but I have no illusions about
how hard this will be. You are not going to wave a magic wand."

Barack Obama rose to sudden national prominence because he painted an
eloquent verbal portrait of the United States that most Americans—the vast
majority outside the ranks of the Republican right—wanted to believe was
a mirror. For some months after the attacks of 9/11, the country had experienced a degree of national unity unknown since World War II and the
immediate postwar period. Obama was telling the country that this period
of shared determination and mutual respect reflected who we really are. Our
nation, he insisted, was far less divided than the media suggested, and we were
far less hostile to each other than manipulative politicians trying to mobilize
their core constituencies wanted us to believe.

Romanticizing the present is no less common than romanticizing the
past. It can't be forgotten that a view of the 1950s as a quiet, consensual
time leaves out a great deal. It sweeps aside McCarthyism, which sought to

marginalize many liberals and all of the left—an approach to politics that lived on long after Joe McCarthy's 1954 censure by the Senate. The 1950s saw the first glimmerings of a dissenting sensibility that would blossom in the 1960s into a counterculture and new engagements with civil rights and women's rights. The civil rights movement, after all, might be said to have commenced its long march on December 1, 1955, when Rosa Parks refused to give up her seat on a Montgomery, Alabama, bus. It found its voice four days later when a twenty-six-year-old pastor named Martin Luther King Jr. rose in the Dexter Avenue Baptist Church to declare that "there comes a time when people get tired of being trampled over by the iron feet of oppression." The Beat Generation went "On the Road" in rebellion against the proprieties of an era that publicly revered religion, the nuclear family, and the virtues of a quiet domestic life. Mainstream critiques of conformity—*The Man in the Gray Flannel Suit, The Lonely Crowd, The Organization Man, The Status Seekers*—also planted the seeds of revolt. And, of course, a new conservatism found a powerful voice when *National Review* published its first issue in the same year that Rose Parks refused to move.

Nonetheless, every era has its tensions, and there is much truth in Arthur Schlesinger Jr.'s elegant summary of the conventional wisdom on the Eisenhower years as a time when conflict went to sleep. "Where his predecessors had roused the people, he soothed them," Schlesinger wrote at the end of Ike's term. "[W]here they had defined issues sharply, he blurred them over." The distinguished historian who was championing John F. Kennedy's presidential candidacy offered his summation of Eisenhower's accomplishments with some impatience but a certain grudging respect for the historical role he had played. "The nation needed an interval of repose to restore its psychological balance," Schlesinger wrote, "and repose was what President Eisenhower gave them."

It was Barack Obama's peculiar role, and the central contradiction of his political promise, that he, too, wanted to soothe the nation while also championing a new era of change and reform. In a sense, he wanted to be Eisenhower and Kennedy at the same time—and, at that, to be even more of a change agent than Kennedy set out to be.

It was first as a soothing presence that he entered the national consciousness on the evening of July 27, 2004, when he offered the Keynote Address to the Democratic National Convention that would send John Kerry into battle against George W. Bush. At that point, Obama was only a state senator from Chicago's South Side. He would not win his seat in the United States Senate until the fall. Not since Ronald Reagan gave "The Speech" in 1964 has a single address accomplished so much for a politician. Just as conservatives and Republicans across the country knew from the moment they saw Reagan on an October night in 1964 that he was destined to be their leader, so did millions of progressives and Democrats suddenly decide that evening that they had discovered a national savior of their own.

The speech was remarkable because it offered its own romantic hope for national unity at a time of deep division—even as it reflected the nation's jangling discords. It was an unapologetically partisan address on behalf of Kerry's presidential candidacy, yet its main theme was how much the country longed to put partisan and ideological fractures behind it. Obama simultaneously sharpened the lines of distinction with Bush's Republican Party and dismissed the philosophical and cultural differences that had set Americans against one another.

In light of how deep the nation's divisions remained more than a decade after Obama gave his speech, it's useful to revisit exactly why it resonated at the time. Early on, he offered a classic progressive view of the costs of inequality to Americans who had once counted on middle-class jobs at middle-class wages. Obama, like Reagan, used stories and concrete examples as his materials to paint an ideologically congenial portrait of the country:

> Fellow Americans, Democrats, Republicans, independents, I say to you, tonight, we have more work to do for the workers I met in Galesburg, Illinois, who are losing their union jobs at the Maytag plant that's moving to Mexico, and now they're having to compete with their own children for jobs that pay seven bucks an hour; more to do for the father I met who was losing his job and choking back the tears wondering how he would pay $4,500 a month for the drugs his son needs without the health benefits that he counted on; more to do for the young woman in East St. Louis, and thousands more like her who have the grades, have the drive, have the will, but doesn't have the money to go to college.

But Obama was well aware of the natural response of Republicans to such rhetoric: to claim that Democrats assumed the need for government plans and programs to remedy the situations of each of these citizens, and millions like them. He thus offered a kind of pre-rebuttal, dismissing the attack before it was launched:

> Now, don't get me wrong, the people I meet in small towns and big cities and diners and office parks, they don't expect government to solve all of their problems. They know they have to work hard to get ahead. And they want to. Go into the collar counties around Chicago, and people will tell you: they don't want their tax money wasted by a welfare agency or by the Pentagon. Go into any inner-city neighborhood, and folks will tell you that government alone can't teach kids to learn.
>
> They know that parents have to teach, that children can't achieve unless we raise their expectations and turn off the television sets and eradicate the slander that says a black youth with a book is acting white. They know those things.

Having dismissed the straw man that Democrats always defaulted to government solutions, he then insisted that government did, indeed, have the wherewithal to ease the nation's burdens. "People don't expect government to solve all their problems," he declared. "But they sense, deep in their bones, that with just a slight change in priorities, we can make sure that every child in America has a decent shot at life and that the doors of opportunity remain open to all. They know we can do better. And they want that choice." Nothing radical here: "just a slight change in priorities" would do the trick.

The lead-in to Obama's famous peroration on behalf of national unity was an assault on the Bush-Rove shameful designs. "Now even as we speak," he said, "there are those who are preparing to divide us, the spin masters and negative ad peddlers who embrace the politics of anything goes." Obama wanted to divide the country between the dividers and everybody else. And then came the words that electrified the country:

> Well, I say to them tonight, there's not a liberal America and a conservative America; there's the United States of America.

There's not a black America and white America and Latino America and Asian America; there's the United States of America.

The pundits, the pundits like to slice and dice our country into red states and blue states: red states for Republicans, blue states for Democrats. But I've got news for them, too. We worship an awesome God in the blue states, and we don't like federal agents poking around our libraries in the red states.

We coach Little League in the blue states and, yes, we've got some gay friends in the red states.

There are patriots who opposed the war in Iraq, and there are patriots who supported the war in Iraq.

We are one people, all of us pledging allegiance to the stars and stripes, all of us defending the United States of America.

In the end, that's what this election is about. Do we participate in a politics of cynicism, or do we participate in a politics of hope?

If the effect of the speech on Obama's career was similar to that of Reagan's on his own trajectory forty years earlier, their respective tactical and emotional purposes were very different. Reagan had intentionally drawn sharp ideological lines—the goal, he said, was to stop "the advance of socialism in the United States," an objective he associated with Lyndon Johnson's Democrats. Reagan wanted to disturb the peace and shake the consensus, precisely because the consensus of the time supported New Deal liberalism.

Obama, by contrast, wanted to reestablish consensus and restore national unity. He saw the nation's divisions over cultural questions and national security as fodder for Republican exploitation and sensed that, if left to itself, the nation's cultural trajectory—"we've got some gay friends in the red states"— would eventually head in a moderately liberal direction. Obama sought to turn Rove's strategy on its head: if the country were united culturally and patriotically, voters like the Maytag worker and the young woman who wanted to go to college would cast ballots in their own economic interests for progressives.

The keynote was the beginning of a four-year effort by Obama to push back against forms of polarization that had empowered the right and weakened the left. Especially notable was his understanding of how liberals and Democrats had alienated themselves from many religious voters, a view reflected in his 2006 speech to the "Call to Renewal" conference of progressive religious leaders. His approach was not so much to attack the religious right as to undercut its appeal by realigning liberal attitudes toward faith.

There were, he said, "some liberals who dismiss religion in the public square as inherently irrational or intolerant, insisting on a caricature of religious Americans that paints them as fanatical, or thinking that the very word 'Christian' describes one's political opponents, not people of faith." After describing his own religious awakening, Obama instructed his allies that "if we truly hope to speak to people where they're at—to communicate our hopes and values in a way that's relevant to their own—then as progressives, we cannot abandon the field of religious discourse."

He argued that "the discomfort of some progressives with any hint of religion has often prevented us from effectively addressing issues in moral terms" and said flatly that "secularists are wrong when they ask believers to leave their religion at the door before entering into the public square."

Obama was not about to alienate liberals and was careful to call on conservatives "to understand the critical role that the separation of church and state has played in preserving not only our democracy, but the robustness of our religious practice." He added: "Whatever we once were, we are no longer just a Christian nation; we are also a Jewish nation, a Muslim nation, a Buddhist nation, a Hindu nation, and a nation of nonbelievers."

But the thrust of Obama's speech was a call for progressives to engage not simply with religion in general, but with the most theologically conservative among their fellow citizens. "If we don't reach out to evangelical Christians and other religious Americans and tell them what we stand for," he said, "then the Jerry Falwells and Pat Robertsons and Alan Keyeses will continue to hold sway."

If religion was one element of the polarizing dynamic that Obama proposed to detoxify, his very identity promised to "turn the page" on the even more vexing problem of racial division. A man of biracial origins who chose to identify himself as black, Obama embodied the very struggle that had torn the nation apart from the time of the arrival of the first African slaves in Jamestown, Virginia, in 1619. Obama could speak a new language on race, which in fact harkened back to the unifying language of civil rights Christianity, which was a multiracial and hopeful creed. Obama's emphasis on hope, his talk of struggle, organizing, and movement-building, his repeated invocations of "the fierce urgency of now"—all openly echoed the vocabulary of a civil rights cause steeped in the Scriptures. In particular, he tended to invoke Martin Luther King Jr.'s most conciliatory themes, not the side of the great civil rights leader capable of expressing great anger over injustice. In trying to move the racial dialogue forward, Obama was drawing it back to a time when so many pastors and rank-and-file believers successfully allied with liberalism.

It was the combination of Obama's acute sensitivity to the promise and the power of civil rights Christianity combined with the country's yearning for a new departure that gave his campaign the feel of a religious revival. In his "Change We Can Believe In" slogan, the word "believe" was at least as important as the word "change."

Obama constantly returned to the paradoxical reality of race in America— exceptional progress combined with continuing discrimination and injustice. "To think clearly about race," he wrote in his pre-campaign book *The Audacity of Hope* in 2006, "requires us to see the world on a split screen—to maintain in our sights the kind of America that we want, while looking squarely at America as it is, to acknowledge the sins of our past and the challenges of the present without becoming trapped in cynicism or despair."

It is an irony that a politician who would find such as large share of the white working class (particularly in the South) opposing him engaged in an ongoing effort to link the struggles of African-Americans and Latinos with those of disadvantaged whites. "These days," he wrote in his book, "what ails working-class and middle-class blacks and Latinos is not fundamentally different from what ails their white counterparts: downsizing, outsourcing, automation, wage stagnation, the dismantling of employer-based health-care and pension plans, and schools that fail to teach young people the skills they need to compete in a global economy." Obama's relentless focus on economics was more successful than is often allowed. In key states such as Ohio, Pennsylvania, and Michigan, he won enough white working-class votes to win in both 2008 and 2012.

Also ironic (painfully so) in light of Obama's multiracial approach to politics was the storm over old sermons from Jeremiah Wright, the pastor who had converted him to Christianity, that emerged in the midst of the primary battle. The very title of Obama's book came from a Wright sermon and Obama had been open about a relationship with Wright that seemed defined by a father-son bond that Obama never had with his natural father. The anti-American anger of some of Wright's comments from his pulpit that ABC News broadcast reflected sentiments utterly at odds with the civil rights Christianity that Obama was preaching. All of them came to be summarized by a single statement by Wright that no candidate for president could be associated with. "God damn America!" Wright had shouted after describing a long string of American injustices and misdeeds.

Obama eventually put the controversy behind him by resorting to what had always been his secret weapon: carefully wrought eloquence in a speech he delivered on March 18, 2008, at the National Constitution Center in Philadelphia. He criticized Wright for having a "profoundly distorted view of this country—a view that sees white racism as endemic, and that elevates what is wrong with America above all that we know is right with America." And he went back to his patented dualism, speaking of "the complexities of race in this country that we've never worked through—a part of our union that we've yet to perfect."

Yet Obama also sought to be true to a kind of secular ministry he had undertaken of explaining black America to white America. There was, he said, a powerful anger in the black community rooted in "memories of humiliation and doubt" that "may not get expressed in public, in front of white co-workers or white friends" but "does find voice in the barbershop or the beauty shop or around the kitchen table. . . . And occasionally it finds voice in the church on Sunday morning, in the pulpit and in the pews."

He declined to disown Wright entirely, saying, "I can no more disown him than I can my white grandmother." But when Wright reemerged on April 28 at the National Press Club and offered even more incendiary comments, including praise for Louis Farrakhan, the Nation of Islam leader, Obama did have to break with him decisively. He pronounced Wright's new statements "outrageous" and "ridiculous."

At the time, I interviewed Obama about the Wright matter and we discussed how Wright's comments were not all that far from angry comments King had made toward the end of his life about the Vietnam War. At his own

Ebenezer Baptist Church in Atlanta on February 4, 1968, King had declared: "God didn't call America to engage in a senseless, unjust war. . . . And we are criminals in that war. We've committed more war crimes almost than any nation in the world, and I'm going to continue to say it. And we won't stop it because of our pride and our arrogance as a nation. But God has a way of even putting nations in their place." King, not unlike Wright, predicted the Almighty's response: "And if you don't stop your reckless course, I'll rise up and break the backbone of your power."

The later King, of course, was also reflecting the disillusionment that had set in after the great hopefulness of the early civil rights years, and he also spoke after the rise of the Black Power movement. In our conversation, Obama made the key historical point that Wright began his career at the pulpit not in the early, upbeat civil rights times, but after the emergence of Black Power and Black Liberation Theology. Wright's angrier tone reflected his formative period. Obama, by contrast, was trying to restore something closer to the old hopefulness of the early 1960s. It represented not a "post-racial" politics that so many touted at the time, but an approach that reflected both the gains the African-American community had made and the troubles it still faced—a politics of racial complexity.

Just how complex was the task Obama was undertaking? At the midpoint of the Wright controversy, on April 6, a recording emerged of comments he had made at what was supposed to be an off-the-record fund-raiser in San Francisco on April 6. The full quotation matters. He said:

> You go into some of these small towns in Pennsylvania, and like a lot of small towns in the Midwest, the jobs have been gone now for twenty-five years and nothing's replaced them. Each successive administration has said that some-how these communities are gonna regenerate and they have not. *So it's not surprising that they get bitter, they cling to guns or religion* or antipathy to people who aren't like them, or anti-immigrant sentiment or anti-trade sentiment as a way to explain their frustrations.

Not surprisingly, the italicized words made big news. The Hillary Clinton campaign used them in its ongoing and successful effort to rally white working-class voters to her side in the later primaries. But they have been used ever since to paint Obama as elitist and out of touch. The irony is that the statement taken whole was a perfect reflection of Obama's analysis of American politics going back to his keynote speech, his "Call to Renewal" address, and his response to Jeremiah Wright: that the white working class had been shortchanged and responded by embracing various forms of social conservatism to protest its conditions. The implication of his argument was that progressives needed to remedy the economic problems that had unleashed the backlash if they wanted the country to move beyond it. But this is not how the quotation looked or sounded—and, to Obama's detriment, it also made him seem distant and detached from the people he was analyzing. That he was "explaining" the white working class to a group of wealthy San Francisco liberals did not help his cause, even if he had made a large part of his political living since 2004 trying to explain different groups of Americans to each other. It says something about race and politics that for many it was easier to accept his explaining African-Americans to whites than to countenance his efforts to explain the white working class to the privileged. The word "cling" didn't help matters.

That these mishaps did not derail Obama in 2008 accounts for his confidence that he could keep his promise to bring red and blue together. He believed—and his victory, with the largest percentage of the popular vote won by a Democrat since 1964, ratified his belief—that he had found the formulas for drawing in not only the Democratic base but also many voters with rather conservative social and religious views.

His own experience taught him that he was good at reaching out to the right. After all, he was elected as the first African-American president of the *Harvard Law Review* with conservative votes. Bradford Berenson, who worked in the Bush White House and was on the law review with Obama, explained to PBS's *Frontline* that at the time, "conservatives were eager to have somebody who would treat them fairly, who would listen to what they had to say, who would not abuse the powers of the office to favor his ideological soul mates and punish those who had different views."

Ultimately, Berenson said, "the conservatives on the review supported Barack as president in the final rounds of balloting because he fit that bill far better than the other people who were running." In the intense environment of the law review, its members got to know each other very well. "You know who the people are who are blinded by their politics," Berenson said. "And you know who the people are who, despite their politics, can reach across and be friendly to and make friends with folks who have different views. And Barack very much fell into the latter category."

Obama was convinced that what he had done at the *Harvard Law Review*, as well as in Illinois Senate, he could do in Washington, D.C.

He thus ran as someone who was at once unifying and transformational. He would bring the country together and still manage to push through profound social and economic changes. The tension within Obama's approach was visible throughout the 2008 campaign and would become problematic once he took office. But it helped him in the primaries by allowing him to campaign simultaneously to Clinton's right *and* left. He could declare himself free of the taint of the political polarization of the Clinton 1990s and insist on his ability to work happily with conservatives and Republicans. Yet he won support from the left for his opposition to the Iraq War, and he unabashedly cast himself as the progressives' answer to Ronald Reagan.

"I think Ronald Reagan changed the trajectory of America in a way that Richard Nixon did not and in a way Bill Clinton did not," he told the *Reno Journal-Gazette* in March 2008. "He put us on a fundamentally different path because the country was ready for it. . . . I think he tapped into what people were already feeling. Which is: we want clarity, we want optimism, we want a return to that sense of dynamism and entrepreneurship that has been missing." The reference to Hillary Clinton's husband did not go unnoticed.

But Clinton got her licks in against Obama and by the end of the primaries, she had fought him to a draw in the popular vote. A comment she made in Toledo, Ohio, on February 24, 2008, captured her skepticism about what Obama was promising. Her words dripped with sarcasm, but they proved prophetic.

"I could stand up here and say: let's just get everybody together, let's get unified," Clinton said. "The sky will open, the light will come down, celestial choirs will be singing, and everyone will know that we should do the right thing, and the world would be perfect."

She added: "Maybe I've just lived a little long, but I have no illusions about how hard this will be. You are not going to wave a magic wand."

★

The excitement of an Obama-Clinton contest that ran right to the end of the primary season allowed Democrats to dominate the public imagination for the first six months of 2008. But it was not simply the historic nature of their confrontation that commanded popular and media attention. Widespread popular disaffection with the Republican Party at the end of the Bush years created a large enthusiasm gap between the two parties. When the primaries ended, Obama had won 17.8 million votes, Clinton 17.7 million. John McCain, the eventual Republican victor, won nearly half of the votes cast in the Republican primaries, but his total reached only 9.9 million.

The paradox of the 2008 contest for the Republican nomination was that while it ended in the nomination of the premier GOP dissident, the flow of the campaign itself would demonstrate the power of right-wing issues and constituents. John McCain won because the more conservative candidates systematically destroyed each other. Yet even in victory, McCain was ultimately forced to bow to forces on the right wing of his party. Thus did he turn Sarah Palin into a national figure.

At the outset, the GOP had an unusual opportunity not only to shake free of Bush but to chart a new philosophical course. Since Vice President Dick Cheney had ruled himself out as a presidential candidate, the party's 2008 field was large and included candidates with records of defying various aspects of conservative orthodoxy. McCain, the original maverick who had dissented from many of Bush's economic policies, was the early favorite. Former New York City mayor Rudy Giuliani, a national hero after 9/11 who held views on social issues that put him on the left end of his party, was often cast as his principal challenger.

Mitt Romney, the former governor of Massachusetts, had allied with Ted Kennedy to get his state to adopt a sweeping health insurance program that would, over time, extend coverage to nearly everyone in his state. Senator Fred Thompson of Tennessee had worked for the famously conciliatory

Senate majority leader Howard Baker. And even the champion of the religious right, former Arkansas governor Mike Huckabee, was a dissenter from conservative economics who spoke of the obligations of Christians to the poor—Compassionate Conservatism Redux.

More than any candidate (other than Ron Paul, the perennial standard-bearer for libertarian Republicans), Huckabee distanced himself from Bush's Iraq policy, and he spoke proudly of his practical achievements as governor. "I'm unapologetic with the conservative evangelicals, and pro-life," he told me when I interviewed him in January 2007. "But if people look at my record, what they're going to see is that the focus of my time as governor was education reform . . . transportation [and] health initiatives." Huckabee's unusual mix of positions and his sunny disposition were strengths the punditocracy and Republican politicians largely underestimated. (It was a less sunny Huckabee who ran for the 2016 nomination. Reflecting perhaps a change in himself but certainly a change in the attitudes of the Republican electorate, he became much harsher—for example, declaring that Obama's nuclear deal with Iran "will take the Israelis and march them to the door of the oven.")

Yet over time, the 2008 Republican field adjusted itself to the reality of an increasingly conservative party. Romney, realizing where the opportunity in the race lay, abandoned the middle-of-the-road posture that had allowed him to win in Massachusetts and ran to McCain's right. So did Thompson, who entered the contest late. Huckabee, despite his independent-mindedness on certain questions, relied primarily on his strong base among the evangelical conservatives.

This left Giuliani and McCain as the two dissenters from orthodoxy. Yet in key respects, they were also the candidates most loyal to the central aspects of Bush's legacy. McCain was the standard-bearer of a neoconservative foreign policy and one of the stoutest defenders of the Iraq War. Giuliani was the symbol of the nation's resiliency after 9/11, and it was his campaign's calling card. "There's only three things he mentions in a sentence: a noun, a verb and 9/11," said Joe Biden, then a senator challenging Clinton and Obama for the Democratic nomination. The wicked line stung because it had the ring of truth. At times Giuliani ran as the moderate he had been, casting himself as the strongest candidate for general election. At other times he moved right, knowing where Republican primary votes lay.

From the beginning, McCain's second campaign for the presidency had a tragic quality. If his first run had been an unruly and joyous romp, the second was carefully planned and meticulously calculated. He very nearly organized and calculated himself out of the nomination.

McCain seemed constantly torn between his desire to resist the Republican powers that be and his need to appease dominant forces in the party. His efforts to pacify the right end of the party muddied his image as a heroic dissident but, in the early going at least, brought him little gain. And if McCain had suffered mightily during the 2000 primaries at the hands of George W. Bush's political operation, he was burdened eight years later by his loyalty to Bush on Iraq. If Bush destroyed McCain's candidacy by design the first time, he threatened to smother him by association the second.

Moreover, no matter how far McCain went to court, soothe, and pamper the right, many in its ranks simply couldn't abide him. He had spoken forcefully in 2000 for campaign finance reform and against "the demands of big-money special interests." The McCain-Feingold law was the largest step in decades toward reform of the campaign money system (before it was eviscerated in 2010 by the Supreme Court). McCain had condemned the "self-appointed" leaders of conservative groups and singled out Jerry Falwell and Pat Robertson as "agents of intolerance." At one point he had called Bush a "Pat Robertson Republican."

In deciding to make up with the president, McCain's chosen vehicle was Iraq, on which he genuinely viewed success in the same terms as the administration. He won over a share of Bush fund-raisers and some Bush operatives, but significant parts of the Bush political family went over to Romney, joining at least a few of McCain's 2000 enthusiasts.

McCain might instead have promised to "build a bigger Republican Party . . . by attracting new people to our cause with an appeal to the patriotism that unites us and the promise of a government that we can be proud of again." Thus spoke the maverick in 2000 in words almost perfectly suited for his party's plight in 2007 and 2008. But McCain made different choices—on principle about Iraq and by calculation for almost everything else. Like Bush, he decided not to challenge the party's drift right.

On July 10, 2007, McCain's campaign cracked up. Longtime adviser and confidant John Weaver and campaign manager Terry Nelson announced their departure, with McCain, as the *Washington Post* reported, expressing "dissatisfaction to his high command over what he regarded as mismanagement of operations and excessive spending in the face of weaker-than-projected fundraising." The impact of the bloodbath went deep. "A staff that once numbered about 120 is now down to about 50," the *Washington Post*'s Dan Balz and Anne Kornblut wrote.

The two main beneficiaries of McCain's decline were Romney and Giuliani. Romney hoped that he could win the Iowa caucuses, where he invested heavily, and supplant McCain as the favorite in New Hampshire, where he owned a summer home and was well-known because much of the state relied on Boston media. To establish his ideological purity, Romney borrowed and reworked a line that Democrat Howard Dean had, in turn, taken from the late Paul Wellstone. Romney declared that he represented "the Republican wing of the Republican Party." (At an October debate, McCain snapped back: "As we all know, when he ran for office in Massachusetts, being a Republican wasn't much of a priority.")

Giuliani stood to gain if McCain floundered because he would be seen as the logical next choice of the moderate and moderately conservative Republican voters, and Independents, too. And Thompson, who did not enter the race until September, thought he could win the hearts of Republicans by reincarnating the good cheer of Ronald Reagan and capitalizing on his standing as a breakthrough candidate in the Republican revolution of 1994. It turned out that Thompson's main function in the race would be to divide the conservative vote and diminish its influence.

The pressure to remain orthodox and very conservative was obvious throughout the debates that fall. In the October encounter where Romney had paraphrased Dean and Wellstone, he and Giuliani sparred over which of them had been the biggest tax cutter—hoping, presumably, that those watching would forget that they had run two of the most liberal, high-tax jurisdictions in the country. And the continuing power of anti-immigrant feeling among Republicans was obvious in a CNN/YouTube debate in November during which Romney and Giuliani each sought to cast the other as a closet liberal.

Romney assailed Giuliani for turning New York into a "sanctuary city" for immigrants. It was, in fact, quite true that in his earlier incarnation as a candidate in New York City, Giuliani had spoken out strongly against nativism. "The anti-immigration issue that's now sweeping the country in my view is no different than the movements that swept the country in the past," Giuliani had said in 1996. "You look back at the Chinese Exclusionary Act, or the Know Nothing movement—these are movements that encouraged Americans to fear foreigners, to fear something that is different, and to stop immigration."

It would have been a mark of courage for Giuliani to repeat those words on that November night. Instead, he accused Romney of having employed illegal immigrants to work on his Massachusetts home, turning it into what Giuliani called a "sanctuary mansion." Romney, in turn, asked Giuliani if he was saying that a person who hired a company for home improvement should be expected to ask someone in the work crew who had "a funny accent" to prove his citizenship. The exchange ennobled neither man, but it showed how they thought Republican primary voters were thinking.

On that evening, it was Huckabee, the Christian conservative, and McCain, the longtime champion of immigration reform, who stood out from the crowd. When Romney attacked Huckabee for an Arkansas program that allowed the children of illegal immigrants to apply for college scholarships, Huckabee was unapologetic and hit back hard: "I'm standing here tonight on this stage because I got an education. If I hadn't had the education, I wouldn't be standing on this stage. I might be picking lettuce.... In all due respect, we're a better country than to punish children for what their parents did." At a lunch with reporters the next day, Huckabee stood his ground. "You can't just pander to anger and hostility," he said. "If that costs me the election, then the country can pick a different guy."

McCain joined in expressing disgust for the discussion's nativist turn. "This whole debate saddens me a little bit," he said. "These are God's children as well, and they need some protections under the law, and they need some of our love and compassion."

Over the long run, the view championed by Huckabee and McCain would get steadily weaker in the Republican Party. By the summer 2015,

Donald Trump could denounce Mexican immigrants as, among other things, "rapists" who were "bringing drugs . . . bringing crime," call for the deportation of all of the estimated 11 million illegal immigrants, and happily watch his campaign take off. It was Giuliani and Romney who correctly sensed where the party was moving. .

But McCain's old authenticity gradually began to work in his favor that fall, after his campaign organization was transformed by financial necessity from a front-runner's behemoth into a scrappy insurgency focused almost entirely on winning the New Hampshire primary.

On a visit to the Granite State that November, I discovered that a campaign that was supposed to be dead was very much alive. This was a real nuisance to McCain's opponents, who had been circling what they thought was his expiring campaign. A *Washington Post*/ABC News survey around that time put him in second place, behind Giuliani, who benefited from his vast name recognition.

The mood of McCain's loyalists in New Hampshire combined relief with the restrained glee that comes from walking away from a car wreck in one piece. Jim Barnett, McCain's state director there, traced McCain's local comeback to his renewed looseness in freewheeling town meeting formats that were his specialty. Barnett pointed to a moment during a mid-October gathering in Hopkinton where McCain had confronted a questioner who spoke—in language that was to become more common on the right during the Obama years—of the "anger the average European Christian, native-born American feels when they see their country turning into a multicultural chaos Tower of Babel."

McCain had been trying to appease his conservative critics on immigration by stressing the need to secure the nation's borders first. But at the Hopkinton meeting, as in the debate, the old, combative, and principled McCain reappeared. He condemned his interlocutor's language and declared that he was "grateful to live in a nation that has been enriched by people coming to our nation from around the world." The applause, Barnett recalled with pride, "went on for a long time."

But the issue on which McCain truly found his voice was the one he cared most passionately about. With Bush having changed strategy in Iraq with the "surge" of more U.S. troops into Iraq, McCain, who had supported the increase, could campaign all out on the idea that abandoning the new approach to the war—and the war itself—amounted to "surrender." Thus began his "No Surrender" tour, a nice double message declaring his opposition to "surrender" in Iraq and his refusal to surrender the nomination to adversaries he considered lightweights.

And just when McCain was ready to surge himself, Giuliani suffered a series of blows that ultimately freed up a new pool of voters. As Dan Balz and Haynes Johnson reported in their excellent account of 2008, Giuliani was embarrassed in November 2007 when Bernard Kerik, his former driver and police commissioner, was indicted on corruption charges. Earlier, Giuliani had pushed Kerik to be secretary of homeland security in the Bush administration, even though it emerged that Giuliani had been briefed on Kerik's potential problems as early as 2004. *Politico*'s Ben Smith then reported that as mayor, Giuliani had "billed obscure city agencies for tens of thousands in security expenses amassed during the time he was beginning an extramarital relationship with future wife Judith Nathan in the Hamptons." Finally, an endorsement he had been expecting from Florida governor Charlie Crist, then a Republican, never materialized, despite Crist's promises. Crist eventually endorsed McCain. (Giuliani would exact his revenge in 2014 by campaigning energetically for Republican governor Rick Scott, who defeated a challenge from Crist, by then politically reborn as a Democrat.)

With Giuliani fatally weakened, McCain was able to occupy all of the party's more moderate ground while the old maverick's more conservative adversaries systematically defeated each other. Romney had invested heavily in winning the January 3 Iowa caucuses, which McCain barely contested. It was money poorly spent. Some 60 percent of Republican caucusgoers were evangelical Christians, and they flocked to one of their own. Huckabee won with 35 percent to 25 percent for Romney. Huckabee demonstrated the continuing power of social conservatism (particularly in low-turnout Republican contests) by building a strong organization that relied on groups not traditionally seen as political powerhouses, including organizations of parents who homeschooled their children. But it's also a certainty that Romney suffered from unease among evangelicals with his Mormonism.

Romney had tried to deal with the religious issue in a speech in December that remains an important document. Its contradictions point to a core tension in contemporary conservatism that continues to bedevil the movement. If Republicans need a strong dose of religious tolerance to regain the ground they have lost with Asians, Muslims, and more secular Millennials, they still find themselves needing to appease Christian conservatives. In his address at the George H. W. Bush Library in College Station, Texas, Romney tried hard to square this circle—and failed.

Romney put forward two propositions: first, that his religious faith should not be a factor in how voters judged him; but, second, that he happened to have a powerful faith in Jesus Christ. The clashing messages led him to make an argument that was, by turns, brilliant and frustrating, inspiring yet also transparently political.

He began with a bracing challenge, calling upon Americans to live up to the demands of pluralism rooted in liberty. "Religious tolerance," he asserted, "would be a shallow principle indeed if it were reserved only for faiths with which we agree." He spoke with perfect pitch about the dangers of subjecting candidates to doctrinal investigations. "There are some who would have a presidential candidate describe and explain his church's distinctive doctrines," Romney said. "To do so would enable the very religious test the Founders prohibited in the Constitution. No candidate should become the spokesman for his faith. For if he becomes president, he will need the prayers of the people of all faiths." He reached for a bit of poetry in declaring "we do not insist on a single strain of religion—rather, we welcome our nation's symphony of faith."

So it was a neck-snapping moment when Romney went on to declare: "What do I believe about Jesus Christ? I believe that Jesus Christ is the Son of God and the Savior of mankind." Romney had every right to declare his faith in Jesus, of course. But with those words, he legitimized the very test that he had just asked voters to reject. And he was insisting that it was an examination on which Christian conservatives should give him an A.

In declaring that "liberty is a gift of God, not an indulgence of government," he was echoing many earlier politicians, including John F. Kennedy. And in saying that "every single human being is a child of God," he was citing a view long invoked by progressive Christians on behalf of social, political, and economic equality. But then he went further. "Freedom," he said, "requires religion, just as religion requires freedom." And to those who see religion as "merely a private affair with no place in public life," he offered this rebuke: "It is as if they are intent on establishing a new religion in America—the religion of secularism. They are wrong."

This was a philosophical mouthful. Religion certainly can be and has been conducive to freedom. But does freedom require religion? Is religion always conducive to freedom? Does freedom not also thrive in far more secular societies than our own? Why not seek solidarity among the lovers of liberty, secular as well as religious? And Romney's knock on the "religion of secularism" was the purest form of pandering to the religious right. Thus did Romney water down his eloquence about "our grand tradition of religious tolerance and liberty." With Romney's defeat in Iowa at the hands of the Christian right, the speech could be rated as a failure, even as a political ploy.

If Huckabee kept Romney from fulfilling the first half of his breakout strategy in Iowa, McCain blocked him from the second, five days later in New Hampshire—and set himself on the path to the nomination. The mathematics of McCain's eventual triumph are important because they show that McCain won the Republican nomination despite his relative moderation rather than because of it. His more conservative foes checked each other's ambitions by dividing the conservative Republican vote. This created the narrow path for McCain.

McCain's New Hampshire victory was not overwhelming, well short of his rout of Bush eight years earlier. He received 37 percent of the vote to Romney's 32 percent. Giuliani's collapse was key; he won less than 8 percent.

Romney finally scored a victory a week later in Michigan, the state of his birth, and won a few days after that in Nevada, with its substantial Mormon population. But the key tests came in South Carolina on January 19 and Florida on January 29.

South Carolina had been McCain's undoing against Bush. This time it provided him with his decisive, if narrow, victory—and here, the splintering of the conservative vote was key. McCain won with just 33 percent, well below the 42 percent he had secured against Bush. His main competitor in a state where religious conservatives are strong was Huckabee, who won 30 percent. Preventing Huckabee from consolidating the right end of the party the way Bush had was Fred Thompson, who drew 16 percent and promptly withdrew from the race. Romney won a little over 15 percent. The more conservative candidates taken together outpolled McCain by nearly 2-to-1.

In Florida, a stronger Giuliani might have hampered McCain the way Huckabee, Romney, and Thompson had blocked each other's way in South Carolina. But by then, Giuliani's campaign was flailing, a fact so obvious that in a January 24 debate in Boca Raton, NBC anchor Brian Williams asked directly: "What has happened to your candidacy?" Gamely, Giuliani replied: "We have them all lulled into a very false sense of security now."

In truth, Florida was a contest between Romney and McCain, and Romney flooded the state with resources and focused the campaign on the economy, an issue that has never been within McCain's comfort zone. With less than a week to go, as Balz and Johnson reported, Romney had fought his way back to a tie in the tracking polls. In the end, McCain pushed the campaign back to Iraq, suggesting (falsely) that Romney favored withdrawal. McCain also drew key last-minute endorsements from Crist and Senator Mel Martinez. Again, he won with a relatively modest share of the vote, beating Romney 36 percent to 31 percent. Giuliani came in at just 15 percent of the vote and Huckabee at 13 percent.

Republican professionals realized quickly that after Florida, there would be no stopping McCain. But for many conservatives, this was a source of alarm. McCain would be the first Republican nominee since Gerald Ford in 1976 to win despite opposition from organized conservatism, and the first whose base in Republican primaries rested on the party's center and its dwindling left. Those who built the American right, from Barry Goldwater in 1964 through the Reagan and Gingrich revolutions, were intensely aware of the dangers a McCain victory portended.

"He is not the choice of conservatives, as opposed to the choice of the Republican establishment—and that distinction is key," declared Rush Limbaugh, the arbiter of orthodoxy, using language that would become popular in the Tea Party years. "The Republican establishment, which has long sought to rid the party of conservative influence since Reagan, is feeling a victory today as well as our friends in the media."

For those outside the conservative movement, such anxiety seems strange. McCain's voting record in the House and Senate has typically won high ratings from conservative groups. His positions on key issues—support for the Iraq War, opposition to abortion, his long-standing criticism of government spending—were those of a conservative loyalist.

But staunch conservatives saw things differently. They knew that in primary after primary, McCain's base had been formed by moderates, liberals, independents, supporters of abortion rights, and critics of President Bush. Conservatives were not his coalition's driving force. Republicans who described themselves as "very conservative" consistently rejected McCain. In the Florida primary, those voters chose Romney over McCain by more than 2-to-1.

Many of the leading Republicans who championed McCain had never been heroes to the right. Giuliani quickly endorsed McCain after Florida. Crist, whose last-minute endorsement in Florida proved important to McCain, appealed at least as much to independents and Democrats as to Republicans. It was no surprise when Crist left the GOP to run for the Senate as an Independent before making his 2014 gubernatorial run as a Democrat. McCain also won the endorsement of Arnold Schwarzenegger, then governor of California, who had veered far from conservatism in working closely with Democrats in the state legislature.

When McCain wrapped up the nomination on February 5, Super Tuesday, the states he lost and those he won told the same story. Huckabee became the champion of the Old South, winning in Arkansas, Tennessee, Georgia, and Alabama, although McCain narrowly won in Missouri and Oklahoma. Romney carried a swath of states in the Midwest and mountain West. McCain lost most of the core Republican states, instead piling up delegates in New York, New Jersey, Connecticut, Illinois, and California—all states Obama would carry handily in November. Once again, McCain prevailed because Huckabee and Romney continued to divide the right.

★

Having never won the ideological heart of his party, McCain made a series of adjustments and overtures to the right, culminating in the choice of Sarah Palin as his running mate. Steve Schmidt, one of McCain's closest campaign aides, insists that her selection was primarily about shaking up a race that clearly seemed to be moving Obama's way. Choosing a forty-four-year-old woman, herself a maverick as Alaska's governor, seemed a perfect complement to McCain, who turned seventy-two that August. The Democrats' rejection of Hillary Clinton's own breakthrough candidacy still bothered—in many cases angered—millions of her supporters. These feelings were aggravated when Obama picked Joe Biden as his running mate rather than Clinton. And in defense of the Palin choice, Schmidt and others who supported it still point out that in the first Gallup poll taken after the Republican convention ended on September 4, McCain took a five-point lead on Obama. He had trailed by three before the convention.

But there were other ways to have shaken up the contest. The one McCain preferred was to put his dear friend Joe Lieberman on the ticket. This would have been a true maverick move, since Lieberman was a Democrat, had been Al Gore's running mate in 2000, and was pro-choice on abortion. This is precisely what sank the idea. It would take a majority in just four state delegations to force a roll call vote, and McCain's aides were certain that conservative pro-lifers would revolt. Senator Lindsey Graham, who favored Lieberman, talked up the possibility, which had the unintended effect of building opposition. As Dan Balz and Haynes Johnson reported, McCain's pollster Bill McInturff further hurt Lieberman's chances—and the prospects of another McCain favorite, Tom Ridge, the pro-labor Republican governor of Pennsylvania—by reporting the results of a survey he did shortly before the convention. It showed that 40 percent of McCain's core supporters would be less likely to vote for him if he chose a pro-choice running mate.

A McCain-Lieberman or McCain-Ridge ticket would have signaled philosophical change in the Republican Party. It was a risk McCain decided he couldn't take. The risk he did take with Palin may have been safe inside his party, but it came to hurt him badly among moderate swing voters who came to see the Obama-Biden ticket as safer. That fall, Representative Debbie Wasserman Schultz, a South Florida Democrat, told me that she had once feared substantial defections of moderate Jewish and traditionally Democratic voters toward McCain. But the Palin choice, she said, unleashed a flood of the people in "my condos"—the vast housing developments where many Jewish voters live—back to the Democrats and Obama. Exit polls ratified Wasserman Schultz's intuition.

Whatever short-term surge McCain enjoyed was, in any event, wiped out over the weekend of September 13, when Lehman Brothers went bankrupt and the Bush administration decided it could not rescue the firm. The Great Recession had begun, even if its full effects were not yet obvious. The episode led eventually to the bank bailout, but in immediate political terms, a strong case can be made that Obama won the election on Wednesday, September 24, when McCain called for a suspension of campaigning and said he would not participate in the first presidential debate two days hence. Shortly after McCain's announcement, Obama calmly told reporters he thought the debate should go forward and that he'd be there. When McCain backed down and agreed to debate after all, Obama, the newcomer, emerged as the victor in a test of strength. McCain appeared impulsive and capricious in the midst of a crisis. In the debate itself, Obama achieved his central objective of showing the country that he was at ease and knowledgeable. A *USA Today*/Gallup Poll found that voters saw Obama as offering "the best proposals to solve the country's problems" by a remarkably wide 52-to-35 percent margin. By 46 percent to 34 percent, they said Obama had turned in the better debate performance, and Obama's overall lead in the presidential race itself was back up to 8 points. There would be no looking back.

The perception that an Obama victory was nearly inevitable did not go down the same way with all Americans. In the afterglow of Obama's historic victory, the bitterness that engulfed substantial parts of the right in the fall of 2008 was largely forgotten. This amnesia distorted subsequent explanations for the rise of the Tea Party and other forms of opposition to Obama once he took office. The Tea Party did not emerge spontaneously and suddenly just because Obama supported a stimulus plan or subsequently proposed health care reforms. The anti-Obama sentiments, rooted in anger, fear, and, in some cases, prejudice, were highly visible on the campaign trail that fall, to the point where McCain himself felt a need at times to push back against them.

"Rage Rising on the McCain Campaign Trail" was the headline on a CNN story published on October 11, 2008. The story, by correspondents Ed Henry and Ed Hornick, recounted a variety of incidents that presaged almost exactly comparable episodes that would become common after Obama was in the White House.

"I don't trust Obama," said a woman at a McCain rally in Minnesota. "I have read about him and he's an Arab." McCain, they reported, shook his head and replied, "No ma'am, no ma'am. He's a decent family man . . . that I just happen to have disagreements with."

One man at the Minnesota rally said he was "scared of an Obama presidency," while at a rally in Waukesha, the heart of the Republican base in Wisconsin, a participant voiced alarm about the mystery of Obama's rise, reflecting a notion that would become popular on the right, that only nefarious forces could have allowed him the success he enjoyed. "We're all wondering why that Obama is where he's at, how he got here," he said. "I mean, everybody in this room is stunned that we're in this position."

"I'm mad. I'm really mad," said another. "And what's going to surprise you, it's not the economy. It's the socialists taking over our country."

McCain seemed "torn" in his response to the attacks on Obama, as CNN put it. On the one hand, he regularly and honorably rebuked audience members for going too far, particularly when one of his supporters labeled Obama a "Muslim." Yet McCain's own campaign ran ads about Obama's neighborhood friendship with Bill Ayers, who had been part of the Weather Underground in the 1960—around the time Obama was eight or nine years old. Later, Ayers became an academic and Obama worked with him in local Chicago charities. The circumstances didn't stop the McCain ad from declaring: "Barack Obama and domestic terrorist Bill Ayers. Friends. They've worked together for years. But Obama tries to hide it." Palin had a convenient shorthand on the Ayers question: She accused Obama of "palling around with terrorists." Palin audiences sometimes responded by shouting "terrorist" and even "Kill him!"

It was to be one of the many paradoxes of Obama's efforts to pull the country out of divisions that had plagued it since the 1990s, and in many cases the 1960s. Precisely because Obama was only nine years old when the sixties ended, he carried none of the generational scars that Clinton did. Most Americans (including most boomers) shared Obama's weariness of living in the past and reprising the 1960s every four years. Yet this posed a real challenge to a certain style of conservative politics, and in their frustration, the right's militants—and, at times, the McCain campaign—reached back even farther, to far-right tropes of the 1950s or even the 1930s.

Thus had the false claims that were the bread-and-butter of the Tea Party and their media allies already emerged in 2008: that Obama was a Muslim, that he trained to overthrow the government, and that he was educated in Wahhabi schools. McCain's campaign did not pick up the most extreme charges, and McCain could not be blamed for the extremists who immediately saw in Obama a chance to earn fame and fortune by concocting lies or half-truths about him. But McCain and his campaign, facing a frustrating, uphill challenge, did occasionally take advantage of such suspicions by suggesting that voters didn't really know who Obama was, thus hinting at a sinister backstory without filling in the details. This was left to the voters' imaginations.

One of the singular defections to Obama's side came when Christopher Buckley, the novelist and former speechwriter for George H. W. Bush, announced he would vote for Obama (his first ballot ever for a Democrat). He referred to words once spoken to him by his late father. "You know," William F. Buckley Jr. had said, "I've spent my entire lifetime separating the right from the kooks."

In the end, nothing worked for McCain, and Obama won handily with 365 electoral votes, 53 percent of the popular vote, and a 9.5 million vote majority. In addition to winning the Kerry states and all of the key swing states (including Ohio, Florida, and Virginia), he carried Indiana, which had not voted for a Democrat since LBJ won it in 1964, and North Carolina, which last went Democratic in 1976 for Jimmy Carter.

Obama's coalition was, in one sense, the traditional Democratic alignment—most of the places and most of the social groups that had voted for Gore and Kerry also supported Obama. But it was also something very new. Obama won by attracting new voters into the electorate, particularly African-Americans and the young. Not only did African-Americans vote in larger numbers, they gave Obama 95 percent of their ballots. Obama also drew a sharp generational line across the country. He carried 66 percent of the voters under the age of 30, up from 54 percent for John Kerry four years earlier and 48 percent for Al Gore in 2000. By contrast, voters 65 and older supported McCain, 53 percent to 45 percent. Young voters enjoyed another breakthrough: they outnumbered older voters, which rarely happens in American elections. Voters under 30 made up 18 percent of the electorate, while voters over 65 accounted for only 16 percent. And the share of ballots cast by white Americans was at its lowest point in history. Obama was clearly the candidate of a new, younger, more diverse America that was on the rise.

What Obama did not and could not change was the ongoing polarization of the country as conservatives and liberals continued to sort themselves according to party. McCain may not have been the first choice of conservatives, but 64 percent of the people who voted for him called themselves conservative. In 1988, by contrast, only 49 percent of George H. W. Bush's voters had called themselves conservative. The Republican Party, in victory or defeat, was now more than ever dependent on the ballots of conservatives, and this would affect the behavior of its leaders. Moreover, as we saw in the previous chapter, Obama's gains over John Kerry were concentrated in the more moderate or progressive parts of the country. The most conservative regions and counties resisted his candidacy, and this fact, too, would affect the choices of Republican politicians. The very nature of the Republican Party would make its leaders highly resistant to explanations of Bush's failures rooted in criticisms of conservative policies (or the Iraq War). Holding the party together required a critique of Bush as too "liberal," too enamored of "big government," and too "Establishment."

It would be equally vital to block Obama's efforts to create a consensual approach to governing, to disrupt his efforts to reduce the power of the social issues, which had brought so many working-class white voters to the Republicans—and, more broadly, to prevent him from keeping his promise to tear down the barriers between red and blue America. If Obama managed to end the bitter political polarization that took root in the Clinton years, the right would be isolated. As gifted as Obama was, he would not succeed in getting a party and a movement to act against its own political interests.

Obama would come to see this eventually, but not before he expended a great deal of energy trying to realize his original vision. The celestial choirs, alas, were not about to sing.

★

In his inaugural address on January 20, 2009, before some 1.6 million people stretched across the National Mall before him, Obama was clearly still hoping he could call those choirs forth, and he struck a strikingly nonpartisan tone. In doing so, he deprived the elated crowd of the applause lines they had become accustomed to during his campaign. "On this day, we gather because we have chosen hope over fear, unity of purpose over conflict and discord," Obama declared. "On this day, we come to proclaim an end to the petty grievances and false promises, the recriminations and worn-out dogmas that for far too long have strangled our politics." There were no celebrations here of partisan victories or ideological triumphs—and no commentary on the shortcomings of the previous eight years that had brought Obama to power and the country to a parlous state.

That evening, an influential group of Republicans came together over dinner to offer each other solace and to plan ahead. The fifteen or so party influentials had been invited to the Caucus Room, a steakhouse and lobbyist hangout nine blocks from the Capitol and seven from the White House, by the Republican pollster Frank Luntz. Fast-talking and unapologetically open in expressing emotion, Luntz was then forty-six years old and had gotten his start as an outsider, advising Pat Buchanan's 1992 presidential campaign. He became famous for providing Republicans with focus-grouped phrases that could make even unpopular conservative policies sound mainstream and serious. The gathering, whose story was well told by the journalist Robert Draper, included Newt Gingrich, who had brought the Republicans back from defeat fourteen years earlier, and three House members who would soon become GOP stars: Paul Ryan, Eric Cantor, and Kevin McCarthy.

While it might be unfair to see the dinner as a celebration of the very "recriminations" and "worn-out dogmas" that Obama had denounced earlier in the day, those whom Luntz brought together had no interest in joining the new president in putting an end to "conflict and discord" or in rethinking conservative ideology. These savvy politicians were determined to get back into power, beginning with victory in the 2010 midterm election. They knew that foiling Obama was essential to that end. "We've gotta challenge them on every single bill and challenge them on every single campaign," McCarthy declared. Among the strategic imperatives agreed upon at the end of four hours of talk, Draper noted, was the need to "show united and unyielding opposition to the president's economic policies." The determined partisans didn't waste any time. As Draper wrote, eight days later, Cantor, the House minority whip, "would hold the House Republicans to a unanimous No against Obama's economic stimulus plan."

Senate Republican leader Mitch McConnell was not at the Caucus Room caucus, but he had reached exactly the same conclusion; it was imperative for Republicans to turn Obama into a failure. He would cause a stir with a sound bite that was repeated endlessly by liberals and Democrats. "The single most important thing we want to achieve is for President Obama to be a one-term president," McConnell would say in an interview with *National Journal* published on October 23, 2010. But he had decided on this strategy long before—around the same time that Luntz's colleagues reached their own combative conclusions.

Senator Bob Bennett, the Utah Republican who in 2010 was one of the first in his party to be denied renomination in the Tea Party purge, spoke to journalist Alec MacGillis about the Senate Republican retreat held in West Virginia in midwinter 2009, just after Obama took office. Bennett's recollection was clear:

"Mitch said, 'We have a new president with an approval rating in the seventy percent area. We do not take him on frontally. We find issues where we can win, and we begin to take him down, one issue at a time. We create an inventory of losses, so it's Obama lost on this, Obama lost on that. And we wait for the time when the image has been damaged to the point where we can take him on.'" MacGillis summarized the strategy: "In other words, wait out Americans' hopefulness in a dire moment for the country until it curdles to disillusionment."

Obama had insisted that "there is a not a liberal America and a conservative America—there is the United States of America." But there *was* a conservative America. Its more assertive and extreme wing had made its feelings known on the campaign trail in October 2008. Its leaders in the House and Senate were in a minority, but they were determined not to remain in that status long, and they were in a fighting mood. Together, the grassroots right and its political leadership would make the new president's life miserable.

11

THE LOGIC OF OBSTRUCTION

Why Conservative Opposition to Obama Was Inevitable

"I want to know: why are you people ignoring his birth certificate?"

The popular assumption about our democracy is that when a new president is elected, he gets a "honeymoon" during which the country, including the political opposition, gives him (and, someday, her) a chance to make proposals and even enact them. In this rationalist view of self-government, a new chief executive's program is given a chance to work. The opposition's job is, after a decent interval, to point out where the president's program has failed and propose alternatives. Voters then get a chance to judge an incumbent's performance, the opposition's response, and cast ballots accordingly.

This highly idealized view has never been fully accurate, since a party that has lost an election turns immediately—which is to say, twenty-four hours after the ballots are cast—to figuring out why it was defeated and how to win the next time. Many of the warm words opposition leaders pronounce on their newly elected adversary are typically, and mostly rightly, written off by voters as hollow niceties. Politics in a democracy never really stops.

Nonetheless, Barack Hussein Obama may be the first president in American history who never got a single day of honeymoon time.

It's true that there was cheering (and self-congratulation) across party lines over the election of the first African-American president in the country's history. The campaign's rough moments when Obama's race did seem to be a problem for many voters were forgotten. Obama himself encouraged the country to give itself a pat on the back. "If there is anyone out there who still doubts that America is a place where all things are possible," he declared in his election night victory speech before a throng of 250,000 in Chicago's Grant Park, "who still wonders if the dream of our founders is alive in our time, who still questions the power of our democracy, tonight is your answer." When they spoke with pollsters, Americans seemed inclined to share in the celebration. Obama's 68 percent approval rating coming into office was much higher than that of nearly all other recent presidents. Only John F. Kennedy at 72 percent approval in 1961, topped him, only Eisenhower tied him, and only Jimmy Carter, at 66 percent in 1977, came close. By contrast, Ronald Reagan and George H. W. Bush took office with the barest majority of public approval at 51 percent. Even Republicans seemed ready to give Obama the benefit of the doubt: 43 percent of them said they approved of Obama, 30 percent disapproved, and 27 percent expressed no opinion.

Yet from the very beginning of his presidency, Obama would be vexed by the peculiar political circumstances of a deeply divided country. To give the invocation at his inauguration, Obama chose Rick Warren, the popular evangelical pastor whose conservative politics had not gotten in the way of his inviting Obama to his mega-congregation at the Saddleback Church in California. Warren had endured much denunciation from the religious right because of Obama's views on abortion, so Obama's invitation was an expression of appreciation. It was also a sign of Obama's determination to demonstrate his openness to theologically conservative white Christians. In the end, Obama took grief for the move from his left because of Warren's views on homosexuality, and got little credit from his right.

When Chief Justice John Roberts botched the words of the oath of office while administering it to Obama, the president's aides decided they simply could not let the error stand. With "birthers" already questioning the right of Obama to be president, because they did not believe he had been born in the United States, it was obvious that some "constitutional conservatives" would question his legitimacy because he had not recited the precise words prescribed in the Constitution. Roberts was invited to the White House to administer the oath again—this time, as Obama put it, "very slowly."

The 57 percent of Republicans who opposed him or had doubts even in that first poll would loom large for other reasons, especially since Obama's benefit of the doubt extended neither to Republican politicians nor to the party's activists. And Obama himself could never take a honeymoon because he had to start governing and make momentous choices involving enormous sums of money even before he took office. He was the "Instant President," as Jonathan Alter called him in *The Promise*, an excellent account of Obama's first year in office.

Obama was inheriting an economy in collapse and he promised rapid action to get the economy moving right after the election. In America's peculiar constitutional system, the new and heavily Democratic Congress took office seventeen days before Obama did. At Obama's direction (though not under his control), it set to work passing a stimulus program aimed at pumping purchasing power into an economy where it was rapidly drying up. While Republicans insisted that they, too, understood the need to stimulate the economy, they were determined to follow Kevin McCarthy's injunction to challenge Obama "on every single bill." In the end, not one House Republican voted for it.

The stimulus saga, including its afterlife, helps to explain much that would happen over the rest of Obama's term. Conservatives would always cite it as Obama's original sin, arguing that it was too big, that Obama had refused to negotiate with them, that he had simply followed the lead of the Democrats in Congress—or some combination of all of these. The stimulus was regularly invoked to account for the rise of the Tea Party. Horror over unprecedented spending was always the go-to explanation for what rallied millions into passionate and frightened opposition to a president who, they insisted, seemed to accept no limits.

The irony is that the stimulus plan proved to be far smaller, and of shorter duration, than the depth of the crisis demanded. The administration itself eventually understood that at least $1.2 trillion would be required to give the economy the boost it needed. Stimulating the economy through a combination of public spending and tax cuts had been a bipartisan habit that Ronald Reagan himself (he combined tax cuts with much stepped-up military spending) had pursued, if not admitted to. George W. Bush had tried to stimulate the economy, too.

Obama and the Democrats decided to keep the stimulus under a trillion dollars for fear of provoking sticker shock, although this did little to protect them from accusations that they were undisciplined deficit spenders. Obama and congressional Democrats also developed what became a dysfunctional relationship, with Obama at times distancing himself from the handiwork of House Speaker Nancy Pelosi and her colleagues and quickly backing down over certain specific Republican criticisms of the stimulus. In some cases, his moves were pragmatic as he tried to rid the package of any provisions that might slow its passage. At other times, though, he seemed eager to preserve his standing as a neither-red-nor-blue, above-the-fray leader. This posture tried the patience of Pelosi, Obama's most loyal ally, and she was eventually direct in expressing her displeasure. "Mr. President, I don't mind your throwing us under the bus," she told Obama toward the end of the stimulus battle. "But I do object to your backing the bus up and running us over again."

In his efforts to keep some distance between himself and the Democrats, Obama played into Republican efforts to split him off from his allies. Their argument, as Alter noted, became: "The president wants to work with us; it's the speaker who's standing in the way." But Obama's efforts to work with the GOP bore no fruit, and by unintentionally feeding the Republican narrative that Pelosi was calling the shots, he weakened his friends in Congress and undercut his own image. Would a strong president let himself be led around by the House Speaker and a bunch of Democratic committee chairs?

Pelosi stayed frustrated with Obama's refusal to recognize publicly that it was Republicans blocking his way and not some nonpartisan entity he regularly referred to simply as "Washington." In his memoir, published in 2015, David Axelrod, Obama's senior adviser, reported on a meeting with Pelosi later that spring in which she took the president to task for his above-the-battle rhetoric. "We can't run against Washington," she told Axelrod. "We *are* Washington." According to Axelrod, Obama sympathized with Pelosi. "Democrats are not the reason things are all gummed up here," the president said. But he would keep trying to cast himself as someone keeping his distance from Washington's partisan mess.

Failing to recognize that the Republicans had decided to let Democrats pass the stimulus on their own had other costs. Obama organized his bargaining strategy around the assumption of at least some goodwill, which began a pattern of what might be called preemptive concession. The president and the Democrats included some $300 billion in tax cuts in the plan, on the theory that they represented at least one form of stimulus the Republicans would be open to. Wouldn't this choice inevitably be seen as a sign of goodwill? When the stimulus finally passed, more than a third of it consisted in tax cuts. But the Democrats' tax cuts took the form of a $400 per individual and $800 per couple refundable tax credit; a temporary increase in the Earned Income Tax Credit for the disadvantaged; and an extension of a program that allowed businesses to recover their capital costs more quickly. Because the Republicans preferred tax rate cuts on incomes and capital gains—and because they had not proposed them—the GOP never accepted the stimulus tax cuts as "real" tax cuts. Proposing no tax cuts at all and letting the Republicans win them as part of a negotiation might have changed the political dynamic. But doing so would have required Obama to admit that he was negotiating with a tough adversary.

The bill eventually cleared the House, but because of McConnell's determination to block anything but tax rate cuts, it needed sixty votes to clear the Senate. The Democrats were one short because future senator Al Franken was still involved in a recount in Minnesota. (He would not take the oath of office until July 7.) And so Obama went into negotiations with the only three Republican senators willing to deal with him: Arlen Specter of Pennsylvania and Maine's two moderates, Susan Collins and Olympia Snowe. (The opposition within the Republican Party that Specter's apostasy unleashed would force him to become a Democrat, and Snowe would retire in frustration.) By the time the bill came out of the House, it had already been cut to $820 billion, and Specter insisted that it be pulled to under $800 billion. It was finally passed at $787 billion, with some potentially popular and visible measures (such as $16 billion in school construction) knocked out at the Republicans' demand. In retrospect, Democrats would have done better to include substantially more infrastructure spending, yet neither Obama nor his party realized how hard it would become to come back for more stimulus—or how difficult it would be to pass even a construction bill, normally the most popular legislation among politicians of all stripes.

Obama signed the stimulus into law on February 17. The speed with which it passed is, in light of usual congressional behavior, astonishing. Yet a bill that materially contributed to saving the American economy turned into both a political albatross and a symptom of Washington dysfunction. It was not the first time that Obama failed to understand the urgency of selling his own program. He often seemed to treat the stimulus, Alter wrote, "as if it was a dog's breakfast concocted by someone else." Because the stimulus was never properly touted or defended—it took journalist Michael Grunwald to write *The New New Deal,* a thoroughgoing brief on its behalf—it was easy to parody or dismiss. Its effects, though broad, were also diffuse, and because the economy was so battered, a full recovery was a long time in coming. Obama faced a problem that FDR did not. Not only did the economy collapse on Herbert Hoover's watch, but the country endured three long years of suffering after 1929 under a Republican president. Voters knew where they wanted to direct their ire. In the Great Recession, the collapse occurred under Bush, but most of its effects were felt after Obama took office.

One of Obama's singular successes, the rescue—or "bailout"—of the auto industry also ran into a wave of opposition, not only from Republicans but also from large parts of a public that blamed the American car companies for failing to produce products they wanted to buy. A CNN poll taken in December 2008, before Obama took office, found that 61 percent of Americans opposed public help for the auto companies; only 36 percent supported it. Yet over time, the auto rescue proved easier to defend because the comeback of the auto industry was quicker and more obvious than the sluggish recovery of the economy as a whole. The benefits of the bailout were concentrated in midwestern states that would be central to the 2012 election and thus were the locus of large-scale advertising touting the policy. The stimulus could never be sold nationwide in the same way.

Any dreams Obama had for a new day in Washington should have vanished during the stimulus battle. The costs of the dysfunctional relationship between the White House and its allies in Congress were ongoing, but their full toll did not become apparent until the 2010 elections wiped out the Democrats' House majority.

The lessons for conservatives and Republicans were obvious: opposition pays. Not only did Republican members of Congress who battled Obama stay within the good graces of the party's conservatives. Their successful branding of the stimulus as a government monstrosity would be highly useful both with the electorate and for right-wing activists itching to organize against Obama.

The Tea Party took off less than a month after the inauguration. Its origin is typically ascribed to a televised rant against mortgage relief programs on February 19, 2009, from the floor of the Chicago Board of Trade—not the usual venue for launching a populist rebellion—by CNBC's Rick Santelli. He charged that the administration was asking his viewers "to pay for your neighbor's mortgage that has an extra bathroom and can't pay their bills." Obama, he said, wanted to "subsidize the losers' mortgages." He compared the American economy to the wreckage of Cuba's economy and then spoke the magic words: "We're having a Chicago Tea Party in July!" He was not calling on the toiling masses to revolt. Presumably they were the "losers" he was condemning. "All you capitalists who want to show up at Lake Michigan," he shouted, "I'm going to start organizing!" Inciting oppressed capitalists to the barricades was not the normal way of starting a revolution. But 2009 was not a normal year.

Santelli clearly struck a nerve on the right, particularly among the stock market mavens who made up much of his audience. CNBC asked visitors to its website: "Would you join Santelli's 'Chicago Tea Party?'" About 170,000 people responded within one day, and 93 percent said yes, Jane Hamsher reported on her liberal website Firedoglake. A CNBC spokesperson told the journalist Arun Gupta that the number of respondents was "much higher" than normal for a CNBC poll. Within eleven days, Gupta reported, "the rant video was the most-watched clip ever on the CNBC website, with nearly 2 million views and another 855,000 hits on YouTube." All those capitalists were ready to march—or, at the least, to click their anger online.

Yet Kate Zernike, the *New York Times* expert on the Tea Party, found that the first Tea Party rally was held three days before Santelli's rant, in the liberal city of Seattle. It was not a political outsider's affair, but the work of twenty-nine-year old Keli Carender, a conservative since high school, a member of Young Republicans, and a regular *National Review* reader. Like many conservatives, Carender had become unhappy at the end of the Bush years and had not much liked any of her party's 2008 presidential candidates. "None of them seemed to understand what conservatives didn't like about Bush," Carender told Zernike, "that it was the spending." She called her rally "The Anti-Porkulus Protest," using Rush Limbaugh's name for the stimulus package. She drew a small crowd, "mostly older people," Zernike reported, "along with a few in their twenties who had supported Ron Paul." Other Tea Party protests followed. At first, Fox News was slow to the party—the movement was given its initial boost by radio talkers. But eventually the network became the Tea party's leading booster. As Zernike noted, Fox searched high and low for all signs of anti-Obama protest, at one point giving coverage to a Florida "rally" organized by a woman named Mary Rakovich that consisted of herself, her husband, and a friend.

These early rumblings are revealing of what the Tea Party was about. It was not a spontaneous uprising of previously apolitical or indifferent voters, although some of them certainly joined in. It was primarily a movement of committed conservatives. A *New York Times* survey later found that 73 percent of Tea Party supporters called themselves conservatives, including 39 percent who said they were "very conservative." (Only 12 percent of all Americans called themselves "very conservative.") Tea Party supporters were twice as likely as the country as a whole to be Republican—54 percent versus 28 percent. This was, for the most part, an activist movement of angry conservative Republicans.

This might go without saying but for the prevalence early on of a romantic portrait of the Tea Party as a spontaneous form of populist protest by hundreds of thousands of Americans who were new to politics. This view was nurtured by the right and picked up at times in the mainstream media.

The conservative media coverage of the anti-Obama movement, including the Tea Party, created a feedback loop: the conservative talkers called for protests, then covered what protest there was, which in turn called out other

conservatives to launch protests of their own, which then created more opportunities for coverage. It was quite brilliant in its way, and very effective.
And as this process rolled forward, mainstream media outlets were pummeled
for not giving the protests enough attention. "This anger has been ignored by
the mainstream media," wrote Scott Johnson on the influential conservative
Power Line blog, echoing criticism that ricocheted across the conservative
media and blogosphere. "It doesn't fit with any narrative that is congenial to
them." Over time, the mainstream media followed the lead of their critics on
the right and gave expansive coverage to the anti-Obama movement.

In certain respects, the Tea Party was simply the old far right with the
added advantages of having on its side a television network of its own, an
army of talk radio hosts, and an activist conservative Web. It also had Sarah
Palin.

The Tea Party allowed Palin to come into her own. If the mainstream
media had called attention to her shortcomings (often simply by interviewing her) in 2008, she would turn the experience into a form of martyrdom in
2009. Attacks on the "lamestream" media were her stock in trade. It was the
media that made her in her second career, as a right-wing spokesperson. For a
period, the mere inclusion of the word "Palin" in a news story or commentary
was enough to make it soar to the top in page views, the newest measure of
media success. On July 4, 2009, she announced her resignation as governor
of Alaska, choosing not to finish out her single term. At the time, she faced
a variety of investigations, but it was also clear that her financial future lay in
large lecture fees and book sales as the figure most sought after by the most
ardent of Obama's foes. She received a $1.25 million advance for her book
Going Rogue. According to *Publishers Weekly*, it went on to sell more than
2,670,000 copies that year.

It said something about the nature of the divisions within the conservative movement and the Republican Party that a significant part of *Going
Rogue* was devoted to attacks on John McCain's campaign. While trying to
be respectful of the senator himself, Palin was unrelenting about what she
described as an overscripted and chaotic campaign that was slow to respond
to the economic catastrophe unfolding that fall and too soft on Obama.
She complained about being muzzled and mishandled. She was especially

tough on Steve Schmidt, even though he was one of the strongest advocates of putting her on the ticket. Schmidt hit back, charging her book was "all fiction."

Melanie Kirkpatrick, the former deputy editor of the *Wall Street Journal*'s reliably conservative op-ed page, tried to be sympathetic in her review of the book, but she found it "disappointing" that Palin devoted "so little of *Going Rogue* to the issues that she and Mr. McCain ran on." But Palin understood her audience. She was against Obama, she was a family woman, she could shoot straight (literally), and the liberal media had gone after her. That was enough.

For the mainstream of the Republican Party and the conservative movement, the rise of this vociferous right would prove both a godsend and a nightmare. In the short run, the appearance of a relentless opposition outside Washington would demonstrate that Obama's election had not meant the death of Republicanism or conservatism, ratify the GOP's insistence that the United States remained a "center-right" country, and show how many Americans believed that Obama was going too far on—well, everything. But in riding the back of the tiger, Republicans ignored the risk that they might end up inside. For the Tea Party did not just view Obama as a "Muslim" and a "socialist." They saw many Republican leaders as big-government sellouts. Their sponsors among Frum's "radical rich" felt much the same way. The new radical right proved quite capable of turning its guns from Obama toward Republicans who had once welcomed their angry insurgency.

From February 2009 through the rest of Obama's first term, the Tea Party and its allies discovered they could say whatever they wished about Obama, no matter how extreme, and count on their charges to win wide coverage— and to escape full-throated repudiation from established Republican leaders. Although their claims that Obama had not been born in the United States were wholly invented, the "birthers" continued to get attention even in the mainstream media, especially when their charges were championed by celebrities such as Donald Trump, who for a while could command the cameras almost as successfully as Palin—and would find himself commandeering them at will six years later.

Planting the doubts about Obama worked. In an April 2010 *New York Times*/CBS News Poll, only 58 percent of Americans replied with certainty that Obama had been born in the United States. Among the rest, 23 percent said they didn't know and 20 percent said he had been born abroad. Among Tea Party supporters, only 41 percent said he had been born in the United States, while 30 percent said he had been born abroad. Other surveys showed that as many as 45 percent of those in the Tea Party thought the president had been born outside the United States.

Whole volumes have been written about the wild charges that were leveled against Obama from the extreme right, both before and during his presidency, so I will not dwell on them at length. Yet it is important to see the powerful role they played on the right in the Obama years, particularly during his first term. The reaction to Obama's election revived a conspiracy-minded right that had been largely dormant—or, at least, largely out of public view—since the 1950s and early 1960s. It drew on many of the themes of the earlier far right and recycled many of its ideas. But it also added new ones specific to Obama and to new worries about radical Islam after 9/11.

An argument that seems like an endless loop has raged over whether opposition to Obama was primarily about his race or his ideology. What is beyond debate is that race played a central role in the various charges about Obama's birth, his father's Kenyan origins, and the insistence of so many that a man whose middle name was Hussein must be a Muslim. Many politicians have been smeared by their opponents, but these charges were unique to Obama. They would not have been made if his background had been different. Many on the left have been accused of "Marxism," but it's hard to find others who were charged with being Muslim Marxists not even constitutionally entitled to be president. All these attacks marked out Obama's "otherness."

The case of Dinesh D'Souza, once a serious conservative intellectual who transformed himself into a wealthy merchant of anti-Obama spleen, is especially revealing. In his 2010 book, *The Roots of Obama's Rage,* D'Souza charged that Obama's politics could be explained by his Kenyan father's allegedly Marxist, anticolonial views. Obama was driven by a "hatred derived from the debris of the anti-colonial wars" and D'Souza wrote of "cases of men who are so preoccupied with their dark dreams that they have difficulty adjusting to contemporary reality." That Obama had almost no relationship with his father and wrote himself about how complicated his feelings about him were was of no consequence. Here was a grand theory that tied Obama back to Africa and cast him as harboring a hidden Marxist agenda. It was a book made to be a far-right bestseller.

In Obama's early years in office, major Republican figures and conservative institutions were quite happy to dabble in this right-wing nonsense themselves. *Forbes* magazine published an excerpt from D'Souza's book while Newt Gingrich pronounced it "brilliant." With Obama, it was possible to propose any theory, as long as it was hostile, and crowds were waiting to proclaim its genius.

Many Republican leaders tried to have it both ways, distancing themselves from the lunatic fringe without actually saying the fringe was wrong. Representative was a February 2011 appearance by John Boehner after he had become House Speaker on *Meet the Press*. NBC's David Gregory played footage of an Iowa focus group run by Republican pollster Frank Luntz that had been broadcast on Sean Hannity's Fox News program.

An unidentified woman says: "I believe that Barack Obama's religious beliefs do govern his foreign policy."

Luntz asks her: "And what are his religious beliefs?"

She replies: "I believe that he is a Muslim."

Luntz then goes around the room and discovers many others who believe Obama is a Muslim. Gregory asked Boehner: "As the speaker of the House, as a leader, do you not think it's your responsibility to stand up to that kind of ignorance?"

"David," Boehner replied, "it's not my job to tell the American people what to think. Our job in Washington is to listen to the American people. Having said that, the state of Hawaii has said that he was born there. That's good enough for me. The president says he's a Christian. I accept him at his word."

Gregory pressed Boehner as to whether he felt some obligation to say, "These are facts. If you don't believe that, it's nonsense." Boehner wouldn't go there: "Listen, the American people have the right to think what they want to think. I can't—it's not my job to tell them."

It falls to Ted Nugent, the heavy metal rocker whose hits included (perhaps appropriately) "Cat Scratch Fever," to offer what might be rated the most compact summary of the far right's charges against Obama. He did so in an interview before attending a gathering on the Washington Mall hosted by the Fox News talker Glenn Beck. Nugent condemned Obama's "Islamic, Muslim, Marxist, communist and socialist agenda." Asked if he really believed Obama was a Muslim, Nugent replied: "You're damn right I do! He says he's a Christian so he can continue with his jihad of America-destroying policies."

Among those "America-destroying" policies, in the eyes of the right, was a health care reform proposal far more cautious than Clinton's. The model for what became the Affordable Care Act was the bill to expand health care coverage championed by Mitt Romney in Massachusetts. The proposals Obama put forward were also similar to the alternative to the Clinton plan introduced in the 1990s by Republican senator John Chafee. It had been cosponsored by a who's who of the GOP, including Bob Dole, the Republican leader; Utah's Orrin Hatch; and Chuck Grassley, the Iowa Republican whose support Obama desperately sought for the Affordable Care Act. The individual mandate to buy insurance had been promoted by conservatives at the Heritage Foundation and many Republican politicians (including Gingrich). They argued, plausibly from a conservative point of view, that Americans who received emergency help when they were sick or injured were "free riders" on those who paid for insurance and on the health care system itself.

But this would not matter to Republicans in Congress whose positions on health care were now well to the right those they held in the 1980s, the 1990s—or, in Romney's case, as recently as 2006. Writing in *Forbes*, Avik Roy, a conservative policy analyst, defended the right's new view but acknowledged that "it's accurate to say that Obamacare was modeled after Romneycare." He also admitted, using nicely diplomatic language, that there had been "an evolution of conservative thinking on the individual mandate." The shift on health care was of a piece with the larger ideological shift in the GOP.

It's ironic that the Affordable Care Act came to be called "Obamacare," since Obama gave Congress such wide leeway in writing the law. The process to produce a bill dragged on precisely because Obama and Senator Max Baucus, the Democratic chair of the Finance Committee, believed that they could win Republican support for the bill. A close friend of Grassley's, Baucus was firmly convinced he could persuade his Iowa colleague to come along and held out hope even longer than Obama did. In the end, Grassley became a fierce critic even of provisions Baucus thought he had agreed to during negotiations.

As the sluggish and meandering legislative process increasingly discredited the health care effort itself, Democrats were desperate to get House and Senate bills out of committee before the summer congressional recess. The House produced its bill, but Baucus's insistence that he could win Republican votes delayed action in the Senate. (He would not move a bill to the floor until October 13.) It was a disastrous failure for the Democrats politically, and nearly fatal to the health care reform effort itself. Opponents of health care reform were ready to pounce on both the ideas being floated and the Democrats' incompetence. The Tea Party Summer would be long and hot, dominated by howls about "socialized medicine" and charges popularized by Palin that the measure included "death panels."

At the end of 2009, the fact-checkers at PolitiFact would declare the death panels charge the "Lie of the Year." (The charge was fabricated out of a provision, which had enjoyed Republican support in the past, providing reimbusements for physicians who provided voluntary counseling to Medicare patients on end-of-life care options, living wills, and advance directives.) But by then death panels had already done their work in damaging the bill's reputation and the Democrats' standing.

★

In that Tea Party Summer, the lives of Mike Castle and Mick Mulvaney were set on very different trajectories as members of Congress confronted angry conservative crowds all over the nation determined to "take our country back." The Castle and Mulvaney stories are parables of the two tracks taken by the right-wing rebellion—a revolt against Republicans deemed insuffi-

ciently ferocious in their opposition to liberalism and all its works, and a push
to replace Democrats with uncompromising champions of the right's true
creed.

A distinguished Republican moderate and former governor of Delaware,
Castle turned seventy that summer and was in his sixteenth year of service
in the House. Tall with an erect bearing, Castle offers just a hint of the aris-
tocratic but keeps it well hidden behind an engaging democratic directness.
Genial in the manner of the elder President Bush—the forty-first president
would later hold a fund-raiser for him at his Kennebunkport, Maine, summer
house—Castle had won every election he contested since 1966. The words
"widely respected" were regularly attached to his name.

At the time, he seemed to be on an easy path to the United States Senate,
the favorite to take the seat vacated by Vice President Joe Biden. Castle had
wide appeal to Democrats who, time after time, had split their tickets on his
behalf. There was no reason to think they would act differently in 2010.

Castle was not accustomed to the treatment he got from voters on the
evening of June 30, 2009, during a town hall meeting in Georgetown, at the
southern end of Delaware. The main town in Sussex County, the most conservative in the state, it still has about it the feel of the Old South. At first
Castle didn't realize the encounter would prove to be more than a single bad
night. "That was the first sign to me that something was amiss," Castle told
me. "We didn't give much thought to it."

For decades, town halls were occasions for members of Congress to take
the pulse of their constituents and for constituents to have the sense that
their voices were being heard. As their name suggests, the exchanges harked
back to tidy white buildings in New England town squares where citizens
engaged in the art of self-rule. Rowdy Congressional town halls were not
unknown. At one particularly acrimonious session in his own district, Barney Frank of Massachusetts had famously shot back at an angry questioner:
"Look, we politicians are no great shakes. But you voters are no day at the
beach either." But such exchanges were not the rule, and they certainly were
not for Castle.

The drama started when a woman rose and waved a plastic bag that turned
out to contain her birth certificate. Her package, she said, was a commentary

on the identity of the president of the United States, whom she could not bring herself to name.

"I have a birth certificate here from the United States of America saying I am an American citizen with a seal on it, signed by a doctor with the hospital administrator's name, my parents, my date of birth, the time, the date," she said, every syllable barked out with anger. "I want to go back to January twentieth, and I want to know: why are you people ignoring his birth certificate? He is not an American citizen. He is a citizen of Kenya. I am here with my father who fought and won World War II with the Greatest Generation in the Pacific Theater. My country—and I don't want this flag to change. I want my country back!"

Castle was clearly flustered but tried to stay in control. "I answered sort-of matter-of-factly," he said later, giving the gist of his response: "I haven't seen his birth certificate, but I will tell you that I am sure that Hillary Clinton, Senator McCain's group, the Republican Party in general all have looked at this pretty carefully. They seem to all come to the conclusion that he was born as an American citizen and I have no reason to doubt that.

"I went on for about three minutes, and they started booing," he said. "It got pretty out of hand . . . it was pretty hellacious."

There was a seemingly spontaneous call for the crowd to pause and recite the Pledge of Allegiance. It was one set of words on which the rationalist congressman and his birther interlocutor could agree. Castle, hand on his heart, joined in.

It was, he said, "the first inkling that there was anything afoot."

A little over a year later, on September, 14, 2010, the state's Republicans delivered shocking news. Castle lost the GOP primary to Christine O'Donnell, a perennial candidate with no obvious qualifications for the office who grabbed hold of the Tea Party banner. It was a sign of the impact the relatively small but committed Tea Party cadre could have that O'Donnell shook national politics by winning with just 30,563 votes—3,542 more than Castle.

The night before the primary, I visited Castle's headquarters at Riverfront Wilmington, the classic sort of bipartisan economic development project that had been Castle's bread and butter. The storefront was welcoming, but only a half-dozen people were working the phones, a brave but paltry band standing against the Tea Party tide.

Later that night, I sat down with Castle at Kelly's Logan House, a watering hole where he has gathered his closest supporters the night before every election since his first victory, for the neighborhood's state legislative seat, forty-four years earlier. He seemed calm and confident, yet almost valedictory as he offered a prescient analysis that would explain what happened the next day.

"There are issues on which, as Republicans and Democrats, we should sit down and work out our differences," Castle said. But Republicans who might be inclined toward the middle of the road are petrified of "quick attacks by columnists and the Sean Hannitys of the world.

"People are very afraid of crossing the line and being called Republicans in Name Only—or worse," he said. "Not too many members are willing to stand up.

"Part of it," he added, "is worry about primaries, and this election has shown the power of very conservative groups."

After the results were in, I spoke with Senator Ted Kaufman, the Democrat appointed to hold Biden's Senate seat pending the outcome of the 2010 election. His analysis was straightforward: Most Mike Castle–style Republicans in northern Delaware weren't Republican anymore. "There was a move of moderate Republicans becoming independents, and independents becoming Democrats," he said. The same pattern could be traced in the nearby Philadelphia suburbs of Montgomery, Bucks, and Delaware counties in Pennsylvania. The forces that had driven Senator Arlen Specter out of the Republican Party in Pennsylvania the year before defeated Castle on the other side of the state line.

In November, O'Donnell went down in a landslide. In the course of the campaign, she did become nationally known, though not in helpful ways. Her best-known public pronouncement, "I am not a witch," came in a general election ad aimed at playing down her past comment that she had "dabbled into witchcraft." New Castle County Executive Chris Coons, the Democrat who everyone had expected would lose a stately sort of contest to Castle, headed off to the Senate in what was one of only a handful of bright spots for his party that evening.

If Castle's town hall experience in Delaware was an intimation of his coming political downfall, Mick Mulvaney's visit to a similar encounter in South Carolina marked the beginning of his successful march to Congress.

You realize quickly when you meet him that Mulvaney, who turned forty-two that summer, feels comfortable engaging with those whose views are radically different from his own; he tosses in good-natured references to himself as a "right-winger" and notes that he often tunes the television in his congressional office to MSNBC. He already knows what the people on Fox will say, he explains.

A staunch conservative with libertarian sympathies, Mulvaney was Tea Party before the fact, although the businessman who graduated from Georgetown and the University of North Carolina Law School doesn't fit Tea Party stereotypes, or at least the ones popular among liberals. A man in a hurry, he was elected to the South Carolina House of Representatives in 2006, served a single term, and then won a state senate seat in 2008.

He traces his decision to run for Congress in 2010 to how he was treated when he tried to attend a town hall held a couple of months after Castle's. It was organized by his district's long-serving member of Congress, John Spratt.

Spratt is the Delaware Republican's Democratic alter ego. Each represents the different form moderation took in his respective party. Both Spratt and Castle won admiration from partisans on the other side, both cared about the details of policy, both saw the search for middle ground not as a poll-tested, split-the-difference electoral ploy but as a necessary governing strategy.

First elected to Congress in 1982, Spratt rose to become chair of the House Budget Committee. This gave him many opportunities to help his district and state, but it also allowed his opponents to hold him responsible for whatever was happening in Washington on fiscal issues. In South Carolina during that Tea Party Summer, having to answer for the stimulus and the Affordable Care Act was a mighty burden.

The then-sixty-six-year-old Spratt carried an additional load. Suffering from Parkinson's disease, he seemed older than his years. His deliberate South Carolina drawl, an emblem of authenticity and thoughtfulness over so many years, was ill-suited to fending off the rapid-fire attacks he would endure from an angry and energized right.

And the onslaught was furious at the September 3, 2009, town hall in

Rock Hill, South Carolina, focused on the health care proposal. Technically, critics of the law asked Spratt questions, but many of the inquiries were barely disguised denunciations.

"There are too many unanswered questions with what you've just described and what I've been reading," one constituent fumed. "Why the rush? Why are we hurrying to get this thing pushed right away through this fall?" And the crowd exploded into applause.

"If this bill passes, will you join us in this health care?" asked a middle-aged woman. More raucous applause and cheering.

A man in a hospital shirt rose to bear witness to his view of government's involvement with health care. "I come here today directly from work. I think my uniform speaks for itself. I have over twenty-plus years of experience inside the health care industry. At fifty-two years of age, I also have had many years of experience seeing the result of government intervention in the private sector. The result of that government intervention has been mostly the result of what I call the reverse Midas Touch. That is, whatever government touches through its control, it mostly turns to crap."

And then a young man with long bushy hair offered the Tea Party's message, undistilled. "Where does it end?" he asked angrily. "Universal health care? Universal housing? Universal food? Universal everything? Where does the government stop and the individual begin? We have a God-given right. . . ." The audience interrupted to cheer. "We in America are individuals. The liberties that the Founding Fathers outlined in those documents are not handouts from the government. They are things that come from within. The pursuit of happiness, life, liberty—these are things that come from the individual, not from the government."

What was a rough night for Spratt was a decisive moment for Mulvaney. His later account of how the event pushed him into challenging Spratt is revealing of how a smart, ambitious young conservative came to see that 2010 would be a year of opportunity.

Mulvaney said he decided to go to Rock Hill because he wanted to check up on reports that such meetings were being disrupted by outsiders—"to see if they really were busing in people from Ohio or Florida, or if the people who were showing up were actually from here."

Then came lesson one: never hassle an elected official who might run against your boss. "I got there and there was a line to check in, so I check in," Mulvaney said. "And the young lady asked me for my identification. And I absentmindedly reached into my bill folder and instead of giving her my driver's license gave her my South Carolina Senate ID."

That wasn't good enough. "I need to know that you live in the district to let you in," he recalled her saying. "I need to see your driver's license."

Although the event was being held just outside his state senate district, Mulvaney eventually got in. But he was furious over his treatment at the door, and says he was immediately struck by how the questioning was organized. Those who had an inquiry were told to put their cards into boxes labeled "for health care reform," "against," and "undecided." He remembers that "98 percent" of the cards were in the "against" box but that the three boxes were treated equally.

One of Mulvaney's sharpest memories was of a woman who asked Spratt: "How can I be sure that this isn't going to be like everything else when government gets involved? It's going to be lower quality, more expensive." Mulvaney recalls Spratt's reply this way: "Madam, I guarantee you, that when the government runs your health care, it will be cheaper than what you have now and better than what you have now."

Mulvaney's account of Spratt's position on Obamacare seems somewhat tendentious. Looking at the tape available of the meeting, the closest Spratt seems to have gotten to such a response was a reply in which he asked rhetorically: "How many people in this room would want to see Medicare disbanded because they can't trust the government?"

Nonetheless, Mulvaney's story captures how defensive Democrats became as Tea Partiers descended on congressional town halls and put Obamacare under siege. In trying to limit attendance to Spratt's constituents, his aides were simply responding to disruptions at comparable events all over the country.

And by then, the Tea Party had broken out of the conservative media into the mainstream. Indeed, the television networks were eager that summer to broadcast the drama of members of Congress who found themselves under siege. "It was relatively easy for citizens to follow the town halls as media coverage was ubiquitous," wrote Jeffrey M. Berry and Sarah Sobieraj in their

2014 book, *The Outrage Industry: Public Opinion Media and the New Incivility*. Berry and Sobieraj cited an August Gallup poll that found 32 percent of Americans following the town halls "very closely" and another 37 percent following them "somewhat closely." They also cited Skocpol and Williamson's study that traced patterns in coverage by tracking Fox News and CNN. Fox News gave the Tea Party extensive attention in the spring and early summer while CNN "generally ignored the movement." But the disruptions of August brought a torrent of CNN air time. The movement had mainstreamed itself—or, perhaps, the mainstream media did the job for it.

And in the usual way of the media, the more raucous the meeting, the more media attention it received. That summer I spoke with frustrated Democrats who felt this approach artificially magnified the voices of right-wing rage.

"The media coverage has done a disservice by falling for a trick that you'd think experienced media hands wouldn't fall for: of allowing loud voices to distort the debate," said Representative Mary Jo Kilroy, who would be defeated in 2010 in her district centered on Columbus, Ohio.

Representative David Price of North Carolina reported that a network stringer who attended a large town hall meeting Price held in Durham told him that he was one of ten journalists who had fanned out to cover the town hall circuses across the country. The reporter, Price said, warned him: "Your meeting doesn't get covered unless it blows up." As it happens, the Durham audience was broadly sympathetic to the health care law. No "news" there.

But the disruptions had their effect, helping to shape the public image of the Affordable Care Act for years afterward.

And Mulvaney was in the race. He insists he really did believe he stood no chance when he persuaded his wife to bless his campaign, but then quickly changed his mind. The turning point came in January 2010, when Republican Scott Brown unexpectedly won the Massachusetts U.S. Senate seat that the late Ted Kennedy had held for nearly five decades.

And by the fall, the tide was clearly running out on Spratt. Focusing on rising deficits, a Tea Party issue that also appealed to country-club Republicans, Mulvaney turned Spratt's past against the incumbent's present, claiming the incumbent had gone from being "the bipartisan John Spratt that you've heard of from the late 1990s and 2000s" to "the John Spratt that voted with Nancy Pelosi 98 percent of the time."

All Republicans ran against House Speaker Nancy Pelosi in 2010, using the San Francisco Democrat as a symbol of Washington and liberalism. The conservative backlash against Obamacare and the stimulus—along with lingering rage over the economic collapse and the bank bailout—set the tone. In 2008, Spratt had been reelected with nearly 62 percent of the vote. Just two years later, Mulvaney beat Spratt by 20,000 votes, 55 percent to 45 percent.

★

Mulvaney was right in seeing Scott Brown's victory in Massachusetts on January 19, 2010, as a sign of things to come. Ted Kennedy died on August 25, 2009, and a special election was called to fill the seat he had held since 1962. Kennedy's endorsement in 2008 had provided a powerful validation of Obama's candidacy, and the liberal lion's struggle with cancer had deprived supporters of universal health care, the cause of his life, of their most powerful and savvy advocate.

To say that the Massachusetts election came at an awkward time for Democrats understates the matter, even if they (and almost all prognosticators) were very slow in seeing Brown's victory coming. Brown proved an excellent campaigner, running as a folksy rebel who traveled the state in a pickup truck. It was the right approach at a time when discontent in the country was widespread—even in the one state that stuck with George McGovern against Richard Nixon in 1972 and had reelected Kennedy eight times. Brown's opponent, state attorney general Martha Coakley, was, by contrast, an overconfident, indifferent campaigner who committed a series of gaffes, including two involving the state's beloved Boston Red Sox.

Obama's approval rating nationally was still positive at the time, but barely so at 50 percent. Republicans who might once have given him a chance had made their decision: only 14 percent of them approved of his performance in office. And as the summer had shown, Republicans were mobilized while Democrats were largely passive, not unhappy with Obama exactly but disappointed that things were not working out better.

Four days before the Massachusetts vote, the U.S. Bureau of Labor Statistics pegged the unemployment rate at 10.0 percent, with 15.3 million Americans out of work. That figure did not include those who had involuntarily left the workforce or were working part-time. Americans hoping to get by the damage of the 2008 crash quickly were disappointed.

At the time, I was reminded of a conversation I had had in June 2008, a few months before the financial implosions began, with two smart financiers about the future of the seemingly shaky American economy.

Defying the moment's conventional predictions that we would muddle through, one offered a dire and uncannily accurate forecast. He explained why banks would blow up, investments would crash, and the federal government would have to spend "at least $300 billion" to bail out financial institutions.

The other expert, a staunch Republican, listened closely, took a sip from his drink, and smiled. "This," he said, "would seem like an excellent time for the Democrats to take power."

It wasn't that he thought Democratic policies would be better in a time of turmoil. As a Republican, he was just hoping that the other side would be in charge to take the blame when things came tumbling down.

That exchange explained Brown's victory better than all the analysis that followed. Conservatives, of course, blamed "liberalism" for Coakley's defeat—big government, big deficits, an overly ambitious health care plan, a stimulus that spent too much, and all the other supposedly left-leaning sins of the Obama regime. The right was especially taken with, and heartened by, the movement of political independents from sympathy for Obama and the Democrats to strong support for Brown's insurgency.

Obama sympathizers countered that the president's approval ratings were quite healthy in light of the unemployment rate and a nearly unprecedented destruction of personal wealth. To cite ideology rather than the economy in explaining the big news for Massachusetts was like analyzing the causes of the Civil War without any reference to slavery, or the rise of the New Deal without mention of the Great Depression.

The Democratic case was strong on the merits—it almost certainly was a Carvillian "It's the economy, stupid" moment. But the success of the conservative narrative pointed to real problems for both liberals and the Obama administration. The president had to own the economic catastrophe much earlier than he should have. Most Americans understood the downturn had happened before Obama took office, yet they were still uneasy that the government had spent so much without an immediate result. The costs of underselling and underexplaining the stimulus and the economy's larger difficulties had come home. Absent a clear and persistent case from Obama for why earlier policies had been mistaken and why he was correcting them, conservatives succeeded in distancing themselves from the very policies that had helped create the downturn—and the resulting big deficits they were bemoaning.

And absent a more robust stimulus, the economy was even slower in coming back than it might have been. Arguing that unemployment would have been more severe without the actions Obama had taken was a hard case to make. As Barney Frank noted, voters rarely responded to the slogan, "It could have been worse."

The raw numbers in the Massachusetts contest told a harrowing story for Democrats that would be prophetic for the fall's midterms. In 2008, Obama had defeated McCain by a wide margin—1,904,098 votes to 1,108,854 for McCain. In 2010, Brown received 1,168,107 votes to Coakley's 1,058,682. Brown had won an enormously significant victory with a little over 59,000 more votes than McCain. Coakley had received nearly 850,000 fewer votes than Obama. The turned-on Obama constituency of 2008 was turned off, or, at best, dormant.

And there was one way in which the rise of the Tea Party reinforced Republican establishment themes—and also the commitments of the broader, supposedly centrist political establishment. At a time when the economy actually needed even more stimulation, the nation's leading voices became obsessed with rising deficits.

Of course the deficit had grown. The downturn itself deprived the government of revenues, and necessary emergency spending added to the red ink. All this was on top of the continuing effect of the Bush tax cuts, which further threw off the balance sheets. But instead of focusing on the urgency of getting the economy moving, established voices highlighted long-term deficit problems related to Social Security and Medicare. All the down-the-road projections, of course, looked much worse because of the downturn. And a large share of the future deficit was explained by soaring inflation in health care costs, one of the problems Obama was trying to solve through his reform.

Nonetheless, conservatives won a major victory early on when the deficit obsession took hold. It shifted the public conversation from the causes and cures of the Great Recession to its aftereffects. If the first subject raised pointed questions about the deregulation of financial markets and the failure of tax-cutting policies to fulfill their promises, the deficit issue made it easy for the right to wage war on "big government."

To a degree that undercut his own priorities, Obama offered a partial but important bow to the antideficit forces. The theory of his political advisers was that the public itself saw the deficits as important, and Obama did not want to be isolated, especially from elites who shared the concern over debt. But failing to challenge the deficit obsession only allowed it to grow, providing Republicans with one of their key campaign themes of 2010.

The highly politicized nature of the fight came into relief in January 2010, when a bipartisan bill to create a deficit reduction commission whose proposals would have to get an up-or-down vote in Congress failed. It received 53 votes, short of a filibuster-proof majority. In an astonishing show of the GOP's determination to oppose Obama even when it agreed with him, six Republicans who had cosponsored the bill actually voted against it after Obama endorsed it. Obama then appointed the commission himself and chose Erskine Bowles, who had served as Bill Clinton's chief of staff, and former Republican senator Alan Simpson as cochairs. Both could be described as moderately conservative.

In the very short term, Obama got a political edge on intransigent Republicans. But the deficit issue had been blessed as a central concern, and Obama was later criticized by deficit hawks when he refused to embrace the commission's findings, some of which he saw, unsurprisingly given his own leanings, as too conservative.

Scott Brown's victory deprived Democrats of their sixtieth vote in the Senate at just the moment when they hoped to pass the health care bill. There were voices in the administration advising Obama to give up on comprehensive reform. Brown's victory in one of the most Democratic states in the union—*for Ted Kennedy's seat*—was the clearest indicator, they argued, of the cost of the health care fight to the administration. Rahm Emanuel, Obama's chief of staff and an instinctive moderate, was quoted by columnists sympathetic to him (to Emanuel's later chagrin) as favoring bailing out on a big bill to pass a smaller one. But Obama decided to fight for the broader plan, with much encouragement from Pelosi.

Now that Republicans had the 41 votes in the Senate that would allow them to kill a new bill that would result from House-Senate negotiations, Democrats had only one option. The Senate had already passed a version of health care reform, so *that* bill could get to the president's desk if the House simply passed it. The Senate bill was imperfect, and less generous than the competing House version. But since the liberal House members who were most unhappy with the proposal Baucus had crafted were also the most committed supporters of universal coverage, they were willing to swallow their objections to get the job done. Then the Senate passed a series of necessary amendments related to financing under what are known as "reconciliation" rules, which bar filibusters on certain budget matters. The arcane process had been used many times before by Republicans (notably to pass Bush's big tax cut), but here the GOP cried foul. Whether the party's objections were sincere or not, they represented shrewd politics, giving conservatives one more opportunity to tarnish the biggest health care achievement since the passage of Medicare.

There were many other legislative victories during the two years in which Obama had a Democratic Congress. The largest besides health care and the stimulus was the reform of Wall Street and financial institutions. The law—known as Dodd-Frank after its cosponsors, Senator Chris Dodd and Representative Barney Frank—also created a new agency to protect the rights of consumers of loans, mortgages, and other financial products where fine print frequently led to exploitation and gouging.

Yet, as Robert Kaiser wrote in *Act of Congress*, his definitive account of the law's enactment, "This big, substantial and consequential new law never penetrated the public consciousness." It was another marker of the Republicans' success in scarring Obama's record and the failure of both the administration and a Democratic Congress to defend their achievements.

The cost was high. That fall, Republicans ran a masterly campaign on three levels that gave its candidates a wealth of advantages in flexibility, deniability, and determination. At the first level, Republicans could be as reasonable or as angry, as moderate or as conservative, as their circumstances required. They had such freedom because outside groups that were flooding the political system with money were pounding their Democratic opponents in commercials for which no one was accountable. And then, on the farther right, Bill O'Reilly, Rush Limbaugh, and Glenn Beck and their media allies continued to cast Obama as the central figure in a conspiracy against America itself, fueling participation by the most extreme 10 percent or 15 percent of the electorate, including the Tea Party's enthusiasts who came out in force that fall. Rather than repudiate these forces, establishment Republicans were happy to ride the wave they helped create.

I visited New Hampshire that fall to watch the strategy in action. At a meeting of New England's largest Rotary Club at the Red Hook Brewery in Portsmouth, Kelly Ayotte, the GOP Senate candidate and former state attorney general, was all charm and reasonableness as she worked her way through the luncheon crowd made up mostly of businesspeople and professionals. She offered the usual Republican criticisms of a Washington that "has been spending too much money" and "not focusing on getting our economy back on track." She committed herself to "lower taxes on small business and less regulation" but also pledged not to be a partisan figure. "Often, I'll be bucking my own party," she promised.

Frank Guinta, the Republican House nominee challenging Carol Shea-Porter, an incumbent Democrat, was also the soul of equanimity, standing foursquare against mindless partisanship while sticking to his party's message on taxes, spending, and jobs. Shea-Porter bravely defended tax increases on upper-bracket earners before a crowd that, judging from their questions, included a great many of them. "We all have a responsibility to do what we can to get out of this debt," she said. Her comment was a telltale about how successfully the Republicans had put the Democrats on the defensive. In the meantime, she stoutly defended her vote for health care reform, asking the crowd if it really wanted to repeal the new law's consumer protections or its tax credit to help small businesses buy insurance. That fall, many Democrats stayed away from the health care law altogether, giving it little support in the public argument because the polls showed it to be unpopular.

The Portsmouth event was a lovely, friendly Rotarian civic moment worthy of Tocqueville—since the work of attacking on the airwaves was in large measure being carried out by groups that could claim no direct connection to the candidates they were helping. Paul Hodes, the Democrat opposing Ayotte—he missed the Portsmouth forum—was being hit hard by American Crossroads, the group associated with Karl Rove. "The guy just can't tell the truth," one ad declared, citing the state's leading conservative newspaper. Shea-Porter was assailed by a mysterious group with a pious name, "Revere America," for her support of "Obamacare." The ad warned ominously: "Your right to keep your own doctor may be taken away."

The experience in New Hampshire was repeated all over the nation. Republicans Ayotte and Guinta both won, part of the broad Republican sweep. Republicans seized control of the House, picking up 63 seats, their largest gain since the 1938 elections. The Democrats maintained control of the Senate, but the Republicans reduced their majority by 6 seats. For the long run, the most significant Republican triumphs were at the state level. Overall, Republicans posted a net gain of 6 governorships, leaving them at the helm in 29 of the 50 states. More important, their candidates took control in pivotal swing states—Ohio, Michigan, Wisconsin, and Iowa in the Midwest, along with Florida, Pennsylvania, and New Mexico.

Worse still for the Democrats, the GOP gained nearly 700 state legislative seats. In Pennsylvania, Ohio, Michigan, Wisconsin, Florida, and North Carolina, the Republicans won uncontested power to draw new congressional and legislative district maps after the 2010 census. They would use that authority shrewdly through aggressive gerrymandering to entrench their majorities.

The single most important difference between 2008 and 2010 was the age composition of the electorate: the Obama base among young voters stayed home, while older conservative voters flocked to the polls. In 2008, as we saw, 18 percent of voters were under 30 and only 16 percent were over 65. But in 2010, just 11 percent of the voters were under 30, while 23 percent were over 65, an astonishing (if not entirely surprising) turn. Moreover, while the entire electorate was more inclined toward the Republicans than the 2008 electorate had been, the sharpest Republican gains were among voters over 60. Voters under 30 gave Republican House candidates 42 percent of their ballots in 2008, a gain of 7 points from two years earlier. But among voters 60 and over, the Republicans rose 10 points, from 48 percent in 2008 to 58 percent in 2010. The Republican landslide was a senior citizen landslide.

The 2010 electorate was also whiter. Ruy Teixeira and John Halpin, voting analysts at the Center for American Progress, noted that the minority share of the electorate fell from 26 percent in 2008 to 22 percent in 2010, "a sharp drop by recent standards." The prospect of the first African-American president had boosted black participation to extraordinary levels in 2008 and raised the Democratic share of the African-American presidential vote to an unprecedented (and almost impossible to repeat) 95 percent. But the decline in the minority vote in just two years was a warning sign: hope needs to be nurtured.

And within the electorate, 2010's voters produced the most conservative Republican majority ever recorded. In the five elections from 1982 to 1990, the Republican share of the vote cast by self-described conservatives in House races averaged just under 66 percent. In 2008, Republicans won 77 percent of the conservatives' votes. In 2010, that figure rose to 86 percent. The dependence of the Republican Party on votes from the right was greater than ever, and this would have consequences.

From Democrats' standpoint, the most important warning sign of 2010 was their anemic showing among white working-class voters. They had been drifting Republican for decades, particularly in the South, but Democrats had recently managed to hold down the GOP's margins. In 2006 and 2008, Democrats lost the white working class by 10 points, and had done much better than that outside the South. But in 2010, Democrats lost the white working class by 29 points.

Finally, it was clear that 2010 was an election about disappointment and anger—far more a "no" vote than a "yes" vote. Many who didn't like the GOP voted for its candidates anyway. The exit poll found that 52 percent of the midterm voters had an unfavorable view of the Republican Party, yet 23 percent of them supported Republican candidates for the House.

This disappointment was the mirror image of the hopefulness that Obama had inspired two years earlier. Even if he and Democrats in Congress could brag of a remarkable legislative record, the president's first two years did not—

and perhaps could not—live up to the dreams and imaginings of the young. The working class was mired in an economic downturn that showed no signs of ending quickly, and this after the years of income stagnation in supposedly good times. These were the voters who cost the Democrats 27 of their 63 lost House seats in the great belt of states that had once constituted the nation's industrial heartland: New York, New Jersey, Pennsylvania, Ohio, Indiana, Illinois, Michigan, and Wisconsin. These defeats more than accounted for the difference between majority and minority status.

Poignant testimony about the causes of the Democrats' defeat came from Ohio Democrat Mary Jo Kilroy, who had been elected in 2008 and then lost her seat two years later. In almost every respect, Kilroy was a middle-American Democrat, in touch with the aspirations of her district and insistent that her role was to represent the poor and the middle class alike.

The party's losses among white working-class voters came as no shock to Kilroy when I spoke with her after the election. "I watched them in the last four years go from being anxious about the future to being worried but also hopeful during the 2008 campaign, to being very angry," she said. To explain, she invoked the world as seen by a person who worked for twenty-five years at Siemens, a large global electronics company that had cut employment in her area.

"You have a son who is a high school basketball player and wants to go to college—and then your factory goes off to Mexico," she said. "And you're a man of a certain age and another factory or another employer won't give you a second look. Think of the despair felt by that person."

Voters in this fix, she said, see Washington as "a place where their interests get sold out." What they want, she said, is "to feel they're being treated as well as the bankers who get bailed out." And, indeed, the exit poll found that 35 percent of the 2010 voters blamed Wall Street rather than either Barack Obama or George W. Bush for the nation's economic problems—and these voters supported Republican House candidates over Democrats by 57 percent to 41 percent.

When critics of Wall Street vote overwhelmingly for the Republicans, something is badly awry in the Democrats' approach. But this would also prove to be a challenge to the new conservative majority. Could a party whose donor base demanded policies tilted heavily toward the affluent represent the disaffected downscale voters who had flocked to Republican candidates? The question would haunt the party's presidential nominee just two years later.

And for all the good news the Tea Party election brought to the GOP in 2010, it also provided much evidence of how a sharp turn rightward could create profound problems for the party in the long run. Christine O'Donnell was soundly defeated in Delaware, but she was not alone among the Tea Party losers. The Republicans also threw away a chance to defeat U.S. Senate majority leader Harry Reid in Nevada by nominating Sharron Angle, who proved too radical for her state. Similarly, the Republicans narrowly lost in Colorado with Ken Buck, another Tea Party favorite, as their nominee. They held on to Alaska only because incumbent Republican senator Lisa Murkowski ran successfully as a write-in candidate after losing the Republican primary to Tea Party favorite Joe Miller. Some Tea Party candidates did pull through, notably Rand Paul in Tennessee—he was more a libertarian than a Tea Partier—and Florida's Marco Rubio, who also had ties to the Republican establishment in his state. And in Utah, Mike Lee, who had defeated incumbent Republican Bob Bennett at the state Republican convention in what might be seen as the first major Tea Party triumph, won handily. But Utah was not a state Republicans were ever in danger of losing.

In the meantime, the scores of new House Republicans included many staunch Tea Party supporters with limited political experience. Others, like Mulvaney, had risen through conventional political paths but were sympathetic to the ideological insurgency. And more traditional Republican politicians who rode the 2010 wave were well aware of the role the Tea Party had played in creating it. They would be reluctant to cross what seemed on Election Day to be the most dynamic force in conservatism. All of this meant that John Boehner, the new Speaker and an old-style Republican conservative, would be leading a caucus so unruly that he would often allow it to lead him—and eventually lead him to leave the Speakership and Congress altogether.

There were twin lessons from this radicalization, and they were contradictory. On the one hand, Republican professionals were furious that the insurgency they courted and built had undermined their capacity to take control of the Senate. They would pay closer attention to primaries in the future. On the other hand, moderates and moderate conservatives in the party had good reason to worry that what had happened to Mike Castle and even to bona fide conservatives like Bob Bennett could happen to them. They could resist the Tea Party in defense of a more middle-ground approach that was palatable to the broader electorate, but only at the risk of losing their own seats in primaries. Few Republicans were willing to lose, which meant that even though the right would continue to complain about a Republican establishment, it became an establishment willing to trade many of its convictions for a continued, if often tenuous, hold on power.

12

THE TEA PARTY OVERREACHES AND REPUBLICANS WAGE CLASS WAR

The Making and Unmaking of Mitt Romney

"They're just vultures. They're vultures that are sitting
out there on the tree limb waiting for the company to
get sick, and then they swoop in, they eat the carcass,
they leave with that and they leave the skeleton."

The Tea Party had every reason to be happy in the first months of 2011. Their success in moving the entire national debate to the right was breathtaking. Their power was not confined to Republicans who feared primaries. Many Democrats also felt obligated to talk their talk and harp on their commitment to reducing the deficit. John Boehner could play the good cop trying to protect the republic by keeping the bad cops of the Tea Party at bay.

That winter, it was hard to believe that the nation's unemployment rate was still at 9 percent, that the wages of those who were working continued to stagnate, and that the United States was facing unprecedented challenges to its economic dominance. Instead, Washington acted as if the only real problem the United States confronted was its deficit and the only test of leadership was whether President Obama was willing to make big cuts in programs for the elderly. If there was any threat to our prosperity, it was seen as coming from public employees.

Gone was talk about how Wall Street shenanigans had tanked the economy in the first place—and in the process made a small number of people very rich. Discussion of the problems caused by concentrated wealth was largely confined to the academic or left-wing sidelines. There were remarkably few stories in the media describing the impact of long-term unemployment on people's lives or the difficulty working-class kids were encountering if they wanted to go to college. There was a lot of talk about how much the government was spending on the elderly but little notice of a report from the Employee Benefit Research Institute finding that Americans over 75 "were more likely than other age groups—including children under 18—to live on incomes equal to or less than 200 percent of poverty." Any analysis of the economic struggles many elderly people were enduring was ignored, since it might get in the way of the "greedy geezer" narrative so popular at the time among those seeking big cuts in Medicare and Social Security benefits.

And the Tea Party was getting its way, at least in the House. That February, the House Republicans passed a budget bill that cut spending on Head Start, Pell grants for college access, teen pregnancy prevention, clean-water programs, K–12 education, and a host of other programs.

Liberals felt under siege, not only from the Republicans but from Obama himself. At a news conference a little over a month after the election catastrophe, Obama infuriated liberals—especially those in Congress who had lost their seats, partly because of their loyal support for his program—by calling them "sanctimonious" and arguing that they longed for the "satisfaction of having a purist position and no victories for the American people."

For those who accused him of negotiating with "hostage-takers" in the Republican Party, Obama was unrepentant. "In this case," he said, "the hostage was the American people, and I was not willing to see them get harmed." Writing in the *Washington Post*, Perry Bacon and Scott Wilson captured the fears such words inspired in many quarters of the Democratic Party. "Acceding to the demands of hostage-takers is generally viewed as unwise because it risks encouraging future hostage-taking," they wrote. "Democratic critics fear that is precisely the cue Republican leaders will take from this standoff—threaten this president and win."

Liberals wondered who Obama thought he could count on when conservatives tried to repeal the health care law, forced cuts in programs he supported, and investigated his administration down to the last pencil, even as the right's hard core continued to denounce him as an un-American Muslim socialist. Many Democrats were deeply suspicious of signals coming from White House aides casting the president as a centrist problem solver. It looked like a new iteration of Bill Clinton's old "triangulation" strategy.

But Obama seemed just as frustrated. He complained that many liberals were so upset that the health care law failed to include a "public option"—a Medicare-like alternative to private health insurance plans—that they overlooked the fact that "we got health insurance for 30 million people." In one sense, Obama's frustration was understandable. At the time, Congress was meeting in a lame duck session that would prove to be one of the most productive in history. Obama and progressives won some major victories that December, including repeal of the military's "Don't Ask, Don't Tell" policy, a major step forward for the rights of gays and lesbians. The START Treaty with Russia was ratified, a food safety bill was passed, and so was a bill to provide free medical treatment and compensation to the first responders to 9/11.

The budget deal disappointed many Democrats because Obama acceded to Republican demands to continue the Bush tax cuts for another two years. But some liberals supported the compromise since it included many provisions they saw as essential to keeping the recovery going. For roughly $100 billion to the rich, Obama got $197 billion in benefits he sought for the nonrich, including a thirteen-month extension of unemployment benefits. He also won $146 billion in business tax cuts to push job creation, plus an extension of a $280 billion middle-class tax cut. Many Democrats insisted that the Republicans would have eventually given in on relief for the middle class; the administration was not so sure.

At the time, I spoke with a House Democrat who was an Obama supporter. He backed the budget deal Obama had made, but his reasoning was hardly a vote of confidence in him or his administration, one reason he asked that his name not be used.

"If I thought they were ready to go twelve rounds on this next year, I'd kill it in a heartbeat," he said. "But if they're going to keep leaving the ring after the first punch, this is the best alternative we've got to keep this recovery going and helping those who are hurting the most." There was no sanctimony or purism here, just a sober and melancholy realism.

Obama was unrepentant on the need to give ground in order to win ground, and at that December news conference, he invoked his race. It was something he rarely did in public, a sign, perhaps, of how agitated he was beneath his customary calm. "This country was founded on compromise," he insisted. "I couldn't go through the front door at this country's founding. And, you know, if we were thinking of ideal positions, we wouldn't have a union."

But what would be the price of compromise, especially with opponents whose most energetic partisans saw compromise as a form of selling out? Then and for years to come, majorities of Democrats and Independents would tell pollsters that they favored compromise even at the cost of giving some principle. Substantial majorities of Republicans, on the other hand, would express a preference for sticking to principle. All negotiations were thus destined to be asymmetric.

The new House Speaker, John Boehner, proved early on (though not later) to be a master of a negotiating style Richard Nixon had characterized as "the madman theory." The approach induces the other side to believe you are capable of dangerously irrational actions and leads it to back down in the hope of avoiding the wreckage your rage might let loose.

In Boehner's variation, the Speaker cast himself as the reasonable man fully prepared to reach a deal to avoid a government shutdown. But, he would explain calmly, he also had to satisfy a band of "wild-eyed bomb-throwing freshmen," as he characterized his new House members in a *Wall Street Journal* interview, comparing them fondly to his younger self.

Thus were negotiators for President Obama and Senate Democrats forced to deal not only with Republican leaders across the table but also with a menacing specter outside the room. As "responsible" public officials, Democrats were being asked to make additional concessions just to keep the bomb-throwers at bay. The bomb-throwers obliged by treating the idea of a government shutdown not only as a normal part of politics but also as an outcome devoutly to be wished for. At a gathering of several hundred Tea Party supporters in April, Representative Mike Pence, then a Republican fire-eater from Indiana (he would become somewhat more soft-spoken as the state's governor), declared that if Senate Democrats refused to accept "a modest down payment on fiscal discipline and reform, I say, 'Shut it down!'" What counted as "modest," of course, was in the eye of the beholder, but Pence had the crowd with him. It erupted, lustily and joyfully: "Shut it down! Shut it down!" There was contempt in the way the crowd shouted the word "it," a reference to the government of the United States.

With the Senate still under the control of Democrats, the early Republican game plan seemed normal, if very conservative. Republicans sought $61 billion in budget cuts and got $38 billion in a deal passed in early April. The Democrats were having to play on Republican turf, but they had been able to moderate Republican demands and structured the package so most of the cuts were in later years, minimizing the immediate drag on the economy. The concessions bothered 59 of Boehner's "wild-eyed" bomb-throwers who voted against the deal—and kept up the pressure on him.

The right wing got something more to its liking the next week when the House passed budget chairman Paul Ryan's fiscal plan that proposed to cut $5.8 trillion over the next decade. "Yesterday we cut billions," a triumphant Representative Kevin McCarthy declared. "Today we cut trillions." The most eye-catching part of the plan (and the part Democrats highlighted) was its proposal abolishing the existing Medicare system over time and replacing it with government support for private insurance premiums. But at least as consequential were the plan's deep cuts in Medicaid, which covers the poor and the disabled, and in other safety net programs. The Center on Budget and Policy Priorities estimated that nearly two-thirds of Ryan's cuts came in programs for low-income Americans.

Ryan's goal, moreover, was not simply to balance the budget but to slash taxes, especially on the wealthy. His design included $2 trillion in tax cuts, including a reduction in the top income tax rate to 25 percent. That would have been the lowest rate since the Hoover administration. Those earning over $1 million a year, according to the Tax Policy Center, would have received an average $265,000 tax break, on top of the $129,00 reduction they were already enjoying courtesy of Bush's tax cuts.

The Ryan budget, even more than Tea Party rants, was a sign of how far to the right the Republican mainstream had moved. Ryan was in no way a political outsider and his temperament was not that of an angry extremist. On the contrary, he was an affable midwesterner with a sunny disposition whose entire career was built inside the conservative end of the Washington establishment. He had started out as a twenty-two-year-old staffer for Wisconsin senator Bob Kasten and, after Kasten's 1992 defeat, became a speechwriter at the blue-chip conservative think tank Empower America, working for movement luminaries Jack Kemp and Bill Bennett. He wrote speeches for Kemp's 1996 vice presidential campaign, and also served as legislative director for Kansas senator Sam Brownback, who would later push through the Tea Party program as his state's governor. Ryan returned home to Wisconsin in 1997 and spent a year at the family construction company preparing to run for Congress. He was elected in 1998 at the age of twenty-eight. Except for that brief sojourn at the family business, Ryan was entirely a creature of Washington.

But this also underscored the problem facing Republican leaders, especially Boehner. The older-style Republicans were now in broad agreement with the farther reaches of the right on policy. If government spending was as monumental a problem as even mainstream Republicans said it was, shouldn't the tactics used by the leadership reflect the urgency of the cause? And if the leadership was simply content with passing a budget through one house and then going back to politics as usual, why shouldn't the ardent Tea Partiers view them as engaging in a thinly disguised sellout? There was also this: if Barack Obama was as corrupt and dangerous as so many in the party's base devoutly believed, how could the Republicans engage him in a normal give-and-take?

There was thus an inevitability to how John Boehner ended up creating a crisis over the debt ceiling in the summer of 2011, a crisis he had said shouldn't happen. "At some point it's clear to me that we have to increase the debt ceiling," Boehner said in late May on CBS's *Face the Nation*. Raising the debt ceiling had never been an issue before. It had been raised repeatedly under Reagan and both Presidents Bush. In the past it had been, at worst, an opportunity for much political posturing. The party out of power would let the party in power do the dirty work, but without obstructing the distasteful but necessary task. The notion that the country would assume debt and then somehow walk away from it had never occurred to anyone as a usable political lever.

It did in the summer of 2011, with serious Republican politicians claiming that there were worse things than defaulting, and that drastically reducing the debt was well worth the risk of doing so.

Boehner and Obama seemed at various points determined to negotiate their way to a solution. In early July, a Boehner-Obama effort to reach a deal was killed by House Majority Leader Eric Cantor. There was a second try, involving Cantor this time, in which Obama, as was his wont, moved more than halfway to accommodate Boehner. Obama initially seemed to bless a deal that included $1.7 trillion in spending cuts in exchange for $800 billion in revenues. Even that modest amount of revenue was to come not from tax rate increases but through "tax reform." And much of the revenue granted by Boehner as a "concession" would have come automatically at the end of 2012 with the expiration of the Bush tax cuts if Obama simply sat tight. It was an astonishingly good deal for the Republicans and would, in fact, have deprived Obama of many of the talking points about taxes and economic justice he would later use in his 2012 campaign.

The deal fell apart for a variety of reasons, though it was never clear that Boehner could have sold it to his conference in any form. Two days after the Boehner and Obama sides seemed close to a deal, a bipartisan group of senators known as the Gang of Six, with three members from each party, came up with an outline worth $3.7 trillion in deficit reduction, including $2 trillion in revenue. Knowing that Democrats would wonder why he had been unable to come up with more revenue than a bipartisan Senate group, Obama asked Boehner if he could find some new revenue in the Senate plan and add it to their deal.

When Jack Lew, Obama's budget director, finally briefed Senate Democrats on what Obama had been cooking up with Boehner, their anger was explosive. They were furious at being left out of the discussions and what they saw as paltry revenue concessions being exchanged for much larger spending cuts. Obama, knowing any deal would need some Democratic support, eventually asked Boehner for $400 billion more in revenue, bringing the total to $1.2 billion. Boehner said the number was impossible, and the talks collapsed.

It was a revealing episode. To begin with, it's astonishing that with unemployment still over 9 percent, the government was obsessed not with restoring job growth but with cutting government—and with very long-term plans that had nothing to do with the immediate crisis. The impact of a radicalized Republican Party was to pull the center of the nation's political conversation far from anything that might once have been recognized as moderation or problem solving. An abstract goal related to the size of government took precedence over the issues that preoccupied Americans at their kitchen tables— employment, wages, mortgages, and defaults. And Washington's centrist elites, themselves focused on long-term deficit reduction, became effective allies of the Republicans by reinforcing their message that deficits mattered most.

Obama was complicit in allowing the Republicans to set the agenda, but he was also responding to a genuine fear. At the time, I regularly asked White House officials why they were so forthcoming in their negotiations with the Republicans. Why were they willing to play on the Republicans' turf and thus reinforce their arguments about the primacy of deficits when Obama and his party knew that economic growth was the more pressing issue? Again and again, I got the same answer: Obama was absolutely convinced that House Republicans were willing to take the country over the cliff. Obama felt he had to do whatever was necessary to prevent default and the resulting economic catastrophe.

This meant that the side prepared to blink was the White House. The madman theory was doing its work.

As for Boehner, opinion was divided in the White House as to whether he was ever serious about making a deal with Obama. The president was convinced that he was, his aides much less so. But a larger truth harmonized these competing assessments: Boehner did not control his own fate. As long as holding on to his job was his main priority, he would have to bend to the right wing of his conference. Estimates of its strength varied, but the Tea Party could count on between 50 and 80 votes, depending on the circumstances. Roll calls suggested that Boehner had 85 to 100 true loyalists. The rest of his 242 members were generally inclined to support Boehner but also deeply fearful of primaries from candidates running to their right. He could not rely on members of this Petrified Caucus, which meant that he could never regard his position as secure.

All of this meant that the country came perilously close to default. A deal was finally struck around a principle unknown to Washington until that point. The "compromise" was based on a simple proposition: politicians would point a fiscal gun to their own heads by assembling a collection of future budget cuts so foolish and nonsensical that neither side would ever allow them to become law. The deal authorized $1.2 trillion in spending caps and then set up a commission to come up with another $1.2 trillion in cuts. If the commission failed, automatic, across-the-board cuts would take hold, half in domestic spending, half in defense. Obama had originally hoped for a difference split, half-and-half between cuts and tax increases. But the GOP's taxophobia made that a nonstarter. The sweeping sequester was hatched precisely because it was such an irrational approach to fiscal discipline. The Obama White House was convinced the defense hawks in the Republican Party would prove more influential than the spending hawks and that "sequestration," as it was known, would never happen. But this assumed a rationality that politics in Washington no longer possessed. Over the long run, the calculation proved flatly wrong. Congress and the White House were still grappling with the results of this deal in Obama's final years in office.

It was a low point for Obama, but also for the Republicans—and above all for the country. The battle over the debt ceiling was a singularly irrational, wasteful, and shameful moment in the political and economic history of the United States. It reflected much of what was wrong with the priorities of the country's political elites and the obsessions of a Republican right that had won itself a kind of veto power over the American government.

The crisis of confidence began with the world hanging on to every development as it fretted over whether Washington's dysfunction would lead to American default and global calamity. Even robustly pro-American commentators and politicians around the world wondered aloud if the United States could still govern itself.

Yet even when default was averted that August, global markets imploded as American political dysfunction joined with the dysfunction inside the European Union to remind everyone of how dangerously fragile the world's economy remained. The portrait of fecklessness was completed when Standard & Poor's, which once happily and profitably stamped triple-A ratings on dubious securities, ended the week by downgrading the federal government's creditworthiness. S&P had once caved in to pressure from Goldman Sachs in its rating of private financial paper, yet it refused even to pause in its dissing of American creditworthiness even though the Obama administration had identified flaws in its numbers and calculations.

The fixation on a deeply ideological debate over government spending seemed strange to a world that was looking to the United States to help power a recovery and provide leadership. What it saw instead was a nation that was suffocatingly inward-looking. Yet ideologues boasted about what they had done. "We weren't kidding around, either," Representative Jason Chaffetz of Utah proudly declared. "We *would* have taken it down." He said this with pride, even though the "it" involved the American economy and America's standing around the globe.

I was visiting London when the debt ceiling endgame came, and it was depressing to hear what even America's staunchest overseas friends were saying about us. They knew the debt crisis was instigated by Obama's opponents, yet they worried about how strong Obama was, and whether he could draw firm lines and seize back the initiative. The shrewdest judgment I encountered came from a leading British Conservative and a member of Prime Minister David Cameron's cabinet. His take on the politics of the debt fight perfectly captured the ambivalence of those who genuinely wished Obama well.

"As a political strategist, he is often underestimated," this politician said of Obama. "He's playing a longer game." While "the Republicans have allowed the Tea Party tail to wag the dog . . . Obama will be able to say, 'I believe in spending cuts, but I also believe that the richest in the country should pay a little more.'" Republicans would counter by arguing for steep cuts in Medicare and other popular programs, but the politician noted that where public opinion was concerned, Obama would hold the higher ground. This proved prophetic.

But the downside of his analysis perfectly described the fix Obama was in. The American president, the British politician said, "seems to be a passive figure at a time when the world needs a leader."

Solving that problem would be essential both to Obama's standing in the world and to his re-election. It was a problem that would crop up again. But with the crisis behind him, Obama set about to seize back the initiative. His self-rescue project would receive a great deal of help from his opponents.

Two speeches, one in the early summer, and one toward the end of the year, sharply defined the choice the voters would face a year later. The first, by Mitt Romney, demonstrated how a former Republican governor whom many had once seen as a moderate was determined not to let the GOP's new Tea Party disposition get in the way of his presidential aspirations. The second, by Obama, marked his abandonment of triangulation and appeasement. He came to realize he could only win by way of a full-throated challenge to the new conservative radicalism.

In light of what eventually came to pass, it is easy to forget how promising Romney's campaign looked on a beautiful Thursday afternoon, June 2, 2011, when he formally announced his presidential candidacy in Stratham, New Hampshire, at a farm owned by one of his supporters. The bales of hay were stacked strategically in the hope that they'd make it into the television screen. The sturdy white barn nearby provided an image worthy of a Christmas card, the symbol of a solid, calm, industrious, and confident country.

The slogan behind the candidate, BELIEVE IN AMERICA, did not invite debate. It was all very reassuring, a sign that despite economic catastrophes and Tea Party rebellions, not everything in politics had been turned on his head. In an age of media flying circuses where it was never clear whether someone was actually running for president and or simply boosting book sales and speaking fees, Romney did it the old-fashioned way. He offered pretty pictures as part of the venerable liturgy of the country's civil religion.

And in a genuinely beautiful speech, Ann Romney captivated the audience by speaking of how her husband had stood by her when she was diagnosed with multiple sclerosis and fought back. She spoke plainly and unsentimentally, which made her testimony all the more powerful. It would astonish me for the rest of the campaign that the Romney apparatus never fully fleshed out the personal side of their candidate, the family man and Mormon leader who had performed many quiet acts of charity and mercy.

But on that lovely announcement day, there were storm clouds, of a political, not meteorological sort. Sarah Palin and Rudy Giuliani showed up in New Hampshire as if to underscore why the punditocracy always seemed to insert the word "putative" before "front-runner" where Romney was concerned.

Romney's travails spoke to the condition of a party that wouldn't let him embrace his actual record and constantly required him—and all other Republicans—to say outlandish things.

Romney's greatest political achievement, the Massachusetts health care law, was a genuinely masterful piece of politics and policy. The *New Yorker*'s Ryan Lizza had written a superb article about how Romney got the plan passed. The article reflected well on both Romney's political skills and his understanding of health care policy. In normal times, Romney's campaign would have reproduced Lizza's piece in bulk. Instead, Romney's lieutenants were no doubt hoping that Republican primary voters never heard about it. Working with those horrid Democrats to pass any sort of forward-looking government program, particularly one that had been a model for the dreaded "Obamacare," was now forbidden.

And so when Romney spoke at Doug and Stella Scamman's Bittersweet Farm, he was guarded in talking about his health plan, saying he "hammered out a solution that took a bad situation and made it better. Not perfect, but it was a state solution to our state's problem." The crowd gave him modest cheers when he got to the part about health care being a *state* problem. Far louder and much more enthusiastic was the response when he pledged "a complete repeal of Obamacare." That's where the GOP's heart was, and Palin and Giuliani both got into most of the stories about Romney's announcement by bashing him on health care. Was it any surprise that a candidate who was constantly forced to tiptoe around his central accomplishments was regularly accused of shifting his shape?

Yet it was Romney himself who exposed contemporary conservatism's core flaw. "Did you know," he asked, "that government—federal, state, and local—under President Obama, has grown to consume almost forty percent of our economy? We're only inches away from ceasing to be a free economy."

Actually, the federal government of which Obama was in charge was "consuming" about a quarter of the economy—and this after a severe recession, when government's share naturally goes up. But even granting Romney his addition of spending by all levels of government, the notion that the United States was "inches away from ceasing to be a free economy" was worse than absurd. It suggested that the only way of measuring freedom was to tote up how much government spent.

This was where the new conservatism led. It implied that we were less "free" than we could be because of the money we spent on public schools and student loans, Medicare and Medicaid, police and firefighters, roads and transit, national defense and environmental protection. The suggestion was that we would be far freer if government spent zero percent of the economy and just stopped doing such things.

It was hard to imagine that Romney, based on his own record, really believed this, but his comment pointed to an underlying argument in American politics about what freedom meant. If freedom came down primarily to counting up how much government spent, then a country such as Sweden would be less "free" than a right-wing dictatorship that had no welfare state and no public schools—but also didn't allow its people to speak, pray, write, or organize as they wished. Many who did "believe in America" also believed that its history had shown that liberty was compatible with an energetic government that had invested in efforts to expand the freedoms from want, fear, and unfair treatment, and the right to self-improvement. Many Republicans—including the Romney who had battled for universal health insurance—had believed in those things, too. But in the Republican Party of 2011 and 2012, liberty could be measured only through a quantitative analysis of government's size.

It was this argument that Obama took on toward the end of the year in what would prove to be one of the most important speeches of his presidency. The venue he chose for his December 6, 2011, address said as much about his purpose as the words he spoke. He traveled to Osawatomie, Kansas, the site of Theodore Roosevelt's legendary "New Nationalism" speech 101 years earlier. TR's speech presaged his 1912 presidential candidacy as a Progressive, after he lost the Republican nomination. But even more, it was the wellspring of twentieth-century American liberalism. It was, in many ways, a radical speech, even if its purpose was to defend capitalism by reforming it and limiting the power of the trusts and the very rich.

TR declared that the "conflict between the men who possess more than they have earned and the men who have earned more than they possess is the central condition of progress." He spoke of "the struggle of freemen to gain and hold the right of self-government as against the special interests, who twist the methods of free government into machinery for defeating the popular will." Roosevelt's conclusion: "At every stage, and under all circumstances, the essence of the struggle is to equalize opportunity, destroy privilege, and give to the life and citizenship of every individual the highest possible value both to himself and to the commonwealth."

And Obama, who, like TR, found himself under attack from both his left and the right, might particularly have appreciated this Roosevelt observation: "Here in Kansas," he said, "there is one paper which habitually denounces me as the tool of Wall Street, and at the same time frantically repudiates the statement that I am a Socialist on the ground that that is an unwarranted slander of the Socialists."

The timing of Obama's speech was also important. He gave it shortly after the Occupy Wall Street movement had captured large-scale media attention and the imaginations of many Americans. Politically, the most surprising aspect of politics after the 2008 Wall Street crash was the absence of a large and organized protest movement on the left. The Great Depression saw a strengthening of both the Socialist and Communist parties, Upton Sinclair's EPIC movement in California, the rise of the labor movement, vast organizations on behalf of old-age pensions, and Huey Long's call to "share the wealth." The lack of a comparable response during the Great Recession was partly a sign of a weakening of the American left (and particularly the decline of organized labor) as well as the ongoing power of the pro-market swing in the intellectual world after the rise of Reagan and the collapse of the Soviet Union. As the historian Daniel Rodgers noted, market metaphors pervaded almost every sphere of life. "Market ideas moved out of the economic departments to become the new standard currency of the social sciences," he wrote in *Age of Fracture*. "To imagine the market now was to imagine a socially-detached array of economic actors, free to choose and optimize, unconstrained by the power of inequalities, governed not by their common deliberative action but only by the impersonal laws of the market."

If Obama often disappointed his allies on the left, it was in part because he was operating in a world in which the market was hegemonic, intellectually as well as financially. And the very radicalization of the right was enabled by a steady moderation on the left side of politics that began to take hold in the Clinton era. One unintended consequence of Third Way politics, as we've seen, was a compression on the left end of the ideological spectrum, which effectively moved the political center and opened further space on the right.

Obama himself did little to encourage the left. On the contrary, his impatience with the left was obvious, and an administration that found itself under constant attack from the right felt it could ill afford progressive opposition. This, too, had unintended consequences: the absence of a strong left made it easier for the right to define Obama as a "left-winger" or "Marxist," even as Wall Street's recovery took place at a much more rapid clip than did the restoration of middle-class incomes. If Obama was a Marxist, he was singularly unsuccessful at it.

Occupy Wall Street partly filled this void. It represented the pent-up frustrations of tens of thousands who longed for an outlet on the left and millions of Americans who wondered why Wall Street had not been held to account for its misdeeds.

Occupy was in no way comparable to the Tea Party. The Tea Party was a highly organized right-wing pressure group that was entirely comfortable operating inside the Republican Party, even if it often cast itself as an insurgency against the party's establishment. Occupy disdained party and even electoral politics. In its mistrust of the very idea of leadership, it resembled some of the more romantic tendencies of the 1960s New Left. It was therefore ill suited for the mainstream political fray. As the *New Yorker's* Hendrik Hertzberg observed: "Ultimately, inevitably, the route to real change has to run through politics, the politics of America's broken, god-awful, immutably two party system, the only one we have." He asked, almost plaintively: "The Tea Partiers know that. Do the Occupiers?"

No, the Occupiers didn't, and yet they fundamentally changed the American political debate by introducing a powerful slogan that stood in for the entire history of American progressive and left-wing thought: they spoke of the power of the "One Percent." Suddenly the country had its attention focused not on the allegedly overweening power of government, but on the raw power of the wealthiest Americans. The issue was not how much the average American had taken out of his or her paycheck in taxes, but how small that paycheck had become relative to the rewards reaped by the very rich, particularly the financiers and hedge fund managers. The problem was not whether government had grown to 40 percent of the GDP, but how large a share of GDP growth had gone to the wealthiest 1 percent—and particularly the superrich 0.01 percent. If the Tea Party spoke of liberty (or the lack thereof), Occupy spoke of equality (and inequality). Occupy had no electoral ambitions, but it altered the terrain of the 2012 election in ways that would badly hurt Mitt Romney and greatly help Barack Obama.

Many spoke at the time of the Tea Party and Occupy movements as representing similar forces of opposition and alienation. But this view was flatly wrong, misreading both movements by trying to pretend that left-right distinctions no longer mattered. Each movement was more than just a protest; both were, in their very different ways, philosophically and politically coherent. A *Washington Post*/Pew Research Center Poll in October 2011 found that while 64 percent of Occupy supporters were Democrats or Democratic-leaning Independents, 71 percent of the Tea Party's supporters were Republicans or Republican-leaning Independents. Among Tea Partiers, 56 percent called themselves conservative, compared with only 21 percent of Occupiers. And partisans of the two movements simply didn't like each other. Among Occupy supporters, 64 percent said they opposed the Tea Party while only 25 percent supported it. The Tea Partiers returned the favor: 52 percent said they opposed Occupy while 34 percent supported it. In all, only one American in ten claimed to support both the Tea Party and Occupy. Comrades in arms they were not.

The Occupy movement set the stage for Obama in Osawatomie. His speech was the inaugural address he never gave—a clear philosophical rationale for his presidency, a straightforward narrative explaining the causes of the nation's travails, and a coherent plan for battle against a radicalized conservatism. He had decided he was more likely to win if the 2012 election was about big things rather than small ones. He sought to turn the campaign from a plebiscite about the state of the economy into a referendum about the broader progressive tradition that made us a middle-class nation. For the second time, he staked his fate on a battle for the future.

This choice had obvious political benefits for an incumbent presiding over a still-ailing economy, and it confirmed Obama's shift from a defensive crouch to an aggressive philosophical attack. It was his boldest move since he decided to go all-out for health insurance reform even after Scott Brown's victory.

In drawing upon TR, Obama tied himself unapologetically to a defense of America's long progressive and liberal tradition. The Republican Roosevelt, after all, drew his inspiration from the writer Herbert Croly, whose book *The Promise of American Life* can fairly be seen as the original manifesto for modern liberalism. Thus did Tea Party's radicalism encourage a shrewd politician to take on a task that Democrats have been reluctant to engage in since Ronald Reagan's ascendancy.

Obama was remarkably direct in declaring that the core ideas of the progressivism advanced by Theodore and Franklin Roosevelt were right, and that the commitments of Reagan-era supply-side economics were wrong. He praised TR for knowing "that the free market has never been a free license to take whatever you can from whomever you can" and for understanding that "the free market only works when there are rules of the road that ensure competition is fair and open and honest."

He also eviscerated supply-side economics as a theory promising that "if we just cut more regulations and cut more taxes—especially for the wealthy—our economy will grow stronger."

"But here's the problem," Obama said. "It doesn't work. It has never worked. It didn't work when it was tried in the decade before the Great Depression. It's not what led to the incredible postwar booms of the fifties and sixties. And it didn't work when we tried it during the last decade."

His attack that day was on the specifics of conservative policies, but also on the fundamentals: "In fact," he said, "they want to go back to the same policies that stacked the deck against middle-class Americans for way too many years. And their philosophy is simple: We are better off when everybody is left to fend for themselves and play by their own rules." He added:

> I am here to say they are wrong. I'm here in Kansas to reaffirm my deep conviction that we're greater together than we are on our own. I believe that this country succeeds when everyone gets a fair shot, when everyone does their fair share, when everyone plays by the same rules. These aren't Democratic values or Republican values. These aren't 1 percent values or 99 percent values. They're American values. And we have to reclaim them.

That brief passage was interrupted three times by applause. Obama had found his message.

A White House that just a few months earlier had been obsessed with the political center was suddenly not at all wary, as a senior adviser put it to me at the time, of extolling "a vision that has worked for this country." But this lieutenant also noted that Obama implicitly contrasted the flexibility of the Rooseveltian progressivism with the rigidity of the current brand of conservatism. The official pointed to Obama's strong commitment to education reform, including his critique in Osawatomie of "just throwing money at education."

"You can embrace [the progressive tradition] if you can make the point that philosophies and political theories can evolve as facts on the ground change," the adviser said. The liberalism Obama advocated thus contained a core of moderation that the ideology of the Tea Party did not. Obama realized that the path toward moderate voters would pass through a wholesale critique of the immoderation of the right.

For months, progressives had asked why Obama had not invoked the populist language of Franklin D. Roosevelt and his attacks on "economic royalists" and "the privileged princes" of "new economic dynasties." What progressives often forgot is that FDR offered these words only when his first term was almost over, in his acceptance speech at the 1936 Democratic National Convention. Roosevelt did not become a full-throated economic populist until the election was upon him—and only after he was pressed by a left and a labor movement that demanded more of him.

Facing his own reelection and pushed by an Occupy Wall Street movement that made economic inequality a driving political issue, Barack Obama discovered both of his inner Roosevelts. It would work for him, as it did for them, and the Republicans did what they could to make it easy.

Some political insurgencies grow out of presidential campaigns. Both the 1964 Goldwater movement in the Republican Party and the 1968 antiwar Democratic campaigns of Eugene McCarthy and Robert Kennedy had long legacies. But the Tea Party was an antipresidential movement. It arose in reaction to both Bush and Obama and was not particularly taken by John McCain's 2008 campaign, even if it had loved his choice of Sarah Palin. Tea Partiers had made their mark in a midterm election, with its smaller and older electorate, and while they had scattered victories in more moderate or liberal states, they were strongest in the reddest of red states.

Nor was there a single designated Tea Party candidate in the 2012 primaries, although Representative Michele Bachmann tried hard to play that role. Romney, the putative front-runner, was not an obvious Tea Party choice, even if he had run to McCain's right in 2008. Yet the Tea Party left an indelible mark on the 2012 Republican contest by creating a mad scramble to the right.

The Romney who opened his campaign on that beautiful day at Bittersweet Farm wanted to use enough antigovernment rhetoric to satisfy the right but otherwise run a relatively mainstream campaign capitalizing on economic discontent. His campaign guru, Stuart Stevens, was much taken by the British Conservative Party's 1979 campaign against an incumbent Labour Party. It was the election that brought Margaret Thatcher to power. In particular, he admired a poster depicting a long unemployment line under the slogan

LABOUR ISN'T WORKING. He openly borrowed the motif, producing a virtual copy of the poster under the heading OBAMA ISN'T WORKING. The theory of the Romney campaign, by no means exotic or irrational, was that there was enough unhappiness in the country to give Obama's Republican opponent an edge. Romney could win the election—as long as the campaign stayed focused on Obama and the economy. And, of course, as long as Romney could win the nomination.

But in a field of right-wing candidates, and with a very conservative electorate, the second objective derailed the first. Romney was forced to move right and had to spend so much time attacking his opponents to keep them at bay that he never got around to building a positive case for himself. Many moderate voters suspected that Romney didn't believe all the right-wing things he was saying. This, in their view, made him a safe alternative to Obama. But many conservative voters also suspected Romney didn't believe all the right-wing things he was saying. His Republican opponents had every interest in aiming straight at this tension in the Romney strategy, and Democrats cheered them on. In the process, Romney made enough mistakes—many of them encouraged by the nature of his party and the state of conservative ideology—that he moved the focus away from Obama and toward himself.

There was a larger problem: the impression the Republican primary candidates made collectively may have created more damage than did any of their individual shortcomings. It gives one a sense of how it felt at the time that even the loyally conservative columnist Charles Krauthammer referred to the Republican contenders as "bumbling clowns." The "minor" candidates became major celebrities because the party scheduled twenty-two debates. These became an unexpected political sitcom hit with an entertaining cast of characters. Herman Cain seemed to tout his "9-9-9" tax plan in every other sentence. At one point, Bachmann confused John Wayne with the serial killer John Wayne Gacy. Rick Santorum accused President Obama of being a "snob" for the great sin of wanting young Americans to attend college. Newt Gingrich, who specialized in political resurrections, had long ago mastered the art of making himself the center of attention under almost any circumstances. Texas governor Rick Perry pledged to abolish three cabinet departments but couldn't remember the third one. Perry said "oops," which pretty well summarized his party's attitude toward the entire exercise when all the debates were over.

The longing of the Republican right for someone other than Romney was obvious from the polls all through 2011 and into early 2012. Tea Party supporters and their allies shifted from one conservative candidate to another as the fortunes of the various alternatives rose and fell. For a significant part of the Republican primary electorate, it was anybody but Romney, and they clearly did mean *anybody*. Every few weeks, a new conservative candidate (they became known as the "non-Romneys") would consolidate enough votes on the right to take the lead in a national poll. Typically, a candidate would rise with a particularly good debate performance or a victory in a straw poll. In Bachmann's case, Fox News' website headlined her triumph in Iowa's straw poll in August 2011—she won 28 percent and nearly 17,000 ballots. The victory, Fox headlined, "cements her top-tier status in GOP race." Imagining Bachmann in the top tier was terrifying to many Republicans and delightful to Democrats, but it was not fanciful. A couple of months earlier, a Zogby poll found Bachmann leading nationwide with 24 percent to 15 percent each for Romney and Cain. That any poll could find Bachmann and Cain with a full third of the Republican electorate said a great deal about the nature of the GOP in 2011. It was a history that would repeat itself in a more spectacular fashion in the summer and fall of 2015 when Donald Trump and neurosurgeon Ben Carson swapped the number one and number two spots in many national and state surveys—and were then challenged themselves by a brief surge from Carly Fiorina, the former Hewlett-Packard CEO.

The clear opening at the right end of the party drew Perry into the 2012 race, and for a while, he seemed the obvious favorite. He combined the executive experience most of the candidates on the right lacked with views highly congenial to the Tea Party. He was certainly the only Republican candidate who had flirted with secession. After a Tea Party event in 2009, he had told an Associated Press reporter that Texas "would be able to leave [the Union] if we decided to do that," and added: "We've got a great union. There is absolutely no reason to dissolve it. But if Washington continues to thumb their nose at the American people, you know, who knows what may come out of that?" Such notions went down well with many conservatives in the Age of Obama.

And shortly after Perry entered the race on August 11, 2011, he surged to the top. The August 17–21 Gallup survey had him at 29 percent to 17 percent for Romney. Bachmann had fallen to 10 percent and Gingrich and Cain held 4 percent each. Ron Paul, holding aloft the libertarian banner, held his core voters no matter what was happening around him. He came in at 10 percent in July, 13 percent in August. Another survey at the time by Public Policy Polling put Perry at 33 percent to 20 percent for Romney. The nomination was Perry's to lose, and lose it he did. After Perry faded, it was Cain's turn to rise, and he found himself briefly in first, with 27 percent to Romney's 23 percent, in an NBC/*Wall Street Journal* poll in October. Tea Partiers and allied religious conservatives were desperate for an alternative, and they would turn anywhere they could find one.

The causes of Perry's collapse were revealing. The accepted wisdom, true to a certain degree, is that his campaign was over after his "oops" moment at the November 9, 2011, Republican debate. Telling Republican voters what they wanted to hear, he promised deep cuts in the federal bureaucracy. "And I will tell you," he declared, "it's three agencies of government when I get there that are gone: Commerce, Education and the—what's the third one there? Let's see." He struggled and struggled until he surrendered. "I can't. The third one I can't. Sorry. Oops." The missing department was Energy, a curious lapse for a Texas governor.

Momentary failures of memory are common enough. But one presumes that a candidate for president making sweeping proposals ponders them carefully, discusses them with advisers, and understands their implications. Forgetting an idea at the heart of your program is not the same as forgetting a phone number, a friend's name, a football score, or the title of a recently read book. Perry's brain-freeze moment seemed to show he wasn't asserting anything that he was truly serious about. And this spoke to the extent that the conservative movement seemed to have been overtaken by what was, quite literally, a mindless opposition to government. Perry thought, correctly, that he had a winning sound bite, if he had managed to blurt it out, because promises to scrap government departments (and three was a nice, round number) always led conservatives to cheer without asking too many questions.

Yet Perry had begun to fall in the polls before his gaffe. He lost ground largely because he was too *liberal* for the Republican primary electorate—on immigration. At a debate in Orlando on September 23, Romney attacked Perry for a Texas policy providing in-state tuition for the children of undocumented immigrants, a replay of the 2008 attacks on Mike Huckabee. Texas's approach, Romney said, meant that illegal immigrants received as much as $22,000 a year in tuition breaks that citizens who lived outside the state did not get. "That just doesn't make sense to me," Romney said.

Perry was passionate in embracing his state's approach to immigrant children and defending his policy. His stout defense of compassionate conservatism redux, at least in this instance, earned him boos from the crowd. "If you say that we should not educate children that have come into our state for no other reason than they've been brought here by no fault of their own, I don't think you have a heart," Perry said. Conservatives, from Goldwater forward, have never taken kindly to being called heartless. Romney and allied Super PACs went after Perry on the issue and his polling numbers sagged. Perry quickly realized that accusing staunch conservatives—his base—of being heartless was a mistake, and he apologized. "I was probably a bit overpassionate in using that word and it was inappropriate," he said in an interview with the right-wing website *Newsmax*. But conservatives suspected that Perry had meant what he said in the first place, and they were almost certainly right. In 2000, after all, another Texas governor had won a Republican nomination primary by embracing immigrants and Latinos. But what had worked for George W. Bush could no longer work in a Republican primary. Conservative hostility to illegal immigrants, already pronounced in 2008, was moving to the plane of litmus test politics.

Romney's need to put down challenges from his right (and Perry's, before his numbers fell to earth, was clearly the most dangerous) pushed him much further on immigration than he needed to go. And at another debate in Orlando, on January 23, 2012, he made his position indelible for Latino voters.

Adam Smith, the political editor of the *Tampa Bay Times*, told Romney he was "confused" about his stance on deportation because Romney had said he did not want to "round up people and deport them, but you also say that they would have to go back to their home countries and then apply for citizenship. So, if you don't deport them, how do you send them home?"

"The answer is self-deportation, which is people decide they can do better by going home because they can't find work here because they don't have legal documentation to allow them to work here," Romney replied. "And so we're not going to round people up."

One can imagine that at the moment, Romney was pleased with this response. "Self-deportation" was a memorable phrase and it seemed a relatively humane alternative to "rounding people up." Yet those words would haunt Romney for the rest of the campaign. The concept seemed bizarre—and it would be remembered by Latino voters. On that January night, Romney set himself up for what would, ten months later, be the weakest performance for a Republican candidate with Latino voters in decades.

Conservatives quickly realized that Cain was not a plausible alternative, especially after the emergence of sexual harassment charges against him. Cain and his defenders initially tried to rally conservatives with the most reliable call in the conservative playbook, assailing the "liberal media" and "the Democrat machine" for going after their man—forgetting what they had said not many years earlier about comparable charges leveled against Bill Clinton. But Cain was never a strong enough candidate to weather such a storm, and he faded.

By mid-December, the Republican right seemed ready to embrace the tried-and-true. Newt Gingrich had never gone away and a Republican campaign dominated by debates was made for a man who loved nothing more than turning phrases and matching wits with any comer. At the time, it was strangely entertaining to witness the apoplectic fear and loathing of so many GOP establishmentarians toward the man who had led them to victory in 1994. Many Republicans treated Gingrich as an alien body.

Gingrich's rise was the revenge of a Republican base that actually took seriously the intense hostility to Obama, the incendiary accusations against liberals, and the Manichaean division of the world between an "us" and a "them" that Gingrich had long been peddling. The right-wing faithful knew that Gingrich had pioneered this style of politics, and they scoffed at efforts to cast the former House Speaker as something other than a "true conservative." The Establishment was happy to use Gingrich's tactics to win elections, but it never expected to lose control of the party to the voters it rallied with such grandiose negativity. The joke was on those who had manipulated the base. The base was striking back, and Newt, for a while, was its weapon.

It's not as if the criticisms being leveled at Gingrich were all wrong. There was always a flamboyant self-importance and an eerie sense of mission about him. "I am a transformational figure," he had said. He also admitted: "I have an enormous personal ambition. I want to shift the entire planet. And I'm doing it." But Gingrich offered the first set of thoughts in 1994 and spoke of shifting the planet way back in 1985. Newt, in other words, had been Newt for a long time. Yet many of the same Republican leaders who found all this so distasteful in 2011 had cheered the very same qualities when he was in his earlier role. Liberals who criticized these traits earlier were tut-tutted for not "getting it," for failing to understand the man's genius. It was only when Gingrich seemed to threaten Republican chances of defeating Obama that party elders decided that what they once saw as visionary self-confidence was debilitating hubris after all. *National Review,* for example, criticized Gingrich for "his impulsiveness, his grandiosity, his weakness for half-baked (and not especially conservative) ideas." Its editors were simply reciting from a catechism that his critics had written long ago. Meet the new Newt, same as the old Newt.

Still, even conservatives who admired him knew that Gingrich was very much yesterday's man, and if he emerged for a while as better than any of the alternatives to Romney, he had hardly secured that role. I visited Iowa in late December 2011 to take stock of a Republican contest that was in shambles. Romney had hung on as the front-runner simply because no single candidate on the right had risen long enough to assume the role of the main challenger. Romney had also built an impregnable fortress in New Hampshire to survive a possible defeat in Iowa. But on January 3, who would Iowa's very conservative caucusgoers anoint as the alternative to him?

At that point, the race was a bookie's nightmare. The contest was becoming less rather than more settled, and anyone among the six major remaining candidates had a reasonable chance of coming in first or second. Libertarian Ron Paul had the energy of a loyal organization and supporters who didn't have much use for anyone else. Romney's opposition was so badly splintered that he had a chance to come in first—but also faced the possibility of lagging far behind. The line between success and failure for him was very thin. Gingrich, the target of millions of dollars of negative advertising, seemed to be surrendering the Iowa lead he had briefly held. He tried to use jujitsu to turn all the negative media in his favor, and when I caught up with him at a factory in Ottumwa, he denounced Romney as "purely dishonest" for refusing to push his Super PAC—theoretically independent of the campaign but closely connected to Romney's supporters—to stop running the ads. It wasn't going to happen. At the time, Gingrich was visiting an enterprise called Al-jon, which, a company official explained, could take a large truck "and in two minutes, it cubes that truck into a bundle the size of a refrigerator." Figuratively speaking, that's what Gingrich's opponents, Romney in particular, were threatening to do to his candidacy.

And thus was the way prepared for Rick Santorum, the former Pennsylvania senator and both devoutly conservative and devoutly Catholic. Santorum's biggest advantage was that he had never yet emerged as the top alternative on the right to Romney, meaning that he had largely avoided attacks from his opponents and the scrutiny they had received. He also understood something important about the Republican Party, and particularly about Iowa caucusgoers: while all the media attention since 2009 had gone to the shiny new object of the Tea Party, the older forces of the religious right had never gone away—and, as we have seen, many Tea Partiers were as conservative on theological and cultural issues as were the followers of Jerry Falwell, Pat Robertson, and their successors. It was a fact that came home to Republicans later in the year when two social conservatives won Republican Senate nominations and make comments about abortion and rape that would cost the party two elections it should have won.

Santorum's awareness of the outsize role of religious voices in the low-turnout caucuses led him to bet his entire candidacy on Iowa. When I heard him speak that December at the Royal Amsterdam Hotel in Pella—a lovely town that honors its Dutch background with windmills—he told an appreciative crowd that he had spent so much time in the state, he could challenge lifelong residents to Iowa trivia contests. Speaking before a banner touting his "Faith, Family, and Freedom" tour, Santorum combined detailed proposals—including tax policies aimed at reviving American manufacturing—with harsh attacks on President Obama. But he sought to close the deal with frankly theological reflections. "I approach every problem in my life through faith and reason," he said. "If your reason is right and your faith is true, you'll end up in the same place." And toward the end of the campaign, he won endorsements from prominent religious conservatives in the state, including Robert Vander Plaats, the CEO of a group called the Family Leader, and Chuck Hurley, another Christian activist. The effect was to create the sense that Santorum was on the move, a valuable signal to anti-Romney conservatives still trying to figure out the most effective vote to cast.

And on caucus night, it was Santorum who rose above the rest of the non-Romneys. His victory was robbed of its immediate significance when party officials declared Mitt Romney the victor by eight votes, giving him needed momentum. Yet a final count more than two weeks later showed that Santorum had actually won Iowa by 34 votes. By forcing a premature announcement, GOP chieftains did Romney a great favor—one time, at least, when the right's complaints against a party establishment had real force. Still, Iowa made Rick Santorum, at least for a while.

If Santorum's victory was a reminder of the continuing power of religious concerns in the Tea Party Republican era, it also underscored another aspect of the GOP coalition that would prove troubling for Romney: the sharp class split between the working-class whites who provided Republican candidates with critical support, and the upscale conservatives most interested in low taxes and pro-business regulatory policies—and who financed the party. The deal within conservatism involved the business end of the party getting its way on economics and the working and lower middle class getting a dose of social conservatism.

But in an economic downturn, social conservatives could not live on values alone. There was economic discontent in the ranks, and Santorum highlighted the class rift with a moving Iowa valedictory speech in which he spoke of his grandfather, who "worked in the mine at a company town, got paid with coupons . . . lived in a shack.

"He ended up continuing to work in those mines until he was seventy-two years old, digging coal," Santorum went on. "I'll never forget the first time I saw someone who had died. It was my grandfather. And I knelt next to his coffin. And all I could do . . . was look at his hands. They were enormous hands. And all I could think was those hands dug freedom for me."

Santorum turned his personal tale into a challenge to his party. He was all for low taxes, he said, but insisted that "we as Republicans have to look at those who are not doing well in our society by just cutting taxes and balancing budgets." Among his proposals was a plan to eliminate corporate taxes altogether on manufacturing, and he used it to take a jab at free-market ideologues: "When Republican purists say to me, well, why are you treating manufacturing different than retail? I say because Wal-Mart's not moving to China and taking their jobs with them." Santorum's message was that blue-collar work and blue-collar values were intimately linked.

Santorum's attempt to graft a distinctive economic appeal onto traditional social conservatism represented something new in the Republican Party. It served as a warning that despite Obama's unpopularity among many lower-income whites, Republicans and conservatives could not count on their unquestioned loyalty. Santorum was filling a void in the Republican Party left by the withdrawal of Tim Pawlenty, the former Minnesota governor, after he was overwhelmed in the Iowa straw poll by Bachmann. Recognizing the importance of blue-collar voters to the Republican coalition, Pawlenty sought to make it "the party of Sam's Club, not just the country club." He hoped to speak for the movement's less privileged voters who shopped at the famous discount outlet. Without adopting Pawlenty's label, Santorum was picking up his role and his strategy.

In one sense, Santorum was reflecting a widespread nostalgia for the America of the 1950s, a longing that affected both the left and the right. Santorum yearned for the family stability and the high levels of religious observance that characterized the immediate post–World War II era. Progressives wanted to bring back strong unions and a time of American economic dominance that kept blue-collar wages high. The two dreams reinforced each other: the family values Santorum promoted had been underwritten by the high wages the left hoped to restore. Santorum failed to pull off the synthesis, partly because he was constrained by conservatism's continued hostility to unions and the limits of its antigovernment, low-tax ideology. (The same had been true of Pawlenty.) Santorum's economic program was inadequate to the task he was taking on, since a tax break for manufacturers would not be enough to restore the old social bargain. But the success he did enjoy was a warning to conservatives: they could not take the support their movement had won among blue-collar voters for granted.

If Santorum represented an intriguing form of dissent on the blue-collar end of the movement, the candidacy of Jon Huntsman Jr., the former Utah governor whom Obama had appointed as his ambassador to China, was the dissent of the moderately conservative upper middle class. The fact that Huntsman had accepted a job from Obama almost certainly doomed his candidacy from the beginning. For most conservatives, working for Obama was a form of partisan and philosophical treason. And the fact that Huntsman first joined the administration and then left abruptly to become an Obama critic smacked of opportunism.

Nonetheless, when Huntsman announced his candidacy in June 2011, he was opening the way for a different kind of conservatism, a correction of the movement's direction. The closest model for Huntsman's approach was British prime minister David Cameron's remake of the British Conservative Party's image. The Tories chose Cameron as their leader in 2005 because they were sick of losing elections and realized they could no longer present themselves as an old, cranky, right-wing party. Cameron was Mr. Nice, Mr. Modern, Mr. Moderate, and Mr. New. And he won.

Huntsman was betting that enough Republicans had concluded that the country needed a less doctrinaire, less extreme, and less angry GOP. Most striking about his announcement in front of the Statue of Liberty (other than a slew of snafus, including the misspelling of his first name on a batch of press passes) was the extent to which his speech was all about hope and promise. It offered a lot about who Huntsman wanted you to think he was and little about what he'd do. With not all that many changes, it could have been a speech delivered by someone announcing a Democratic primary challenge to Obama—and, in some ways, by Obama himself.

"We have the power, we have the means, we have the character to astonish the world again by making from adversity a new and better country; this inexhaustible land of promise and opportunity," he declared. "We're choosing whether we are to be yesterday's story or tomorrow's."

His slogan might have been: Platitudes with a purpose. Or perhaps: Change we can believe in. Still, the upbeat rhetoric contrasted sharply with a party characterized by a sense of doom about the nation's cultural direction, ideological rigidity, and a reflexive less-government, lower-taxes response to every problem.

It was a sign of how rancid politics had become that the biggest "news" in the speech came in these sentences: "And I respect the president of the United States. He and I have a difference of opinion on how to help a country we both love. But the question each of us wants the voters to answer is who will be the better president; not who's the better American." It was actually brave for a Republican candidate to declare that the president was a good American who loved his country.

Huntsman's hopes rested largely on New Hampshire, where independents could cast ballots in the Republican primary, and in other states where Democrats as well as independents could cross over. Huntsman hoped for a repeat of the 2000 and 2008 victories of another relatively moderate maverick, John McCain.

In December 2011, I stopped by a Huntsman talk to a Rotary Club meeting at the Monadnock Country Club in Peterborough, New Hampshire, a town that had once served as a stately home to old-fashioned moderate-to-progressive New England Republicanism. It was revealing that when Dennis Allen, the club's president-elect, introduced Huntsman, he mentioned that his earlier diplomatic posts came from George H. W. and George W. Bush, but omitted the name of the president who gave Huntsman the China job.

Huntsman's moderate rhetoric made him quite popular among Democrats and moderate independents, but his Rotary speech underscored what they tended to overlook—and what Huntsman hoped Republicans would notice: that on core economic issues, the genial candidate was solidly right of center. He noted that he had "embraced" Representative Paul Ryan's budget as "a very aggressive approach" to the deficit. He endorsed term limits for members of Congress, promised "no more bailouts," condemned "Obamacare" and the Dodd-Frank financial overhaul, and criticized the "regulatory barriers" to business. He boasted of praise he has won from the *Wall Street Journal*'s editorial page, the arbiter of conservative economic orthodoxy.

Yet there was just enough heterodoxy for the moderates. Huntsman said he wanted to break up the biggest banks and put an end to the idea of "too big to fail." He said he would pull American troops out of Afghanistan. And he spoke longingly of national unity, mourning that the country was "more divided than at any point in history."

The orientation of the Republican primary electorate made it hard for Huntsman to run straight out as a middle-of-the-roader, which sent a mixed message to the state's voters, as Steve Duprey, a Republican National Committee member from New Hampshire, told me at the time: "He started running as a moderate, and now he's saying he's a conservative. That's confusing."

At an earlier moment in Republican history, Huntsman might have connected with parts of the right with a more consistently center-right argument. But any link to Obama was toxic in a Republican primary in 2012, and just as it took the British Conservative Party three election defeats before it was willing to turn to Cameron, so it would take more time for the Republicans to be open to the likes of Huntsman. As it was, the 2012 mood in large parts of the party may have been best captured in a question Santorum was asked during an appearance in Windham, New Hampshire: Did he think the Tenth Amendment allowed states to nullify federal laws. To his credit, Santorum did not pander to the nullifier. "We had a Civil War about nullification," Santorum said with a smile. "I'm not sure I want to go there."

When the returns came in on January 10, Huntsman's bet on New Hampshire did not look foolish, but he did fall short. Romney, who had built a powerful organizational firewall in the state, won overwhelmingly with 39 percent, to 23 percent for Ron Paul. Huntsman came in third with 17 percent. Paul's showing reflected the powerful libertarian strain that runs through the state with "Live Free or Die" on its license plates. Pure libertarianism was a minority view, but it was a big enough minority to keep Huntsman out of second place. Gingrich and Santorum ran virtually even, at just over 9 percent each, fourth and fifth respectively, well behind Huntsman.

In political terms, it was a nearly perfect result for Romney: Gingrich and Santorum, the two main competitors to his right, were weakened, but neither had managed to knock the other out. Paul was never going to threaten Romney for the nomination. And the wild-card challenge from Huntsman was definitively derailed.

Yet there have been many moments when presidential candidates lost their immediate battles but foreshadowed the future. Goldwater has entered history as such a figure. While the 2012 Huntsman and Santorum campaigns will never enjoy the cache of Goldwater's glorious defeat, the two stood in for the debate Republicanism and conservatism will need to have in the coming decades.

Huntsman was a forceful economic conservative but also resolutely modern. He was a defender of science and a hard-eyed realist on foreign affairs who rejected neoconservative moralism and interventionism. He spoke the language of the moderately conservative wing of the upper middle class that preferred politics to focus on economic growth, deficits, and our future competition with China rather than on the social issues of abortion and gay rights. Huntsman's core vote, such as it was, came from less intensely religious economic rationalists who do not perceive culture wars as breaking out all over.

Santorum championed the Republican working class. He was a Catholic on one side of a long-standing debate in the church about how to build a decent society. In contrast to the more liberal social justice Catholics who found a voice again in Pope Francis, Santorum was what Republican strategist Steve Wagner labeled a "social renewal" Catholic. Such Catholics saw opposition to abortion as a foundational matter and opposition to gay marriage as essential to protecting the family. They viewed the federal government less as a guarantor of social fairness than as "inflicting harm on the nation's moral character," as Wagner put it. It was a brand of Catholicism that sought an alliance with evangelical Christians who viewed the social issues as paramount.

Yet Santorum, like Pawlenty, also struggled to find an economic program that would speak to the interests as well as the values of those on the right who were not invited to join country clubs. Their specific proposals were inadequate to the task, but they were right in their insight that conservatives could no longer take the white working-class vote for granted. It would fall to other conservatives to try to answer the need they identified but did not meet.

The future of conservatism depends on the willingness of conservatives to recognize that Huntsman's modernist critique and Santorum's traditionalist critique each point to long-term problems facing their coalition and their creed. If conservatives want to focus primarily on economic issues, they will have to engineer the movement toward social moderation that Huntsman began. And if they want to maintain the support of middle-income and working-class voters who have been so vital to their victories, conservatives will have to pay heed to the discontent among working-class conservatives with whom Santorum identified.

In 2012, the issue of class would not go away, and class warfare against Romney was initially injected into the campaign not by Obama and the Democrats, but by Republicans themselves. Occupy Wall Street was hardly a conservative movement, but Mitt Romney's opponents saw a chance for victory in the language of lower Manhattan's Zuccotti Park.

With Romney emerging after New Hampshire as the clear front-runner, it was nothing short of astonishing that GOP rivals *running to his right* sought to place the nature of modern capitalism at the center of the Republican debate. Their interest was not theoretical. They decided, in line with one of Karl Rove's famous dictums, that the best way to undercut an opponent was to attack him in his area of perceived strength. Romney's central claim was that his experience in business, including venture capital, prepared him to be the nation's premier job creator. This message would run into difficulty if he came to be seen as a job destroyer. And that's exactly the case his opponents made.

What if a certain class of capitalist made scads of money not by building up companies but by tearing them down? What if there was a distinction between the capitalist who created a good product and hired people to make and market it, and another kind of capitalist who took over a company, pulled out all the cash he could, and then abandoned it to die? These questions were raised not by a Marxist intellectual writing in an obscure journal. They underlay the way Rick Perry chose to describe Romney's line of work at a town hall meeting in Fort Mill, South Carolina, on January 10, 2012. He did it more colorfully than the average academic.

"They're just vultures," Perry declared. "They're vultures that are sitting out there on the tree limb waiting for the company to get sick, and then they swoop in, they eat the carcass, they leave with that, and they leave the skeleton." The late Molly Ivins, the Lone Star State's legendary populist scribe, must have been smiling in a People's Heaven.

The day before, Newt Gingrich had made a similar case while visiting the right's media citadel. On Fox News, he told Sean Hannity: "I think there's a real difference between people who believed in the free market and people who go around, take financial advantage, loot companies, leave behind broken families, broken towns, people on unemployment."

Rarely had class warfare been so explicit in the conservative world. And the strategy of the non-Romneys right made tactical sense. Romney was clearly the candidate of the best-heeled Republicans. In New Hampshire, the exit polls found he had done best among voters earning more than $200,000 a year, next best with those whose incomes were between $100,000 and $200,000. He was weakest among those taking home less than $50,000 annually. A privileged candidate was sitting atop a relatively privileged base. The available votes were elsewhere.

Romney hit back, and would eventually force his rivals to relent, by insisting that they were putting "free enterprise on trial," and he would be proud to defend it. His language fit more comfortably within the conservative worldview. But damage was being done, and non-Republican blue-collar voters started noticing.

Indeed, one of the very toughest ads against Romney's business past during the 2012 campaign was produced by the Super PAC supporting Gingrich and funded by Sheldon Adelson, the casino billionaire. It was not subtle. Titled "King of Bain: When Mitt Romney Came to Town," it included interviews in which those who had lost jobs at companies that Romney's Bain Capital had taken over. The ad, drawn from a documentary, intermingled their accounts of pain and suffering, which they attributed to Bain, and images of Romney's "$12 million California beach house."

"Who am I?" a man in a Vietnam veteran's hat says. "I'm Bob Stafford. Mitt Romney and those guys, they don't care who I am."

The film's producer, Barry Bennett, said he wanted Republicans to be aware of the political risks they would run with Romney. "David Axelrod is going to have a heyday with this," Bennett told the *New York Times,* referring to Obama's top strategist, "and Republicans need to know this story before we nominate this guy." Bennett was entirely right, although he also made Axelrod's job easier. In his 2015 memoir, Axelrod called the video "vicious" and said it played into the campaign's plans to make Romney's activities at Bain "ground zero for an economic values argument." The Obama forces would pick up the Bain critique in May and start running their own ads on Romney and his company in June.

The attacks on Romney helped Gingrich to overwhelm him in the January 21 South Carolina primary. Gingrich won more than 40 percent of the vote, to just under 28 percent for Romney and 17 percent for Santorum. Gingrich beat Romney by 20 points among Tea Party supporters and by 5 points among voters who said they were neutral about the Tea Party. Romney carried Tea Party opponents, 32 percent to 19 percent for Gingrich. But this group amounted to all of *8 percent* of South Carolina primary voters, 64 percent of whom said they supported the Tea Party. Gingrich also drew a class line across South Carolina, once again confirming Romney's weakness among working-class and middle-class voters, even in Republican primaries. The exit polls found Romney carrying only one income group: voters earning more than $200,000 a year. Voters earning less than $100,000 a year went strongly for Gingrich.

But Romney was blessed with weak opponents. With his challengers whittled down to Gingrich and Santorum (even as Ron Paul continued to gather up votes from faithful libertarians), Romney appealed to enough Republicans, even those who didn't much like him, as the only plausible president on the ballot. After launching fierce attacks on Gingrich, Romney recovered his footing in the January 31 Florida primary, taking 46 percent to 32 percent for the former Speaker. Santorum trailed both. Romney's victory was in large part a negative verdict on Gingrich, who was viewed unfavorably by 40 percent of those who cast ballots. After months of campaigning, nearly 40 percent of Florida's voters still said they wished that someone else would seek the nomination. Even Romney's supporters had doubts about him: he won 46 percent of the Florida vote, but only 34 percent of the same electorate saw him as the Republican candidate who "best understands the problems of average Americans." Roughly a quarter of Romney's own voters, Republican primary voters, denied him this distinction. It was a problem that Obama's team would notice. In the fall election, voters who said the most important characteristic they sought in a president was that he "cares about people like me" would vote for Obama over Romney, 81 percent to 18 percent.

Florida put Romney on the road to the nomination, but not before he was tested for another two months. He profited from the refusal of either Gingrich or Santorum to give way to the other. In many states, their combined vote, from the right end of the party, was larger than Romney's share. In very conservative states, one or the other would defeat Romney. (In the end, Santorum carried eleven states and Gingrich two.) In more moderate states, where they could not afford to split conservative ballots, Romney won.

As the primaries rolled on, the candidates regularly underscored contradictions in the conservative argument. Both Romney and Santorum opposed President Obama's rescue of the auto industry, a form of direct government intervention whose success Republicans (though not, it turned out, voters in Michigan and Ohio) had a hard time acknowledging. But Santorum raised a good question during a debate at the Detroit Economic Club. "Governor Romney supported the bailout of Wall Street and decided not to support the bailout of Detroit," Santorum said. "My feeling was that . . . the government should not be involved in bailouts, period. I think that's a much more consistent position."

Indeed it was. Romney could offer all sorts of rationales for the distinction he made between the two bailouts, but once he backed the Wall Street rescue, he could no longer claim free-market purity. And the financial bailout, however necessary, might be seen as creating the very "dependency" and "sense of entitlement" within the privileged classes that Romney condemned when it came to the less well-off.

For his part, Romney (through his Super PAC) attacked Santorum for regularly voting to increase the debt ceiling when he was a senator from Pennsylvania. This was the same Santorum who heaped praise on congressional conservatives when they had tried to block a debt ceiling increase in pursuit of more budget cuts. "We cannot continue to write blank checks that our nation cannot cash," Santorum said—referring to the very blank checks he freely authorized when he was in the Senate.

Romney defeated a spirited Santorum challenge in Michigan, and promptly touted his tax cut program, structured pretty much like every other conservative tax cut plan put forward over the previous three decades. Romney promised to enact an "across-the-board, 20 percent rate cut for every American," pledged to "repeal the alternative minimum tax," and said he'd abolish the "death tax," conservative-speak for the estate tax paid by only the most affluent Americans. He also proposed to cut the corporate tax rate to 25 percent. Absent steep spending cuts, his plan would have increased the deficit—remember the deficit?—by some $3 trillion.

The "across-the-board" part was meant to sound fair and balanced, but its impact certainly was not. A Tax Policy Center study the previous November, when Romney began floating his ideas, found that a 20 percent across-the-board rate cut would cut the taxes of the wealthiest 0.1 percent of Americans by $264,000. Those in the middle of the income distribution would see a reduction of $791, and the poorest 20 percent would get $78. It was not exactly "Ask not what your country can do for you," but these ideas clearly appealed to Romney's most faithful constituency in the primaries. Republicans earning more than $200,000 a year repeated the pattern of the earlier primaries and backed Romney over Santorum by 2-to-1 in Michigan. Romney had temporarily beaten back the attacks on Bain, but the class self-portrait he helped his opponents paint was clear enough to most voters.

Romney's Mormonism was never an open issue in the 2012 primaries. Indeed, Romney was so wary that his devotion to the Church of Jesus Christ of Latter-day Saints might damage his standing with evangelicals—as it had in Iowa in 2008—that he did little to call attention to his faith or to the acts of service and charity it had inspired. This flattened Romney's image and gave him little to call on when he was painted as a heartless financier first by his Republican opponents and then by Obama. He had reason to worry about theological issues, since he never did well in the primaries with evangelical Republicans. But his church membership may have been less important with these voters than the sense that he had flip-flopped on social issues, including abortion. Many religious conservatives may also have suspected that like many Republicans at the high end of the class structure, he was a closet moderate, a view that Gingrich tried hard to reinforce. This suspicion helped Romney throughout the primaries among Republicans who were bona fide moderates—they regularly voted for him over his more conservative adversaries—but left the religious conservatives cold.

The exit polls made this clear. In ten states that had voted before the Illinois primary on March 20, pollsters asked Republican voters how important it was for a candidate to share their religious beliefs. On average, Romney received only 23 percent from voters who said a candidate's religious views mattered a "great deal" to them. When Virginia (where Romney faced only Ron Paul) and Arizona (with its substantial Mormon population) were excluded, Romney's average among these voters dropped to 17 percent. By contrast, Santorum averaged 46 percent among voters who said a candidate's religious views mattered a great deal.

And in sixteen of the states that voted before Illinois, exit pollsters asked whether voters were white evangelical or born-again Christians. In the states that went for Santorum, evangelicals averaged 71 percent of the electorate. In the states Romney won, they averaged only 33 percent of the electorate (and only 31 percent if Virginia is excluded). In the two states Gingrich carried, South Carolina and Georgia, evangelicals made up 64 percent of the vote.

The primaries for other offices underscored how a focus purely on the Tea Party's small-government, antispending commitments obscured how important social issues such as abortion and gay marriage still were to the movement's core constituency of older, white, and religious voters. In 2012, this would saddle the Republicans with two Senate candidates who would astonish even staunch conservatives with their insensitivity.

In May, Senator Richard Lugar, a thirty-five-year Senate veteran and one of the body's most respected foreign policy voices, lost the Indiana Republican primary to state treasurer Richard Mourdock by a 3-to-2 margin. Mourdock had strong support from outside conservative groups, including the Club for Growth, while the eighty-year old Lugar refused to adjust his approach to campaigning or to apologize for his history of working with Democrats, including Obama. That Lugar's overall record was, by most standards, solidly conservative did not help him. In a CNN interview that May, Mourdock illustrated how defining compromise out of the conservative playbook was a new imperative on the right.

"What I've said about compromise and bipartisanship," Mourdock said, is that "I hope to build a conservative majority in the United States Senate so bipartisanship becomes Democrats joining Republicans to roll back the size of government, reduce the bureaucracy, lower taxes and get America moving again." When the interviewer noted that this didn't sound like compromise, Mourdock replied: "Well, it is the definition of political effectiveness." It certainly was an effective position to take for a Republican primary in the Tea Party era.

It was only much later that the costs of nominating Mourdock would become clear. Two weeks before the 2012 election, he was asked about his opposition to exceptions to an abortion ban, for example in the case of rape. He replied: "I think even when life begins in that horrible situation of rape, that's something God intended to happen."

At that point in the campaign, Mourdock was favored to defeat Democratic representative Joe Donnelly. But on Election Day, even as Obama was losing Indiana to Romney by 10 points, Donnelly defeated Mourdock by 6, and a margin of nearly 150,000 votes.

Something similar happened in the August Republican Senate primary in Missouri. Representative Todd Akin, a staunch conservative Christian—he had once said that "at the heart of liberalism really is a hatred of God"—upset two opponents who had been running well ahead of him, former state treasurer Sarah Steelman, who had Sarah Palin's endorsement, and John Brunner, a businessman who was a favorite of the Chamber of Commerce and spent more than $7 million of his own money on his campaign. All three had been running ahead of incumbent Democratic senator Claire McCaskill in the polls, but Akin's lead was the smallest and he was universally regarded as the weakest general election candidate.

Democrats knew this, and shrewdly intervened in the GOP primary on Akin's behalf. McCaskill's campaign ran an ad "attacking" Akin, but in the context of the Republican primary McCaskill was trying to influence, it was anything but an attack. The ad noted that Akin was a "true conservative," "the most conservative congressman in Missouri," and a "crusader against bigger government" with "a pro-family agenda." These were magic words of praise with Missouri's very conservative Republican primary electorate, and the ad provided Akin with additional air cover he could not have afforded himself.

In the meantime, Majority PAC, a Super PAC dedicated to helping Democratic Senate candidates, spent nearly $1.2 million going after Brunner, the most moderate candidate and thus the most dangerous foe to McCaskill.

The Democrats got the foe they wanted: Akin won the August 7 primary. And their investments paid off quickly and handsomely. On Sunday, August 19, a St. Louis TV station asked Akin a similar question to the one Mourdock would eventually face: why his opposition to abortion extended even to women who had become pregnant because of rape. His answer astounded the nation and sent Republicans, including Romney, scurrying away in horror.

"From what I understand from doctors, that's really rare," Akin said. "If it's a legitimate rape, the female body has ways to try to shut that whole thing down. But let's assume that maybe that didn't work or something, I think there should be some punishment, but the punishment ought to be of the rapist, and not attacking the child."

The next day, Romney declared that Akin's comments were "insulting, inexcusable, and, frankly, wrong." The stray "frankly" in Romney's statement may have reflected his frank realization of how politically damaging Akin's comment was to the party as a whole. Two Republican senators urged Akin to withdraw from the race and statements by both the Senate Republican leader, Mitch McConnell, and Senator John Cornyn, who headed the Republican Senate campaign arm, were clearly aimed at the same result.

But Akin refused to drop out, and the result was predictable. While Romney carried Missouri by 9 points, McCaskill overwhelmed Akin by 15 points and received more votes than Romney.

It was astonishing enough that two different Republican candidates in the same year would entangle themselves in impossible controversies because of their peculiar statements on rape. But the lessons of the 2012 primaries extended well beyond Akin and Mourdock and pointed to how the conservative movement's radicalized wings might not only cause problems with the larger electorate, but also devour each other.

Conservatism has always had to struggle with real and principled differences among its various tendencies. *National Review*'s fusionist consensus worked well as long as parties to the agreement did not ask too many questions and did not press each other too hard. At a practical level, economic conservatives such as George W. Bush could side with opponents of abortion and win their votes as long as they were allowed to press their case quietly, using soothing language about "building a culture of life" and seeking indirect, longer-term victories through Supreme Court appointments. But abortion's foes had watched the practice take deep hold in the country in the four decades after *Roe v. Wade* and wanted more than they had been given by conservative politicians whose energies mainly focused on low taxes and deregulation. It was thus not surprising that they turned to more uncompromising candidates such as Akin and Mourdock in the primaries, and demanded stronger and stronger legislation at both the state and national levels—intrusive requirements for ultrasounds for those seeking abortions became the most controversial. Loyalty and high turnouts needed to be requited.

But the radicalization of conservatism on economic issues was problematic for the very working-class and middle-class constituencies that were drawn rightward not because they were particularly pro-business but because they disliked the liberals for their views on social issues or civil rights, or because they felt government policies indulged the lazy—and illegal immigrants. It was one thing for Reagan to propose across-the-board tax cuts when the top income tax rate was (in theory if not in practice) 90 percent. It was quite another to argue for lower income tax rates when the top rate was down to 35 percent, and the rate on capital gains was only 15 percent. The benefits of these policies were not obvious to social conservatives with middle- or working-class incomes.

There was always a certain cynicism in the conservative strategy of gaining the votes of the less well-to-do for economic policies that did little for them in exchange for what was often mere lip service to their views on religious and cultural matters. In early 2015, Ralph Reed, the veteran religious right leader, illustrated this cynicism, no doubt unconsciously, when in an interview with the *New York Times* he instructed wealthy, pro-business conservatives on the importance of evangelical voters.

"You're not going to get your tax cut if this vote doesn't turn out," Reed said. "If evangelicals don't pour out of the pews and into the voting precincts, there isn't going to be any successful business agenda." In other words: pay attention to God and the prayerful, or your taxes will go sky-high.

Moreover, the Great Recession was widely seen, even among many rank-and-file conservatives, as having been caused in whole or in part by Wall Street financiers who had made their money much as Mitt Romney had. The objection to the Wall Street bailout for many street-corner conservatives was less that it violated free-market norms than that it had protected the wealthy and connected while leaving Americans like themselves exposed to economic hardship. "Where's my bailout?" was a slogan that appealed across ideological lines. And many middle Americans of all political views did not need to look at statistical tables to know that the rewards in the economy had shifted sharply away from them and toward the very well-off. Working-class voters who had supported Nixon and Reagan in the years when the term "middle Americans" was popular felt they had a great deal to lose at a time when industrial wages were high, a large share of the workforce was unionized—and the full effects of globalization had not yet been felt.

Some of these voters might still respond to arguments against spending their tax dollars on the "takers" unwilling to work as hard as they were. But these appeals were less persuasive when they came from a millionaire venture capitalist. Many toward whom they were directed began to suspect that the greatest threat to their standard of living came not from below but from above. If the core contradiction of the old Roosevelt coalition had been race, the central contradiction of the conservative coalition in the twenty-first century was class. Barack Obama may have caused offense by talking about working-class voters who "cling to guns or religion." But he understood this contradiction perfectly. Romney would pay the price.

13

SAYING YES AND
NO TO OBAMA

The Two Electorates and the Cycles of Dysfunction

"The House GOP's incredible, amazing discovery:
Most Americans aren't entrepreneurs."

Mitt Romney had barely secured the Republican nomination when the Obama campaign picked up where his primary opponents had left off. The Obama calculus was based on a classic principle of modern political consulting: elections can be either a referendum on an incumbent or a choice between two candidates. Obama's lieutenants were determined to make the election a choice between Barack Obama and Mitt Romney.

The Romney campaign was based on a simple and logical proposition: that economic discontent and impatience with Obama would help Republicans twice over. Swing voters who had elected Obama in 2008 because of their dissatisfaction with Bush would turn back to the Republicans because of their unhappiness with the president's economic stewardship. And voters in Obama's base, particularly young people and African-Americans, would not turn out in the same strength as they had in 2008 because he had disappointed their very high expectations—and because many of them were suffering in the slow recovery. It was the classic referendum theory, embodied in the Stuart Stevens's "Obama Isn't Working" poster, and it had a certain historical logic on its side. Two of the most consequential presidents in American history, Franklin Roosevelt and Ronald Reagan, initially won office in classic referendum elections. Both were ideologically transformative, but they won largely because the country was so unhappy with first Herbert Hoover and then Jimmy Carter.

Yet in 2012, the referendum theory had core weaknesses. The biggest: most Americans didn't blame Obama for the economic mess. In September 2012, after Obama had been in office for nearly four years, a CNN/ORC poll found that 57 percent of voters blamed George W. Bush and the Republicans for the country's economic problems; only 35 percent blamed Obama and the Democrats. If his party had been able to run against Herbert Hoover for decades, Obama could run against Bush for at least one more election.

Moreover, most Americans thought the economy was better than it had been, even if it was not yet good enough. Republican pollster David Winston was shrewd in warning his party that Reagan's classic question—"Are you better off now than you were four years ago?"—would not work for Romney as it had for Reagan because the public had a genuinely nuanced view of the nation's economic situation.

Winston asked a question of his own that gave voters three options. The results were revealing. The largest group, 39 percent, said the economy was better but that the amount of progress it had made was unacceptable; 29 percent said it was better and that level of progress was acceptable. Only 31 percent said flatly that the economy was not getting better. Romney's campaign was geared to the third group, which was not nearly large enough to elect him. Obama's campaign pocketed the second group and directed its efforts toward persuading the largest share of the electorate that his policies, rather than Romney's, were more likely to speed the improvement these voters were looking for. Romney's advisers were a sophisticated bunch, but their view was clearly influenced by two core beliefs of the right and far right: that Obama was a dangerous and miserable failure, and that most Americans shared this view. They were entitled to the first view as a matter of opinion, but the second was a factual matter on which they turned out to be wrong.

The attacks on Romney, first from his own primary opponents and then from the Democrats, were important because if he were successfully branded as a wealthy and out-of-touch capitalist who had made money destroying rather than creating jobs, his economic program—especially if its provisions disproportionately benefited wealthy Americans like himself, which they did—would be suspect. Romney would be crippled in the campaign's most important game-within-a-game for the hearts of the largest group of voters, those looking primarily toward the future.

Thus did the Obama campaign go on the air on May 15, 2012, with a two-minute ad called "Steel." It ran in only a few markets but received wide attention. It told the story of GST Steel in Kansas City, Missouri, and opened with the testimony of Joe Soptic, who had worked there. "I was a steelworker for thirty years. We had a reputation for quality products. It was something that was American made. And we weren't rich but I was able to put my daughter through college. . . . That stopped with the sale of the plant to Bain Capital." The ad contained footage of Romney on the stump declaring: "I know how business works. I know why jobs come and why they go." Soptic comes back: "They made as much money off it as they could and they closed it down and filed for bankruptcy without any concern for the families or the community." If Rick Perry had called Romney-style capitalists "vultures," another worker in the ad, Joe Cobb, chose a different villain. "It was like a vampire. They sucked the life out of us."

The ad concluded with Soptic reciting words the Obama campaign hoped would stick in the minds of voters—and the media: "He's running for president, and if he's going to run the country the way he ran our business, I wouldn't want him there. He would be so out of touch with the average person in this country. How could you care? How could you care for the average working person if you feel that way."

The *Washington Post*'s Dan Balz highlighted the ad in his book on the campaign, *Collision 2012*, because it kicked off what may have been the decisive period of the contest in May and June. That is when Romney lost any chance he had for a referendum election. And because that groundwork was laid, Romney's "47 percent" comments later were seen in the worst possible context—the context partially set by Joe Soptic.

In late May, the pro-Obama Super PAC Priorities USA would run one of the most devastating ads of the entire campaign. It was about another company Bain had owned, Ampad. Mike Earnest, a worker at the company's plant in Marion, Indiana, describes how he and some fellow workers were asked to build a stage. It was from that stage that plant managers announced they were shutting the factory down. "Turns out that when we built that stage," Earnest said, "it was like building my own coffin—and it just made me sick."

On June 21, Tom Hamburger of the *Washington Post* cited Securities and Exchange Commission documents for a story in which he reported that during Romney's nearly fifteen years at Bain, "it owned companies that were pioneers in the practice of shipping work from the United States to overseas call centers and factories making computer components."

The Obama campaign couldn't move fast enough to create a new ad. "What a president believes matters," it declared. "Mitt Romney's companies were pioneers in outsourcing U.S. jobs to low-wage countries. He supports tax breaks for companies that ship jobs overseas. President Obama believes in insourcing. He fought to save the U.S. auto industry and favors tax cuts for companies that bring jobs home. Outsourcing versus Insourcing. It matters."

A choice was being framed. Mitt Romney's referendum was on permanent hold. And a class war that conservatives had long waged on social and religious issues would be waged instead around—class.

★

At the midpoint of 2012, it was startling how far the nation's political conversation had moved in just a year.

In the summer of 2011, the country was focused on budget deficits, the new Republican Congress, the debt ceiling fiasco, and the threat of default. Republicans were on offense, Obama was reactive, and progressive voices in the country were still or ignored.

Republicans had reason to believe they had not only prevented the progressive realignment that Democrats had dreamed of the day Obama was elected but had also reversed the tide. The sweep in the 2010 midterms could only be a portent of that long-elusive conservative majority. And this time, with the Tea Party giving the movement spine and electoral muscle, it would be a majority led by full-throated conservatives. Government really would be rolled back. Even the great monuments of the New Deal and the Great Society, Social Security and Medicare, would be contained and set, if not on a path to extinction, then at least toward much lower spending levels in the long run. Establishment Republicans, witnessing the fate of their more moderate colleagues, were edging steadily right.

In state governments around the country, full Republican control had ushered in some of the most conservative approaches to policy since the 1920s. In Wisconsin, Governor Scott Walker had vastly reduced the power of public employee unions—and, in what conservatives hoped was a portent for the fall, beat back the unions' effort to recall him from office in June 2012.

As it was in Wisconsin, so it was in states as diverse as North Carolina, Kansas, Ohio, Arizona, and Pennsylvania, where state budgets were slashed and taxes cut. In many states where Republicans held both the executive and the legislature, new restrictions on abortion were passed and "voter protection" measures were enacted. Justified in the name of preventing voter fraud—of which there was scant evidence—these measures had the effect of making access to the ballot box more difficult for many voters, particularly members of minority groups and younger Americans. They were the very groups that had swelled Obama's margins in 2008. Some of the laws involved voter ID requirements. Others shortened early voting periods and complicated voter registration efforts. At least one Republican admitted the political motivation behind the measures. In Pennsylvania, the Republican House majority leader Mike Turzai ticked off a series of his party's legislative accomplishments at a Republican State Committee meeting and proudly included the state's new voter requirement on the list. "Voter ID, which is going to allow Governor Romney to win the state of Pennsylvania, done." Not for nothing did Democrats and civil rights leaders see these measures as the return of voter suppression. They were one of many marks of a conservative movement not only on the move, but also determined to use the power it had to lock in its advantages for the future.

Yet in the seven months from the rise of Occupy Wall Street and Obama's Osawatomie speech through the strange Republican primary journey, the issue landscape was transformed. If the country was skeptical of how government worked, it was also skeptical of how economic elites had managed the nation's business. When the focus shifted from the first to the second, progressives, including Obama, regained the advantage.

Obama was again fully engaged, reflecting the peculiar rhythms of his political life. He was up and energetic during campaigns, but restrained and curiously passive in his public performances when the campaign was over—except when his back was against a wall and his competitive inclinations, learned on basketball courts and in all other games with winners and losers, drove him to seek victory.

His senior political adviser David Axelrod had prepared a video for Obama, shown at the first major planning meeting for the reelection campaign on September 17, 2011. It included parts of the 2004 convention speech, Axelrod wrote in his memoir, "in which he so eloquently gave voice to the hopes and struggles of hardworking Americans he had met while traveling in Illinois," and highlights of inspiring moments from the 2008 campaign. "I finished with more recent footage, documenting a restrained president sharing the details of his deficit reduction policies and what they would mean for some distant fiscal year," Axelrod wrote. "It was a clinical and bloodless performance, lacking both passion and a sense of advocacy."

"We need you to be *that* guy again," Axelrod said, referring to the earlier Obama who had been "passionate and purposeful."

Obama's old friend was right about the president's need to get back on his game, but the point was about more than performance. Obama was always stronger when making an affirmative case that challenged conservative assumptions and policies. With the right determined not only to defeat him but also to roll back the larger progressive project, falling back on bromides about the need to end partisanship and discord would neither answer its challenge nor mobilize his own supporters. It was bound to be a loser's strategy, and Obama did not want to lose.

Romney, of course, wanted to win, too. He had turned back his primary foes by accusing them of being enemies of free enterprise, and he tried to do the same when Obama gave him an opening. Speaking in front of a fire station in Virginia on July 13, Obama tried to channel a comment by Harvard professor Elizabeth Warren that had become a Web sensation earlier in the year; Warren declared that "there is nobody in this country who got rich on his own" because everyone, perhaps especially the wealthy, depended on government for the provision of social goods. Thriving entrepreneurs, she noted, moved their products "on the roads the rest of us pay for," hired workers whom "the rest of us paid to educate," have their property protected by police and firefighters that the rest of us also pay for—and that was just for starters. Obama made the same point by saying, "If you were successful, someone along the line gave you some help." He went on with this theme for a while, and then got to a somewhat garbled passage: "Somebody invested in roads and bridges. *If you've got a business—you didn't build that.*"

When the fact-checkers looked back after the italicized sentence became a Republican cause célèbre, they concluded that what Obama was saying the businessperson didn't build were those roads and the bridges. Obama was *not* referring to the businesses themselves. This didn't detain the Republicans. Romney hit back with a Web ad. If Obama's ads included workers, Romney's ads, as was only appropriate given his worldview, included the voices of management and ownership. "Through hard work and a little bit of luck, we built this business," Jack Gilchrist, a New Hampshire metal plant owner, said in the ad. "Why are you demonizing us for it? It's time we had somebody who believes in us."

Republicans were so certain they had found the key to the election—definitive proof, as many saw it, of Obama's "socialism"—that they made attacks on the phrase a centerpiece at their national convention and a mainstay of the campaign.

In his book *The Center Holds,* Jonathan Alter recounted how Obama's "you didn't build that" comment drove respectable Republican politicians and scholars to distraction. Writing under the headline "Un-American" on the American Enterprise Institute's blog, prominent conservative author Charles Murray grumbled: "That's the thing about Obama. Time and again, he does things and says things that are un-American. Not evil. Not anti-American. Just un-American." John Sununu, the former New Hampshire governor, echoed this language. "I wish the president would learn how to be an American," he said. As Alter observed, "These were not Internet trolls attacking the president's patriotism but prominent conservatives." There were now two streams of conservative radicalism. At the edges were those who saw Obama as a Muslim, a foreign interloper who had no right to be president. But within the Republican establishment, there were many who had so turned against public provision by the state, particularly when the state was run by Obama, that even a defense of the idea that prosperity depended on a reasonably active government had become "un-American." Alexander Hamilton, Henry Clay, and Abraham Lincoln would all have been surprised to have been read out of the American experiment. The Tea Party view had entered the right's mainstream.

Obama, of course, had issued more than his share of encomiums to entrepreneurs. But the episode showed how far conservatism had strayed from the emphasis that both Nixon and Reagan placed on working people. The Reagan Democrats were southerners, to be sure, but also factory workers in states such as Pennsylvania, Ohio, and Michigan. Partisans of the new conservative ideology were so obsessed with the "job creators," a term repeated thousands of times at hundreds of Republican rallies, that they forgot entirely about those who held the jobs. Far from upending Obama, the attention Romney and his party gave to the "you didn't build that" line only reinforced the sense that they looked at the world entirely from the perspective of the boss, the investor, the boardroom, and the front office.

Only after the election did conservatives come to terms with how absurd this approach was, as a political matter no less than as a factual matter. In early 2014, the conservative *Washington Examiner*'s lead political writer, Byron York, reported on a speech by then–majority leader Eric Cantor. The *Examiner*'s puckish headline: "The House GOP's incredible, amazing discovery: Most Americans aren't entrepreneurs." Cantor had, indeed, stated an obvious truth: "Ninety percent of Americans work for someone else. . . . Their dream is to have a good job, with an income that will allow them to support their family. We shouldn't miss the chance to talk to these people." But in 2012, they did miss their chance. The obvious can get lost in a cloud of ideology.

Romney's choice of Representative Paul Ryan as his running mate reinforced his image as a hard economic conservative. The turn to Ryan said a lot about Romney, some of it good. Romney was not about to saddle the country (or himself) with a gimmicky and patently unqualified running mate. He and the party had learned from its Sarah Palin experience. Ryan knew Washington well, having worked there since his early twenties. He was bright and affable with a young man's smile and a devotion to personal fitness. He was the face and voice of a new generation of conservatives. In a laudatory profile pushing Ryan as the logical VP pick, the *Weekly Standard*'s Stephen Hayes called the Wisconsin congressman "the intellectual leader of the Republican Party." Hayes quoted the legendary Democratic strategist James Carville declaring that Ryan would be "a clarifying choice" and would make the contest "about big issues."

This proved to be absolutely true. Precisely because Ryan, then forty-two, was representative of the new generation on the right, he espoused—in a folksy and friendly way—its radicalism on taxing, spending, and the purpose of government. Like many young conservatives, he had been influenced in college by the radical individualism of Ayn Rand, whose works included a book with the brutally candid title *The Virtue of Selfishness*. In 2005, Ryan addressed the Atlas Society, named after Rand's most influential book, at an event honoring the hundredth anniversary of her birth. He told the assembled Randians that *Atlas Shrugged* "inspired me so much that it's required reading for all my interns and my staff." If Bill Buckley tried to read Rand out of the conservative movement, Ryan and a great many others on the younger right never got the message.

Although Ryan tried to distance himself from Rand in subsequent years, his speech in October 2011 at the Heritage Foundation reflected how profound her influence had been. Like Rand, Ryan divided the world sharply between the productive and the unproductive—between the "makers" and the "takers." The formulation would haunt the Romney campaign, and still haunts the American right.

"We're coming close to a tipping point in America where we might have a net majority of takers versus makers in society and that could become very dangerous if it sets in as a permanent condition," Ryan declared. "Because what we will end up doing is we will convert our safety net system—which is necessary I believe to help people who can't themselves, to help people who are down on their luck get back onto their feet—into a hammock that ends up lulling people into lives of dependency and complacency which drains them of their incentive and the will to make the most of their lives."

The "hammock" metaphor drove home what Ryan was saying. The poor receiving government benefits (especially the working poor on food stamps who labored long hours for low pay) would have been surprised to learn that they were living pleasant lives on the dole, comfortably swinging between trees. But the passage explained all of Ryan's budgets with their tax cuts for the "makers" and their sharp program cuts for the "takers." The theory seemed to be that the rich responded to incentives that offered them more money and the poor responded to incentives that offered them less. Ryan's greatest fear was not that American society was becoming unequal but that government was coddling the less productive and thus weakening the economy and the social fabric. Ryan insisted that as a Catholic, he believed in Christian charity. Late in the campaign, in an effort to align himself with a compassionate conservatism that had largely disappeared from the public dialogue, Ryan gave a moving speech warmly embracing the work of faith-based and community groups in alleviating poverty. But it was hard to miss Ayn Rand's worldview beneath it all, a philosophy tinged with the Gilded Age Social Darwinism of William Graham Sumner, who had scorned charity as destructive because it interfered with a "natural" process through which the fittest survived and prospered.

Ryan's "makers" and "takers" riff would prove to be a disastrous backdrop to the tale of the greatest error of Romney's campaign. It was not an error he was even aware of, since it came during a speech on May 17, 2012, to a group of donors in Boca Raton that Romney thought was private and would never be heard by the larger electorate. But thanks to Scott Prouty, who worked as a caterer at the event and put a small camera on the bar near where Romney spoke, the whole world would eventually learn what Romney said that night. Prouty eventually got the recording to David Corn of *Mother Jones* magazine, and it went online on September 17, 2012. Here are Romney's words that upended his candidacy:

There are 47 percent of the people who will vote for the president no matter what. All right, there are 47 percent who are with him, who are dependent upon government, who believe that they are victims, who believe that government has a responsibility to care for them, who believe that they are entitled to health care, to food, to housing, to you name it. That that's an entitlement. And the government should give it to them. And they will vote for this president no matter what. And I mean, the president starts off with 48, 49, 48—he starts off with a huge number. These are people who pay no income tax. Forty-seven percent of Americans pay no income tax. So our message of low taxes doesn't connect. And he'll be out there talking about tax cuts for the rich. I mean that's what they sell every four years. And so my job is not to worry about those people—I'll never convince them that they should take personal responsibility and care for their lives.

After the campaign, Romney told the *Washington Post*'s Dan Balz that he thought he was just engaging in rather uncontroversial electoral analysis. Romney translated the passage this way: "Look, the Democrats have 47 percent, we've got 45 percent, my job is to get the people in the middle, and I've got to get the people in the middle." But Romney had said much more than this and his words reflected Ryan's stark division of the world between "makers" and "takers." The contempt for the needy—those who "believe that they are victims, who believe that government has a responsibility to care for them, who believe that they are entitled to health care, to food, to housing, to you name it"—was astonishing. Worse still was the arrogance in the line: "I'll never convince them that they should take personal responsibility and care for their lives." A declaration that the less affluent 47 percent of the country did not "take responsibility" for their own lives reflected a view so out of touch with the day-to-day struggles of a large part of the country as to disqualify Romney from the presidency, which is exactly what many voters did when they heard about his comments. Romney's very definition of the 47 percent was revealing for how blind the right could be on the matter of who actually paid the most in taxes. To define taxpayers as only those who paid income tax ignored the extent to which middle-class and poor Americans often paid a *larger* share of their income in taxes than did the best-off because of regressive payroll, sales, and property levies. The very rich typically paid low capital gains rates, which is why Warren Buffett could say that his secretary paid proportionately more in taxes than he did.

Politically, Romney may have taken the biggest hit for his statement, "my job is not to worry about those people." The idea that a president would not "worry" about nearly half the country was shocking, too, although this, at least, fits with Romney's claim that he was only engaging in electoral analysis.

Romney is certainly a more caring man than his 47 percent moment suggested, given his record of extensive acts of personal charity. But this is also why his statement was so important, and so damning of what conservative ideology had become. Conservatives were aware of the damage Romney's statement had done, which is why many of them disowned it, some during the campaign and many more afterward. This was not about how Romney *felt*. It was about how he *thought*. Romney did not invent any of the ideas contained in his statement. As David Frum argued, it really did reflect the view of the new "radical rich," who had come to see decades of social provision as promoting only dependency and who saw themselves as the primary productive class in the United States. Those who failed to join their ranks had missed out not because of bad luck, discrimination, economic change, or social injustice. They were failures and moochers who were unprepared "to take personal responsibility and care for their lives."

After the 47 percent moment, only once did Romney genuinely threaten Obama's lead. The president's performance in their first debate on October 3 in Denver—the scene of his nomination four years earlier—was disastrous. It was obvious from the debate's first moments that Romney was not only well prepared, with a clear strategy to execute, but also warm, at ease, and ready to fight. As for Obama, Axelrod, his loyal friend and partisan, captured the president's failure that night as candidly as anyone. "While he defended his record to a fault, indulging in esoterica, Obama was remarkably passive, seldom challenging Romney or, especially, Romney's cynical reinvention of himself," Axelrod wrote in his memoir. "Worse, the president looked disengaged, in stark contrast with a challenger who was in command of the moment." Romney's victory was so overwhelming that Obama's partisans stopped even trying to defend the president's performance on Twitter, the new spin room of American politics. A consensus formed early, and it was bleak for the Democrats. The Republicans were joyously triumphant, and not a little surprised.

But Axelrod pointed to an important aspect of the evening that was largely lost in the pummeling Obama legitimately took. At that very late hour in the campaign, Romney was trying to pivot away from the right and recapture his image as a moderate, after so many years of running away from it. Having campaigned hard on a tax proposal that called for $5 trillion in tax cuts, he said flatly: "I don't have a tax cut of the scale that you're talking about." Romney, it seemed, was for his tax plan before he was against it, though no one was talking about this much that night.

Romney's whole approach was moderate, practical, and terribly concerned about the middle class. The candidate who had repeatedly attacked regulations was quick to insist: "Regulation is essential. . . . You have to have regulations so that you can have an economy work." He reiterated his criticism of the Dodd-Frank Wall Street reform legislation, but the scourge of big government during the primaries took care to make clear that whatever his running mate's reading habits might be, he was not about to turn the United States into Ayn Rand's utopia.

Having hidden his Massachusetts health care plan behind "Repeal Obamacare" rhetoric in the primaries, Romney finally embraced (or reembraced) it, without explaining why repealing a national health care system modeled after the one of which he was now so proud would be consistent with his view. He repeatedly used the word "crushed" to describe the impact of the president's policies on Americans' well-being and returned to Stuart Stevens's favorite theme. "We know that the path we're taking is not working," Romney said late in the debate. "It's time for a new path."

In the early going that night, Obama seemed reluctant to go on offense and backed away from several opportunities to engage Romney. The president appeared far more interested in explaining than attacking, more concerned with scoring policy points than with raising larger questions about his opponent's approach. The words "47 percent" did not come up.

Obama did return repeatedly to a central point: the vagueness of Romney's proposals on taxes and health care. He charged that Romney was hiding the details of those plans because they would prove unpopular with and harmful to the middle class. Several times, using different language, Obama effectively asked: if Romney's ideas were genuinely helpful to average voters, wouldn't he be shouting their particulars from the rooftops? And at several moments, Obama spoke of the baleful impact that Paul Ryan's budget cuts would have on Medicare, student loans, and community colleges. Only in the last minutes did Obama find a stronger voice in describing his achievements. He contrasted his willingness "to say no to things" with Romney's refusal to say no to "the more extreme parts of his party." But Obama never managed to put Romney on the defensive, and in truth, never really tried. He contented himself with telling voters what he himself had done and why. Pollsters and pundits had long pondered whether Obama might suffer on Election Day from an "enthusiasm gap" on the part of his supporters. That night, said political writer Matt Bai, there certainly was an enthusiasm gap. It was Obama's own.

The schedule provided for a thirteen-day gap between the first and second presidential debates. These were very long days for Obama's supporters, who got something of a reprieve when Vice President Joe Biden cheerfully pummeled Paul Ryan and his budgets in the single vice presidential debate on October 11. As has always been his way, Obama performed best when he was on the ropes. In debate two, it was Obama on the offensive and Romney forced to be defensive. And the heart of Obama's attack was a moment that distilled the essence of the critique of Romney, pioneered by Perry, Santorum, and Gingrich and driven home by the Democrats. After Romney had described his five-point economic plan, Obama pounced:

> Governor Romney doesn't have a five-point plan. He has a one-point plan. And that plan is to make sure that the folks at the top play by a different set of rules. That's been his philosophy in the private sector, that's been his philosophy as governor, that's been his philosophy as a presidential candidate. You can make a lot of money and pay lower tax rates than somebody who makes a lot less. You can ship jobs overseas and get tax breaks for it. You can invest in a company, bankrupt it, lay off workers, strip away their pensions, and you still make money. That's exactly the philosophy that we've seen in place for the last decade. That's what's been squeezing middle-class families.

Neatly, Obama wrapped together criticisms of Romney's views and his business habits, threw a punch at the Bush legacy (without a mention of Bush's name), and drove home a progressive critique of conservative economics, including the sorts of tax cuts that Romney and Ryan favored. A campaign that had been headed Obama's way before the first debate resumed its earlier trajectory.

Fox News commentators, reflecting the opinion bubble in which so many on the right lived, were absolutely certain of a Romney victory—certain because Americans could not possibly be happy with Obama, and certain that Obama's own supporters could not help but be disillusioned. Romney himself shared this certainty. It was a belief driven in part by data—but the data came from the 2010 election. Surely, many conservatives reasoned, turnout in 2012 would be more demographically similar to 2010, the most recent election, than to 2008, wouldn't it?

This proved to be entirely wrong, as the best pollsters knew it would be. In fact, exit polls found that the makeup of the 2012 electorate was even *more* congenial to Obama than 2008's had been. Voters ages 18–29 had made up 18 percent of the 2008 electorate, only 12 percent of the 2010 electorate, but 19 percent of the 2012 electorate. Nonwhites made up 26 percent of the 2008 electorate, 23 percent of the 2010 electorate, but 28 percent of the 2012 electorate. The Obama constituency had mobilized after all. Indeed, the percentage of eligible African-American voters who went to the polls exceeded that of whites, and the African-American vote appeared to increase in battlegrounds such as Ohio and Virginia. Voter suppression efforts not only backfired; they increased the determination of African-Americans to cast ballots. If the reduction in early voting hours meant having to stand in longer lines, this is what they did.

And Romney paid dearly for his anti-immigration comments in the primaries, including his unforgettable "self-deportation" idea. Not only was the Latino share of the electorate up from 2008, but in an election where Obama's overall support dropped by 2 percentage points, he saw his percentage of the Latino vote rise by 4. Romney's 27 percent of the Latino vote was the lowest for a Republican since 1996—and a warning sign that the party's nativist noises could keep it uncompetitive in presidential elections for years to come.

Even more shocking for Republicans was Obama's 73 percent share of the Asian-American vote, up from 62 percent four years earlier. Historically, Asian-Americans had been open to Republican candidates. Even in defeat in 1992, George H. W. Bush had secured 55 percent of the Asian-American vote against Bill Clinton, according to the network exit poll. Here again, the costs of nativism to the Republicans were evident, and perhaps also the costs of the highly visible public role played by the more extreme among the older, white, conservative Christians in the Tea Party.

The diversity of the American electorate made an even bigger difference to Obama in 2012 than in 2008 because his share of the white vote declined, from 43 percent in 2008 to 39 percent in 2012. Obama's percentage of the white vote was lower than Michael Dukakis's share in his 1988 defeat, as Ruy Teixeira and John Halpin noted in a careful analysis of the election. The vast demographic changes in the country that had been important to Obama's election were essential to his reelection. One clear warning sign for Democrats: Obama, who had lost white college graduates by only 4 points in 2008, lost them by 14 in 2012. And his deficit among white working-class voters rose from 18 points in 2008 to 25 points in 2012.

However, his share of the white vote generally and white working-class vote in particular was significantly higher in swing and industrial states such as Ohio, Michigan, and Pennsylvania. In general, Obama's vote among whites was much higher in states where he actively campaigned and advertised. On the other hand, among white southerners, according to *New York Times* voting analyst Nate Cohn, Obama won only 28 percent. And in the Deep South states—Louisiana, Georgia, Alabama, Mississippi, South Carolina, Tennessee, Arkansas, and Texas—he won just 16 percent among white voters. The new Solid South was as Republican as ever. The two southern states Obama carried, Florida and Virginia, have seen large-scale in-migration of non-southerners and were the least culturally southern states in the South. North Carolina, which he carried narrowly in 2008 and lost narrowly in 2012, had similarly been transformed by immigration from outside the South and outside the country.

Finally, the exit polls left no doubt that if the 2012 election was in large part a war over class issues, Obama won it handily. The pollsters asked voters if they thought the policies of each candidate would "generally favor" the rich, the middle class, or the poor. Their ruling on Obama: only 10 percent said his policies favored the rich, 44 percent said his policies favored the middle class, and 31 percent said they favored the poor. Obama overwhelmingly won the last two groups. Romney's numbers were very different: 54 percent said his policies favored the rich while only 34 percent said they favored the middle class. A paltry 2 percent said Romney's policies favored the poor. Especially important was Obama's 10-point advantage over Romney as the candidate of the middle class. Game and match to Obama.

Moreover, a majority of voters rejected a core Republican proposition: that the economy works on behalf of everyone. The voters were asked: "Do you think the U.S. economic system generally favors the wealthy, or is fair to most Americans?" The exit poll found that 55 percent said the economy favors the wealthy, while only 39 percent said it was fair to most Americans. Romney won three-quarters of the ballots of those who thought the economy was fair; Obama won nearly as big a margin within the larger group that said it favored the wealthy.

Thus did Obama become the first Democratic president since Franklin Roosevelt to win two consecutive elections with a majority of the vote. His share was down, and so was his total: from 69.5 million votes in 2008 to 65.9 million in 2012. But most of his losses appear to have come from past supporters who abstained rather than from those who switched to Mitt Romney. Romney received only 948,667 more votes than John McCain had four years earlier, and, appropriately perhaps, 47 percent of the vote. (Libertarian Gary Johnson won 1.275 million votes, while Jill Stein, the Green Party candidate, won just under 470,000.)

Democrats did very well in the Senate races, picking up two seats. The struggles Akin and Mourdock had in discussing rape explained some of the Democrats' strength. But their Senate victories were comprehensive. They had the satisfaction of seeing Scott Brown, who caused them so much grief in 2010, defeated by Elizabeth Warren, the Harvard professor who had perfected populist language and policies. Even before her election, she had become the most powerful progressive voice in national life. Democrats not only won competitive races in Virginia, Ohio, and Connecticut, but also won contests in North Dakota and Montana, states where Obama was soundly beaten.

They were less fortunate in the House. Democratic House candidates outpolled Republicans by 1.4 million votes nationwide, but gerrymandering and the packing of Democrats in urban districts meant that this lead translated into only 201 seats, to 234 for the Republicans—a Democratic gain of just 8 seats. The effects of the gerrymander were especially pronounced in states such as Pennsylvania, Ohio, North Carolina, and Wisconsin, where Republicans won a much larger share of seats than they did votes. In Pennsylvania, to pick a particularly stark case, Democrats edged out Republicans in the popular vote in all House races, but they won only 5 seats to the Republicans' 13. The cost of losing control of states in midterm elections right before redistricting years was very high.

The long-term trend toward a steadily less white electorate in the presidential years bodes well for the Democrats in battles for the White House. But the wide variation in the makeup of presidential and midterm electorates points to the likelihood of sharply divergent outcomes between presidential years and off-years for some time to come. The United States Election Project found that 40 million fewer Americans voted in 2010 than in 2012. And at 48 million, the drop-off from 2012 to 2014 was even more dramatic. This trend is likely to continue until much of the current Millennial generation reaches its mid-thirties or early forties, the time in life when most people begin to develop more stable residential habits (which, because of complicated voter registration rules in many states, makes regular voting easier) and a higher degree of ongoing political engagement.

This rise of the two electorates will lead to more gridlock in Washington until the Republicans moderate, or until one or both parties fully adapt to the new demographic realties. The Democrats' task is to increase their share of the white working-class vote and also their percentages among voters over the age of 65, who loom very large in the midterms. The second may, to at least some degree, happen naturally: the next group of Americans approaching retirement is somewhat more liberal and Democratic than current retirees. Obama lost those over 65 by 8 points to John McCain and by 12 points to Mitt Romney. But among voters ages 45 to 64, Obama led McCain by a point in 2008 and trailed Romney by only 4 in 2012.

For Republicans, restoring their ability to win presidential elections almost certainly depends on cutting their deep losses among nonwhites. There are many reasons why the African-American vote is likely to remain overwhelmingly Democratic for some time to come, although Obama's share is certainly a peak, much as the Democrats' share of the Catholic vote peaked in John F. Kennedy's election in 1960. But the GOP's opportunity among Latinos is much greater, as George W. Bush showed in 2000 and 2004. And the party must certainly do better among Asian-Americans, who include many nationalities that once had an affinity for the party.

After Romney's loss, some conservatives argued that there was nothing wrong with the party that couldn't be cured by an even higher share of the white vote. On its face, this seems absurd, given that the white vote will continue to decline as a share of the electorate—and since it is difficult to imagine the Democratic share of the white vote falling much lower than it did in 2012.

But there is a strain of something important in this line of analysis, as the respected voting analyst Sean Trende has shown. One of the most important facts about 2012 was the decline in white voting. Trende estimates that some 5 million fewer whites voted in 2012 than in 2008. Most of them lived in the North and were less well-to-do.

Trende's analysis pointed, first, to the downside of nominating a venture capitalist after a Wall Street–induced crash, the costs of Romney's 47 percent comment and other statements that made him appear out of touch, and the success of both his Republican foes and the Obama campaign in branding him as an enemy of working-class aspirations. It seems likely that Obama's advertising and messaging—typified by the succinct summary of the case against Romney he offered in the second debate—may have led voters in this group who could not vote for his reelection to stay home. But the missing downscale whites also pointed to the larger cost of the Republicans' ties to corporate interests, tax policies that favor the wealthy, and their growing economic radicalism. Appealing to these missing white voters, Trende argued, "means abandoning some of its more pro-corporate stances." He went on: "This GOP would have to be more 'America first' on trade, immigration and foreign policy; less pro–Wall Street and big business in its rhetoric; more Main Street/populist on economics." It would be a complicated mix, but Trende identifies the same working-class problem for conservatives that emerged during the primaries, and that Obama exploited so effectively. When Donald Trump ran for president, he campaigned as if he had read Trende's analysis.

There is another challenge—to the political system generally and to Republicans in particular—that arises from the emergence of the two electorates and the dominance of Republicans in the House of Representatives. The political scientist Thomas Schaller identified it in his important 2015 book, *The Stronghold.* Republicans, he said, were in the process of becoming "a party anchored to and defined by its congressional wing, and its House caucus in particular." Schaller sees in this a potential vicious cycle for Republicans. As the party became more conservative, it also became more Congress-centered. But as the party relies more and more on its congressional stronghold, it is likely to become *more conservative still,* given the number of Republicans who represent very conservative districts, and another large group that fears primaries from the right and the ongoing pressures from right-wing donors and media. The danger, said Schaller, is that the GOP's congressional stronghold could become a "chokehold." He was referring to the chokehold on the party, but we are in danger of its becoming a chokehold on governing itself.

14

THE FEVER THAT WOULDN'T BREAK

When Winning Two Elections Isn't Enough

"Interesting things happen in the fourth quarter."

Obama spoke over and over during the 2012 campaign of how his victory might finally "break the fever" in Washington. If the Republicans had operated during his first four years with the sole purpose of foiling his program and defeating him, they might see in his reelection a sign that the voters had rejected their approach. They might try something different. Surely two consecutive presidential majorities would mean something for him, as they had for Ronald Reagan.

The first order of business after the election was the matter of Bush's expiring tax cuts. Obama had kicked the issue down the road, partly from perceived political necessity and partly because tax increases during a sluggish recovery did not seem wise. But he had drawn the line on 2012. And his hand was strong. Unless Congress gave him a bill that he could sign, it would be enabling one of the largest tax increases in history. Taxes across the board would rise as all the Bush tax cuts expired. Obama was seeking only the restoration of the higher tax rates of the Clinton era for families earning more than $250,000 a year.

Between Obama's theory of the fever breaking and Schaller's theory of a vicious cycle, the vicious cycle largely prevailed. House Speaker Boehner's caucus was no less unruly after the election than it had been before. Boehner continued to resist any deal that Obama could plausibly reach, and the Speaker could not get Republicans to accept that failing to act meant a huge tax increase. He tried to push through his own "Plan B," providing for tax increases only for those earning more than $1 million a year. Even that was unacceptable to his members. His most radical members continued to assert their right to use any means at their disposal to impose their views on the country. But in the process, they marginalized the House from any serious negotiations. It would fall to Democrats to get something done with a rump of Republicans. That was kind of, sort of, like breaking the fever—but only when Obama was wielding a mighty weapon of a large tax increase no Republican could stomach. The situation recalled George H. W. Bush's 1990 deficit reduction deal with Democrats after a conservative rebellion had brought down his initial bill. Little had changed, except that Bush's defeat only hardened the conservative view. Obama was living with the results.

Eventually, Obama sent Joe Biden to negotiate a deal with Senate Minority Leader Mitch McConnell. And Boehner actually let it through with mostly Democratic votes: 172 Democrats voted for it, only 85 Republicans did.

It wasn't a bad deal. It settled an argument that progressives had been having with conservatives since the beginning of the Bush presidency, and the progressives won. The top income tax was back up to 39.6 percent, though the increase applied on family incomes of $450,000 or more, not the lower level Obama had sought. This meant the bill didn't raise nearly as much revenue as Obama knew was needed—it secured $620 billion over a decade, less than half of what he had sought. Capital gains taxes, cut repeatedly since the 1970s, were also raised. The deal extended unemployment benefits and various refundable tax credits that are especially helpful to lower-income people. And it set the estate tax at 40 percent on fortunes of more than $5 million, still low by historical standards, but better than the zero rate envisioned by the original Bush's proposal.

The real cost involved Obama's surrendering of all of his leverage for limited gains. Some 82 percent of Bush's tax cuts were now permanent. Obama's hopes that Congress might eventually agree to more revenue were as forlorn as his original hopes for an end to the divide between red and blue. This was his big chance. He won a principle. He got some money. But he would not get much later—except for a government shutdown.

On December 14, the cost of the nation's permissive firearms laws was brought home when twenty children and six staff members were gunned down at Sandy Hook Elementary School in Newtown, Connecticut. Obama himself was shaken, well aware, as Alter pointed out, that he had declined to push through the tougher restrictions he knew the nation needed after a 2012 mass shooting at a movie theater in Aurora, Colorado, when twelve people were killed. This had clearly been a political calculation: the shooting came during an election year, and Obama felt he faced enough political challenges without igniting the gun issue. After Newtown, he acted, putting forward a comprehensive, if still relatively cautious, set of proposals, including some he adopted directly through executive orders. This time was different, or so nearly everyone said. The national outpouring of sympathy for the victims and their families, and particularly for the schoolchildren, seemed to rattle even the gun lobby.

But it would not be rattled for long. Led by the National Rifle Association, one of the most powerful constituencies on the right, the pro-gun forces rallied once again. And once again, fear of the gun lobby would engulf moderate Democrats no less than Republicans. It would trump the outrage of a vast majority of Americans.

Obama's Inaugural Address on January 20, 2013, was the speech of a victor and a survivor. He used it to make a broad case for a progressive view of government, and for the particular things that government should do in our time. It was in the tradition of Franklin Roosevelt's second inaugural and Ronald Reagan's first. All three speeches were unapologetic in offering arguments for a set of philosophical commitments and explanations of the policies that naturally followed from them.

Obama was combative in directly refuting conservative ideas, and one pas-sage pointedly alluded to Paul Ryan's signature distinction. Obama insisted that social insurance programs *encouraged* rather than discouraged risk-taking, and thus a more, not less, dynamic society. "The commitments we make to each other—through Medicare, and Medicaid, and Social Security—these things do not sap our initiative; they strengthen us," Obama said. "They do not make us a nation of takers; they free us to take the risks that make this country great."

He rooted his egalitarian commitments in the promises of the founding. The Declaration of Independence was the driving text—as it had been for Abraham Lincoln and Martin Luther King Jr.

Obama's refrain was "We, the people," a reminder that "we" is the first word of the Constitution and that a commitment to community and the common good is as American as Washington, Adams, Madison, and Jeffer-son. The passages invoking that phrase spoke of shared responsibility—"we, the people, understand that our country cannot succeed when a shrinking few do very well and a growing many barely make it." "We, the people, still believe that our obligations as Americans are not just to ourselves, but to all posterity." Obama was saying a powerful "no" to the radical individualism at the heart of so much of Tea Party and makers-and-takers conservatism.

It was notable, and his critics noted it, that Obama abandoned the lofty and nonpartisan ground he had once made his own. He did not pretend that the previous four years hadn't happened and he did not walk away from the forceful case he had been making since Osawatomie.

Neither Roosevelt nor Reagan had given in to philosophical timidity, ei-ther. Each represented poles in the long national argument on which Obama chose to take sides.

"We of the Republic pledged ourselves to drive from the temple of our ancient faith those who had profaned it," FDR had said in 1937. "[W]e rec-ognized a deeper need—the need to find through government the instrument of our united purpose to solve for the individual the ever-rising problems of a complex civilization. . . . We refused to leave the problems of our common welfare to be solved by the winds of chance and the hurricanes of disaster."

Reagan's answer in 1980: "In the present crisis, government is not the solution to our problem. . . . It is time to check and reverse the growth of government which shows signs of having grown beyond the consent of the governed. It is my intention to curb the size and influence of the Federal establishment and to demand recognition of the distinction between the powers granted to the Federal Government and those reserved to the States or to the people."

Like those two bold predecessors, Obama offered his fellow citizens the "why" behind what he thought and what he proposed to do. The argument he had hoped to avoid when he sought to subsume red into blue was upon him, and he had reason to believe that his reelection had given him a chance to win it.

But the National Rifle Association had other ideas. Newtown had necessarily changed Obama's agenda, and the nation's. After years of defeat at the hands of the gun lobby, advocates of modest, sane restrictions on the use of firearms had reason for hope. Bravely, two senators known for sympathy for the gun lobby, Senators Joe Manchin, a conservative West Virginia Democrat, and Pat Toomey, a conservative Pennsylvania Republican, joined forces on a bill requiring background checks for gun purchasers. It was well short of gun registration, let alone a renewal of the ban on assault weapons. But passing anything would be a sign that the NRA and its even more extreme allies could be defeated. (It is hard for liberals to believe: there are more extreme groups than the NRA.)

The extremism of the American gun lobby always comes as a shock to the rest of the democratic world, which sees the regulation of guns as no less normal than the regulation of cars or consumer products that are far less lethal. The radicalization of the NRA is of a piece with the radicalization of the rest of the right, and the gun issue has provided a way for opponents of regulations of all kinds—environmental, financial, workplace safety, consumer protection—to create a mass libertarian base ready to go on the attack at the mere hint of government action. Working-class and middle-class gun owners around the nation might not be ready to rally on behalf of Wall Street or a polluting business, but they could not countenance interference with their firearms. No wonder the weapons industry is the least-regulated enterprise in the country. Nor is it an accident that many of the most prominent leaders of other parts of the conservative movement have rallied to the NRA. The NRA's board has been a who's who of conservative leaders, politicians and celebrities. A partial list: Grover Norquist, John Bolton, Ollie North, David Keene, Chuck Norris, Ted Nugent, Larry Craig, Jim Gilmore, Ken Blackwell, and Joe Allbaugh.

Opposition to gun control also provides the right with a second set of cultural issues alongside its arsenal of religious concerns. The gun lobby has been remarkably effective at casting its foes as coastal big-city cultural elitists who neither understand nor respect rural culture. That former New York City mayor Michael Bloomberg, one of the richest men in the world, poured resources into the gun safety movement gave the NRA and its friends a new and convenient target.

The gun ideology is built around a reading of the Second Amendment that the Courts largely rejected until a 5-to-4 conservative majority in the 2008 *Heller* case affirmed an individual right to bear arms. The awkwardly worded amendment reads in its entirety: "A well-regulated militia, being necessary to the security of a free state, the right of the people to keep and bear arms, shall not be infringed." The gun lobby's view of the amendment largely endorsed in *Heller* ignores its opening reference to "a well-regulated militia, being necessary to the security of a free state." As Michael Waldman recounts in his fine book, *The Second Amendment: A Biography*, Justice John Paul Stevens in his *Heller* dissent returned to James Madison and the original debates over the amendment to argue that, as Waldman put it, "the militias were— and still are—the protected party." Stevens wrote that "there is no indication that the Framers of the Amendment intended to enshrine the common-law right of self-defense in the Constitution." But Waldman rightly lays heavy stress on how Justice Antonin Scalia's majority opinion, which abandoned this history, arose not primarily from a clash of legal briefs but from years of political agitation by gun rights absolutists. The Court's ruling, he wrote, "reflected a popular consensus won by focused activists."

And a great deal of that activism played into both the most paranoid elements of the far right and the more elevated concerns of those who called themselves "constitutional conservatives." Liberals regularly tried to win over gun owners by visibly toting their firearms, entering duck blinds or hiking through forests in search of deer. But most NRA members instruct such liberals that hunting is not what matters. The point of an armed citizenry is to be prepared for the moment that demands a stand against tyranny. And in the Obama era, there were many Americans who were convinced that tyranny was just around the corner. The NRA and the weapons manufacturers were highly successful in persuading gun owners that confiscation of their weapons was a real possibility. Even though the proportion of American households with firearms has been dropping, gun sales soared under Obama. It was one of the unheralded ways in which he increased the nation's GDP.

Opponents of measures such as background checks are a small minority of the country—generously, a third of Americans, and on some gun control measures, even fewer. But particularly in rural states, the NRA strikes fear in politicians, particularly moderate Democrats who are always on the hunt for more conservative votes. Such Democrats are essential to the party's ability to hold the Senate, a body gerrymandered by the Constitution itself to favor rural interests. Republicans of more moderately conservative views also worry about the NRA's power in primaries, especially with the Tea Party providing their potential enemies additional ballast.

And so it was that even the deaths of twenty schoolchildren could not tame the gun lobby. When the Manchin-Toomey proposal came up for a vote on April 17, it was supported by 54 Senators representing some two-thirds of the American population. But under the new supremacy of the filibuster, 54 votes were not enough, and the measure was defeated. The flight of both moderate Democrats and moderately conservative Republicans was impressive testimony to the gun lobby's power to intimidate. Democratic "no's" came from Max Baucus, Mark Begich, Heidi Heitkamp, and Mark Pryor—respectively from Montana, Alaska, North Dakota, and Arkansas. Republicans who prided themselves on their reputations for reasonableness, including Lamar Alexander, Kelly Ayotte, Bob Corker, and Johnny Isakson, also cast their lot with the NRA. Only four Republicans voted yes: Susan Collins of Maine, Mark Kirk of Illinois, John McCain of Arizona, and Toomey. Two courageous "yes" votes came from Democrats Mary Landrieu of Louisiana and Kay Hagan of North Carolina. Both faced reelection in 2014 in states Obama had lost in 2012—and both would go down to defeat.

It was an enormous, dispiriting loss, a sign that Obama's reelection and the Democrats' continued control of the Senate would not make things easier. The fever remained unbroken. And things would get worse.

Even the good news for Obama was bad news that year. In the Senate, a significant group of Republicans was determined to repair the damage the party had done with Latino voters and pass comprehensive immigration reform. A startling and brutally honest postelection report commissioned by the Republican National Committee and issued in March under the rubric of the "Growth and Opportunity Project" had suggested as much. The authors noted bluntly that "if Hispanics think we do not want them here, they will close their ears to our policies." Its authors added: "We are not a policy committee, but among the steps Republicans take in the Hispanic community and beyond, we must embrace and champion comprehensive immigration reform."

And many GOP senators did. On June 27, 2013, after months of negotiation, the Senate passed an immigration reform bill by an overwhelming vote, 68 to 32. All the Democrats voted for it, and so did 14 Republicans. Among the Republican supporters was a favorite of the Tea Party and one of the party's young conservative hopes, Senator Marco Rubio of Florida. Not only did Rubio vote for the bill; he was closely involved in the discussions leading up to it. For once Obama could bring back his one-America theme and describe something that had actually happened in Washington with support from both parties. "The bipartisan bill that passed today was a compromise," he said. "By definition, nobody got everything they wanted. Not Republicans. Not Democrats. Not me."

And then the bill died. Repeatedly, Speaker John Boehner signaled the White House that he wanted to act on immigration reform. But nothing happened. Republican senators representing relatively large constituencies—including those, like Rubio, a Cuban-American whose White House dreams made him think of the largest constituency of all—could think not only about GOP primary electorates, but also about the party's need to make peace with Latinos. And many of them, particularly John McCain, had long supported immigration reform on principle. They thought their party might be ready to join them after Mitt Romney's Hispanic and Asian shellacking.

But the Republican House was a different creature. There the Tea Party influence remained strong, and the Tea Party's supporters were resolutely against any measure they saw as rewarding the lawbreaking of illegal immigrants. Boehner, however much his pro-business Republicanism inclined him toward a bill that the party's corporate interests and Chamber of Commerce members longed for, was not about to threaten his own job by putting a bill on the floor that would enrage his right wing. Immigration reform's supporters said repeatedly, and they were right, that the Senate bill could almost certainly have passed the House because there were enough Republicans—albeit a minority in their party—ready to join almost all of the Democrats to push it through. Boehner wouldn't do it. And Rubio, suddenly finding himself under a scalding attack from his onetime allies in the Tea Party, steadily backed off his own creation and leaned further away still as the primary campaign went on.

Nothing would happen on immigration until Obama acted unilaterally. And, to the growing consternation of his Latino allies, he would wait to act until after the 2014 election. The Tea Party had won another one.

In the summer and fall of 2013, the fevers returned to Washington in full force, once again sparked by budget matters, although the budget itself was not really the central issue. At stake was the Republicans' determination to repeal the Affordable Care Act.

That the House felt obligated to vote dozens of times to repeal "Obamacare" was a source of amusement to critics of conservatism. Why wasn't once enough? But there was a logic to their grand quest. As a political matter, the health law was Obama's largest policy monument. The reforms of Dodd-Frank were important—Republicans wanted to repeal those, too—but they were complicated, not widely understood, and still subject to a bureaucratically intricate rule-making process. The stimulus, which they had demonized with great success, was a thing of the past. But if Obamacare endured and succeeded, it would be an achievement that Democrats would keep pointing back to, much as they touted Social Security and Medicare. All would be seen as decisive uses of government to reduce the anxieties created by the workings of a market economy.

And if Obamacare endured, it would represent a major extension of the American welfare state. The Affordable Care Act's Medicaid expansion was a direct government program, unmediated by insurance exchanges and private insurances companies. Many conservative governors continued to resist it, empowered by the 2012 Supreme Court decision that upheld Obamacare's constitutionality but allowed states to turn down the Medicaid expansion without losing the rest of their Medicaid funds. The Court had upheld the Affordable Care Act and partly gutted it at the same time.

The Medicaid expansion was also, from a conservative point of view, insidiously attractive, since it was paid for almost entirely with federal funds. As one Republican governor after another decided to buck conservative ideologues and take the money to support their local hospitals and insure their neediest citizens, the dangers loomed ever larger. And the plan's market-oriented part, involving subsidies for the purchase of private insurance, could easily be expanded gradually. The trajectory that many on the left foresaw was also visible to the right: over time, government would have to play a larger and larger role in the provision of health care.

And the 2012 elections brought a new voice to Washington who was determined to be the hero of Obamacare's demise. Senator Ted Cruz of Texas had defeated a more moderate conservative in the Republican primary and stormed into Washington set upon making himself the loudest and most insistent voice of uncompromising Tea Party conservatism—all by way of preparing for the presidential run he would launch in March 2015. Cruz quickly saw that his boisterous and self-promoting ways did not sit well with his Republican Senate colleagues. One might fairly ask: how is Cruz any different and what would the Senate be without self-promotion? Cruz's colleagues would readily answer that self-promotion is perfectly acceptable as long as it is carried out under certain rules of decorum and with due regard for the political interests of colleagues. Cruz was apparently never shown the rulebook.

And so he allied himself with the most fervent conservatives in the House, crossing over to the other side of Capitol Hill to meet with them at Tortilla Coast and other House watering holes and dining venues. If this did not sit well with Cruz's Senate colleagues, it did not please John Boehner, either. The Speaker didn't much like the community organizer in the White House, and he surely did not want a Senate-based community organizer inciting House colleagues who were ready to rebel without any additional encouragement.

Cruz himself embodied the conservatives' double-sided message on Obamacare. They had to insist that it wasn't working and could not possibly work. But their real fear was that it would *succeed*. In an interview on Fox News in July, Cruz gave the game away. After ritualistically declaring that "Obamacare isn't working," he said this: "If we're going to repeal it, we've got to do so now or it will remain with us forever." Why? Because once the administration gets the health insurance "exchanges in place . . . the subsidies in place," people will get "hooked on Obamacare so that it can never be unwound." Keeping uninsured Americans with obviously addictive personalities from getting "hooked" on Obamacare was an urgent task.

The Cruz-led patriots of the Tea Party thus engineered a government shutdown that began on October 1, 2013. Their position: they would not vote to fund the federal government unless the bill in question repealed or postponed Obamacare. Boehner warned his colleagues that the shutdown was a bad idea and wouldn't work. But when they wouldn't listen, he ran to the head of the army he thought was moving in the wrong direction and led them off the cliff. It was the beginning of what the conservative writer Marc Thiessen called "The Seinfeld Shutdown" because it really was, in the end, about nothing.

The episode represented a very curious way to approach, or perhaps to avoid, governing. Repealing Obamacare the normal way—the constitutional way, as Tea Partiers might have said under other circumstances—required passing a bill in two houses and getting the president to sign it. There was virtually no chance of the Senate passing such a bill and absolutely no chance that Obama would repeal his own program. Only extraordinary means could get the job done. Therefore, in the peculiar logic of the right, financing government in the normal, constitutional way came to be seen as a "concession" because anything that kept Obamacare on the books was a "concession." Many nonradical conservatives fully understood how bizarre this approach was. "It's a dead end," said Representative Peter King, the crusty Long Island Republican who had no patience for the foolishness.

But this confrontation was different from others in the earlier Obama years because Republicans were badly divided while Democrats were united. In this sense, the political temperature had dropped, even if the fever was not entirely broken. Many Republicans had buyer's remorse even before the adventure began.

It was also different because the GOP had caused fiscal chaos over an issue quite apart from normal budget wrangling and made a demand that most of them knew would never be met. The new health care system was up and running the very day the shutdown began. This would cause problems later, but at the time, it undercut the Republicans' case. And Republicans had no coherent strategy, as many of them privately acknowledged. As one adviser to the leadership put it to me at the time, they were laying track just ahead of the train as it roared forward.

Finally, it was different because Obama was different. In the past, he had always been ready to negotiate and typically went out of his way never to cast showdowns in partisan terms. This time, he freely called out "House Republicans" as the culprits and confidently asserted that serious talks could take place only if Republicans stopped using threats to the country's well-being as bargaining levers.

During the shutdown, 800,000 government employees were furloughed and 1.3 million had to report to work without knowing how they'd be paid. In response to pressure, Republicans announced they would pay the furloughed workers for having done no work. It was an odd contradiction for the small-government party, and another way in which the shutdown was about nothing.

In the Senate, Mitch McConnell stated the obvious: the House's strategy, he said, had gone "awry." The affair finally ended on October 16 when the House passed a Senate bill that reopened the government. All 198 Democrats who voted favored it. Among Republicans, 87 voted yes and 144 voted no—the latter being, in effect, a vote to continue the shutdown. Once again, the Republican leadership had to rely mostly on Democrats to get itself out of a scrape and to carry out the duties of governing.

And so the shutdown reached its inevitable failure for all who had promoted it, and for a leadership that had acquiesced to it. The turning point may have been an NBC News/*Wall Street Journal* poll released on October 10 showing the Republican Party's positive rating at 24 percent, its lowest ever to that point, while President Obama's rating had risen slightly, to 47 percent. And Republicans were staring at a potential political catastrophe in 2014: By a margin of 47 percent to 39 percent, the public said it preferred a Democratic Congress to a Republican Congress. In July, the two parties had been tied.

Beneath these numbers was another instructive shift. Positive feelings toward the Tea Party fell to 21 percent, down from 34 percent at the movement's peak in June 2010. The Tea Party had lost well over one-third of its friends.

Democrats were elated, but their elation did not last long. The Health Care.gov website had crashed on its very first day of operation, October 1. But the problems with the website emerged slowly and did not become fully obvious until after the shutdown ended. They promptly took over the news. Day after day, stories about unconscionable delays, crashes, recriminations among officials and contractors dominated the airwaves and the newspapers. Obamacare's foes came off defense and were suddenly back on the attack— and this time, the administration's mishandling of the rollout gave them live ammunition.

On October 21, Obama went to the Rose Garden to admit the obvious. "Of course, you've probably heard that HealthCare.gov—the new website where people can apply for health insurance, and browse and buy affordable plans in most states—hasn't worked as smoothly as it was supposed to work," he said with mild understatement. He spoke for a half hour, trying hard to defend the Affordable Care Act and to describe the benefits and relief it was bringing to so many Americans. But his defensiveness was palpable. "Let me remind everybody that the Affordable Care Act is not just a website," he said almost plaintively. "It's much more."

Although the website was eventually fixed and the ACA went on to cover tens of millions, the damage done in that period was incalculable. Politically, the snafu immediately moved the spotlight away from Republican dysfunction and toward the administration's failures. There was no telling whether the strong Democratic poll numbers immediately after the shutdown would have persisted into the 2014 campaign, but the ACA's troubles guaranteed they would not. The fact that government had failed in one of the basic tasks of setting up access to an insurance system ratified classic conservative complaints about bureaucratic failure and incompetence. Not for the first time did liberals learn that they had more of an interest than anyone in promoting government efficiency and performance.

And the website crash was the administration's second self-inflicted blow that fall. The first came in late August and early September when it emerged that Syria had used chemical weapons against its internal foes. At a news conference on August 20, 2012, Obama had said that "we have been very clear to the [Bashar al-] Assad regime, but also to other players on the ground, that a red line for us is [if] we start seeing a whole bunch of chemical weapons moving around or being utilized." The president had resisted getting the United States deeply engaged in Syria's civil war—it would emerge that Secretary of State Hillary Clinton favored stronger American intervention—but on August 20, the president spoke what would prove to be fateful words about the use of chemical weapons: "That would change my calculus. That would change my equation."

A little over a year later, he was stuck with his red line, and he announced that he planned air strikes against Syria. And to the surprise of many, including Congress, he also said he would seek congressional authorization for his action. He won almost immediate support from Boehner and Eric Cantor, but widespread opposition to giving Obama the authority he sought emerged quickly, particularly in the House. Resistance came not only from dovish Democrats but also from many Republicans. Some were opposed because they held broadly anti-interventionist views, others simply because they mistrusted Obama. In the end, the issue was never directly joined because Obama picked up on a Russian proposal to negotiate a voluntary surrender of chemical weapons by the Assad government.

The episode was deeply harmful to Obama over the long run and ended the long advantage he had enjoyed on foreign policy. Americans approved of his two most visible accomplishments: the withdrawal from Iraq and the killing of Osama bin Laden. But after the confusion around Syria, some foreign governments began expressing doubts about Obama's steadfastness even as his fellow citizens began to question his overall approach. This would hurt him later when the Islamic State emerged, out of nowhere for most Americans and to the surprise of the administration itself, as a new threat.

The year 2013 ended far less merrily for Obama than it had begun. Julie Pace of the Associated Press captured the mood when she asked him at his year-end news conference in December, "Has this been the worst year of your presidency?"

Obama declined to give a direct answer, though the distinction probably belonged to 2011, or at least its first eight months, when the president emerged from the summer looking weak after the debt ceiling fiasco in which he had operated from a position of fear. Yet the knocks Obama took in 2013 were real. They included the defeat of background checks, the bottling up of immigration reform, the website disaster, and the costs of his Syrian jumble. The gaudy progressive hopes of his Inaugural Address had gone largely unfulfilled.

But there was also this: in 2013, at least, conservatives had also absorbed heavy blows. The Tea Party began to decline in both real and perceived power, and Republicans began a slow retreat from the politics of absolutism.

At year's end, Democratic senator Patty Murray and Paul Ryan did something that had not happened since the Republican takeover of the House in 2010: they quietly negotiated a middle-of-the-road budget deal that more or less split the differences between the parties. This was big news because compromise itself had come to be viewed as a violation of conservative ideals and was a new dividing line between the parties. Yet if compromise was now a countercultural activity for conservatives, Ryan and Boehner correctly calculated they could get away with it because their colleagues were still dealing with the political wreckage from the shutdown and had no stomach for another fight.

Boehner himself even spoke out against the party's new alternative establishment, the well-funded outside groups such as FreedomWorks, Heritage Action, and Americans for Prosperity, for opposing the Ryan-Murray deal "before they even saw it." He accused them of "using our members and using the American people for their own goals." It was a recognition that a counter-establishment, bolstered by conservative radio talkers, Fox News, and right-wing money, was in direct competition with the party's elected leaders for control not only over its message but also over its approach to governing.

Yet there was no letting up on Obama. All year long, Republicans searched in vain for a conspiracy behind the killing of four Americans, including Christopher Stevens, the American ambassador to Libya, at the diplomatic compound in Benghazi on September 11, 2012. Mere mention of the word "Benghazi" was enough to incite conservative crowds and it became the new shorthand on the right for all that was wrong with both Obama and Secretary of State Hillary Clinton. Republicans insisted that the administration was covering up its failures and had not done everything it could have to save American lives. The focus on Benghazi did not dissipate even when a report from the House Intelligence Committee—released, conveniently, after the 2014 elections—cleared the administration of such charges. Still the Benghazi obsession eventually had a political payoff for Republicans. The never-ending congressional inquiry into Benghazi led, at least indirectly, to the revelation in 2015 that Hillary Clinton had avoided sending email on a State Department account and used a private server in her home instead. It would be the first major controversy of her campaign for president, and it would drag her down in the polls throughout the summer of 2015. She would win a reprieve only in late September of 2015, when Kevin McCarthy bragged on Fox News of the investigation's impact on Clinton's poll numbers. His admission of a political motive enraged his colleagues, helped doom his candidacy for Speaker—and was a lifeline to Clinton. Her strong performance at a House investigative committee hearing in the face of Republican badgering strengthened her further. Like her husband, she was, for a while at least, the beneficiary of Republican and conservative overreach.

Conservatives also took on their favorite target, the Internal Revue Service, for allegedly targeting conservative political groups seeking tax-exempt status under the "social welfare" provision of the tax code. With the loosening of campaign finance rules by the Supreme Court, the IRS took on new responsibilities to regulate these groups. It emerged that the IRS did not single out conservative organizations but also challenged progressive groups—and that most of the conservative groups received the tax status they were seeking anyway. In the end, even Representative Darrell Issa, the scourge of the Obama administration, could not find any participation by the White House in the screening and vetting process. Issa's report was left to claiming that "President Obama's rhetoric against conservative-oriented groups" had "influenced how the IRS engaged with them." Both the Benghazi and IRS stories provided many hours of entertaining outrage for Fox News viewers and created moments of embarrassment for public officials. But they did not produce the Watergate moment Republicans longed for.

★

Was 2014 the year the "Republican establishment" put the Tea Party in its place? Or was it the year when the Establishment went over to the Tea Party?

The first narrative was popular in the media because the Republican Party did far better in 2014 than in the previous two election cycles at preventing the nomination of obviously extreme candidates. Incumbents were more prepared for challengers, and those challengers were, on the whole, less formidable than some of the earlier Tea Party standard-bearers. In the case of Mississippi's Thad Cochran, as we saw in Chapter One, Republicans had to import Democratic voters into their primary to fend off Chris McDaniel in the year's strongest Tea Party challenge. But other incumbents had it easier, and 2014 was the first year since 2008 in which conservative insurgents failed to dislodge a single Republican incumbent. Besides Cochran, the victors included the Senate Minority Leader Mitch McConnell and Senators Lamar Alexander, Lindsey Graham, Pat Roberts, and John Cornyn.

Yet the scorecard did not reflect the entire game. L. Brent Bozell III, a leading voice on the right, told the *Washington Post*, "What I find to be the greatest irony of them all is everybody has one thing in common—everybody is running as a conservative." In fact, the Tea Party's greatest victory was not electoral. It was to change the nature of the party and the definition of conservatism. Despite Boehner's grumbling at the end of 2013, the distinction between the Establishment and the Tea Party was now blurred.

This was obvious in the contests that did not involve incumbents. Most of these could not be characterized as fights between "the grass roots" and "the big guys." Rather, they were clashes between competing establishment factions with vast sums to spend. They had little to do with the long-term philosophical direction of the party, since rich ideological donors, along with Tea Party groups, had already seen to the task of moving it rightward. Political correctness of an extremely conservative kind was the rule in 2014, meaning that some Republican politicians experienced indigestion as they were forced to eat old words acknowledging a human role in climate change. Except for the year-end budget agreement, they shunned deal-making with Obama.

The May primary for an open seat in Nebraska was revealing. Ben Sasse, a university president who held a variety of jobs in George W. Bush's administration, won it handily. His success was broadly taken as a triumph for the Tea Party, which just a week earlier had been said to have suffered a defeat in North Carolina. There, Thom Tillis, the Speaker of the state House of Representatives and the so-called establishment candidate, faced opponents perceived to be to his right. Yet Tillis would prove to be one of the most right-wing candidates on any ballot in 2014. In the legislature, he had worked happily with the most conservative forces in the state.

An instructive way to look at the Nebraska result was suggested by *Wall Street Journal* writer Reid Epstein. Sometimes news stories are like good poems that convey meaning through artful—if not always intentional—juxtaposition.

Epstein noted that Sasse was "backed by more than $2.4 million in ad spending, either praising him or attacking his opponents, from organizations such as the small-government Club for Growth and the Senate Conservatives Fund, which targets Republicans it deems insufficiently conservative."

Yet in the very next paragraph, Epstein quoted a Facebook post from Senator Ted Cruz, the Tea Party hero who supported Sasse. The Texas Republican declared that "Ben Sasse's decisive victory is a clear indication that the grass roots are rising up to make D. C. listen."

So, was this really the grass roots speaking to Washington? Or was it a cadre of conservative groups, largely working out of Washington, spending vast sums of cash to persuade voters to listen to them? It was hard to see Nebraska's primary as a mass revolt, since turnout amounted to just 316,124 out of 1,152,180 registered Nebraskans. Sasse won with about 110,000 votes. And the grassroots claim was problematic given Sasse's Washington experience and also because many Nebraska-based Tea Party groups backed one of his opponents, former state treasurer Shane Osborn. *Salon*'s Jim Newell noted that FreedomWorks, one of the Washington-based operations that latched on to the Tea Party early, initially endorsed Osborn but switched to Sasse. The local Tea Party faithful who preferred Osborn resented the machinations of the big-money groups headquartered in the nation's capital, whose competition resembled a *Game of Thrones* power struggle. As the *Atlantic*'s Molly Ball put it, "Sasse actually represents less the Tea Party's anti-incumbent rage than the sort of fusion candidate who can unite the party establishment and base—a well-credentialed insider who can convince the right wing he's on their side."

In one of the most insightful and important articles of the election cycle, Rich Lowry and Ramesh Ponnuru of *National Review* introduced "Establishment Tea" into the political conversation. "The tea parties have almost since their inception been attacking the party establishment for not standing for anything, and the establishment has been complaining for nearly as long that tea party candidates are not ready for prime time. This primary season, each side seems to be learning the others' lesson." Sasse fit this bill, they argued because he "campaigned on a full-throated anti-Obamacare and anti-Washington message" yet "was a former Bush official who didn't scare anyone."

Establishment Tea meant this: the Establishment was moving right to survive, and the Tea Partiers, at least when they were not facing incumbents, were finding themselves a better bunch of candidates.

Tea Party rebels did achieve one victory that shocked the political class—and perhaps even the Tea Party itself. House Majority Leader Eric Cantor could be forgiven for thinking that in unseating him, the Tea Party had gone after a friend. After all, in November 2010, he had declared that "[t]he Tea Party [is] . . . an organic movement that played a tremendously positive role in this election. I mean, certainly, it produced an outcome beneficial to our party when you're picking up at least 60-some seats." Cantor fell to the very forces he and his colleagues unleashed and encouraged.

Immigration was a central issue used against Cantor by David Brat, the insurgent professor who defeated him by 11 percentage points. It was a reminder of how powerful the issue is for the Republican right. If there had ever been any chance that Boehner would act on his promises to Obama about immigration reform, Cantor's defeat almost certainly closed it off. Cantor's loss made holding a fearful and fractious GOP caucus together an even more central preoccupation.

Cantor's loss was also a blow to conservatives who were trying to reform the movement. He recognized, as we've seen, that employees and not just entrepreneurs deserved the party's attention, and he had sponsored efforts to strengthen thinkers in the movement who were trying to come up with plausible policies. His defeat helps explain why he and his allies worried so much about being too bold in their new ideas venture.

There was an irony in the race, and it related to gerrymandering. Cantor's district was changed to give him more Republican voters—and he lost especially badly in the primary among the new and very conservative voters who had been moved in to strengthen him in the general election.

For Democrats entering the fall of 2014, the election was set up badly, and then things would get darker still. Most of the key Senate races were in states Obama lost in 2012, and the two seats the party thought it might pick up from the GOP were in Romney states, too. Democratic incumbents were in trouble from the start in Louisiana, Arkansas, North Carolina, and Alaska. Open seats held by Democrats who had left or retired in Montana, South Dakota, and West Virginia also looked very vulnerable. Every one of these seats fell to the Republicans, although North Carolina and Alaska were close. And Democrats fell far short of picking up targeted seats in Kentucky—McConnell's seat—and Georgia.

Democrats lost two other seats they should have won. In Colorado, Senator Mark Udall, a respected environmentalist, had the misfortune of watching as the party establishment successfully pushed out a Tea Party candidate and replaced him with the smoother but still very conservative Cory Gardner. And in Iowa, Representative Bruce Braley was caught on tape telling a trial lawyers' group that they should be horrified at the thought of Iowa Senator Charles Grassley, "a farmer," becoming chairman of the Judiciary Committee. The two obvious problems with the statement: the race was for a seat in Iowa, and Iowa has a lot of farmers. Braley lost to Republican Joni Ernst, a state senator who made her name in the primary with an ad in which she boasted about castrating hogs. Ernst was a "fusion" Establishment–Tea Party candidate like Sasse, although in a very different way. Her endorsers in the primary, as *Politico* put it, were "an eclectic coalition of Republicans" that included Sarah Palin, Mitt Romney, and Marco Rubio. All of them campaigned for her.

At a national level, Democrats were tongue-tied. Senate Majority Leader Harry Reid and the party's top strategic thinker, Senator Charles Schumer of

New York, put together a package of economic issues under the rubric of "A Fair Shot for Everyone." They pledged to make the campaign a battle for the middle class—not unlike the campaign that had worked for Obama in 2012. Their key issues included a minimum wage increase, equal pay for women, college affordability, child care, and incentives for companies to invest in the United States. Lacking Romney as a convenient moneyed foil, they regularly assailed the Koch brothers for trying to buy the election for right-wing corporate interests.

What the Democratic Party could not figure out was a national message about Obama's presidency and how to talk about an economic recovery that had finally begun to gather steam. With Republicans making opposition to the president their central and in some ways their only issue, these were not trivial shortcomings. Because Obama's popularity was down and because he was especially unpopular in the key Romney states Democrats hoped to win or hold in the Senate, many in his party feared that mounting a defense of the president would backfire. In an environment in which Obama was under constant attack, the lack of a defense only made the Democrats' situation worse. And the failure to defend Obama was depressing to his support base, whom Democrats, even in red states, needed. It was a conundrum the Democrats never resolved.

Obama himself was restrained, partly because embattled red state Democrats wanted him to be. He postponed executive actions on immigration that he had promised to undertake if the Republican House failed to act. Democrats feared that any move to legalize undocumented immigrants would create a backlash against incumbent red state Democratic senators. In the event, they lost anyway, and Obama's failure to act enraged many Latinos and held down their turnout.

And on the economy, Democrats were torn three ways. Some Democrats, particularly in the White House, believed the party should proudly tout the economy's rescue from near collapse, its steady comeback, and the job creation that was finally picking up steam. But Democratic pollsters warned that with so many Americans still hurting, robust praise of economic conditions would only make the party look out of touch with the large number of voters whom the recovery had still not yet reached. The further complication was the Democrats' insistence that changes in the economy had shortchanged the middle class to the benefit of the wealthy. Obama often said these things himself. Yet this, too, was in its way a depressing message that did not necessarily reflect well on a party that had held the White House for nearly six years.

And beyond the actual campaign was the flow of disconcerting news voters were absorbing on television, online, and in their newspapers. In the months before the election, the world seemed to be flying out of control. The spate of bad news was part of the Republicans' good luck in 2014. In the summer came the surge of Latin American children, fleeing violence in their home countries, across the United States' southern border. The mass movement of immigrants had started the previous October but it hit the media as a major development that summer. Then came the rise of the Islamic State, a new, strange, and thoroughly terrifying group that routed the Iraqi army in northern Iraq and called into question Obama's policies. Within two weeks in August and early September, the group put out gruesome videos of its beheadings of two American journalists, James Foley, a photographer, and Steven Sotloff.

As if these horrors were insufficient, the Ebola outbreak in Africa hit the news in September and October, punctuated by scare stories about a handful of Americans who contracted the disease. By 2015 it was clear that the Obama administration as well as local governments had handled the Ebola problem skillfully. But this was not obvious in the weeks before the election as health officials scrambled to deal with a very new problem.

These crises gave the Republicans' their closing theme, and they linked them to their favorite issues, particularly the need to "secure" the southern border against immigrants. Typical was the closely fought Senate race in New Hampshire. "We have a border that's so porous that anyone can walk across it," said Scott Brown, who had moved across another border, from Massachusetts to the Granite State, to challenge incumbent Democrat Jeanne Shaheen. "I think it's naïve to think that people aren't going to be walking through here who have these types of diseases and or other types of intent, criminal or terrorist."

In an ad that was montage of frightening images, Brown declared, implausibly, that "[r]adical Islamic terrorists are threatening to cause the collapse of our country." Democrats, he said, just didn't get it. "President Obama and Senator Shaheen seem confused about the nature of the threat," he said. "Not me. I want to secure the border, keep out the people who will do us harm, and restore America's leadership in the world." Even the obligatory tagline sounded like a reprise of old Republican campaign messages from 2002 and 2004: "I'm Scott Brown, and I approved this message because protecting the homeland is the first step to making America strong again."

Margaret Talev of *Bloomberg Politics* reported that in the period October 21–25 alone, ads invoking Ebola ran 734 times.

On Election Day, the voters of an edgy, unhappy country who did show up routed the Democrats. A record number didn't vote at all, and in many respects, the year was even worse for Democrats than 2010. This time the Republicans took control of the Senate and won their largest number of House seats since 1928, the last election before the Great Depression. It was, perhaps, Hoover's revenge. Democrats were trounced in contests for state legislative seats as well as governorships. Right-wing Republican governors who were thought to be in grave peril in Kansas and Maine survived while Democrats lost governorships in their usually loyal bastions of Massachusetts, Maryland, and Illinois. Republicans now controlled 31 governorships and 68 of the country's 99 legislative chambers. After 2014, Democrats held full control—meaning the governorship and both houses of the legislature—in only 8 states. Republicans had full control in 24. There was a red America and a blue America on the night of November 4, 2014. The red one was much bigger.

At 35.9 percent, turnout in 2014 was the lowest since 1942, an election held during World War II, when many Americans were abroad in the service. And as in 2010, Democratic-leaning groups were the stay-at-homes. Some 13 percent of 2014 voters were 18–29 years of age, sharply down from their 19 percent share in 2012. As voting analysts Ruy Teixeira and John Halpin noted, the 6-percentage-point fall "was identical to the drop-off in young voter representation from the 2008 to 2010 elections." On the other hand, older voters stormed the polling places: 22 percent of 2014 voters were 65 and older, up from their 17 percent share of the electorate in 2012 and even a point above their 21 percent share in 2010. Teixeira and Halpin noted that

2012 marked "the highest share of seniors in the electorate since 1988." And seniors were now a very Republican group.

Aggravating the Democrats' problems was the decline in participation among ethnic and racial minorities. Nonwhites had made up 28 percent of the 2012 electorate but were 25 percent of 2014's voters. The African-American share of the vote was down one point from the presidential election, and the Latino share dropped by two. Obama's delays in acting on immigration extracted a price. Teixeira and Halpin also noted a drop in the female share of the electorate, from 53 percent to 51 percent. Thus did "a substantially older, whiter, and less-female electorate" hand the Democrats their drubbing.

A postelection survey by the Public Religion Research Institute, which reinterviewed 1,399 respondents who had been contacted before the election, underscored the Democrats' turnout troubles. Latinos comprised just 8 percent of all voters in the overall sample—but 22 percent of nonvoters. Whites, on the other hand, made up a much larger share of those who voted (73 percent) than of those who didn't (56 percent).

The nonvoter pool was also overwhelmingly young: Millennials, those of ages 18–34, made up 47 percent of the nonvoters but just 17 percent of voters. On the other hand, 54 percent of those who reported voting were over the age of 50. The electorate also skewed by class. Among nonvoters, 44 percent made less than $30,000 a year; among voters, only 26 percent had incomes that low. At the other end of the scale, those earning $100,000 or more annually accounted for 7 percent of nonvoters, but 17 percent of voters. This time the battlefield of class tilted toward the best-off.

All this had an ideological effect. Liberals accounted for 26 percent of nonvoters and 25 percent of voters. But conservatives constituted a much larger share of the voter pool relative to their numbers: while 34 percent of nonvoters called themselves conservative, 42 percent of voters did. Republicans called on Obama's opponents to use their votes to register their unhappiness with the president. The president's foes readily accepted the invitation.

★

It was less curious than it seemed that Obama was liberated by the defeat. No longer did he have to worry about Democrats trying to win in states where he was disliked, including some where he was loathed. He had been cautious, as many of the Democrats in those battlegrounds had wished—and they had lost anyway. With the election over, he was freer to make a case for his achievements, especially after the continuing improvement of the economy began to brighten the outlook even of Americans who had, only a few months earlier, believed that the recovery would never reach them. The sense of economic progress began to move his polling numbers upward.

And there were, again, the strange rhythms of Obama's own competitiveness. He was a fourth-quarter player whose energies often kicked in fully only when the threat of losing was upon him. It was after the disastrous summer of 2011 that he began to take the aggressive moves that his reelection would require and to make the case against the ideas of his conservative adversaries. He offered the sports metaphor himself during his 2014 year-end news conference. "My presidency is entering the fourth quarter," he said brightly. "Interesting things happen in the fourth quarter." The 2014 defeat—and the calendar—reminded him that he needed to get done what he could, but also to advance ideas and arguments that would strengthen the chances that his allies could sustain his policies beyond the life of his presidency.

And so he moved quickly to act unilaterally where he had the power, and to lay down markers. He used executive action to legalize the situations of up to 5 million undocumented immigrants. There was exultation in a Latino community that had only recently excoriated Obama's caution, and this helped bump up his polling numbers as disaffected parts of the community returned to the fold. He reached an agreement with China setting ambitious targets to reduce greenhouse gases, a signal that acting on climate change would be a central focus of his final two years in office. He upended fifty-three years of American policy by opening diplomatic relations with Cuba.

And his 2015 State of the Union address made clear he had come to understand that winning the long-term argument with his partisan and ideological opponents took priority over hoping that the celestial choirs Hillary Clinton had mocked would finally start singing. He was at long last dealing with the Republican Party he had, not the one he once thought he could persuade.

He was unabashed in saying, about as clearly as a president could in an address of that sort, that his opponents had been flatly wrong. "At every step, we were told our goals were misguided or too ambitious," he declared, "that we would crush jobs and explode deficits. Instead, we've seen the fastest economic growth in over a decade, our deficits cut by two-thirds, a stock market that has doubled, and health care inflation at its lowest rate in fifty years."

His analysis of the nature of his political opposition, in turn, dictated the approach he took in the rest of the speech. There was no point in hedging on his wishes, constraining his hopes, and compromising in advance. At earlier points in his administration, he often seemed inclined to begin a negotiation by offering his interlocutors their asking price up front and then moving backward from there. No more.

Instead, he laid out what he would do if he had a more cooperative Congress. Obama's agenda was specifically organized around the interests of middle-class American workers. Thus did he offer redistributive tax proposals—cuts for the middle class, increases for the very wealthy—even as he called for guaranteed sick leave for all, expanded child care, free and universal access to two years of community college, and equal pay for equal work.

He even offered encouraging words to organized labor. "We still need laws that strengthen rather than weaken unions," he said, "and give workers a voice." And his single most combative line came in renewing his support for an increase in the minimum wage. "If you truly believe you can work full-time and support a family on less than $15,000 a year," he told the assembled members of Congress, "go try it."

Yet he ended a pugnacious speech by revisiting and defending his signature notion that "there wasn't a liberal America or a conservative America."

"Over the past six years, the pundits have pointed out more than once that my presidency hasn't delivered on this vision," he said. "How ironic, they say, that our politics seems more divided than ever. It's held up as proof not just of my own flaws—of which there are many—but also as proof that the vision itself is misguided, naïve, that there are too many people in this town who actually benefit from partisanship and gridlock for us to ever do anything about it."

He stuck by his notion in principle, but did so in a way that was an implicit rebuke to his opponents on the farther ends of the right, calling for moderation in the face of polarization, even on an issue as divisive as abortion. "We still may not agree on a woman's right to choose," he said, "but surely we can agree it's a good thing that teen pregnancies and abortions are nearing all-time lows, and that every woman should have access to the health care that she needs."

And on immigration, he asked his opponents to embrace an idea that many of them could never accept. "Passions still fly on immigration," he said, "but surely we can all see something of ourselves in the striving young student, and agree that no one benefits when a hardworking mom is snatched from her child, and that it's possible to shape a law that upholds our tradition as a nation of laws and a nation of immigrants."

The reponse from Obama's opponents was not encouraging.

Mitch McConnell, Obama's most wily adversary, embodied the contradictions of a Republican Party and a conservative movement aware that their election victory would require them to demonstrate their ability to "govern"— even though they could not let go of their conviction that stymieing Obama was still their most important task.

On election night, McConnell, a veteran of thirty years in the Senate, savored a reelection margin far wider than the pundits and the pollsters expected. Having spent the previous six years doing all he could to obstruct Obama's program, his appointments, and his political standing, McConnell's reward was to achieve his lifelong ambition of leading a Republican majority in the United States Senate.

And so McConnell tried hard the day after he won to sound the notes of conciliation that were once standard currency among legislative leaders. "When the American people choose divided government, I don't think it means they don't want us to do anything," he said, promising no government shutdowns and debt ceiling disasters on his watch. "I think they want us to look for areas of agreement."

But such graciousness had been missing from his victory speech the night before. "For too long, this administration has tried to tell the American people what's good for them—and then blamed somebody else when their policies didn't work out," he told his raucous supporters.

And the man who has spent the vast majority of his working life in the nation's capital added this: "What the current crowd in Washington is offering is making us weaker both at home and abroad. . . . Friends, this experiment in big government has lasted long enough!"

His election night roar was, perhaps, McConnell's final tribute to a campaign stump speech riff that came to him by reflex. But the contrast in tone and purpose between his two sets of remarks defined the choice McConnell and his party would need to make—not only about its attitude toward Obama's final two years but also about the future.

When McConnell declared that "this experiment in big government has lasted long enough," he was obviously describing his view of the Obama presidency, but he also sounding a conservative battle cry that went back to the Goldwater years. The conservative movement had been resisting "this experiment in big government" since the Roosevelt administration. Again and again, conservatives were promised that this election victory, and then the next, and then the next, would finally rout the statists and return the nation to the smaller government they were certain our Founders had in mind. And again and again, conservatives were disappointed. Neither Nixon nor Reagan nor either President Bush could fulfill a promise that, in truth, most Americans did not want kept.

And in the second decade of the twenty-first century, conservatives were forced to grapple with a problem that their own doctrine was ill-suited to confront. With inequality rising, wages stagnating, and upward mobility stalling, the economic market itself was failing to live up to the promises conservatives regularly made on its behalf. These class discontents broke through in the 2012 Republican primaries and were central to Romney's defeat.

Republicans realized these issues could no longer be swept aside. And so they at least began talking about them. Thus did Speaker Boehner open the new Congress declaring that "too many are working harder only to lose ground to stagnant wages and rising costs." Thus did Jeb Bush launch the first stages of his presidential campaign by setting up a fund-raising organization called "Right to Rise PAC," whose double meaning involved his hope for a conservative revival and his promise to put forward ideas that would help "all Americans to rise up" and "to move up the income ladder." Thus did Marco Rubio advance his own presidential aspirations with a book called *American Dreams* and a promise to end what he called "opportunity inequality."

The skeptic might write off such pronouncements as a tribute to the miracles that focus groups and polling can call forth. And as Obama argued in his

State of the Union address, the strengthening economic recovery undercut the Republicans' claims that his policies had failed to restore the economy's health, so his conservative critics had to focus their criticisms on the tasks still to be completed.

Yet the Republican Congress that took over in 2015 did not seem to take this rhetoric particularly seriously. Its opening efforts focused on yet more attempts to repeal or gut Obamacare; an all-out attempt to block the president's executive actions on immigration; building an oil pipeline; and chopping away at the Wall Street reforms. The shutdown habit died hard and the new Republican Congress went right to the edge of temporarily shuttering the Department of Homeland Security in its campaign to block Obama on immigration. But the filibuster, the Senate Republicans' friend during Obama's first six years, was now a Democratic weapon. Senate Democrats refused to vote for a funding bill that undercut the president's immigration moves. Republicans, knowing they now held the copyright on the word "shutdown," also knew they had to back off. In early March, they did. There was no shutdown, and Republicans hoped conservative judges would block Obama's efforts on behalf of immigrants.

Later that month, the budget bills passed by the House and Senate hardly sent a signal that conservatives were taking a new approach to inequality. On the contrary, they included many of the same old cuts, many magic tricks to claim a deficit reduction total of $5 trillion over a decade, and an effort to finesse a fight between deficit hawks and defense hawks by moving military spending outside the boundaries of the old sequestration targets. The Center on Budget and Policy Priorities estimated, once again, that more than two-thirds of the cuts came in programs for low- or middle-income Americans.

The new talk about inequality thus had no connection to what was happening on the floor of the Republican Congress, but it did mean something. One of the most revealing indicators in politics is when one side of the political debate is forced to talk about the problems that the other side defines as most pressing. The side engaged in such code-switching reinforces the worldview of its opponents and suggests a retreat from its own ideology. This is exactly what happened after Ronald Reagan's victory, when Democrats peppered their speeches with praise for "markets" and "entrepreneurship" and redefined social spending as "investments in human capital."

In his 1984 book on the era, *The Neo-Liberals*, Randall Rothenberg pointed to one of the key slogans of the revisionist Democrats who were arguing that their party needed to reach beyond the ideas of Franklin D. Roosevelt. "The solutions of the thirties," they said, "will not solve the problems of the eighties." Was this beginning to happen in reverse? Would conservatives begin to acknowledge that the solutions of the eighties would not solve the problems of the second decade of the twenty-first century?

Bold talk of a new "reform conservatism" suggested a willingness to modernize and moderate, but the right had been there before with compassionate conservatism, a slogan full of promise but short on detail. The question was whether the right was offering a new gloss on old ideas or seeking a genuine breakthrough.

To the surprise and consternation of party leaders who continued to hope they could ride but contain the anger on the right that they stoked, an entirely new threat to their power emerged in the summer of 2015. The rage among grass-roots conservatives had not dissipated and neither had the disaffection among working-class Republicans. Donald Trump, the billionaire deal-making television star, would emerge as the unlikely champion of both groups. Freely criticizing his foes inside and outside the party as "losers" and "morons," Trump seized Reagan's old promise to "make America great again" as his own. He even tried to trademark it. The earnest efforts of policy specialists and intellectuals to tweak the old ideology would confront a skilled twenty-first-century carnival barker for whom policy details were far less important than a personality the media could not get enough of and an eagerness to exploit the deep and angry pessimism that burned inside so many Republican partisans and conservative loyalists.

15

REFORMING CONSERVATISM OR TRUMPING IT

A New Conservatism, a New Pizza Box, or Something Completely Different?

"The average conservative reformist output consists of about three articles bashing liberal statism for every one questioning Republican dogma."

After LBJ's 1964 landslide victory over Barry Goldwater and during the rush of progressive legislation that followed, Republican congressional leaders decided they needed to respond with some proposals of their own. It was the high tide of Great Society liberalism, and Johnson had created a vogue for legislative creativity and national solutions to public problems. Republicans, who had not yet made their decisive move rightward, did not want to be left out, and they hoped that some of their ideas might moderate and ultimately halt LBJ's juggernaut.

Thus arose the movement for Constructive Republican Alternatives. Liberals have always claimed that the original idea was for "Constructive Republican Alternative Policies," until someone realized how unfortunate the acronym would be. But in truth, the conservative, moderate, and liberal Republicans (there were liberal Republicans then) who put their minds to formulating new policies were a creative bunch. The torrent of ideas came from the liberals at the Ripon Society, the libertarian wing of Young Americans for Freedom, and mainstream members of Congress such as Al Quie from Minnesota, Melvin Laird from Wisconsin, Charles "Mac" Mathias from Maryland, and Bob Ellsworth of Kansas. They included a volunteer military, the establishment of revenue sharing with the states (an idea that can be traced back to Henry Clay and the Whigs), the negative income tax (broached early by the conservative economist Milton Friedman) to supplement poor people's incomes, block-granting programs to the states (still popular on the right), and the vogue for tax credits as an alternative to direct government spending, a method Bill Clinton freely applied when the era of big government had supposedly ended. Republicans were also essential to the enactment of the great civil rights and voting rights acts.

Now the trumpet summons Republicans again. A loose, informal confederation of conservative thinkers and legislators has come together in what they label the "conservative reform project." They call themselves "reform conservatives." They are not the Constructive Republicans of old—the absence of liberal Republicans means the intellectual compass of this group points farther right. But these Reformicons do have ambitions.

Some are sharply critical of the Tea Party. Others embrace it. Many maintain a diplomatic silence or keep their criticism implicit. To reduce the chance that they will be seen as hostile to the party's right-wing factions, they often say that they are simply trying to fill a policy void on the right created by four and a half years of largely defensive and negative politics directed against President Obama.

Several refer to Mitt Romney's 2012 campaign as an object lesson in what Republicans should not do, pointing especially to Romney's failure to speak to the vast majority of Americans who are employees, not "job creators." There are conservative reformers who hint at nudging the GOP to the left of where it is now and specifically emphasize the importance of shedding radical antigovernment rhetoric. But a very strong strain of reform conservatism seems most interested in wrapping the old small-government precepts in appealing language about reviving "civil society" and relying on local communities to solve problems. This allows them to make many of the same antiliberal, antigovernment arguments, but freshens them with warm references to community redolent of Edmund Burke or Alexis de Tocqueville. Here are the 1970s ideas of Peter Berger and Richard Neuhaus proving useful yet again. Here also is a split similar to the pro- and antigovernment divide that hobbled compassionate conservatism.

Indeed, even supporters of the Tea Party sought to march under the reform banner. Michael Needham, chief executive officer for the Heritage Foundation, took to the pages of *National Affairs*, a quarterly journal that has become an intellectual meeting place for reform conservative intellectuals and policy specialists, to argue that the Tea Party should be seen as an effort to "disrupt the status quo" and that its efforts should be welcomed by those "eager to shake up a stale Republican agenda." Senator Mike Lee—he had won the first big Tea Party intra-Republican fight against then-Senator Robert Bennett in Utah—also waved the reform standard in an April 2013 speech at the Heritage Foundation, urging conservatives to embrace words like "compassion" and "community" but insisting that "collective action doesn't only—or even usually—mean government action."

Yuval Levin, the lead conductor of the reform conservative orchestra, criticizes the left's "prescriptive, technocratic approach" as "a poor fit for American life." Where conservatives revere "the space occupied by families, communities, civic and religious institutions, and the private economy," progressives, he says, have always viewed these "mediating institutions that stand between the individual and the government with suspicion, seeing them as instruments of division, prejudice and selfishness or as power centers lacking in democratic legitimacy." Such talk underscores the insistence of many Reformicons that they are not dissidents. Levin says that while he and his allies want to offer "a positive vision of what government is for," their approach would "inevitably lead to a smaller government because it just envisions a larger society and a smaller state."

When it comes to the Tea Party, you might say that Levin is fair and balanced. "I'm certainly not an anti–Tea Party voice," he told me in a 2014 conversation. "I think it brought a lot of energy to Republican politics. I think it focused on a lot of the right problems. But it hasn't been focused on policy-oriented conservatism. I think that's where things need to change." He added: "There are a lot of members of Congress, most of them elected in the last four years, who just don't think they're here to make policy, and I disagree."

Ronald Reagan is a challenging figure for the reformers. The younger ones (and it tends to be a younger movement) are especially inclined to say that the conservative movement must free itself from Reagan nostalgia. But others see the road to the Promised Land passing through a reembrace of Reaganism— properly understood, of course. The Reagan they have in mind is the one who created Reagan Democrats because he could speak to working-class voters, a gift Romney obviously didn't possess.

The reform conservatives can already claim a significant success: almost all of God's conservative children seem to want to take up the reform banner. This can arouse suspicions as to whether there is any there here. The word "reform" polls very well. It was not surprising to see Karl Rove praise the movement in a March 2014 *Wall Street Journal* column. It was Rove who shrewdly rebaptized George W. Bush as "A Reformer with Results" to fend off John McCain in 2000. "Reform" is a word that only machine politicians relish taking on.

It puts the current reform conservatism in context to see McCain as this era's first reform conservative and to notice that many of the positions he took were far more adventurous and well to the left of where most of today's reform conservatives are willing to venture. McCain was a passionate campaign finance reformer in a party that is now committed to tearing down all barriers to big money in politics. He acknowledged the human causes of global warming and introduced what would now be seen as sweeping legislation to curb carbon emissions. He opposed the Bush tax cuts with populist language that is familiar to today's progressives. And he worked hard for immigration reform, an issue that divides the Reformicons.

Today's reform conservatives are operating in a highly constrained environment. Some of them confront the Tea Party's extreme opposition to government directly. But the Reformicons generally choose to accept the limits placed on them by the increasingly conservative Republican primary electorate, the shift in the GOP's geographical center of gravity toward the South, and the rightward drift within the business community. As long as these boundaries on their thinking hold, it is unlikely that they will leave behind as many policy monuments as the earlier Constructive Republicans did.

There is another constraint as well. While it is an article of faith among conservatives that Barack Obama has pursued a left-wing agenda, the reality is that Obama has picked up on many policy ideas that are conservative in origin and might, in a different world, be deployed by the reform conservatives themselves. Example number one, as we've seen, is the Affordable Care Act, the chief object of Republican scorn. Its much-maligned complexity is built around ideas that were developed on the right and are designed to keep the private market in health insurance intact. Had Obama supported a single-payer system or some other more government-oriented plan, one could imagine reform conservatives endorsing something that looked like Obamacare—which is what Mitt Romney did in Massachusetts. It's the conundrum that has confronted progressives since the Clinton Era: in trying to be practical, moderate, and reasonable, they may have helped shrink the philosophical space in which policies are formulated and arguments are carried out.

Obama strongly advocates income supplement plans such as the Child Tax Credit and the Earned Income Tax Credit, which often figure in conservative alternatives to more elaborate government programs and to increases in the minimum wage. Oh, yes, and income taxes under Obama are still lower than they were when Bill Clinton was president.

Reform conservatives are leery of acknowledging any of this. If Obama is socialism personified, then any idea he supports, no matter its genealogy, is suspect. This is the lesson we learn from the ritualistic attacks on the president for having "extended the power of the federal government to an unprecedented degree," for having engineered "a federal regulatory takeover of health insurance," and for pursuing policies that "set a high-water mark for the size and reach of the federal government." These words came from an otherwise quite bold—and at times scathing—critique of the Tea Party's view of government by Michael Gerson and Peter Wehner, who served with Gerson in the Bush administration. Describing what he called the "Reformish Conservatives," the liberal journalist Ryan Cooper noted that members of this tribe seem inclined to produce "about three articles bashing liberal statism for every one questioning Republican dogma."

So what is serious here, and what amounts to repackaging? David Frum, the conservative heretic, argues that many on the right know that their product is not selling well. He uses the analogy of a failing pizza chain to frame the key question: how much are they willing to change the pizza inside, and how much are they merely changing the box?

The answer turns out to be complicated. At times, reform conservatism does seem more concerned with the box than its contents—more infatuated with the idea of new ideas than with new ideas. There is also a great deal of orthodoxy in the ongoing imperative to propose new tax cuts for the very wealthy, usually bundled into a package touted as "tax reform." But it's also true that the Obama years produced such a sharp lurch to the right within conservatism that many Reformicons accept the need for readjustment and for something that resembles a governing agenda.

Michael Strain, an economist at the American Enterprise Institute, speaks of an "unemployment crisis," particularly for the long-term jobless, and is willing to entertain Keynesian remedies. It is a sign that progressive arguments about inequality have gained sufficient purchase that Marco Rubio is willing to acknowledge that "from 1980 to 2005, over 80 percent of the total increase in income went to the top 1 percent of American earners," and that "70 percent of children born into poverty will never make it to the middle class."

Some on the right have taken the Tea Party's antigovernment attitudes head-on. In their essay, Gerson and Wehner pointed to "the inadequacy of the oppositional and negative approach to the question of the government's purpose and role." And a few have broken with conservative conventional wisdom altogether, as columnist Josh Barro did in supporting the Affordable Care Act. It is, however, a mark of the boundaries of conservative orthodoxy that many conservatives do not see Barro as one of them. His hard-to-classify ideology led the writer Andrew Sullivan (who is himself ideoligially eclectic) to label Barro a "conservative Whig." Barro became a contributor to the *New*

York Times' online feature, "The Upshot," hardly a redoubt of conservative ideology.

Although McCain's maverick years suggest that some conservatives have long been aware of the need for new departures, the reformist impulse blossomed in the final years of the Bush presidency in response to its failures. The early reform conservatives saw an opening for an approach focused on problem solving. They hoped to speak to the less well-off voters who rejected the right and Bush. But their early efforts were buried under the Tea Party insurgency.

Bookish types were important to the early rumblings of reform conservatism. And some of the earliest books on the need to rethink conservatism quickly put their authors on a conservative Index of Forbidden Thinkers.

Frum might be seen as a "premature reformer," in the manner of those whom parts of the old left once labeled as "premature anticommunists" because they broke with the Popular Front before most of their allies. Frum's criticisms of his own camp (beginning with his open disgust at McCain's choice of Sarah Palin as a running mate in 2008) led many on the right to excommunicate him. Although the story is told differently by different sides, Frum's dissidence had something to do with his departure from (or his being asked to leave) the American Enterprise Institute in 2010. His break with AEI happened to come only a few days after he lambasted the Republican Party for its failure to negotiate with the Obama White House over the Affordable Care Act. Frum's heresy included acknowledging that the ACA had "a broad family resemblance to Mitt Romney's Massachusetts plan," building on "ideas developed at the Heritage Foundation in the early 1990s that formed the basis for Republican counter-proposals to Clintoncare in 1993–1994."

Against Republican outcries that Obama was leading the nation to socialism, Frum insisted (correctly) that "the gap between this plan and traditional Republican ideas is not very big." He earned the opprobrium of many a conservative talk show host—and coined a highly useful term—by declaring the bill's passage "a huge win for the conservative entertainment industry." Their "listeners and viewers," he wrote, "will now be even more enraged, even more frustrated, even more disappointed in everybody except the responsibility-free talkers on television and radio." The conservative talk show world doesn't take to anyone who coins a term as evocative as "the conservative entertainment industry."

An earlier apostate was Bruce Bartlett. A founder of supply-side economics, he rebelled against the Bush administration's budget policies. The title of his 2006 book, *Imposter: How George W. Bush Bankrupted America and Betrayed the Reagan Legacy*, explains why he became persona non grata among Republicans (and also why he was fired by the National Center for Policy Analysis, a generally pro-Bush think tank). The book summarizes rather well the views that many Tea Party Republicans were to come to a few years later. Bartlett got there too early, and he has subsequently moved away from the right altogether and become one of its sharpest critics.

If Frum and Bartlett were rebels, two younger men who published a reformist book in 2008 are among the Founders of Reform Conservatism. Ross Douthat and Reihan Salam (both born in 1979) have managed to stay a few steps ahead of the reform curve while still remaining inside the conservative family. Appropriately for their generation, both were influential bloggers. Douthat later became the youngest-ever *New York Times* columnist, and Salam has written for a variety of publications and is a columnist for *Slate*. Their *Grand New Party* carried a subtitle that captured their central preoccupation: *How Republicans Can Win the Working Class and Save the American Dream*. The book grew out of their 2005 article in the *Weekly Standard*, "The Party of Sam's Club," in which they sought to put policy seriousness behind former Minnesota governor Tim Pawlenty's evocative sound bite, the basis for his ultimately short-lived 2012 Republican presidential campaign.

Like Frum, Douthat and Salam acknowledged the challenges and problems created by globalization. Most distinctive about the Douthat-Salam thesis was its criticism of the Republican Party for having relied over many years on white working-class voters without delivering many tangible benefits to a constituency that had reason to "feel more insecure." Working class voters had flocked to Reagan in the 1980s and to Newt Gingrich's revolution in the 1990s, they wrote, but quickly became "disillusioned with conservative governance and returned to the Democratic column" because Republicans failed to do much for them. Republicans ruined the courtship, they charged, "by confusing being pro-market with being pro-business . . . and by shrinking from the admittedly difficult task of reforming the welfare state so that it serves the interests of the working class rather than the affluent."

Their prime policy antidote served as a prototype of the stance later reformers would come to. Republicans like to fiddle the tax code downward, and they proposed a large expansion of the Child Tax Credit to $5,000 (a policy that alleged socialist Obama embraced in a more modest form) as well as pension and tuition credits for stay-at-home parents. They argued that means-testing of Social Security benefits (a long-standing conservative goal) should be linked to payroll tax cuts for lower-income workers (a direct, immediate benefit for the working class). They pushed a version of expanded charter schools and, in a bow to Bill Clinton, proposed federal help to assist communities in hiring more police. Some of their ideas were altogether outside the box, including a suggestion that farm subsidies be scrapped in favor of "subsidies for carbon removal and other environment-friendly agricultural ventures."

But in all this, their cardinal concern was the breakdown of the working-class family, a catastrophe that aggravates inequality and stifles mobility and opportunity. This worry about the state of the American family—quite different from opposition to gay marriage—might be seen as a Reformicon growth stock. Charles Murray, the libertarian conservative whose 1984 book, *Losing Ground,* was a manifesto for cutting welfare, influenced many beyond the right with *Coming Apart* in 2013, a warning about the cost to lower-income Americans of family decay. But he was far from alone in his focus. At its worst, blaming "culture" for inequality can be seen as an alibi for avoiding any confrontation with injustices within the economic system and a way to beat back proposals that challenge existing privileges. But the best of the reformers, Douthat and Salam among them, are willing to flip the causal arrows and acknowledge that the economic struggles of the working class have made the task of forming and maintaining stable families more difficult, thus their emphasis on new tax benefits keyed to parents.

In their worries over the state of the family, they were joined by *National Review* writer Ramesh Ponnuru, who originally advocated the large Child Tax Credit, and *New York Times* columnist David Brooks. Ponnuru has never shied away from pointing out weaknesses in conservative arguments and was one of the first on the right, within days of the 2012 election, to score Republicans for a narrow focus on the heroism of entrepreneurs to the exclusion of the vast majority of voters who work for wages and salaries. Brooks has long been a conservative dissident (Charles Krauthammer, speaking only partly in jest, once labeled Brooks his favorite "liberal columnist") and he frequently invokes the Whig tradition of Henry Clay and Abraham Lincoln to defend large-scale federal investment in infrastructure, research, development, and education. The chaos that followed the collapse of Kevin McCarthy's candidacy for House Speaker led Brooks to protest that the Republican Party had "abandoned traditional conservatism for right-wing radicalism" and had adopted a tone that was "bombastic, hyperbolic and imbalanced."

Two other early ventures in reform conservatism are worthy of note. Levin (born in 1977) is a University of Chicago PhD who founded *National Affairs.* His goal, he told me in 2014, is straightforward. "You have to offer a vision of what government looks like to you," he said, "and what it ought to be doing about the particular set of problems we have now." He speaks hopefully of a desire, through the magazine and the reform movement, to "inject some different priorities and different arguments and different visions" into the discourse between left and right.

"There's not a lot of connection with the fact that people in the middle class are seeing stagnant wages, are finding themselves pessimistic about their children's future, are under all kinds of pressures that are not about the one percent, but they're not about their tax rates either," he said. "It doesn't seem like anyone is talking about them, or anyone is offering a plausible story about what is going on."

In his 2014 book, *The Great Debate: Edmund Burke, Thomas Paine, and the Birth of Right and Left,* Levin chided "today's conservatives" for being "too rhetorically strident and far too open to the siren song of hyperindividualism." He suggested that conservatives could learn from "Burke's focus on the social character of man," his "thoroughgoing gradualism," and "his emphasis on community and on the sentiments."

In an important 2006 article for the *Weekly Standard* prefiguring these arguments, Levin acknowledged, as few conservatives have been willing to do, the deep tensions between the market and the family:

> The market values risk-taking and creative destruction that can be very bad for family life, and rewards the lowest common cultural denominator in ways that can undermine traditional morality. Traditional values, on the other hand, discourage the spirit of competition and self-interested ambition essential for free markets to work, and their adherents sometimes seek to enforce codes of conduct that constrain individual freedom. The libertarian and the tradition-alist are not natural allies.

The last thought, of course, threatened to blow up the "fusionist" consensus that Bill Buckley and Frank Meyer built, although it was their awareness of the problem Levin identified that led them to work so hard to square the philosophical circles.

Levin acknowledged that the policy fixes he proposed then (they included health care portability, long-term care insurance, and school choice) were "barely a start" to what needs to be done for those in "the parenting class." This admission points to an ongoing problem for the Reformicons: even when they face up to the contradictions in conservative ideology and acknowledge the market's shortcomings, their solutions rarely challenge the market's priorities and are thus much smaller than the problem they're addressing. Levin deserves credit for treading where many conservatives feared to go.

Michael Gerson's 2007 *Heroic Conservatism*, as we've seen, was a hold-out's case for compassionate conservatism at a time when most conservatives had passed it by. It was also an early marker for reform conservatism, and there are important overlaps between yesterday's battlers for compassion and today's advocates of reform. Gerson mourned the decline of the alliance between evangelicalism and the cause of social justice, asking, "Where does someone belong who is pro-life and pro-poor?" And he has reserved some of his toughest polemics for libertarians. "If Republicans run in future elections with a simplistic anti-government message, ignoring the poor, the addicted, and children at risk," he warned, "they will lose, and they will deserve to lose."

Gerson was right about 2012, although in 2010, Republicans did run on "a simplistic anti-government message" that did ignore "the poor, the addicted and children at risk"—and they won. What mattered, declared Representative Mike Pence—elected governor of Indiana in 2012—was steering the Republican Party "back to the principles of limited government, fiscal discipline, and traditional moral values."

The key word is "back." The Tea Party's call for a "constitutional conservatism," based on a remarkably skewed reading of the Founders' intentions, was, for a while, the only "reform" conservatism that counted. The question "What Would the Founders Do?" is, of course, popular across ideological lines, as the historian David Sehat pointed out in his 2015 book, *The Jefferson Rule: Why We Think the Founding Fathers Have All the Answers*. But tendency to invoke "constitutionalism" is especially strong within American conservatism, and it goes back a very long way—to Calhoun in the nineteenth century, to critics of progressive initiatives under both Roosevelts at the turn of the century and in the 1930s, and to southern resistance to civil rights beginning in the 1940s.

In their inclination to return to the Founders, many Reformicons are at one with their Tea Party brethren. In an essay in the Reformicons' 2014 manifesto, "Room to Grow," Ramesh Ponnuru explicitly defended "political constitutionalism" and argued: "In America, what conservatism chiefly means is the conservation of our political inheritance from the Founders."

And while the reform conservatives did not match the Tea Party in the harshness of their criticism of Obama, they rarely spoke out against its extreme rhetoric, and most of them fell in line behind criticisms of the stimulus and the health care law—to which many of them had objections anyway. The increasingly conservative Republican mood made it lethal for potential conservative reformers to find common ground or seek compromise with Obama even on issues where their views overlapped.

The 2010 elections certainly had a chilling effect on the reform project, yet the 2012 primaries and Romney's campaign illustrated the continuing costs of an unchallenged orthodoxy. The party's dominant ideas about "makers and takers" and the primacy of "job creators" left little room for initiatives on behalf of working-class voters in pivotal states such as Ohio, Wisconsin, and Pennsylvania. Romney's political problem was also an intellectual problem.

This is why his defeat enabled a reform conservative comeback. In the wake of the 2012 election and the strategic fiasco of the Republican shutdown of government in the fall of 2013, reform conservatives were in a position to say, "I told you so." Tea Party slogans would not be enough.

One sign of the shift was a strategic repositioning by Republicans and conservatives who had once broadly accepted the "job creators" and "makers and takers" formulations but now embraced something more, well . . . compassionate. Arthur Brooks, who had once warmed to the "makers and takers" idea, published an article in the February 2014 issue of *Commentary* titled "Be Open-Handed Toward Your Brothers." He called on conservatives to accept the idea of a social safety net, supported increases in the Earned Income Tax Credit, and favored new ways of helping the unemployed, including Strain's proposals for subsidies to help them move to more promising job markets. Brooks didn't break with his past positions, but his emphasis was entirely different.

He elaborated on these themes in *The Conservative Heart: How to Build a Fairer, Happier and More Prosperous America*, published in 2015, which laid heavy stress on the moral imperative to fight poverty. The tactical movement within at least parts of conservatism can be seen in the contrast with the book Brooks (who is no relation to the *New York Times* columnist) published five years earlier, *The Battle: How the Fight Between Free Enterprise and Big Government Will Shape America's Future*. The earlier work was a far more aggressive attack on liberalism and argued that the fight between capitalism and its enemies was the new American "culture war." Brooks, a genial and religious man, had absorbed some of the lessons of 2012. Still, he signaled in his second book that he was less interested in rethinking conservative premises— not suprising, really, from the head of the nation's premier conservative think tank—than in selling the conservative idea more effectively. In concluding that "we've got to improve the way we *make our case* to the American people" (my italics), he underscored the centrality of Frum's pizza box question.

Because of electoral reality, Republicans were also thinking once again about the working class. One of the boldest Reformicon thinkers, Henry Olsen of the Ethics and Public Policy Center, was devastating in his description of the 2012 campaign:

Obama effectively asked: Which do you like better? Would you prefer the Republican alternative as exemplified by the candidacy of Mitt Romney and the policies he and his party have proposed in Congress and on the stump? ... One would have thought that Romney would actively join the debate. In a way he did, for he often emphasized that America was a land where anyone could start from scratch and build a business. The subtle implication, however, was that people who did so were the best Americans and everyone else was just along for the ride. It is in that sense that the phrase "you built that" and laments about "makers" versus "takers" were the essence of Romney's America.

Republicans lost a debate they had never joined because they forgot a core constant in American politics that involves, Olsen argued, "the willingness to use government power to help individuals advance in life." He concluded: "If American principles simply require hands-off government, then American principles have not been part of our politics for a very long time. A hands-off approach is not what American politics and principles require; it is a parody of what America and American conservatism mean."

Olsen offered what may be the ultimate conservative heresy: "The painful truth is that President Obama's rhetoric was closer to Reagan's than the rhetoric of Romney and many other leading Republicans in 2012."

Olsen has been the most insistent Reformicon in learning the lessons Reagan taught. These, he argued, included "a profound respect for the aspirations of the common person" and acceptance of "the federal government's potential as a means of helping these people." There is certainly a romanticism in Olsen's vision on Reagan. He plays down some of Reagan's strongest antigovernment ambitions and policies—including Reagan's attack on unions—that sped the long decline of blue-collar wages. Yet Olsen is among those in the movement who have taken on the essential task of reminding conservatives that however much they properly revere Reagan, the Reagan era is well and truly over.

The headline of a November 2014 article in *Commentary* he coauthored with Peter Wehner was "If Ronald Reagan Were Alive Today, He Would Be 103 Years Old." Much of the article is an encomium to Reagan, but they nonetheless insisted that "Reagan was not a man for all seasons or causes" and warned: "Republicans need to be careful not to be trapped by Reagan as Democrats allowed themselves to become trapped by FDR and JFK. It's difficult to grow while living in someone else's shadow. . . . Reagan, while conservative to the bone, would never have allowed himself to become captive to the past."

Injecting the conservative movement with some bracing doses of realism has been the reform conservative movement's greatest contribution. Yet Walter Mondale's old question applies: Where's the beef? Do the ponderings of the Reformicons have any resonance among Republican politicians who write budgets and pass laws? And are reform conservatives really willing to challenge them? So far, the results have been less than overwhelming.

Although there were exceptions, it's significant that the reform conservatives were not, on the whole, sharply critical of the steep cuts in both taxes and spending that House Republicans repeatedly proposed after 2010. Indeed, most reform conservatives consider Paul Ryan, the architect of the cuts, an ally. Levin, for example, praised the new Republican Congress in 2012 for having "put a stop to the explosion of liberal activism that characterized President Obama's first two years in office" and in particular Paul Ryan's budgets for managing "to restrain the growth of spending." In one sense, Levin was simply being who he is, a conservative. But his stance suggested that he and his colleagues were operating largely inside the existing conservative consensus. The Reformicons were far less willing than Clinton's New Democrats to challenge their own side's orthodoxy.

Rubio, who emerged as one of the strongest Republican presidential contenders and is close to the Reformicons, has received credit for facing some of the facts about inequality and obstacles to mobility. "Our modern-day economy has wiped out many of the low-skill jobs that once provided millions with a middle-class living," Rubio said in a January 2014 speech. "Those that have not been outsourced or replaced by technology pay wages that fail to keep pace with the cost of living."

Fair enough. Then what? Rubio dismissed the importance of raising the minimum wage, arguing that "having a job that pays $10 an hour is not the American Dream." Perhaps not, but it's $2.75 closer than $7.25 an hour.

We need to foster more growth, Rubio said as he offered conservative boiler-plate: concern about our "dangerous and growing national debt," support for a "tax code that incentivizes investment," and criticism of "regulations that prevent employers from expanding."

Rubio's approach reflects the Reformicon focus on culture and family is-sues. A child born into a broken family, living in a bad neighborhood, and attending a dysfunctional school, he said, "is, in all likelihood, not going to have the same opportunity to succeed as a child growing up in a stable home, in a safe neighborhood, and attending a good school," Rubio said. Yes, and then what?

Rubio's big ideas include turning "Washington's anti-poverty programs—and the trillions spent on them—over to the states" and creating a "revenue-neutral Flex Fund" out of the proceeds. He has also called for replacing the Earned Income Tax Credit (EITC) with a federal wage enhancement for qualifying low-wage jobs that "appl[ies] the same to singles as it would to married couples and families with children."

Rubio's "Flex Fund" idea was just a super block grant, harking back to Rea-gan's 1976 proposal for devolving responsibilities to the states, which helped Gerald Ford beat him for the nomination. Moreover, as Sharon Parrott of the Center on Budget and Policy Priorities pointed out, his approach threatens to obliterate the role of various entitlements as automatic economic stabiliz-ers during downturns. And block grants are invitations to future cuts. It's much easier to rally opposition to throwing large numbers of children off food stamps than to cutting a big, abstract number.

As for Rubio's plan to replace the EITC, it was a form of progress that he and other reform-oriented conservatives were endorsing income transfer pro-grams that Republicans in Congress had tried to cut. And he was right that the EITC is insufficiently generous to single workers without families. One person who agreed with him on this is President Obama, who has included an expansion in his budgets.

But then there was the question of financing. Unless Rubio planned to spend much more on his wage program than was spent already on the EITC, Parrott noted, "his proposal would have to dramatically cut the earnings supplements that the EITC now provides to low-income working families with children." Thus did Rubio's policy contributions underscore one of the Reformicons' core difficulties: even when they acknowledged that there are problems that only government can solve, they have been reluctant to put enough money behind their responses to make a material difference.

This may be because many of the reformers still want to cut taxes—a lot. A 2014 tax plan that Rubio introduced with Senator Mike Lee was estimated to cost $2.4 trillion over a decade, substantially more than the Bush tax cut. Rubio's 2015 reworking of the plan for his campaign was even broader in its scope, to the point where the liberal Citizens for Tax Justice estimated the plan could add an astonishing $11.8 trillion to the debt.

Rubio and Lee's proposal could hardly have been more generous to the wealthy. It not only ended taxation of capital gains, dividends, and interest, but also eliminated the estate tax, now paid only on very large fortunes. It cut the business tax rate to 25 percent and included a variety of other benefits for companies. This is classic supply-side tax cutting. The proposal's major bow to reform conservative concerns was a new $2,500 per Child Tax Credit. Rubio's plan was especially parsimonious in its benefits to the middle class.

As the liberal writer Jonathan Chait noted, "The new Rubio-Lee plan would surpass anything George W. Bush or Mitt Romney ever proposed to do in its ambitions to relieve the richest Americans of their tax burdens." Noting that reform conservatives such as Ponnuru and Levin had enthusiastically praised the plan, Chait wondered what this said about the movement's real objectives. "Perhaps the reform conservatives have capitulated completely in the name of party unity," he wrote. "Or maybe they were misunderstood from the beginning and never proposed to deviate in any substantive way from the traditional platform of massively regressive, debt-financed tax cutting." Chait's critique raises once again the central question the reformers have still not answered: how much does their approach represent any real break with the conservatism of the last twenty-five—or fifty—years? Ponnuru, at least, diplomatically recognized that the more costly campaign version of the Rubio plan—he put the price tag at $6 trillion—went "too far in the right direction."

Jeb Bush also had ties to the reformers and his willingness to court opposition from the Republican base, mentioned earlier, was reciprocated. His support for immigration reform and his defense of the "Common Core" education standards (once supported by many conservatives but later relabed by the right, unsurprisingly, as "ObamaCore") were his most obvious deviations. Yet the detailed tax proposal he issued in September 2015 was orthodoxy itself, signaled by his decision to unveil it in an op-ed piece for the *Wall Street Journal,* whose editorial page is the home church for supply-side economics. Bush tried to cast the plan as populist because it eliminated some tax loopholes, but it was plainly the opposite. Its key features included cutting the top income tax rate from 39.4 percent to 28 percent and eliminating the estate tax. The Tax Foundation concluded that the top 1 percent of earners—those making more than about $406,000—would see their after-tax incomes increase on average by 11.6 percent, even as the average increase for all income levels would be only 3.3 percent. Bush's critics gleefully noted that Jeb Bush's plan would be especially beneficial to Jeb Bush. The liberal Center for American Progress estimated that Bush's plan would cut his own taxes by $773,677 while *Washington Post* columnist Catherine Rampell figured Bush's windfall at $789,137. As for Donald Trump, he talked a good game on tax fairness, but his actual plan was very generous to best-off.

The fact that Republicans never tried to pass an alternative to Obamacare is also a commentary on reform conservatism's limits. Levin himself had focused on health care when he worked in George W. Bush's administration and he regularly made proposals designed mainly to reduce government's role in health insurance regulation and focusing on tax credits. Two Republican presidential candidates who put out the rudiments of health care plans, Scott Walker (before he dropped out) and Rubio, both proposed to turn Medicaid into a block grant, hardly an innovative proposal (and one that would over time almost certainly reduce spending on health insurance for the poor). Both, as the *New York Times* reported, favored "a much less regulated insurance market" and were "much less concerned about ensuring health care access for the poor." Both favored tax credits to help people buy insurance, which, of course, is a central part of Obamacare. But Walker based his credits on age rather than income. The impact of this difference was clear. Walker's plan "would tend to work out well for some middle- and upper-income people, because right now they don't qualify for much—or any—financial assistance for the government," wrote health care analysts Jeffrey Young and Jonathan Cohn. "But less affluent people would lose assistance, to the point that large numbers of Americans would no longer be able to afford comprehensive coverage at all, and those who *could* afford it would face much more punishing bills." Once again, conservative redistribution would go upward.

CNBC's John Harwood confronted Walker directly on the issue. "Given the trends of income disparity in the country," Harwood asked, "why is this the right time for that kind of redistribution?"

Walker's reply did not deny the redistributive impact of his plan. He just declared it a nonproblem ("It's not about a redistribution of wealth issue") and fell back on the conservative ideological boilerplate. "Our system's purely about freedom," he said. "It's about giving people the freedom." Including, it would appear, the freedom not to afford health insurance.

Similar critiques applied to Rubio's plan, which continued to raise the question: why are the Republicans the only conservative party in any of the wealthy democracies to oppose a universal guarantee of access to health insurance? And why, in particular, has the success of Mitt Romney's health care effort in Massachusetts not made his approach more attractive to the wider conservative movement? The obvious answer: Obamacare is too much like Romneycare.

The closest political ally of the Reformicons before his primary defeat was Eric Cantor, and his unsuccessful foray into health care politics was an indicator of just how toxic that issue is on the right. In 2013, he gave a speech entitled "Make Life Work" in which he was unusually explicit for a conservative in acknowledging government's responsibility "to ensure [that] every American has a fair shot at earning their success and achieving their dreams."

Cantor brought to the House floor one of the proposals from his speech. It would have transferred money out of the Affordable Care Act's disease prevention account to pay for high-risk pools for Americans who had difficulty obtaining regular insurance. He lost. Conservative Republicans did not want to cast any votes that might be seen as even indirectly endorsing Obamacare. Cantor's defeat on an idea that by any fair reading was intended to undercut Obamacare raised once more the fundamental problem facing Reformicons: they could come up with all the new policy they wanted, but as long as congressional Republicans remained locked into obstruction and opposition, even repackaging—let alone rethinking—was in danger of remaining an isolated project championed primarily by a few intellectuals and journalists.

Their great hope was that Republican presidential candidates, including Rubio and Bush, could champion reform ideas in the 2016 presidential campaign, much as Bill Clinton had championed the New Democrat project in 1992. But the reform conservative ideas were hardly catching fire among Republican voters. At least in the early going, the energy in the contest was with outsiders far removed from, and even disdainful of, Washington's policy deliberations. And one of them was especially loud.

★

Donald Trump did not make his mark with tax credits or education reform proposals or bold ideas to balance the budget. He did it by trashing Mexicans and endorsing the mass deportation of illegal immigrants. No worries about whether getting 11 million people out of the country would be complicated, let alone cruel. He told ABC News' George Stephanopoulos: "George, it's called management. . . . They would be out really fast, immediately." He said he'd build a border wall with Mexico—and make Mexico pay for it.

He did it by condemning the leadership of the United States in terms everyone could understand. "We are led," he declared, "by very, very stupid people." He criticized Carly Fiorina, the former CEO of Hewlett-Packard and the only woman in the Republican presidential contest, for her looks. "Look at that face!" Trump said. "Would anyone vote for that?"

He did it by saying that because he was tough and made a lot of real estate deals, he could negotiate the United States out of any difficulties it now had with Russia, China, Iran, or anyone else. He did it by saying that the United States had become "a hell hole" and "a third-world country" and promising to "make it great again." He did it by endorsing a national registry for Muslims after the Paris terrorist attacks in November of 2015, before backing away.

He also did it by saying that rich people got too many tax breaks. "The hedge fund people make a lot of money and they pay very little tax." Of himself, he said: "I do very well. I don't mind paying a little more in taxes." He did it by saying: "I will protect your Social Security. I will protect your Medicare and Medicaid."

He did it by saying that while he was against Obamacare, single-payer health care had worked well—in "Scotland," for example. He did it by attacking Republican orthodoxy on free trade, condemning the flow of American jobs overseas. He did it by denouncing the role of big money in the political system. His opponents, Trump said, are "controlled by lobbyists, controlled by their donors, they're controlled by special interests." In late July 2015 he tweeted: "While I'm beating my opponents in the polls, I'm also beating lobbyists, special interests & donors that are supporting them with billions." And he did it by saying of CEO pay: "You see these guys making an enormous amount of money, it's a total and complete joke."

Trump's surge into first place in the summer and early fall of 2015 mystified Republican leaders and upended the party's established candidates. His strength was a measure of the depth of disillusionment and radicalization in the Republican Party, as was support for Dr. Ben Carson, an African-American neurosurgeon who found himself in second place in September— and in first place, ahead of Trump, in many polls before Carson confronted questions about how he described his past. Carson built on a manner as quiet as Trump's was flamboyant. Carson had created a conservative following by saying outlandish things about Obamacare ("the worst thing that has happened in this nation since slavery") and about Barack Obama (he said those who want to understand him should "read *Mein Kampf* and read the works of Vladimir Lenin"). But his personal story was remarkable and his manner dignified. He won strong support from evangelicals by being a deeply and, on all the evidence, sincerely devout Christian. Carson seemed to pick up his support from voters who wanted to support an outsider protest candidate, but someone less glitzy, less egocentric, and less bombastic than Trump. Carly Fiorina turned the outsider sweepstakes into a three-way competition with a strong performance in the second Republican debate in September. She took Trump on directly for sexism and was the first of his adversaries to inflict real damage.

The abandonment of traditional politicians by Republicans in the campaign's first stages was underscored by a CNN/ORC Poll taken September 4–8, 2015. The survey found that 54 percent of Republicans favored a candidate for president who had never held public office. Trump led with 32 percent, followed by Carson at 19 percent. Fiorina was backed by an additional 3 percent, equal to the support won by Senators Paul and Rubio. Among the politicians, Jeb Bush ran first—with all of 9 percent, followed by Ted Cruz at 7 percent and Scott Walker and Mike Huckabee, both at 5 percent. With Trump decimating his early support, Walker eventually dropped out after an indifferent performance in the second encounter.

There were many reasons why Republicans could blame themselves for the Trump phenomenon. The party had created the rough beast it was suddenly trying to slay.

Many of Trump's Republican foes took to condemning how mean and nasty he was. Trump, in Rick Perry's formulation, was "throwing invectives in this hyperbolic rhetoric out there." Yet the party had not worried about invective or hyperbole in the days when Trump directed both against Obama in challenging his right to be president. "Now, he doesn't have his birth certificate or he's not showing it," Trump said in a representative comment on CNN in 2011. "So it's a very strange situation. . . . The fact is, if he wasn't born in this country, he shouldn't be the president of the United States." Even when Obama produced his certificate in late April of that year, Trump did not back off, because, he explained, "a lot of people do not think it was an authentic certificate."

Were Republicans backing away from Trump then? Some did, but most wanted to hug Trump close and, as Trump noted, seek his campaign contributions. When he accepted Trump's endorsement during the 2012 Republican primaries, Mitt Romney was positively giddy about how cool it was to be with the man who emblazons his name on gaudy hostelries.

"There are some things that you just can't imagine happening in your life," Romney enthused when he got Trump's backing at the Trump International Hotel in Las Vegas. "This is one of them. Being in Donald Trump's magnificent hotel and having his endorsement is a delight. I am so honored and pleased."

Romney was even ready to endorse Trump's self-image as a great gift to public policy. Romney praised The Donald for his "extraordinary ability to understand how our economy works and to create jobs" and for being "one of the few who has stood up to say China is cheating" on trade. For Republican leaders, Trump was a genius—until he wasn't.

The party's establishment paved the way for Trump in another way. Since 2006, many of the GOP politicians had courted the votes of Americans strongly opposed to immigration reform, evidenced by John Boehner's refusal to take up the Senate-passed bipartisan bill. Recall also that in the Republican primaries, Mitt Romney had deployed resentment over immigration first against Rudy Giuliani in 2008 and then against Rick Perry in 2012. Republican Congressional leaders were happy enough to have Tea Party candidates ride the issue when it helped the party win and then hold their majority in the House. Republicans had repeatedly complained about an insecure border, even though border security vastly increased under Obama and net immigration from Mexico actually fell to zero, a decline also partly explained by the economic downturn.

It's true that Trump's most outrageous comments about Mexican immigrants ("They're bringing drugs. They're bringing crime. They're rapists.") went far beyond anything most Republican politicians had said. His call for the deportation of all illegal immigrants was well outside the mainstream discussion as well and made Romney's "self-deportation" remark look comparatively humane.

Some Republicans—Jeb Bush, Rubio, Paul, Senator Lindsey Graham, and Perry before he dropped out of the race—criticized Trump and Bush made opposition to Trump central to his campaign. He repeatedly warned that Trump's rhetoric and his ideas risked deepening the party's deficits among Latinos and Asian-Americans. But many in the Republican field played to Trump as a way of reaching his constituency. Walker had already reversed his support for immigration reform and said Trump's immigration plan was "similar to what I brought up about four or five months ago." After Trump's "rapist" remark, Ted Cruz—who saw himself as the second choice of many Trump backers—went out of his way to say positive things about his rival. "I like Donald Trump," Cruz said. "I think he's terrific, I think he's brash, I think he speaks the truth."

Trump did not invent anti-immigration feeling in the Republican Party.

He just went several steps further in exploiting it. Nor was he in the least bit innovative in harping on border security. If security was as bad as Republican politicians had been saying—recall the alarm about the border that had played a big role in the 2014 mid-terms—Trump would propose measures as extreme as the scare rhetoric.

Where Trump began to be innovative, in a retro—and, in certain respects, frightening—way was by reaching back into Republican history for Richard Nixon's rhetoric. "The silent majority is back," Trump declared, "and we're going to take the country back." Speaking in Nashville at the end of August, Trump courted a potential backlash against "Black Lives Matter" and other groups protesting police killings of unarmed African-Americans.

"I know cities where police are afraid to even talk to people because they want to be able to retire and have their pension," Trump said. Discussing the riots in Baltimore that followed a funeral service for Freddie Gray, a twenty-five-year-old African-American who died of a severe spine injury while in police custody, he added: "That first night in Baltimore, they allowed that city to be destroyed. They set it back 35 years in one night because the police weren't allowed to protect people."

And then came the magic words: "We need law and order!"

The racial tinge in Trump's appeal was unmistakable and had a very long pedigree.

Finally, Trump's appeal to less affluent Republicans reflected his skill at filling the void in Republican politics that Rick Santorum had identified in 2012. A September 7–10 *Washington Post*/ABC News poll found that Trump's strongest support came from Republican voters without a college degree and those with incomes below $50,000. The GOP's forgotten working class found a champion in a billionaire. By breaking with Republican conventional wisdom on such a long list of issues—trade, taxes, the political power of the wealthy, the excesses of CEO pay—he spoke to cultural conservatives who had never fully bought into the party's economic assumptions and to the disaffected and angry voters who were no fonder of the rich and powerful than Bernie Sanders was.

Among the Reform Conservatives, it was Ross Douthat who saw the depth of Trump's challenge to the Republican Party most clearly. "So far,"

Douthat wrote, "he's running against the Republican establishment in a more profound way than the Tea Party, challenging not just deviations from official conservative principle but the entire post-Reagan conservative matrix." Trump, he added, had the special appeal of a candidate "campaigning as a traitor to his class" and had managed to unite a significant share of Tea Party supporters with moderate but disaffected working-class voters.

Douthat warned that if Republicans found "a way to crush Trump *without* adapting to his message . . . the pressure the Donald has tapped will continue to build—and when it bursts, the GOP as we know it may go with it."

★

The Trump movement and the Carson surge ought to wake Republicans and conservatives up to the challenges they face, to the depth of the disaffection among their supporters, and to the costs of the cycle of disappointment and betrayal. Conservative reformers—both inside the formal Reform Conservative movement and beyond it—will be required to do more than offer a few tax credits and speak warmly about civil society. They will need to respond far more creatively and substantively to the seething unhappiness among the Republican Party's long-suffering working-class supporters.

It's true that liberals will always see the Reform Conservatives as falling short simply because, as Salam observed, "Conservative reformism is conservative." This, says Douthat, is why the movement "strikes many liberals as disappointing, counterproductive, or woefully insufficient." From a progressive perspective, the Reformicons are timid in their approaches to economic injustice and inequality and too willing to look away from the structural problems in the economic system. Except for criticizing "corporate welfare," they rarely challenge the reward structure of the modern corporate economy or the reward structures it promotes. Even when the reform conservatives and liberals agree, as they do on the value of the EITC and the Child Tax Credit, most of the Reformicons (there are exceptions like Salam) are reluctant to make common cause with progressives to expand these programs. Even when they acknowledge the need to spend public money, whether on some forms of the safety net or on infrastructure investments, they often engage in "rob Peter to pay Paul" budgeting by calling for sharp reductions in programs progressives see as necessary. Reformicons typically support steep long-term cuts in programs such as Medicare, Medicaid, and Social Security.

Might the Reformicons and progressives find common ground? Some of the most productive left-right conversations have been around the issues of prison and sentencing reform, a cause that drew together Senators Cory Booker and Rand Paul and grass roots movements on both the left and the right. Yet the rise of a new "law and order" politics on the right that Trump broached and that other Republicans quickly seized upon could block even these promising initiatives.

There is a large opportunity for convergence on the question of how family breakdown and the decline of marriage have aggravated economic inequalities. As stable marriage has become far more widespread in the upper middle class than among lower-income Americans, the life chances of children are even more defined by social class than they were in the past. Conservatives point to family dissolution as a genuine problem for low-income Americans. Progressives insist that economic insecurity bred by the decline of well-paying blue-collar work has placed unbearable pressures on families. Even two-parent families are challenged by workplace practices that have not adjusted to the explosion in the number of households in which both members of the couple join the labor market by choice, necessity, or both. In principle, both sides ought to able to recognize what Robert Putnam, the author of the 2015 book *Our Kids: The American Dream in Crisis,* has called "the red problem" (the crisis in families) and "the blue problem" (declining wages and the disappearance of well-paid blue collar work). Each contributes to rising inequality and declining life chances for low-income children.

But unless both problems are recognized, what must be a shared quest for sensible and compassionate policies could become instead another shouting match about culture and values. Focusing the conversation about Americans in great distress on family difficulties alone would be the equivalent of telling a severe depressive to "snap out of it." If social justice depends on improving family lives, improving family lives depends upon greater social justice. For some conservatives, embracing the second imperative will prove difficult.

Despite Levin's claims, most progressives value civil society institutions as much as conservatives do. What they object to, as Mike Konczal of the

Roosevelt Institute has argued, is the idea that these voluntary forms of community can replace essential government services. As Konczal noted, private charity can respond to social problems "with targeted and nimble aid for individuals and communities" but cannot be expected to shoulder "the huge, cumbersome burden of alleviating the income insecurities of a modern age." Strengthening society's mediating structures is a worthy goal. Invoking mediating structures as cover for reducing government's commitment to promoting greater equality of opportunity and condition is simply to dress the old conservatism in finery. It did not work during compassionate conservatism's opening run. It will not work any better now.

How do we judge the Reformicons? Frum offers a demanding standard. He argues that conservatives need "an economic message that is inclusive" and in which "middle-class economic performance is at the core." This would include providing "various kinds of benefits to middle-class people outside the market." Unapologetic about his Obamacare heresy, Frum argues that conservatives as well as progressives should make "removing health care as a haunting concern" a priority. Conservatives also need a "modern cultural message," he says, and they should abandon their insistence on making abortion illegal. Instead they should seek to reduce the incidence of abortion and pledge "to cut the number of abortions by two-thirds over the next ten years." Republicans should be "just banishing the idea that the purpose of your party is to regulate the intimate behavior of women." Frum thinks Republicans need to be more environmentally conscious, and, against the libertarian leanings of Rand Paul, insists that Republicans must maintain their position as advocates of military strength and engagement abroad.

While some of the Reformicons share Frum's leanings toward neoconservative views on international issues, the movement is focused on domestic policy, and this is where it will make its mark. To do so, it needs to take Frum's domestic agenda seriously. His call for an economic approach willing to go "outside the market" to ease the struggles of low-income and middle-class Americans is the acid test of the movement's seriousness.

A true reform conservatism would move Republicans out of a comfort zone that sees deregulated markets and even more rewards for investors as elixirs for all economic ailments.

It would halt and reverse the right's retreat on a broad range of issues, including health care and climate change. Where Republican politicians of the center-right once proposed robust plans to provide for near-universal access to health insurance, they are now so focused on repealing Obamacare that they have largely given up on enacting realistic alternatives. On the environment, conservatives once offered market-based ideas for dealing with the human causes of climate change. Now much of the right has joined with the energy industry lobbies in denying the problem altogether. And even when conservatives such as Rubio offer modest tax measures to lift the incomes of lower-income Americans, they join them with large tax reductions for the wealthy that dwarf their redistributive efforts and worsen inequalities.

The Reformicons also need to be bolder in asserting that to have a future, conservatism cannot view an increasingly diverse and tolerant America as a horror. A Burkean traditionalism honors the gifts diverse communities bring to a nation.

Both reform conservatism and compassionate conservatism arose from an intuition among thoughtful and self-aware center-right thinkers that their side of politics needs a governing philosophy responsive to the problems of our moment. Yet both movements have operated within the severe constraints imposed by an asphyxiating orthodoxy and a Republican coalition resistant to change. Reform conservatism must still prove itself to be more than a slogan, more than a marketing campaign, more than the new pizza box. It needs to respond to the crisis of confidence among the conservative rank and file reflected by the rise of Carson and Trump. The Reformicons can settle for being sophisticated enablers of more of the same, or they can be part of the historic correction the conservative movement badly needs. But to do so, they will have to challenge not only the tactics of the Tea Party but also the turn conservatism took during the Goldwater revolution. It was once common for conservatives to say that liberals needed to free themselves from the 1960s. That is now the imperative for the American right.

16

UP FROM GOLDWATERISM
The Conservative Challenge and America's Future

"Neither a wise man nor a brave man lies down on the tracks
of history to wait for the train of the future to run over him."

In his commentary on the French Revolution, Edmund Burke wrote that at certain dangerous moments, "Moderation will be stigmatized as the virtue of cowards, and compromise as the prudence of traitors." He could have been describing the spirit that has overtaken much of the American right.

It is no accident that the turn away from Burkean moderation began in the 1960s when an attractive and compelling man warmed the hearts of his followers by preaching against precisely this virtue. "I would remind you that extremism in defense of liberty is no vice," Barry Goldwater declared at the 1964 Republican National Convention. "And let me remind you also that moderation in pursuit of justice is no virtue."

We have not been the same since Goldwater's version of conservatism became the philosophy's dominant form, and a narrative of disappointment and betrayal became the movement's signature story. Loyal conservatives have been upset that promises made over and over again were not kept, and this is neither surprising nor malign. But by continuing to pledge to achieve what they could not deliver and by responding to their own failures by further escalating political conflict, conservative political leaders have only aggravated this discontent.

They have also created the vicious cycle in our politics that Thomas Schaller described. It is a cycle that conservatives themselves must break. Doing so will be difficult precisely because the forces set loose by the Goldwater rebellion have created an increasingly homogeneous Republican Party that is less and less open to course corrections. The pressures on Republican elected officials are almost uniformly from the right. That earlier Republican regimes failed to satisfy the yearnings of the conservative movement's base led not to a rethinking of its objectives but to a doubling down on a more radical posture. If citizens are told over and over that certain outcomes are inevitable if only they stay true and work hard enough for the next victory, their natural response to failure will be to search for scapegoats and conspiracies. They are given good reason to blame the "morons" and "losers" of Trumpian demonology.

But the real conspiracy is a conspiracy of silence over the inevitability of a rather large government and the need for regular fine-tuning to a market system that is highly productive but requires regulation to function well, and adjustments to spread the riches it produces more fairly. This is part of the Trump Paradox: He gained a following not only because of the disappointments of the Tea Party Right but also because many less affluent Republicans welcomed the moments when he gave voice to protests against the power of the very wealthy that have not been heard within the GOP for decades. Ross Douthat is right that Republicans ignore the significance of the Trump Rebellion at their peril.

Conservatives repeated this pattern in response to cultural change. Yes, one of conservatism's central tasks is to remind us that not all cultural change is good or positive or beneficial. But it's also true that not all cultural change is evil, decadent, or sinful. Especially when it involves recognizing the claims of previously marginalized and excluded groups, cultural change is an expression of justice.

It is not as if all Republicans or all conservatives have been blind to the problems their movement faces. I have recounted the history of post-

Goldwater conservatism not only to emphasize that a narrow focus on the rise of the Tea Party misses how its ideology has been with us for decades, but also to show that leading conservatives often tried to move their cause toward a more realistic approach, only to be foiled by those who preferred ideological purity.

Richard Nixon was always torn between his earlier commitments to the Modern Republicanism of the Eisenhower years and his awareness of the political advantages of the Southern Strategy and a turn right on the social issues. His administration created major monuments to progressive governance and foreign policy realism. Pushed by his dissident liberal adviser Daniel Patrick Moynihan, Nixon even tried, for a while at least, to establish a guaranteed national income, a longtime progressive goal. Yet the New Majority he built was rooted in a conservative analysis of the electorate first conceived by southern segregationists such as Charles Wallace Collins and Goldwater conservatives such as William Rusher and Ralph de Toledano. And when Nixon went down in Watergate, conservatives in large numbers—particularly those, like Rusher, who never trusted him in the first place—were quick to insist that his failures had nothing to do with conservative doctrine. They removed him from a conservative pantheon where his place had always been tenuous.

Ronald Reagan left behind an ambiguous legacy whose contradictions still bedevil his followers. His governing side was far more moderate than the words he regularly spoke. He was willing to compromise when he had to, and boldly broke with the right on the driving issue of his life. He realized, ahead of most, that Mikhail Gorbachev really was a different kind of communist leader, and acted accordingly.

Conservatives were able to evade Reagan's apostasies because they transferred his ideological sins entirely to George H. W. Bush. Bush tried to create a sustainable form of conservatism by acknowledging the fiscal realities of the modern state. He was willing to raise taxes to pay for the government he knew voters wanted. Reagan had been willing to raise taxes, too, but all the political costs fell to Bush, and they were very high.

Bush embraced an affirmative role for government in other areas. In 1990 he became the pioneer of a new civil rights movement by signing the Americans with Disabilities Act. He fulfilled his pledge to be "an environmental president" by signing a strong Clean Air Act. In foreign policy he was a prudent and realistic activist, managing the end of the Cold War with exceptional skill. He evicted Saddam Hussein's forces from Kuwait—and prudently declined to follow him to Baghdad because he understood the impossible costs of occupying Iraq.

He was defeated in 1992 largely because of an economic downturn, the country's weariness after twelve years of Republican rule, and the political shrewdness of Bill Clinton. Bush's defeat strengthened the Right's control of the party. The Republican sweep of 1994 enshrined the dominance of the coalition conceived by Goldwater and his allies. The conversion of the white South to the Republican Party came in stages—from Strom Thurmond States' Rights campaign in 1948 to Goldwater's showing in 1964 to George Wallace's insurgency in 1968 and Nixon's sweep in 1972. The 1994 election extended the coalition's reach to Congress. The midterm elections of the Obama years decisively shifted southern governorships and state legislative seats the Republicans' way, completing what Goldwater and Gingrich had set in motion. Lincoln's party became the party of Dixie.

Yet the years after 1994 also showcased the key weaknesses of the new conservative disposition. Clinton restored his standing by taking on the most extreme and dangerous reaches of the right after the Oklahoma City bombing and won his battle over Republican budget cuts and a government shutdown. The Gingrich Congress failed to understand a tendency in the electorate that has reasserted itself again and again: Americans often respond to antigovernment arguments in theory, but in practice value the services government provides. Thus was Clinton's mantra in defense of "Medicare, Medicaid, Education, and the Environment" a shrewd riposte to his conservative adversaries. He moved the ground of the debate from abstractions to particulars. As Clinton suggested, ideology would consistently founder on "the laws of arithmetic." And the conservative calculation that popular mistrust of government would lead a majority to cheer when it was shut down proved flatly wrong, time after time.

It was ironic that this revolution was led by Gingrich, who had once been a Rockefeller Republican. And when Gingrich fell, many conservatives were eager to see him go because they saw him as too open to compromise with Clinton. It was as if his Rockefeller past had finally caught up with him. It said a great deal about the state of conservatism that Gingrich came to be viewed as too moderate.

The impeachment saga was a mark of how far frustrated conservatives would go in trying to undercut progressive advances. The controversy over the effort to remove Clinton from office combined with what many liberals saw as a power grab in the Supreme Court's *Bush v. Gore* decision in 2000 to give American politics a much harder edge. Assumptions of good faith, essential to the workings of any democratic political system, continued to break down.

George W. Bush is a paradoxical figure who initially accepted the need for conservatism to change but backed away from the challenge of transforming it, partly by choice and partly because of circumstances. The turn to compassionate conservatism was a promising acknowledgment that a majority of Americans expected their government to be socially generous. It also offered conservatives a path toward strengthening religious charities and other institutions of civil society that they extolled, following Burke, as society's "little platoons." Bush expanded the federal government's role in education by pushing through the No Child Left Behind law and he added a comprehensive and expensive prescription drug benefit to Medicare. He tried to bring a large share of the nation's Latinos into the Republican fold by welcoming immigrants and supporting immigration reform.

But Bush's party turned its back on his immigration plans, thereby pushing both Hispanic and Asian-Americans toward the Democrats. Bush's defeat, standing in contrast to Reagan's victory in securing passage of the Simpson-Mazzoli immigration law in 1986, suggested how far the right had moved toward restrictionist immigration policies. Opposition to immigration reform would be one of the central passions of the Tea Party. Donald Trump made the cause his own and took it in an even more radical direction.

Compassionate conservatism was already in retreat when the attacks of September 11, 2001, abruptly shifted the focus of Bush's presidency. Its importance diminished further as the wars that followed in Afghanistan and Iraq took the bulk of his attention. The Iraq adventure was a decidedly unconservative approach to foreign policy. The war's underlying purpose was to reorder the Middle East by installing a democratic regime in Iraq that would be a model for the transformation of the region. In pursuing the war, Bush broke with his father's prudent approach and ignored a core conservative insight: that large actions by government can have major and sometimes destructive unintended consequences. This rule proved as apt abroad as it can be at home.

But even without the wars, Karl Rove's sense of what had gone wrong in the 2000 election led him to give priority to base mobilization over efforts to broaden support for the Republicans at the center of the electorate. Polarization was doing its work in politics long before it became a national obsession. And within the conservative base, compassionate conservatism never won broad legitimacy. Bush's own administration was always divided as to how forcefully to push it, knowing that many conservatives resented the suggestion that they lacked compassion (just as Goldwater had been unhappy with Richard Nixon's insistence that conservatives needed to show "heart"). Republicans in Congress were reluctant to back initiatives associated with the compassion agenda—"particularly," as Gerson noted drily, "if they cost money." Finally, Bush never resolved the contradiction between those who turned to compassionate conservatism as a way of dismantling the state and those who saw it as a supplement and corrective to traditional programs.

Once again, conservatives who sought to alter conservatism's post-Goldwater trajectory confronted a wall of resistance.

Outside the Republican Party, Bush's travails led to a turn toward the center-left, first in the 2006 midterm elections and then in Barack Obama's sweeping victory in 2008. But inside the GOP, Bush's failures were used to discredit his moves toward moderation, opening the way for the Tea Party to restore the uncompromising commitments of Goldwaterism, supplemented with a strong streak of nativism. By 2010 the Republican Party had moved far to the right of where Bush once hoped to lead it.

This was the conservatism Obama confronted. It was rooted in Goldwater's creed but had advantages Goldwater never enjoyed—the new institutions of talk radio and Fox News and financing from a group of very wealthy champions whose power was vastly expanded by misguided Supreme Court decisions. The reach of the new right-wing rich far exceeds the influence of the financial angels behind Goldwater or Reagan. Charles and David Koch are representative figures. They were more expansive in their means and more ambitious in their ends than their father, Fred, the John Birch Society National Council member, had ever been. Conservative media institutions and funders pressed for conformity. They usually got it. With an increasingly homogeneous Republican primary electorate always threatening dissidents with defeat, the reformist currents in the movement and the party's so-called Establishment found it as far easier to appease these forces than to challenge them.

The vast demographic gap between Americans who vote in presidential elections and the smaller group that casts ballots in midterm elections created an additional barrier to change, as did gerrymandered districts in many states. Over the next decade or so, very conservative Republicans are likely to maintain their bastion in the House. They will have more than a fighting chance every two years to win the Senate. Given the nature of the districts and states that Republicans represent, they have far more incentive to resist rethinking than to promote it. But staying on their current path will make it increasingly difficult for Republicans to win the presidency as the nonwhite share of the presidential electorate continues to grow.

This demographic gap, as long as it persists, will make governing very difficult whenever Democrats control the White House and Republicans control Congress. A narrowly based Republican Party with an ideology far removed from the political center is ill-suited to compromising with a Democratic Party of the center-left. The sharply divergent attitudes toward compromise itself within the two parties make this process even more difficult. This partisanship increasingly influences the Supreme Court, where, as Emory University political scientists Alan Abramowitz and Steven Webster noted, "the justices now divide along party lines on major cases with greater frequency than at any time in recent history."

Thus the story told in this book, and it leads to two questions: Short of an extended period of unified party control of our government, how will we govern ourselves? And if, as I have argued, effective government depends on the rise of a more moderate brand of conservatism, how—given all the constraints I have described—will the movement reform itself?

★

There is, of course, no reason to imagine that conservatives would have any particular interest in changing their movement on the advice of a liberal. In fact, liberals have been urging conservatives to rediscover the virtues of Burke since the rise of a more militant right in the 1950s—without much effect. Given the Republican Party's long-term prospects of maintaining a strong position in Congress and the fact that a relatively small swing in their favor could give Republicans the White House, why should conservatives even consider changing?

Part of the answer is in the hands of progressives and Democrats—in the arguments they advance, in their skill at calling out extremism, and in their ability to maintain their presidential majority. Over the long run, a conservative movement that continually loses the presidency will tire of an almost entirely defensive and oppositionist role in American politics.

But to challenge the gridlock created by the two electorates, progressives will need to win back white working-class voters who look to government to reduce economic insecurity and expand opportunity—yet have lost confidence in government's capacity to succeed.

For progressives, the lessons of the last fifty years are paradoxical. It's certainly true that liberalism needed the updating and the course corrections that Bill Clinton undertook in the 1990s. His "Opportunity, Responsibility, Community" slogan helped free Democrats and progressives from the stereotypes that had attached to liberalism. His campaigning against false choices—between feminism and the family, between environmentalism and economic growth, between worry over crime and a concern about the social causes of crime—transformed a stale debate. He showed that fiscal responsibility was not the enemy of progressive goals, and that progressives gave a higher priority to fiscal prudence than conservatives did. On budgets, he really was an Eisenhower Republican. His battle with the Republicans in 1995 was based on a defense of the core purposes of government, and he prevailed. And the period of soaring economic growth and job creation after Clinton and a Democratic Congress raised taxes decisively undercut the claims of supply-side economics, even if the supply-siders continued to sell their wares well into the new century.

But Clinton also gave up ground, some rhetorical and some substantive. There was no need for him to say, "The era of big government is over," a statement that was both flatly untrue and surrendered a large point of principle about government's role in American life. Having defended government so effectively against the Gingrich revolutionaries, he then conceded to their core critique of the American state for the purposes of a single line in an election-year State of the Union message. It may have been only a momentary gift to the right, but given the centrality of the debate about government in the ongoing political battle, it had lasting consequences.

Clinton too easily embraced Wall Street's view of the benefits of financial deregulation. Since the New Deal, liberals had rightly insisted on the need to regulate finance, to keep banking a boring business, and to limit the dangers that speculation could pose to the larger economy. Deregulation not only opened the way the crash of 2008. It also helped fuel a sharp shift in the reward structure of the economy in favor of the very wealthy, and particularly those in the financial sector. It is not surprising that Bernie Sanders, a democratic socialist senator from Vermont, gained a wide following for a presidential campaign that reasserted his party's traditional belief in the imperative of checking the economic power of the very wealthy. In a sense, Sanders was taking Obama's Osawatomie speech to its logical conclusion. Hillary Clinton understood that new economic circumstances and new forms of inequality demanded serious revisions and updates in the now old New Democrat playbook. If Republicans need to recognize that the problems of the the new century are different from those of the 1980s, Democrats need to accept the formulas for success now will be different from those championed by Bill Clinton in the prosperous 1990s.

Moreover, the Democrats' eager embrace of a centrist form of liberalism helped open space on the right end of politics. At its best, centrism can involve the very sort of balanced politics that Eisenhower preached. But there are moments when the primary political task is to move the center to a new place—or, at the least, to keep it from being dragged in the wrong direction. By the time of Clinton's election, the American center had clearly veered well to the right. This is an achievement that Goldwater and Reagan can both claim. For liberals, chasing the moving center meant acquiescing as it shifted ever rightward. In the middle of the Goldwater campaign, Irving Howe, the distinguished left-wing intellectual, offered an axiom that was prescient about the entire period that followed. "A law might be here advanced about recent American politics," he wrote: "the more housebroken the left, the more adventuresome the right."

The Obama years offer a similar message. Obama was at his most effective when he was on offense, advancing not only an agenda but also an argument. His weakest moments came when he seemed excessively eager to compromise. Over time, Obama learned this lesson. Days before he stepped down as Obama's senior adviser in 2015, Dan Pfeiffer described to *New York* magazine's Jonathan Chait the president's conversion to a more aggressive approach. "There's very little we can do to change the Republicans' political situation because they are worried about a cohort of voters who disagree with most of what the president says," Pfeiffer argued. "We don't have the ability to communicate with them—we can't even break into the tight communication circles to convince them that climate change is real. They are talking to people who agree with them, they are listening to news outlets that reinforce that point of view, and the president is probably the person with the least ability to break into that because of the partisan bias there."

Chait went on to note that the "original premise of Obama's first presidential campaign was that he could reason with Republicans—or else, by staking out obviously reasonable stances, force them to moderate or be exposed as extreme and unyielding. It took years for the White House to conclude that this was false."

The greatest irony of an Obama presidency that began with a pledge to tear down ideological barriers is that, as Chait noted, his "most politically successful maneuvers . . . have all been unilateral and liberal." Pfeiffer underscored the point: "Whenever we contemplate bold progressive action, whether that's the president's endorsement of marriage equality, or coming out strong on power-plant rules to reduce [carbon] pollution, on immigration, on [Inter]net neutrality, you get a lot of hemming and hawing in advance about what this is going to mean: Is this going to alienate people? Is this going to hurt the president's approval ratings? What will this mean in red states?" Yet in the end, "there's never been a time when we've taken progressive action and regretted it."

The one exception to this pattern in a sense proves the rule. Among Obama's many victories in 2015 was passage of fast-track authority to negotiate an Asian trade deal—and trade was the rare issue on which the president was closer to Republicans and conservatives than to members of his own party. Even on this issue, some conservatives who would normally have endorsed free trade opposed the trade bill because Obama was doing the negotiating. They labeled it "Obamatrade," which for some conservatives was enough to settle the argument. But on trade, most Republicans voted with Obama not because he compromised but because he endorsed the long-standing position of a majority of conservatives.

And if 2015 was one of the best years of Obama's presidency, all its other achievements came in the face of Republican opposition, from the new Cuba policy to the Supreme Court victories on gay marriage and the Affordable Care Act and his own big steps on climate change. The continued drop in the unemployment rate into the early fall of 2015 reflected the combined success of his own policies and a broadly Keynesian approach by the Federal Reserve. If the economy was still not delivering the wage growth Democrats (and wage earners themselves) sought, it had been rescued from catastrophe. And the historic nuclear deal with Iran confronted unanimous opposition from Republican Senators. It was saved entirely by Democratic votes.

The lesson for progressives is to recognize what the liberal writers Paul Starr and Robert Kuttner observed, and what Obama eventually learned: "The idea of transcending partisan differences works only when there is some basic agreement on the ends." But this does not mean that simply standing their ground is sufficient for liberals. The most ambitious parts of their agenda require Congressional action and the Democrats' loss of both houses of Congress means that liberals must, for now, play a largely defensive game.

To have any hope of regaining the political terrain they have lost in the state houses and in the House and Senate, progressives need to pay far more attention than they do to making government work effectively. Nothing did more damage to the Affordable Care Act than the collapse of its website, an entirely avoidable problem. This was not a failure of ideology but of procurement, performance, and management. Obama also lost an opportunity when he did not try to convert the enthusiasm of the young for his campaign in

2008 into a generational commitment to public service. Creating a sense of energy and possibility in government, key achievements of both Franklin Roosevelt and John F. Kennedy, is essential to repairing both its image and its performance. The seemingly mundane task of reforming how government recruits and hires is actually a critical component of any effort to revive progressivism and to encourage a form of conservatism more open to public endeavor.

And if Mitt Romney had problems with working-class voters, so did Barack Obama. Obama's race is often cited as the main reason for his difficulties with the white working class. There is no doubt that racial reaction cost him votes—and, as we have seen, played an important role long before Obama was born in the formation of the conservative coalition he confronted. The problems liberals and Democrats have with working-class voters predate him. Their difficulties are tied in part to social issues, and there is good reason for liberals to pay respectful heed to the values of working-class voters, especially their religious commitments. Democrats face difficult coalition management problems around religion because their core constituency includes very religious African-Americans and Latinos alongside middle- and upper-middle-class (and largely white) secular voters. Winning also requires the party to seek more support from middle-ground Catholics who happen to be swing voters in the swing states of the Midwest. Democrats need to defend religious freedom and tolerance while showing that their commitment to tolerance and openness extends to those for whom religion plays a central role in their lives. Pope Francis has opened possibilities here that did not exist before.

But on many specific issues, progressives have no reason, political or substantive, to abandon their social liberalism, especially since polling shows that younger white working-class voters are more socially liberal than their elders. Over time, conservatives are playing a losing hand on these questions, particularly on gay rights.

The major difficulty progressives face is that—except in the final years of the Bill Clinton–era economic boom—they have not delivered on their promises to lift working-class wages and to close the opportunity gap between the children of the well-off and those from families of modest means.

My purpose here is not to outline a full-scale economic program, although the Inclusive Prosperity Commission of the Center for American Progress, of which I was a part, made an important start at doing so, as did "Rewriting the Rules of the American Economy," a report written by Joseph Stiglitz and the Roosevelt Institute. This is the issue on which progressives will stand or fall, something Hillary Clinton recognized in a campaign kickoff speech in June 2015 that laid heavy stress on the need "to make the economy work for everyday Americans, not just those at the top." She elaborated on these themes in a series of detailed policy speeches that drew on both reports and other ideas that have gained broad support among progressives.

The paradox, as the Democratic pollster Stanley Greenberg has argued, is this: both the party's core constituencies and whites with lower incomes who have been drifting Republican are seeking government policies that could help them shore up their living standards and improve their job prospects and family lives. Yet they are skeptical about how government works and wary of the influence of the well-heeled and well-connected.

"Democrats," Greenberg argued, "have not addressed the profound wage stagnation and the special interest corruption of government that leaves the middle class out in the cold. That leaves the Democrats' potential majority without a reason to stay consistently engaged—and leaves Democrats short on white working-class votes as well." Voters the Democrats need to mobilize and those they need to win over "are ready for government to help—if the stables can be cleaned."

Progressives not only need to defend the rights of minorities whose access to the ballot box is being challenged by conservatives in many states through modern-day voter suppression measures; they also should take the offensive by easing access to the polls, particularly for lower-income Americans whose work schedules often make voting difficult. Clinton's call in 2015 for a renewal of a Voting Rights Act gutted by the Supreme Court, automatic voter registration, at least twenty days of early voting, and other reforms pointed in the right direction. Stopping efforts to make voting more difficult is good; making voting easier and more conveninent is better.

Above all, progressives need to challenge their conservative adversaries directly to accept that America's demographic and social changes are part of the ongoing history of a nation that stays young and vibrant because of its openness. Restricting ballot access for these new constituencies may have short-term electoral advantages for conservatives, but it is not a viable long-term strategy in a pluralistic and democratic society.

Obama's best moments have come when he insisted on a definition of our nation based not on a deification of a static past but on a celebration of its capacity to transform itself. Standing before the Edmund Pettus Bridge in Selma, Alabama, in 2015 to celebrate the fiftieth anniversary of the great voting rights march, Obama delivered one of the best speeches of his presidency. "America is a constant work in progress," he declared. "[L]oving this country requires more than singing its praises or avoiding uncomfortable truths. It requires the occasional disruption, the willingness to speak out for what's right and shake up the status quo." Americans, he said, are "strong enough to be self-critical," and he urged Americans not to flee the nation's diversity but to celebrate it:

> We're the immigrants who stowed away on ships to reach these shores, the huddled masses yearning to breathe free—Holocaust survivors, Soviet defectors, the Lost Boys of Sudan. We're the hopeful strivers who cross the Rio Grande because we want our kids to know a better life. That's how we came to be. We're the slaves who built the White House and the economy of the South. We're the ranch hands and cowboys who opened up the West, and countless laborers who laid rail, and raised skyscrapers, and organized for workers' rights.

In the short run, progressives will need to mobilize far more effectively than they do now if they are to end the great divide between midterm and presidential electorates. But in the long run, the trends are on the side of progressives.

And that is the strongest incentive for conservatives to change and reform. There is a time limit on the ability of conservatism in its current form and Republicanism in its current incarnation to win elections. A movement rooted in a fifty-year-old ideology, dependent on an aging constituency, and closed to the kind of nation the United States is becoming may win short-term victories, but it will ultimately wither. And some very practical Republicans know it.

★

Jim Brulte, California's Republican state chairman, had sobering but useful words for his party when I spoke with him in the spring of 2015. "California is the leading edge of the country's demographic changes," Brulte said. "Frankly, Republicans in California did not react quickly enough to them, and we have paid a horrible price."

One measure of the cost: In the three presidential elections of the 1980s, California voted twice for Ronald Reagan and once for George H. W. Bush. The state has not gone Republican since.

California telescoped the demographic changes the nation is going through, so its transformation from Ronald Reagan's base to a Democratic bastion ought to be an alarming portent for conservatives. "The one thing no one can stop," said Representative Ted Lieu, a Los Angeles–area Democrat who was elected to Congress in 2014, "is that every month, the rest of America looks more like California."

Republicans made the mistake of alienating Latinos, Asian-Americans, and African-Americans in a state whose population is already a majority nonwhite. The passage of Proposition 187 in 1994 with the strong support of Republican governor Pete Wilson—the ballot measure barred illegal immigrants from a variety of state services—simultaneously turned off Hispanic voters from the GOP and mobilized many of them into the political process.

The same thing is now happening nationally as the Republican Party is pressured by its political base to repeat the California GOP's mistake on immigration—or, in Trump's case, to go even farther. Brulte urges Republicans to emblazon these facts on a wall in every party headquarters: "In 2012, Mitt Romney carried 59 percent of the white vote and he carried independents. In 2004, this would have elected him president. In 2000, it would have given him an Electoral College landslide. In 2012, it gave him second place."

Republican pollster Whit Ayres hails from North Carolina and has enjoyed great success in helping Republicans win across the South. But as we saw earlier, he shares Brulte's views on the imperative of changing his party. "Unfortunately for Republicans, the math is only going to get worse," he wrote in the *Wall Street Journal* in March 2015. "Groups that form the core of GOP support—older whites, blue-collar whites, married people and rural residents—are declining as a proportion of the electorate. Groups that lean Democratic—minorities, young people and single women—are growing." He added: "The challenge is obvious: Republicans can't win a presidential election by trying to grab a larger piece of a shrinking pie." Ayres's solution—for the party to nominate "a candidate who can speak to minorities, especially Hispanics, and offer a vivid and compelling vision of expanded economic opportunity at home and a stronger America abroad"—came naturally to an adviser to Marco Rubio, whose presidential candidacy precisely met these specifications. But Ayres' broader point applies well beyond a single candidacy.

Perhaps the right candidate fronting the old ideology would be enough to pull Republicans and conservatives through their demographic difficulties. But Rubio's own experience on immigration—having to back away from the reform bill he helped negotiate in order to appease the Tea Party—suggests that the pull of the movement's current orientation is not easy to overcome. The party's demographic problems are plainly intertwined with its ideological orientation, and the immigration issue is not the only concern that pushes Latinos away from the Republicans. Latinos have been among the strongest supporters of Obamacare, reflecting both the large number of Hispanics who lack health coverage and their general support for social insurance. Bush's compassionate conservatism was targeted partly at these voters; a harder-right ideology has little to say to them. A Republican Party that cannot answer the Latino community's desire for public programs aimed at relieving economic stresses and enhancing opportunities for mobility will remain at a long-term disadvantage. And a failure to deal with barriers to mobility will eventually haunt conservatives among white working-class voters as well.

Conservatism as it is now understood places the movement in a policy straitjacket, which is precisely why compassionate and reform conservatives alike have been unable to achieve their potential. As long as conservatism is dedicated to lower taxes as one of its unbreakable public commitments, its proposals aimed at easing inequality and promoting mobility will be small, largely symbolic, and ineffective. Republican leaders may have felt obliged to discuss wage stagnation and rising inequality after the 2014 election because these were problems on the public's mind. They may have publicly abandoned the "makers" and "takers" idea. But their budgets continued to be rooted in this understanding of how the world works.

As has been clear since the Reagan era and the dramatic budget confrontations of the Clinton years, Republican budgets whose central aim is to reduce taxes on the wealthy will never pass the test of simple arithmetic. Such plans require either deep program cuts that that majorities of the voters reject or the very ongoing deficits that conservatives regularly denounce. At some point conservatives face a reckoning with the fiscal contradictions of their ideology.

There is, finally, the question of whether conservatives want to continue to seek power based on a strategy that might be seen as Marxist, in its approach if certainly not its goals: Heightening the tensions in our democracy has been at the heart of the conservative approach throughout Obama's time in office.

Sometimes, it worked. Its payoff was obvious in the midterm elections of 2010 and 2014, and this is not suprising. As the party that insists on government's ability to solve problems and foster social improvement, Democrats need to prove government can work. Gridlock and polarization serve the interests of antigovernment conservatism by proving the opposite: that government is destined to fail and that the public sphere is rife with conflict. This in turn can lead to an abandonment of the quest for public solutions to public problems. Citizens come to feel that the best they will ever be able to do is fall back on their own individual resources. For some on the right, this would be a positive outcome.

But the costs of this style of politics to our democratic system are enormous. Conservatives have an obligation to their own tradition and to their nation to ask whether promoting a politics of showdowns and crises based on thoroughly unrealistic expectations is consistent with the highest callings of their philosophy. John Boehner, for one, decided he had had enough of this. His resignation as Speaker in the fall of 2015 was an effort to appease right-wing members of his caucus who thought he, too, had sold out conservatism. He hoped offering his head would forestall another shutdown. Boehner was yet another victim of the cycle of disappointment and betrayal, created by promises made that could not be kept.

This is how Boehner himself saw the matter. "The Bible says, beware of false prophets," he told CBS's John Dickerson on *Face the Nation* two days after he announced his departure. "We have got groups here in town, members of the House and Senate here in town who whip people into a frenzy believing they can accomplish things that they know, they know are never going to happen." In accepting the Speakership, Paul Ryan has now bet his career on the proposition that he can break this cycle.

Over the decades, the United States has taken on an obligation beyond the inescapable duties of preserving the security of its own people and advancing their prosperity: to provide a model for the world of self-rule within a democratic republic. Few would make a case that we are doing so now.

In fact, most of the world's democracies confront contradictions that are undermining faith in public endeavor and unraveling old loyalties. Nearly all the democracies have seen dissident movements on the left and the right not unlike the Trump insurgency. In the United States, the decline of trust in traditional political parties has curiously been accompanied by a rise in partisanship. A broad desire for governments to reduce the levels of economic insecurity and expand opportunity is constrained by a loss of confidence in the capacity of government to succeed. Intense demands for change are accompanied by fears that much of the change that is occurring will make life worse for individuals and families.

This is creating a very sour mood. Abramowitz and Webster are right when they argue that "one of the most important trends in American politics over the past several decades has been the rise of negative partisanship in the electorate." It occurs, they write, when "supporters of each party perceive supporters of the opposing party as very different from themselves in terms of their social characteristics and fundamental values." Our current form of partisanship leads us to dislike not only the other side's politicians, but also each other.

Conservatives would argue, with some merit, that they are not solely responsible for these developments. Yet their own flight from moderation gravely aggravates the problem. A politics of "us versus them" is further encouraged by the far right's proclivity toward the demonization of illegal immigrants and cultural liberals, the Republican Party's dependence on an ethnically homogeneous coalition, and the mainstream right's still-implicit "takers" rhetoric.

In our time, advocates and apologists for antidemocratic regimes argue that the democracies are no longer capable of managing their problems or creating a sense of social dynamism. The democracies are cast as sclerotic, inefficient, and ungovernable. In all the democratic nations, and especially our own, politicians of all parties have an obligation to counter this critique of democracy by proving once again that free governments can grapple with the problems that confront us—much as the United States did in the 1930s when the forces of dictatorship were on the march around the globe.

Nurturing tolerance, harmony, social generosity, and optimism have been particular obligations of conservatism going back to Burke. Dwight Eisenhower was certainly being romantic about America's past when he declared that our history "has been characterized by cooperation, and not by fighting among ourselves or refusing to see the other fellow's viewpoint." A country that went through a civil war has had more than its share of disharmony. Nonetheless, he was right in what he said next: "It has been a group effort, freely undertaken, that has produced the things of which we are so proud and which are represented in the American way of life." Preserving "the American way of life"—including all that we have built since the Progressive Era, the New Deal, and the civil rights years—would seem a worthy object of a philosophy that calls itself "conservative."

Our nation needs a new conservatism that finally breaks with the direction the philosophy took in the Goldwater years, and the search for a path forward must begin with an examination of the alternative form of conservatism that the partisans of Goldwaterism were rejecting. So powerful is the ongoing effect of the Goldwater revolution that we forget there were other paths.

The central object of right-wing ire in the 1950s and early 1960s was not the liberal adversary in the Democratic Party, but those inside the Republican Party who preached a more moderate form of conservatism willing to make peace with the New Deal order while seeking to curb its excesses. It was, as we saw in Chapter One, the approach of Dwight D. Eisenhower and it went under the name of Modern Republicanism.

From the beginning, as John Judis wrote, William F. Buckley Jr.'s *National Review* was "utterly contemptuous of Eisenhower and his policies." Eisenhower, *National Review* wrote, "is a man more distinguished for his affability and skills in reconciling antagonisms than for a profound knowledge of his country's institutions." Buckley told his friend Alistair Horne, the British historian: "Eisenhower was above all a man unguided and hence unhampered by principle. Eisenhower undermines the Western resolution to stand up and defend what is ours."

Early in *The Conscience of a Conservative*, Goldwater singled out Modern Republicanism and its leading interpreter, Arthur Larson, an Eisenhower aide, for opprobrium. Goldwater was vexed by a passage from Larson's 1956 book, *A Republican Looks at His Party*, asserting that the "underlying philosophy" of Modern Republicanism was a belief that "if a job has to be done to meet the needs of the people, and no one else can do it, then it is the proper function of the federal government."

Larson's formulation was simply a restatement of the first Republican president's dictum. The legitimate object of government, Abraham Lincoln said, was "to do for the people what needs to be done, but which they cannot, by individual effort, do at all, or do so well, for themselves." But Goldwater equated Larson's view with that of Democrat Dean Acheson, Truman's secretary of state, who had said that the New Deal "conceived of the federal government as the whole people organized to do what had to be done." Goldwater saw both men guilty of "an unqualified repudiation of the principle of limited government," and provided the Tea Party with its text. "There is no reference by either of them," Goldwater wrote, "to the Constitution, or any attempt to define the legitimate functions of government." Thus was Lincoln Republicanism cast as the enemy of constitutional conservatism.

Larson had defined Eisenhower's alternative conservative approach this way:

Now we have as much government activity as is necessary, but not enough to stifle the normal motivations of private enterprise. And we have a higher degree of government concern for the needs of people than ever before in our history, while at the same time pursuing a policy of maximum restoration of responsibility to individuals and private groups. This balance, together with a gradual restoration of a better balance between federal and state governments, is allowing all these elements of society to make their maximum contribution to the common good.

Larson certainly lacked Buckley's fluency and dash, but he was describing a sober yet hopeful form of conservatism that had taken hold across much of the West at the time—in Harold Macmillan's Conservative Party in Britain, for example, or in the Christian Democratic Party of Konrad Adenauer in West Germany. After a dreadful depression, a world war, and genocide in Hitler's Germany, moderation was a very attractive disposition. The democratic right across the West accepted a role for government in tempering the workings of a market economy that all participants in politics at the time knew was capable of hurtling toward chaos.

In a 1955 speech, Gabriel Hauge, an assistant to Eisenhower who later became a leading New York bank executive, defined "the economics of Eisenhower conservatism." Ike, he said, stressed "free markets and private initiative" and "the tradition of incentive and reward." But he also recognized that programs from the New Deal era "met real needs" and had thus "been integrated into the American way." Eisenhower's conservatism, Hauge said, was "neither standpattism nor reaction" and did not "seek to stop the clock of progress or turn it back."

Eisenhower himself offered the clearest definition of his philosophy in his Farewell Address on January 17, 1961. The speech is best known for his warning against the power of "the military-industrial complex," which, as libertarian conservatives would note, was a caution against big government and its alliance with big business. But the speech as a whole was a powerful plea for balance and prudence. Ike was unapologetic in using the word "balance" over and over. He called for "balance in and among national programs—balance between the private and the public economy, balance between the cost and hoped-for advantages—balance between the clearly necessary and the comfortably desirable; balance between our essential requirements as a nation and the duties imposed by the nation upon the individual; balance between the actions of the moment and the national welfare of the future."

He concluded: "Good judgment seeks balance and progress; lack of it eventually finds imbalance and frustration."

This was thoroughly Burkean and so, too, was his rejection of the idea that "some spectacular and costly action could become the miraculous solution to all current difficulties." In facing down communism, he argued that the country needed "not so much the emotional and transitory sacrifices of crisis, but rather those which enable us to carry forward steadily, surely, and without complaint the burdens of a prolonged and complex struggle." Ike was not afraid to talk about complexity, or patience.

In a passage that many libertarians can still appreciate, he warned of the lure of government money and how it could affect the freedom of intellectuals. He feared the "prospect of domination of the nation's scholars by Federal employment, project allocations, and the power of money" and worried that "public policy could itself become the captive of a scientific-technological elite." His fiscal conservatism showed through with his insistence that the nation "avoid the impulse to live only for today, plundering for our own ease and convenience, the precious resources of tomorrow." And he defended the role of negotiations in foreign policy, urging nations to "the conference table," which, "though scarred by many past frustrations, cannot be abandoned for the certain agony of the battlefield."

He concluded with the hope that "in the goodness of time, all peoples will come to live together in a peace guaranteed by the binding force of mutual respect and love."

Commenting on Eisenhower's speech, William Galston, who had served as an aide to Bill Clinton, recalled that "in a moment of exasperation, the president I served once complained that we're all Eisenhower Republicans now." Galston's conclusion: "We could do worse."

And so could today's conservatives. It is a mark of how much conservatism has changed that even to cite Eisenhower as anything but a "moderate" or even a "liberal" seems strange. Many conservatives still cannot accept in their ranks a man who declared: "Should any political party attempt to abolish social security, unemployment insurance, and eliminate labor laws and farm programs, you would not hear of that party again in our political history."

But in thinking about their political ancestors, conservatives need to ponder the costs of their sharp turn away from his legacy. He was certainly fiscally prudent, reducing the debt as a share of GDP from 71.4 percent when he took office to 60.4 percent when he left. Yet within the framework of prudence and balance, he was willing to use the federal government in substantial and innovative ways to solve postwar problems. He left lasting monuments by inaugurating the Interstate Highway System and establishing the first student loan program under the National Defense Education Act, following the model of the GI Bill in broadly expanding access to higher education. It's worth noting that long before the rise of the religious right, Eisenhower presided over a much larger public role for religion. As noted earlier, it was under Eisenhower that "Under God" was inserted into the Pledge of Allegiance and "In God We Trust" became the nation's motto. Yet Eisenhower-style public religion lacked the hard edge that religious conservatism would develop later.

In political terms, Eisenhower's victories were national in scope and he made large inroads into traditionally Democratic constituencies, including Catholics, Jews, and working-class voters. The South began to drift toward the Republicans under Eisenhower—he carried Texas, Louisiana, Florida, Tennessee, and Virginia—but his strategy for winning the South did not focus on racial reaction. On the contrary, while carrying those southern states, Ike also won 39 percent of the nonwhite vote. Eisenhower did not have a Southern Strategy. He had a national strategy.

Reading Eisenhower back into the conservative tradition is not a magical solution to what ails the American right, and he is not an infallible guide, especially in his attitude toward the deportation of immigrants. But reengaging Eisenhower is a necessary first step toward opening the conservative mind, sparking the conservative imagination, and restoring moderation as a conservative virtue. Eisenhower shows that in the postwar period, there was another way to be conservative, Republican, and successful. He proposed a far less polarizing approach to governing, to political foes, and to electoral victory. Eisenhower's conservatism rejected the radicalism entailed in promises to overthrow the country's inheritance from the New Deal. Here, too, is a lesson for conservatives. Writing of our time, the political theorist Greg Weiner noted that "[t]he New Deal regime has been an integral part of American society for more than seventy-five years," while the Great Society has "extended its reach into American institutions for fifty—more than a fifth of US constitutional history. It is here. Expectations have formed around it." The conservative tradition that evolved from Burke does not have to "acquiesce" to this order, Weiner wrote, but it should certainly "approach its modification with a degree of caution and regard." In his 2013 book *The Right Path*, Joe Scarborough explicitly praised Eisenhower for traits many movement conservatives saw as grave sins. "Unlike most GOP activists in 1952," Scarborough wrote, "Eisenhower knew that no conservative president—no matter his popularity—would be able to eliminate Social Security and a bevy of other popular New Deal programs. It was a political pragmatism that frustrated conservatives like William F. Buckley, but it was a shrewd approach embraced even by the likes of Margaret Thatcher three decades later."

There is something strange about the linkage of the words "conservative" and "revolutionary" and something decidedly unconservative about trying to break with three-quarters of a century of our history. A conservatism that accepted the responsibility of conserving the genuine achievements of progressive reform would be truer to its own tradition than a form of reaction dedicated to rooting out all vestiges of the liberal governance that shaped the America that exists now.

And this goes to the larger conservative problem. Many contemporary conservatives have trouble being at home in the raucous, pluralistic, multicultural country that has come into being during precisely the period when their creed moved right. Obama inspired opposition not just for what he did but for who he was and what he represented. It was not only that he was the first African-American president, but also the son of a Kenyan immigrant and a white mother who spent his youth in Hawaii and Indonesia—and was raised in part by grandparents from Kansas. He embodied diversity, and combined this with an Ivy League education and a cosmopolitan worldview.

Obama *was* different from what Americans have been used to in their president. He leads a changing country, and his coalition represents this change: young, multicultural, multiracial, urban, and near-suburban. It links some of the poorest Americans with educated professionals.

The problem for conservatives is that their distance from the new America has made many in their ranks sour about America itself—not the abstract ideal of the America they celebrate but the actual, living America of the early twenty-first century. This, in turn, has created a deep pessimism in a movement that reached its high point in the glow of Ronald Reagan's radiant optimism. As an electoral matter, angry pessimism rarely triumphs. As a disposition for governing, it will neither unite nor inspire.

The currently dominant brand of conservatism is still rooted in the fusionism of Buckley and Frank Meyer, a marriage of traditionalism and free-market economics. In recent years, fusionism has taken the form of an alliance between social and religious conservatives, right-leaning libertarians and business interests, financed increasingly by David Frum's "radical rich." Only once since 1992 has this alliance produced a popular vote majority in a presidential election, a narrow one for George W. Bush in 2004 that was powered more by national security concerns in the wake of 9/11 than by the country's ideological mood.

The fusionist coalition is fraying, and it blew apart dramatically in the spring of 2015 when Indiana passed a "religious freedom" law that effectively opened the way for discrimination against gays and lesbians. To the shock of the measure's supporters, who saw it as a relatively painless way to satisfy religious conservatives, the bill created an uproar. In a sign of how deeply gay rights and marriage equality were becoming embedded in mainstream American life, both Indiana and Arkansas, which passed a similar bill, came under intense pressure from businesses ranging from Apple to Wal-Mart to repeal or dilute it. Within days, Republican governors in both states reversed themselves, fearing that keeping the law on the books would lead to business and tourist boycotts.

The episode hurt the Republican Party's image outside the ranks of religious conservatives, particularly among younger voters who strongly support gay rights. But the religious conservatives felt betrayed by politicians who had caved in to pressure from those whom Gary Bauer, a leading social conservative, called "corporate insiders." It will not be the last fight of this sort.

Conservatism thus faces twin challenges. It must modernize on cultural issues lest it lose the next generation and continue facing hostility from educated professionals. Yet as the 2012 election showed, it also has reason to fear defections—if not always to the Democrats then to abstention—from working-class voters who do not see their interests represented by conservative politicians who spend so much of their energy advocating tax cuts for the wealthy and regulatory relief for business. For less affluent voters who have up to now supported Republicans, social issues will not be enough—and, as the Indiana episode showed, Republicans will find it increasingly problematic to deliver on their conservative social promises.

Earlier, I noted that the two poles of the party's challenge were embodied in two failed but instructive candidacies in 2012. Jon Huntsman was the upscale candidate of cultural modernization. Rick Santorum was the candidate of working-class social conservatives. Huntsman and Santorum, it would seem, point Republicans and conservatives in opposite directions. But in another sense, each suggests ways in which conservatives must seek a more moderate path. Huntsman's campaign was based on defanging the social issues and moving away from polarization. Santorum—like the reformist thinkers Henry Olsen, Ross Douthat, and Reihan Salam—was telling Republicans that their near-total focus on the interests of "job creators" and the very wealthy was leading them to ignore the concerns of the working-class voters who were essential to their electoral victories. Donald Trump's initial success in rallying less-affluent Republicans by speaking out against unfair distributions of both economic and political power underscored the urgency of this task.

A turn toward moderation and an embrace of those who have been left-out—these are the tasks essential to the conservative future.

Conservatives rightly revere those who came before us, but they will not prosper if they continue to yearn for a past they will never be able to call back to life. They may win some elections, but they will not govern effectively on the basis of an ideology rooted in the struggles of a half-century ago. They will not succeed if they celebrate only the America that once was, not the vibrant nation that is being born. In his homely but direct way, Eisenhower put the challenge to conservatives of every generation plainly: "Neither a wise man nor a brave man lies down on the tracks of history to wait for the train of the future to run over him." This generation of conservatives must be willing to face the future with confidence, and with hope.

AFTERWORD

Why Trump Happened
2016 and the Conservative Reckoning

"We are mad, and we've been had. They need to get used to it."

It was sudden and it was shocking. On May 4, 2016, the contest for the Republican presidential nomination just stopped. Donald Trump was the only candidate left standing.

Less than a month earlier, as voters prepared to cast ballots in Wisconsin, Trump was floundering. His campaign manager had been charged with assault. Trump had said he was, and then said he wasn't, for punishing women who had abortions. He set off another round of backlash among women by insulting Senator Ted Cruz's wife, Heidi. Wisconsin's powerful conservative talk-show hosts assailed Trump, and the state's Republican governor, Scott Walker, campaigned against him. It appeared that the anti-Trump forces had finally mustered their courage and found their voices. When Cruz crushed Trump in the Wisconsin primary, talk of a divisive and contested national convention reached a crescendo.

But Wisconsin turned out to be an outlier. Trump overwhelmed his remaining foes, John Kasich and Ted Cruz, in the New York primary two weeks later. He carried every county in the state except his home base of Manhattan. A week after that, Trump swept through Connecticut, Maryland, Delaware,

Pennsylvania, and Rhode Island. Then came May 3 and the Indiana primary. It was the state where Cruz was supposed to stall Trump. Instead, Indiana coronated Trump with a 53 percent to 37 percent victory over Cruz, who suspended his campaign that night. Kasich followed suit the next day.

It was over. What Republicans often claimed was their best field of potential nominees in years—Kasich and Cruz, Jeb Bush and Marco Rubio, Chris Christie and Scott Walker, Lindsey Graham and Rand Paul—all fell before a man who was, by almost any reckoning, the least prepared person in generations to serve as president. But how did it happen?

Trump's primary victories were made possible by a Republican Party leadership that professed to be horrified by the results, even if so many Establishmentarians meekly fell into line behind Trump after he had beaten them. Step-by-step, they had capitulated to a politics of unreason, to a policy of silence toward the most extreme and wild charges against President Obama, and to the lifting up of rage and rancor over ideas and solutions as the party's lodestars.

John F. Kennedy once warned that "those who foolishly sought power by riding the back of the tiger ended up inside." This, roughly, is what happened to the leaders of contemporary conservatism and of the Republican Party.

A showdown had been required *before* the steady, large-scale defection of moderate voters from the party. When party leaders finally needed moderate voters to stop Trump and Cruz, the moderates were no longer there—and many of those left inside the party preferred Trump to the available alternatives. Instead of battling the impulses that inspired Trump's legions, GOP honchos exploited them: They fanned nativist feeling by claiming that illegal immigrants were flooding across our borders, even when net migration from Mexico had fallen below zero. They promised radical reductions in the size of government, knowing that no Republican president, including Ronald Reagan, could pull this off. They pledged to "take our country back," leaving vague the identity of the people (other than Obama) from whom it was to be reclaimed. Politicians whose rhetoric brought the right's loyalists to a boiling point complained that they don't much like the result. But it was a little late for that.

And with Trump, the angriest voters in the party felt they at least knew what they were getting. "We are mad, and we've been had," declared Sarah Palin. "They need to get used to it." And slowly they would.

★

Why the Right Went Wrong, published thirteen days before the Iowa Caucuses when the first votes in the Republican contest were cast, made the case that American conservatism is in a deep crisis of its own making. Trump was the utterly unexpected but entirely logical product of this crisis. He instinctively understood it, he stoked it, and he exploited it.

I was gratified that many reviewers and commentators described the book as prophetic and timely. Adele Stan, writing in the *American Prospect*, kindly observed that a GOP race that had come down in the end to Trump and Cruz stood as "proof" of its thesis about the right's radicalization. Fareed Zakaria in the *Washington Post* and Nicholas Kristoff in the *New York Times* both argued that the 2016 campaign ratified the book's core theme that the sense of disappointment and betrayal among Republican base voters was bound to lead to a political conflagration. The betrayal theme, laid out in the very first sentence of the book, won direct empirical support over and over again from surveys of primary voters in the winter and spring of 2016. As Jonathan Martin observed in the *New York Times*, "In every state where the question was asked in exit polls during the primary season, 50 percent or more of Republicans said they felt betrayed by their leaders."

Garry Wills, one of the wisest observers of our politics and someone who knows conservative history from the inside, shared my view that one could not understand what was happening in 2016 without going back to 1964 and reengaging the longer story of right-wing extremism.

To all these writers and many others who wrote generously about *Why the Right Went Wrong*, I offer my gratitude, but I was particularly appreciative of a review by Henry Olsen in *National Review*, the flagship magazine of American conservatism that plays such an important role in these pages. Given my criticisms of the magazine's history, I had no reason to anticipate as respectful an engagement with my argument as I received. Olsen began his review with the obvious and legitimate point that it would be "easy for conservatives to dismiss . . . a book on the Right by a man of the Left, and one that therefore suffers from the usual sins of omission and commission." But then I got my happy surprise when he added: "Easy, but wrong."

Olsen, like Wills, shared my view on the importance of going back to Goldwater, arguing that the book "correctly identifies why conservatives either fail to win power or, when we do, do not use that power to transform America." He continued: "Conservatives who want to win and effectively use political power must, then, come to grips with the central question Dionne poses: Does the intellectual legacy of Barry Goldwater prevent conservatism from being an effective governing movement?"

His conclusion was similar to my own: "A conservatism that pays lip service to the Goldwaterite ideal of welfare-state rollback will neither succeed politically nor be effective in providing a principle that explains why we want what we say we want, a government that gives Americans a Better Deal, one that gives us more for less." My book, he said of conservatives, "clarifies the challenge we face," which is exactly what I had hoped it would do.

Olsen did take me to task for believing that "conservatism is, at its heart, at worst racist and at best racially tinged." He argued that "the story of what happened in the rural, conservative South is much more complicated than progressives such as Dionne want to admit." Interestingly, in a warm and thoughtful review in the *Washington Post*, the historian Heather Cox Richardson thought I committed the opposite sin of understating the role of race. While acknowledging that I had noted "the racism inherent in Goldwater conservatism" and Nixon's Southern Strategy, she argued that I had avoided "the reality that conservative media has saturated the country with racist and sexist rhetoric to attack government activism."

I certainly won't claim that these criticisms from opposing political standpoints show that I found some golden analytical mean on the role of race in the formation of the contemporary conservative coalition. But I retain the view that when it comes to racial backlash, two things are true simultaneously: The conservative creed and the movement are too complicated and conservatives themselves are too diverse in their views to reduce everything about contemporary conservatism to race. (Contra Olsen, I do not believe I say otherwise in the book.) At the same time, as Richardson would insist, conservatives need to acknowledge the continuing role of racial reaction and outright racism in building support for candidates of the right. The presidential candidate who spoke of Mexican immigrants as "rapists," who proposed to build a wall with Mexico, and who channeled old law-and-order rhetoric in opposing the Black Lives Matter movement was well aware of this. From his past of claiming that Barack Obama had not been born in the United States to his present, Trump has freely and, in the Republican primaries at least, quite successfully courted the backlash vote.

And lest anyone forget the role of racism in Trump's rise, the candidate created a crisis for himself in June when he declared that Judge Gonzalo Curiel, who was presiding over a civil lawsuit against Trump University, had "an absolute conflict" in handling the case because he was "of Mexican heritage." At other times, Trump simply referred to the Indiana-born judge as "a Mexican."

Even Republicans who had capitulated to Trump realized the problem they confronted, and he forced some of them into remarkable moral contortions. House Speaker Paul Ryan, who had endorsed Trump just before the Curiel episode, said Trump's remarks were "the textbook definition of a racist comment," and yet he reiterated his endorsement of Trump, saying "we have more common ground on the policy issues of the day." An edition of the *New York Daily News* wickedly but accurately summarized Ryan's comments with a blaring front cover headline: "I'm With Racist!"

But the Curiel episode prompted other Republican politicians to withdraw earlier Trump endorsements, and his response to the mass shooting at the Pulse nightclub in Orlando on June 12 prompted further defections. Trump's initial reaction was to make the murder of forty-nine people about himself: he bragged on Twitter about "being right on radical Islamic terrorism." At a moment when he might have made a turn toward being presidential and unifying, he became instead more divisive, broadening his call for a ban on Muslim immigration, implying that American Muslims were holding back information about potential terrorists, and darkly suggesting that President Obama had secret motives when it came to Islam.

Calls on Republican delegates to ignore the primary results and find a way to block Trump's nomination grew more urgent and widespread as Hillary Clinton surged past him in the polls and his campaign operation fell into chaos. But Republicans knew that even if Trump alienated a majority of the electorate, he and his views were still popular in the GOP. Dumping him would have a high price. His Muslim ban was rejected by 62 percent of the entire electorate but supported by 56 percent of Republicans, according to a June CBS News survey. A *Washington Post*/ABC News Poll in the same period found that 70 percent of Americans had an unfavorable view of Trump—but 65 percent of Republicans viewed him favorably. Republican leaders had created their own Jurassic Park: they animated and exploited the anxieties and conspiracy theories of the ultra-right, and then lost control over what they had created.

Many readers have asked if I saw Trump coming when I began researching the book in 2014. In truth, I had no idea that this strange, self-involved man would so grab the attention of his adopted party and the nation. But his emergence in the summer of 2015 fit seamlessly with the argument here—updating was required, but no major rewriting. Trump was already a presence in the early drafts, and he was a central figure in my argument in the final draft, from the second page forward. As I argued in the chapter entitled "Reforming Conservatism or Trumping It," Trumpian passion overtook the small tweaks of the old conservative agenda that conservative reformers had undertaken. In particular, they offered little to the voters who were hurting most.

This remains a problem. Bravely, *National Review* took a strong stand against Trump in January 2016, declaring him "a philosophically unmoored opportunist who would trash the broad conservative ideological consensus within the GOP in favor of a free-floating populism with strong-man overtones." The editorial included this observation about Republicans: "If they cannot advance a compelling working-class agenda, the legitimate anxieties and discontents of blue-collar voters will be exploited by demagogues."

Yes, indeed, and that agenda is still very much missing. Another central argument of this book is that conservative politicians have relied on the votes of white working-class Americans for decades without offering policies to improve their lives. I noted that conservative thinkers—most prominently Ross Douthat and Reihan Salam—had warned long ago that absent such proposals, conservatism could confront a political explosion. They were right. That explosion produced Donald Trump.

★

Trump split and challenged the conservative coalition in so many ways that it's common for analysts and partisans to focus on whichever aspect of his ascendancy best fits their worldview or their political goals. He is confounding because he represents continuity with conservative history in some respects and a sharp break in others.

Progressives naturally focused on the strong support he won from working-class voters, those with less formal education whose living standards had been flattened by globalization and technological change. Trump himself spoke of their importance to his coalition in one of the year's most notable sound-bites: "I love the poorly educated." As I note in Chapter Fifteen, Trump broke with Republican economic orthodoxy in many ways, particularly through his assaults on free trade agreements and his repeated pledges not to cut Social Security or Medicare. He said he was willing to raise taxes on the wealthy, even though his own tax plan cut them steeply. Rhetorically, Trump often sounded like Bernie Sanders, and Trump's support base in Midwestern industrial states hit hard by trade, particularly Michigan, bore similarities to Sanders's constituency. When Hillary Clinton secured the Democratic nomination, Trump made clear he would try to bring some of Sanders's supporters his way, and his apostasies on trickle-down economics—even if more rhetorical than substantive—were the clearest indication of a conservative ideological crack-up.

But economics were only part of Trump's draw, and not necessarily the most important part. His unique contribution was to import many of the themes of the European far right into American politics. He combined economic nationalism with opposition to immigration, strident attacks on Islam (including his proposed ban on admitting Muslims to the United States), and an authoritarian style.

One of the most disturbing aspects of the strange political year of 2016 was the extent to which the strong-man theme caught on with a large part of the electorate. A survey by PRRI released in June 2016 asked voters if they agreed or disagreed with this statement: "Because things have gotten so far off track in this country, we need a leader who is willing to break some rules if that's what it takes to set things right." Americans were split down the middle: 49 percent partly or completely agreed with the statement, while 50 percent partly or completely disagreed. Among those who agreed with the break-the-rules sentiment, 33 percent had a favorable view of Trump; among those who disagreed, only 17 percent did.

Trump was seen by some analysts as the Tea Party incarnate and by others as presiding over the death of the Tea Party. There was something to each of these claims. On the one hand, his critique of immigration and his nostalgic call to "Make America Great Again"—the word "again" was key—spoke to a large share of those who had rallied to the Tea Party. On the other, many in the Tea Party preferred Cruz, an antipolitician but a politician nonetheless. The Tea Partiers were torn about what mattered most: traditional conservative ideology or strong leadership, immigration or the old social issues. The PRRI's rule-breaking question illustrated the division, splitting opinion among Tea Party sympathizers exactly fifty-fifty. Those hungering for a strong leader were lined up against those loyal to what they regularly extolled as "constitutional conservatism."

A similar divide was visible among white evangelical conservatives. Here again, by taking a significant share of the religious right, Trump doomed Cruz's chances and blew apart another important piece of the conservative coalition. The struggle for the political souls of the devout pitted those still motivated by the old-time issues of abortion and same-sex marriage (they rallied to Cruz or, in some cases, to Marco Rubio's relatively short-lived campaign) against those who identified with Trump's brand of identity politics. Trump's religious supporters wanted to strike back hard against a culture they saw as dominated by liberals and an increasingly diverse America in which they no longer felt at home. The PRRI question about a leader who was willing to break the rules was again telling: 59 percent of white evangelicals who liked the idea of such a leader had a favorable view of Trump, but he was viewed favorably by only 33 percent of white evangelicals who rejected rule-breaking leadership.

But another piece of the Trump constituency did not fit easily into standard analyses of his ascendancy: middle-of-the-road Republicans. Remember that Trump carried New York and Massachusetts as well as Alabama, Arkansas, and Tennessee. He brought together some of the staunchest conservatives in the party with a large number of those who consider themselves moderate. Democratic pollster Stan Greenberg pointed out that many moderates backed Trump because they saw him as less committed to social conservatism (especially on abortion and family planning) than anyone else in the Republican field. The fact that Trump seemed entirely opportunistic on these matters may have helped him with the GOP's moderate minority: They saw him as fundamentally indifferent to these issues. They calculated that the deal maker would be willing to deal on just about everything.

★

It was remarkable how quickly resistance to Trump among Republican politicians dissipated once his nomination became a virtual certainty. Even politicians who at first declared him utterly unacceptable for the presidency suddenly discovered reasons why he might be qualified after all. The go-to rationales (or rationalizations) involved hostility to Hillary Clinton and the likelihood of a liberal Supreme Court emerging under a Democratic president.

But there were holdouts. Neoconservatives could not abide his "America First" foreign policy. It combined bombastic threats of force with commitments to noninterventionism. Economic conservatives did not trust him on trade or spending. Libertarians mistrusted his authoritarianism. And a range of Republicans, including but not limited to moderates, were alarmed over his outbursts on, among other things, torture, immigration, race, women, Latinos, Muslims, Vladimir Putin, and John McCain's military service. Trump's comments on Judge Curiel expanded the community of dissenters.

In the meantime, Republicans in Congress tried to act as if Trump wasn't there—and, as much as they could, as if President Obama wasn't there, either. For the most part, Republicans in the House and Senate tried to position themselves on Trump based less on principle than on their best sense of what might help them the most—or hurt them the least—electorally.

Trump's triumph exposed profound weaknesses in our political system, in the media, among conservatives, and among mainstream Republican politicians. He was able to convert fame and outrage into votes without a moment of apprenticeship in public service. The utter contempt toward government that conservative ideology encouraged made this easier. As *National Review*'s

Ramesh Ponnuru noted of his fellow conservatives: "We have come to reward the expression of resentment and anger more than the mastery of public policy."

Trump also capitalized on the fragility of the media system. Throughout Obama's tenure, he was a Fox News and talk-radio hero: birtherism was a calling card that kept him in the news and forged a strong connection with the angriest parts of the far right. But once he became a candidate, the mainstream media became his echo chamber. In its thirst for ratings, television could not get enough of him. The *New York Times* reported that the tracking firm mediaQuant estimated that as of mid-March 2016 Trump had received close to $1.898 billion worth of free media time, more than double the $746 million that Hillary Clinton had received to that point and nearly *nine times* as much as Jeb Bush, the number two Republican in media attention.

Only after Trump had secured the Republican nomination did media coverage of him truly toughen up and he began to be held more accountable for what he had said and done. Hillary Clinton previewed the attacks and the mockery Trump would face with a powerful speech in early June that declared him "temperamentally unfit to hold an office that requires knowledge, stability, and immense responsibility."

The sharper critiques of Trump emerged too late to stop his romp through the primaries because the Republican Party and its candidates largely failed to take Trump on in the early going for fear of alienating his supporters. For the candidates, it was a classic tragedy of the commons: they had a collective interest in defeating Trump, but each assumed that Trump would eventually fall and wanted to inherit his supporters. Alternatively, each gambled that he would be the last man standing against Trump. Both proved to be very bad bets. The party, in the meantime, gyrated back and forth among complacency, indifference, panic, timidity, and, finally, resignation.

Trump's rise is testimony to a profound distemper in our politics and to the depth of the conservative crisis. I concluded *Why the Right Went Wrong* with a plea for conservatives to take a turn toward moderation and to embrace those who have been left out. The experience of 2016 makes these imperatives all the more urgent.

ACKNOWLEDGMENTS

My first thanks go to a group of conservative and Republican politicians, thinkers, strategists, and writers who agreed to long conversations with me when I set out to write this book. The people I spoke with knew I was a liberal trying to understand what had happened to the American right—and also knew they were unlikely to convert me to their cause. All were forthcoming, generous with their time, and candid not only about their hopes for their movement but also about the difficulties it faces. They helped me see nuances and complexities I might otherwise have missed (although I am sure I missed some anyway).

So my gratitude to Whit Ayres, Haley Barbour, Jim Brulte, Pat Buchanan, Dave Camp, Mike Castle, Chris Chocola, Ed Crane, Tom Davis, David Frum, Michael Gerson, Kevin Hassett, Doug Holtz-Eakin, Charles Krauthammer, William Kristol, Raoul Labrador, Steve LaTourette, Yuval Levin, Mick Mulvaney, Grover Norquist, Steve Schmidt, Craig Shirley, Vin Weber, and David Winston. The usual disclaimer—that the conclusions in this book are my own and that the many people who helped me should not be blamed for them—applies especially to this group.

Other conservative friends and colleagues have enriched my understanding of politics over many years of dialogue and argument. Exchanging views with David Brooks (weekly on NPR's *All Things Considered* and occasionally on PBS's *The News Hour*) is an enormous personal and professional joy. I will not implicate all of my conservative and libertarian interlocutors, but I should mention and thank Spencer Abraham, Saul Anuzis, Michael Barone, David Boaz, Glen Bolger, Karlyn Bowman, Arthur Brooks, John Buckley, Stuart Butler, Christopher Caldwell, Alex Castellanos, Matt Continetti, Michael Cromartie, Linda DiVall, Ross Douthat, Terry Eastland, John Engler, Tony Fabrizio, Frank Fahrenkopf, John Feehery, Andrew Ferguson, Newt Gingrich, Hugh Hewitt, Peter King, Brink Lindsey, Kevin Madden, Eddie Mahe, Mary Matalin, Bill McInturff, Ed Morrissey, Kate O'Beirne, Henry Olsen, Ramesh Ponnuru, Reihan Salam, Michael Strain, John Sununu (father and son), Lance Tarrance, and George F. Will. For their insights over a long period, many others should be named here, too, but at least some of them might be just as happy to be left off my list.

The late Robert Novak hid his kindness beneath his proudly gruff exterior, and the late William F. Buckley Jr. was very generous to me over the years, even though I cannot claim to have known him well.

Given my views, it's not surprising that I treasure the conversations I have had with moderate and liberal Republicans. I should say a special thanks to Jim Leach, William McKenzie, Connie Morella, Jack Quinn, and Chris Shays.

Many on all sides of politics helped me during reporting trips—those undertaken specifically for this book and during my political travels across the country over many years. I want to single out the staffs of the *Courier-Journal* in Kentucky and the *Clarion-Ledger* in Mississippi for their warm collegiality during my 2014 travels by way of underscoring how important state and local reporting remain in our new and challenging media system.

I have been criticized in the past, with justice, for the epic length of my acknowledgments. To save readers from an ungainly burden, I ask all who were thanked in my earlier books to consider themselves thanked again. A variety of political writers, historians, and political scientists whose work was so helpful to me are acknowledged in my bibliographic note. I'm grateful to them all.

In writing about the Democratic side of the 2008 and 2012 campaigns and the legislative and political struggles of the Obama years, I was informed by many people, only some of whom I can list here. They included David Axelrod, Melody Barnes, Joel Benenson, Bob Borosage, Bill Burton, James Carville, Bill Daley, Brendan Daly, Brian Deese, Rosa DeLauro, Shaun Donovan, Mo

Elleithee, Rahm Emanuel, Brian Fallon, Barney Frank, Al Franken, Geoff Garin, Anna Greenberg, Stan Greenberg, Mandy Grunwald, Peter Hart, Matt House, Cam Kerry, Tom Kahn, Celinda Lake, John Lawrence, Jack Lew, Bernadette Meehan, Mark Mellman, Guy Molyneux, Cecilia Munoz, David Obey, Peter Orszag, Jen Palmieri, Sharon Parrott, Dan Pfeiffer, David Price, Wendell Primus, Chuck Schumer, Gene Sperling, Neera Tanden, Chris Van Hollen, Kelly Welsh, Fred Yang, and Jeff Zients.

Bob Greenstein and his colleagues at the Center on Budget and Policy Priorities are indispensible guides to policy, budgets, and getting numbers right. They were extraordinarily helpful to me on all the budget fights described in this book.

Thanks to Robby Jones and Dan Cox of PRRI, brilliant and careful students of public opinion and partners on many joint polling projects. Thanks also to my Brookings Institution partner on those studies, Bill Galston, who teaches me new things about politics and philosophy every day. My friends at the Pew Research Center, among them Mike Dimock, Carroll Doherty, Scott Keeter, Claudia Deane, and Alan Cooperman, are always generous in responding to inquiries for data, including my sometimes complicated cross-tabulation requests. Exactly the same is true of the great polling staff at the *Washington Post*. Great thanks to Peyton Craighill and Scott Clement. The late Andy Kohut, who founded Pew, was a dear friend and a model for deeply engaged but utterly unbiased social science research. I miss him still.

This book is built on reporting and reflection over many years of writing about American politics. For the opportunity to see American political life up close, to crisscross our nation over and over, and to meet politicians, activists, and citizens in almost every state, I thank both the *New York Times* and the *Washington Post*. From 1975 through 1989 (with some time out in Europe and the Middle East between 1983 and 1986), I wrote about various levels of politics for the *Times*, and I will always be grateful for the experience. Some of my reporting in those years—on the complicated fight inside the Democratic Party in 1976 that led to Jimmy Carter's victory, the rise of Ronald Reagan and George H. W. Bush's triumph in 1988—is important to this account. I found a home at the *Washington Post* in 1990, first as a political reporter and then, after 1993, as a columnist.

This book had an interactive relationship with my column and my work at the *Post*. Some of my reporting for the *Post* was extremely important to this account, notably key parts of a long interview with George W. Bush in 1998 for the *Washington Post Magazine*. At various points, I also draw on conclusions from my columns, since the reporting they involved gave me a courtside seat to many of the events described here. At the same time, reporting undertaken specifically for this book and made possible by a modest but very helpful book advance—particularly my road trips in 2014, research into the history of conservatism, and my interviews with conservative leaders and thinkers—fed back into columns that I could not have written had I not been working on this volume.

The list of people to whom I owe debts at the *Post* is long, and I have enumerated many of them in earlier books. I reiterate my thanks to two old friends, Steve Luxenberg and David Ignatius, who were essential to making my time at the *Post* a great blessing; to the late Ben Bradlee, Len Downie, and Bob Kaiser for bringing me on; to the entire political staff whose brilliant guide over many years has been my friend Dan Balz; to the extraordinary people at the Washington Post Writers Group, who syndicate my column and edit it with me twice a week in a truly cooperative spirit: Alan Shearer, the maestro of the whole operation, and Richard Aldacushion, Karen Green, Sophie Yarborough, and, until they retired, Jim Hill and Anna Karavangelos. Thanks to the late Meg Greenfield for giving me the chance to write the column; to editorial page editor Fred Hiatt for good advice and the opportunity to offer my views to one of the world's most politically engaged audiences; to the deputy editorial page editor Jackson Diehl; and to Michael Larabee, our smart and level-headed op-ed editor, and Autumn Brewington, his excellent predecessor. The editors who make up the op-ed staff are hugely skilled; they are also a joy to deal with, week after week.

Thanks to my friends at *Democracy* journal, where I serve as chair of the editorial committee, particularly to Mike Tomasky and Elbert Ventura, superb editors and friends, and also to the magazine's founders, Ken Baer and Andrei Cherny. The first words written for this book, about Reform Conservatives, first saw light of day in *Democracy* and some of them appear in Chapter 15. I appreciated the opportunity, and the excellent first round of editing.

Thanks also to Harold Meyerson and my friends at *The American Prospect;* to Paul Baumann and his colleagues at *Commonweal;* and for many kindnesses, to Katrina vanden Heuvel of *The Nation.*

Two other institutions are central to my life: Georgetown University and the Brookings Institution. Thanks to all my colleagues at both places. At Georgetown, I owe particular debts to the university's president, Jack DeGioia, to the former dean of Georgetown Public Policy Institute, Judy Feder, and to the current dean of the McCourt School of Public Policy, Ed Montgomery. At Brookings, my debts to all my colleagues are legion. I should say a particularly thank you to Tom Mann and Brookings former president Michael Armacost for bringing me in; to its current president, Strobe Talbott; and to the vice president and director of Governance Studies, Darrell West (who shares my diehard devotion to Boston sports and to the politics of southeastern New England).

I especially need to underscore my debt and (let's just say it) love for Tom Mann. He is as fine and generous a friend and colleague as it's possible to find. He and Norm Ornstein (another dear and brilliant friend to whom I also owe many debts) wrote a brave book, *It's Even Worse Than It Looks,* that described the radicalization of the Republican Party and brought wide attention to the essential idea of asymmetric polarization. My thanks to Tom and Norm for sharing their ideas—and, in Norm's case, for also sharing a constant stream of new jokes.

My assistant, Elizabeth Thom, has gone through the book so many times that she could probably recite large parts of it from memory. She is a brilliant editor, thinker, researcher, organizer, diplomat, and political sage. I cannot say enough good things about her, but can't say all of them here except: my deepest thanks. Many thanks also to Elizabeth's predecessor, Ross Tilchin, who did great work in helping me organize the early stages of research and interviewing. He is great, too, as are Emily Luken and Korin Davis.

An exceptional group of interns helped me throughout the time I was working on this book. Thanks to Sarah Engell, Sean Foley, Natalie Gould, Luke Hill, Ben Huber, Megan Rogers, Alexander Snowdon, Laura Sorice, and Jeremy Waldron. Thanks also to research assistants at Georgetown, Janou Gordon and Sean Long, and also Jacob Lupfer.

I am very grateful to Anton Mueller of Bloomsbury USA for his flexibility and deep thoughtfulness, and to my agent, Gail Ross, who first broached the thought of my doing this book in a conversation with Alice Mayhew at Simon & Schuster. Gail is hands-on, very smart about politics as well as the book business, and she has a profound loyalty to her authors that all of us appreciate. Thanks to her for making this book possible.

At Simon & Schuster, let me first thank Carolyn Reidy, the CEO; Jonathan Karp, president and publisher; Stuart Roberts, assistant editor to Alice, who was with this book from beginning to end and is exceptionally energetic, careful, smart, and engaged; Tom Pitoniak, my copy editor; Phil Metcalf, a truly amazing production editor who went to extraordinary lengths to accommodate many rounds of revisions that let me keep up with a fast-moving story as Donald Trump rose and the Republican side of the House fell into turmoil; to the designers who did such a lovely job on the book, Ruth Lee-Mui and Jackie Seow; and to Julia Prosser, Stephen Bedford, and Richard Rhorer, who are working hard to get the word out.

This book is dedicated to my editor Alice Mayhew with love and admiration. We became friends many years before I had writing books in mind through our friends Peter and Peggy Steinfels and Harvey Cox. When I first met Alice, I had no idea what a legend she already was in publishing. I just liked her immediately because of her passion for ideas, history, books, people, and politics, and for her directness. A decade later, it was Alice who signed up my first book, *Why Americans Hate Politics*, and then two others. This time around, it was her idea that it was an excellent time for a book explaining the strange journey of the American right, and I thank her for reestablishing our partnership. Working with her on this project was a particular joy and she was engaged at every level. She not only had views on every political controversy discussed here, but extraordinary insight and knowledge (down to the precinct level, you might say), and a brilliant sense of how to organize an argument. I owe her a great debt, and it is an honor to offer this book to her.

Thanks to my sister, Lucie-Anne Dionne Thomas, for so many things, not the least being that we shared very nearly identical political trajectories, and for the same reasons; and also to her husband, Drew, and their wonderful daughter, my niece, Kim Dionne Thomas.

The usual thing is to thank your immediate family for living through a book with you, and mine was, indeed, magnificently encouraging whenever I retreated to my office to write, and cheerfully tolerant whenever I announced triumphantly that I had finally done final revisions—which never seemed to stay final.

Mary Boyle and I first met twenty-nine years ago on public transit, a fine thing for liberals to do and the surest sign of the extent to which my life has been a series of unearned blessings. This one brought many other blessings, including friendship with Mary's truly remarkable mother, Helen; her brothers Brian, Kevin, Mark, Chris, and Terry; and a splendid clan of nephews and nieces. It also brought us our children, James, Julia, and Margot.

I have been over the top about Mary and our kids (who are no longer kids) for many years. James, Julia, and Margot would disapprove of my doing it again here. To Mary, I'll simply express my abiding love, admiration, and gratitude, and my profound appreciation for your unerring instincts—political, philosophical, personal, literary, and moral. James, Julia, and Margot, you know how much delight and wonder you've brought us. You have taught me more than I will ever learn from any other source, and you inspire me to keep my mind open about politics, music, sports, books, religion, and everything else. My faith in the future comes from the knowledge that you'll be there to shape it.

A BRIEF
BIBLIOGRAPHIC ESSAY

It took time for academia and large parts of the journalistic world to take conservatism seriously. By way of underscoring liberal blindness to their very existence, conservatives are fond of citing the observation of Lionel Trilling, the great literary critic, in 1954. "In the United States at this time liberalism is not only the dominant but even the sole intellectual tradition," Trilling wrote in *The Liberal Imagination.* "For it is the plain fact that nowadays there are no conservative or reactionary ideas in general circulation."

Yet Trilling had a point: conservatism *was* largely marginalized in the academy and the intellectual world at the time he wrote, and New Deal ideas were still dominant in politics. William F. Buckley Jr. founded *National Review* a year later precisely to fill the void on the right that Trilling described. Why else would a magazine declare that it "stands athwart history, yelling Stop"?

Conservatism was, in fact, much stronger in the mid-1950s than either Trilling or Buckley allowed. But it took years for scholarship and journalism to catch up with what was happening. The rise of Ronald Reagan was the break point, a kind of shock to the system. Since 1980, there has been an outpouring of fine writing and research on conservative politics and conservative ideas. I have drawn, with gratitude, on this good work. While I have cited much of this work in my text and have included extensive notes to make my debts as clear as possible, I thought it useful to highlight books that were especially important to me in writing this one and also to include works that

I did not draw on directly but influenced my understanding over the years. Some of them might be of interest to those who want to explore different aspects of the rich conservative story, and my accounting includes books that offer points of view very different from my own. I would underscore that this brief essay does not cover all the works I cite, and it is by no means exhaustive. For brevity's sake, I have only included subtitles where I felt they were important in identifying the subject of a book.

At the outset, I honor conservative magazines that were essential to this work, particularly *National Review*, the *Weekly Standard*, *National Affairs*, the *Public Interest*, *Commentary*, and the *American Conservative*. I cannot cite all of the political journalists and bloggers who regularly enlighten me. On the progressive side, Jonathan Chait, Greg Sargent, Jonathan Cohn, Steve Benen, Joan Walsh, Paul Waldman, Tim Noah, Greg Dworkin and his colleagues at *Daily Kos*, and Ed Kilgore are a few of the legion of bloggers and political writers I have relied on. *National Review*'s "The Corner" and its political writers, particularly Ramesh Ponnuru, provide a constant flow of opinion and insight into conservative thinking. Others who have been helpful include *RedState.Com*; *HotAir.com*, particularly Ed Morrissey; Jennifer Rubin; and Hugh Hewitt. Three now-defunct libertarian magazines, *New Individualist Review*, the *Libertarian Review*, and *Inquiry*, are lively sources on that movement's origins and development. The volumes produced from the transcripts of the quadrennial campaign managers' conferences organized since 1972 by the Institute of Politics at the John F. Kennedy School of Government at Harvard are an exceptional source of postelection insight on presidential contests.

I leaned regularly on the very informative websites Vox, The Upshot at the *New York Times*, *The Atlantic*, and Wonkblog at the *Washington Post*, particularly Ezra Klein, Matt Yglesias, David Leonhardt, Emma Green, and Chris Ingraham.

There can be no understanding of the Goldwater-Reagan right absent of an awareness that many of its ideas and some of its organizational structures had their origins in anti–New Deal politics in the 1930s, spearheaded by business leaders in the Liberty League and other groups. Kim Phillips-Fein's *Invisible Hands: The Making of the Conservative Movement from the New Deal to Reagan* (Norton, 2009) was a breakthrough reminder of this past. Early on, the historian James T. Patterson provided a rich understanding of the old right in *Congressional Conservatism and the New Deal* (Praeger, 1981) and in his biography of Robert Taft, *Mr. Republican* (Houghton Mifflin, 1972). Richard Norton Smith's *Thomas E. Dewey and His Times* (Simon & Schuster, 1982) is a fine portrait of Taft's major protagonist in those early Republican fights. Leo Ribuffo told the story of *The Old Christian Right* (Temple University Press, 1983), covering the period from the Depression to the Cold War. Kevin M. Kruse's *One Nation Under God* (Basic Books, 2015) tells the little-known prehistory of the religious right in the 1950s.

Crucial to understanding the rise of conservatism in the New Deal Era is Ira Katznelson's extraordinary *Fear Itself: The New Deal and the Origins of Our Time* (Norton, 2013). Katznelson is especially enlightening on the role of race in the early decay of the New Deal coalition and pointed me toward Joseph E. Lowndes's essential book, *From the New Deal to the New Right: Race and the Southern Origins of Modern Conservatism* (Yale, 2008). Lowndes is especially important on Charles Wallace Collins's role in the Dixiecrat revolt. Also important on southern conservatism is Joseph Crespino, *In Search of Another Country: Mississippi and the Conservative Counterrevolution* (Princeton, 2007). A fine collection of essays from a left-of-center perspective is *The Rise and Fall of the New Deal Order, 1930–1980*, edited by Steve Fraser and Gary Gerstle (Princeton, 1989).

The best general and sympathetic introduction to postwar conservative thought is George H. Nash, *The Conservative Intellectual Movement in America: Since 1945* (Basic, 1979). I have gone back to Nash's essential book again and again over the years. Also helpful is Patrick Allitt's *The Conservatives: Ideas and Personalities Throughout American History* (Yale, 2009). From a very different point of view, a brilliant, deeply critical examination of American conservatism is Corey Robin's *The Reactionary Mind* (Oxford, 2011).

William F. Buckley Jr. wrote too many books to cite them all here. I would note that his Blackford Oakes thrillers provide an exceptionally entertaining look at the Cold War conservative mind and his *Flying High: Remembering Barry Goldwater* (New York: Basic Books, 2008) is an affecting and very personal look at Goldwater's rise. John Judis's *William F. Buckley Jr.* (Simon

& Schuster, 1988) is a superb biography that reflects a feeling for Buckley himself, for the movement he was building, and for the broad currents of American politics. I'd also recommend Judis's *The Paradox of American Democracy* (Routledge, 2001), an underappreciated work on the movement of business and the Establishment rightward. It can be seen as foreshadowing today's world of Super PACs. Two other helpful books on Buckley are Carl T. Bogus's *Buckley* (Bloomsbury, 2011) and Lee Edwards's brief *William F. Buckley Jr.: The Maker of a Movement* (ISI, 2010). Kevin J. Smant, *Principles and Heresies* (ISI, 2002), is a useful and sympathetic biography of Frank Meyer, the architect of conservative "fusionism."

Two books from the Goldwater period, both long out of print, illustrate the stakes of the battles of 1964 well. Ralph de Toledano's *The Winning Side* (Macfadden, 1964) made the case for Goldwater and included electoral analysis that proved very wrong in the short run but rather more accurate for the longer term. George F. Gilder and Bruce K. Chapman offered an eloquent argument for progressive Republicanism and a powerful critique of Goldwaterism in *The Party That Lost Its Head* (Knopf, 1966). Princeton University Press deserves praise for bringing Barry Goldwater's classic, *The Conscience of a Conservative*, back into print in 2007.

As I make clear in the text, Rick Perlstein is the author of the most definitive and also the liveliest account of the Goldwater campaign, *Before the Storm* (Nation Books, 2009). The cliché words of praise—anyone interested in American conservatism should read this book—are absolutely true of *Before the Storm*. I am indebted to Perlstein's account in many ways. One of the most important: his book encouraged me to find the controversial and especially revealing 1964 "Choice" ad for Goldwater on YouTube. I also found his *Invisible Bridge: The Fall of Nixon and the Rise of Reagan* (Simon & Schuster, 2014) extremely helpful. I truly wish that the conservative writer Craig Shirley had not—wrongly in my view—accused Perlstein of plagiarism; Perlstein, I thought, went out of his way to acknowledge Shirley's work on the 1976 campaign, *Reagan's Revolution: The Untold Story of the Campaign That Started It All* (Nelson Current, 2005). That book and Shirley's volume about the 1980 campaign, *Rendezvous with Destiny: Ronald Reagan and the Campaign That Changed America* (ISI Books, 2009) are both important and deeply researched, as Shirley used his standing as a conservative activist to gain access to important players. I appreciated the work Shirley did and also an off-the-record lunch he had with me early on in this project. A fine recent account that sees the 1964 contest as seminal for much that came later is Jonathan Darman's *Landslide: LBJ and Ronald Reagan at the Dawn of a New America* (Random House, 2014).

Geoffrey Kabaservice's *Rule and Ruin* (Oxford, 2012) is an enormous contribution to the history of American politics and the Republican Party, and it was important to me as I was writing this one. Kabaservice brings back to life the largely forgotten leaders of the Republican center and left—there was a Republican left back then—and he explains in compelling detail how the modern right buried Modern Republicanism. An excellent earlier look at the Republican center-left is Nicol C. Rae, *The Decline and Fall of Liberal Republicans* (Oxford, 1989). Bringing helpful attention to a figure largely lost to us today, David L. Stebenne's *Modern Republican: Arthur Larson and the Eisenhower Years* (Indiana University Press, 2006) tells the story of the man who tried to codify Eisenhower's worldview into a useable Republican ideology.

The first full accounting of the neoconservative movement, Peter Steinfels's *The Neoconservatives* (Simon & Schuster, 1979; new edition 2013), is still one of the best books on the subject. Two other fine treatments are Gary J. Dorrien, *The Neoconservative Mind* (Temple, 1989), and *Neoconservatism* by Justin Vaisse (Harvard, 2010). *The Neoconservative Persuasion* (Basic Books, 2011) is a comprehensive collection of essays by the late Irving Kristol, who is fairly called the Godfather of Neoconservatism. Brian Doherty's *Radicals for Capitalism* (PublicAffairs, 2007) is lively and stands as the definitive history of the modern libertarian movement.

Too many broad biographical works were helpful to me to list them all here. Sean Wilentz's *The Age of Reagan* (Harper, 2008) was especially useful as I wrote this account. Other fine biographical works include: Richard Reeves's *President Kennedy, President Nixon,* and *President Reagan* (Simon & Schuster, 1993, 2001, and 2005); Steven Ambrose's two volumes on *Eisenhower* (Simon & Schuster, 1983 and 1984) and his three volumes on *Nixon* (Simon & Schuster, 1988, 1989, and 1992); Robert Dallek, *Flawed Giant:*

Lyndon Johnson and His Times, 1961–1973 (Oxford, 1988); and Doris Kearns Goodwin, *Lyndon Johnson and the American Dream* (St. Martin's Griffin paperback, 1991). Matthew Dallek broke important ground in his account of Ronald Reagan's 1966 election as governor of California, *The Right Moment: Ronald Reagan's First Victory and the Decisive Turning Point in American Politics* (Free Press, 2000). Chris Matthews wrote two important books involving unlikely juxtapositions, *Kennedy & Nixon* (Simon & Schuster, 1996) and *Tip and the Gipper* (Simon & Schuster, 2013).

The pioneer of books recounting the drama of presidential elections is Theodore H. White, and his *Making of the President* series on the elections of 1960, 1964, 1968, and 1972 is still essential and engrossing reading. A truly remarkable book on the 1968 campaign is *An American Melodrama* (Viking, 1969), by Lewis Chester, Godfrey Hodgson, and Bruce Page. Jules Witcover wrote the essential book on 1976, *Marathon: The Pursuit of the Presidency, 1972–1976* (Viking, 1977). Witcover and Jack Germond wrote very helpful books on the campaigns of 1980, 1984, 1988, and 1992.

Patrick J. Buchanan's *The Greatest Comeback* (Crown Forum, 2014) is an excellent inside look at the 1968 campaign and a guide to the divided mind of Richard Nixon. It added greatly to my understanding of the forces at work inside the Republican Party, and I thank Buchanan for an exceptionally enlightening interview. From a different point of view, Stephen Hess's delightful *The Professor and the President* (Brookings, 2014) illustrates Nixon's complexity by examining his relationship with Daniel Patrick Moynihan. Greg Weiner's book *American Burke: The Uncommon Liberalism of Daniel Patrick Moynihan* (University Press of Kansas, 2015) helped crystallize some of my intuitions about conservatism and also about Nixon and Moynihan.

Two shrewd ventures in electoral analysis during the Nixon years saw and understood how conservative victories would be won, and shaped popular and activist views of politics for decades: Kevin Phillips, *The Emerging Republican Majority* (originally published in 1969; republished by Princeton, 2014); and Richard M. Scammon and Ben J. Wattenberg, *The Real Majority* (Coward-McCann, 1970). By 1982, Phillips was describing the instability of the Reagan Coalition in *Post-Conservative America* (Random House, 1982). These books clearly inspired John B. Judis and Ruy Teixeira to offer *The Emerging*

Democratic Majority (Scribner, 2002) at a time when few saw the possibility. Although Judis developed some second thoughts about their thesis in 2015, the book foresaw the Obama Coalition.

In writing about the Clinton years, I kept going back to John F. Harris's definitive *The Survivor* (Random House, 2005), an extraordinarily complete and lively account; and to Steven M. Gillon's *The Pact* (Oxford, 2008), which focuses on the Clinton-Gingrich relationship.

A fine early look at George W. Bush's presidency is the collection of historical essays edited by Julian E. Zelizer, *The Presidency of George W. Bush* (Princeton, 2010). Thomas B. Edsall's *Building Red America* (Basic Books, 2006) is a shrewd and extremely well-reported examination of the realignment strategy Bush and Karl Rove hoped to execute, written just before the strategy went awry. Also enlightening is Lou Cannon and Carl M. Cannon, *Reagan's Disciple: George W. Bush's Troubled Quest for a Presidential Legacy* (PublicAffairs, 2008).

For differing perspectives on compassionate conservatism, see Michael Gerson's *Heroic Conservatism* (HarperOne, 2007); Marvin Olasky's *Renewing American Compassion* (Regnery, 1987) and *Compassionate Conservatism* (Free Press, 2000); David Kuo, *Tempting Faith* (Free Press, 2007); and John J. DiIulio, *Godly Republic* (University of California Press, 2008).

I am especially indebted to my friends and colleagues Dan Balz and Haynes Johnson. Their book *The Battle for America 2008* (Viking, 2009) was essential to me here, as was Balz's excellent volume on Obama's reelection, *Collision 2012* (Viking, 2013). Both books tell the story of both elections straight and with great insight. I worked closely with Dan in the early 1990s; he is, quite simply, one of the most generous and warmhearted people in journalism. John Heilemann and Mark Halperin's *Game Change* (Harper, 2010) is a jaunty insider account of 2008 saga that provides particular insight on the rise of Sarah Palin.

Another debt obvious in these pages is to Jonathan Alter's two indispensable works on the Obama presidency, *The Promise* and *The Center Holds* (Simon & Schuster, 2010 and 2013). These books will provide guide posts to historians for many years to come. Two good looks at Obama's economic policies are Michael Grunwald's *The New New Deal* and Noam Scheiber's *The*

Escape Artists (both Simon & Schuster, 2012). Chuck Todd's *The Stranger: Barack Obama in the White House* (Little Brown, 2014) is a deeply reported, critical view of Obama's use of power. The long-term trend toward political polarization and its impact in the Obama years is brilliantly documented in Alan I. Abramowitz, *The Disappearing Center* (Yale, 2010). James T. Kloppenberg's *Reading Obama* (Princeton, 2010) is a brilliant look at how the president thinks.

Kate Zernike's *Boiling Mad: Inside Tea Party America* (Times Books, 2010) shows how a good beat reporter can provide timely insight into a new movement even when it baffles so many. Two important early academic studies of the Tea Party are Theda Skocpol and Vanessa Williamson, *The Tea Party and the Remaking of American Conservatism* (Oxford, 2011), and Matt A. Barreto and Christopher S. Parker, *Change They Can't Believe In* (Princeton, 2014). A sympathetic view of the Tea Party is provided in Scott Rasmussen and Doug Schoen, *Mad as Hell: How the Tea Party Movement Is Fundamentally Remaking Our Two-Party System* (HarperCollins, 2010). Robert Draper's *When the Tea Party Came to Town* (Simon & Schuster, 2013) is an essential book on the Republican House elected in 2010 and was very helpful to me here. Alec Magillis's *The Cynic: The Political Education of Mitch McConnell* (Simon & Schuster, 2014) is also invaluable. Thomas F. Schaller's *The Stronghold* (Yale, 2015) is extremely insightful on how Republicans built their congressional bastion and the problems this creates for them.

Several general histories cover overlapping parts of the story told here. A thoughtful and provocative history of the United States from 1945 to the George W. Bush years that I draw on at key points is Joshua B. Freeman, *American Empire* (Penguin 2012). A valuable political history that points to links between Roosevelt and Reagan is Michael Barone's *Our Country* (Free Press, 1990). Everyone who cares about our nation's story should read Godfrey Hodgson's *America in Our Time* (Doubleday, 1976), which covers the period from the end of World War II to Nixon's presidency. Heather Cox Richardson's *To Make Men Free: A History of the Republican Party* (Basic Books, 2014) is an interesting revisionist view that stresses the role of "Lincoln Republicans" such as Teddy Roosevelt and Dwight Eisenhower and how their efforts to use government to promote economic opportunity were regularly foiled by the party's conservative wing.

Two valuable looks at the Great Society are G. Calvin Mackenzie and Robert Weisbrot, *The Liberal Hour: Washington and the Politics of Change in the 1960s* (Penguin, 2008), and Julian E. Zelizer, *The Fierce Urgency of Now* (Penguin, 2015). On the New Left, Todd Gitlin's *The Sixties* (Bantam, 1987) is masterly and essential; also important is Maurice Isserman and Michael Kazin, *The Civil War of the 1960s* (Oxford, 2011). A critical view of the 1960s that greatly influenced George W. Bush is Myron Magnet's *The Dream and the Nightmare: The Sixties' Legacy to the Underclass* (Encounter Books, 2000). Jefferson Cowie offers a rich account of cultural and economic change in the 1970s in *Stayin' Alive: The 1970s and the Last Days of the Working Class* (New Press, 2012). Daniel T. Rodgers's *Age of Fracture* (Belknap, 2011) is an unparalleled intellectual history of our time.

Memoirs from politicians and their top aides are underrated as sources of historical knowledge. Yes, memoirs reflect the view of those who write them and are typically selective in the slices of history they report. But they can still be richly informative. For this book, I found the following memoirs especially helpful: Richard Nixon's *RN* (Simon & Schuster, 1978); Bill Clinton's *My Life* (Knopf, 2004); Michael Waldman's *POTUS Speaks: Finding the Words That Defined the Clinton Presidency* (Simon & Schuster, 2000); Robert Novak, *The Prince of Darkness* (Three Rivers Press, 2007); Michael Gerson's *Heroic Conservatism;* George W. Bush's *Decision Points* (Broadway Paperbacks, 2010); Karl Rove's *Courage and Consequence* (Threshold Editions, 2010); and David Axelrod's *Believer* (Penguin Press, 2015). David Frum's many analytical writings as well as his reflections on his White House experience were also very instructive. His *Dead Right* (Basic Books, 1994) was an early warning to conservatives about the problems they faced.

Memoirs of conservative activists take us inside the mind of the movement and how it strategized its victories (and defeats). William A. Rusher's *The Rise of the Right* (William Morrow, 1984), which doubles as a history and a personal reminiscence, is a celebratory but candid account that helped guide me here. Two important contemporary memoirs of Goldwater's defeat from the inside are Stephen Shadegg's *What Happened to Goldwater?* (Holt, Rinehart & Winston, 1965) and F. Clifton White (with William J. Gill), *Suite 3505: The Story of the Draft Goldwater Movement* (Arlington House, 1967).

Scholarly views of conservatism in the 1950s and early 1960s often focused on the rise of the far right, and an important group of academics, notably Richard Hofstadter and Seymour Martin Lipset developed theories around the "status anxiety" experienced by supporters of right-wing movements. This view, carried too far, could be simply dismissive and may have contributed to the academy's difficulties in hearing what conservatives were saying and seeing why conservatism was on the rise. Christopher Lasch, one of Hofstadter's greatest students, said that "instead of arguing with opponents," advocates of this view "simply dismissed them on psychiatric grounds." Nonetheless, these scholars also provided important insights into extremism—their work received wide new attention after the rise of the Tea Party—and their insistence that the radical right represented "pseudo-conservatism" still has relevance for today. The definitive collection of their essays is Daniel Bell, ed., *The Radical Right* (Anchor Books, 1964). Also important are Richard Hofstadter, *The Paranoid Style in American Politics* (first published as an essay in 1964, reissued by Vintage, 2008); and Seymour Martin Lipset and Earl Raab, *The Politics of Unreason: Right-Wing Extremism in America, 1790–1977* (originally published by Harper & Row in 1970; updated edition, Chicago, 1978).

The rise of Reagan let loose a new wave of historical scholarship on conservatism that tended to take the movement on its own terms, even when the works were critical or partly so. One of the best collections of the work of these new historians is Bruce J. Schulman and Julian E. Zelizer, eds., *Rightward Bound: Making America Conservative in the 1970s* (Harvard, 2008). See also Mary C. Brennan, *Turning Right in the Sixties: The Conservative Capture of the GOP* (University of North Carolina, 1995); Lisa McGirr's *Suburban Warriors: The Origins of the New American Right* (Princeton, 2001), a careful examination of the rise of the right from the bottom up in California's Orange County; Dan T. Carter, *The Politics of Rage: George Wallace, The Origins of the New Conservatism, and the Transformation of American Politics* (Simon & Schuster, 1995); Jonathan Reider, *Canarsie: The Jews and Italians of Brooklyn Against Liberalism* (Harvard, 1985); David T. Crichlow, *The Conservative Ascendancy: How the GOP Right Made History* (Harvard, 2007); and Steven M.

Teles, *The Rise of the Conservative Legal Movement* (Princeton, 2008). This list only scratches the surface, and those interested in a much fuller accounting of the new scholarship exploring the American right should consult Kim Phillips-Fein, "Conservatism: A State of the Field," in the *Journal of American History* (December, 2011). Fein rightly notes that over the past two decades, the study of conservatism "has been one of the most dynamic subfields in American history."

It may be a harbinger of a new period of conservative self-scrutiny that another revival of interest in the thought of Edmund Burke is under way. My views on Burke were especially influenced by a recent book from a Conservative member of the British Parliament, Jesse Norman, *Edmund Burke: The First Conservative* (Basic Books, 2013). Yuval Levin offered *The Great Debate: Edmund Burke, Thomas Paine, and the Birth of Right and Left* (Basic Books, 2014). Levin is the informal leader of the Reform Conservative movement and his book offers insight into the background assumptions of the new disposition. David Bromwich's *The Intellectual Life of Edmund Burke* (Harvard, 2014) is a major new scholarly work on the complexity of Burke's thinking.

Joe Scarborough's *The Right Path: From Ike to Reagan, How Republicans Once Mastered Politics—and Can Again* (Random House, 2013) is a lively look at the GOP and especially important for being the rare book by a conservative that reads Eisenhower back into the history of conservatism. My friend John Kenneth White recently published *What Happened to the Republican Party? And What It Means for American Presidential Politics* (Routledge, 2016). The perspective he offers in his fine extended essay is quite compatible with my own.

Several recent works on American politics influenced my overall view, as is clear from my text. Thomas E. Mann and Norman Orenstein's *It's Even Worse Than It Looks* (Basic, 2012) is one of our era's most important books on politics and opened many eyes to the asymmetric nature of polarization. Both are dear and generous friends who have shared their insights over many years. Two books by Jacob S. Hacker and Paul Pierson, *Off Center* (Yale, 2006) and *Winner-Take-All Politics* (Simon & Schuster, 2010), are essential to understanding the radicalization of the right. Two eloquent polemics reflect the frustrations this radicalization has called forth from thinkers who hold broadly moderate views: Sam Tanenhaus's *The Death of Conservatism* (Random House, 2009) and Alan Wolfe's *Return to Greatness* (Princeton, 2005).

And despite my skepticism about developments on the right over the last fifty years, I turn regularly to two books that remind me of my underlying respect for conservative thought: Robert A. Nisbet's *Tradition and Revolt* (Vintage, 1970) and William F. Buckley Jr.'s *Gratitude: Reflections on What We Owe Our Country* (Random House, 1990).

I got a copy of Phyllis Schlafly's *A Choice Not an Echo* (Pere Marquette Press, 1964) when I was a preteen fascinated by politics. It has been sitting on my bookshelves for more than fifty years. Few brief, highly polemical tracts have done more to change the trajectory of American politics and American history. To say I disagree with Schlafly is an understatement. But I'm glad I kept the book.

NOTES

INTRODUCTION

2 "The Republican Party created Donald Trump": Erick Erickson quoted in Molly Ball, "Donald Trump and the Search for the Republican Soul," *Atlantic* (August 13, 2015).

3 The numbers tell the story: NBC News/Wall Street Journal Survey, January 2015.

4 "unity of purpose over conflict and discord": President Barack Obama, Inaugural Address, January 21, 2009.

4 On the roots of contemporary conservatism in the reaction of conservative business groups to the New Deal, the definitive account is Kim Phillips-Fein, *Invisible Hands: The Making of the Conservative Movement from the New Deal to Reagan* (New York: Norton, 2009). An earlier look at the role of the anti–New Deal backlash in creating contemporary American conservatism is Michael W. Miles, *The Odyssey of the American Right* (New York: Oxford University Press, 1980). There is a rich scholarship on the rise of the conservative movement. A good brief overview is Mary C. Brennan, *Turning Right in the Sixties: The Conservative Capture of the GOP* (Chapel Hill: University of North Carolina Press, 1995). An excellent look at the rise of the right from the bottom up in California's Orange County is Lisa McGirr's *Suburban Warriors: The Origins of the New American Right* (Princeton: Princeton university Press, 2001). A fine recent account that sees the 1964 contest between Lyndon Johnson and Barry Goldwater as seminal for much that came later is Jonathan Darman's *Landslide: LBJ and Ronald Reagan at the Dawn of a New America* (New York: Random House, 2014). Matthew Dallek broke important ground in his account of Ronald Reagan's 1966 election as governor of California in *The Right Moment: Ronald Reagan's First Victory and the Decisive Turning Point in American Politics* (New York: Free Press, 2000). An affecting and very personal look at Goldwater's rise is William F. Buckley Jr.'s *Flying High: Remembering Barry Goldwater* (New York: Basic books, 2008). Dan T. Carter, *The Politics of Rage: George Wallace, The Origins of the New Conservatism, and the Transformation of American Politics* (New York: Simon & Schuster, 1995), is essential to understanding the role of race—and George Wallace in particular—in the rise of the new conservative coalition. Also see Patrick Allitt, *The Conservatives: Ideas and Personalities Throughout American History* (New Haven: Yale University Press, 2009).

5 when the right was at its turning point: Clinton Rossiter, *Conservatism in America*, 2nd ed., revised (Cambridge, MA: Harvard University Press, 1962), p. 180.

5 "as a bland moderate": Joe Scarborough, *The Right Path: From Ike to Reagan, How Conservatives Once Mastered Politics—and Can Again* (New York: Random House, 2013), p. 18.

6 "radical rich": David Frum, "Crashing the Party," *Foreign Affairs*, September/October 2014.

6 "the insurgent outlier in American politics": Thomas Mann and Norman Ornstein, *It's Even Worse Than It Looks: How the American Constitutional System Collided with the New Politics of Extremism* (New York: Basic Books, 2012), p. 185.

7 But radicalization: One Republican strategist acutely aware of this problem is Whit Ayers, who detailed his party's challenges in his book *2016 and Beyond: How Republicans Can Elect a President in the New America* (Alexandria, VA: Resurgent Republic Press, 2015). Ayers writes: "Demographic groups that form the core of Republican support—older whites, blue-collar whites, married people and rural residents—are declining as a proportion of the electorate. Demographic groups where the party is weak—minorities, young people, single women—are growing" (p. 7). My thanks to Ayers for a series of enlightening conversations. As a loyal Republican and conservative, he will no doubt disagree with many of my conclusions in this book, although we agree on the GOP's long-term demographic problem.

8 only 39 percent of conservatives were over fifty: The Pew Research Center calculated these numbers for me from their surveys. My thanks to Michael Dimmock, Carroll Doherty, and Scott Keeter for their assistance here and for other very helpful polling information. And thanks to Andy Kohut, the founder of the center, for help on polling matters over more than three decades.

9 revealing term "Establishment Tea": Rich Lowry and Ramesh Ponnuru, "Establishment Tea," *National Review,* July 7, 2014.

9 "the current Republican majority in the Senate": Jacob S. Hacker and Paul Pierson, "No Cost for Extremism," *American Prospect,* Spring 2015, pp. 71, 72.

10 Republicans won in 2010 and 2014: On the tendency of midterm nonvoters to be in more Democratic groups see Lindsey Cook, "Midterm Turnout Down in 2014," *U.S. News & World Report,* November 5, 2014.

12 Richard Nixon's health care initiatives: Ben Stein, "RN's Health Care Plan More Comprehensive than Obama's," April 1, 2010, blog posting at http://www.nixonfoundation.org.

12 In 2014, the Pew Research Center: Andrew Kohut, "Are the Democrats Getting Too Liberal?," *Washington Post,* February 28, 2014.

12 Among Democrats, 59 percent: "Support for Compromise Rises, Except Among Republicans," Pew Research Center, January 17, 2013, http://www.people-press.org/files/legacy-pdf/01-17-13%20Political%20Release.pdf.

12 27 percent of Democrats saw Republicans: Carroll Doherty, "Which Party Is More to Blame for Political Polarization? It Depends on the Measure," Pew Research Center, June 17, 2014, http://www.pewresearch.org/fact -tank/2014/06/17/which-party-is-more-to-blame-for-political-polarization-it-depends-on-the-measure/.

13 the Republicans have turned much more: Christopher Ingraham, "This Astonishing Chart Shows How Moderate Republicans Are an Endangered Species," *Washington Post* Wonkblog, June 2, 2015, http://www .washingtonpost.com/blogs/wonkblog/wp/2015/06/02/this-astonishing-chart-shows-how-republicans-are-an -endangered-species/.

13 traditional Washington habit: Thomas Mann and Norman Ornstein, "Let's Just Say It: The Republicans Are the Problem," *Washington Post,* April 27, 2012.

13 "Over the past five years": David Frum, "Don't Knock the Reform Conservatives," *Atlantic,* July 10, 2014.

14 conservatism . . . is primarily interested: Corey Robin, *The Reactionary Mind: Conservatism from Edmund Burke to Sarah Palin* (New York: Oxford University Press, 2011), p. 7.

14 conservatism is a "disposition": Philip Wallach and Justus Myers, "The Conservative Governing Disposition," *National Affairs,* Summer 2014, p. 128.

16 movement bestseller: Phyllis Schlafly, *A Choice Not an Echo* (Alton, IL: Pere Marquette Press, 1964), quotations from the cover material and p. 6; Taft defeat, pp. 33–68.

17 metaphors related to the market: On the power of market metaphors, see Daniel T. Rodgers, *Age of Fracture* (Cambridge, MA: Belknap Press of Harvard University Press, 2011), pp. 41–76. The book is a superb marriage of intellectual and political history.

18 Dwight Eisenhower won: Eisenhower votes from Gallup 1956 poll and Nixon votes from Gallup 1960 poll.

19 As recently as 2004: Ibid.

19 In 2012, Mitt Romney: "Latino Voters in the 2012 Election," Pew Research Center, November 7, 2012.

24 "What has happened to our party?": Kasich quoted in Daniel Strauss, "Kasich Lashes Out: 'What Has Happened to the Conservative Movement?'" *Politico,* October 28, 2015.

1. THE AMBIGUOUS HERO

28 "There is something a bit strange": Chris McDaniel's primary night speech, June 24, 2014, http://www.c-span .org/video/?320130-3/chris-mcdaniel-primary-night-speech.

28 "That's not an easy vote to cast": "Mississippi 2014 Senate Election: Anatomy of a Takedown," *Politico,* June 2014, http://www.politico.com/story/2014/02/mississippi-2014-election-thad-cochran-chris-mcdaniel-103644 _Page2.html.

28 "The preservation of liberty and freedom": Sons of Confederate Veterans website, http://www.scv.org/.

29 $3.07 back from the federal government: John Kiernan, "2015's States Most & Least Dependent on the Federal Government," WalletHub, http://wallethub.com/edu/states-most-least-dependent-on-the-federal-government /2700/.

29 It ranks number one: Richard Borean, "Monday Map: Federal Aid as a Percentage of State General Revenue," Tax Foundation, June 18, 2013, http://taxfoundation.org/blog/monday-map-federal-aid-percentage-state-gen eral-revenue.

30 Between the primary and the runoff: Nate Cohn, "Big Jump in Turnout is Key in Thad Cochran's Victory," *New York Times,* June 25, 2014.

31 On Walker and Cruz and Reagan: K Biswas, "God and Guns and the Grand Old Party," *New Statesman* (September 4–10, 2015); on Rubio as Reagan's heir: Paul Kengor, "Marco Rubio Seizes the Reagan Mantle," *American Spectator* (May, 19, 2015), http://spectator.org/articles/62763/marco-rubio-seizes-reagan-mantle.

31 Reagan . . . raised taxes: Jon Perr, "Ronald Reagan, the President Who Really Negotiated with Terrorists," Daily Kos blog, June 1, 2014, http://www.dailykos.com/story/2014/06/01/1303690/-Ronald-Reagan-the-President -who-really-negotiated-with-terrorists#.

32 "They confuse tactics with principles": Craig Shirley, "Reagan, Then and Now: Commentators and Politicians and Underestimating Him—Again," *National Review*, June 4, 2014, http://www.craigshirley.com/article/reagan-then-and-now/

32 totaling $2.8 trillion: Peter Beinart, "Think Again: Ronald Reagan: The Gipper Wasn't the Warhound His Conservative Followers Would Have You Think," *Foreign Policy*, June 7, 2010, http://foreignpolicy.com/2010/06/07/think-again-ronald-reagan/.

32 "Those sons of bitches": Barron Youngsmith, "New Republic: The Romney Doctrine," NPR, November 28, 2011, http://www.npr.org/2011/11/28/142843202/new-republic-the-romney-doctrine.

33 "in the use of military power": Rand Paul, "Buckley's Realist Foreign Policy," *National Review*, April 22, 2014, http://www.nationalreview.com/article/376307/buckleys-realist-foreign-policy-sen-rand-paul.

33 Grenada gave him: Beinart, "Think Again."

33 grumbled that Reagan: Duncan Currie, "Whose Reagan Is It, Anyway?," *National Review*, July 2, 2009, http://www.nationalreview.com/corner/184200/whose-reagan-it-anyway-duncan-currie.

33 "like a punctured balloon": Beinart, "Think Again."

33 Paul argued that Reagan: Rand Paul, "America Shouldn't Choose Sides in Iraq War," *Wall Street Journal*, June 19, 2014, http://www.wsj.com/articles/sen-rand-paul-america-shouldnt-choose-sides-in-iraqs-civil-war-1403219558.

34 And then came the swipe: Rick Perry, "Isolationist Policies Make the Threat of Terrorism Even Greater," *Washington Post*, July 11, 2014, http://www.washingtonpost.com/opinions/rick-perry-isolationist-policies-make-the-threat-of-terrorism-even-greater/2014/07/11/6dbfba4a-06f0-11e4-bbf1-cc51275e7f8f_story.html.

35 Reagan was always: Rand Paul, "Rick Perry Is Dead Wrong," *Politico*, July 14, 2014, http://www.politico.com/magazine/story/2014/07/rick-perry-is-dead-wrong-108860.html#.VRmtI_nF8kR.

36 "All sides take": Jonathan Chait, "Rand Paul, Rick Perry Holding a Reagan-Off," *New York*, July 14, 2014, http://nymag.com/daily/intelligencer/2014/07/rand-paul-rick-perry-holding-a-reagan-off.html.

37 "I bet the hard-liners": Lou Cannon, "Gorbachev Sincere, Reagan Tells Aides," *Washington Post* (November 23, 1985), http://www.washingtonpost.com/archive/politics/1985/11/23/gorbachev-sincere-reagan-tells-aides/64b0b373-0343-4373-9f39-d12b17530ec7/.

37 "not a contagious disease": Reagan 1978 op-ed reprinted in Gerald Magliocca, "Ronald Reagan and Gay Rights, concurringopinions.com (October 18, 2010), http://concurringopinions.com/archives/2010/10/ronald-reagan-and-gay-rights.html.

2. IN THE SHADOW OF GOLDWATER

38 "in the reaction against the New Deal": Kim Phillips-Fein, *Invisible Hands: The Making of the Conservative Movement from the New Deal to Reagan* (New York: Norton, 2009), pp. xii and 10–11.

39 "the wingnut sun": Rick Perlstein, "The Grand Old Tea Party: Why Today's Wacko Birds Are Just Like Yesterday's Wingnuts," *Nation*, November 25, 2013, http://www.thenation.com/article/177018/grand-old-tea-party#

39 "yelling stop": William Buckley Jr., "Our Mission Statement," *National Review*, November 19, 1955, http://www.nationalreview.com/article/223549/our-mission-statement-william-f-buckley-jr.

40 "two main strands of conservatism,": Kevin Smant, *Principles and Heresies: Frank S. Meyer and The Shaping of the American Conservative Movement* (Wilmington, DE: ISI Books, 2002), p. 94.

40 Donald Devine, a conservative: Donald Devine, quoted in Dionne, *Why Americans Hate Politics* (New York: Simon & Schuster, 1991), p. 161.

41 "monopoly on sophisticated information": Sam Tanenhaus, *The Death of Conservatism* (New York: Random House Paperbacks, 2001), 46.

42 "We cannot reestablish": Dan Smoot Report, YouTube video, https://www.youtube.com/watch?v=1NvLsKeOlmY&app=desktop.

42 "over a million gave": Rick Perlstein, *Before the Storm: Barry Goldwater and the Unmaking of the American Consensus* (New York: Nation Books, 2009), p. 475.

42 bestseller list: *New York Times* bestseller list, July 27, 2014, http://www.nytimes.com/best-sellers-books/2014-07-27/hardcover-nonfiction/list.html.

43 "maneuvered into nominating": Phyllis Schlafly, *A Choice Not an Echo* (Washington, DC: Regnery, 1964), p. 25.

44 "deprived the American people": Ralph de Toledano, *The Winning Side: The Case for Goldwater Republicanism* (New York: Macfadden Books, 1964), p. 196; "The dominant consensus of this country": p. 11; "the Democratic coalition formed:" pp. 8–9; "In its economic principles" and reference to Calhoun: p. 29; later reference in chapter to Electoral College votes for Rockefeller and Goldwater: pp. 81–83.

45 CIO unions in particular: Ira Katznelson, *Fear Itself: The New Deal and the Origins of Our Time* (New York: Norton, 2013). Southern Democrats defecting and all other references come from Chapter 5, "Jim Crow Congress," pp. 156–94.

45 In late 1937: James T. Patterson, *Congressional Conservatism and the New Deal* (Lexington: University of Kentucky Press, 1967), p. 205.

46 "We insist upon": Ibid.

46 "new meanings to old words": Charles Wallace Collins, *Whither Solid South* (New Orleans: Pelican, 1947). The

story of this book is told well in Joseph E. Lowndes, *From New Deal to the New Right* (New Haven: Yale University Press, 2008), pp. 11–45; see also Katznelson, *Fear Itself,* pp. 139–44.

47 "the strongest party in the country": Lowndes, *From New Deal to the New Right,* 25.

47 "the advanced race": "Why the South Must Prevail," editorial, *National Review,* August 24, 1957, http://adam gomez.files.wordpress.com/2012/03/whythesouthmustprevail-1957.pdf.

48 "In the South": William F. Buckley Jr., *Up from Liberalism* (New York: Hillman Books, 1961), pp. 146–47.

49 Rusher proudly noted: William A. Rusher, "Crossroads for the GOP," *National Review,* February 12, 1963. My thanks to *NR*'s Ramesh Ponnuru for asking the magazine's library to retrieve this article for me, which its staff kindly did. Rusher discusses the article and its impact in his enlightening history-cum-memoir, *The Rise of the Right* (New York: William Morrow, 1984), pp. 137–38.

49 yet his map: de Toledano, *The Winning Side,* pp. 72–85.

50 "It has been the dominating ambition": Buckley Jr., *Up from Liberalism,* 114.

51 the heart of Goldwaterism: Barry Goldwater, *The Conscience of a Conservative* (1960; reprint, Princeton: Princeton University Press, 2007), p. 15.

51 plenty of specifics: Ibid., pp. 19, 61, 83, and 85–86.

51 immediately ordered 2,500 copies: Perlstein, *Before the Storm,* p. 62.

55 Goldwater salvaged only: 1964 Presidential General Election Results from the U.S. Election Atlas, http://uselectionatlas.org/RESULTS/national.php?year=1964.

56 whether the GOP would be best served: Rusher, "Crossroads for the GOP," *National Review,* February 12, 1963.

57 "With your help": Charles Mohr, "Goldwater Hits U.S. Moral 'Rot,'" *New York Times,* October 11, 1964, http://www.nytimes.com/1964/10/11/goldwater-hits-us-moral-rot.html?_r=1.

57 They called it: "Choice," https://www.youtube.com/watch?v=xniUoMiHm8g.

58 The outcry against: Perlstein, *Before the Storm,* p. 496.

58 Goldwater's key moneymen: Theodore H. White, *The Making of the President 1964* (New York: Atheneum, 1965).

60 "the trouble with": Ronald Reagan's "A Time for Choosing" speech, October 27, 1964.

62 "No modern precedent exists": George F. Gilder and Bruce Kerry Chapman, *The Party That Lost Its Head* (New York: Knopf, 1966), p. 213.

62 takeover of the party: Edward Brooke, *The Challenge of Change: Crisis in Our Two-Party System* (Boston: Little, Brown, 1966), p. 14.

62 The conservative southern: Ibid., p. 15.

63 "desperate condition": White, *The Making of the President 1964,* p. 385.

64 "The future of the Birch Society": Alan Westin, "The John Birch Society: 'Radical Right' and 'Extreme Left' in the Political Context of Post World War II," in *The Radical Right,* ed. Daniel Bell (New York: Anchor Books, 1964), p. 267.

3. FROM RADICALISM TO GOVERNING

67 During Dwight Eisenhower's presidency: See Arthur Larson, *A Republican Looks At His Party* (1956; reprint, Westport, CT: Greenwood Press, 1974), quotation on p. 10. Larson finally received the historical attention he deserves in David L. Stebenne, *Modern Republican: Arthur Larson and the Eisenhower Years* (Bloomington: Indiana University Press, 2006). An excellent look at the losing struggle of moderate and liberal Republicans is Nicol C. Rae, *The Decline and Fall of Liberal Republicans: From 1952 to the Present* (New York: Oxford University Press, 1989).

68 Chris Matthews's joint biography: Chris Matthews, *Kennedy and Nixon: The Rivalry That Shaped Postwar America* (New York: Simon & Schuster, 1996), p. 17.

68 Nixon was never: Richard Nixon's "The Silent Majority" speech, November 3, 1969.

69 Samuel Lubell, the public opinion: Sam Lubell, *The Future of American Politics* (New York: Harper, 1952), p. 200.

70 "were determined to capitalize on the underlying fragility": Julian Zelizer, *The Fierce Urgency of Now: Lyndon Johnson, Congress, and the Battle for the Great Society* (New York: Penguin Press, 2015), p. 247; "didn't believe that opposing": p. 250; Reagan and open housing: 254–255. Zelizer offers an excellent account of the breakdown on the civil rights coalition, the political impact of the period's riots, and the reaction against fair-housing laws on pp. 228–247. His account of the 1966 midterm campaign is on pp. 247–261.

70 But Geoffrey Kabaservice: Geoffrey Kabaservice, *Rule and Ruin: The Downfall of Moderation and the Destruction of the Republican Party, from Eisenhower to the Tea Party* (New York: Oxford University Press, 2012), p. 223.

71 The research-and-writing team: Patrick J. Buchanan, *The Greatest Comeback* (New York: Crown Forum, 2014), pp. 280–81.

72 Bell urged Nixon: Ibid.

72 Yet Nixon was torn: Ibid., pp. 281–82.

73 McGovern was tagged: Timothy Noah, "Acid, Amnesty, and Abortion: The Unlikely Source of a Legendary Smear," *New Republic,* October 22, 2012.

73 It came to light: Robert Novak, *The Prince of Darkness: 50 Years Reporting in Washington* (New York: Three Rivers Press, 2007), p. 226.

73 But the conservative rebels: Jeffrey Bell, William F. Buckley Jr., William Rusher, et al., "We Suspend Our Support," *National Review*, August 10, 1971.

73 Representative John Ashbrook of Ohio: "Chronology of Political Events: Jan. 1971–Nov. 1972," *CQ Almanac*, http://library.cqpress.com/cqalmanac/document.php?id=cqal72-1249975#.

74 He took to the op-ed pages: William Rusher, "The Nixon-McGovern Choice Is No Choice for Conservatives," *Los Angeles Times*, April 28, 1972.

74 Savoring in retrospect: Richard Nixon, *RN: The Memoirs of Richard Nixon* (New York: Simon & Schuster, 1978), pp. 761–64.

76 "The liberal wing of the Republican Party": Rick Perlstein, *The Invisible Bridge: The Fall of Nixon and the Rise of Reagan* (New York: Simon & Schuster, 2014), p. 670.

77 "Christine Jorgensen of the Republican Party": See Carl M. Cannon, "Jenner's Trail Was Blazed by Christine Jorgensen," *RealClearPolitics*, June 3, 2015.

78 He gave conservatives a rallying cry: James H. Broussard, *Ronald Reagan: Champion of Conservative America* (New York: Routledge, 2014), p. 87.

78 "Without Reagan's 1976 campaign": Craig Shirley, *Reagan's Revolution: The Untold Story of the Campaign That Started It All* (Nashville: Nelson Current, 2005), p. xxvii.

79 "When it comes to the Canal": Perlstein, *The Invisible Bridge*, p. 633.

79 He cited David Keene: Ibid.

80 "The conservative challenge": Kabaservice, *Rule and Ruin*, p. 347.

80 "We are going to forget the use of the word *détente*": Gerald Ford, *Public Papers of the Presidents of the United States: Gerald R. Ford, 1976–1977*, p. 185. See also Sean Wilentz, *The Age of Reagan* (New York: HarperCollins, 2008), p. 64, and Kabaservice, *Rule and Ruin*, p. 347.

80 Fearing that whatever: Kabaservice, *Rule and Ruin*, p. 347.

80 Reagan might have won: See Kabaservice, *Rule and Ruin*, p. 347; Perlstein, *The Invisible Bridge*, p. 594.

81 But there was a catch: Kabaservice, *Rule and Ruin*, p. 347.

82 Los Angeles County home values: Robert Kuttner, *Revolt of the Haves: Tax Rebellions and Hard Times* (New York: Simon & Schuster, 1980), pp. 51–55; "When inflation blended with": Kuttner, p. 93. A fascinating recent look at tax revolts in American history is Isaac William Martin, *Rich People's Movements: Grassroots Campaigns to Untax the One Percent* (New York: Oxford University Press, 2013).

83 In a three-way race: 1980 Presidential General Election Results, U.S. Election Atlas, http://uselectionatlas.org/RESULTS/national.php?year=1980.

85 "a community of values": Ronald Reagan, speech in acceptance of the Republican nomination for president, July 17, 1980.

86 "Capitalism begins with giving": George Gilder, *Wealth and Poverty* (New York: Bantam Books, 1981), p. 23.

86 "The highest goal of the political economy": Michael Novak, *The Spirit of Democratic Capitalism* (New York: AEI/Simon & Schuster, 1982), p. 357.

87 "I feel like we have sort of an amazing inheritance": MSNBC promotional video featuring Rachel Maddow, filmed in 2011.

88 The historian Joshua Freeman summarizes Reagan's fiscal legacy: Joshua Freeman, *American Empire: The Rise of a Global Power, the Democratic Revolution at Home* (New York: Penguin Books, 2012), pp. 374–75.

88 "weak claims, rather than weak claimants": Alice Rivlin and Isabel Sawhill, *Restoring Fiscal Sanity: How to Balance the Budget* (Washington, DC: Brookings Institution Press, 2004), p. viii.

89 Reagan failed to make a significant dent: Freeman, *American Empire*, p. 375.

89 "the poor and the urban working class": Ibid.

89 The national debt rose: See table from Treasury Direct website, https://www.treasurydirect.gov/govt/reports/pd/histdebt/histdebt_histo4.htm.

89 It fell back further: See the Office of Management and Budget Historical Tables on the budget, https://m.whitehouse.gov/omb/budget/Historicals.

90 But the tax cuts and the military spending: Freeman, *American Empire*, p. 380.

91 "People want to believe": Rick Perlstein, *Before the Storm: Barry Goldwater and the Unmaking of the American Consensus* (New York, Nation Books, 2009), p. 804.

91 "he changed course, moved on": Perlstein, *The Invisible Bridge*, p. 409.

91 Perlstein notes that: Ibid.

91 "thrived . . . on contradictions": Freeman, *American Empire*, p. 381.

92 "stabbed in the back": Sean Wilentz, *The Age of Reagan* (New York: HarperCollins, 2008), p. 148.

92 "governing as he had done": Ibid.

93 "If voters see a race as a nice-guy": E. J. Dionne Jr., *Why Americans Hate Politics* (New York: Simon & Schuster, 1991), p. 296.

4. THE END OF THE REAGAN MAJORITY

94 Lee Atwater: The fullest biography of Atwater is John Brady, *Bad Boy: The Life and Politics of Lee Atwater* (Reading, MA: Addison-Wesley, 1997).

95 "hooked up to jumper cables": E. J. Dionne Jr., "Fierce GOP Partisan Harvey Lee Atwater," *New York Times*, November 18, 1988.

96 Atwater knew exactly: Atwater spoke very candidly at the Harvard Institute of Politics Election Conference. See also David Runkle, ed., *Campaign for President: The Manager's Look at '88* (Dover, MA: Auburn House, 1989), pp. 33–34.

96 "Guess what? They would have": Runkle, ed., *Campaign for President*, p. 112.

98 But in an interview shortly before his death: "Gravely Ill, Atwater Offers Apology," *New York Times*, January 12, 1991, original interview from *Life*, February 1991.

99 Bush's approval rating hit an astonishing: "Presidential Approval Ratings," Gallup Historical Statistics and Trends, http://www.gallup.com/poll/116677/presidential-approval-ratings-gallup-historical-statistics-trends.aspx.

99 His reasoning was explained: Charles Pope, "Cheney Changed His View on Iraq," *Seattle Post-Intelligencer*, September 28, 2004.

99 After his 1991 highs: "Presidential Approval Ratings," Gallup Historical Statistics and Trends, http://www.gallup.com/poll/116677/presidential-approval-ratings-gallup-historical-statistics-trends.aspx.

100 "Read my lips": No new taxes: George H. W. Bush, speech in acceptance of the Republican nomination for president, August 18, 1988.

101 The result on October 5, 1990, was a humiliation: David Rosenbaum, "Budget Plan Fails First House Test by 254–179," *New York Times*, October 5, 1990.

101 Democrats, on the other hand: See final roll call votes on the Omnibus Budget Reconciliation Act of 1990: http://clerk.house.gov/evs/1990/roll475.xml.

101 The elder Bush: Beth Marlowe and Chris Cillizza, "George H. W. Bush Backs Romney, Criticizes Gingrich," *Washington Post*, December 22, 2011.

102 "It is a philosophy of progressive moderation": Prescott Bush, Lincoln Day speech, 1950s.

104 Clinton's policy balance: From a Clinton 1992 campaign speech.

105 "was not one thing or another": Sean Wilentz, *The Age of Reagan* (New York: HarperCollins, 2008), pp. 325–26.

105 "neither a set of public positions nor a psychological dysfunction": Ibid., 326.

106 "A disturbing trend": Ross Perot, *Not for Sale at Any Price: How We Can Save America for Our Children* (New York: Hyperion, 1993), p. 75.

106 A Gallup poll in early June 1992: "U.S. Presidential Election Center," Gallup poll from June 11, 1992, http://www.gallup.com/poll/154559/us-presidential-election-center.aspx.

107 "The people are concerned": "'Honored to Accept': Excerpts from Perot's News Conference," *New York Times*, October 2, 1992.

107 Bush's 37.4 percent: "Federal Elections 92: Election Results for the U.S. President, the U.S. Senate and the U.S. House of Representatives," Federal Election Commission, June 1993, http://www.fec.gov/pubrec/fe1992/federalelections92.pdf.

107 Exit polls showed that if Perot had not: Steven A. Holmes, "The 1992 Elections: Disappointment—News Analysis: An Eccentric but No Joke; Perot's Strong Showing Raises Questions on What Might Have Been, and What Might Be," *New York Times*, November 5, 1992.

109 "Not only did he epitomize": Joshua Freeman, *American Empire: The Rise of a Global Power, the Democratic Revolution at Home* (New York: Penguin Books, 2012), p. 431.

109 John Bricker, his running mate: William Chafe, *The Unfinished Journey: America Since World War II* (New York: Oxford University Press, 1986), p. 93.

109 "Clinton faced a well-funded conservative effort": Freeman, *American Empire*, p. 431.

109 "I believe this program": Quote from the *Congressional Record*, April 6, 2000.

110 "Clearly this is a job killer": CNN interview with Dick Armey, August 2, 1993.

111 They fit the Napoleonic: Joshua Green, "Karl Rove in a Corner," *Atlantic*, November, 2004.

112 Peter Mandelson, one of the central architects: Michael White, "Peter Mandelson Has not Lost the Knack of Infuriating His Enemies," *Guardian*, January 26, 2012.

112 "I hope you're all aware we're Eisenhower Republicans here": Freeman, *American Empire*, p. 420.

114 While Kristol nodded to various policy objections: See William Kristol's memorandum to Republican leaders, "A Serious Threat to the Republican Party," December 2, 1993.

115 As the *Los Angeles Times*: Tom Petruno, "Thrills, Chills: The 'Real Economy' Enters the Center Ring," *Los Angeles Times*, January 1, 1995.

116 The 1994 Republican takeover: Adam Clymer, "G.O.P. Celebrates Its Sweep to Power; Clinton Vows to Find Common Ground," *New York Times*, November 9, 1994.

117 Especially alarming for Democrats: Richard Morin, "The Forgotten Majority," *Washington Post*, May 29, 2000.

119 When Obama's top political adviser David Axelrod: Mike Allen and Jim VandeHei, "Under Fire, President Obama Shifts Strategy," *Politico*, September 1, 2009.

122 In what has become a hallowed formulation: Richard Reeves, "Thou Shalt Not Attack Other Republicans ... Except, Maybe, in '76," *New York*, March 10, 1975.

123 "Government is the enemy": E. J. Dionne Jr., "Bailing Out the Capitalists," *RealClearPolitics*, March 18, 2008.

5. THE GINGRICH REVOLUTION AND CONSERVATISM'S SECOND CHANCE

124 As Clinton explained: Bill Clinton, *My Life* (New York: Knopf, 2004), p. 660.

125 He'd be helped: Ibid., p. 632.

125 "I think we all agree": President Bill Clinton, State of the Union address, January 24, 1995.

126 On November 10: Clinton, *My Life*, p. 681.

127 After a fruitless: Ibid., 682.

127 "We made a mistake": Ibid., p. 694.

128 Representative David Funderburk: See "Congressional Record Proceedings, Debates of the U.S. Congress," from November 20, 1995, https://www.congress.gov/congressional-record/1995/11/20/house-section/article /H13348-2.

128 "The balanced budget": E. J. Dionne Jr., "For Many Republicans, A Balanced Budget Isn't—And Never Was— The Real Goal," *Philadelphia Inquirer*, January 10, 1996.

130 "I chose to bomb": "McVeigh's April 26 Letter to Fox News," Fox News, April 26, 2001, http://www.foxnews .com/story/2001/04/26/mcveigh-apr-26-letter-to-fox-news.html.

131 He urged Americans: Doyle McManus, "Clinton Calls for Purge of 'Dark Forces,'" *Los Angeles Times*, April 24, 1995.

131 "It was the nation's": Michael Waldman, *POTUS Speaks: Finding the Words That Defined the Clinton Presidency* (New York: Simon & Schuster, 2000), p. 145.

131 And in honoring the dead: Bill Clinton, Address in Oklahoma City, Oklahoma, April 23, 1995, http://www .presidentialrhetoric.com/historicspeeches/clinton/oklahomacity.html.

131 "found his voice": Peter Keating, "Remembering Oklahoma City, and How Bill Clinton Saved His Presidency," *New York*, April 19, 2010.

133 "The era of big government is over": President Bill Clinton, State of the Union address, January 23, 1996.

133 "If Dole wins": "Commercials Target Economy, Gingrich," *Los Angeles Times*, August 22, 1996.

134 "We're the new liberals": Katharine Seelye, "In Visit to Arizona, Senator Emphasizes Goldwater Roots," *New York Times*, February 25, 1996.

135 He'd say they were: He used this phrase in public speeches and in conversations with the author.

135 For a useful and laudatory biography of Kemp, see Morton Kondracke and Fred Barnes, *Jack Kemp: The Bleeding-Heart Conservative Who Changed America* (New York: Sentinel, 2015).

136 "It is so very important": "Vice Presidential Debate in St. Petersburg, Florida," CNN, 1996, http://www.cnn .com/ALLPOLITICS/1996/debates/transcripts/1009/index5.shtml.

137 "My head says yes": John F. Harris, *The Survivor: Bill Clinton in the White House* (New York: Random House, 2005), p. 237, and especially chapters 22, pp. 30–35.

138 In the final Pew poll: "Final Pew Center Survey—Clinton 52%, Dole 38%, Perot 9%," Pew Research Center for the People and the Press, November 2, 1996.

138 "It is a reminder": Harris, *The Survivor*, pp. 252–53.

139 What the elections did: John F. Cogan and David Brady, "The 1996 House Elections: Reaffirming the Conservative Trend," Hoover Institution, March 1, 1997.

140 a sign of how starved Washington was: E. J. Dionne Jr., "Budget Deal Is a Political Classic," *Washington Post*, August 1, 1997.

140 the agreement was reached: Ibid.

141 Heritage's analyst argued: Scott A. Hodge, "The 1997 Budget Agreement: The Return of Big Government," Heritage Foundation, May 12, 1997.

142 Gingrich, however, was effusive: John F. Harris and Eric Pianin, "Bipartisanship Reigns at Budget Signing," *Washington Post*, August 6, 1997.

142 A Gallup poll in mid-January: "Presidential Approval Ratings—Bill Clinton," Gallup.

142 The United States Supreme Court had set it all in motion: "Green Light for Jones," CNN, May 27, 1997.

143 The details of the encounter: David Brock, "His Cheatin' Heart," *American Spectator*, January 1994.

143 The reporting on Clinton's personal life: Neil A. Lewis, "Almost $2 Million Spent in Magazine's Anti-Clinton Project, but on What?," the *New York Times*, April 15, 1998.

143 It rejected the idea: *Clinton v. Jones* (95-1853), 520 U.S. 681 (1997).

143 In a largely deserted White House: David Finkel, "How It Came to This," *Washington Post*, December 13, 1998.

144 The Jones case and the president's affair: Kenneth Starr, "The Starr Report," *Washington Post*, 1998.

144 Unbeknownst to the president: What came under the heading "Whitewater" referred to a development along Arkansas's White River in which the Clintons invested, invited into the deal by James McDougal, a colorful

figure described by John Harris as "a political and financial impresario." The controversy over the deal went on for years, starting with a *New York Times* story early in the 1992 campaign, Jeff Gerth, "Clintons Joined S.&L. in an Ozark Real Estate Venture," *New York Times,* March 8, 1992. Starr did not bring any charges in connection with Whitewater. For a good brief description of Whitewater, see Harris, *The Survivor,* pp. 102–9. For the definitive and painstakingly fair account of the entire Clinton impeachment controversy, see Ken Gormley, *The Death of American Virtue: Clinton vs. Starr* (New York: Broadway Books, 2011).

144 The story of Starr's: Ibid.
144 the reaction of Clinton partisans: E. J. Dionne Jr., "Even Clinton Supporters Are Floored by Accusations," *Washington Post,* January 23, 1998.
145 Clinton's famous reply: Howard Kurtz, "Dick Morris, High on the Critical List," *Washington Post,* February 3, 1999.
145 the statement that would never be forgotten: Martin Kettle, "Clinton Takes Up Fight," *Guardian,* January 26, 1998.
145 Clinton's approval rating: "Presidential Approval Ratings—Bill Clinton," Gallup.
146 The conservatives' frustration: William J. Bennett, *The Death of Outrage: Bill Clinton and the Assault on American Ideals* (New York: Touchstone, 1998).
146 a popular collection of traditional stories teaching moral lessons: William J. Bennett, *The Book of Virtues* (New York: Simon & Schuster, 1996).
147 "It is said that private character": Bennett, *The Death of Outrage,* pp. 8–9.
148 By 2000, after the boost: "Election Gave Cable News a Wild Ratings Ride, but Now It Needs an Encore," *Chicago Tribune,* December 19, 2000.
149 Starr called Brill: Howard Kurtz, "Starr Defends 'Background' Talk," *Washington Post,* June 14, 1998.
149 a five-minute address to the nation: President Bill Clinton, remarks to the nation in response to Lewinsky scandal, August 17, 1998.
150 Gingrich saw none of this coming: Steven Gillon, *The Pact: Bill Clinton, Newt Gingrich, and the Rivalry That Defined a Generation* (Oxford: Oxford University Press, 2008), p. 256.
150 Gingrich himself: Ibid., pp. 254–56.
151 "Gingrich looked": Ibid.
151 Ken Starr delivered: Ibid., p. 241.
151 The report itself was thus defensive: "Testing of a President; Response of President's Lawyers to Independent Counsel's Report," *New York Times,* September 13, 1998.
152 Blair, who loved synthesizing concepts: E. J. Dionne, "'Third Way' Politics," *Washington Post,* September 29, 1998.
152 "We have to take the world as we find it": James Bennet, "With Nation Glued to Television, Clinton Sticks with His Peers," *New York Times,* September 21, 1998.
154 A young Florida congressman named Joe Scarborough: Jerry Gray, "Gingrich Offers an Agenda, but the Christian Coalition Attacks Sharply," *New York Times,* March 7, 1997.
154 As Gillon observed: Gillon, *The Pact,* p. 260.
155 He urged Clinton: Alison Mitchell, "Impeachment: The Overview—Clinton Impeached; He Faces a Senate Trial, 2D in History; Vows to Do Job Till Term's 'Last Hour,'" *New York Times,* December 20, 1998.
155 When it finally acted on February 12, 1999: "How Senators Voted on Impeachment," CNN, February 12, 1999.
157 nicely summarized by Hillary Clinton: Steven M. Teles, "The Eternal Return of Compassionate Conservatism," *National Affairs,* Fall 2009.
158 "we had too many people in prison": Jeremy Diamond, "Bill Clinton Concedes Role in Mass Incarceration," *CNN.com* (May 7, 2015).
158 Clinton's rhetorical concessions to the right: President Bill Clinton, State of the Union address, January 23, 1996.
158 approval ratings in the Gallup Poll: "Presidential Approval Ratings—Bill Clinton," Gallup.

6. PUT ON A COMPASSIONATE FACE

162 "We should not ignore the potential for suffering": E. J. Dionne Jr., "The New Bleeding Hearts: The Prospect Is Enough to Make a Liberal's Day," Brookings Institution, February 16, 1997.
162 Berger and Neuhaus emphasized: Peter L. Berger and Richard John Neuhaus, *To Empower People: The Role of Mediating Structures in Public Policy* (Washington, DC: AEI Press, 1977), p. 158.
164 "For too long in modern America": E. J. Dionne, *Community Works: The Revival of Civil Society in America* (Washington, DC: Brookings Press, 1998), p. 102.
164 "take the side of people": Ibid., p. 106.
165 "Instead of embracing": Steven M. Teles, "The Eternal Return of Compassionate Conservatism," *National Affairs,* Fall 2009.
165 "the idea that a society": Ibid.
166 Kuo's lesson to liberals was simple enough: David Kuo, "Poverty 101: What Liberals and Conservatives Can Learn from Each Other," Brookings Institution, Fall 1997.

166 Marvin Olasky: For Olasky's view of compassionate conservativism, see Marvin Olasky, *Conservatism: What It Is, What It Does, and How It Can Transform America* (New York: Free Press, 2000). The book was published as Bush's campaign for president was in full swing, and Bush contributed a foreword that reflected his own careful balancing between the compassionate conservative camps. Bush called for a "government that knows its limits and helps people show what's in their hearts," and added: "Government will not be replaced by charities but it can welcome them as a partner." Reflecting a certain pragmatism that naturally comes to someone who has suddenly emerged as an adviser to a presidential candidate, Olasky expresses his preference for cutting back on government, but urges conservatives to take an "all-or-something" approach: "try to cut back on government, but when that does not happen, work to have improved programs." It should be said that there is no doubt about Olasky's sincerity as a Christian who believes his approach to poverty is the best. But it is difficult to see how his call for returning to an approach to poverty that preexisted the Progressive Era and the New Deal would lead to anything but a radical reduction in the standard of living of the poorest Americans.

166 "time for Congress to increase the pressure": Marvin Olasky, *Renewing American Compassion* (Washington, DC: Regnery, 1997), pp. 98–108.

167 "placing in the hands of state officials": Michael Gerson, *Heroic Conservatism* (New York: HarperCollins, 2007), p. 168.

169 "He's not looking over your shoulder": Interview with author.

169 "to make sure that there are consequences": E. J. Dionne Jr., "Getting Good Press," *Chicago Tribune*, October 27, 1998.

169 "That means somebody's got": E. J. Dionne Jr., "Getting Good Press," *Chicago Tribune*, October 27, 1998.

170 "A Bush victory": E. J. Dionne Jr., "In Search of George W.," *Washington Post*, September 19, 1999.

170 Ibid, Dionne, "Getting Good Press."

171 "I heard Bush say over and over": Karl Rove, *Courage and Consequence* (New York: Threshold Editions, 2010), pp. 121–22.

171 Ibid., p. 158.

175 In 1999, *National Journal* magazine: J. A. Barnes (August 7, 1999).

175 Bush, in his own words. *National Journal, 31*, 2275-2279. Errata, corrections 8/14/1999.

176 In April 1996: Governor George W. Bush, "We Need a Renewal of Spirit in this Country," remarks delivered April 10, 1996.

176 Bush memorably proposed: George W. Bush, campaign speech in Indianapolis, July 22, 1999.

177 "Reducing problems to economics is simply materialism": Governor George W. Bush, second inaugural address as governor of Texas, January 19, 1999.

177 Now consider another speech: President Herbert Hoover, radio address, February 12, 1932.

7. DOUBLE-EDGED "STRATEGERY"

179 Dan Simon, writing in *Forbes*: Dan Simon, "5 Differences Between Strategy and Strategery," *Forbes*, September 11, 2012.

182 Without mentioning the forty-second president: Frank Bruni, "The 2000 Campaign: The Texas Governor; Bush Calls On Gore to Denounce Clinton Affair," *New York Times*, August 12, 2000. A fascinating take on Bush's approach is offered by Lou Cannon and Carl M. Cannon, *Reagan's Disciple: George W. Bush's Troubled Quest for a Presidential Legacy* (New York: PublicAffairs, 2008). Cannon, father and son, argue that Bush sought a "melding" of his father's "'kinder and gentler' impulses" with "Reagan's conservatism on taxes, social policy and America's place in the world." There is much truth here, and the Cannons' account underscores the son's abiding conservatism. They also candidly describe the problems he faced in Iraq. I lay heavier stress than they do on the extent to which the successes of Clinton years forced Bush and Rove—at least during the 2000 campaign—to reach past the legacies of both the first President Bush and Reagan.

182 to Gore, wrote: John F. Harris, *The Survivor: Bill Clinton in the White House* (New York: Random House, 2005), p. 385.

182 "Not only do immigrants help build our economy": Elise Foley, "George W. Bush: Immigration Reform Needed to Boost Economy," *Huffington Post*, December 4, 2012.

183 Bush echoed, word for word: Terry M. Neal and Juliet Eilperin, "Bush Faults House GOP Spending Plan," *Washington Post*, October 1, 1999.

183 Dan Balz, the *Washington Post*'s top political reporter: Dan Balz, "Bush Shows a Shadow of Clintonism," *Washington Post*, October 7, 1999.

183 As Rove explained the strategy to *Washington Post*: Thomas B. Edsall, *Building Red America* (New York: Basic Books, 2006), p. 51.

183 Education, he wrote: Karl Rove, *Courage and Consequence* (New York: Threshold Editions, 2010), p. 159.

183 voters who considered education: Ibid., pp. 238–39.

184 "Bush talked about education endlessly": Ibid., p. 239.

184 in the New Hampshire primary: Ibid., p. 140.

184 Even in the face of Bush's defeat: Elizabeth Armet, "Poll Analysis: New Hampshire, Where Underdogs Have a Chance," *Los Angeles Times*, January 23, 2000.

184 He was later attacked: Juliet Eilperin and Hana Rosin, "Bob Jones: A Magnet School for Controversy," *Washington Post*, February 25, 2000.

184 In his memoir: Rove, *Courage and Consequence*, p. 146.

185 Thus did Bush's campaign suggest: R. W. Apple Jr., "The 2000 Campaign: The Electorate; Bush Redefined McCain and Retained the Right," *New York Times*, February 21, 2000.

185 "that McCain was a closet liberal": R. W. Apple, "Bush Redefined McCain and Retained the Right," *New York Times*, February 20, 2000.

185 Not only did conservatives make up: See CNN election results: http://www.cnn.com/ELECTION/2004/pages /results/states/US/P/00/epolls.0.html.

186 It was no surprise that he loved capitalism: Mark Silva, "As War Slows, Bush Returns to Other Goals," *Orlando Sentinel*, January 27, 2002.

187 "The Gore Coup": David Tell, "The Gore Coup," *Weekly Standard*, November 27, 2000.

187 The upshot, as the historian Gary Gerstle put it: Gary Gerstle, *The Presidency of George W. Bush: A First Historical Assessment*, ed. Julian E. Zelizer (Princeton: Princeton University Press, 2010), p. 278.

187 Dowd's memo "allowed Republican leaders": Edsall, *Building Red America*, p. 52.

188 the strategy that emerged from Rove's dual quest: Gerstle, ed., *Presidency of George W. Bush*, p. 278.

188 His short and elegant inaugural address: President George W. Bush, Inaugural Address, January 20, 2001.

189 First came the Economic Growth: See the Economic Growth and Tax Relief Reconciliation Act of 2001, text from the Tax Policy Center, http://www.taxpolicycenter.org/legislation/upload/EGTRRA-2001.pdf.

189 "some interesting incentives": Paul Krugman, "Reckoning: Bad Heir Day," *New York Times*, May 29, 2001.

190 The second tax cut was tilted: John F. Dickerson, "Confessions of a White House Insider," *Time*, January 10, 2004.

190 cost the Treasury another $350 billion: Glenn Kessler, "Revisiting the Cost of the Bush Tax Cuts," *Washington Post*, May 10, 2011.

190 "Floor Statement of Senator John McCain on Jobs and Growth Tax Relief Reconciliation Act, 2003," Office of Senator John McCain, May 23, 2003.

190 "Increasingly, I find myself in disagreement": Christopher Graff, "Jeffords Leaves Republican Party," *Washington Post*, May 24, 2001.

191 "Why isn't everyone": Howard Kurtz, "Republican Right Rips Jeffords," *Washington Post*, May 24, 2001.

191 The *New York Post* portrayed the senator: Deborah Orin, "Jeffords Hounded by Death Threats," *New York Post*, June 1, 2001.

191 "He is a liberal": E. J. Dionne Jr., *Stand Up, Fight Back: Republican Toughs, Democratic Wimps, and the Politics of Revenge* (New York: Simon & Schuster, 2004), p. 22.

192 The law passed the House overwhelmingly: See No Child Left Behind Act of 2001, https://www.govtrack.us /congress/bills/107/hr1.

192 Democrats were already blaming Bush: Jim VandeHei, "Education Law May Hurt Bush," *Washington Post*, October 14, 2003.

192 VandeHei cited the findings: Robert Maranto, Tom Lansford, and Jeremy Johnson, *Judging Bush* (Stanford: Stanford University Press, 2009), p. 203.

193 Senator Hillary Clinton strongly opposed: E. J. Dionne Jr., "The Democrats' Dilemma on the Prescription Drug Bill," *Washington Post*, June 25, 2003.

194 After much arm-twisting: See Medicare Prescription Drug, Improvement and Modernization Act of 2003, https://www.govtrack.us/congress/bills/108/hr1.

194 "I don't mean to be an alarmist": E. J. Dionne Jr., "The Democrats Take a Dive," *Washington Post*, November 25, 2003.

195 And in 2003 enacted the largest expansion: Barry Goldwater, *The Conscience of a Conservative* (Princeton: Princeton University Press, 2007), pp. x–xx.

196 After an extensive review of policy: President George W. Bush, "Stem Cell Science and the Preservation of Life," delivered August 12, 2001.

196 This, Bush said in a nationally televised: Katharine Q. Seelye, "The President's Decision: The Overview; Bush Gives His Backing for Limited Research on Existing Stem Cells," *New York Times*, August 10, 2001.

196 Even Gerson, a strong defender: Michael Gerson, *Heroic Conservatism* (New York: HarperCollins, 2007), p. 166.

196 "Bin Laden Determined": "Transcript: Bin Laden Determined to Strike in US," CNN, April 10, 2004.

8. "I CAN HEAR YOU"

197 "Freedom itself": President George W. Bush, remarks in response to September 11 attacks, September 11, 2001.

197 "The president had vital": Karl Rove, *Courage and Consequence* (New York: Threshold Editions, 2010), p. 260.

198 During a videoconference: George W. Bush, *Decision Points* (New York: Random House, 2010), p. 135.

198 Gerson saw the address: Michael Gerson, *Heroic Conservatism* (New York: HarperCollins, 2007), p. 69.

198 "Just three days": President George W. Bush, remarks at national prayer service, September 14, 2001.

198 "the president had misspoken": Gerson, *Heroic Conservatism*, p. 72.

198 "I can hear you": George W. Bush, remarks at Ground Zero, September 14, 2001.

199 "The face of terror": George W. Bush, remarks at the Islamic Center in Washington, D.C., September 17, 2001.

199 The 9/11 attacks: "Presidential Approval Ratings—George W. Bush," Gallup.

200 Americans endorsed the war: David W. Moore, "Eight of 10 Americans Support Ground War in Afghanistan," Gallup, November 1, 2001.

201 Representative Tom Davis: E. J. Dionne Jr., "A New and Improved George W.," *Washington Post*, October 12, 2001.

201 Eight days after: "A New Presidency," *Wall Street Journal*, September 19, 2001.

202 "We have no choice": Rush Limbaugh, "Clinton Didn't Do Enough to Stop Terrorists," *Wall Street Journal*, October 4, 2001.

202 "The Clinton curbs": E. J. Dionne Jr., *Stand Up Fight Back* (New York: Simon & Schuster, 2004), p. 59.

202 "During the Clinton years": Charles Krauthammer, "The Real New World Order," *Weekly Standard*, November 7, 2001.

202 "We now pay the wages": Charles Krauthammer, "Paying for Our Holiday from History," *Houston Chronicle*, February 15, 2003.

203 Cheney warned Daschle: Brian Montopoli, "Schlep to Judgment," *Washington Monthly*, September 2003.

203 But even the families: Dionne, *Stand Up Fight Back*, p. 60.

203 "Unless responsibility is": David Firestone, "2 Senators Say White House Is Thwarting 9/11 Inquiry," *New York Times*, October 12, 2002.

203 Cheney denounced: "Cheney Cautions Democrats Criticizing Bush," Associated Press, May 17, 2002.

203 the partisan construction of national identity: Melinda Lawson, *Patriot Fires: Forging a New American Nationalism in the Civil War North* (Lawrence: University Press of Kansas, 2002), p. 77. The Julian quotation appears on p. 65. The "partisan construction of national identity" is described in chapter 3, pp. 65–97. The story of Rove's interest in Lawson's book is told in Kurt M. Campbell and Michael E. O'Hanlon, *Hard Power: The New Politics of National Security* (New York: Basic Books, 2006), pp. 1–2.

204 Scowcroft took to: Brent Scowcroft, "Don't Attack Saddam," *Wall Street Journal*, August 15, 2002.

204 While 56 percent: "ABC News Nightline Poll: Iraq Update 8/29/02: Support for Military Action Against Iraq Declines," ABC News, released September 3, 2002.

205 "concerned about a go-it-alone strategy": Dionne, *Stand Up Fight Back*, p. 69.

205 as would Senator John Kerry: John Kerry, "We Still Have a Choice on Iraq," *New York Times*, September 6, 2002.

206 "What I am opposed": Barack Obama, remarks denouncing the Iraq War, October 2, 2002.

206 "If I were running": George W. Bush, remarks by the president in meeting with Central African leaders, September 13, 2002.

206 The war resolution passed: "Roll Call Vote in House on Iraq Resolution," *New York Times*, October 10, 2002.

206 The Senate passed: "Senate Roll Call: Iraq Resolution," *Washington Post*, October 11, 2002.

207 "I thought maybe": E. J. Dionne Jr., "Wellstone Had Passion for Politics, People," *Philadelphia Inquirer*, October 29, 2002.

208 Bush campaigned on: David E. Thigpen, "Indiana House: By Foot and by Humvee," *Time*, September 30, 2002.

208 "I think people are very uneasy": Dionne, *Stand Up Fight Back*, p. 73.

209 Chocola won the race: "The 2002 Elections: Midwest; Indiana," *New York Times*, November 6, 2002.

209 Republican senators filibustered: William M. Welch, "Daschle Condemns Bush on Iraq Debate," *USA Today*, September 26, 2002.

209 The ad claimed: Mark Z. Barabak, "The Democrats' 'Poster Boy,'" *Los Angeles Times*, July 18, 2004.

209 "I served my country": Bootie Cosgrove-Mather, "Who's More Patriotic?," *CBS Evening News*, October 31, 2002.

210 "A decorated and disabled": Dionne, *Stand Up Fight Back*, p. 63.

211 "They don't believe there": Senator Zell Miller, remarks at the Republican National Convention, September 1, 2004.

211 Conservatives saw the: Karl Rove, remarks to the New York Conservative Party, June 22, 2005.

211 The first Gallup poll: "Presidential Approval Ratings—George W. Bush," Gallup.

211 Every prediction the administration: *Meet the Press*, "Transcript for September 14, 2003," NBC News.

212 the reason most Americans: Wolf Blitzer, "Searching for the 'Smoking Gun,'" CNN, January 10, 2003.

212 His approval rating: "Presidential Approval Ratings—George W. Bush," Gallup.

212 the 2004 Democratic National Convention: "Kerry Makes Gains on Issues, Bush Maintains Leadership Image Advantage," Pew Research Center, August 12, 2004, http://www.people-press.org/files/legacy-pdf/221.pdf.

213 Regnery, the conservative: John E. O'Neill and Jerome E. Corsi, *Unfit for Command* (Washington, DC: Regnery, 2004).

213 "How do you ask": "Flashback: A Rare Broadcast of John Kerry's 1971 Speech Against the Vietnam War Before the Senate," Democracy Now!, July 30, 2004.

213 A lengthy *New York Times*: Kate Zernike and Jim Rutenberg, "Friendly Fire: The Birth of an Anti-Kerry Ad," *New York Times*, August 20, 2004.

213 *Los Angeles Times:* "These Charges are False," *Los Angeles Times*, August 24, 2004.

213 He endorsed: Elisabeth Bumiller, "Same Sex Marriage: The President; Bush Backs Ban in Constitution on Gay Marriage," *New York Times*, February 25, 2004.

214 New Mexico and Iowa: "U.S. Electoral College: Historical Election Results 2000–2008," National Archives and Records Administration.

215 A single exit poll: "National Election Pool Exit Poll 2004," CNN, http://www.cnn.com/ELECTION/2004/pages/results/states/US/P/00/epolls.0.html.

215 Bush increased his share: Ibid.

216 "They also control a majority": Fred Barnes, "Realignment, Now More than Ever," *Weekly Standard*, November 22, 2004.

216 "I earned capital": Richard W. Stevenson, "Confident Bush Outlines Plan for Second Term," *New York Times*, November 5, 2004.

217 The Bush program: Stephen Moore, "Bold Deal for Social Security," Cato Institute, May 12, 2000.

217 "I guess you could argue": Lori Montgomery, "Social Security Enters Elections," *Washington Post*, October 25, 2006.

218 Bush lobbied hard: Jonathan Weisman, "Immigration Bill Dies in Senate," *Washington Post*, June 29, 2007.

218 The bill's supporters, he explained: Robert Pear and Carl Hulse, "Immigration Bill Fails to Survive Senate Vote," *New York Times*, June 28, 2007.

218 The very religious president: Gary Gerstle, *The Presidency of George W. Bush: A First Historical Assessment*, ed. Julian E. Zelizer (Princeton: Princeton University Press, 2010).

219 The rejection of the 2007 immigration: E. J. Dionne, "Is the Tea Party Out to Banish Bush-Style Conservatism?," *Washington Post*, November 18, 2010.

219 "The Republican base": Sean Trende, "What Cantor's Loss and Graham's Win Mean," *RealClearPolitics*, June 11, 2014.

220 Schiavo had suffered severe: David Brown and Shailagh Murray, "Schiavo Autopsy Released," *Washington Post*, June 16, 2005.

222 Suburbanites, the ultimate swing: "Portrait of the Electorate: Table of Detailed Results," *New York Times*, November 6, 2010, http://www.nytimes.com/interactive/2010/11/07/weekinreview/20101107-detailed-exitpolls.html.

224 "One Nation Under God": Kevin Kruse sheds a powerful new light on the politics of religion in the Eisenhower years in his *One Nation Under God: How Corporate America Invented Christian America* (New York: Basic Books, 2015).

225 Trende offered the familiar litany: Trende, "What Cantor's Loss and Graham's Win Mean."

226 By a margin of 57 percent: "57% of Public Favors Wall Street Bailout," Pew Research Center, September 23, 2008.

226 This more pointed and arguably: Matthew Benjamin, "Americans Oppose Bailouts, Favor Obama to Handle Market Crisis," Bloomberg, September 23, 2008.

227 Representative Jeb Hensarling: "Hensarling 'Unconvinced' on Treasury Plan," CBS News/*Politico*, September 19, 2008.

227 Representative John Culberson: Chris Isidore, "Bailout Plan Rejected—Supporters Scramble," *CNN Money*, September 29, 2008.

227 Four days later: David Herszenhorn, "Bailout Plan Wins Approval; Democrats Vow Tighter Rules," *New York Times*, October 3, 2008.

228 discretionary spending grew by only 2 percent: Michael Gerson, *Heroic Conservatism* (New York: HarperCollins, 2007), p. 157. Gerson also argues that "the Golden Age of austerity under Reagan is a myth," noting that "[d]uring the Reagan years, big government got bigger" (p. 159).

228 "No president, of any party": Michael Gerson, "Obama's Mosque Duty," *Washington Post*, August 16, 2010.

228 Joe Scarborough, the "Morning Joe": Ben Craw, "Joe Scarborough Takes on Newt Gingrich Mosque Comments: 'It's Deplorable, It's Sick Politics,'" *Huffington Post*, August 18, 2010.

229 "In that Oval Office meeting": Gerson, *Heroic Conservatism*, p. 8.

229 "A retreat from idealism": Ibid., p. 10.

229 "From tax cuts to Medicare": Alan Cooperman and Jim VandeHei, "Ex-Aide Questions Bush Vow to Back Faith-Based Efforts," *Washington Post*, February 15, 2005.

230 Kuo, who died of cancer in 2013: David Kuo, *Tempting Faith: An Inside Story of Political Seduction* (New York: Simon & Schuster, 2006), p. 289.

230 Noting that 9/11: Steven M. Teles, "The Eternal Return of Compassionate Conservatism," *National Affairs*, Fall 2009.

231 Citing Walter Dean Burnham: Barnes, "Realignment, Now More than Ever."

232 Bush produced a net 1.1 million jobs: Job report figures are from the U.S. Bureau of Labor Statistics, cited in this post from FactCheck.org: http://www.factcheck.org/2011/08/reid-wrong-on-bushs-economic-record/.

233 "Don't get me wrong": Eric Cantor, Kevin McCarthy, and Paul Ryan, *Young Guns: A New Generation of Conservative Leaders* (New York: Simon & Schuster, 2010), pp. 20–21, 24.

234 But his indictment involved: Ibid., p. 150.

235 Jeb, rather bravely, courted: Michael J. Mishak, "Jeb Bush's 'Lose the Primary to Win the General' Could Just Mean 'Lose the Primary,'" *National Journal*, June 15, 2015, http://www.nationaljournal.com/2016-elections/jeb-bush-s-lose-the-primary-to-win-the-general-could-just-mean-lose-the-primary-20150615.

235 "The Bushes have always underestimated": Ingraham quoted in Ed O'Keefe and Robert Costa, "How Jeb Bush's Campaign Ran off Course Before It Even Began," *Washington Post*, June 10, 2015.

235 He drew 26 percent: McClatchy-Marist poll, March 9, 2015, http://maristpoll.marist.edu/wp-content/misc/usapolls/us150301/2016/Complete%20March%202015%20McClatchy_Marist%20Poll_2016_Release%20and%20Tables.pdf.

9. THE NEW, NEW, OLD RIGHT

237 "I'll tell you the expression": Jeff Zeleny, "A Proud 'Lobbyist' and 'Southerner' Weighs 'President,'" *New York Times*, March 21, 2011.

238 *New York Times* reporter Kate Zernike: Kate Zernike, *Boiling Mad: Inside Tea Party America* (New York: Times Books, 2010).

238 A year later, the British academic: Dominic Sandbrook, *Mad as Hell: The Crisis of the 1970s and the Rise of the Populist Right* (New York: Random House, 2011).

238 Alan Crawford, a conservative: Alan Crawford, *Thunder on the Right* (New York: Pantheon, 1981), p. 5.

239 Groups facing such displacement: Matt A. Barreto and Christopher S. Parker, *Change They Can't Believe In: The Tea Party and Reactionary Politics in America* (Princeton: Princeton University Press, 2014), p. 4.

239 "true believers in the Tea Party": Ibid., p. 247.

239 What concerned them: Theda Skocpol and Vanessa Williamson, *The Tea Party and the Remaking of Republican Conservatism* (Oxford: Oxford University Press, 2011), p. 56.

240 Nonetheless, the two: Ibid., p. 69.

240 "Grassroots activists": Ibid., p. 13.

241 It is no accident: Jacob Hacker and Paul Pierson, "No Cost for Extremism," *American Prospect*, Spring 2015, p. 74.

241 Radio talkers on the progressive side: On the bias of owners toward the right-wing talkers, see Bill Press, *Toxic Talk: How the Radical Right Has Poisoned America's Airwaves* (New York: St. Martin's Press, 2011) pp. 242–49. A good academic study of conservative talk is Kathleen Hall Jamieson and Joseph N. Cappella, *Echo Chamber: Rush Limbaugh and the Conservative Media Establishment* (New York: Oxford University Press, 2008).

241 "highest non-sports cable program": Chris Ariens, "24 Million Watch GOP Debate on Fox News; Most-Watched Cable News Program Ever," TV Newser wedbsite, *adweek.com* (August 7, 2015).

242 "Ailes built Fox": Gabriel Sherman, *The Loudest Voice in the Room* (New York: Random House, 2014), p. xix.

242 "I've never seen anyone": Ibid., p. 342.

242 A PRRI/ Brookings Institution survey: Daniel Cox, E. J. Dionne, William A. Galston, Robert P. Jones & Juhem Navarro-Rivera, "What Americans Want from Immigration Reform in 2014," PRRI/Brookings Institution, p. 34.

244 "is going to win by more than five points": "Dick Morris: 'Romney Will Win in a Landslide,'" *RealClearPolitics*, October 31, 2012.

244 "I was fired": CNN Political Unit, "Dick Morris: 'I Was Wrong at the Top of My Lungs,'" CNN, February 7, 2013.

245 "Republicans have been fleeced": Dylan Byers, "Republicans Lied to by 'Conservative Entertainment Complex,'" *Politico*, November 9, 2012.

245 "If leaders of the Republican Party are not setting": Jackie Calmes, "'They Don't Give a Damn About Governing: Conservative Media's Influence on the Republican Party," paper published by the Shorenstein Center on Media, Politics and Public Policy (July, 2015), p. 4.

245 "They really didn't know what to do": Gabriel Sherman in interview with Steve Malzberg on Newsmax TV (August 28, 2015), http://www.newsmax.com/t/newsmax/article/672378.

246 "epistemic closure": Julian Sanchez, "From, Cocktail Parties and the Treat of Doubt" (March 26, 2010), http://www.juliansanchez.com/2010/03/26/frum-cocktail-parties-and-the-threat-of-doubt/. Quoted in Calmes, pp. 35–36.

246 Skocpol and Williamson: Skocpol and Williamson, *The Tea Party and the Remaking of Republican Conservatism*, p. 13.

246 When he founded the John Birch Society: Justin Dart was a drugstore magnate who later in life became active on behalf of the disabled. Reagan awarded him the Presidential Medal of Freedom posthumously in 1987. Holmes Tuttle was seen as the informal head of Reagan's "kitchen cabinet," having encouraged him to run for governor of California in 1966. He made his fortune with a chain of auto dealerships. Alfred Bloomingdale made his money in the credit card industry. Reagan appointed him to the Foreign Intelligence Advisory Board.

Joseph P. Coors built his grandfather's beer company into a major enterprise and was a leading funder of many conservative causes, including the Heritage Foundation at its founding.

246 The quintessential business organization: John Judis, *The Paradox of American Democracy* (New York: Routledge, 2001).

247 In the 1970s: Ibid., p. 110.

247 A Virginia lawyer named Lewis Powell: Lewis F. Powell, "Attack on American Free Enterprise System," confidential memorandum to Eugene Sydnor, August 23, 1971.

248 As Judis noted: Judis, *The Paradox of American Democracy*, p. 131.

248 And businesses opposed: For an excellent report and analysis on business's role in the health care reform battle, see John Judis, "Abandoned Surgery: Business and the Future of Health Care Reform," *American Prospect*, Spring 1995, pp. 65–73.

249 "We want to be seen as the tax cut": Conor Friedersdorf, "How Republicans Get Declared RINOs," *Atlantic*, May 16, 2012.

250 Specter barely survived: Janet Hook, "Specter Barely Survives Primary," *Los Angeles Times*, April 28, 2004.

250 The Koch brothers': Brian Doherty, *Radicals for Capitalism* (New York: PublicAffairs, 2007), p. 410.

251 When libertarian dissidents: Ibid., p. 418.

251 A 2007 *Washington Post*: Michael Abramowitz and Steven Mufson, "Papers Detail Industry's Role in Cheney's Energy Report," *Washington Post*, July 18, 2007.

252 *New Yorker* writer Jane Mayer: Jane Mayer, "Covert Operations," *New Yorker*, August 31, 2010.

252 Writing in *Foreign Affairs* magazine: David Frum, "Crashing the Party," *Foreign Affairs*, September/October 2014.

252 "from the epicenter of progressive thought": Tom Perkins, "Progressive Kristallnacht Coming?," *Wall Street Journal*, January 24, 2014.

243 Perkins was not the only: Frum, "Crashing the Party."

254 "Conservatism is something more": Russell Kirk, quoted in George H. Nash, *The Conservative Intellectual Movement in America* (New York: Basic Books, 1979), p. 81.

254 "The religious person is entitled": Terry Eastland, "In Defense of Religious America," *Commentary*, June 1, 1981.

254 "may be on the offensive": Nathan Glazer, "Fundamentalism: A Defensive Offensive," in Richard John Neuhaus and Michael Cromartie, eds., *Piety and Politics* (Lanham, MD: University Press of America, 1987), p. 255.

255 "The New Right": James Reichley, *Faith in Politics* (Washington, DC: Brookings Institution Press, 2002), p. 296.

255 More generally, religious conservatives: Richard John Neuhaus, *The Naked Public Square* (Grand Rapids, MI: Eerdmans, 1984).

256 "Whites in Mississippi": The next several paragraphs are based on Joseph Crespino's excellent account of the controversy, "Civil Rights and the Religious Right," in Bruce Schulman and Julian Zelizer, eds., *Rightward Bound: Making America Conservative in the 1970s* (Cambridge, MA: Harvard University Press, 2008), pp. 90–105. See also Joseph Crespino, *In Search of Another Country: Mississippi and the Conservative Counterrevolution* (Princeton: Princeton University Press, 2007), pp. 253–56.

258 The *New York Times* published: "Electoral Shifts," *New York Times*, April 14, 2011. http://www.nytimes.com /interactive/2008/11/05/us/politics/20081104_ELECTION_RECAP.html?_r=0.

258 The cultural feel: "Portrait of the Electorate: Table of Detailed Results," *New York Times*, November 6, 2010, http://www.nytimes.com/interactive/2010/11/07/weekinreview/20101107-detailed-exitpolls.html.

258 "There's no other explanation": Adam Nossiter, "For South, a Waning Hold on National Politics," *New York Times*, November 10, 2008.

259 only 19 percent said: "Polling the Tea Party," *New York Times*/CBS News, April 10, 2010.

259 opposition to illegal immigration: On the Tea Party and immigration, the *New York Times*/CBS News poll and many other surveys have shown Tea Party supporters to be strongly motivated by opposition to immigration reform. See Daniel Cox, "Why Loyalty to Their Tea Party Constituents Is Holding Back House Republicans on Immigration Reform," Public Religion Research Institute, August 8, 2014, http://publicreligion.org/2014/08 /why-loyalty-to-their-tea-party-constituents-is-holding-back-house-republicans-on-immigration-reform/. See also Christopher Parker, "The (Real) Reason Why the House Won't Pass Comprehensive Immigration Reform," Brookings Institution FixGov blog, August 4, 2014, http://www.brookings.edu/blogs/fixgov /posts/2014/08/04-immigration-tea-party-constituencies-parker?utm_campaign=Brookings+Brief&utm _source=hs_email&utm_medium=email&utm_content=13705896&_hsenc=p2ANqtz-9O34zJ_UZgzKolEF funsJ70vK0Cf28Pn7RceUYvTmhq2-Dh6ZkYaUDDKsn2i28aDHA321R55Vxtqo1wvT9OoxhIOnGjw& _hsmi=13705896.

259 A PRRI/Brookings Institution survey: E. J. Dionne and William A. Galston, "The Old and New Politics of Faith: Religion and the 2010 Election," PRRI/Brookings Institution, November 17, 2010.

260 "People who could not even spell": Jonathan Raban, "At the Tea Party," *New York Review of Books*, March 25, 2010.

10. DREAMS OF CELESTIAL CHOIRS

262 It found its voice four days later: Dr. Martin Luther King Jr., "Address to First Montgomery Improvement Association Mass Meeting," 1955.

262 "Where his predecessors had roused the people": Arthur Schlesinger, *The Politics of Hope and the Bitter Heritage* (Princeton: Princeton University Press, 2008), p. 110.

263 Obama, like Reagan, used stories: Barack Obama, Democratic National Convention keynote address, July 27, 2004.

265 Reagan had intentionally drawn: Ronald Reagan, "A Time for Choosing," address delivered October 27, 1964.

266 267"some liberals who dismiss": Senator Barack Obama, Speech on Faith and Politics, June 28, 2006.

267 "To think clearly about race": Senator Barack Obama, *The Audacity of Hope* (New York: Three Rivers Press, 2006), p. 233.

268 He criticized Wright: Senator Barack Obama, Speech on Race, March 18, 2008, http://www.nytimes.com/2008 /03/18/us/politics/18text-obama.html?pagewanted=all.

268 He declined to disown Wright: Peter Slevin and Darryl Fears, "Obama Calls Minister's Statements 'Outrageous,'" *Washington Post*, April 30, 2008.

269 "God didn't call America": E. J. Dionne, "Another Angry Black Preacher," *Washington Post*, March 21, 2008.

269 "You go into some of these small towns": David Axelrod, *Believer: My Forty Years in Politics* (New York: Penguin Press, 2015), p. 267.

270 "conservatives were eager": Bradford Berenson, "Harvard Law Days," *Frontline*, http://www.pbs.org/wgbh /pages/frontline/choice2008/obama/harvard.html.

271 "I think Ronald Reagan changed": Senator Barack Obama, "In Their Own Words: Obama on Reagan," *New York Times*, January 16, 2008.

271 "I could stand up here": Julie Bosman, "Clinton Turns from Anger to Sarcasm," *New York Times*, February 24, 2008.

273 "I'm unapologetic": E. J. Dionne, "A Dark Horse's War Edge," *Washington Post*, January 16, 2007.

273 "will take the Israelis": Mike Huckabee quoted in "Huckabee: Obama Marching Israelis to 'Door of Oven,'" *Breitbart* (July 25, 2015).

273 "There's only three things": Sean Sullivan, "Joe Biden's Greatest (and Not-So-Greatest) Debate Hits," *Washington Post*, October 10, 2012.

274 McCain had condemned: Mike Glover, Associated Press, "McCain Condemns Pat Robertson," *Washington Post*, February 28, 2000.

274 McCain might instead: "Sen. John McCain Attacks Pat Robertson, Jerry Falwell, Republican Establishment as Harming GOP Ideals," CNN, February 28, 2000, http://transcripts.cnn.com/TRANSCRIPTS/0002/28/se .01.html.

275 And on July 10: Dan Balz and Anne E. Kornblut, "Top Aides Leave McCain Campaign," *Washington Post*, July 11, 2007.

275 "dissatisfaction to his high command": Ibid.

275 Romney declared that he: Marc Santora, "Candidates Spar Over Who Is a Real Republican," *New York Times*, October 14, 2007.

276 "You look back at the Chinese Exclusionary Act": New York City mayor Rudolph Guiliani's address to a conference on immigration at the University of Minnesota, September 30, 1996. See full transcript provided by the *New York Times*: http://www.nytimes.com/1996/10/01/nyregion/excerpt-from-address-on-immigration.html.

276 "I'm standing here tonight": Michael Cooper, "G. O. P. Rivals Trade Jabs in Debate," *New York Times*, November 28, 2007.

276 "This whole debate saddens me": Clyde Haberman, "Sanctuary Was a Lovely Word. Then The G.O.P. Got a Hold of It," *New York Times*, November 30, 2007.

277 "rapists" "bringing drugs"; Donald Trump quoted in Michelle Ye Hee Lee, "Donald Trump's False Comments Connecting Mexican Immigrants and Crime," *Washington Post* online (July 8, 2015).

277 McCain had confronted a questioner: Holly Ramer, "Voter Confronts McCain on Immigration," *Washington Post*, October 14, 2007.

278 Giuliani suffered in November: Dan Balz and Haynes Johnson, *The Battle for America 2008* (New York: Viking, 2009), p. 267.

278 Giuliani had 'billed obscure city agencies": Ben Smith, "Giuliana Billed Obscure Agencies for Trips," *Politico*, November 28, 2007.

278 Some 60 percent of Republican caucusgoers: "Election 2008: Iowa Caucus Results," *New York Times*, http:// politics.nytimes.com/election-guide/2008/results/states/IA.html.

279 "Religious tolerance": Mitt Romney, "Faith in America," address delivered December 6, 2007.

280 McCain's New Hampshire victory: "Election 2008: New Hampshire Primary Results," *New York Times*, http:// politics.nytimes.com/election-guide/2008/results/states/NH.html.

281 McCain won with just 33 percent: "Election 2008: South Carolina Primary Results," *New York Times*, http:// politics.nytimes.com/election-guide/2008/results/states/SC.html.

281 Giuliani's campaign was flailing: Michael Cooper and Michael Luo, "At Debate on the Economy, Republicans Become the Kindest of Candidates," *New York Times*, January 25, 2008.

281 he won with a relatively modest: "Election 2008: Florida Primary Results," *New York Times*, http://politics.ny times.com/election-guide/2008/results/states/FL.html.

281 "He is not the choice": E. J. Dionne, "The McCain Divide?," *Washington Post*, February 1, 2008.

283 McCain took a five-point lead: "Gallup Daily: McCain 48%, Obama 43%," Gallup, September 10, 2008, http://www.gallup.com/poll/110212/Gallup-Daily-McCain-48-Obama-43.aspx?utm_source=&utm_medium =&utm_campaign=tiles.

283 McCain's pollster Bill McInturff: Balz and Johnson, *The Battle for America 2008*, pp. 330–31.

284 voters saw Obama as offering: Jill Lawrence, "Poll: Obama Outperformed McCain in Debate," *USA Today*, September 28, 2008.

285 "Rage Rising on the McCain Campaign Trail": Ed Henry and Ed Hornick, "Rage Rising on the McCain Campaign Trail," CNN, October 11, 2008.

285 didn't stop the McCain ad from declaring: Andy Barr, "McCain Launches Ayers Ad," *Politico*, October 9, 2008.

286 "I've spent my entire lifetime": Howard Kurtz, "*National Review* Boots Buckley Son for Obama Boost," *Washington Post*, October 15, 2008.

286 nothing worked for McCain: Federal Election Commission, "Federal Elections 2008: Election Results for the U.S. President, the U.S. Senate, and the U.S. House of Representatives," http://www.fec.gov/pubrec/fe 2008/tables2008.pdf.

287 Young voters enjoyed: "Young Voters in the 2008 Election," Pew Research Center, November 13, 2008.

287 In 1988, by contrast: My thanks to Jon Cohen and later Peyton Craighill, both of them directors of polling at the *Washington Post*, for finding these and other polling data for me. These figures were first published in a story by Dan Balz.

288 "On this day, we gather": President Barack Obama, First Inaugural Address, delivered January 20, 2009.

289 Among the strategic imperatives: Robert Draper, *When the Tea Party Came to Town* (New York: Simon & Schuster Paperbacks, 2012), pp. xi–xviii.

289 "The single most important thing": Major Garrett, "Top GOP Priority: Make Obama a One-Term President," *National Journal*, October 23, 2010.

289 "Mitch said, 'We have a new president'": E. J. Dionne Jr., "Hope's in Need of Hope Today," *Washington Post*, November 2, 2014.

11. THE LOGIC OF OBSTRUCTION

292 "If there is anyone out there": President-elect Barack Obama, postelection victory speech, November 4, 2008.

292 Obama's 68 percent approval rating: Jeffrey M. Jones, "Obama's Approval Ratings in Historical Context," Gallup, January 26, 2009.

293 "Instant President": Jonathan Alter, *The Promise: President Obama, Year One* (New York: Simon & Schuster, 2011), pp. 77–99.

294 "backing the bus up": I was told this by Pelosi staffers. A version of the story was first reported by Maureen Dowd of the *New York Times*. Maureen Dowd, "Potomac's Postpartisan Depression," *New York Times*, February 7, 2009. Dowd reports that Pelosi told Obama: "I don't mind you driving the bus over me, but I don't appreciate your backing it up and running over me again and again."

294 "The president wants to work with us": Alter, *The Promise*, p. 118.

294 "We can't run against Washington,": David Axelrod, *Believer: My Forty Years in Politics* (New York: Penguin Press, 2015), p. 415.

295 When the stimulus finally passed: Statistics from the U.S. government's official website on the American Recovery and Reinvestment Act: http://www.recovery.gov/arra/About/Pages/The_Act.aspx.

296 "as if it was a dog's": Alter, *The Promise*, p. 129.

296 Because the stimulus: Michael Grunwald, *The New New Deal: The Hidden Story of Change in the Obama Era* (New York: Simon & Schuster, 2012).

296 A CNN poll: Paul Steinhauser, "Six in 10 Oppose Auto Bailout, Poll Shows," CNN, December 3, 2008.

297 The Tea Party took off: Michael Barone, "The Transformative Power of Rick Santelli's Rant," *National Review*, June 10, 2010.

297 He charged that the administration: Ron Elving, "6 Years On, Is the Tea Party Here to Stay?," NPR, February 25, 2015.

297 About 170,000 people responded: Jane Hamsher, "Rick Santelli, Angry White Male 2.0," Firedoglake, February 20, 2009.

297 "the rant video was the most-watched clip": Arun Gupta, "The Tea Party: The New Populism," Political Research Associates, August 1, 2011.

297 Kate Zernike, the *New York Times* expert on the Tea Party: Kate Zernike, *Boiling Mad: Inside Tea Party America* (New York: Times Books, 2010), pp. 13–19.

298 Tea Party supporters were twice as likely: 73 percent called themselves conservative etc. Zernike helpfully

includes details from the *New York Times*/CBS News poll on the Tea Party poll in an appendix to *Boiling Mad*, pp. 195–227.

299 "This anger has been ignored": Scott Johnson, "Hannity Joins the Party," Power Line blog, March 27, 2009.

299 According to *Publishers Weekly*: "Facts & Figures 2009 Revised," *Publishers Weekly*, April 5, 2009.

300 Schmidt hit back: Andy Barr and Jonathan Martin, "McCain Camp: Palin Account 'All Fiction,'" *Politico*, November 13, 2009.

300 she found it "disappointing": Melanie Kirkpatrick, "Her Side of the Story," *Wall Street Journal*, November 16, 2009.

301 April 2010 *New York Times*/CBS News poll: Dalia Sussman and Marina Stefan, "Obama and the 'Birthers' in the Latest Poll," *New York Times*, April 21, 2010.

302 Obama was driven by: Dinesh D'Souza, *The Roots of Obama's Rage* (Washington, DC: Regnery, 2010), pp. 1–127.

302 Newt Gingrich pronounced it "brilliant": David Weigel, "Newt is Nuts!," *Slate*, September 13, 2010.

302 a February 2011 appearance by John Boehner: "*Meet the Press* Transcript for February 13, 2011," NBC News, updated February 16, 2011, http://www.nbcnews.com/id/41536793/ns/meet_the_press-transcripts/ns/meet_the_press-transcripts#.VRqyxfnF-1Y.

303 Nugent condemned Obama's: John Avlon, *Wingnuts: Extremism in the Age of Obama* (New York: Daily Beast Books, 2014), p. 123.

303 Avik Roy, a conservative policy analyst: Avik Roy, "The Torturous History of Conservatives and the Individual Mandate," *Forbes*, February 7, 2012.

304 the fact-checkers at PolitiFact: Angie Drobnic Holan, "PolitiFact's Lie of the Year: 'Death Panels,'" *PolitiFact*, December 18, 2009.

305 "Look, we politicians are no great shakes": This story was told to me by Frank and others in Massachusetts.

306 "I have a birth certificate here": Elizabeth Kolbert, "The Things People Say," *New Yorker*, November 2, 2009.

306 It was a sign: Federal Election Commission, "Official Election Results for United States Senate: 2010 U.S. Senate Campaigns," http://www.fec.gov/pubrec/fe2010/2010senate.pdf.

307 "There are issues": E. J. Dionne Jr., "Mike Castle's Defeat—and the End of Moderate Republicanism," *Washington Post*, September 16, 2010.

307 Her best-known public pronouncement: Elyse Siegel, "Christine O'Donnell in New Ad: 'I'm Not a Witch,'" *Huffington Post*, October 4, 2010.

310 "It was relatively easy for citizens": Jeffrey M. Berry and Sarah Sobieraj, *The Outrage Industry: Public Opinion Media and the New Incivility* (Oxford: Oxford University Press, 2014), p. 169.

311 "The media coverage": E. J. Dionne Jr., "Extremism in Media's Glare," *Washington Post*, September 3, 2009.

311 the tide was clearly running out on Spratt: Katharine Q. Seelye, "After 28 Years, a Congressman on the Ropes," *New York Times*, October 12, 2010.

312 Spratt had been reelected: "Election 2010: South Carolina Results," *New York Times*, http://elections.nytimes.com/2010/results/south-carolina.

312 Obama's approval rating: "Presidential Approval Ratings—Barack Obama," Gallup, http://www.gallup.com/poll/116479/barack-obama-presidential-job-approval.aspx.

313 the U.S. Bureau of Labor Statistics pegged: Bureau of Labor Statistics, "Labor Force Statistics from the Current Population Survey," data accessed March 31, 2015. The figure is for December 2009, the last report before the special election; http://data.bls.gov/timeseries/LNS14000000.

314 As Barney Frank noted: Frank said this to me in an interview and repeated variations on it over the years. See, for example, "Ezra Klein Interviews Barney Frank," *Washington Post*, September 27, 2009.

314 Obama had defeated McCain: "Election Center 2008: President: Massachusetts," CNN, http://www.cnn.com/ELECTION/2008/results/individual/#mapPMA.

314 In 2010, Brown received: "Senate Race 2010: Town-by-Town Results," *Boston Herald*, http://www.boston.com/news/special/politics/2010/senate/results.html.

315 It received 53 votes: Eric Naing, "Senate Rejects Deficit Reduction Commission," *Open Congress*, January 26, 2010.

316 Yet, as Robert Kaiser wrote: Robert G. Kaiser, *Act of Congress* (New York: Knopf, 2013), p. 384.

317 She offered the usual Republican criticisms: E. J. Dionne Jr., "GOP's Election Strategy Lets Others Do Its Dirty Work," *Washington Post*, October 18, 2010.

318 "The guy just can't tell the truth" and other advertising references: Dionne, "GOP's Election Strategy."

318 the age composition of the electorate: Ruy Teixeira and John Halprin, "Job Loss and Liberal Apathy," *New Republic*, November 6, 2010.

319 Republicans won 77 percent: "Portrait of the Electorate: Table of Detailed Results," *New York Times*, November 6, 2010, http://www.nytimes.com/interactive/2010/11/07/weekinreview/20101107-detailed-exitpolls.html.

319 In 2006 and 2008: Jonah Goldberg, "Obama and the White Working Class," *National Review*, March 8, 2011.

319 The exit poll found: "Portrait of the Electorate: Table of Detailed Results," *New York Times*, November 6, 2010, http://www.nytimes.com/interactive/2010/11/07/weekinreview/20101107-detailed-exitpolls.html.

320 "I watched them in the last four years": E. J. Dionne Jr., "Can Democrats Step Up Their Game?," *Washington Post*, December 6, 2010.

320 the exit poll found that: "Portrait of the Electorate: Table of Detailed Results," *New York Times*, November 6, 2010, http://www.nytimes.com/interactive/2010/11/07/weekinreview/20101107-detailed-exitpolls.html.

12. THE TEA PARTY OVERREACHES AND REPUBLICANS WAGE CLASS WAR

324 little notice of a report: Employee Benefit Research Institute, "EBRI Databook on Employee Benefits," http://www.ebri.org/pdf/publications/books/databook/db.chapter%2006.pdf.

324 Obama infuriated liberals: President Barack Obama, press conference, December 7, 2010.

325 "Acceding to the demands of hostage-takers": Perry Bacon Jr. and Scott Wilson, "Obama Calls Liberal Critics 'Sanctimonious,'" *Washington Post*, December 8, 2010.

325 "we got health insurance": Justin Frank, *Obama on the Couch: Inside the Mind of the President* (New York: Free Press, 2011), p. 138.

326 "This country was founded": President Barack Obama, press conference, December 7, 2010.

326 "he also has to satisfy": Naftali Bendavid and Janet Hook, "GOP Aims to Tame Benefits Programs," *Wall Street Journal*, March 4, 2011.

327 At a gathering of several hundred Tea Party supporters: E. J. Dionne Jr., "The High Cost of Hating Government," *Washington Post*, April 10, 2011.

327 "Yesterday we cut billions": Carl Hulse, "House Approves Republican Budget Plan to Cut Trillions," *New York Times*, April 15, 2011.

328 "At some point": E. J. Dionne, "The Symbolic Battle Over the Debt Ceiling," *Washington Post*, May 18, 2011.

332 "We weren't kidding around": E. J. Dionne, "Can America Still Lead," *Washington Post*, August 7, 2011.

334 The *New Yorker's* Ryan Lizza: Ryan Lizza, "Romney's Dilemma," *New Yorker*, June 6, 2011.

334 he was guarded in talking about his health plan: Philip Rucker, "Mitt Romney Announces 2012 Presidential Bid," *Washington Post*, June 2, 2011.

335 "We're only inches away": Mitt Romney, campaign announcement speech, Stratham, New Hampshire, June 2, 2011.

336 "conflict between the men who possess": President Theodore Roosevelt, "New Nationalism," speech delivered August 31, 1910.

336 "Here in Kansas": President Barack Obama, "Remarks by the President on the Economy in Osawatomie, Kansas," December 6, 2011.

337 "Market ideas moved out": Daniel T. Rodgers, *Age of Fracture* (Cambridge, MA: Harvard University Press, 2011), pp. 10 and 76.

338 "Ultimately, inevitably, the route to real change": Hendrik Hertzberg, "Occupational Hazards," *New Yorker*, November 7, 2011.

338 A *Washington Post*/Pew Research Center poll: *Washington Post*/Pew Research Center, "Support for Occupy Wall Street and Tea Party Movements," October 24, 2011, http://www.washingtonpost.com/politics/support-for-occupy-wall-street-and-tea-party-movements/2011/10/24/gIQAJyFxDM_graphic.html.

339 The Republican Roosevelt: Herbert David Croly, *The Promise of American Life* (Cambridge, MA: Belknap Press of Harvard University Press, 1965).

339 He praised TR for knowing: Obama, "Remarks by the President on the Economy in Osawatomie, Kansas."

341 In particular, he admired a poster: "Romney Campaign Ad Uses Theme 'Obama Isn't Working,'" *BBC News*, May 8, 2012.

342 "bumbling clowns": Jonathan Alter, *The Center Holds* (New York: Simon & Schuster, 2013), p. 178.

343 a Zogby poll found Bachmann: Stephen Dinan, "Poll: Bachmann Surges to Primary Lead," *Washington Times*, June 21, 2011.

343 "would be able to leave [the Union]": "Gov. Rick Perry: Texas Could Secede, Leave Union," Associated Press, May 16, 2009.

344 The August 17–21 Gallup survey: Jeffrey M. Jones, "Perry Zooms to Front of Pack for 2012 GOP Nomination," Gallup, August 24, 2011.

344 Another survey at the time by Public Policy Polling: Mark Blumenthal, "Poll Shows Rick Perry Surging Ahead of GOP 2012 Pack," *Huffington Post*, August 24, 2011.

344 in an NBC/*Wall Street Journal* poll in October: Mark Murray, "NBC/WSJ Poll: Cain Now Leads GOP Pack," NBC News, October 13, 2011.

344 "it's three agencies of government": Amanda Terkel, "Rick Perry Forgets Which Three Agencies He Would Eliminate as President," *Huffington Post*, November 9, 2011.

345 "That just doesn't make sense to me": Jim Rutenberg and Jeff Zeleny, "Perry and Romney Come Out Swinging at Each Other in G.O.P. Debate," *New York Times*, September 22, 2011.

345 "I was probably a bit overpassionate": Martin Gould and Ashley Martella, "Rick Perry to Newsmax: I Regret 'Heartless' Comment on Immigration," *Newsmax*, September 28, 2011.

345 Adam Smith, the political editor of the *Tampa Bay Times*: Lucy Madison, "Romney on Immigration: I'm for 'Self-Deportation,'" CBS News, January 24, 2012.

347 "I am a transformational figure": E. J. Dionne Jr., "Newt and the Revenge of the Base," *Washington Post*, December 18, 2011.

347 criticized Gingrich: *National Review* Staff, "The Gingrich Editorial," *National Review*, December 15, 2011.

349 "I approach every problem": E. J. Dionne Jr., "The GOP's Iowa Caucus," *Washington Post*, December 21, 2011.

349 economic discontent in the ranks: Former senator Rick Santorum, Iowa Caucus address, delivered January 3, 2012.

350 the importance of blue-collar voters: Reihan Salam, "The Crisis of 'Sam's Club' Republicans," *Los Angeles Times*, January 11, 2005.

351 "We have the power": Jon Huntsman, presidential candidacy announcement, June 21, 2011.

353 "He started running as a moderate": E. J. Dionne Jr., "GOP Candidates in Circular Firing Squad," *Washington Post*, January 8, 2012.

354 less as a guarantor of social fairness: E. J. Dionne Jr., "Santorum, Huntsman and the Future of Conservatism," *Washington Post*, January 4, 2012.

356 "They're just vultures": Arlette Saenz, "Perry Likens Romney's Bain Capital to 'Vultures,'" ABC News, January 10, 2012.

356 "there's a real difference": Newt Gingrich on *Hannity*, Fox News, January 9, 2012.

356 "free enterprise on trial: Josh Lederman, "Romney Hits Obama for Wanting to 'Put Free Enterprise on Trial,'" *The Hill*, January 11, 2012.

356 "King of Bain": Winning Our Future, "King of Bain: When Mitt Romney Came to Town," released January 11, 2012.

357 "Republicans need to know": Trip Gabriel and Nicholas Confessore, "PAC Ads to Attack Romney as Predatory Capitalist," *New York Times*, January 8, 2012.

357 Axelrod called the video "vicious": David Axelrod, *Believer: My Forty Years in Politics* (New York: Penguin Press, 2015), p. 454.

357 The attacks on Romney: "South Carolina Republican Primary," *New York Times*, January 21, 2012, http://elections.nytimes.com/2012/primaries/states/south-carolina.

357 taking 46 percent to 32 percent: "Florida Republican Primary," *New York Times*, January 31, 2012, http://elections.nytimes.com/2012/primaries/states/florida.

357 Romney's victory: E. J. Dionne Jr., "Mitt Romney Won in Florida but Lost Overall," *Washington Post*, February 1, 2012.

358 "best understands the problems": Ibid.

358 In the fall election: "Portrait of the Electorate: Table of Detailed Results," *New York Times*, November 6, 2010, http://www.nytimes.com/interactive/2010/11/07/weekinreview/20101107-detailed-exitpolls.html.

358 "Governor Romney supported the bailout": Richard A. Oppel Jr., "In Detroit, Santorum Defends Opposition to Auto Industry Bailout," *New York Times*, February 17, 2012.

358 "We cannot continue": E. J. Dionne Jr., "Ideological Hypocrites," *New York Times*, February 19, 2012.

359 Romney promised to enact: Katrina Trinko, "Romney Proposes 20 Percent Tax Cut," *National Review*, February 22, 2012.

360 On average, Romney received: E. J. Dionne Jr., "Religion Continues to Play a Strong Role in the GOP Campaign," *Washington Post*, March 21, 2012.

360 And in sixteen of the states: Ibid.

360 The primaries for other offices: Ibid.

360 In May, Senator Richard Lugar: Ibid.

361 "What I've said about compromise": Jonathan Miller, "Mourdock: Compromise is Democrats Agreeing with Republicans," *National Review*, May 9, 2012.

361 "even when life begins": Associated Press, "Richard Mourdock: Rape, Pregnancy, and God's Plan," *Politico*, October 23, 2012.

361 spent over $7 million: Michael Beckel, "Outside Groups Spend $2.2 Million in Missouri Senate Race," Center for Public Integrity, August 7, 2012.

361 The ad noted: Akin Ramesh Ponnuru, "McCaskill Tries to Pick Her Opponent," *National Review*, August 2, 2012.

362 "From what I understand from doctors": John Eligon and Michael Schwirtz, "Senate Candidate Provokes Ire with 'Legitimate Rape' Comment," *New York Times*, August 19, 2012.

362 Romney declared: Rachel Weiner, "Insulting, Inexcusable, and, Frankly, Wrong," *Washington Post*, August 20, 2012.

364 "You're not going to get your tax cut": Alan Rappeport, "Memo to the G.O.P. in 2016: Have Faith in the Faith-Based," *New York Times*, January 29, 2015. http://www.nytimes.com/politics/first-draft/2015/01/29/today-in-politics-85/.

13. SAYING YES AND NO TO OBAMA

366 57 percent of voters blamed George W. Bush: CNN/ORC Poll, released September 13, 2012, http://i2.cdn.turner.com/cnn/2012/images/09/13/rel10c.pdf.

366 "Are you better off": Alexander Burns, "GOP Pollster Winston: 'Better Off Now?' May Not Be the Right Ques-
     tion for 2012," *Politico*, September 24, 2012.
366 largest group, 39 percent, said the economy: Winston shared his polling results with me. My thanks to him for
     many helpful conversations, even if he will disagree with many parts of this book. A good analysis based in part
     on Winston's numbers is David M. Drucker, "In 2012, 'Blame Bush' Worked Again," *Roll Call*, December 4,
     2012.
367 If Rick Perry had: Obama for America, "Steel," released May 15, 2012.
367 The *Washington Post*'s: Dan Balz, *Collision 2012* (New York: Viking, 2013), pp. 246–47, 277.
368 It was from that stage: Priorities USA, "Stage," ad released June 23, 2012.
368 Tom Hamburger: Tom Hamburger, "Romney's Bain Capital Invested in Companies that Moved Jobs Over-
     seas," *Washington Post*, June 21, 2012.
368 "He fought to save the U.S. auto industry": Obama for America, "Believes," ad released July 3, 2012.
369 "Voter ID, which is going to allow": State representative Mike Turzai, remarks before Pennsylvania Republican
     State Committee, July 23, 2012.
370 "We need you": David Axelrod, *Believer: My Forty Years in Politics* (New York: Penguin Press, 2015), p. 443.
371 Thriving entrepreneurs: Reihan Salam, "Elizabeth Warren's Quote," *National Review*, September 22, 2011.
371 He went on with this theme: President Barack Obama, "Remarks by the President at a Campaign Even in
     Roanoke, Virginia," delivered July 13, 2012.
371 "Through hard work": Romney for President, "These Hands," ad released July 19, 2012.
371 Republican politicians: Charles Murray, "Un-American," American Enterprise Institute, July 18, 2012, also
     found in Jonathan Alter, *The Center Holds* (New York: Simon & Schuster, 2013), p. 288.
371 John Sununu: Grace Wyler, "John Sununu: 'I Wish This President Would Learn How to Be an American,'"
     Atlantic, July 17, 2012.
371 "These were not Internet trolls": Jonathan Alter, *The Center Holds* (New York: Simon & Schuster, 2013), p. 289.
372 The *Examiner*'s puckish: Byron York, "The House GOP's Incredible, Amazing Discovery: Most American's
     Aren't Entrepreneurs," *Washington Examiner*, January 31, 2014.
373 Hayes quoted the legendary: Stephen F. Hayes, "Man with a Plan," *Weekly Standard*, July 23, 2012.
373 He told the assembled Randians: Representative Paul Ryan, "Paul Ryan and Ayn Rand's Ideas: In the Hot Seat
     Again," Atlas Society, April 30, 2012.
373 "We're coming close": Paul Ryan, "The American Idea," delivered October 26, 2011.
374 "There are 47 percent of the people": David Corn, "Secret Video: Romney Tells Millionaire Donors What He
     Really Thinks of Obama Voters," *Mother Jones*, September 17, 2012.
375 Romney translated the passage: Dan Balz, *Collision 2012: Obama vs. Romney and the Future of Elections in
     America* (New York: Viking, 2013), pp. 346–47.
376 "While he defended his record": Axelrod, *Believer*, p. 467.
377 Having campaigned: Mitt Romney, remarks during the first presidential debate, October 3, 2012.
378 "Governor Romney doesn't": President Barack Obama, remarks during the second presidential debate, Octo-
     ber 16, 2012.
379 Voters ages 18–29: "Portrait of the Electorate: Table of Detailed Results," *New York Times*, November 6, 2010,
     http://www.nytimes.com/interactive/2010/11/07/weekinreview/20101107-detailed-exitpolls.html.
379 And Romney paid dearly: Lucy Madison, "Romney on Immigration: I'm for 'Self-Deportation,'" CBS News,
     January 24, 2012.
379 Romney's 27 percent: Jordan Fabian, "Analysis: Romney Done in by GOP's Latino Problem," ABC News,
     November 7, 2012.
380 Even more shocking: Sean Sullivan, "The Republican Party's Broad Trouble with Minority Voters, in 2 Charts,"
     Washington Post, March 5, 2013.
380 George H. W. Bush had secured 55 percent: "Portrait of the Electorate: Table of Detailed Results," *New York
     Times,* November 6, 2010, http://www.nytimes.com/interactive/2010/11/07/weekinreview/20101107-detailed
     -exitpolls.html.
380 The diversity: Ronald Brownstein, "Bad Bet: Why Republicans Can't Win with Whites Alone," *National Jour-
     nal,* September 5, 2013.
380 One clear warning sign for Democrats: "Portrait of the Electorate: Table of Detailed Results," *New York Times,*
     November 6, 2010, http://www.nytimes.com/interactive/2010/11/07/weekinreview/20101107-detailed-exit
     polls.html.
380 Obama won only 28 percent: Nate Cohn, "No, Obama Didn't Win One-Third of White Voters in the Deep
     South," *New York Times*, April 24, 2014.
381 Especially important was: David Rohde, "Why Obama Is Winning the Battle for Middle America," *Atlantic*,
     April 13, 2012.
381 The exit poll found: E. J. Dionne Jr., "Mitt Romney's Class Problem," *Washington Post*, November 7, 2012.
382 Democratic House candidates: W. Gardner Selby, "Republicans Won More House Seats than More Popular
     Democrats . . . ," PolitiFact, November 26, 2013.

382 40 million fewer Americans: United States Election Project, "Voter Turnout Data," http://www.electproject.org /home/voter-turnout/voter-turnout-data.

382 Obama led McCain by a point: Pew Research Center, "Young Voters Supported Obama Less, but May Have Mattered More," published November 26, 2012, http://www.people-press.org/2012/11/26/young-voters-supported-obama-less-but-may-have-mattered-more/.

383 5 million fewer whites: Sean Trende, "The Case of the Missing White Voters, Revisited," *RealClearPolitics*, June 21, 2013.

384 The political scientist Thomas Schaller: Thomas Schaller, *The Stronghold: How Republicans Captured Congress but Surrendered the White House* (New Haven: Yale University Press, 2015). Schaller summarizes his very important argument on pp. ix–xi, and 297–302. The "chokehold" quotation is on p. 302.

14. THE FEVER THAT WOULDN'T BREAK

386 Obama sent Joe Biden: Janet Hook, Corey Boles, and Siobhan Hughes, "Congress Passes Cliff Deal," *Wall Street Journal*, January 2, 2013.

388 "The commitments we make": President Barack Obama, Second Inaugural Address, January 20, 2013.

388 "We of the Republic pledged": President Franklin D. Roosevelt, Second Inaugural Address, January 20, 1937.

388 "In the present crisis": President Ronald Reagan, First Inaugural Address, delivered January 20, 1981.

390 "the militias were": This and the Stevens quotation are from Michael Waldman, *The Second Amendment: A Biography* (New York: Simon & Schuster, 2014), p. 127; "reflected a popular consensus," p. 174.

392 "if Hispanics think": Republican National Committee, "Growth and Opportunity Project," p. 8.

392 Senate passed an immigration reform: 113 Congress, S.744, June 27, 2013.

392 "The bipartisan bill": Statement by President Obama on Senate passage of immigration reform, June 27, 2013.

395 "Obamacare isn't working": "Cruz: Democrats 'Want People Hooked on Obamacare So it Can Never Be Unwound,'" *RealClearPolitics*, July 24, 2013.

395 "The Seinfeld Shutdown": Marc A. Thiessen, "The Seinfeld Shutdown," *Washington Post*, October 4, 2013.

395 "It's a dead end": Rosalind Helderman and Ed O'Keefe, "Less-Conservative Republicans May Be Key to Solving Federal Fiscal Drama," *Washington Post*, October 1, 2013.

396 800,000 government employees: Brad Plumer, "The Nine Most Painful Impacts of a Government Shutdown," *Washington Post*, October 3, 2013.

396 All 198 Democrats: Clerk of the House of Representatives, "Final Vote Results for Roll Call 550," October 16, 2013.

396 The turning point: "Study #13413," NBC News and *Wall Street Journal*, October 10, 2013, http://online.wsj.com /public/resources/documents/WSJNBCpoll10072013.pdf.

397 "Of course, you've probably": President Barack Obama, "Remarks by the President on the Affordable Care Act," delivered October 21, 2013.

398 At a news conference: Chris Good, "President Obama's 'Red Line': What He Actually Said About Syria and Chemical Weapons," ABC News, August 26, 2013.

399 Julie Pace of the Associated Press: "Reporter to Obama: Has This Been the Worst Year of Your Presidency?," *RealClearPolitics*, December 20, 2013.

399 Boehner himself: Matt Berman, "Boehner: Conservative Groups' Reaction to Budget Deal is 'Ridiculous,'" *National Journal*, December 11, 2013.

400 Issa's report: Michael Hiltzik, "Issa's Big Dud: No White House Connection to IRS 'Scandal,'" *The Los Angeles Times*, December 24, 2014.

401 "What I find to be the greatest": Sean Sullivan and Robert Costa, "The Tea Party's Senate Primary Hopes Down to One Final Faceoff in Tennessee," *Washington Post*, August 7, 2014.

402 backed by more than $2.4 million: Reid J. Epstein, "Tea Party–Backed Ben Sasse Wins Nebraska GOP Senate Primary," *Wall Street Journal*, May 14, 2014.

402 316,124 out of 1,152,180 registered Nebraskans: Office of Secretary of State John A. Gale, "17 Nebraska Counties Exceed 50 Percent Turnout in Primary," May 14, 2014.

402 Sasse won with: E. J. Dionne Jr., "The Two GOP Establishments," *Washington Post*, May 14, 2014.

402 *Salon*'s Jim Newell: Jim Newell, "Tea Party's Next Big War: Nebraska's Confusing GOP Senate Primary," *Salon*, May 13, 2014.

402 As the *Atlantic*'s Molly Ball: Molly Ball, "What Ben Sasse's Win in the Nebraska Republican Primary Means," *Atlantic*, May 14, 2014.

403 "This primary season": Rich Lowry and Ramesh Ponnuru, "Establishment Tea," *National Review*, July 7, 2014.

403 The Tea Party as "organic movement": Chris Wallace, "Key Republican Lawmakers on GOP Agenda for New Congress," Fox News, November 7, 2010.

404 And in Iowa, Representative Bruce Braley: "Braley Scoffs: Grassley Just an Iowa farmer Who Never Went to Law School," YouTube video, https://www.youtube.com/watch?v=QH51LNpqZ94.

404 Her endorsers in the primary: James Hohmann, "Joni Ernst Wins Iowa GOP Senate Primary," *Politico*, June 3, 2014.

404 "A Fair Shot for Everyone": "Senate Democrats Unveil 2014 Agenda: 'A Fair Shot for Everyone,'" Democratic Policy and Communications Center, March 26, 2014.

406 "We have a border that's so porous": Greg Sargent, "Scott Brown: Anyone with Ebola Can 'Walk' Across Our 'Porous' Border," *Washington Post*, October 14, 2014.

407 Ebola ran 734 times: Margaret Talev, "Ebola Spikes in Campaign Ads Ahead of Midterms," *Bloomberg Politics*, October 28, 2014.

407 At 39.5 perenct turn out in 2014: "2014 November General Election Turnout Rates," United States Elections Project, last updated December 30, 2014, http://www.electproject.org/2014g.

407 Some 13 percent of 2014: Ruy Teixeira and John Halprin, "The Political Consequences of the Great Recession," Center for American Progress, November 6, 2014.

408 A postelection survey: Robert P. Jones, Daniel Cox, Juhem Navarro-Rivera, E. J. Dionne Jr., and William A. Galston, "What Americans Want from Immigration Reform in 2014," PRRI/Brookings, June 2014.

409 He offered the sports metaphor: "Obama: 'My Presidency Is Entering the Fourth Quarter and Interesting Stuff Happens in the Fourth Quarter," *RealClearPolitics*, December 19, 2014.

409 "At every step": President Barack Obama, State of the Union address, delivered January 20, 2015.

411 "When the American people": Benjamin Landy, "McConnell Urges Compromise Amid Divided Government," MSNBC, November 5, 2014.

411 "For too long": Stephen Dinan, "Landslide! Republicans Capture Senate and Prized Governorships," *Washington Times*, November 4, 2014.

412 "too many are working harder": E. J. Dionne Jr., "What Change Sounds Like," *Washington Post*, January 18, 2015.

412 "all Americans to rise up": Peter Beinart, "Do Americans Have a 'Right to Rise'?," *Atlantic*, January 8, 2015.

412 *American Dreams:* Marco Rubio, *American Dreams: Restoring Economic Opportunity for Everyone* (New York: Penguin Group, 2015).

414 "The solutions of the thirties": Randall Rothenberg, *The Neo-Liberals: Creating the New American Politics* (New York: Simon & Schuster, 1984), p. 27.

15. REFORMING CONSERVATISM OR TRUMPING IT

417 "disrupt the status quo": Michael A. Needham, "Building a Real Reform Mandate," *National Affairs* (Winter, 2015), http://www.nationalaffairs.com/publications/detail/building-a-real-reform-mandate.

417 criticizes the left's: Yuval Levin, "A Conservative Governing Vision," *National Review*, May 28, 2014.

418 to see Karl Rove praise the movement: Karl Rove, "The New Republican Reformers," *Wall Street Journal*, March 26, 2014.

419 This is the lesson: Michael Gerson and Peter Wehner, "A Conservative Vision of Government," *National Affairs*, Winter 2014.

419 critique of the Tea Party's view: Ryan Cooper, "Reformish Conservatives," *Washington Monthly*, May/June 2013.

420 "unemployment crisis": Michael R. Strain, "A Jobs Agenda for the Right," *National Affairs*, Winter 2014.

420 progressive arguments about inequality: Senator Marco Rubio, "Reclaiming the Land of Opportunity: Conservative Reforms for Combatting Poverty," delivered January 8, 2014.

420 Some on the right: Gerson and Wehner, "A Conservative Vision of Government."

420 Barro a "conservative Whig": "Ask Josh Barro Anything: The Recent Revolution of Conservatism," *The Dish*, June 5, 2013.

421 Frum's heresy included: David Frum, "Waterloo," *Frum Forum*, March 21, 2010.

422 An earlier apostate was Bruce Bartlett: Bruce Bartlett, *Imposter: How George W. Bush Bankrupted America and Betrayed the Reagan Legacy* (New York: Doubleday, 2006).

422 The book grew out: Ross Douthat and Reihan Salam, "The Party of Sam's Club," *Weekly Standard*, November 14, 2005.

422 Douthat and Salam acknowledged the challenges: Ross Douthat and Reihan Salam, *Grand New Party: How Republicans Can Win the Working Class and Save the American Dream* (New York: Anchor Books, 2009), pp. 2–11.

423 "subsidies for carbon removal": Ibid., p. 217.

423 the libertarian conservative: Charles Murray, *Losing Ground: American Social Policy, 1950–1980* (New York: Basic Books, 1984); Murray, *Coming Apart: The State of White America, 1960–2010* (New York: Crown Forum, 2013).

424 His 2014 book: Yural Levin, *The Great Debate: Edmund Burke, Thomas Paine, and the Birth of Right and Left* (New York: Basic Books, 2014), p. 229.

424 In an important 2006 article: Yuval Levin, "Putting Parents First," *Weekly Standard*, December 4, 2006.

424 Ibid.

425 a holdout's case for compassionate conservatism: Michael Gerson, *Heroic Conservatism* (New York: Harper-Collins, 2007), p. 287.

425 steering the Republican Party: E. J. Dionne Jr., "Can the GOP Find its Center?," *Washington Post*, November 28, 2006.

426 an essay in the Reformicons' 2014 manifesto: Ramesh Ponnuru, "Room to Grow: Conservative Reforms for a Limited Government and a Thriving Middle Class," YG Network.

427 Arthur Brooks, who had once embraced: Arthur C. Brooks, "Be Open-Handed Toward Your Brothers," *Commentary*, February 1, 2014.

427 He elaborated on these themes: Arthur Brooks, *The Conservative Heart: How to Build a Fairer, Happier, and More Prosperous America* (New York: Broadside Books, 2015); and *The Battle: How the Fight Between Free Enterprise and Big Government Will Shape America's Future* (New York: Basic Books, 2010).

427 "make our case": Brooks, *The Conservative Heart*, p. 215.

427 One of the boldest Reformicon thinkers: Henry Olsen, "Conservatism for the People," *National Affairs*, Winter 2014.

428 The headline of a November 2014 article: Henry Olsen and Peter Wehner, "If Ronald Reagan Were Alive Today, He Would Be 103 Years Old," *Commentary*, Winter 2014.

429 "put a stop to the explosion of liberal": Yuval Levin, "In Praise of the House," *Weekly Standard* (January 2, 2012), http://m.weeklystandard.com/articles/praise-house_614770.html?nopager=1. See also Levin, "A Tale of Two Budgets," *Weekly Standard* (April 2, 2012), http://m.weeklystandard.com/articles/tale-two-budgets_634420 .html?nopager=1.

429 "Our modern-day economy": Senator Marco Rubio, "Reclaiming the Land of Opportunity: Conservative Reforms for Combatting Poverty," delivered January 8, 2014.

430 Sharon Parrott of the Center on Budget and Policy Priorities: Sharon Parrott, "Rubio Proposal to Replace EITC Would Likely Come at Expense of Working-Poor Families with Children," Off the Charts, January 9, 2014.

431 add an astonishing $11.8 trillion to the debt: Citizens for Tax Justice, "Marco Rubio's Tax Plan Gives Top 1% an Average Tax Cut of More Than $220,000 a Year," November 3, 2015, http://ctj.org/ctjreports/2015/11 /marco_rubios_tax_plan_gives_top_1_an_average_tax_cut_of_more_than_220000_a_year.php#.VjkM_GviNSE.

431 "The new Rubio-Lee plan": Jonathan Chait, "The Fight for the Soul of the Republican Party Is Over: The Rich Have Won Again," *New York* (March 5, 2015).

431 "too far in the right direction": Ramesh Ponnuru, "Marco Rubio's $6 Trillion Problem," *Bloomberg View*, October 28, 2015, http://www.bloombergview.com/articles/2015-10-28/marco-rubio-s-6-trillion-problem.

431 the detailed tax proposal he issued: Jeb Bush, "My Tax Overhaul to Unleash 4% Growth," *Wall Street Journal* (September 8, 2015).

432 on average by 11.6 percent: John D. McKinnon, "Top 1% Are Biggest Winners in Jeb Bush's Tax Plan," *Wall Street Journal*, September 10, 2015.

432 Jeb Bush cuts his own taxes: Harry Stein, "Jeb Bush Wants to Cut Taxes for Jeb Bush," Center for American Progress Action Fund (September 11, 2015), https://www.americanprogressaction.org/issues/tax-reform/news /2015/09/11/120930/jeb-bush-wants-to-cut-taxes-for-jeb-bush/; Catherine Rampell, "Jeb Bush's Tax Plan Is Great for Jeb Bush," *Washington Post* (September 10, 2015), https://www.washingtonpost.com/opinions/how-jeb -bush-would-reduce-his-own-tax-bill/2015/09/10/e5ed6744-57dd-11e5-8bb1-b488d231bba2_story.html.

432 "a much less regulated insurance market": Margot Sanger-Katz, "Health Proposals by Walker and Rubio Are Much Less Concerned About the Poor," "The Upshot," *New York Times* (August 18, 2015), http://mobile.ny times.com/2015/08/20/upshot/walker-and-rubio-health-proposals-are-less-concerned-about-poor.html?re ferrer=&_r=0.

432 Walker plan and the poor: Jeffrey Young and Jonathan Cohn, "Scott Walker and the Trouble with Obamacare Replacement Plans," *Huffington Post* (August 18, 2015), http://www.huffingtonpost.com/entry/scott-walker -obamacare-replacement_55d32f11e4b0ab468d9e4aa4?kvcommref=mostpopular.

432 Walker on "freedom": John Harwood, "10 Questions with Scott Walker," *cnbc.com* (September 1, 2015), http:// www.cnbc.com/2015/09/01/10-questions-with-scott-walker.html.

432 His "Make Life Work" address: Representative Eric Cantor, "Make Life Work," delivered February 5, 2013.

434 "George it's called management": Carl M. Cannon, "Stupid Is as Stupid Says," *RealClearPolitics* (September 13, 2015), http://www.realclearpolitics.com/articles/2015/09/13/stupid_is_as_stupid_says_128055.html.

434 "We are led" and "Look at that face!": quoted in Cannon.

434 Trump quotations: "This country is a hellhole": quoted in "Trump's America" (editorial), *Economist* (September 5, 2015); "a third world country": YouTube (June 16, 2015), https://m.youtube.com/watch?v=elTq6 VZdaQQ&autoplay=1; "the hedge fund people make a lot of money": "Donald Trump: Tax the Rich More," *CNN Money* (August 28, 2015), http://money.cnn.com/2015/08/27/news/economy/donald-trump-economy -tax-plan/; "I will protect your social security": Sahil Kapur, "How Donald Trump Is Winning Over Anti-Wall Street Republicans," *Bloomberg Politics* (September 1, 2015), http://www.bloomberg.com/politics/articles/2015 -09-01/how-donald-trump-is-winning-over-anti-wall-street-republicans; "controlled by lobbyists": Daniel Strauss, "Donald Trump's New Pitch: I'm So Rich I Can't Be Bought," *Politico* (July 28, 2015), http://www.po litico.com/story/2015/07/donald-trumps-so-rich-i-cant-be-bought-120743; CEO pay "a joke": "Trump Says CEO Pay Is Disgraceful a Joke," Reuters (September 13, 2015), http://uk.mobile.reuters.com/article/idUK L1N11J0DQ20150913?irpc=932.

435 CNN/ORC Poll available at i2.cdn.turner.com.

435 For Perry and Romney on Trump and links to their statements, see E. J. Dionne Jr., "Trump Has the GOP Establishment's Number," *Washington Post* (July 22, 2015), https://www.washingtonpost.com/opinions/trump-has-the-gops-number/2015/07/22/60ec49e6-309d-11e5-8353-1215475949f4_story.html.

437 Walker on Trump plan being "similar to his: Daniel Strauss, "Scott Walker: Trump and I Have Similar Immigration Proposals," *Politico* (August 17, 2015), http://www.politico.com/story/2015/08/scott-walker-donald-trump-similar-immigration-policies-121445; Cruz "I like Trump": Tim Mak, "Cruz, Trump in Secret Talks," *The Daily Beast* (August 19, 2015), http://www.thedailybeast.com/articles/2015/08/19/ted-cruz-s-secret-trump-strategy.html.

437 Trump on the silent majority and law and order: Steve Benen, "Trump Claims to Champion 'Silent Majority,'" MSNBC, July 13, 2015; James Hohmann, "Trump, in Tennessee, Downplays Police Brutality, Promises to Get Rid of Gangs," *Washington Post*, August 29, 2015.

438 Trump's supporters: Dan Balz and Scott Clement, "Poll: Trump, Carson Top GOP Race; Clinton Leads Dems but Support Drops," *Washington Post*, September 14, 2015.

438 Douthat on Trump: Ross Douthat, "Donald Trump, Traitor to His Class," *New York Times*, August 29, 2015. See also Ross Douthat, "Trump, Taxes and the G.O.P.," *New York Times*, August 31, 2015.

439 "Conservative reformism is conservative": Reihan Salam, "Conservative Reformism is Conservative," *National Review*, May 28, 2013.

440 Mike Konczal of the Roosevelt Institute: Mike Konczal, "The Conservative Myth of a Social Safety Net Built on Charity," *Atlantic*, March 24, 2014.

16. UP FROM GOLDWATERISM

443 "Moderation will be stigmatized": Edmund Burke, *Reflections on the Revolution in France* (London: J. Dodsley, 1793), p. 361.

443 "I would remind you": Barry Goldwater, speech in acceptance of the Republican nomination for president, July 16, 1964.

445 For an excellent, brisk account of Moynihan and Nixon's Family Assistance Plan, see Stephen Hess, *The Professor and the President* (Washington, DC: Brookings Institution Press, 2015); see also Greg Weiner, *American Burke: The Uncommon Liberalism of Daniel Patrick Moynihan* (Lawrence: University Press of Kansas, 2015), pp. 76–79.

445 He fulfilled his pledge: Glen Sussman and Bryon W. Daynes, *George W. Bush: Evaluating the President at Midterm* ed. Bryan Hilliard, Tom Lansford, and Robert P. Watson (Albany: State University of New York Press, 2004), p. 55.

446 Clinton's mantra: President Bill Clinton, address regarding the government shutdown, November 14, 1995.

447 The turn to compassionate conservatism: Ben James Taylor, "The 'Big Society' and the Politics of Paternalism: Edmund Burke's Influence on the Government Is Clear," London School of Economics and Political Science, June 24, 2013. http://blogs.lse.ac.uk/politicsandpolicy/edmund-burke-the-big-society-and-the-politics-of-paternalism/.

449 partisanship increasingly influences: Alan Abramowitz and Steven Webster, "All Politics Is National: The Rise of Negative Partisanship and the Nationalization of U.S. House and Senate Elections in the 21st Century," paper for the Annual Meeting of the Midwest Political Science Association, April 2015.

450 An excellent early example of a liberal contrasting Burkean conservatism with the new right that began rising in the United States in 1950s is Arthur M. Schlesinger Jr.'s "The Politics of Nostalgia," published in 1955. It is reprinted in Schlesinger, *The Politics of Hope* (Boston: Houghton Mifflin, 1963), pp. 72–80.

450 Ibid, President Bill Clinton, State of the Union address, 1996.

452 "A law might be here advanced": Irving Howe, *Steady Work: Essays in the Politics of Democratic Radicalism 1953–1966* (New York: Harcourt, Brace & World, 1966), p. 224.

452 "There's very little we can do": Jonathan Chait, "How the White House Learned to Be Liberal," *New York*, March 8, 2015.

453 The idea of transcending partisan differences: Paul Starr and Robert Kuttner, "What We Know Now," *American Prospect*, Spring 2015, p. 5.

455 outline a full-scale economic program: Lawrence H. Summers, Ed Balls, et al., "Report of the Commission on Inclusive Prosperity," Center for American Progress, January 15, 2015; Joseph E. Stiglitz et al., "Rewriting the Rules of the American Economy: An Agenda for Growth and Share Prosperity," Roosevelt Institute, May 2015.

455 a campaign kickoff speech: "Hillary Clinton Campaign Rally Speech Transcript," *Politico*, June 13, 2015, http://www.politico.com/story/2015/06/hillary-clinton-campaign-rally-speech-transcript-118973.html.

455 "Democrats," Greenberg argued, "have not addressed": Stanley B. Greenberg, "A New Formula for a Real Democratic Majority," *American Prospect*, Spring 2015, pp. 66–70.

456 Obama's best moments: President Barack Obama, "Our March Is Not Yet Finished," address in Selma, Alabama, March 7, 2015.

458 "Unfortunately for Republicans": Whit Ayres, "A Daunting Demographic Challenge for the GOP in 2016," *Wall Street Journal*, March 4, 2015. He offered a similar argument in an interview with me.

458 Latinos have been among: Michael Oleaga, "Obamacare News Today: Latinos Increasingly Favor Affordable Care Act, Likely to Influence Election 2016," *Latin Post*, April 18, 2015.

460 "beware of false prophets": John Boehner, "Face the Nation Transcripts Sept. 27: Boehner, Sanders & Kasich," CBS News website (September 27, 2015), http://www.cbsnews.com/news/face-the-nation-transcripts-september-27-boehner-sanders-kasich/.

461 "It has been a group effort": Quoted in Clinton Rossiter, *Conservatism in America* 2nd ed., revised (Cambridge, MA: Harvard University Press, 1962), p. 193.

462 "utterly contemptuous": John B. Judis, *William F. Buckley, Jr.: Patron Saint of the Conservatives* (New York: Simon & Schuster, 1988), p. 136.

462 Goldwater singled out Modern Republicanism: Barry Goldwater, *The Conscience of a Conservative* (Princeton: Princeton University Press, 2007), p. 7.

463 "Now we have as much government": Arthur Larson, *A Republican Looks at His Party* (1956; reprint, Westport, CT: Greenwood Press, 1974), p. 10.

463 In a 1955 speech: Gabriel Hauge, "The Economics of Eisenhower Conservatism," speech at The Commonwealth Club, San Francisco, California (October 14, 1955). Thanks to John Hauge for pointing me to this speech and making it available.

463 "the military-industrial complex": President Dwight D. Eisenhower, Farewell Address to the Nation, January 17, 1961.

464 "in a moment of exasperation": William Galston, "Why I Miss President Eisenhower," *New Republic*, January 20, 2011.

464 share of GDP: "The U.S. Economy from Presidents Eisenhower to Carter," Macrohistory and World Timeline, http://www.fsmitha.com/h2/ch37-econ1d.htm.

465 Ike also won 39 percent: Election Polls—Vote by Groups, 1952–1956, Gallup, http://www.gallup.com/poll/9451/election-polls-vote-groups-19521956.aspx.

465 "[t]he New Deal regime": Greg Weiner, *American Burke: The Uncommon Liberalism of Daniel Patrick Moynihan* (Lawrence: University Press of Kansas, 2015), p. 132.

466 "Unlike most GOP activists in 1952": Joe Scarborough, *The Right Path: From Ike to Reagan, How Conservatives Once Mastered Politics—and Can Again* (New York: Random House, 2013), p. xv.

467 religious conservatives felt betrayed: Laura Meckler and Ana Campoy, "Arkansas Governor Calls for Changes to 'Religious Freedom' Bill," *Wall Street Journal*, April 1, 2015.

468 "Neither a wise man": "Foreign Policy: Ike," *Time*, October 6, 1952.

INDEX

ABOUT THE AUTHOR

E.J. DIONNE JR. grew up in Fall River, Massachusetts. He attended Catholic schools, graduated from Harvard University, and received a D.Phil. in sociology from Oxford University, where he was a Rhodes Scholar. In 1975, he went to work for the *New York Times* covering state, local, and national politics and also serving as a foreign correspondent. He reported from more than two dozen countries, including extended periods in Paris, Rome, and Beirut. His coverage of the Vatican was described by the *Los Angeles Times* as the best in two decades. He joined the *Washington Post* in 1990 as a political reporter and has been writing a column for the *Post* since 1993. It is syndicated by the Washington Post Writers Group and appears in more than 240 newspapers. He is a senior fellow at The Brookings Institution and University Professor in the Foundations of Democracy and Culture at Georgetown University, where he teaches in the McCourt School of Public Policy and the Government Department. Dionne analyzes politics weekly on NPR's *All Things Considered* and is regular analyst for MSNBC. In 2014–2015, he was vice president of the American Political Science Association and is chair of the editorial committee of *Democracy* journal. He is the author of six books and edited or coedited six other volumes. His *Why Americans Hate Politics* won the Los Angeles Times Book Prize and was a National Book Award nominee. He lives in Bethesda, Maryland, with his wife, Mary Boyle. They have three children, James, Julia, and Margot.